QUANTITATIVE METHODS FOR BUSINESS AND MANAGEMENT

Visit the *Quantitative Methods for Business and Management*
Companion Website at **www.pearsoned.co.uk/buglear** to find
valuable student learning material including:

- Guidance on using Excel, SPSS and Minitab
- Fully worked solutions to the Review Questions

PEARSON | **QUANTITATIVE METHODS FOR BUSINESS AND MANAGEMENT** JOHN BUGLEAR

Welcome to the Companion Website for Quantitative Methods for Business and Management.

Students - select from the links in the drop-down menu above or the resource link below to access the student study materials.

- **Student resources** including:
  - Guidance on using Excel, SPSS and Minitab
  - Fully worked solutions to the Review Questions

Instructors - visit the Instructor Resource Centre to access password-protected resources accompanying this title.

PEARSON

At Pearson, we take learning personally. Our courses and resources are available as books, online and via multi-lingual packages, helping people learn whatever, wherever and however they choose.

We work with leading authors to develop the strongest learning experiences, bringing cutting-edge thinking and best learning practice to a global market. We craft our print and digital resources to do more to help learners not only understand their content, but to see it in action and apply what they learn, whether studying or at work.

Pearson is the world's leading learning company. Our portfolio includes Penguin, Dorling Kindersley, the Financial Times and our educational business, Pearson International. We are also a leading provider of electronic learning programmes and of test development, processing and scoring services to educational institutions, corporations and professional bodies around the world.

Every day our work helps learning flourish, and wherever learning flourishes, so do people.

To learn more please visit us at: www.pearson.com/uk

QUANTITATIVE METHODS FOR BUSINESS AND MANAGEMENT

John Buglear

Nottingham Trent Universiy

PEARSON

Harlow, England • London • New York • Boston • San Francisco • Toronto • Sydney
Auckland • Singapore • Hong Kong • Tokyo • Seoul • Taipei • New Delhi
Cape Town • São Paulo • Mexico City • Madrid • Amsterdam • Munich • Paris • Milan

Pearson Education Limited

Edinburgh Gate
Harlow
Essex CM20 2JE
England

and Associated Companies throughout the world

Visit us on the World Wide Web at:
www.pearson.com.uk

First published 2012

© Pearson Education Limited 2012

ISBN: 978-0-273-73628-8

British Library Cataloguing-in-Publication Data
A catalogue record for this book is available from the British Library

Library of Congress Cataloging-in-Publication Data
A catalog record for this book is available from the Library of Congress

10 9 8 7 6 5 4 3 2 1
15 14 13 12

Typeset in 9.5/13 pt ITC Charter by 73
Printed and bound by Rotolito Lombarda, Italy

Contents

15.4 Non-probabilistic sampling methods   339

16 **Test driving – sampling theory, estimation and hypothesis testing**   **342**
    Reality check: Business use of small sample inference, the origins
    of the *t* distribution and testing population proportions   343
    16.1 Introduction   344
    16.2 Sampling distributions   344
    16.3 Statistical inference: estimation   351
    16.4 Statistical inference: hypothesis testing   363
    Review questions   376

17 **High performance – statistical inference
    for comparing population means and bivariate data**   **381**
    Reality check: Business use of contingency analysis and ANOVA   382
    17.1 Introduction   382
    17.2 Testing hypotheses about two population means   382
    17.3 Testing hypotheses about more than two population means –
          one-way ANOVA   387
    17.4 Testing hypotheses and producing interval estimates for quantitative
          bivariate data   393
    17.5 Contingency analysis   404
    Review questions   412

18 **Going off-road – managing quantitative research for projects
    and dissertations**   **418**
    18.1 Introduction   419
    18.2 Using secondary data   420
    18.3 Collecting primary data   421
    18.4 Presenting your analysis   428

    Appendix 1 Statistical and accounting tables   **433**
    Table 1 Present values   434
    Table 2 Binomial probabilities and cumulative binomial probabilities   435
    Table 3 Poisson probabilities and cumulative Poisson probabilities   436
    Table 4 Random numbers   437
    Table 5 Cumulative probabilities for the standard normal distribution   438
    Table 6 Selected points of the *t* distribution   440
    Table 7 Selected points of the *F* distribution   441
    Table 8 Selected points of the chi-square distribution   442

Supporting resources

Visit **www.pearsoned.co.uk/buglear** to find valuable online resources

Companion Website for students
- Guidance on using Excel, SPSS and Minitab
- Fully worked solutions to the Review Questions

For instructors
- Fully worked solutions to the Review Questions
- Additional questions for each chapter with fully worked solutions

For more information please contact your local Pearson Education sales representative or visit **www.pearsoned.co.uk/buglear**

List of Self-assembly guides

Introduction: the Quantitative Methods road map

Driving to *distinction*, not *distraction*

My name is John Buglear. I have taught quantitative methods (QM) on business degree programmes for some years and I have used this experience in writing this book.

Any serious learning is a journey and studying QM is no exception. It is a bit like learning to drive a car; it may not be easy but the end result is very useful.

Although I enjoy teaching QM the honest truth is that not all my students are keen on learning it. Many of them are mortified to find that although they were studying business, 'maths' was on the menu. Despite this initial wariness I am pleased to say that the great majority persevered and passed their QM modules, often doing far better than they expected. So, put any negative experiences of maths at school behind you; this book is all about quantitative methods for business, which is a whole new ball game. It covers techniques that businesses use to understand numbers and analyse problems. This is important for you as a business student; companies always generate numbers in the course of doing business so understanding this subject will give you a cutting edge in your future career.

I haven't always been an academic. Earlier in my career I worked in electronics, engineering, and the travel industry. Since becoming a lecturer I have undertaken collaborative work with major organisations in the energy, housing and professional services sectors. From this experience I can assure you that the techniques described in this book are widely used in the 'real' world.

To guide you through these techniques at the start of each chapter there is a **Bare bones** contents outline after the **Chapter objectives.** Beneath this is a list of related features on the supporting website at **www.pearsoned.co.uk/buglear**.

There are **Reality check** sections early in all chapters except the first and last. These are intended to show how the techniques have been used in business.

Some techniques are important but can be tricky. To help you with these there are **Self-assembly guides** which provide a step-by-step approach to using them.

At the end of the chapters are **Review questions** to help you consolidate your understanding. These are classified from 'basic' to 'challenging'. After these there is a **Debrief** which reiterates the key themes from the chapter.

A book can help, and I do hope you find this one useful, but in the final analysis it's up to you. If you are anxious about studying QM don't let it become one of your demons; crack it and you will be a far more effective future manager.

Guided tour

Clear **Chapter objectives** open every chapter

The bare bones describes what you will find in the chapter and on the companion website

Reality check boxes show you where these quantitative methods are used in real-life scenarios

Self-assembly guides give you simple step-by-step instructions to follow, enabling you to apply the techniques you learn

Once we have come to a recommendation for the later course of action we assume that the decision-maker would follow our advice at that stage and hence we need only incorporate the preferred strategy in the subsequent analysis. We work out the EMV of each decision open to the decision-maker at the earlier stage and recommend the one with the highest EMV.

EXAMPLE 11.12

Find the EMV for each decision that Sam, the market trader in Example 11.10, could take concerning the offer made to her by the supplier.

Solution

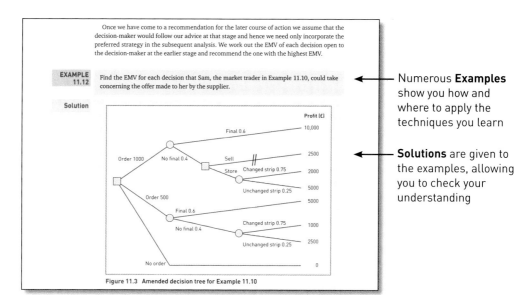

Figure 11.3 Amended decision tree for Example 11.10

*Numerous **Examples** show you how and where to apply the techniques you learn*

***Solutions** are given to the examples, allowing you to check your understanding*

☆★★ **More testing questions**

2.5 Following a crash, the owner of the Skorrost Courier Service has to purchase a new van. The make and model have already been decided, but there is a choice between petrol and diesel versions. The petrol version costs £10,000 to buy and will incur fuel costs of £0.12 per mile. The diesel version costs £11,000 and will incur fuel costs of £0.08 per mile. What is the minimum number of miles that the vehicle must travel to make purchasing the diesel version the more economical choice?

2.6 Samocat Automotive wants to move the production of its motor scooters to a purpose-built new plant that will cost £24m to construct. The scooters sell for £1850 and variable costs of production amount to £1100 per scooter.

(a) What is the break-even point for scooter production at the new plant?
(b) How will the break-even point change if the costs of the new plant rise to £30m?

2.7 Holly buys a hot dog stall for £360. In addition she has to pay a fixed charge of £200 to the local council to secure her pitch. She plans to sell her hot dogs at £1 each and the cost of preparing each one is £0.60.

(a) How many hot dogs will she need to sell to break even?
(b) She finds a supplier that can provide cheaper hot dog sausages, enabling her to save 10p per hot dog on the preparation cost. What effect does this have on the break-even point?

2.8 Roo Satellite Systems manufactures two types of broadcast receiving system, the 'Soap Dish' and the 'Houston'. The production process for each includes wiring, assembly and inspection, the times in hours required in each section are:

	Soap Dish	Houston
Wiring	3.0	3.0
Assembly	1.2	3.0
Inspection	0.4	0.5

*Graded **Review questions** enable you to test your knowledge with questions of varying difficulty*

THE DEBRIEF

Key things to remember from this chapter

→ Some business costs vary in non-linear ways with output or activity level.
→ Differential calculus is a useful tool for finding at what output or activity level costs are at a minimum.
→ In the EOQ model differential calculus is used to find the quantity that should be purchased to minimise costs.
→ Although the original EOQ model has serious shortcomings it is the foundation of much more sophisticated approaches to stock control so understanding EOQ is probably the best way of understanding key tools of modern inventory management.

***The Debrief** provides a concise summary of the material in the chapter*

Acknowledgements

I would like to thank Allison for her creative insights and critical assessment, and Max and Tom for their patience during the many hours I spent writing this book. My thanks also to the academic colleagues past and present for the part they have played in shaping my thinking about the teaching of quantitative methods, especially Helen Knight, Jan Lincoln and Hristo Nikolov. I am very grateful to Rufus Curnow, Matthew Walker and their colleagues at Pearson without whose considerable efforts this work would not have been published.

Publisher's acknowledgements
We are grateful to the following for permission to reproduce copyright material:

Text
Exercises 8.3, 8.10 from Office for National Statistics, Crown Copyright material is reproduced with permission under the terms of the Click-Use Licence

Picture Credits
The publisher would like to thank the following for their kind permission to reproduce their photographs:

Cover images: *Front:* **Alamy Images**

All other images © Pearson Education

Every effort has been made to trace the copyright holders and we apologise in advance for any unintentional omissions. We would be pleased to insert the appropriate acknowledgement in any subsequent edition of this publication.

CHAPTER 1

Rules of the road – the basic techniques

CHAPTER OBJECTIVES

This chapter will help you to:

→ Make full use of this book

→ Apply arithmetical procedures

→ Appreciate the importance businesses attach to quantitative methods

THE BARE BONES

What you will find in this chapter . . .

- An explanation of why numbers are important in the world of business
- An introduction to the general approach and style we use in this book
- Key words that are used frequently in quantitative methods and what they mean
- Guidance on the basic numerical skills you will need to use in studying quantitative methods
- The technological support, calculators and computer software available to help you with numerical work
- Review questions so you can test your understanding

. . . and on the supporting website (www.pearsoned.co.uk/buglear)

- How to get started with Minitab and SPSS
- Calculators and links to calculator instructions on the web
- Fully worked solutions to the review questions
- More review questions

1.1 Introduction

Beginning a new programme of study is always something of a challenge. To help ease you into the study of quantitative methods this chapter begins with an outline of the importance of numbers in business life (section 1.2). Following this is an overview of this book and ways in which it can help you in your studies (section 1.3). Finally, section 1.4 provides guidance on arithmetical procedures that feature in the techniques you will meet in later chapters.

1.2 Quantitative methods, numbers and business

If you are studying business or are interested in any aspect of business you need to know about quantitative methods, or 'QM' as it is often termed. Why? Because business is all about quantities: quantities of goods produced and services provided, quantities of inputs and costs, quantities of revenues and profit, and so on.

How many times have you seen a TV news programme that does *not* mention numbers? Look at stories about companies or the economy on the internet; they are full of figures. Numbers are integral to our way of life, our understanding of the world around us. This is especially so of the business world that, now and in the future, we relate to as customers, employees and suppliers.

Consider how numbers played a part in the publisher's decision to produce this book. It was interested in the size of the potential market, which meant looking at the number of students on business courses. It needed to set a price, which led it to consider the prices of rival texts on the one hand and its own production costs on the other. The production costs would depend in turn on the number of pages in the book and the number of copies to be produced.

You may feel rather uncomfortable at the prospect of studying numerical subjects. Perhaps memories of Mathematics at school have left a legacy that leads you to associate analysing numbers with mental numbness. If this is what happened to you, it is best to try to put it behind you. For one thing, the focus you will find here is on applications and interpretation rather than on proof and derivation. It may help to bear in mind that employers consistently identify numerical and problem-solving skills as highly desirable qualities in potential employees, so try to think of your quantitative studies as building a valuable career asset. For example, the Confederation of British Industry lists both of these skill areas in their profile of graduate employability (CBI, 2009: 8). Google's Chief Economist, Hal Varian, predicts that this area of experience is of increasing importance, suggesting that 'the sexy job in the next 10 years will be statisticians' (Lore, 2009).

If you are worried about studying QM you may be tempted to think that this is a subject that really doesn't matter because it is of no use to businesses. It might be comforting to think that the subject is irrelevant because this would excuse you not bothering with it. In fact the subjects that you will meet in this book have, in many cases, been forged in and grown up with the business world. The origins of many of the techniques described in this book are embedded in the history of business sectors as diverse as brewing and insurance.

It is not only people who teach quantitative methods who say this; a number of researchers have investigated the use that companies make of these methods. Usually these studies are aimed at finding out how widespread is the use of a particular type of technique, but occasionally researchers canvass the application of the spectrum of techniques that comprise quantitative methods. One comprehensive study was a survey of American companies undertaken in the 1980s (Kathawala, 1988).

Kathawala surveyed US companies that were in the 'Fortune 500' list. *Fortune* is an American business magazine that periodically compiles lists of the most prominent companies in the USA. He sent questionnaires to firms in the manufacturing and service sectors, as well as a random sample of small companies. Respondents were asked about the extent to which they used a variety of quantitative techniques, 13 of which feature in this book. Approximately half or more of the respondents' organisations used them to a moderate, extensive or frequent extent. Some were very widely used; in the case of forecasting only 6% of respondents reported little or no use.

Kathawala found that, in general, large companies were more likely to use quantitative methods than small companies. He also found that some techniques were widely used in certain sectors; for example, all respondents from the retailing sector reported that they used stock control methods, whereas all the life insurance companies said they used computer simulation.

An interesting aspect of Kathawala's study is the list of reasons companies gave for *not* using quantitative techniques. Foremost among these were that managers lacked knowledge of them. In other words, many respondents who reported that particular techniques were not used said that it was because they had no training in them, not that the techniques were considered to be of no value.

The comprehensive nature of the study makes Kathawala's work interesting, but it is now over 20 years old. However, in the years since it was published the quality and availability of computer software that performs quantitative analysis has vastly improved, suggesting that the use to which businesses put quantitative methods has increased rather than decreased.

1.3 What's in this book?

- This first chapter is essentially a platform for your quantitative methods studies. It is designed to give you an idea of the relevance of the subject, an outline of the structure and approach used in this book, and a refresher course in the basic 'tools of the trade'.

- Chapters 2 and 3 cover simple *deterministic* models that can help to represent and understand business operations. Deterministic means that the numbers used in such models are fixed or *predetermined*.

- Chapters 4 to 9 introduce *descriptive* techniques, which are ways of arranging and analysing numbers so that the situation under investigation can be *described*. These are important because typically numbers in business do vary and the *way* in which they vary is of interest.

- Chapters 10 to 14 deal with techniques and models that allow the risk inherent in business situations to be reflected in the analysis of them.

- Chapters 15 to 17 are about *inferential* techniques, ways of making *inferences* or drawing conclusions about a general situation using relatively limited data.

- Chapter 18 will assist you in dealing with the quantitative aspects of the project or dissertation that you may well have to produce in your final year.

- There is a wide range of additional materials at **www.pearsoned.co.uk/buglear**

This book covers material from the fields of Business Mathematics, Operational Research and Statistics that make up a tool-kit of techniques used for investigating situations and solving problems. Like any tool-kit, knowing how to use it depends on understanding what the tools do and how use them. The book will enable you to gain this understanding by showing how the techniques are applied using business contexts and scenarios.

To help you appreciate the wider relevance of the methods you will meet, there are sections at the beginning of each of the other chapters called **Reality checks**. These outline applications of the techniques in the business world. They are intended to reassure you that these techniques are important and so your study of them is not in vain. Some of the sources on which these are based were published some time ago and describe pioneering work with the techniques concerned; in such cases the use of a technique has become so commonplace that it no longer merits publication. In other cases commercial confidentiality means that illustrative rather than actual data has had to be used. These published accounts of the applications of quantitative methods are really only the tip of a sizeable iceberg; the everyday use of the techniques you will be studying is vast, but largely unseen.

In the body of each chapter techniques are described and illustrated using worked examples. We explain calculations in words before introducing symbols to represent the procedures. Detailed instructions on carrying out the more elaborate procedures are given in **Self-assembly guide** sections. Solutions to the worked examples are given precisely or accurate to three decimal places, unless it says otherwise.

The technical aspects of quantitative methods, producing the right answers to calculations, are important, but there is far more to this subject. It is essential that you can interpret the results you get and are able to convey the meaning of them to others. In your working life you may or may not need to carry out quantitative analysis, depending on your career direction. Whatever you do almost inevitably you will have to understand and explain the results of such analysis, even to decide whether the techniques used to generate them are appropriate. With this in mind the book not only describes and illustrates the use of techniques, it also discusses the various results that you could get and what each of them means.

Each chapter, except Chapter 15 and the final one, ends with review questions that you can use to confirm your understanding of the methods and ideas featured in the chapter. You can find answers to these questions at the back of the book alongside which you will find references to examples in the chapter. In each case the example is very similar to the question, so that if you do not obtain the correct answer you can refer to the example for guidance. The review questions are grouped by the level of difficulty. One star ☆☆★ denotes basic questions that should be straightforward once you have studied the material in the chapter. Two stars ☆★★ denote questions that are more testing; if you can do these you have 'got it'. Three stars ★★★ denote challenging questions; if you can do these you have really mastered the topic.

All numerical answers to the review questions are precise or accurate to at least three decimal places unless stated otherwise. After the review questions there is a short **Debrief** section that sums up the knowledge and skills you should have acquired from the chapter.

1.4 Key arithmetical procedures

Certain numerical operations feature in many of the techniques that you will meet later on, so this section is designed to remind you of them and introduce you to some you may not have met.

1.4.1 Addition and subtraction

Addition, symbolised by $+$, the plus sign, means putting two or more figures together to produce a sum or total. If all the figures being added are positive, i.e. greater than zero, the total grows as more are added.

EXAMPLE 1.1

A sales manager has to drive to a regional office from the company headquarters. The route involves driving 7 miles to a motorway junction, 15 miles along the motorway, 4 miles along a major road, and finally 3 miles across a city. What is the total length of the journey?

Solution

You can get the answer by adding together the distances for the four parts of the journey.

$$\text{Total distance} = 7 + 15 + 4 + 3 = 29 \text{ miles}$$

You will have met addition before but you may not know that the Greek letter 'sigma', Σ, is also used in addition. It is the Greek equivalent of capital S and stands for 'the sum of'. Using an s makes sense because the word 'sum' begins with an s.

There are several Greek letters that you will come across in studying quantitative methods. This is probably because when many of the techniques were invented Greek and Latin were common features of university education. The distinctive Greek alphabet was a ready source of symbols for the people who pioneered these techniques.

Although it may seem that the use of letters and symbols by mathematicians is a conspiracy to intimidate the rest of the world, actually they distil the essence of an operation from what would otherwise be a mass of words. It is a form of shorthand that is used for convenience. Letters are used in numerical subjects to represent quantities, to abbreviate a procedure involving specific numbers and to represent a procedure in general. For instance,

$$\sum x \text{ is 'the sum of a set of numbers, each one represented by the letter } x\text{'.}$$

It is often important to specify exactly which among a set of numbers must be summed. To signify this, the letter 'i' is used as a counter, for example,

$$\sum_{i=1}^{4} x_i \text{ is 'sum the first to the fourth in the set of numbers'.}$$

The statement '$i = 1$' underneath the sigma sign means start with the first number and add the next numbers. The '4' above the sigma means keep adding the numbers together up to and including the fourth one.

EXAMPLE 1.2

For the sales manager's journey in Example 1.1, the total distance travelled (which we will represent using 'D') is the sum of the distances of the four stages of the journey. Using d_1 to represent the first stage, d_2 to represent the second stage and so on, the total distance is:

$$D = \sum_{i=1}^{4} d_i = d_1 + d_2 + d_3 + d_4 = 7 + 15 + 4 + 3 = 29$$

If we want to specify that all the numbers in a set must be summed but we don't know how many there are, we use 'n' to represent the last number in the set, so

$$\sum_{i=1}^{n} x_i \text{ is 'the sum of the first to the last of the numbers'.}$$

Using these symbols and letters in this way may seem odd at first, but stick with them; they are invaluable 'shorthand' devices that are very useful to you in later work.

Subtraction, symbolised by $-$, the minus sign, means subtracting or 'taking away' one or more figures from another. If the figures being taken away are positive, i.e. greater than zero, the result gets lower as more figures are subtracted.

EXAMPLE 1.3

A small general store had a stock of 49 bottles of 'Electric soup' vodka at the beginning of February. Sales were 11 bottles in the first week of the month, 6 bottles in the second, 9 bottles in the third week and 13 bottles in the final week. How many bottles are left in stock at the end of the month?

Solution

To get the answer subtract the orders from the initial stock:

$$\text{Stock at the end of the month} = 49 - 11 - 6 - 9 - 13 = 10$$

An alternative approach is to start by adding the sales figures together then subtracting the total sales from the initial stock. This would be written as:

$$\text{Stock at the end of the month} = 49 - (11 + 6 + 9 + 13)$$
$$= 49 - 39 = 10$$

The brackets signify that the procedure within them must be conducted first. They show the priority of the operations.

Addition and subtraction are usually straightforward, but sometimes they can be trickier. This is true if they involve negative amounts or the figures are in more difficult measurement units such as minutes or hours.

If a negative figure is added into a sum, the sum will be reduced.

EXAMPLE 1.4

A customer purchases four items in a supermarket: a pizza costing £2.50, milk costing £1.50, and two deodorants costing £3 each. The deodorants are on a 'two-for-one' special offer. What is the total bill the customer should expect?

Solution

Because the till adjusts for the special offer after the second deodorant has been scanned, the answer might be written as:

$$\text{Total bill} = £2.50 + £1.50 + £3 + £3 + (-£3) = £7$$

In Example 1.4 brackets are used to draw attention to the presence of the negative number and to show that dealing with it is the first priority. But how should we cope with what seems to be a contradiction; the '+ −' combination of signs? Actually the minus sign 'trumps' the plus sign; adding a negative figure is simply the same as subtracting a figure. The expression used to find the sum in Example 1.4 produces the same result as the following:

$$\text{Total bill} = £2.50 + £1.50 + £3 + £3 - £3 = £7$$

How about subtracting a negative figure? Actually if we subtract a negative figure we get the same result as if we add a positive one.

EXAMPLE 1.5

The till operator notices that the deodorants the customer has selected are not those on special offer. How will this change the total bill?

Solution

The special offer reduction of £3 has to be taken away from the previous total:

$$\text{Total bill} = £7 - (-£3) = £10$$

This is the same answer as we would get if we added the £3.

It may help to think of one minus sign cancelling out the other and simply leaving an addition; to put it another way 'two minuses make a plus'. This is similar to the interpretation of double negatives in the English language where, for instance the sentence 'I won't do it for nothing' means 'I want something'. You could take a more philosophical approach to this; that taking away a negative is something positive.

Addition and subtraction where units of time are involved can be problematic because, for example, there are 60 minutes in an hour and 60 seconds in a minute. When we use the 24-hour clock it is even trickier.

EXAMPLE 1.6

A parcel delivery driver has to deliver packages to four customers. From the depot it takes 45 minutes to reach the first, a further 40 minutes to reach the second, a further 10 minutes to reach the third, and a further 27 minutes to reach the fourth. It takes 1 hour 25 minutes (i.e. 85 minutes) to reach the depot from the last customer. How long does the trip take?

Solution

We can start by expressing all of these times in minutes.

$$\text{The total duration of the trip} = 45 + 40 + 10 + 27 + 85 = 207 \text{ minutes}$$

It is probably more useful to express the answer in hours and minutes. To get this we have to ascertain the number of 60-minute lots in 207 minutes. Since three times 60 is 180 but four times 60 is 240 there are three. This leaves a residue of 27 minutes. The total duration is therefore 3 hours 27 minutes.

EXAMPLE 1.7

If the driver in Example 1.6 sets off at 10am, when will she get back to the depot? For simplicity we will assume that the time for delivering packages from the van is negligible.

Solution

Start with the hours, then introduce the minutes:

$$\text{Arrival time} = 10 + 3 \text{ hours} = 1\text{pm} + 27 \text{ minutes} = 1.27\text{pm}$$

What time is this on the 24-hour clock?

Add 12 to the pm time, because the arrival time is after midday:

$$\text{Arrival time} = 1.27 + 12 = 13.27$$

What time would the driver return to the depot if she set out at 10.45am?

This is more complex as the time of departure and the total duration of the trip are in minutes as well as hours. Getting the answer involves dealing with the hours first. Add the number of hours in the start time and the number of hours in the duration:

$$10 + 3 = 13$$

Next, add the minutes in the starting time to the minutes in the duration:

$$45 + 27 = 72$$

This is obviously longer than 60 minutes and so more than one hour. We cannot leave it as it is. It must be put in hours and minutes. Once we have done this we simply add the result to the total hours:

$$72 \text{ minutes} = 1 \text{ hour and } 12 \text{ minutes}$$

$$13 + 1 = 14 \text{ hours} + 12 \text{ minutes}$$

$$= 14.12, \text{ or } 2.12\text{pm}$$

1.4.2 Multiplication and division

Multiplication, often referred to as 'times-ing', is symbolised by either an asterisk '*' or the 'times' sign '×'. It involves multiplying two or more figures together to get what is termed the *product*. When a figure is multiplied by another which is more than one, the product is bigger than the first figure.

EXAMPLE 1.8

A domestic heating supplier is replacing old boilers in a housing estate. The new boilers can supply up to 15 litres of hot water a minute. According to the original specifications an old boiler could supply up to 14 quarts of hot water per minute. There are 1.137 litres in a quart. Will a new boiler supply hot water at a greater rate than an old one?

Solution

We need to convert the quarts given for an old boiler into litres by multiplying the number of quarts by the conversion rate:

$$\text{Litres per minute} = 14 * 1.137 = 15.918$$

We can conclude that a new boiler will not supply hot water at a greater rate than an old one.

In Example 1.8 the product, the number of litres, is greater than the number of quarts because the conversion figure, 1.137, is more than one. The multiplication results in a larger number.

In contrast, if we multiply a figure by another lower than one, we get a product less than the first figure. This is illustrated in Example 1.9.

EXAMPLE 1.9

An exporter needs to send a package weighing 20 pounds abroad. The airfreight company he uses requires the weight to be given in kilograms. If one pound is 0.4536 kilograms, what is the weight of the package in kilograms?

Solution

Find the answer by multiplying the number of pounds by the conversion rate:

$$\text{Weight in kilograms} = 20 * 0.4536 = 9.072$$

But what if the multiplication involves negative numbers? Multiplying a positive figure by a negative one results in a negative product. On the other hand multiplying two negative figures results in a positive product:

$$4 * (-2) = -8 \text{ and } (-4) * (-2) = 8$$

In the second of these cases the two negatives 'cancel each other out' when they are multiplied together.

If more than two negative figures are multiplied together, whenever the number of figures is *odd* the result is negative but when the number of figures is *even* the result is positive:

$$(-3) * (-2) * (-2) = -12 \text{ but } (-3) * (-2) * (-2) * (-2) = 24$$

Division is conventionally symbolised by the '÷' sign, the *obelus*, or by a horizontal line with the amount being divided, the *dividend* or *numerator* above and the amount by which it is divided, the *divisor* or *denominator* below. These days we use a forward slash '/' instead of a horizontal line to fit the expression on one line, which is much more convenient for word-processing. Dividing involves establishing how many lots of one figure 'go into' another.

When the figure we divide by is more than one, the result is smaller than the first figure.

**EXAMPLE
1.10**

A small design partnership makes a profit of £94,200. If the profit is shared equally be-tween the six partners in the business, how much should each partner receive?

Solution

Find the answer by dividing the profit by the number of partners.

$$\text{Profit share} = £94,200/6 = £15,700$$

Note that this could have been written as

$$£94,000 \div 6 \text{ or } \frac{£94,000}{6}$$

When we divide one figure by another which is lower than one, the result is larger than the first figure.

**EXAMPLE
1.11**

A businessman from the Netherlands travels 341 miles in the UK. On his return he must enter the number of kilometres he has travelled on his expense claim.

A kilometre is 0.62 of a mile (to 2 decimal places), so how many kilometres should he record?

Solution

To get this we divide 341 by 0.62:

$$\text{Kilometres travelled} = 341/0.62 = 550$$

1.4.3　Squares, powers and roots

Finding the square of a figure involves multiplying the figure by itself. It is symbolised by writing the figure with a superscript of 2 alongside it, for instance four squared is 4^2. This means multiply four by four.

When the figure to be squared is greater than one, the result is bigger than the figure, for example four squared is 16. If, on the other hand the figure to be squared is smaller than one the result is less than the figure, for instance a half squared is a quarter.

**EXAMPLE
1.12**

A company changes its logo and must order a new square brass plate measuring 65cm long by 65cm wide for the main office. The cost of the plate will be based on the area of the plate. There are two possible suppliers: Boldazbrass, who need the area in square centi-metres, and Striking Plates, who need the area in square metres. What figures should be given to the suppliers?

Solution

To find an area multiply the length by the width. Here because the plate is square, that is, the length and width are the same, we can simply square 65 to get the figure for the first supplier:

$$\text{Plate area for Boldazbrass} = 65^2 = 4225 \text{ square centimetres}$$

To get a figure in square metres for the second supplier we have to divide 65 by 100 so that the dimensions are expressed in metres before we square them:

$$\text{Plate area for Striking Plates} = 0.65^2 = 0.4225 \text{ square metres}$$

A positive figure squared is always positive, but so is a negative figure squared. This is because multiplying one negative figure by another always produces a positive result. So,

$$4^2 = 16 \text{ and } (-4)^2 = 16$$

Try to remember this because it is part of some of the techniques you will come across during your quantitative studies.

The number 2 in 4^2 is known as the *power* to which 4 is *raised*, which means the number of fours that have to be multiplied together. Four to the power three indicates that 4 should be *cubed*, in other words four fours should be multiplied together:

$$4^3 = 4 * 4 * 4 = 64$$

Multiplying with numbers expressed in powers involves adding the powers, so:

$$4^2 * 4^3 = 4^5$$

Four to the power five ($4 * 4 * 4 * 4 * 4$) is 1024, which is another way of representing 16 (4^2) times 64 (4^3). At first sight it might seem odd to be *adding* something when the sign '*' says multiply but in adding the powers (two plus three to give five) we are simply counting the number of fours that would have to be multiplied together to get the answer.

Before electronic calculators became widely available powers were used to carry out multiplication because adding powers was easier. This is what logarithms were all about; converting numbers into powers of 10 meant that any multiplication, no matter how complex could be undertaken using only addition.

Whilst our access to calculators today means that we have no such need for logarithms for arithmetical convenience, you may find powers of 10 used when very large numbers are shown in calculator displays and output from computer software.

<table>
<tr><td>**EXAMPLE 1.13**</td><td>An economist wants to find how much it would cost to give every resident of the UK half a million pounds, assuming the UK population is 60 million.</td></tr>
</table>

Solution

If you multiply 60 million by half a million on your calculator ($60{,}000{,}000 * 500{,}000$) it will probably show something like:

$$3.0^{13} \text{ or } 3.0 * {}^{10}13 \text{ or } 3.0\text{E} + 13$$

The calculator produces the answer 30000000000000 but has insufficient space to fit in all the zeroes, so it uses powers of ten to represent them and expresses the answer as 3 times 10 to the power 13. The power, 13, is the number of times you would have to multiply 3 by 10 to get $30{,}000{,}000{,}000{,}000$. The letter E in the third version of the expression stands for *exponent*, another word for power.

Large numbers like the result in Example 1.13 are quite common in the business world, for example the Gross Domestic Product (GDP) of a country or the earnings of a large corporation. Such numbers are sometimes expressed in billions, but be careful because in US terms a billion is one thousand million (10^9) whereas the convention in the UK is that a billion is one million squared, i.e. a million million (10^{12}). The answer in Example 1.13 would therefore be 30,000 'US billion' or 30 'UK billion'. When you use published figures that are quoted in billions, check which definition has been used. You will probably find that in business and economic figures the US usage prevails.

You will also meet negative powers or exponents in calculator and computer work. To understand negative powers it helps if you are aware that dividing with numbers involving powers means subtracting powers, for instance:

$$4^3 \div 4^2 = 4^{3-2} = 4^1$$

This is another way of saying four cubed (64) divided by four squared (16) is four; the result is four to the power one since a number raised to the power one is simply the number itself.

If we use the same approach to divide four cubed by four cubed, we get four to the power zero:

$$4^3 \div 4^3 = 4^{3-3} = 4^0$$

Four cubed is 64, so this is the same as dividing 64 by 64, which gives us one. So four to the power zero is one; in fact any number to the power zero is one.

If we divide four squared by four cubed we get a negative power:

$$4^2 \div 4^3 = 4^{2-3} = 4^{-1}$$

Here we are dividing 16 (4^2) by 64 (4^3), which gives us a quarter.

A number raised to the power minus one is one divided by the number, which is known as the *reciprocal* of the number.

A number raised to the power minus two is one over the square of the number:

$$4^2 \div 4^4 = 4^{2-4} = 4^{-2}$$

This is another way of saying that 16 (4^2) divided by 256 (4^4) is one-sixteenth, or one over the square of four.

In the same way as positive powers of 10 are used in calculator displays and computer software to represent very large numbers, negative powers of 10 are used to represent very small numbers.

EXAMPLE 1.14

Half a kilogram of a hazardous chemical is deposited by accident in a tank holding 800 million litres of water. If the chemical disperses throughout the contents of the tank, how much will there be per litre of water?

Solution

If you divide one-half by 800 million on your calculator ($0.5 \div 800000000$) you will probably see:

$$6.25^{-10} \text{ or } 6.25 * {}^{10} - 10 \text{ or } 6.25E - 10$$

The answer is 0.000000000625 kilograms per litre but there is not enough room for all the zeroes, so the calculator uses negative powers of 10 and the answer is shown as 6.25 divided by 10 to the power 10, in other words 6.25 divided by 10, ten times.

Taking the square root of a number means finding what has to be squared to produce the number. The radical sign, $\sqrt{}$ represents this process, for instance $\sqrt{16}$, means the square root of 16, which is 4, since 4 multiplied by 4 is 16. Note that $\sqrt{16}$ is also -4, because -4 multiplied by -4 is also 16, although in business contexts it is usually the positive root that matters.

EXAMPLE 1.15

A mobile phone retailer has been sent a pack of merchandising material that has to be assembled in the shop window for the launch of a new 'Square Deal' product. At the heart of the display is a fluorescent mosaic in the shape of a square that must be made up of centimetre square stickers. If the pack contains 234 stickers, what are the maximum dimensions of the mosaic square, assuming that the stickers cannot be cut?

Solution You can determine the answer by taking the square root of 234:

$$\text{Length/width} = \sqrt{234} = 15.297$$

The maximum dimensions would be 15 centimetres long by 15 centimetres wide. Although $\sqrt{234}$ is also -15.297 the concept of negative dimensions makes no sense here.

An alternative form of representing the square root of a number is to show the number to the power of a half, so:

$$\sqrt{3} = 3^{1/2}$$

If you square the square root of a number you get the number itself, so:

$$\sqrt{3} * \sqrt{3} = 3$$

We get the same result adding powers:

$$3^{1/2} * 3^{1/2} = 3^1 = 3$$

1.4.4 Fractions, proportions and percentages

These three terms seem to differ considerably, but actually fractions, proportions and percentages are merely contrasting ways to express one part of an amount relative to the whole. For instance, suppose a company employs 100 people of whom 25 are women, we could express this as:

- women make up one-quarter of the labour force, or
- women make up 0.25 of the labour force, or
- women make up 25% of the labour force.

In this list the quarter is the fraction, 0.25 is the proportion and 25% is the percentage. Each of these has the same meaning as four quarters make a total of one, four times 0.25 is one and four times 25% is 100%. Note that all of them are numbers smaller than 1, including 25% which at first sight seems larger than one. To avoid any confusion over this remember that %, *per cent,* means *per hundred,* so 25% is actually 25/100.

EXAMPLE 1.16 A bookshop gets £20 for every copy of a particular book sold, 70% of which is paid to the publisher. The publisher pays 10% of the 70% it gets to the writer of the book. If the bookshop sells 270 copies, how much will the writer get?

Solution The bookshop gets

$$270 * £20 = £5400$$

To work out how much of this the publisher will get you may be tempted to multiply £5400 by 70 and get £378,000. Although the publisher would be delighted by your result it far exceeds the amount the bookshop received for the books! The result is distorted because we have multiplied by 70 not 70%.

To do it properly we need to multiply by 0.7, the proportion form of 70%, or by 70/100, the fraction form of 70%:

$$£5400 * 0.7 = £3780 = £5400 * 70/100$$

To find the amount the writer will get we need to take 10% or one-tenth of this, £378. We could represent the whole procedure as:

$$270 * 20 * 0.7 * 0.1 = £378$$

Proportions are the easiest form of numbers less than one to deal with because they are 'calculator friendly', but you may occasionally come across arithmetical operations involving fractions.

Addition and subtraction with fractions is straightforward if the figures below the line, the denominators, are the same:

$$\frac{1}{5} + \frac{2}{5} = \frac{3}{5}$$

But if the denominators are different we need to make them compatible. The easiest way of doing this is to multiply them together to find a compatible or *common* denominator, a unit that can be used for both numbers.

EXAMPLE 1.17

A third of visitors to an internet site use the Alpha service provider and a quarter use Omega. What fraction of visitors uses Alpha or Omega?

Solution

To find this we need to add a quarter to a third,

$$\frac{1}{3} + \frac{1}{4}$$

But these are incompatible; thirds are not the same as quarters. If we multiply three by four we get 12. Since both a third and a quarter can be expressed in twelfths (4/12 and 3/12 respectively), we can conduct the addition using twelfths:

$$\frac{4}{12} + \frac{3}{12} = \frac{7}{12}$$

Subtracting fractions also involves identifying a common denominator, so:

$$\frac{1}{3} - \frac{1}{4} = \frac{4}{12} - \frac{3}{12} = \frac{1}{12}$$

To multiply two fractions, multiply the figures above the line, the numerators, and divide the result by the product you get from multiplying the denominators together, so:

$$\frac{2}{5} * \frac{3}{4} = \frac{2*3}{5*4} = \frac{6}{20}$$

It is better to express fractions in the smallest denominator possible. Here we could divide both the numerator and denominator by two (doing the same thing top and bottom does not alter the value of the expression), giving the answer as 3/10.

Dividing is the reverse of multiplying. If you multiply a number by two then divide the result by two you get the number you started with. Bear this in mind when you divide fractions, as it involves 'reversing' or inverting the second fraction and then multiplying:

$$\frac{1}{4} \div \frac{2}{5} = \frac{1}{4} * \frac{5}{2} = \frac{1*5}{4*2} = \frac{5}{8}$$

1.4.5 Approximation and rounding

Some people find mental arithmetic, working out numbers in their head, easy whereas others find it impossible. In fact, like many other skills it is a matter of practice and technique.

The key to using mental arithmetic is to round the figures first before using them to work out a rough figure that you can then refine if necessary.

Rounding is something people often do intuitively. Suppose you are asked how old you are. You'd probably respond by saying '19' or whatever is appropriate. This is rounding; your exact age might be 19 years, 4 months and 17 days but you wouldn't be that precise. Instead you approximate your age by rounding it down to the nearest whole year. Similarly, suppose you need to check how much cash you have with you. You'd probably just check the notes and perhaps the larger coins, and estimate. Unless you are worried that you may not have enough cash for your needs you are you unlikely to count it all.

Approximation and rounding are therefore probably familiar to you. They make it easier to handle figures and to identify errors in numerical work.

EXAMPLE 1.18

You go to a sandwich bar to get lunch for yourself and some friends. You have a list of things to order but little idea what the total cost will be. Above the counter there is a display of prices so you check how much the things you want cost. The tuna mayo is £3.19, the cheese and pickle £2.99, the BLT is £3.69, the cold drink is £1.99, and the hot drink is £1.79.

What is the total cost?

Solution

To get a rough estimate, round every price to the nearest £:

$$\text{Estimated cost} = £3 + £3 + £4 + £2 + £2 = £14$$

This is a simple addition but produces a very approximate figure. To be more precise we could round to the nearest 10 pence:

$$\text{Estimated cost} = £3.20 + £3.00 + £3.70 + £2.00 + £1.80 = £13.70$$

In this approximation every one of these five figures has been increased by one penny. The exact total is 5 pence less than this estimated cost, £13.65.

1.4.6 Significant figures and decimal places

In describing a situation using numerical information total precision is not always necessary. Rounding enables us to provide more useful and accessible figures in these cases. The number of *significant figures* is the extent to which you round a figure. Round *up* if the figure to the right of the number of significant figures is 5 or over and *down* if it is under 5. For example, how we round to three significant figures depends on the fourth figure.

EXAMPLE 1.19

An internet search produces a total of 2,915,386 hits. Use rounding to express this figure to:

(a) four significant figures

(b) three significant figures

Solution

(a) The fifth figure is 3 so round down to 2,915,000

(b) The fourth figure is 5 so round up to 2,920,000

When you round amounts that have numbers after, i.e. to the right of, the decimal point, the extent of rounding is termed the number of *decimal places*.

EXAMPLE 1.20

A bureau de change offers an exchange rate of 3.2856 for one currency against another. Express this figure to:

(a) three decimal places

(b) two decimal places

(c) one decimal place

Solution   (a) 3.286

(b) 3.29

(c) 3.3

In Example 1.19 the noughts to the right of the last *significant* figure are included but in Example 1.20 they are excluded. The reason for this is that in Example 1.19 the noughts signify the magnitude of the amounts.

When you are working with numbers involving decimals you will need to work to a certain number of decimal places, in other words a certain degree of precision, but exactly how many decimal places? To ensure that your work is not too approximate, avoid rounding until you have reached the answer, and express the answer to one more place of decimals than the original figures were in. For example, if the numbers you start with are given to two places of decimals, give your answer to three places of decimals.

1.4.7 The precedence of arithmetical operations

Often you will find that the forms of arithmetical operations we have looked at in this chapter are used in combination. An expression may for instance involve addition, multiplication and squaring. If this is the case it is important that you carry out the operations in the right sequence, with some operations preceding others. This sequence is known as *BoDMAS* (**B**rackets, powers **o**f, **D**ivision, **M**ultiplication, **A**ddition and **S**ubtraction).

SELF-ASSEMBLY GUIDE

Using BoDMAS

◆ First carry out any operations in **B**rackets.

◆ Then do any powers **o**f, e.g. squaring and square rooting.

◆ Then **D**ivision and **M**ultiplication.

◆ Finally, **A**ddition and **S**ubtraction.

The priority given to brackets is particularly important because they can be used to change the sequence of other operations completely for example:

$$4 + 7 + 2 * 3 = 17 \quad \text{but} \quad (4 + 7 + 2) * 3 = 39$$

In the first case the multiplication is carried out before the additions. The effect of the brackets is to prioritise the addition over the multiplication. Addition would normally be undertaken after multiplication, but enclosing the additions in brackets makes them 'jump the queue' ahead of the multiplication.

You may find *nested* brackets used to specify a sequence of operation, for instance:

$$((3 + 2) * 4)^2 = (5 * 4)^2 = 20^2 = 400$$

You need to carry out this sort of sequence by starting inside the innermost brackets and working outwards. Note that without the brackets we would get a completely different answer:

$$3 + 2 * 4^2 = 3 + 2 * 16 = 3 + 32 = 35$$

If you come across an expression involving operations with equal priority, carry them out from left to right, for example:

$$16/2 * 4 = 8 * 4 = 32, \text{ not } 16/2 * 4 = 16/8 = 2$$

If we wanted to specify that the multiplication should be undertaken first, we should use brackets:

$$16/(2 * 4) = 16/8 = 2$$

EXAMPLE 1.21

A contractor has to prepare an estimate for resealing the damaged floor of a square swimming pool that has an area measuring 17 metres by 17 metres. The cost of sealing materials is £15 per square metre. He estimates the job will take three days. The cost of labour will be £80 per day and equipment hire will cost £50 per day. He adds a mark-up of 35% to the total cost to cover overheads and profit. Work out his estimate.

Solution

$$\text{Total cost} = 17^2 * 15 + 3 * 80 + 3 * 50$$

The mark-up of 35% means that to get the estimate we must take the total cost and increase it by 35%. We can do this by taking 135% of the total cost, in other words multiplying by 135/100 or 1.35. Since we should only do this after the total cost has been worked out, we will use brackets to clarify the sequence:

$$1.35 * (17^2 * 15 + 3 * 80 + 3 * 50)$$

Start inside the brackets, squaring first:

$$\text{Estimate} = 1.35 * (289 * 15 + 3 * 80 + 3 * 50)$$

Then multiplying:

$$\text{Estimate} = 1.35 * (4335 + 240 + 150)$$

Then adding:

$$\text{Estimate} = 1.35 * (4725)$$

Finally the multiplication outside the brackets:

$$\text{Estimate} = £6378.75$$

The rules about precedence apply where capital sigma (Σ) is used to represent addition. You may find the process of taking a set of numbers and multiplying them in turn by a set of related numbers before adding up the resulting set of products is expressed as:

$$\sum_{i=1}^{n} x_i y_i$$

Here the x values, x_1 to x_n, are the numbers in the first set and the y values, y_1 to y_n, are the numbers in the second set. When you see something like this remember that the multiplication must be carried out before the addition. Bear in mind that when we use letters to represent numbers, as we have done here, the multiplication is implicit or assumed because the y_i is written right after the x_i. This convention avoids the confusion that might arise from using one 'x' to represent a number and another 'x' to represent multiply.

| EXAMPLE 1.22 | A cinema manager checks the revenue, R, from the screening of a film by working out: |

$$R = \sum_{i=1}^{3} p_i q_i$$

The p values are the ticket prices; p_1 is the adult price of £10, p_2 the children's price of £5, p_3 is the concessionary price of £6 for pensioners. The q values are the quantities of tickets sold; q_1 the number of adult tickets, q_2 the number of children's tickets and q_3 the number of concessionary tickets. What is the revenue from a screening attended by 25 adults, 32 children and 15 pensioners?

Solution

$$R = \sum_{i=1}^{3} p_i q_i = p_1{}^* q_1 + p_2{}^* q_2 + p_3{}^* q_3$$

$$= 10 * 25 + 5 * 32 + 6 * 15$$

$$= 250 + 160 + 90 = £500$$

The review questions at the end of this chapter cover the techniques dealt with in this section. You may like to use them to consolidate your understanding.

Whilst this section has covered the arithmetical material you will need in order to follow and apply the techniques you will encounter later in the book, it is not intended to be a comprehensive guide to basic maths. If you would like to look at these topics in greater detail you might find Lawler (2003) or Curwin and Slater (2000) useful.

REVIEW QUESTIONS

Answers to these questions are on page 443. There are tips and hints to help you with them on the supporting website at **www.pearsoned.co.uk/buglear**, where you will also find the fully worked solutions.

☆☆★ Basic questions

1.1 Match the expressions listed below on the left to the answers listed to the right. Try it without a calculator first then use your calculator to check your solutions.

(i)	$4 + 3 + 8 * 2 - 5$	(a)	14
(ii)	$15/3 * 2 - 4 + 6$	(b)	8 or -8
(iii)	$3 * 8/6 + 1 - 5$	(c)	1.5 or -1.5
(iv)	$(4 + 3 + 8) * 2 - 10$	(d)	48
(v)	$(2 * 8) + (3 - 5)$	(e)	20
(vi)	$(((5 - 2) + 7) * 4)$	(f)	0
(vii)	$(6 - 2)^2 * 3$	(g)	18
(viii)	$\sqrt{64}$	(h)	12
(ix)	$\sqrt{36}/4$	(i)	3 or -3
(x)	$\sqrt{(36/4)}$	(j)	40

1.2 Pair up the expressions listed below on the left to the alternative forms of them listed on the right.

(i)	0.00000045	(a)	$4.5 * 10^{10}$
(ii)	45	(b)	$4.5 * 10^{-7}$
(iii)	450,000	(c)	$4.5 * 10^{1}$
(iv)	$\sqrt{45}$	(d)	$4.5 * 10^{-1}$
(v)	0.0045	(e)	$4.5 * 10^{0}$
(vi)	45,000,000,000	(f)	$4.5 * 10^{1/2}$
(vii)	4.5	(g)	$4.5 * 10^{-3}$
(viii)	0.45	(h)	$4.5 * 10^{5}$

1.3 Match the operations on the left below to the answers on the right.

(i)	40% of 200	(a)	120
(ii)	$2/3 * 3/5$	(b)	2/15
(iii)	120% of 100	(c)	5/3
(iv)	$5/4 \div 3/4$	(d)	8%
(v)	$1/5 + 1/4$	(e)	80
(vi)	$1/3 - 1/5$	(f)	9/20
(vii)	20% of 40%	(g)	2/5

1.4 Annual world wine output recently was 6,875,396 thousand gallons, of which Italy produced 1,439,911 thousand gallons, the USA produced 543,408 thousand gallons, and Australia produced 197,035 thousand gallons.

(a) Express the total production and the production of Italy, the USA and Australia to (i) four significant figures, (ii) two significant figures.

(b) What is the proportion of world output produced by each of these countries, to three decimal places?

☆★★ More testing questions

1.5 A summary of payroll data for a retail store contains the following list:

Department	Number of operatives	Weekly wage per operative
(1) Goods received	5	£230
(2) Sales – Electricals	8	£310
(3) Sales – Furniture	3	£300
(4) Sales – Textiles	6	£280
(5) Cleaning	4	£200

If x represents the number of operatives in a department and y represents the weekly wage of an operative, find

(a) $\sum_{i=1}^{n} x_i$, the total number of operatives

(b) $\sum_{i=2}^{4} x_i$, and explain what your answer means

(c) $\sum_{i=1}^{n} x_i y_i$, the total weekly wage bill for the operatives.

1.6 You are to fly from London to Tokyo. The plane is due to depart at 17.30 and you have to check in two hours before take off. You reckon that it will take an hour and a quarter to drive to the airport and a further 30 minutes to get from the car park to the check-in desk.

(a) What time should you start your journey to the airport?

(b) The flight is scheduled to take eleven and a half hours. Going through passport control and baggage collection should take an hour. If local time is nine hours ahead of UK time, when should the person meeting you aim to be at the airport in Tokyo?

1.7 An insurance company claims department reports that 45% of the claims they dealt with over the last month related to motor policies, and 30% of those involved drivers under 25 years of age. The claims department dealt with 2400 claims last month, so how many were motor policy claims involving drivers under 25?

1.8 The loyalty card scheme operated by a retail grocery chain offers customers one point for every £10 of purchases. Occasionally double or triple points are offered on some products. If a customer spent £3700 over a year, of which £290 worth earned double points and £130 worth earned triple points, how many points would he have accumulated?

★★★ Challenging questions

1.9 According to college regulations, to pass a module a student must get at least 40% of the credit for the module, and at least 35% in each assessed element. In one module the assessment consists of an essay worth 40% of the total credit for the module and an exam worth the remaining 60% of the credit for the module. The following students have completed the module and the marks awarded are listed below. Determine who will pass and who will fail the module, identifying the reason for each failure.

Student	Essay mark (%)	Exam mark (%)
Alexander	57	47
Bukhtar	68	38
Ciani	43	36
Dalkiro	65	33
Elchin	51	39
Franklin	40	37

1.10 The price of a new Sabaka car purchased from a car supermarket is £12,500. Against this a customer is offered a trade-in of £1700 for her current vehicle. Later the customer visits a brand dealership where the same car is on sale at the full list price of £14,995. The salesperson is prepared to offer a discount of 8% off this price. What is the least that the customer should accept as a trade-in price for her current vehicle to make it worth her while to buy the car from the dealership?

1.11 A UK courier delivery service uses vans that will soon need to be replaced and the fleet manager has obtained details of a new van that is currently only available in continental Europe. The fuel economy is given as 8.2 litres of fuel per 100 kilometres travelled. What is the fuel economy of the van in miles per gallon? (There are 4.546 litres in a gallon and 1.609 kilometres in a mile, both to three decimal places.)

1.12 A visitor to a Central Asian republic is offered a new vehicle for 600,000 zoom, the national currency. She can buy zoom from a bank at the official exchange rate of 150 zoom per US dollar, but in the bazaar she could get 200 zoom to the dollar. If one dollar is worth 63 pence, what is the cost of the vehicle in pounds:

(a) if she buys zoom at the official rate?

(b) if she uses the bazaar?

THE DEBRIEF

Key things to remember from this chapter

→ Quantitative Methods is an important part of the business curriculum.

→ Sigma notation; Σ means add up.

→ Fractions, proportions and percentages have the same function.

→ Rounding numbers; the meaning of 'significant figures' and 'decimal places'.

→ BoDMAS, the 'pecking order' of arithmetic.

References

CBI (2009) Future fit: Preparing graduates for the world of work [online]. Available at: http://www.cbi.org.uk/pdf/20090326-CBI-FutureFit-Preparing-graduates-for-the-world-of-work.pdf

Curwin, J. and Slater, R. (2000) *Improve Your Maths: A Refresher Course*, London: International Thomson Business Press.

Kathawala, Y. (1988) 'Applications of quantitative techniques in large and small organisations in the United States: an empirical analysis', *Journal of the Operational Research Society*, 39(11), pp. 981–9.

Lawler, G. (2003) *Understanding Maths: A Practical Survival Guide for Students in Further and Higher Education* (2nd edn), London: Studymates.

Lore, S. (2009) For Today's Graduate, Just One Word: Statistics, New York Times [online]. Available at http://www.nytimes.com/2009/08/06/technology/06stats.html?_r=3

CHAPTER 2

Straight ahead – linear models

CHAPTER OBJECTIVES

This chapter will help you to:

→ Plot and solve linear equations

→ Apply basic break-even analysis

→ Interpret inequalities

→ Undertake simple linear programming using graphs

THE BARE BONES

What you will find in this chapter . . .

- Equations of straight lines and how to plot them
- Two ways of solving simultaneous equations
- Modelling costs with linear equations in order to find break-even points
- Using linear programming to work out the best way of using limited amounts of resources
- Review questions to test your understanding

. . . and on the supporting website (www.pearsoned.co.uk/buglear)

- How to use the Solver linear programming tool in Excel
- Fully worked solutions to the review questions
- More review questions

REALITY CHECK

Business use of break-even analysis and linear programming

◆ Break-even analysis is a well-established technique used to assess the viability of business operations.

◆ Ciftci (2010) explains its application to Ford and General Motors in the aftermath of the difficulties both companies experienced in 2008.

◆ Reinhardt (1973) describes its use in negotiations between Lockheed and the US government about the costs of the Lockheed Tri Star aircraft.

◆ Shanmugandandam (2009) shows how it is used to establish a minimum capacity utilisation level in the Indian textile industry.

◆ Linear programming was invented in the 1940s by George Dantzig, a US Department of Defense planner. He used it to plan military training, logistics and deployment (Dantzig, 1999). The Esso Standard Oil Company (the forerunner of Exxon) began using Dantzig's technique in the early 1950s in oil refining. One application concerned pitch, a product of crude oil distillation. This could be combined with flux to make fuel oil or used to make tar. There were constraints on viscosity and quantity of flux. Pitch, fuel oil and tar yield different amounts of profit. The aim was to decide how much pitch should be used for fuel oil and how much for tar in order to maximise profits (Symonds, 1955: 4–11).

◆ Wardle (1965) describes how the UK Forestry Commission used linear programming in managing the New Forest in Hampshire. They wanted to find the optimal felling pattern for the mature hardwood stock in the forest; how much should be felled and replaced with pine, how much felled and regenerated, and how much should be retained. The aim was to maximise the net return. The constraints included restrictions on the total area planted with conifers, and their total felling capacity.

◆ Heroux and Wallace (1975) recount the use of linear programming in designing the Highlands property development in New York State. The developer could build different types of houses and service buildings (commercial and social), each type generating different amounts of profit. The objective was to maximise the developer's profits. The constraints included the total area available for development, maximum school population and maximum local employment opportunities.

◆ The Turkish Ministry of Tourism commissioned a linear programming model for allocating public funds to tourism development projects that involved restoring ruins, improving transport access and building accommodation (Swart et al., 1975). The model was designed to decide which among a set of projects should be supported with public funds. The main constraint was the amount of funds. The objective was to maximise 'tourist attractiveness'.

2.1 Introduction

This chapter is intended to introduce you to the use of algebra in solving business problems. For some people the very word 'algebra' conjures up impressions of abstract and impenetrable jumbles of letters and numbers that are the preserve of mathematical boffins. Some aspects of algebra are complex, but our concern here is with algebraic techniques that help to represent or *model* business situations.

In doing this we are following in the footsteps of the 'father of algebra', Mohammed ibn-Musa al-Khwarizmi. In the ninth century al-Khwarizmi wrote *Al-jabr wa'l-muqabala*, which might be translated as 'Calculation Using Balancing and Completion'. The first part of the Arabic title gives us the word algebra. Although al-Khwarizmi was a scholar working at the House of Wisdom in Baghdad, he saw his task in very practical terms, namely to focus on

> ... what is easiest and most useful in arithmetic, such as men constantly require in cases of inheritance, legacies, partitions, law-suits, and trade, and in all their dealings with one another...
>
> (Cited in Boyer, 1968: 252)

In the course of this chapter we will confine our attention to simple algebra and how you can use it to solve certain types of business problem. We will focus on linear equations, which are those that are straight lines when they are plotted graphically. They form the basis of linear models that assist business problem-solving.

2.2 Linear equations

Central to algebra is the use of letters, most frequently x and y, to represent numbers. Doing this allows us to deal systematically with quantities that are unknown yet of importance in an analysis. These unknown quantities are often referred to as *variables*, literally things that vary over a range of numbers or *values*. Sometimes the point is to express a quantitative procedure in a succinct way, and the use of letters merely constitutes convenient shorthand.

EXAMPLE 2.1

A sales agent is paid a basic wage of £200 per week plus 10% commission on sales. The procedure for working out her total wage could be written as:

$$\text{Total wage} = 200 + 10\% \text{ of sales}$$

It is often more useful to abbreviate this by using letters. If y is used to represent the total wage and x to represent sales we can express the procedure as:

$$y = 200 + 0.1x$$

Using this we can find the total wage for a week when sales were £1200:

$$y = 200 + 0.1 * 1200 = 200 + 120 = £320$$

These types of expression are called equations because of the equals sign, '=', which symbolises equality between the quantity to its left and the quantity to its right. An equation is literally a state of equating or being equal.

An equation that involves just two unknown quantities can be drawn as a line or a curve on a graph. Each point along it represents a combination of x and y values that satisfies, or fits, the equation.

To plot an equation, start by setting out a scale of possible values of one unknown along one *axis*, or dimension, and a scale of the possible values of the other unknown along the other axis. Ensure the scales cover the range of plausible values, and start them at zero unless interest in the line is limited to part of it well away from zero. Plot the x values along the horizontal axis, known as the x axis, and the y values along the vertical axis, known as the y axis. This conveys that y depends on x.

Once each axis has been prepared, portraying an equation in its graphical form involves finding two points that lie along the line that will represent the equation. This means you have to identify two pairs of x and y values both of which satisfy the equation. The way to do this is to specify an x value and use the equation to work out what value y would have to take in order to satisfy the equation, then repeat the process for another x value. To ensure that your line is accurate it is important to take one x value from the far left-hand side of the horizontal axis and the other from the far right-hand side.

EXAMPLE 2.2

Plot the equation that represents the procedure for working out the weekly wage for the sales agent in Example 2.1.

Solution

The equation is:

$$y = 200 + 0.1x$$

where y represents the wage and x the sales.

To help us design the *x axis* let us suppose that the maximum sales revenue the agent could achieve in a week is £5000. Using the equation we can use this to find the maximum wage:

$$y = 200 + 0.1 (5000) = 700$$

This means the highest value we need to include in the scale on the *y axis* is £700.

We are now in a position to construct the framework for our graph, which might look like Figure 2.1.

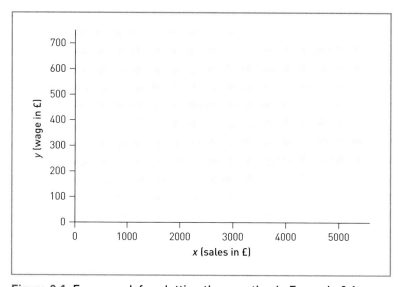

Figure 2.1 Framework for plotting the equation in Example 2.1

To plot the line that represents the equation we need to find two points that lie on the line. One of these should be on the left-hand side. The lowest number on the left of the horizontal axis is zero, so we could use the equation to work out the wage when sales are zero:

$$y = 200 + 0.1 (0) = 200$$

When sales are £0 the wage is £200. This pair of values gives us the position, or *coordinates* of one point on the line. The sales value, 0, positions the point along the horizontal axis and the wage value, 200, positions the point along the vertical axis.

To get a second set of coordinates we should take a sales figure from the right-hand side of the horizontal axis, say the maximum figure of 5000, and work out the wage when sales are £5000, again using the equation:

$$y = 200 + 0.1 (5000) = 700$$

When sales are £5000 the wage is £700. The point we plot to represent this pair of values will be positioned at 5000 along the horizontal axis and at 700 along the vertical axis. We can now plot both points as in Figure 2.2:

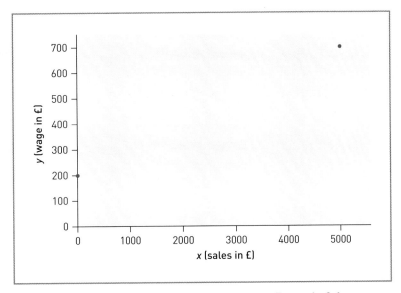

Figure 2.2 Points on the line of the equation in Example 2.1

If plotting an equation is new to you, or just something you haven't done for a while, it is a good idea to plot a third point between the first two. A third point should lie in line with the first two so it is a good way of checking that you have plotted the other points correctly. A suitable position for our third point in this case might be when sales are £2000 and the wage will be:

$$y = 200 + 0.1\,(2000) = 400$$

The point that represents these coordinates, sales of £2000 and a wage of £400, has been plotted in Figure 2.3.

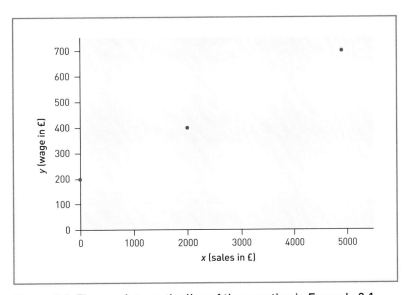

Figure 2.3 Three points on the line of the equation in Example 2.1

Solution cont

The final stage in plotting the equation is to draw a straight line linking the plotted points. This is shown in Figure 2.4.

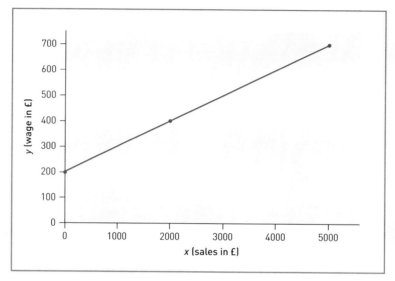

Figure 2.4 The line of the equation in Example 2.1

Lines that represent simple linear equations, such as the one plotted in Figure 2.4, have two defining characteristics: a starting point, or *intercept*, and a direction, or *slope*. We can think of the intercept as specifying the point at which the line begins, and the slope as specifying the way in which the line travels. In Figure 2.4 the line begins at 200, when sales are zero, and travels upwards at a rate of 0.1 for every one-unit increase in sales, reflecting the fact that the sales agent receives an extra £0.10 for every additional £1 of sales.

Different lines will have different intercepts and slopes. It will help you interpret results of this type of analysis if you can associate basic types of intercept and slope in linear equations with their plotted forms. To illustrate this we can extend the sales agent example to include contrasting approaches to wage determination.

EXAMPLE 2.3

Suppose the basic wage of the sales agent in Example 2.1 is increased to £300 and the commission on sales remains 10%. Express the procedure for determining the wage as an equation and plot it.

Solution

The total wage (y) in terms of sales (x) is now:

$$y = 300 + 0.1x$$

The line representing this has an intercept of 300 and a slope of 0.1. It is the upper line in Figure 2.5.

You can see two lines plotted in Figure 2.5. The lower is the line plotted in Figure 2.4, the original formulation for finding the wage. The upper represents the equation from Example 2.3, where the basic wage is increased to £300. It is higher because the intercept is 300 compared to the 200 in the original equation but note that the two lines are parallel since they have exactly the same slope. Lines that have the same slope will be parallel whatever their intercept.

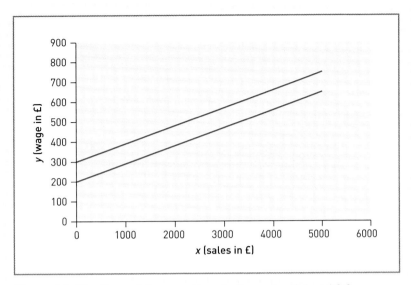

Figure 2.5 The lines of the equations in Examples 2.1 and 2.3

Identify the equation that would express the calculation of the wages of the sales agent in Example 2.1 if there was no basic wage and the commission rate remained at 10%.

Solution   The total wage would be:

$$y = 0 + 0.1x$$

This is plotted in Figure 2.6 together with the equations from Examples 2.1 and 2.3.

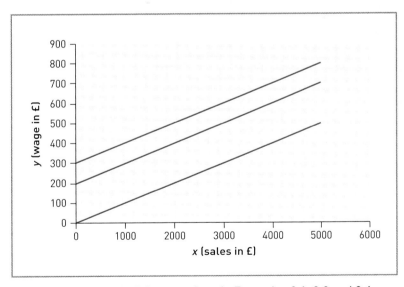

Figure 2.6 The lines of the equations in Examples 2.1, 2.3 and 2.4

The bottom line in Figure 2.6 represents the equation from Example 2.4. It starts from the point where both wage and sales are zero, known as the *origin*, since the intercept of the line is zero. It is parallel to the lines above it because it has the same slope as them.

EXAMPLE
2.5 The basic wage of the sales agent in Example 2.1 is to remain at £200, but the rate of commission increases to 20%. Express the procedure for determining the wage as an equation and plot it.

Solution The total wage (y) in terms of sales (x) is now:

$$y = 200 + 0.2x$$

The line representing this has an intercept of 200 and a slope of 0.2. It is plotted in Figure 2.7 together with the equation from Example 2.1.

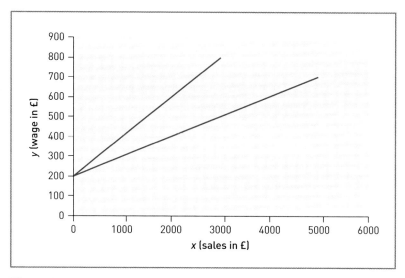

Figure 2.7 The lines of the equations in Examples 2.1 and 2.5

The equations plotted in Figure 2.7 have the same intercept, 200, but different slopes. This means they start at the same point on the left-hand side of the graph but their paths diverge. The upper, steeper line represents the equation from Example 2.5. It has a slope of 0.2, twice the slope of the line representing the equation in Example 2.1 (0.1), reflecting the greater rate at which commission is earned, 20% rather than 10%. The slope is twice as steep since the same sales will result in the sales agent earning double the commission.

EXAMPLE
2.6 Identify the equation that would express the calculation of the wages of the sales agent in Example 2.1 if the basic wage is £200 and there is no commission.

Solution The total wage would be:

$$y = 200 + 0x$$

This is plotted in Figure 2.8 together with the equation from Example 2.1.

The equation in Example 2.6 is plotted as the bottom, horizontal line in Figure 2.8. It has a zero slope; literally it goes neither up nor down. Whatever the level of sales the wage will be unaffected.

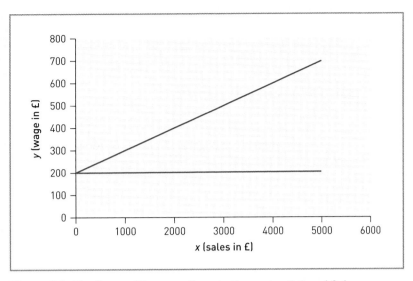

Figure 2.8 The lines of the equations in Examples 2.1 and 2.6

The slopes in the equations we have looked at so far have been upward, or *positive*, and in the case of Example 2.6, zero. You will also come across equations that have *negative*, or downward slopes.

EXAMPLE 2.7

The company that employs the sales agent in Example 2.1 believes that its sales vary according to the price charged for its product. It summarises the relationship in the form of the following equation:

$$y = 800 - 10x$$

where y represents the number of units sold and x the price at which they are sold in £. The equation is plotted in Figure 2.9.

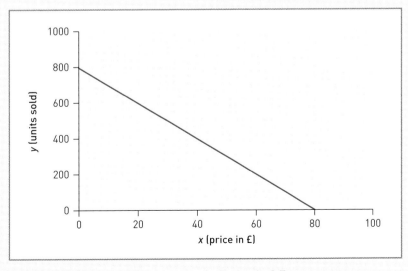

Figure 2.9 The line of the equation in Example 2.7

In Figure 2.9 the line slopes downwards because the slope, –10, is negative. It means that for every increase of £1 in the price of the product the number of units sold will decrease by 10. At this point you may find it useful to try **Review question 2.1** at the end of the chapter.

2.3 Simultaneous equations

In the previous section we looked at how linear equations can be used to show the connection between two variables. Such equations represent the relationship in general terms; they are in effect recipes or formulae that specify how the value of one quantity can be established with reference to another quantity. This is how a wage that consists of a basic component plus sales commission can be calculated or how a phone bill made up of a fixed charge plus a cost per unit can be worked out. In each case a single linear equation provides a clear numerical definition of the process involved and can be used to work out the appropriate y value for any given x value.

Sometimes it is necessary to consider two linear equations jointly, or simultaneously, hence the fact that such combinations of equations are known as *simultaneous equations*. Typically the aim is to find a pair of specific values of x and y that satisfy both equations. You can achieve this by plotting both equations on the same pair of axes and identifying the point where the lines cross.

EXAMPLE 2.8

The sales agent in Example 2.1, currently receiving a wage of £200 plus 10% commission on sales, is offered the alternative of receiving 20% commission on sales with no basic wage. What is the minimum level of sales the agent would have to reach to make the alternative commission-only wage attractive?

Solution

The existing arrangement can be represented as:

$$y = 200 + 0.1x$$

where y represents the wage and x the sales.

The alternative can be expressed as:

$$y = 0 + 0.2x$$

Both equations are plotted in Figure 2.10.

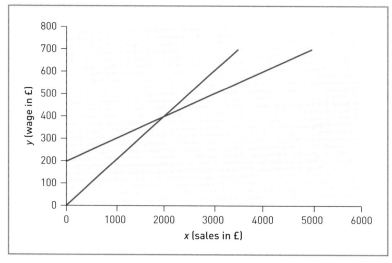

Figure 2.10 The lines of the equations in Example 2.8

In Figure 2.10 the lines cross at the point representing sales of £2000 and a wage of £400. The line representing the current method of determining the wage is the higher line when sales are below £2000, indicating that it would be the better arrangement for the agent when sales are less than £2000. The line representing the alternative arrangement is the higher line when sales are greater than £2000, indicating that it would be the better arrangement when sales exceed £2000. The minimum level of sales the agent would have to reach to make the alternative commission-only wage attractive is therefore £2000.

Finding values that fit both of two equations is known as solving simultaneous equations. In Example 2.8 the point where the lines cross meets the requirements of both equations because it is a point on both lines. The fact that it is the only point where the lines cross tells us that it represents the only combination of wage level and sales that fits both equations.

You can solve simultaneous equations without plotting their lines on a graph using a method known as *elimination*. As the name implies this involves removing or eliminating one of the unknown quantities with the intention of leaving a numerical value for the other.

SELF-ASSEMBLY GUIDE

Solving simultaneous equations by elimination

◆ Arrange the equations so that the unknown quantities (e.g. x and y) and the factors applied to them, their coefficients (e.g. the 4 in '$4x$'), are located on the left-hand side of the equals sign and the intercept, or constant, appears to its right.

◆ This may involve rearranging the equations. If this is necessary make sure that any change does not disturb the equality inherent in the equation. Keep the balance by performing any operation in exactly the same way on both sides of the equation.

◆ Next we can remove or *eliminate* one of the unknown quantities, either x or y.

◆ This is straightforward if the number of x's or y's in both equations is the same. Simply subtract one equation from the other to leave you with an expression which has just one unknown on the left of the equals sign and a number on its right. (If the number of x's or y's in both equations is not the same use the approach illustrated in Example 2.10 below to make either the number of x's or y's the same.)

◆ Use appropriate multiplication or division to find the value of this unknown, which is one of the pair of x and y values that fits both equations.

◆ Having found one of the pair of values substitute it into one of the original equations to find the value of the other unknown. This, together with the value of the first unknown, satisfies the original equations jointly, or *simultaneously*.

**EXAMPLE
2.9**

In Example 2.8 the sales agent is presented with two possible wage arrangements represented as:

$$y = 200 + 0.1x \text{ (the original arrangement)}$$

and

$$y = 0 + 0.2x \text{ (the commission-only alternative)}$$

where y represents the wage and x the sales.

Solution

We will start by rearranging both equations so the components, or *terms*, involving x and y are on the left of the equals sign and the 'stand-alone' numbers are on the right. In the case of the first equation, representing the original arrangement, this entails moving the $0.1x$ from the right of the equals sign over to the left. In doing this we have to reverse the sign in front of it, as strictly speaking we are subtracting $0.1x$ from both sides of the equation, and hence preserving the balance:

$$y = 200 + 0.1x$$

Subtract $0.1x$ from both sides:

$$y - 0.1x = 200 + 0.1x - 0.1x$$

to get:

$$y - 0.1x = 200$$

For the second equation:

$$y = 0 + 0.2x$$

subtract $0.2x$ from both sides:

$$y - 0.2x = 0 + 0.2x - 0.2x$$

to get:

$$y - 0.2x = 0$$

We can now set these rearranged equations alongside each another and subtract one from the other to eliminate y:

$$
\begin{array}{rcr}
y - 0.1x &=& 200 \\
y - 0.2x &=& 0 \\
\hline
+ 0.1x &=& 200
\end{array}
$$

We can break this operation down into three parts:

$$y - y = 0y$$
$$-0.1x - (-0.2x) = +0.1x$$
$$200 - 0 = 200$$

giving us:

$$0.1x = 200$$

This tells us that one-tenth of x is 200. If we multiply both sides of this by 10 we find that a 'whole' x is worth 2000:

$$0.1x * 10 = 200 * 10, \text{ so } 1x = 2000$$

In other words, both wage determination models produce the same wage when sales are £2000. But what will the wage be? To find this put the sales figure of 2000 into the equation representing the original arrangement:

$$y = 200 + 0.1 * 2000 = 200 + 200 = 400$$

The original approach to establishing the sales agent's wage will produce a wage of £400 when sales are £2000. The alternative, commission-only formulation will of course yield the same wage when sales are £2000:

$$y = 0 + 0.2 * 2000 = 400$$

The values of 2000 and 400 for sales and wages respectively therefore satisfy both wage determination equations simultaneously.

Applying elimination in Example 2.9 was made easier because in both equations there was only one 'y', that is the coefficient on y in each equation was one. If the coefficients on an unknown are different you have to apply multiplication or division to one or both equations to make the coefficients on the unknown you wish to eliminate equal before you can use subtraction to remove it.

EXAMPLE 2.10

Find the level of wages at which the two procedures for determining the sales agent's wage in Example 2.8 result in the same wage by eliminating x, the level of sales.

Solution

The equations representing the procedure, as rearranged in Example 2.9, are:

$$y - 0.1x = 200$$
$$y - 0.2x = 0$$

If we multiply the first equation by two we get:

$$2y - 0.2x = 400$$

Subtract the second equation from this:

$$
\begin{array}{r}
2y - 0.2x = 400 \\
\underline{y - 0.2x = 0} \\
y = 400
\end{array}
$$

Again we find that the wage level at which the two wage determination models produce the same result is £400. If we substitute this value of y into the equation representing the original arrangement we can find the level of sales that will yield a wage of £400:

$$400 - 0.1x = 200$$

Subtract 400 from both sides:

$$400 - 400 - 0.1x = 200 - 400$$
$$-0.1x = -200$$

Multiply both sides by minus one:

$$(-1) * (-0.1x) = (-1) * (-200)$$
$$0.1x = 200$$

Multiply both sides by 10:

$$x = 2000$$

The level of sales at which both approaches to wage determination will produce a wage of £400 is therefore £2000.

Not all pairs of equations can be solved simultaneously. These are either cases where one equation is a multiple of another, such as:

$$3x + 2y = 10 \text{ and } 6x + 4y = 20$$

or cases where one equation is inconsistent with the other, such as:

$$2x + y = 14 \text{ and } 2x + y = 20$$

In the first case the equations are the same; if you try to plot them you will find they produce the same line. In the second case plotting them produces lines that are parallel and therefore do not cross.

At this point you may find it useful to try **Review question 2.2** at the end of the chapter.

2.4 Break-even analysis

The type of linear model that we have looked at in the previous section can be used to analyse the relationship between the costs and revenue of a company. The aim in doing this is to identify the point at which the revenue matches the costs, known as the *break-even point*, the output level at which the company makes neither profit nor loss but breaks even.

In setting up a break-even analysis we need to make several definitions and assumptions. First we assume that there are two types of cost, fixed and variable. Fixed costs, as the name implies, are those costs that are constant whatever the level of production. These might be the costs of setting up the operation such as the purchase of machinery as well as expenses, such as business rates, that do not vary with the level of output. Variable costs on the other hand are costs that change in relation to the amount produced, such as the costs of raw materials and labour. We can define the total costs (TC) as the sum of the total fixed costs (TFC) and the total variable costs (TVC):

$$TC = TFC + TVC$$

The total variable costs depend on the quantity of output. We will assume that the variable cost of producing an extra unit is the same however many units we produce; in other words, it is linear or varies in a straight line with the amount produced. We can therefore express the total variable cost as the variable cost per unit produced, known as the average variable cost (AVC), multiplied by the quantity produced (Q), so the total cost is:

$$TC = TFC + AVC * Q$$

The total revenue (TR) is the price per unit (P) at which the output is sold multiplied by the quantity of output (Q):

$$TR = P * Q$$

Once we have defined the total cost and total revenue equations we can plot them on a graph and look at exactly how total revenue compares to total cost. This is a key comparison as the total revenue minus the total cost is the amount of profit made:

$$Profit = TR - TC$$

The point at which the lines representing the two equations cross is the point at which total cost is precisely equal to total revenue, the break-even point.

**EXAMPLE
2.11**

The Ackrana Security Company intends to manufacture video security cameras. The costs of acquiring the necessary plant and machinery and meeting other fixed costs are put at £4.5 million. The average variable cost of producing one of its cameras is estimated to be £60 and the company plans to sell them at £150 each. How many will it need to produce and sell in order to break even?

Solution

$$\text{Total cost, TC} = 4{,}500{,}000 + 60Q$$

$$\text{Total revenue, TR} = 150Q$$

These equations are plotted in Figure 2.11. Conventionally the money amounts, cost and revenue are plotted on the vertical or *y* axis and the output is plotted on the horizontal or *x* axis. This arrangement reflects the assumption that the money amounts depend on the output and makes it easier to interpret the diagram.

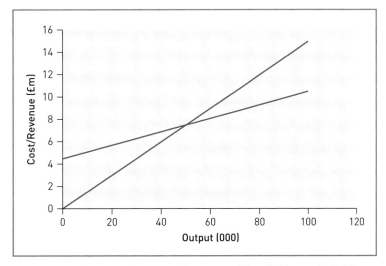

Figure 2.11 Total cost and total revenue lines in Example 2.11

In Figure 2.11 the steeper line that starts from the origin represents the total revenue equation and the other line represents the total cost equation. You can see that the lines cross when output is about 50,000 units. At this level of production both the total cost and total revenue are equal, at about £7.5 million. This is the break-even point, at which costs precisely match revenues.

We can verify the break-even point by solving the total cost and total revenue equations simultaneously:

$$\text{TC} = 4{,}500{,}000 + 60Q \text{ so TC} - 60Q = 4{,}500{,}000$$

$$\text{TR} = 150Q \qquad\qquad \text{so TR} - 150Q = 0$$

When total cost and total revenue are equal, subtracting one from the other will leave us with an expression in which the only unknown is the level of output, Q:

$$\text{TC} - 60Q = 4{,}500{,}000$$
$$\underline{\text{TR} - 150Q = \qquad\qquad 0}$$
$$+90Q = 4{,}500{,}000$$

Dividing both sides by 90 means that the level of output at which total cost and total revenue are equal is 50,000:

$$4{,}500{,}000/90 = 50{,}000$$

The total cost and total revenue when 50,000 units are produced will be:

$$\text{TC} = 4{,}500{,}000 + 60 * 50{,}000 = 4{,}500{,}000 + 3{,}000{,}000 = £7{,}500{,}000$$

$$\text{TR} = 150 * 50{,}000 = £7{,}500{,}000$$

Break-even analysis can be extended to illustrate the levels of output that will yield a loss and those that will yield a profit. A level of output less than the break-even level, and hence to the left of the position of the break-even point along the horizontal axis of the graph, will result in a loss. A level of output higher than the break-even level, to the right of the break-even point on the horizontal axis, will yield a profit.

At any point to the left of the break-even point the total cost line is the higher line indicating that total cost is higher than total revenue; the greater the difference between the two lines, the larger the loss. At any point to the right of the break-even point the total revenue is the higher line, which means that the total revenue is higher than the total cost; the bigger the difference between the two lines, the larger the profit. The areas representing loss and profit are shown in Figure 2.12.

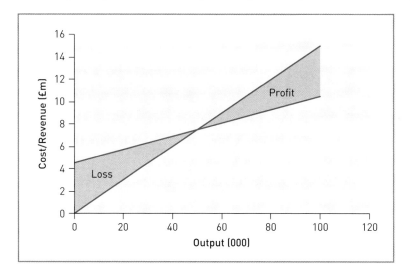

Figure 2.12 Break-even graph for Example 2.11 with areas representing profit and loss

Using Figure 2.12 you can establish how much profit or loss will be achieved at a particular level of production. If for instance production were 30,000 units the graph suggests that the total cost would be £6.3 million and the total revenue would be £4.5 million resulting in a loss of £1.8 million.

We expect that a company would seek to operate at a level of production at which it would make a profit. The difference between the output it intends to produce, its *budgeted output*, and the break-even level of output is its *safety margin*. This can be expressed as a percentage of the budgeted output to give a measure of the extent to which the company can fall short of its budgeted output before making a loss.

EXAMPLE 2.12

If the Ackrana Security Company in Example 2.11 aims to produce 80,000 cameras what profit should it expect and what is its safety margin?

Solution

$$TR = 4,500,000 + 60 * 80,000 = 9,300,000$$
$$TC = 150 * 80,000 = 12,000,000$$
$$Profit = 12,000,000 - 9,300,000 = 2,700,000, \text{ that is £2.7 million}$$

In Example 2.11 we found that their break-even point was 50,000 cameras so its safety margin is:

$$\frac{\text{Budgeted output} - \text{break-even output}}{\text{Budgeted output}} * 100 = \frac{80,000 - 50,000}{80,000} * 100 = 37.5\%$$

The break-even analysis we have considered is the simplest case, where both costs and revenue are assumed to be linear, that is to form straight lines when plotted graphically. In practice companies might find that with greater levels of production come economies of scale that mean their variable cost per unit is not constant for every unit produced but falls as output increases. Furthermore, they may have to reduce their price if they want to sell more products so that their total revenue would not have a linear relationship to their output level.

Despite these shortcomings the basic model can be a useful guide to the consequences of relatively modest changes in output as well as a framework for considering different levels of initial investment, pricing strategies and alternative sources of raw materials.

At this point you may find it useful to try **Review questions 2.3 and 2.5 to 2.7** at the end of the chapter.

2.5   Inequalities

So far we have concentrated on the use of equations to model business situations. Under some circumstances it is appropriate to use *inequalities*, also known as *inequations*, expressions of relationships in which one or more unknowns are not necessarily equal to a specific numerical value.

The basic forms of inequalities are *not equal* ($\neq$), *less than* ($<$), and *greater than* ($>$):

$$x \neq 10 \text{ means } x \text{ must take a value other than 10}$$

$$x < 10 \text{ means } x \text{ must be less than 10}$$

$$x > 10 \text{ means } x \text{ must be greater than 10}$$

It may help you to distinguish between $<$ and $>$ if you think of the sharp end of each symbol as pointing to the lesser quantity and the open end to the greater. In $x < 10$ the sharp end points to x so it is the smaller quantity and 10 is the larger quantity whereas in $x > 10$ the sharp end points to 10 so that is the smaller quantity and x is the larger.

There are two types of composite inequality that you will meet later in this chapter. These are *less than or equal to* ($\leq$) and *greater than or equal to* ($\geq$). In both cases the lines beneath the $<$ and $>$ signs signify that the possibility that the two sides in the relationship are equal is included.

These composite inequalities are useful for representing ways in which business operations might be limited or constrained by factors such as the amount of raw material or time available for the production of different products or services. In such cases all or some of the limited resource might be used, but it is not possible to use more than the amount on hand. The available quantity of resource is a ceiling or *constraint* on the business activity. An inequality can be used to represent the relationship between the amounts of the resource required for the products and the quantity in stock so that we can tell which combinations of products or services can be produced with the given materials, in other words what output levels are *feasible*.

EXAMPLE 2.13

The Sirdaria Citrus Company produces juices using exotic fruits including two made from hoormah, 'Anelle' and 'Emir'. Fruit concentrate for these products is imported and the supply is erratic. Sirdaria has 4000 litres of hoormah concentrate in stock. The Anelle brand consists of 8% concentrate. Emir, the luxury product, consists of 10% concentrate.

Represent the fruit concentrate constraint as an inequality.

Solution

Since we don't know exactly how much of each product can be produced, indeed we want an inequality to identify what the possibilities are, we must start by defining the key variables: the amounts of each product produced. We will use x to represent the amount of Anelle produced and y to represent the amount of Emir produced.

Anelle requires 0.08 litres of concentrate per litre, so if we produce x litres of Anelle we will need $0.08x$ litres of concentrate. Emir requires 0.1 litres of concentrate per litre so producing y litres of Emir will use up $0.1y$ litres of concentrate. Whatever the volume of Anelle and Emir produced the amount of concentrate needed will be the amount required for Anelle production added to the amount required for Emir production:

$$\text{Concentrate required} = 0.08x + 0.1y$$

The concentrate required must be balanced against the available supply of 4000 litres. To be feasible the output of products must not give rise to a demand for concentrate that exceeds the available supply, in other words the demand must be less than or equal to the available supply:

$$0.08x + 0.1y \leq 4000$$

Inequalities, like equations, represent the connection or relationship between amounts either side of the appropriate sign. Like equations they can also be represented graphically, but whereas the graphical form of an equation is a line the graphical form of an inequality is an area bounded or limited by a line. To portray an inequality graphically you have to start by plotting the line that bounds the area. If the inequality is a composite type the line to plot is the line for the equation that represents the limits of feasibility, output combinations that use up all of the available resource.

EXAMPLE 2.14

Show the inequality in Example 2.13 in graphical form.

Solution

If all the hoormah concentrate that the Sirdaria Citrus Company has in stock is used then the amounts of concentrate required for Anelle and Emir production will equal 4000 litres:

$$0.08x + 0.1y = 4000$$

The best way to plot this equation is to work out how many litres of each product could be produced using this amount of concentrate if none of the other product were made. You can work out how many litres of Anelle could be produced from 4000 litres of concentrate by dividing 4000 by the amount of concentrate needed for each litre of Anelle, 0.08 litres:

$$4000/0.08 = 50,000$$

So if only Anelle were made, 50,000 litres could be produced using the 4000 litres of concentrate, but there would be no concentrate remaining for Emir production. The point on the graph representing 50,000 litres of Anelle and zero litres of Emir is the intercept of the line of the equation on the x axis.

If all the concentrate were committed to the manufacture of Emir the number of litres produced would be:

$$4000/0.1 = 40,000$$

At this level of output there would be no concentrate available for Anelle production. The point on the graph representing 40,000 litres of Emir and zero litres of Anelle is the intercept of the line on the y axis.

The line can be plotted using these two points.

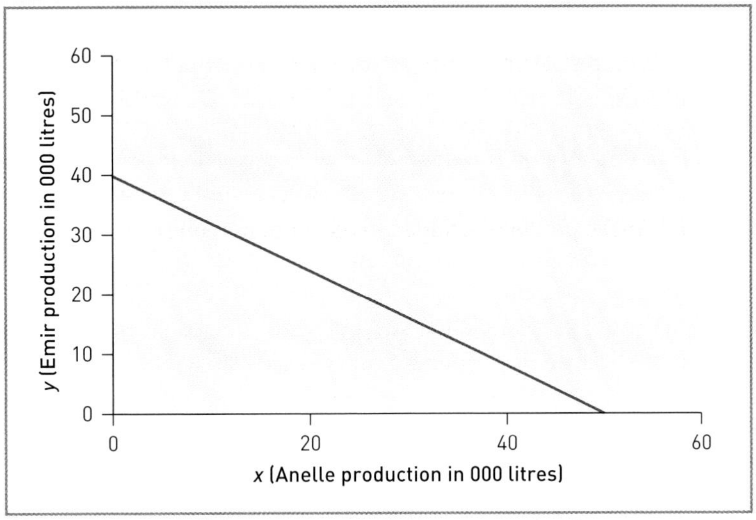

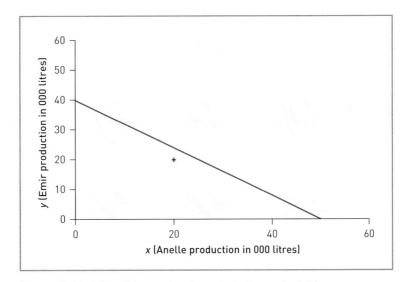

Figure 2.13 The line of the equation in Example 2.14

Each point on the line plotted in Figure 2.13 represents a combination of Anelle and Emir output that would use up the entire stock of concentrate. It is of course feasible to produce output combinations that require a lesser amount of concentrate than 4000 litres, for instance producing 20,000 litres of each product would require only 3600 litres of concentrate. We can confirm this by putting these output levels in the expression representing the concentrate requirement in Example 2.13:

$$\text{Concentrate required} = 0.08x + 0.1y$$

For 20,000 litres of both products:

$$\text{Concentrate required} = 0.08 * 20,000 + 0.1 * 20,000 = 1600 + 2000 = 3600$$

Look at Figure 2.14 and you can see that the point representing this combination lies below the line.

Figure 2.14 A feasible production mix in Example 2.14

Solution cont

The line represents all production combinations that use precisely 4000 litres of concentrate. All the points below it represent combinations that require less than 4000 litres of concentrate. All the points above it represent combinations that require more than 4000 litres of concentrate and are therefore not feasible. An example of this is the manufacture of 30,000 litres of each product, which would require:

$$0.08 * 30,000 + 0.1 * 30,000 = 2400 + 3000 = 5400$$

Clearly 5400 litres of concentrate is considerably higher than the available stock of 4000 so it is simply not possible to produce these quantities.

The graphical representation of the inequality that expresses the constraint is therefore the line that defines the limits to the production possibilities and the area underneath it. In Figure 2.15 the shaded area below the line represents the output combinations that are feasible given the amount of concentrate available.

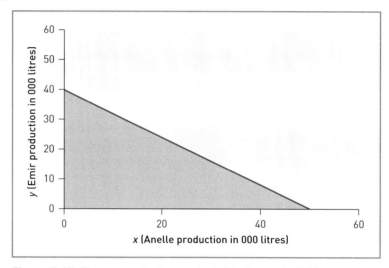

Figure 2.15 The concentrate constraint in Example 2.14

The constraint analysed in Examples 2.13 and 2.14 is an example of a *less than or equal to* form of inequality. Other constraints might take a *greater than or equal to* form of inequality.

EXAMPLE 2.15

The Sirdaria Citrus Company has a contractual obligation to produce 10,000 litres of Anelle for an important customer.

This is a constraint on production because it obliges Sirdaria to produce at least 10,000 litres of Anelle. If x represents the litres of Anelle produced then the inequality for this constraint is that x must be greater than or equal to 10,000 litres:

$$x \geq 10,000$$

Given this limitation any output mix is feasible if it involves producing 10,000 or more litres of Anelle. Were it to produce only 8000 litres, for instance, the company would have insufficient to fulfil its commitment to the customer.

Solution

To represent this constraint on a graph we need to plot the limit to the constraint ($x = 10,000$) and identify which side of it represents production combinations that are feasible.

In Figure 2.16 the vertical line represents the lower limit on Anelle production resulting from the contractual commitment. Any point to its left would result in too little Anelle being produced to meet the commitment. Any point to its right enables the company to fulfil its obligation and is therefore feasible.

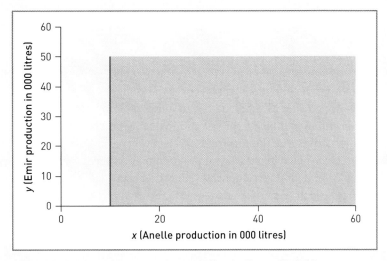

Figure 2.16 The contractual constraint in Example 2.15

Typically companies face not one single constraint on their operations but several. It can be helpful to display the constraints in a single diagram rather than separately.

EXAMPLE 2.16

Show the two constraints faced by the Sirdaria Citrus Company, the 4000 litres of concentrate available and its contractual commitment to produce 10,000 litres of Anelle, in graphical form. Identify the production combinations that would be possible taking both constraints into account.

Solution

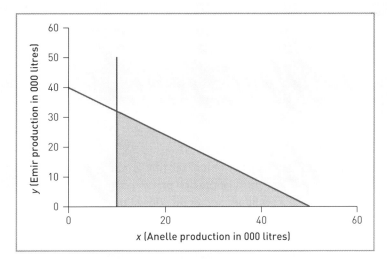

Figure 2.17 Feasible output combinations in Example 2.16

The shaded area in Figure 2.17 represents the production mixes that meet both constraints. There are some output combinations for which it has sufficient concentrate that do not allow the company to satisfy its contractual commitments, such as producing 40,000 litres of Emir and no Anelle. Other combinations allow it to produce enough to fulfil its contract but require more concentrate than it has available, such as producing 30,000 litres of each product.

2.6 Linear programming

The inequalities we considered in the last section are important ways of representing the factors that can constrain or limit business operations, but they only demonstrate the possibilities open to a company. They do not indicate which possible or *feasible* arrangement would be best for the company.

To provide guidance on making the best choice between the available alternatives we need to bring the intentions or objectives the company wants to achieve into the analysis. This can be done using a technique called *linear programming* that is designed to solve problems of *constrained optimality*, problems in which a best, or *optimal* choice, has to be made from the alternatives that the constraints collectively permit, the *feasible solutions*.

As the name implies, linear programming assumes that the problem to be solved involves linear or straight-line relationships. Constraints in linear programming are portrayed as inequalities in exactly the same way as we used in the examples in the previous section. Figure 2.17 is the sort of diagram that forms the basis for solving linear programming problems by graphical means.

The constraints we have considered so far reflect tangible limitations to operations. There are also *non-negativity* constraints that reflect the logical limitation that the output quantities cannot be negative. They simply state that each variable representing output of a product must be more than or equal to zero: for instance if x represents the quantity of a product made, then $x \geq 0$.

Once the constraints have been plotted and the area representing all the operational possibilities that the constraints collectively allow, the *feasible region*, has been identified, the company objective can be brought into consideration. To do this we need to specify it in algebraic form, as what is called an *objective function*. We assume that the company objective might involve maximising something, like profit or revenue, but it could be to minimise something, such as cost.

If the company whose operations are being modelled wants to maximise its profit it will want to select the feasible solution that yields the most profit. To help it find this we need to know the amount of profit generated from units of the different products it can produce with its limited resources. These figures are key components of the objective function.

The objective function is the profit per unit from the first product multiplied by the quantity of that product made, added to the profit per unit of the second product multiplied by the quantity of the second product made. Since we do not know the level of output for each product when we represent or *formulate* the problem, indeed the point of the analysis is to establish exactly what are the best levels of output, we have to use symbols for the amounts produced. An objective function will look like:

Maximise: $ax + by$

where a is the profit per unit of the first product
        x is the quantity of the first product made
        b is the profit per unit of the second product
        y is the quantity of the second product made

Whatever the level of output, we can use the objective function to find the resulting profit.

EXAMPLE 2.17

The Sirdaria Citrus Company wants to maximise profits from its production of Anelle and Emir juices. It makes a profit of £0.20 per litre on Anelle and £0.30 per litre on Emir.

Set out the objective function for the company and use it to find the total profit it would make by producing 10,000 litres of Anelle and 20,000 litres of Emir.

Solution

The objective function is:

Maximise: $0.20x + 0.30y$

where x is the number of litres of Anelle produced
     y is the number of litres of Emir produced

When the value of x is 10,000 and the value of y is 20,000 total profit will be:

$$0.20 * 10,000 + 0.30 * 20,000 = 2000 + 6000 = 8000$$

Producing 10,000 litres of Anelle and 20,000 litres of Emir will yield a total profit of £8000.

Formulating the objective function is one thing, but how can we use it to find the best feasible solution, the optimal solution? There are two ways of doing this: either using the objective function to work out the total profit for each feasible solution, or plotting the objective function graphically. We will look at both methods.

The first approach seems daunting because there are simply so many feasible solutions that working out the total profit for each one would be laborious. In fact the vast majority of feasible solutions can be ruled out because logically they cannot be the optimal solution. These are the feasible solutions that are inside, as against on the edges of, the feasible region. Any solution within the feasible region is surrounded by other feasible solutions, including solutions with higher output levels of one or both products. As long as the products yield a profit, a higher level of output of them will yield a higher profit, so a feasible solution inside the feasible region can always be bettered.

**EXAMPLE
2.18**

If you look at Figure 2.18 you can see point P inside the feasible region for the Sirdaria Citrus Company problem. If the company were producing the output combination represented by P, it would have fruit concentrate spare to increase Anelle production and move to somewhere like point Q, or to increase Emir production and move to somewhere like point R, or to increase output of both products and move to somewhere like point S. Combinations Q, R and S will all yield a higher profit than combination P, so P cannot possibly be the optimal, maximum profit solution.

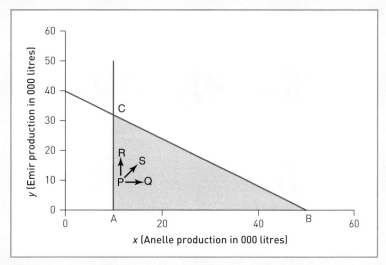

Figure 2.18 The feasible region in Example 2.18

Excluding the solutions inside the feasible region still leaves us with all the solutions along its edges, which still amount to so many that working out the profit for each one of them would be tedious. Fortunately we can ignore the vast majority of these because the optimal solution will be located at one of the corners of the feasible region, except in special circumstances that we will consider later. Because the corners are fundamental to solving the problem they are referred to as *basic feasible solutions*.

Since one corner will be the optimal solution we need only work out the total profit for the output mixes represented by the corner points. The optimal solution is the one that results in the highest profit.

EXAMPLE 2.19

In Figure 2.18 the corners of the feasible region are labelled A, B and C. Identify the production mixes they represent, work out how much profit each of them will yield, and find the optimal solution.

Solution

Corner	Output (litres)		Profit (£)		Total profit (£)
	Anelle	Emir	Anelle	Emir	
A	10 000	0	2 000	0	2 000
B	50 000	0	10 000	0	10 000
C	10 000	32 000	2 000	9 600	11 600

The optimal solution is point C, which represents the production of 10,000 litres of Anelle and 32,000 litres of Emir, and yields a profit of £11,600.

To understand why the solution is one of the corner points rather than somewhere along an edge of the feasible region we can consider the points between points B and C in Figure 2.18. If the company were producing the output represented by corner B, 50,000 litres of Anelle and no Emir, but wanted to produce some Emir it would have to reduce the amount of Anelle produced. It would have no concentrate available for producing Emir as producing 50,000 litres of Anelle would use up all 4000 litres of concentrate at its disposal. Reducing Anelle production to allow some Emir to be produced would amount to moving from corner B in Figure 2.18 along the edge of the feasible region in the direction of corner C.

Would it be worth doing this? Yes, because the profit will increase. Suppose the company decreased Anelle production by 100 litres. Since each litre of Anelle requires 0.08 litres of concentrate, this reduction will release 8 litres of concentrate. This is enough to make 80 litres of Emir, as each litre of Emir requires 0.1 litres of concentrate. The company would lose £0.20 profit for each litre less of Anelle it produces, a total of £20 profit lost for the 100 litres decrease, but it will gain £0.30 profit for each litre of Emir produced, a total of £24 on the 80 litres it produces. The substitution of Emir production by Anelle production would be worth doing and should be continued as far as possible, which is all the way to corner C. Corner B cannot be the optimal solution because from point B swapping Anelle production for Emir production increases profit. Any point between B and C represents a better solution than B, but none will be as good as corner C.

The only case where the optimal solution will not be a corner of the feasible region will be when the ratio of the profits per unit for the products are the same as the ratio of the scarce resource usage. If, for instance, the profit per litre from Emir were £0.25 the amount of profit gained from producing 80 litres would be only £20, exactly the same as the profit from the 100 litres of Anelle that the company would have sacrificed to make the Emir. With these profits per litre all the solutions along the edge running from B to C in Figure 2.18 would produce the same total profit, so there would be no unique optimal solution.

Instead of working out the total profit for each corner of the feasible region it is possible to identify the optimal solution by plotting the objective function. This approach is more elegant and can be quicker, especially when the feasible region has more corners. But before you can do this you have to assign a value to the objective function.

EXAMPLE 2.20

The objective function in Example 2.17, $0.20x + 0.30y$, cannot be plotted on a graph in its current form because it is not an equation, but a general definition of total profit. It has no equals sign or right-hand side. Without these we can't identify points on a graph to use to plot a line.

To get us out of this difficulty we need only specify a figure for the total profit. In Example 2.17 we can't plot:

$$0.20x + 0.30y$$

but we can plot:

$$0.20x + 0.30y = 12,000$$

The figure of 12,000 is an arbitrary one that happens to be a convenient round number that is easy to divide by both 0.2 and 0.3. We could choose 15,000 or 18,000, or indeed any other figure to make our *general* objective function into a *specific* equation. These specific values of the objective function are plotted in Figure 2.19. As you can see they are parallel to each other and the higher the profit, the higher the line representing it.

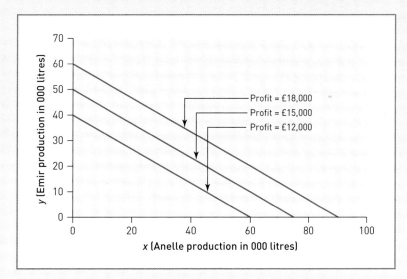

Figure 2.19 Values of the Sirdaria Citrus Company objective function

When an objective function is given a value and plotted the resulting line is called an *iso-profit line*. The points on such a line all have one thing in common: they represent output combinations that yield exactly the same profit. The prefix iso- means equal so an iso-profit line shows production mixes that give equal profit, in the same way as isobars on weather maps link places with the same level of atmospheric pressure. In Figure 2.19 the points along the lower line are all different ways in which the company could make a profit of £12,000.

By plotting an iso-profit line that runs through the feasible region we can identify those feasible combinations giving that level of profit. You can use such a line to see how far above it you can go without leaving the feasible region; the furthest you can go is the optimal solution.

However, you may find it easier to plot a value of the objective function that is above the feasible region and look for the point on the feasible region that is nearest to the plotted iso-profit line. This point is the optimal solution. Once we have identified it we can find the levels of production it represents by reading from the graph or solving simultaneously the equations of the lines that cross at the optimal solution.

Plot the iso-profit line showing product combinations yielding a profit of £12,000 for the Sirdaria Citrus Company and use it to identify the optimal solution. Confirm the levels of output at which profit will be maximised by solving the relevant equations.

Solution

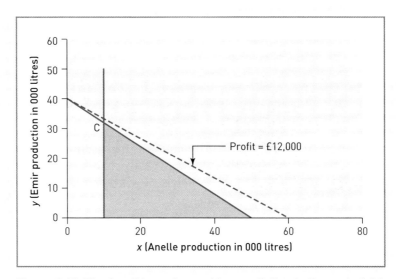

Figure 2.20 The feasible region and iso-profit line in Example 2.21

In Figure 2.20 the iso-profit line is an unattainable level of profit because nowhere across its length does it even touch the feasible region, so it is not possible for the company to make a profit of £12,000. The nearest we can get to it is to produce combination C, where the lines representing the limits of the contractual obligation to produce 10,000 litres of Anelle and the concentrate constraint meet. At point C:

$$x = 10,000 \text{ (contract)}$$

and
$$0.08x + 0.1y = 4000 \text{ (concentrate)}$$

The first expression defines the Anelle output at point C. To find the Emir output, substitute 10,000 for x in the concentrate equation:

$$0.08 * 10,000 + 0.1y = 4000$$
$$800 + 0.1y = 4000$$

subtract 800 from both sides

$$0.1y = 4000 - 800$$
$$= 3200$$

multiply both sides by 10

$$y = 32,000$$

This confirms that point C, the optimal solution, depicts the production of 32,000 litres of Emir as well as 10,000 litres of Anelle.

Plotting an iso-profit line to identify the optimal solution is particularly useful if the problem is a little more complex.

EXAMPLE 2.22

The Sirdaria Citrus Company has encountered another factor that limits its operations; it only has 480kg of sweetener. A litre of Anelle requires 8 grams and a litre of Emir requires 15 grams.

Show this constraint graphically, and identify the feasible region that results when it is combined with the concentrate and contract constraints. Use the iso-profit line for £12,000 to find the optimal solution, verify it by solving the relevant equations, and work out how much profit the company would make by producing the optimal output mix.

Solution

Using x to represent the litres of Anelle produced and y to represent the litres of Emir, the sweetener constraint is:

$$0.008x + 0.015y \leq 480$$

The equation representing the limits of this constraint is:

$$0.008x + 0.015y = 480$$

This is represented by the black line in Figure 2.21.

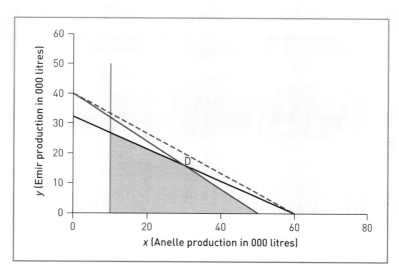

Figure 2.21 The feasible region in Example 2.22

The feasible region is now rather smaller than it was in Figure 2.20. There are production combinations that previously were feasible but are now not possible because they require too much sweetener. Among these is the previous optimal solution. You can check this by working out how much sweetener would be needed to produce 10,000 litres of Anelle and 32,000 litres of Emir:

$$0.008 * 10,000 + 0.015 * 32,000 = 80 + 480 = 560\,kg$$

Since the company only has 480kg it needs to look for a new optimal solution. The point on the feasible region that is closest to the iso-profit line for £12,000 represents the combination of 30,000 litres of Anelle and 16,000 litres of Emir, marked as point D in

Solution cont

Figure 2.21. We can check the exact production levels by solving simultaneously the equations of the lines that cross at that point:

$$0.08x + 0.1y = 4000 \text{ (concentrate)}$$
$$0.008x + 0.15y = 480 \text{ (sweetener)}$$

Multiply the sweetener equation by 10 and subtract from it the concentrate equation:

$$0.08x + 0.15y = 4800$$

less $$0.08x + 0.1\ y = 4000$$

gives $$0.05y = 800$$

Multiply both sides by 20 $$y = 16{,}000$$

Substitute this in the concentrate equation:

$$0.08x + 0.1 * 16{,}000 = 4000$$
$$0.08x + 16{,}000 \quad = 4000$$

Subtract 1600 from both sides:

$$0.08x = 2400$$

Divide both sides by 0.08:

$$x = 2400/0.08 = 30{,}000$$

This confirms that the optimal solution is to produce 30,000 litres of Anelle and 16,000 litres of Emir. The profit the company would make is:

$$0.20 * 30{,}000 + 0.3 * 16{,}000 = 6000 + 4800 = £10{,}800$$

Note that the amount of Anelle produced is above that specified in the contract constraint, 10,000. This type of constraint, one that does not actually constrain the solution, is known as a *slack* constraint. In contrast concentrate and sweetener are *tight* constraints.

At this point you may find it useful to try **Review questions 2.4 and 2.8 to 2.11** at the end of the chapter.

2.6.1 Minimisation problems

The examples in the previous section featured a maximisation problem, one in which the company was seeking to maximise its profits. There are also linear programming problems in which the objective is to minimise something, typically total costs.

The approach to solving a minimisation problem is essentially the same as that we use for a maximisation problem. We start by formulating the problem, i.e. defining the variables, then setting out the constraints and the objective function. We can then proceed to represent the problem graphically, indicate the feasible region, and use the objective function to find the optimal solution.

Apart from the contrasting form of the objective the main difference between maximisation and minimisation problems is the type of constraint involved. In maximisation problems the constraints are typically 'less than' constraints that impose upper limits on outputs that generate profits. In minimisation problems the constraints are usually 'more than' constraints that impose lower limits on inputs that incur costs.

EXAMPLE 2.23

The Pamoch Aid Agency has to evacuate the residents of a volcanic island and their belongings by boat. The island's small harbour can only handle small boats. There are two types of boat the agency can hire locally: the Lotka and the Soodna. A Lotka can take 25 passengers and 10 tons of cargo, and costs £800 per day to charter. A Soodna can take 40 passengers and 4 tons of cargo, and costs £1000 per day to charter. The agency needs capacity for at least 2000 passengers and 440 tons of cargo. How many of each type of boat should be chartered to minimise the agency's costs per day, and what is the minimum daily cost?

Solution

If we define x as the number of Lotkas they charter and y as the number of Soodnas they charter then their objective is to minimise:

$$800x + 1000y$$

Subject to the following constraints:

$$25x + 40y \geq 2000 \text{ (passengers)}$$
$$10x + 4y \geq 440 \text{ (cargo)}$$
$$x \geq 0 \text{ and } y \geq 0$$

Figure 2.22 shows the constraints and the feasible region. You can see that the feasible region is above the plotted constraints, which is typical for a minimisation problem. Note that it has no upper boundary.

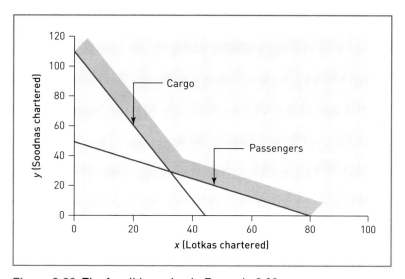

Figure 2.22 The feasible region in Example 2.23

The objective is to minimise cost, so a specific value of the objective function line that we plot is called an *iso-cost* line. The value we choose should be easy to divide by the coefficients in the objective function, in this case 800 and 1000, and should be large enough to position the line near the edges of the feasible region. The iso-cost line for £80,000 will meet both requirements; it is the dashed line in Figure 2.23.

Much of the iso-cost line passes through the feasible region, which means that the agency can charter sufficient capacity for £80,000, but much of the feasible region lies below the iso-cost line, which suggests they can do better than that. Finding the optimal solution means locating the point in the feasible region that is as far *below* the iso-cost line as possible as we are trying to find the lowest possible cost.

$\rightarrow$

Solution cont

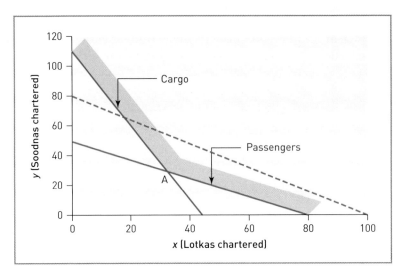

Figure 2.23 The feasible region and iso-cost line for £80,000 in Example 2.23

The lowest cost combination is represented by point A and entails chartering 32 Lotka and 30 Soodna boats. (You could verify these figures by solving simultaneously the equations that cross at point A.) Putting these figures into the objective function will give us the minimum total cost:

$$800 * 32 + 1000 * 30 = 25,600 + 30,000 = £55,600$$

At this point you may find it useful to try **Review question 2.12** at the end of the chapter.

2.6.2 The application and limitations of linear programming

If you want to read more about linear programming you may find Wisniewski (2001) helpful. Gass offers a range of pioneering uses of the technique (1970: 158–68), and Taha has a good general discussion of the types of use to which it can be put (1997: 39–53). Chvatal (1983) presents a thorough technical guide.

The optimal solution to a linear programming problem like the result we obtained in Example 2.23 is fixed or *static*. As long as the constraints and objective function stay the same so will the optimal solution.

In practice businesses operate in environments that are *dynamic*. The profit levels in an objective function may need to change because new competition is squeezing margins. Constraints may relax if new sources of supply can be located. To cope with such eventualities and answer questions beginning 'what if', we can use *sensitivity analysis* to explore around the optimal solution of a linear programming problem.

We have assumed that profits and resource use are both linear. But is this always so? In the case of profits, a company may offer discounts for purchases or enjoy discounts from suppliers for bulk orders or incur disproportionately higher selling costs in achieving high sales. All of these will alter profit margins. In the case of resource use a company may benefit from economies of scale at high volumes of output or have to meet new set-up costs if production is expanded beyond a certain point.

The products a company produces may compete with one another, implying that increasing production of one will reduce profit margins on others. Perhaps it would be costly or difficult to stop and start production in the short term. The technique takes no account of sequencing production. It may be desirable to have a sustained presence in a market even if it means making a loss, indicating that a company may well have several objectives rather than one. There may indeed be uncertainty about the market for the product.

Despite these shortcomings linear programming is an important technique. It is not only immensely useful in its own right, but it is the basis of other techniques of *mathematical programming* such as *integer programming*, which allows for options to be limited to whole numbers of products, and *transportation*, which is used to find optimal routes for goods to be moved between numbers of sources and numbers of destinations. You will find a good coverage of these in Taha (2008), and Bronson and Naadimuthu (1997).

REVIEW QUESTIONS

Answers to these questions are on pages 443–4. There are tips and hints to help you with them on the supporting website at **www.pearsoned.co.uk/buglear**, where you will also find the fully worked solutions.

☆☆★ Basic questions

2.1 The current system for allocating budgets for the local depots of a national office-cleaning company gives each depot a fixed sum of £35,000 plus an extra £500 for each corporate client in the area the depot covers.

(a) Express the budget allocation model as an equation and portray it graphically.

(b) Use your equation from (a) to work out the budget allocations for the following depots:
  (i) Ashford, which has 43 corporate clients
  (ii) Byfleet, which has 29 corporate clients
  (iii) Carlton, which has 66 corporate clients

(c) A new accountant at the company head office wants to alter the budget allocation model by reducing the fixed sum to £20,000 and increasing to £800 the extra for each corporate client. What changes will these alterations mean for the depots in (b)?

2.2 Solve each of the following pairs of simultaneous equations by elimination:

(a) $3x + 2y = 7$
     $x + y = 3$

(b) $5x + 3y = 19$
     $2x - y = 1$

(c) $2x + 7y = 3$
     $4x + 3y = 17$

(d) $6x + 6y = 27$
     $4x + 5y = 22$

2.3 The Pasuda Porcelain Company is about to launch a new luxury tableware range. The selling price for a set will be £90. To make the range the company has invested £319,000 in new equipment. Variable production costs will be £35 per set.

(a) What number of sets must it sell to break even?

(b) What profit will it make if it sells 6000 sets, and what is its safety margin?

2.4 A company making lubrication products for vintage cars produces two blended oils, Smazka and Neftianikov. They make a profit of £5 per litre of Smazka and £4 per litre of Neftianikov. A litre of Smazka requires 0.4 litres of heavy oil and 0.6 litres of light oil. A litre of Neftianikov requires 0.8 litres of heavy oil and 0.2 litres of light oil. The company has 100 litres of heavy oil and 80 litres of light oil. How many litres of each product should they make to maximise profits and what level of profit will they achieve?

☆★★ More testing questions

2.5 Following a crash, the owner of the Skorrost Courier Service has to purchase a new van. The make and model have already been decided, but there is a choice between petrol and diesel versions. The petrol version costs £10,000 to buy and will incur fuel costs of £0.12 per mile. The diesel version costs £11,000 and will incur fuel costs of £0.08 per mile. What is the minimum number of miles that the vehicle must travel to make purchasing the diesel version the more economical choice?

2.6 Samocat Automotive wants to move the production of its motor scooters to a purpose-built new plant that will cost £24m to construct. The scooters sell for £1850 and variable costs of production amount to £1100 per scooter.

(a) What is the break-even point for scooter production at the new plant?

(b) How will the break-even point change if the costs of the new plant rise to £30m?

2.7 Holly buys a hot dog stall for £360. In addition she has to pay a fixed charge of £200 to the local council to secure her pitch. She plans to sell her hot dogs at £1 each and the cost of preparing each one is £0.60.

(a) How many hot dogs will she need to sell to break even?

(b) She finds a supplier that can provide cheaper hot dog sausages, enabling her to save 10p per hot dog on the preparation cost. What effect does this have on the break-even point?

2.8 Roo Satellite Systems manufactures two types of broadcast receiving system, the 'Soap Dish' and the 'Houston'. The production process for each includes wiring, assembly and inspection, the times in hours required in each section are:

	Soap Dish	Houston
Wiring	3.0	3.0
Assembly	1.2	3.0
Inspection	0.4	0.5

Each month the company has 4500 hours of wiring labour, 3000 hours of assembly labour and 600 hours of inspection labour available. It makes a profit of £16 from each Soap Dish and £12 from each Houston. How many of each system should it make per month in order to maximise its profit, and what is the maximum profit?

★★★ Challenging questions

2.9 The Ooze Haircraft Corporation makes two brands of hair treatment: Volossy, which is produced under licence, and its own products Sedina. The company is in dispute with its supplier of colourant and solidifier as a result of which the supplier is no longer taking its orders. An alternative source of supply cannot be arranged for a month and Ooze must plan production for the month with its stock of 480 litres of colourant and 900 litres of solidifier.

A bottle of Volossy requires 3 millilitres of colourant and 9 millilitres of solidifier. A bottle of Sedina requires 4 millilitres of colourant and 6 millilitres of solidifier. The licensing agreement restricts production of Volossy to no more than 60,000 bottles a month and commitments to existing customers mean that at least 20,000 bottles of Sedina must be produced.

The company makes £0.40 profit per bottle of Volossy and £0.20 profit per bottle of Sedina.

(a) How many bottles of each product should it produce and how much profit will it make?

(b) Identify which constraints are tight and which are slack.

2.10 The Reklama Advertising Agency has a client who wants to buy TV advertisement slots. The client wants to reach the largest possible target audience within its budget of £3m. Reklama has been offered peak and off-peak slots by one network. These slots reach 14 million and 4 million people respectively. A peak slot costs £150,000 and an off-peak slot £50,000. The network has only 12 peak slots available within the timescale the client wants and they insist that at least 10 of the slots they sell to Reklama are off-peak.

(a) How many of each type of slot should Reklama book to maximise the audience for the client, and what is the maximum total audience?

(b) Independent analysis suggests that the audiences are actually 12 million for the peak and 5 million for the off-peak slots. How, if at all, should Reklama change its bookings in the light of this new information?

2.11 Tapachki & Sons produces handmade clogs in Lancashire. The company produces two types of clog, the Nelson and the Oldham. The profits per pair are £10 and £12 respectively. It employs two leather-cutters, four sole-makers and three stitchers. Each works a 40-hour week. The amount of labour time in hours required for a pair of each type of clog is:

	Nelson	Oldham
Leather-cutting	0.40	0.25
Sole-making	1.00	0.80
Stitching	0.80	0.50

Work out the optimal weekly production mix for the company to make the highest level of profit possible and state the maximum weekly profit they can expect.

2.12 Kolbasnik the pig farmer needs to add 36kg of protein and 10kg of vitamin to the pig feed. There are two possible additives. The cost and protein and vitamin content of each are:

Additive	Cost per kg (£)	Protein content	Vitamin content
Seelni-swine	20	60%	40%
Vita-sosiska	15	90%	10%

How much of each additive should be used in order to minimise costs, and what is the lowest cost of ensuring that the protein and vitamin requirements are met?

THE DEBRIEF

Key things to remember from this chapter

→ Linear equations can be used to model business costs.

→ Break-even analysis involves plotting costs and revenues to find the break-even point: the operating level at which costs equal revenues.

→ Linear programming is a technique for finding the best output combination where two or more products or services deliver different returns and use different amounts of the same resources.

→ Sensitivity analysis is a way of exploring linear programming results to investigate the impact of changes on the solution.

References

Boyer, C.B. (1968) *A history of mathematics*, New York: Wiley.

Bronson, R. and Naadimuthu, G. (1997) *Operations research* (2nd edn), New York: McGraw–Hill.

Chvatal, V. (1983) *Linear Programming*, New York: W.H. Freeman.

Ciftci, B. (2010) Break even point for the US domestic auto industry 2010 [online]. Available at http://ezinearticles.com/?Break-Even-Point-For-The-US-Domestic-Auto-Industry&id=3511968

Dantzig, G.B. (1999) *Linear programming and extensions*, Princeton, NJ: Princeton University Press.

Gass, S.I. (1970) *Illustrated Guide to Linear Programming*, New York: McGraw–Hill.

Heroux, R.L. and Wallace, W.L. (1975) 'New community development with the aid of linear programming', in H.M. Salkin and J. Saha (eds), *Studies in linear programming*, Amsterdam: North-Holland, pp. 309–22.

Reinhardt, U.E. (1973) 'Break-even analysis for Lockheed's Tri Star: An application of financial theory', *Journal of Finance*, 28(4), pp 821–38. Available at: http://www.estg.ipleiria.pt/files/350738_BREAKEVE_4628e59997e2a.pdf

Shanmugandandam, D. (2009) 'How to estimate break-even utilisation for spinning mills?', *The Indian Textile Journal*, Nov. 2009 [online]. Available at: http://www.indiantextilejournal.com/articles/FAdetails.asp?id=2422

Swart, W.W., Gearing, C., Vas, T. and Cann, G. (1975) 'Investment planning for the tourism sector of a developing country with the aid of linear programming', in H.M. Salkin and J. Saha (eds), *Studies in linear programming*, Amsterdam: North-Holland, pp. 227–49.

Symonds, G.H. (1955) *Linear programming: The solution of refinery problems*, New York: Esso Standard Oil Company.

Taha, H.A. (2008) *Operations research: An introduction* (8th edn), Harlow: Pearson Education.

Wardle, P.A. (1965) 'Forest management and operational research: a linear programming study,' *Management Science*, 11(10), pp. B260–B270.

Wisniewski, M. (2001) *Linear programming*, Basingstoke: Palgrave.

CHAPTER 3

Around the bend – dealing with the curves

CHAPTER OBJECTIVES

This chapter will help you to:

→ Deal with types of non-linear equations

→ Interpret and analyse non-linear business models

→ Apply differential calculus to non-linear business models

→ Use the Economic Order Quantity (EOQ) model for stock control

THE BARE BONES

What you will find in this chapter . . .

- The difference between equations of straight lines and equations of basic types of curves
- Quadratic and hyperbolic equations
- Identifying maximum and minimum points using differentiation
- The application of differential calculus to find optimal inventory decisions; the Economic Order Quantity (EOQ) model
- Review questions to test your understanding

. . . and on the supporting website (www.pearsoned.co.uk/buglear)

- Fully worked solutions to the review questions
- More review questions

Business use of the EOQ model

◆ The Economic Order Quantity (EOQ) model, based on non-linear analysis of business costs, is a well-established technique that dates back about a century. Its invention is usually credited to Ford Whitman Harris, who worked for Westinghouse, a US electrical goods company. In his 1913 article in the journal *Factory, The Magazine of Management* Harris described his approach to finding the optimal output levels for copper components at Westinghouse. He used mathematics to identify the least-cost production run by balancing storage costs with set-up costs (Harris, 1990).

◆ Some years later R.H. Wilson applied essentially the same model to find the optimal quantity to buy, rather than the optimal quantity to make (Wilson, 1934). Both models involve storage costs, but in the Wilson model these are balanced against the cost of making an order.

◆ According to Wilson the Western Electric Company developed a model similar to his some time earlier (Wilson, 1934: 122, fn4). Western Electric was then the largest electrical equipment manufacturer in the USA.

◆ Other US manufacturers adopted the EOQ model. It was attractive because it reduced the chances of being out of stock whilst avoiding holding too much. Berk and Berk (1993), who are highly critical of the model, concede that: 'For most of America's manufacturing history, industry has followed the economic ordering quantity (or EOQ for short) philosophy of inventory management' (Berk and Berk, 1993: 186).

◆ The EOQ model was a key benchmark for a US pioneer of just-in-time production management, Dennis Butt, manager of the US Kawasaki Heavy Industries plant. The plant manufactured motorcycles, jet skis and snowmobiles and had a troubled early history. Butt's approach is described in Schonberger (1982). Hall (1987) provides a fuller account of the improvements introduced at the Kawasaki factory.

3.1 Introduction

In the last chapter we looked at how linear equations, equations that represent straight lines, can be used to model business situations and solve business problems. Although important, their limitation is that the relationships they are used to model need to be linear for them to be appropriate. There are circumstances when this is not the case, for instance the models economists use to represent the connection between volume of production and cost per unit. In such a model economies of scale mean that the average cost of production per unit gets lower as output increases. The equation representing the situation would be non-linear and we might be interested in analysing it to find the least cost level of output.

In this chapter we will look at the features of basic non-linear equations and use them to analyse business operations. Following this we will consider how to find optimal points in non-linear business models using simple calculus. Later in the chapter you will meet the Economic Order Quantity (EOQ) model, a non-linear business model that organisations can use in determining their best stock ordering policy.

3.2 Simple forms of non-linear equations

One thing you might have noticed about the linear equations that featured in Chapter 2 was the absence of powers. We met terms like 60Q and 0.08x but not 3Q^2 or 3/x. The presence of powers (or for that matter other non-linear forms like sines and cosines, although we will not be concerned with them here) distinguishes a non-linear equation. In order to appreciate why, consider two possible relationships between x and y:

$$y = x$$
$$y = x^2$$

In the first case we have a linear equation: y will increase at the same pace with x however big x is. If x is 4, y will be 4. If x goes up to 5, so will y. If x is 10 and goes up to 11, so will y. Even if we had something that looks more elaborate, the effect on y that is caused by a change in x is the same, whether x is small or large.

EXAMPLE 3.1

A train operating company sets ticket prices using the equation:

$$y = 0.8 + 0.2x$$

where y is the ticket price in £ and x is the number of miles travelled.

To use this equation to work out the cost of a ticket for a 4-mile journey we simply substitute the 4 for x:

$$y = 0.8 + 0.2 * 4 = 0.8 + 0.8 = £1.60$$

The cost of a 5-mile journey will be:

$$y = 0.8 + 0.2 * 5 = 0.8 + 1.0 = £1.80$$

The cost of a 10-mile journey will be:

$$y = 0.8 + 0.2 * 10 = 0.8 + 2.0 = £2.80$$

The cost of an 11-mile journey will be:

$$y = 0.8 + 0.2 * 11 = 0.8 + 2.2 = £3.00$$

Notice that the difference an extra mile makes to the cost, £0.20, is the same whether the difference is between 4 and 5 miles or between 10 and 11 miles. This is because the equation is linear; the slope is constant so the rate at which the value of y changes when x is changed is the same however big or small the value of x. The equation is plotted in Figure 3.1.

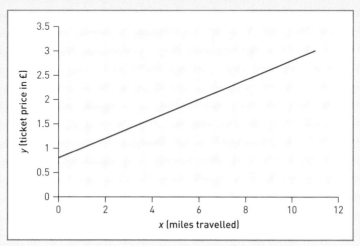

Figure 3.1 The ticket price equation in Example 3.1

If an equation is not linear the size of the change in y that comes about when x changes depends on how big x is. With a non-linear equation a one-unit increase in x when x is small may result in a modest change in y whereas a one-unit change in x when x is large may cause a much larger change in y.

EXAMPLE
3.2

The inventor of the new Slugar household labour-saving gadget prepares a business plan to attract investors for the venture. She anticipates that over time sales of the product will grow according to the equation:

$$y = 2 + x^2$$

where y is the sales in thousands of units and x is the number of years elapsed since the product launch.

Show the expected sales growth over nine years graphically.

Solution

To plot a linear equation you only need two points since the line is straight. To plot a non-linear equation we need a series of points that track the path of the curve that represents it. This entails calculating y values using the range of x values in which we are interested, in this case from 0 (product launch) to 9.

x (years since product launch)	y (sales in 000s)
0	2
1	3
2	6
3	11
4	18
5	27
6	38
7	51
8	66
9	83

These points are plotted in Figure 3.2.

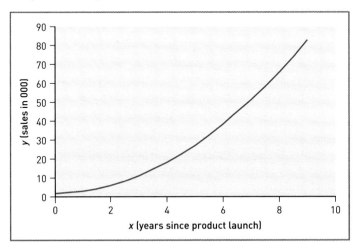

Figure 3.2 The sales growth equation in Example 3.2

An equation that includes x to the power two is called a *quadratic* equation, derived from the Latin word *quadrare*, which means to square. Similarly an equation that includes x to the power three is known as *cubic*. You may also meet reciprocal or *hyperbolic* equations. These include x to a negative power, for instance:

$$y = x^{-1} = 1/x$$

EXAMPLE 3.3

An economist studying the market for a certain type of digital camera concludes that the relationship between demand for the camera and its price can be represented by the equation:

$$y = 800/x$$

where y is the demand in thousands of units and x is the price in £.

To plot this equation we need a series of points such as the following:

x (price in £)	y (demand in 000s)
100	8.000
200	4.000
300	2.667
400	2.000
500	1.600
600	1.333
700	1.143
800	1.000

The equation is plotted in Figure 3.3.

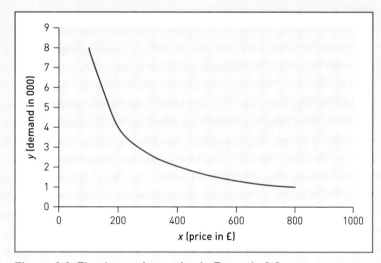

Figure 3.3 The demand equation in Example 3.3

Some curves feature peaks and troughs, known as maximum and minimum points respectively. These sorts of points are often of particular interest as they may represent a maximum revenue or a minimum cost: indeed later in the chapter we will be looking at how such points can be identified exactly using *calculus*.

EXAMPLE 3.4

The project manager of the new Machinar car plant suggests to the board of directors that the production costs per car will depend on the number of cars produced according to the equation:

$$y = x^2 - 6x + 11$$

where y is the cost per car in thousands of pounds and x is the number of cars produced in millions.

Example 3.4 cont

The equation is plotted in Figure 3.4.

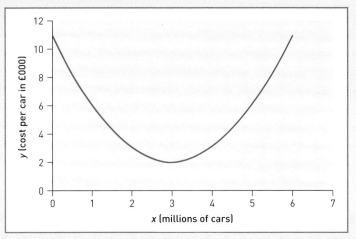

Figure 3.4 The curve representing the equation in Example 3.4

Figure 3.4 shows the sort of curve that economists might use to represent economies of scale. The minimum point represents the minimum cost per unit and the point below it on the horizontal axis the level of output that should be produced if the firm wants to produce at that cost. Other models economists use include maximum points.

EXAMPLE 3.5

Pustinia plc sells adventure holidays. The company accountant believes that the relationship between the prices at which it could sell its holidays and the total revenue that the firm could earn is defined by the equation:

$$y = -x^2 + 4x$$

where y is the total revenue in millions of pounds and x is the price per holiday in thousands of pounds.

The equation is plotted in Figure 3.5.

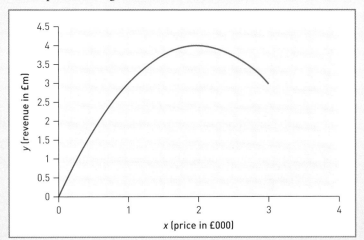

Figure 3.5 The curve representing the equation in Example 3.5

The maximum point in Figure 3.5 represents the maximum revenue the firm could earn and the point below it on the horizontal axis the price the firm should set in order to maximise its revenue.

At this point you may find it useful to try **Review questions 3.1 and 3.2** at the end of the chapter.

3.3 Basic differential calculus

We can find the approximate location of the maximum and minimum points in Examples 3.4 and 3.5 by studying the graphs carefully, marking the maximum or minimum point then identifying the values of x and y at which the point is located using the scales along the axes. At best this would give us an idea of where the point lies in relation to x and y, but it is almost impossible to pinpoint it accurately by inspecting the graph.

To find the precise location of maximum and minimum points we can use techniques from the branch of mathematics known as calculus. The word calculus conveys an impression of mystery to some people. In fact like the word calculate, it is derived from the Latin word *calculare* which means to reckon with little stones, a reflection of the method of counting in ancient times. *Calculare* is related to the Latin word *calx* which means a stone, the source of the word calcium.

Calculus has two branches, *differential* calculus and *integral* calculus. The former, which involves the process of *differentiation*, is about finding how curves change, whereas the latter is about finding areas underneath curves. Our concern in this section is with differentiation. If you would like to find out about integration you may find Croft and Davison (2006) helpful.

Differentiation is concerned with slopes, and slopes in equations reflect the way that the x variable changes the y variable. In a simple equation such as:

$$y = 5 + 3x$$

the slope, $+3$, tells us that an increase of one in the value of x will result in the value of y increasing by three. The slope is the *rate of change* in y that is brought about by a unit change in x. The other number in the equation, 5, is a constant or fixed component; whatever the value of x, the amount added to three lots of x to get y is always 5.

The slopes of more elaborate equations are not so straightforward. If you look carefully at Figure 3.5 you will see that the slope changes as the line moves from left to right across the graph. It begins by climbing upwards then reaches a maximum before altering course to descend. To start with it has a positive slope then at the maximum it has a zero slope, it 'stands still', and finally it has a negative slope. The nature of the slope therefore depends on where we are along the horizontal scale, in other words, the value of x. For the lower values of x the slope is positive, for the higher ones it is negative.

Figure 3.4 shows a similar pattern. To begin with the slope is downwards, or negative, then it 'bottoms out' at a minimum and finally becomes upwards, or positive. In this case the minimum is the point where the slope is momentarily zero: it is a point of transition between the negative-sloping and positive-sloping parts of the curve. The maximum point in Figure 3.5 is a similar point of transition, or *turning point* in the line.

Some of the equations you may have to differentiate will consist of several different parts, not necessarily all involving x. For the types of equation we shall look at you need only deal with the parts one at a time to reach the differential.

Note that in Example 3.6 the constant of 11 is not represented in the derivative. The derivative tells us how y changes with respect to x. When x changes so will x^2 and $6x$ but the constant remains 11.

EXAMPLE 3.6

The production cost equation for the car plant in Example 3.4 was:

$$y = x^2 - 6x + 11$$

where y is the cost per car in thousands of pounds and x is the number of cars produced in millions. Differentiate this equation.

Solution

$$\frac{dy}{dx} = 2x^{2-1} - 6x^{1-1} = 2x - 6$$

Applying differentiation

◆ Differentiation is a fairly mechanical procedure that is applied to all the components in an equation that contains x in one form or another. This might be in a simple form like $3x$, or perhaps raised to a power like x^2.

◆ To differentiate take the power to which x is raised and make it the new coefficient on x then reduce the original power by one.

◆ If we apply this to x^2 we get $2x$. Put the power, 2, in front of the x, to be the coefficient and reduce the power from 2 to 1, i.e. x^2 becomes $2x^{2-1}$, which is simply $2x$.

◆ For the equation $y = x^2$ this means that the rate y changes in response to a unit change in x, is $2x$. This is the difference that a change in x makes to y. It is known as the *differential* of the equation and written as dy/dx:

$$y = x^2 \qquad \frac{dy}{dx} = 2x$$

◆ You may find it helpful to think of *differ*entiation as finding such a *differ*ence. A more exact definition is that it is the marginal change in y resulting from an infinitely small marginal change in x.

◆ Because the differential is *derived* from the original equation it is also known as the *derivative*.

◆ If the expression already includes a coefficient for x, like $2x^2$, we multiply the power by the existing coefficient to give us the new coefficient:

$$y = 2x^2 \qquad \frac{dy}{dx} = 2 * 2x = 4x$$

◆ In this case the differential includes x, so the slope of the equation depends on the size of x; whatever x is, the rate of change in y arising from a change in x is four times the value of x.

◆ If we differentiate $3x$, the result is a constant, 3. In carrying out the differentiation of $3x$ remember that $3x$ is three times x to the power one so the power reduces to zero, and that any quantity raised to the power zero is one:

$$y = 3x^1 \qquad \frac{dy}{dx} = 1 * 3x^{1-1} = 3x^0 = 3$$

◆ In this case the slope is simply 3, and does not depend on the value of x; whether x is small or large the slope will always be 3.

◆ What about cases where x is raised to a negative power, such as the reciprocal of x, $1/x$? It helps if you remember that $1/x$ can be written as x^{-1}, $1/x^2$ as x^{-2} and so on.

◆ The process is the same, take the original power and multiply it by the existing coefficient then reduce the power by one:

$$y = \frac{2}{x^2} = 2x^{-2} \qquad \frac{dy}{dx} = (-2) * 2x^{-2-1} = -4x^{-3} = \frac{-4}{x^3}$$

◆ When you differentiate expressions like this remember that a constant divided by x raised to a positive power is simply the constant multiplied by x raised to the negative power. Taking x above the line makes the power negative.

At this point you may find it useful to try **Review question 3.5** at the end of the chapter.

When an equation has a turning point, a maximum or a minimum, we can use the differential to find the exact position of the turning point. At the turning point the slope is zero, in other words the differential, the rate of change in y with respect to x, is zero. Once we know the differential we can find the value of x at which the slope is zero simply by equating it to zero and solving the resulting equation.

EXAMPLE 3.7

Find the location of the turning point of the production cost equation for the car plant in Example 3.4.

Solution

From Example 3.6 we know that the derivative is:

$$\frac{dy}{dx} = 2x - 6$$

The value of x at which this is equal to zero is the position of the turning point along the horizontal axis:

$$2x - 6 = 0 \quad \text{so} \quad 2x = 6 \quad \text{and} \quad x = 3$$

The turning point is located above 3 on the horizontal axis. If you look back to Figure 3.4 you can see that the plotted curve reaches its minimum at that point. We can conclude that the minimum production cost per car will be achieved when 3 million cars are produced.

The cost per car at that level of production is something we can establish by inserting the value of x at the turning point into the original production cost equation:

$$y = x^2 - 6x + 11$$
$$\text{Minimum cost } = 3^2 - 6 * 3 + 11 = 9 - 18 + 11 = 2$$

If 3 million cars are produced the cost per car will be £2000.

In Example 3.7 we were able to refer back to Figure 3.4 and see from the graph that the turning point was a minimum. But what if the cost equation had not been plotted, how could we tell that it was a minimum and not a maximum? We take the derivative and differentiate again to produce a *second derivative*. If the second derivative is positive the turning point is a minimum, if it is negative the turning point is a maximum. It may help to think that after a minimum the only way to go is up, so the second derivative is positive whereas after a maximum the only way to go is down, so the second derivative is negative.

EXAMPLE 3.8

Find the second derivative of the production cost equation from Example 3.4.

Solution

The first derivative of the cost equation was:

$$\frac{dy}{dx} = 2x - 6$$

If we differentiate this again we get 2, which is of course positive, confirming that the turning point is a minimum.

To distinguish the second from the original or first derivative the notation representing it is:

$$\frac{d^2y}{dx^2} = 2$$

The inclusion of the 2s on the left-hand side signifies that the process of differentiation has been applied twice in reaching the result.

EXAMPLE 3.9

The total revenue for the firm in Example 3.5 was:

$$y = -x^2 + 4x$$

where y is the total revenue in millions of pounds and x is the price per holiday in thousands of pounds.

Find the first order derivative and use it to locate the turning point. Confirm that the turning point is a maximum by finding the second derivative, and work out the maximum revenue.

Solution

The first derivative is:

$$\frac{dy}{dx} = -2x + 4$$

The turning point location is:

$$-2x + 4 = 0$$
$$-2x = -4$$
$$x = 2$$

Revenue will be maximised when the price is £2000.
The second derivative is:

$$\frac{d^2y}{dx^2} = -2$$

Since the second derivative is negative, the turning point is a maximum.
The revenue when the price is £2000 is:

$$y = -(2)^2 + 4*2 = -4 + 8 = 4$$

The maximum revenue is £4 million.

At this point you may find it useful to try **Review questions 3.3, 3.6, 3.7, and 3.9** at the end of the chapter.

3.4 The Economic Order Quantity (EOQ) model

An important application of the calculus we looked at in the previous section occurs in a technique companies use to manage inventories, the Economic Order Quantity (EOQ) model. This model was developed to help companies manage stocks of materials and components, specifically by enabling managers to work out the quantity to order each time if they want to minimise costs.

Before we look at the model in detail it is worth reflecting on the reasons companies keep stocks or inventories. Most companies keep some stock of the materials they need for their operations; a bus company will probably have a stock of diesel fuel, a furniture maker will probably have a stock of wood. Such stocks are important because being without the material would disadvantage the company. On the other hand, if a company keeps a large amount of stock the costs of holding it are likely to be very high. The stock would have to be stored somewhere, perhaps under certain temperature or security constraints, and these facilities will have a cost.

For sound business reasons then a company will not want to run out of stock, yet will not want to hold too much. To resolve this, a company might consider placing small, regular orders with its supplier. Whilst this would mean that stock would never be very high, and hence stock-holding costs would be modest, it will probably cost money every time an order is made; a requisition may have to be processed, a delivery charge met, a payment authorised. The company would find that the more orders it made, the higher the cost of making them.

The dilemma it faces is to decide how much material should be ordered each time it places an order, the order quantity, so that the combined costs of making the orders and holding the stock, the *total stock cost*, is at a minimum. To see how this can be resolved we need to start by examining how the total stock-holding costs and the total order costs vary in relation to the quantity ordered.

We shall concentrate on the simplest EOQ model, in which we assume that the rate at which the material is used is constant. The amount used in one week is the same as the amount used in any other week. We also assume that once an order is placed the material will be delivered right away, there is no time lag for delivery. This latter assumption means that the company can wait until its stock runs out before placing an order for its replenishment.

Taking these assumptions together we can conclude that the highest amount that could be in stock would be the order quantity, which we will refer to as Q, the amount that is ordered every time an order is placed. The lowest level of stock will be zero, since it doesn't need to order more until it runs out. The rate of use is constant, so the fluctuations in the stock level will follow the pattern shown in Figure 3.6.

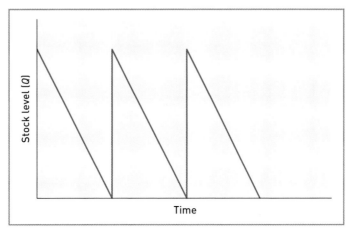

Figure 3.6 Stock levels over time

The repeating saw-tooth pattern that you can see in Figure 3.6 consists of a series of vertical lines each of which represents a delivery of the order quantity, Q. The stock level peaks at Q at the point of each delivery and then declines at a constant rate as the material is taken out of the store and used until the stock level is zero and another delivery comes in. The level of stock fluctuates between Q and 0. The even rate of depletion means that the average stock level will be midway between these extremes, half of Q.

If we use S to represent the cost of storing one unit of the material for a year then the cost of storing an average of $Q/2$ units in stock for a year, the total annual stock-holding cost, is:

$$\frac{SQ}{2}$$

The implication of this expression is that the bigger the order quantity, the larger the average stock and hence the greater the total annual stock cost.

The other part of the total stock cost is the total order cost, which again we shall express for a whole year. If we use Y to represent the number of units of the material that are used over a year, then the number of orders made during a year will be Y divided by the amount that is ordered on each occasion, the order quantity, Q:

$$\frac{Y}{Q}$$

If we use C to represent the cost of making an order, the total order cost for a year will be the number of orders multiplied by the order cost:

$$\frac{CY}{Q}$$

The implication of this expression is that the larger the order quantity the fewer the number of orders and hence the lower the total annual order cost. Note that the total order cost for the year is the total cost of making the orders and not the total purchase cost of the items bought. We will assume for the time being that the purchase cost of the individual items will be the same whether they are bought 10 at a time or a 100 at a time.

The total stock cost for a year is the sum of the total annual stockholding cost and the total annual order cost:

$$\text{Total stock cost} = \frac{SQ}{2} + \frac{CY}{Q}$$

This total cost will vary according to the size of Q, the order quantity. We assume that in any given context the other factors, the storage cost, annual demand and so on, are fixed, so we can focus on how big the order quantity should be if the total stock cost is to be minimised.

EXAMPLE 3.10

The Cheesty Cleaning Company uses 200 gallons of floor cleaner over a year. The company would like to find out how many gallons of floor cleaner it should order at a time to minimise its total stock costs. Storage costs are £50 per gallon per year and the order cost is £12.50.

Solution

The cost of storing one gallon of floor cleaner for a year is £50. We will begin by showing graphically how the total annual stock-holding costs are related to the quantity ordered.

$$\text{The total annual stock-holding cost} = \frac{SQ}{2} = \frac{50Q}{2} = 25Q$$

Using this expression we can work out the total annual stock-holding cost for a given order quantity, for instance if the order quantity is 5 the total annual stock-holding cost will be £125. The expression is plotted in Figure 3.7.

The cost of processing an order for a consignment of floor cleaner is £12.50. We can show graphically how the total annual order costs are related to the quantity ordered.

$$\text{Total annual order cost} = \frac{CY}{Q} = \frac{12.50 * 200}{Q} = \frac{2500}{Q}$$

From this we can find the total annual order cost for a given order quantity. If, say, the order quantity is 5 gallons the total annual order cost will be 2500/5, £500. The expression is plotted in Figure 3.8.

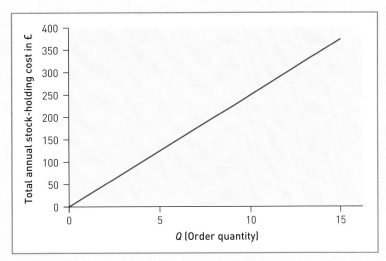

Figure 3.7 Total annual stock-holding cost and order quantity in Example 3.10

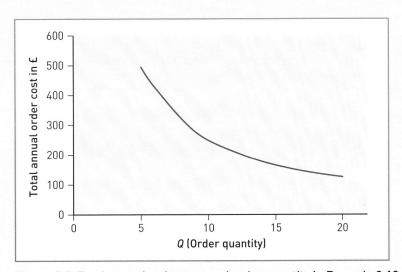

Figure 3.8 Total annual order cost and order quantity in Example 3.10

The company will have both stock-holding and order costs so we need to see how these costs combined, the total annual stock cost, are related to the order quantity.

$$\text{Total annual stock cost} = \frac{CY}{Q} + \frac{SQ}{2} = \frac{12.5 * 240}{Q} + \frac{50Q}{2} = \frac{3000}{Q} + 25Q$$

We can use this to determine the total annual stock costs for a specific order quantity, for instance 5 gallons:

$$\text{Total annual stock cost} = \frac{3000}{5} + 25 * 5 = 600 + 125 = £725$$

Figure 3.9 shows the relationship between total annual stock cost and order quantity.

The uppermost line in Figure 3.9 represents the total annual stock cost. The lower straight line represents the total annual stock-holding cost, the lower curve represents the total annual order cost. These lines reflect the fact that as the order quantity is increased the holding costs will rise and the order costs will fall.

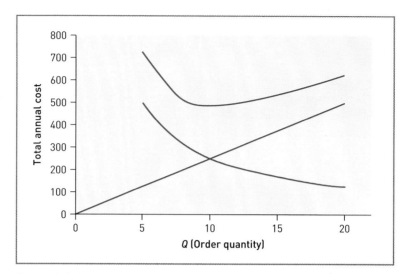

Figure 3.9 Total annual stock cost and order quantity in Example 3.10

If you look carefully at Figure 3.9 you will see that the curve representing the total annual stock cost does reach a minimum when the order quantity is about 10 gallons.

To ascertain the exact position of the minimum point of the total stock cost equation we can differentiate it:

$$\text{Total annual stock cost} = \frac{CY}{Q} + \frac{SQ}{2} = CYQ^{-1} + \frac{SQ}{2}$$

$$\frac{\text{dCost}}{\text{d}Q} = -CYQ^{-2} + \frac{S}{2} = \frac{CY}{Q^2} + \frac{S}{2}$$

At the minimum point of the curve this derivative will be equal to zero:

$$-\frac{CY}{Q^2} + \frac{S}{2} = 0$$

We can rearrange this to obtain a definition of the least-cost order quantity:

$$\frac{S}{2} = \frac{CY}{Q^2}$$

$$\frac{S}{2CY} = \frac{1}{Q^2}$$

$$\frac{2CY}{S} = Q^2$$

$$\sqrt{\frac{2CY}{S}} = Q$$

So Q, the least cost or *economic order quantity* is:

$$Q = \sqrt{\frac{2CY}{S}}$$

This is the EOQ model.

Of course, the square root can in theory be either positive or negative, but since only a positive order quantity makes practical sense the positive root is the only relevant one.

We can confirm that at this value of Q the total stock cost is at a minimum by finding the second derivative of the total stock cost equation:

$$\frac{d^2\text{Cost}}{dQ^2} = (-2) - CYQ^{-3} = \frac{CY}{Q^3}$$

If this is positive it means that the turning point is indeed a minimum. This will be the case because C, the order cost, and Y, the annual demand for the item, and all plausible values of Q will be positive so the second derivative will always have a positive value.

EXAMPLE 3.11

Use the EOQ model to find the order quantity Cheesty Cleaning Company should use in purchasing its supplies of floor cleaner, and find out the total annual stock costs it will incur by implementing that stock control policy.

Solution

The order cost, C, in this case is £12.50, the annual demand, Y, is 200 gallons and the stock holding cost, S, is £50. The economic order quantity is:

$$Q = \sqrt{\frac{2CY}{S}} = \sqrt{\frac{2 * 12.50 * 200}{50}} = \sqrt{\frac{5000}{50}} = \sqrt{100} = 10$$

To minimise its total stock costs the company should order 10 gallons of floor cleaner at a time.

The total annual stock costs when Q is 10 will be:

$$\text{Total annual stock cost} = \frac{CY}{Q} + \frac{SQ}{2} = \frac{12.50 * 200}{10} + \frac{50 * 10}{2} = 250 + 250 = £500$$

Note that in Example 3.11 both elements of the total annual stock cost, the total annual order cost and the total annual stock-holding cost, are equal when the amount ordered is the economic order quantity. This is no accident; in the EOQ model the minimum point of the total annual stock cost curve is always directly above the point where the lines representing the total annual order cost and the total annual stock-holding cost cross. You can see this if you look back at Figure 3.9.

At this point you may find it useful to try **Review questions 3.4, 3.8, 3.10 and 3.11** at the end of the chapter.

3.4.1 Limitations of the EOQ model

Despite its widespread use the EOQ model has serious limitations, both practical and attitudinal. The practical limitations arise because some of the assumptions on which the original EOQ model is based are simply unrealistic. The attitudinal limitations arise because in assuming certain factors are fixed, when in reality they are not, managers' attitudes to stock control could become too blinkered.

One assumption is that demand is constant. There are situations where this may be true, such as items used on a consistent basis by maintenance departments, but typically demand for items is variable rather than fixed. This is a criticism that Wilson himself recognised:

> This system is not intended to apply to stock control of style, seasonal, or perishable goods, but has found its chief application in the field of routine orders and of goods not subject to the vagaries of fashion.
>
> (Wilson, 1934: 116)

In practice, forecasting the demand for the item concerned became an important adjunct of the EOQ model.

Another assumption is that delivery of the item by the supplier is immediate. In practice there is a time lag between placing an order and its being delivered, and to complicate matters further the lag could vary. To allow for this uncertainty the idea of a reorder level, a volume of stock at which the placing of a new order was triggered, was built into the model.

More complications arise in applying the model when the costs of running out of stock are high, perhaps the loss of important customers. This is simply not catered for in the EOQ model. It also did not allow for the common practice of securing a discount for buying in bulk, as it excludes the purchase price of the item. Such a saving might be so significant that it outweighs the costs that are the focus of the EOQ model.

Most organisations of any size are likely to store many different items at many different locations, perhaps involving different costs of capital. This makes it very difficult to identify even an approximate storage cost for a given item.

The limitations in the EOQ model meant that it came to be regarded as a rough guide to stock control policy rather than the source of a definitive solution. This is in part because the optimal order policy shown in a diagram like Figure 3.9 is at the bottom of a shallow curve, particularly along the section to the right of the minimum point on the curve. This suggests that even if the actual order quantity is a little higher than the EOQ, the resulting increase in total stock costs is modest.

To find out more about the practical limitations of the EOQ model, and how it was adapted to deal with some of them, you may find Lewis (2001) helpful.

The philosophical limitations of the EOQ model relate not to the assumptions, but to the influence it had on stock control management. One of the things the model assumes is that delivery times are outside the control of the purchasing organisation, whereas it may be possible to negotiate the reduction or even eradication of delivery lags with a supplier, especially if the purchasing organisation is a particularly important customer for the supplier.

At this point you may find it useful to try **Review question 3.12**.

REVIEW QUESTIONS

Answers to these questions are on page 444. There are tips and hints to help you with them on the supporting website at **www.pearsoned.co.uk/buglear**, where you will also find the fully worked solutions.

☆☆★ Basic questions

3.1 Crassney Cosmetics Inc. produces a wide range of lipsticks, including the Soska shade that was worn by a woman involved in a political scandal during her testimony at the official inquiry into the affair. When a picture of her wearing the lipstick appeared in the newspapers demand for the lipstick rocketed. The sales in thousands of units, y, were related to the days since the publication of the picture, x, in the form

$$y = 3 + 2x^2$$

Plot the sales for the 10 days after the picture was published.

3.2 The Phoney Fabrics company recently launched a new protective product for mobile phones, the 'MobyCosy'. According to the Marketing department the sales revenue (in £m), y, depends on the price (in £), x, in the following way:

$$y = -3x^2 + 24x$$

Work out the sales revenues for prices of £1, £2, £3, £4 and £5. Use your results to sketch the line of the equation.

3.3 Glazoptics plc performs laser eye surgery in a purpose-built facility. The cost per operation in £, y, depends on the number of operations conducted per week, x, as follows:

$$y = \frac{x^2}{2} - 36x + 1300$$

(a) How many operations should be undertaken per week to minimise the cost per operation?
(b) Confirm by means of the second derivative that the cost equation will reach a minimum when this many operations are performed.
(c) What is the minimum cost per operation?

3.4 Doroga City Council Highways Department uses 2000 litres of yellow road paint a year at a constant rate. It costs the council £50 per litre to store the paint for a year. Each time a purchase order for paint is processed the cost to the council is £20. What is the optimal order quantity of paint that will allow the council to minimise its total stock cost?

☆★★ More testing questions

3.5 Differentiate each of the equations listed below on the left and match your answers to the derivatives listed on the right.

(i) $y = 3x$

(a) $\dfrac{dy}{dx} = \dfrac{-1}{x^2}$

(ii) $y = 4x^2$

(b) $\dfrac{dy}{dx} = 2x^3$

(iii) $y = 2x^3$

(c) $\dfrac{dy}{dx} = 8x$

(iv) $y = \dfrac{1}{x}$

(d) $\dfrac{dy}{dx} = 2x + 4$

(v) $y = \dfrac{x^4}{2}$

(e) $\dfrac{dy}{dx} = \dfrac{-10}{x^3} - 1$

(vi) $y = 3x^3 + 2$

(f) $\dfrac{dy}{dx} = 3$

(vii) $y = x^2 + 4x$

(g) $\dfrac{dy}{dx} = 6x^2$

(viii) $y = \dfrac{5}{x^2} - x$

(h) $\dfrac{dy}{dx} = \dfrac{-2}{3x^2} + 10x$

(ix) $y = \dfrac{2}{3x} + 5x^2$

(i) $\dfrac{dy}{dx} = 16x^3 + 9x^2$

(x) $y = 4x^4 + 3x^3$

(j) $\dfrac{dy}{dx} = 9x^2$

3.6 The Mashinar Garage provides an exhaust system replacement service for the Bistri car. The revenue from this operation in thousands of pounds, y, depends on the price of the service in £, x, in line with the equation:

$$y = -\frac{x^2}{5} + 10x - 90$$

(a) How much should it charge for this service to maximise its revenue from it?

(b) Find the second derivative and use it to show that the revenue equation will be at a maximum at the price established in (a).

(c) What is the maximum revenue it can expect?

3.7 Peridatt Audio manufactures specialist sound amplifiers. The company has identified the following expressions to represent the demand for its products and the total cost of its operations:

$$\text{Price (£)} = 500 - 3x$$

$$\text{Cost (£)} = 150 + 20x + x^2$$

where x is the number of amplifiers produced and sold. (Production is to order only.)

(a) Determine the profit equation for the company.

(b) Use the profit equation to find the profit maximising level of output and price, and the optimum profit.

(c) Find the second derivative of the profit equation and use it to confirm that the output level in (b) does occur at a maximum.

3.8 The annual demand for dog biscuits at Dogwatch Security amounts to 1690kg. The cost of the manager going to collect a supply of dog biscuits in her company car is reckoned to be £40 per trip. The cost of storing the biscuits is estimated to be £8 per kilogram per year. The dog biscuits come in sealed packs and last indefinitely. How many kilograms of dog biscuits should the manager collect at a time to minimise the total stock costs?

★★★ Challenging questions

3.9 Avaria Autosports sells rally-driving adventure weekends to companies looking for incentive gifts for staff. Careful study of its past sales suggests that the price per weekend is based on the number of weekends sold, x, in line with:

$$\text{Price (£)} = 635 - 3x$$

Their costs depend on the weekends sold according to the expression:

$$\text{Cost (£)} = 450 + 5x + \frac{x^2}{2}$$

(a) Obtain the profit equation for the company.

(b) Use this equation to find the number of sales and the price at which it would maximise its profit, as well as the maximum profit.

(c) By means of the second derivative of the profit equation demonstrate that the sales level in (b) is at a maximum point on the profit equation.

3.10 The kitchen at a children's hospital used 12,800kg of ice cream last year and expects to use approximately the same amount this year. The storage costs incurred by keeping 1kg of ice cream in the freezer for a year are estimated to be £7. The cost of processing an order to the supplier is £28.

(a) Use the EOQ formula to ascertain how much ice cream (to the nearest kg) should be ordered each time to minimise costs.

(b) Scrapping obsolete equipment means that maximum storage capacity has recently been reduced to 350kg. Will this be sufficient for the stocks that will accumulate if your recommendation in (a) is implemented?

(c) The storage cost has been recalculated to be £10 per kilogram per year. What is the new EOQ?

3.11 Aptieka Chemicals uses 80 litres of a solvent per week in a continuous process. Storing the solvent in accordance with fire and safety requirements costs £5 per litre per annum. The cost of administering an order is £26.

(a) Assuming the process operates for all 52 weeks of the year, how much of the solvent should the company order each time if total stock costs are to be minimised?

(b) How will a 25% increase in the price of the solvent affect the EOQ?

3.12 The manager of a garden centre expects that sales of barbecue fuel will reach 16,000 bags for the year. The cost of keeping a bag of barbecue fuel in stock for a year is put at £5 and the administrative and other costs associated with implementing an order amount to £25.

(a) Use the EOQ model to advise the proprietor how many bags should be ordered each time an order is made.

(b) What will be the average stock level if the proprietor does as you advise in (a)?

(c) In the light of the assumptions on which the EOQ model is based, how valid is its application to this case?

THE DEBRIEF

Key things to remember from this chapter

→ Some business costs vary in non-linear ways with output or activity level.

→ Differential calculus is a useful tool for finding at what output or activity level costs are at a minimum.

→ In the EOQ model differential calculus is used to find the quantity that should be purchased to minimise costs.

→ Although the original EOQ model has serious shortcomings it is the foundation of much more sophisticated approaches to stock control so understanding EOQ is probably the best way of understanding key tools of modern inventory management.

References

Berk, J. and Berk, S. (1993) *Total Quality Management*, New York: Sterling.

Croft, A. and Davison, R. (2006) *Foundation Maths* (4th edn), Harlow: Prentice Hall.

Hall, R.W. (1987) 'Kawasaki USA', in C.A. Voss (ed.), *Just-in-time Manufacture*, Bedford: IFS, pp. 339–64.

Harris, F.W. (1990) 'How many parts to make at once', *Operations Research*, 38(6), pp. 947–50.

Lewis, C. (2001) *Inventory Control*, Basingstoke: Palgrave.

Schonberger, R.J. (1982) *Japanese Manufacturing Techniques*, New York: Macmillan.

Wilson, R.H. (1934) 'A scientific routine for stock control', *Harvard Business Review*, 13, pp. 116–28.

CHAPTER 4

Filling up – fuelling quantitative analysis

CHAPTER OBJECTIVES

This chapter will help you to:

→ Understand key technical terms
→ Distinguish between primary and secondary data
→ Recognise different types of data
→ Arrange data using basic tabulation and frequency distributions

THE BARE BONES

What you will find in this chapter . . .

- Definitions of words that are commonly used in quantitative analysis
- The difference between 'first-hand' and 'second-hand' data
- NOIR: how to distinguish between nominal, ordinal, interval and ratio data
- Using classification methods to organise qualitative and quantitative data
- Comparing sets of data using grouped frequency distributions
- Review questions to test your understanding

. . . and on the supporting website (www.pearsoned.co.uk/buglear)

- How to use EXCEL, Minitab and SPSS to arrange data
- Fully worked solutions to the review questions
- More review questions

4.1 Introduction

In previous chapters we focused on techniques or models involving single values that are known with certainty. Examples of these are break-even analysis and linear programming, which we looked at in Chapter 2, and the EOQ model featured in Chapter 3. In break-even analysis the revenue per unit, the fixed cost and the variable cost per unit are in each case a specified single value. In linear programming we assume that both profit per unit and resource usage are constant amounts. In the EOQ model the order cost and the stock-holding cost per unit are each known single values. Because these types of models involve values that are fixed or *predetermined* they are called *deterministic* models.

Deterministic models can be useful means of understanding and resolving business problems. Their reliance on known single value inputs makes them relatively easy to use but is their key shortcoming. Companies simply cannot rely on a figure such as the amount of raw material used per unit of production being a single constant value. In practice, such an amount may not be known with certainty, because it is subject to chance variation. Because of this company managers may well need to study the variation and incorporate it within the models they use to guide them. Studying variation is what the subject of *Statistics* is all about.

Models that use input values that are uncertain rather than certain, values that are subject to chance variation rather than known, are called *probabilistic* models, after the field of *probability*, which involves the measurement and analysis of chance. We shall be dealing with probability in later chapters.

Before you can use probability to reflect the chance variation in business situations you need to know how to get some idea of the variation. To do this we have to start by ascertaining where relevant information might be found. Having identified these sources you need to know how to arrange and present what you find from them in forms that will help you understand and communicate the variation. In order to do this the right way it is important that you know the different types of data you may meet.

The purpose of this chapter is to acquaint you with the essential preliminaries for studying variation. We will start with definitions of key statistical terms, before considering sources of data and the different types of data. After that we shall look at ways of arranging data.

4.2 Important statistical terms

There are several important words that you will find mentioned frequently in this and subsequent chapters. They are listed in Table 4.1 with their definitions.

Table 4.1 Key statistical terms

Term	Definition
Data	Facts; things that are known or 'given'. These might consist of numbers, e.g. employees' wages, or categories, e.g. employees' job titles.
Data set	The names of the variables studied in an investigation and all observed values of them that were collected.
Distribution	The pattern formed when observations of a variable are arranged by size.
Element	A single component of the population, e.g. one of the cars sold at a car showroom.
Observed value/ observation	An *actual* value of a variable. Conventionally depicted by a lower case letter with a suffix, e.g. $x_1 = 87$ means that the number of incoming calls in the first hour was 87. If 101 were received in the second hour, $x_2 = 101$.
Population	All the things/people/occurrences of interest in an investigation, e.g. all the cars sold at a showroom.
Random	Chance or unplanned.
Random sample	A set of elements drawn from a population using a random process.
Random variable	A variable whose values occur by chance. Sales volume per month at a car showroom is a random variable. The days in each month is a variable (31 for some, 30 for others etc.) but its values are fixed not random.
Sample	A set of elements drawn from a population.
Value	A *possible* quantity of a variable, e.g. 123 could be the number of incoming calls to a call centre in one hour.
Variable	Something that varies. Conventionally represented by a capital letter, e.g. X is the number of incoming calls to a call centre per hour.

A typical quantitative investigation of a business problem might involve defining the *population* and specifying the *variables* to be studied. Following this a *sample* of *elements* from the *population* is selected and *observations* of the *variables* for each element in the sample recorded. Once the *data set* has been assembled work can begin on arranging and presenting the data so that the patterns of variation in the *distributions* of values can be examined.

At this point you may find it useful to try **Review question 4.1** at the end of the chapter.

4.3 Sources of data

The data that forms the basis of an investigation might be collected at first hand in response to a specific problem. This type of data, collected by direct observation or measurement, is known as *primary data*. The procedures used to gather primary data are surveys, experiments and observational methods. A survey might involve asking consumers their opinion of a product. A series of experiments might be conducted on products to assess their quality. Observation might be used to ascertain the hazards at building sites.

The advantages of using primary data is that they should match the requirements of those conducting the investigation and be up to date. The disadvantages are that gathering such data is both costly and time-consuming.

An alternative might be to find data that has already been collected by someone else. This is known as *secondary data*. A company looking for data for a specific study will have access to internal sources of secondary data, but as well as those there are a large number of external sources; government statistical publications, company reports, academic and industry publications, and specialist information services such as the Economist Intelligence Unit. The advantages of using secondary data are that it is usually easier and cheaper to obtain. The disadvantages are that it could be out of date and may not be entirely suitable for the purposes of the investigation.

4.4 Types of data

Collecting data is usually not an end in itself. Collected data is in a 'raw' form, a state that might lead someone to refer to it as 'meaningless data'. The next stage is to begin turning data into *information*, literally to enable it to *inform* us about the issue being investigated.

There is a wide range of techniques that you can use to organise, display and represent data. Selecting which to use depends on the nature of data. The type of the raw material you are working with determines your choice of tools. Scissors are fine for cutting paper but no good for cutting wood. A saw will cut wood but is useless for cutting paper. It is therefore essential that you understand the type of data you want to analyse before embarking on the analysis. In this section we will look at ways of distinguishing the different types of data.

The different data types arise because of the different ways of gathering facts. Data takes the form it does because in some cases things can be clearly categorised but in other cases data is collected by counting or measuring on a scale.

EXAMPLE 4.1

Individual shareholders in a large oil business are generally regarded as 'rich', but what exactly does 'rich' mean?

Solution

To investigating this we might:

- *categorise* the shareholders by socio-economic class
- *count* the homes they own
- *measure* their annual salaries.

Perhaps the most important way of contrasting data types is on the basis of the scales of measurement used in obtaining them. The acronym *NOIR* stands for *Nominal, Ordinal, Interval, Ratio*; the four basic data types. Nominal is the 'lowest' form of data, which contains the least amount of information. Ratio is the 'highest' form of data, which contains the most amount of information.

The word nominal comes from the same Latin root as the word name. Nominal data is data that consists solely of names or labels. These labels might be numeric, such as a bank account number, or they might be non-numeric, such as gender. Nominal data can be categorised using the labels themselves to establish, for instance, the number of males and females. It is possible to represent and analyse nominal data using proportions and modes (the modal category is the one that contains the most observations), but carrying out more sophisticated analysis such as calculating an average is inappropriate; for example, adding a set of telephone numbers together and dividing by the number of telephone numbers to get an average would be meaningless.

Like nominal data, ordinal or 'order' data consist of labels that can be used to categorise the data, but order data can also be ranked. Examples of ordinal data are academic grades and finishing positions in a horse race. An academic grade is a label (an 'A' grade student) that also belongs to a ranking system ('A' is better than 'B'). Because ordinal data contains more information than nominal data we can use a wider variety of techniques to represent and analyse it. As well as proportions and modes we can also use *order statistics*, such as identifying the middle or *median* observation. However, any method involving arithmetic is not suitable for ordinal data because although the data can be ranked the intervals between the ranks are not consistent. For instance, the difference between the horse finishing first in a race and the one finishing second is one place. The difference between the horse finishing third and the one finishing fourth is also one place, but this does not mean that there is the same distance between the third- and fourth-placed horses as there is between the first- and second-placed horses.

Interval data consist of labels and can be ranked, but in addition the intervals are measured in fixed units so the differences between values have meaning. It follows from this that unlike nominal and ordinal, both of which can be either numeric or non-numeric, interval data is always numeric. Because interval data is based on a consistent numerical scale, techniques using arithmetical procedures can be applied to it. Temperatures measured in degrees Fahrenheit are interval data. The difference between 30° and 40° is the same as the difference between 80° and 90°.

What distinguishes interval data from the highest data form, ratio data, is that interval data is measured on a scale that does not have a meaningful zero point to 'anchor' it. The zero point is arbitrary, for instance 0° Fahrenheit does not mean a complete lack of heat, nor is it the same as 0° Celsius. The lack of a meaningful zero also means that ratios between the data are not consistent, for example 40° is not half as hot as 80°. (The Celsius equivalents of these temperatures are 4.4° and 26.7°, the same heat levels yet they have a completely different ratio between them.)

Ratio data has all the characteristics of interval data – it consists of labels that can be ranked as well as being measured in fixed amounts on a numerical scale. The difference is that the scale has a meaningful zero and ratios between observations are consistent. Distances are ratio data whether we measure them in miles or kilometres. Zero kilometres and zero miles mean the same – no distance. Ten miles is twice as far as five, and their kilometre equivalents, 16 and 8, have the same ratio between them.

| EXAMPLE 4.2 | Identify the data types of the variables in Example 4.1. |

| Solution | The socio-economic classes of shareholders are ordinal data because they are labels for the shareholders and they can be ranked. |

The numbers of homes owned by shareholders and the incomes of shareholders are both ratio data. Four homes are twice as many as two, and £60,000 is twice as much income as £30,000.

At this point you may find it useful to try **Review question 4.9** at the end of the chapter.

Data can be described as either *qualitative* or *quantitative*. The former is based on characteristics that are observed and are always either nominal or ordinal. The analysis of qualitative data is based on the categories by which the characteristics can be grouped. Quantitative data on the other hand arises from measurement or counting and is always interval or ratio. The analysis of quantitative data is based on the scale against which the measurements are made.

Quantitative data can be either *discrete* or *continuous*. Quantitative data is discrete if the set of possible values it can take is limited. This is because it arises from measuring on a scale that comprises discrete stages. In this context the word discrete means separate or distinct.

When quantitative data is discrete it is for one of three reasons. It may be data that can only have some values because others are impossible. An example is the number of cars a dealer sells each week. This might 35 in one week and 27 in a second week: 31.4 car sales is impossible as 0.4 of a car makes no sense. This data is discrete by definition.

The second case is where it has become customary for data to have only some of the values that could conceivably occur. An example is the volumes by which draught beers are sold in UK pubs. There is no theoretical reason why a customer cannot order a quarter of a pint of beer, but it would be impractical; they would be told that the minimum amount that can be served is half a pint.

The third case is where it is convenient for values that don't actually have to be discrete to be rounded. People usually do this when giving their age; they quote the age they reached at their last birthday. Weather forecasts give temperatures that are rounded up or down to the nearest degree. The distances given on road signs are to the nearest kilometre or mile. Such data are actually *continuous*.

Typically discrete data consists of values in whole numbers but there are exceptions. A car park will contain a whole number of cars, but the sizes of women's garments in the UK are even numbers.

A good way of remembering the difference between discrete and continuous data is to think of discrete data as having gaps between the possible values, which is the reason it is also known as *discontinuous* data. Continuous data is not constrained in this way; it is measurements made using continuous scales, scales that have no gaps like weight or height. The only thing that limits the degree of precision of continuous data is the technology of the measurement process. If we weigh materials using kitchen scales we will not get the same precision as if we use laboratory equipment.

In the same way as data might be discrete or continuous, variables can be either discrete or continuous. The difference is straightforward; the values of a *discrete variable* are discrete and the values of a *continuous variable* are continuous.

EXAMPLE 4.3

A motoring website uses the variables listed below to define vehicles:

Vehicle type e.g. saloon, SUV

Number of passengers that can be carried

Gearbox type: Automatic or manual

Fuel efficiency in miles per gallon.

Which of these variables are qualitative and which quantitative? Which quantitative variables are discrete and which continuous?

Solution

Vehicle and gearbox types are qualitative; number of passengers and fuel efficiency are quantitative.

Number of passengers is discrete, fuel efficiency is continuous.

At this point you may find it useful to try **Review question 4.5** at the end of the chapter.

Your first experience of data analysis will most likely be limited to studying the observations of just one variable. This is known as *univariate* analysis, where the prefix uni- means one, as in unicycle. In later work you will probably also want to analyse one variable in relation to another, e.g. to investigate the link between the distance a vehicle travels and the fuel it uses.

Work of this type is known as *bivariate* analysis, where the prefix bi- means two, as in biped and bicycle. You may also meet *multivariate* analysis, which involves exploring relationships between more than two variables.

Data is sometimes referred to as either *hard* or *soft*. Hard data is facts, measurements or characteristics arising from situations that actually exist or were in existence. Temperatures recorded at a weather station and the nationalities of tourists are examples of hard data. Soft data is about beliefs and attitudes. Asking consumers what they know about a product or how they feel about an advertisement will yield soft data. The implication of this distinction is that hard data can be subjected to a wider range of quantitative analysis. Soft data is at best ordinal and therefore offers less scope for quantitative analysis.

A further distinction you need to know is between *cross-section* and *time series* data. Cross-section data is data collected at the same point in time or based on the same period of time. Time series data consist of observations collected at regular intervals over time. The volumes of wine produced in European countries in 2010 are cross-section data whereas the volumes of wine produced in Italy in the years 2001 to 2010 are time series data.

At this point you may find it useful to try **Review question 4.6** at the end of the chapter.

4.5 Arranging data

The arrangement or *classification* of data in some sort of systematic way is the first stage you should take in transforming data into information, and hence getting it to 'talk to you'. The way you approach this depends on the type of data you wish to analyse.

4.5.1 Classifying qualitative data

Dealing with qualitative data is fairly simple if the number of categories involved is small. It is more complicated with more categories but merging them makes the job easier.

The most basic form of classification of qualitative data involves *tabulation*, literally arranging it in a table. Tabulation is a way of summarising data so such a table is called a *summary table*. There are two components; the categories of the data, and the numbers of people or items in each category. This is the category's *frequency*. Actually, compiling a summary table is no more than counting how many elements in the study fall into each category.

EXAMPLE 4.4

Imagine you have been asked to investigate the numbers of different types of retailers in a city that sell watches.

You draw up a list of shops that sell watches by using internet directories. The list is too long to be presented as it is, so compiling a summary table, with the types of shops and the numbers of them, is a better way of conveying your findings.

Table 4.2 Numbers of shops selling watches by type of shop

Type of shop	Frequency	Relative frequency (%)
Jewellery shops	12	27.9
Fashion shops	11	25.6
Superstores	8	18.6
Other	12	27.9
Total number of outlets	43	100.0

Note that the types of shop in Table 4.2 are examples of *qualitative* data; each type of shop is qualitatively different from the other types of shop.

To keep Table 4.2 to a reasonable size there is a catch-all category, 'Other', which includes every other type of shop selling watches, e.g. sports stores and gift shops.

In the third column of Table 4.2 the *relative frequency* of each type of shop is listed. This is the number of shops of that kind as a percentage of all the shops. A relative frequency is a more convenient way of expressing the proportion of shops in each of the categories of shop; it is easier to say that 25.6% are fashion shops rather than 11/43rds of them are fashion shops, although they have the same meaning.

Summary tables can be used to summarise two sets of categories or *factors*. The aim of doing this is usually to investigate possible links between the factors. These two-way tables are called *contingency tables* as they are means of finding if one factor is connected to, or *contingent* upon, the other.

EXAMPLE 4.5

Three holiday companies each sell package tours through high street travel agents and on the internet. The following contingency table shows the bookings of each company by sales channel:

Table 4.3 Holiday bookings by sales channel

Company	Travel agent bookings	Internet bookings	Total bookings
Atdikat	511	170	681
Booyaneet	264	295	559
Canniculae	313	489	802
Total	1088	954	2042

The figures in Table 4.3 reveal a considerable contrast between the companies with Canniculae taking the majority of its booking through the internet and Atdikat taking most of its bookings through agents.

At this point you may find it useful to try **Review questions 4.2, 4.7 and 4.10** at the end of the chapter.

4.5.2 Classifying quantitative data

The nature of quantitative data is different from qualitative data so there are different ways of classifying them. Having said that, the best way to classify simpler sets of quantitative data is the same as the approach we used to classify qualitative data. This is the case if we are dealing with a discrete quantitative variable with very few feasible values. We use the values as the basis for classifying the data in exactly the same way as we used the categories in classifying qualitative data. List the feasible values and count how many times each occurs. Because the resulting table shows how often, or frequently, each value in the distribution crops up it is known as a *frequency distribution*.

We can use Table 4.4 to display the data in Example 4.6 as there are so few different values that occur; 0, 1, 2 and 3. Sometimes there are simply too many different values for this method of tabulation. Suppose in Example 4.6 there were customers who spent all day in the

EXAMPLE
4.6

A department store café offers free refills when customers purchase hot beverages. The numbers of refills taken by 20 customers were:

0 1 3 1 2 0 2 2 0 1 0 3 1 0 1 2 1 1 0 2

These figures can be tabulated as follows:

Table 4.4 Number of hot beverage refills taken

Number of refills	Number of customers
0	6
1	7
2	5
3	2
Total number of customers	20

café and drank up to 20 cups of coffee each. To accommodate such relatively large values the table would have too many rows to be of use.

At this point you may find it useful to try **Review question 4.3** at the end of the chapter.

The solution would be to *group* the observations into a smaller number of categories or *classes*. This entails producing a *grouped* frequency distribution, a table that specifies how may observations there are in each of the classes.

EXAMPLE
4.7

The numbers of package holidays sold in one week by each of 27 independent travel agents were:

46 13 23 6 7 31 49 11 13

47 5 36 16 71 3 26 4 95

33 11 57 9 73 19 22 34 67

Produce a grouped frequency distribution to present these data.

Solution

Holidays sold	Frequency
0–19	12
20–39	7
40–59	4
60–79	3
80–99	1
Total frequency	27

At this point you may find it useful to try **Review question 4.4** at the end of the chapter.

Producing a grouped frequency distribution requires a little judgement. There are many different lists of classes you might use for a given data set but not all of them will be appropriate. To be viable the set of classes you use must have classes that don't overlap or have gaps between them. As well as this the first one must begin at a value lower than the lowest observed value and the last one must end with a value higher than the largest observed value.

To illustrate the first of these rules consider using classes 0–20, 20–40, 40–60 and so on in Example 4.7. This wouldn't work because we could well have a value of 20, which we could put into the first (0–20) or second (20–40) class, or even both. Such ambiguity, which arises because of the overlaps between the classes, is something to avoid.

As far as the second rule is concerned the classes in Example 4.7 do have gaps between them; the first class ends at 19, the second starts with 20 and so on. This does not break the second rule because the gaps are not 'real' in the sense that there is no possible value that could fall into the gaps. The number of holidays sold is discrete; they must be a whole number. A value like 19.2, which would fall in the gap between the first two classes, is simply impossible.

The third rule is that the range between the beginning of the first class and the end of the last must be wider than the range of values. The classes used in Example 4.7 do meet this requirement; the first class starts at zero but the smallest value is 3 and the last class ends at 99 and the largest value is 95.

As a general guide when you look at a grouped frequency distribution it must be absolutely clear where every possible value goes. Each feasible observation should belong to one and only one class. For the avoidance of any doubt there is a general purpose type of class set that you can use, based on the wording 'and under'. Applying this to Example 4.7 we would use:

0 and under 20
20 and under 40
40 and under 60
60 and under 80
80 and under 100.

This set of classes do not overlap, for instance 20 must go in the class '20 and under 40' not '0 and under 20'. There are no gaps; the classes are seamless.

These rules are particularly important for continuous quantitative data. You can use the 'and under' formulation but if you don't you must ensure each class's beginning and ending is given to the same level of precision as the observations themselves.

EXAMPLE 4.8

'Meelar' shower gel is sold in 250ml bottles. A quality control check involved measuring precisely the contents (in millilitres) of a sample of 30 bottles. The results were:

250.30 250.05 250.06 249.82 250.09 249.85 249.98 249.97 250.28 250.01
249.92 250.03 250.17 249.95 250.23 249.92 250.05 250.11 250.02 250.06
250.21 250.04 250.12 249.99 250.19 249.89 250.05 250.11 250.00 249.92

Arrange these figures in a grouped frequency distribution.

Solution

Shower gel (ml)	Frequency
249.80–249.89	3
249.90–249.99	7
250.00–250.09	11
250.10–250.19	5
250.20–250.29	3
250.30–250.39	1
Total frequency	30

SELF-ASSEMBLY GUIDE

What classes should I use?

◆ The number of classes you use is linked to the key question of how wide they will be.

◆ The fewer classes you use the wider they will be and conversely the more classes you use the narrower they will be.

◆ Few, wide classes give only a basic idea of the distribution of the observations but a lot of narrow classes may give so much detail we don't get the big picture.

◆ What is the right balance? To get a general idea find the square root of the number of observations in the data set.

◆ In Example 4.7 we had 27 observations. The square root, $\sqrt{27} = 5.2$ to one decimal place. This is between 5 and 6. We have to round this up or down as the number of classes must be a whole number; 0.2 of a class doesn't make sense. The result, 5.2 is nearer to 5 than to 6 so it makes sense to round it down to 5.

◆ There are five classes in Example 4.7, the sort of number our square root method suggests.

◆ Now the number of classes is decided, how wide should they be?

◆ Unless there is good reason to do otherwise make all classes equally wide. This makes it much easier to do further work with your distribution.

◆ Your classes must collectively include every observed value from the lowest to the highest. This is useful for determining the class width.

◆ Take the smallest observed value away from the largest. The resulting difference is the range of the distribution.

◆ Find the minimum possible width of your classes by dividing the range by the number of classes you have decided to use.

◆ In Example 4.7 the range is $95 - 3 = 92$. If we divide this by 5 we get 18.4. This means that if we want a set of five equally wide classes to cover the range 3 to 95, each one has to be 18.4 or more units wide.

◆ 18.4 is a rather ungainly number. By rounding it to a tidier figure the grouped frequency distribution will be easier to read and interpret.

◆ The figure to use is 20. Five classes each of which is 20 units wide are enough to cover the range.

◆ These classes together span a range of 100. Since the range is less than this, 92, we have some leeway in choosing the beginning of the first of the classes.

◆ The first of our classes has to start at or below the smallest of the observations in the set, which means for Example 4.7 the class must begin with 3 or a lower number.

◆ We could start our set of classes with 3. If the class width is 20 the first one would be '3–22', the second '23–32' and so forth.

◆ This would work but is not as elegant as using '0–19', '20–39'and so on. The beginnings of these classes, 0, 20, 40 etc. are tidier than 3, 23, 43 etc.

◆ If you start each class with a round number the grouped frequency distribution and any diagram you base on it has a 'neater' framework.

At this point you may find it useful to try **Review questions 4.8 and 4.11** at the end of the chapter.

Grouped frequency distributions are very useful for comparing two or more sets of data because the classes provide a common framework. The best way of using grouped frequency distributions in this way is to calculate the relative frequencies of the number of observations in every class for each set of data.

EXAMPLE 4.9

A rival brand of shower gel to 'Meelar', 'Tyela', is also sold in 250ml bottles. The contents in millilitres of a sample of 26 bottles of this product were:

250.19 249.92 250.22 250.39 249.95 250.15 250.12 250.25 249.94
249.88 249.92 250.23 249.86 250.34 250.37 250.38 250.34 250.08
250.23 250.05 249.86 249.92 250.35 250.07 249.93 250.14

Classify the data using the classes from Example 4.8 and work out the relative frequencies for both distributions.

Solution

Contents (ml)	Frequency (Meelar)	Relative frequency (%) (Meelar)	Frequency (Tyela)	Relative frequency (%) (Tyela)
249.80–249.89	3	10.0	3	11.5
249.90–249.99	7	23.3	6	23.1
250.00–250.09	11	36.7	3	11.5
250.10–250.19	5	16.7	4	15.4
250.20–250.29	3	10.0	4	15.4
250.30–250.39	1	3.3	6	23.1
Total	30	100.0	26	100.0

The use of relative frequencies in Example 4.9, given in percentages to one place of decimals, makes direct comparison of the two sets of data much easier. Saying for instance that 3.3% of the sample of Meelar and 23.1% of the sample of Tyela contained 250.3ml or more is more straightforward than comparing 1/30 with 6/26.

At this point you may find it useful to try **Review question 4.12** at the end of the chapter.

REVIEW QUESTIONS

Answers to these questions are on page 445–6. There are tips and hints to help you with them on the supporting website at **www.pearsoned.co.uk/buglear**, where you will also find the fully worked solutions.

☆☆★ Basic questions

4.1 Match the definitions listed below on the right-hand side to the words listed on the left-hand side.

(a) distribution
(b) element
(c) random
(d) sample
(e) population
(f) observation

(i) something that occurs by chance
(ii) a subset of a population
(iii) a complete set of things to study
(iv) a value of a variable that has occurred
(v) a systematic arrangement of data
(vi) a single member of a population

4.2 On a single day 360 customers used an ATM machine. Half of them only withdrew cash, a quarter only checked their account balance and one tenth only made a deposit. The remainder used the machine for more than one type of transaction, e.g. checking their balance and withdrawing cash.

Compile a summary table of the types of transaction and numbers of customers conducting them.

4.3 The 'To Let' column in the accommodation pages of a local newspaper contains details of 20 houses available to rent. The numbers of bedrooms in these properties are:

$$
\begin{array}{cccccccccc}
2 & 3 & 5 & 2 & 4 & 2 & 4 & 4 & 4 & 3 \\
2 & 5 & 3 & 2 & 3 & 4 & 4 & 3 & 2 & 4
\end{array}
$$

Arrange this data into a frequency distribution.

4.4 The number of business trips abroad taken in the last year by each of a sample of 41 executives were:

$$
\begin{array}{ccccccccccc}
3 & 11 & 1 & 10 & 14 & 14 & 12 & 6 & 1 & 10 & 7 \\
11 & 9 & 2 & 7 & 11 & 17 & 12 & 13 & 2 & 0 & 14 \\
6 & 4 & 3 & 12 & 14 & 8 & 7 & 11 & 9 & 6 & 9 \\
15 & 0 & 4 & 9 & 7 & 10 & 4 & 5 & & &
\end{array}
$$

Arrange this data into a frequency distribution and classify it into a grouped frequency distribution using the classes 0–2, 3–5, 6–8, 9–11, 12–14 and 15–17.

☆★★ More testing questions

4.5 Indicate which of the variables below are qualitative, discrete quantitative or continuous quantitative.

   (a) Duration of telephone calls
   (b) Modes of travel to work
   (c) The alcohol contents of beers
   (d) Sizes of theatre audiences
   (e) Places of birth of passport applicants
   (f) Numbers of websites found in a search

4.6 Select which of the statements listed below on the right-hand side best describes each of the terms on the left-hand side.

   (a) time series data   (i)   concerns attitudes and beliefs
   (b) nominal data   (ii)   is limited to distinct numerical values
   (c) hard data   (iii) consists of values of two variables
   (d) discrete data   (iv)   is collected at regular intervals
   (e) cross-sectional data (v)   is factual
   (f) bivariate data   (vi)   is based on a scale with an arbitrary zero
   (g) soft data   (vii) is only labels
   (h) interval data   (viii) relates to a specific point or period of time

4.7 A total of 127 people applied for several jobs at a new clothing retail outlet. Seventy-four applicants were female, and of these 32 had previous experience of clothing retail and 19 had no previous retail experience. A total of 45 applicants had previous retail experience but not in the clothing sector. Of the males only 9 had no previous retail experience.

Use the information given to construct a contingency table showing the breakdown of applicants by gender and experience.

4.8 The prices (in £s) of 27 second-hand 'Krushenia' cars on sale at a car hypermarket are:

4860	1720	2350	2770	3340	4240	4850	4390	3870
2790	3740	2230	1690	2750	1390	4990	3660	1900
5200	4390	3690	1760	4800	1730	2040	4070	2670

Create a frequency distribution to present this data.

★★★ Challenging questions

4.9 Identify the type of scale of measurement (nominal, ordinal, interval or ratio) appropriate for each of the following types of data:

(a) Star ratings of hotels
(b) Sales revenues of companies
(c) Grades of officers in armed forces
(d) House numbers in a street
(e) Prices of cars
(f) Classes of accommodation on passenger flights
(g) Passport numbers
(h) Numbers in a rating scale on a questionnaire
(i) Index numbers such as the FTSE 100 ('Footsie')

4.10 A hotel had 1360 bookings for accommodation in a month. Of these 940 were for one night. Business bookings amounted to 813 of the total number, all but 141 being for one night. Leisure bookings amounted to a further 362, the remaining bookings being associated with functions (weddings etc.). Only 23 of these latter bookings were for more than one night.

Draw up a two-way table for these figures with rows for the types of booking and columns for the length of stay. Deduce the figures that are not given by using the information provided.

4.11 The hourly wages (in £s) of 32 jobs offered by an employment agency are:

6.28	4.90	4.52	5.11	5.94	5.82	7.14	7.28
8.15	7.04	4.41	4.67	6.90	5.85	5.65	5.50
4.12	5.27	5.25	6.43	5.73	4.65	5.37	4.24
6.45	4.70	5.09	4.82	6.23	5.40	6.48	5.26

Construct a grouped frequency distribution for these figures.

4.12 A leisure company operates three amusement arcades in the UK: at Redcar, Skegness and Torquay. As part of a performance review the duration in minutes of the period spent in the arcades by each of a sample of customers visiting was recorded. The durations of visits made by 21 customers visiting the Redcar arcade were:

23	8	39	72	73	13	44
74	37	21	21	27	27	34
31	32	43	74	44	36	23

The figures for 18 customers visiting the Skegness arcade were:

31	51	69	12	53	28	36	28	36
35	45	48	25	9	32	60	66	30

The figures for 18 customers visiting the Torquay arcade were:

3	19	1	15	219	7	20	10	2
6	2	11	37	106	10	14	3	5

(a) Classify the three sets of data into grouped frequency distributions.

(b) Calculate the relative frequency for each class of all three distributions.

(c) The company expects customers to spend at least 20 minutes on visits to its arcades. Use your relative frequency figures to compare the performances of the arcades in this respect.

THE DEBRIEF

Key things to remember from this chapter

→ There are different types of data: qualitative/quantitative, discrete/continuous quantitative data, cross-section/time series.

→ The methods used to arrange or classify data depend on the type of data.

→ Classify qualitative data using a summary table based on the categories of characteristics or factors that occur in the data.

→ Classify simple discrete quantitative data in a frequency distribution using the values that occur.

→ Classify continuous quantitative data or more complex discrete data in a grouped frequency distribution using classes of values.

→ Use relative rather than absolute frequency to discuss the results of classification.

References

Greenwood, Major (1941) 'Medical statistics from Graunt to Farr', in E.S. Pearson and M.G. Kendall (eds), *Studies in the History of Statistics and Probability*, London: Griffin, pp. 47–73. [Originally published in *Biometrika*, 32 (1941), pp.101–27.]

Kendall, M.G. (1960) 'Where shall the history of statistics begin?', in E.S. Pearson and M.G. Kendall (eds), *Studies in the History of Statistics and Probability*, London: Griffin, pp. 45–6. [Originally published in *Biometrika*, 47 (1960), pp. 447–9.]

Tesco PLC (2010) *Annual Review and Financial Statement 2010,* Cheshunt, Hertfordshire: Tesco PLC. Available at: http://ar2010.tescoplc.com/~/media/Files/T/Tesco-Annual-Report-2009/Attachments/pdf/Full-Review.pdf

CHAPTER 5

Good visibility – pictorial presentation of data

CHAPTER OBJECTIVES

This chapter will help you to:

→ Illustrate qualitative data using pictographs, bar charts and pie charts

→ Portray quantitative data using histograms, cumulative frequency charts and stem and leaf displays

→ Present bivariate quantitative data using scatter diagrams

→ Display time series data using time series plots

THE BARE BONES

What you will find in this chapter . . .

- Constructing charts to display qualitative data
- Displaying quantitative data from frequency distributions
- Compiling stem and leaf displays from raw data
- Using stem and leaf displays to compare distributions
- Using scatter diagrams to portray bivariate data
- Using time series plots to show time series data
- Review questions to test your understanding

. . . and on the supporting website (www.pearsoned.co.uk/buglear)

- How to use EXCEL, Minitab and SPSS to present data
- Fully worked solutions to the review questions
- More review questions

Business use of pictorial presentation

◆ The techniques considered in this chapter are very widely used in a range of documents produced by and for businesses.

◆ The use of visual tools to display data goes back as far as the origins of modern business organisations. An early pioneer was the Scottish draughtsman William Playfair (1759–1823), who worked for the Birmingham engineering firm Boulton & Watt. He produced charts that he used to depict, among other things, the trading fortunes of the East India Company and the balance of trade (see Holmes, 1991: 13–18; Tufte, 2001: 32–4).

◆ Company annual reports often describe company operations using pie charts, bar charts and histograms as well as depicting the progress of the company using time series charts. For examples of this see the annual reports of Tata Motors (2010) and the Vodafone Group (2010).

5.1 Introduction

In the last chapter we looked at arranging and tabulating data, the initial stages in getting information from data. In the process of doing this we can find something meaningful, information from things that may appear to have no meaning, the raw or unprocessed data. In this chapter we continue this theme by considering various ways of portraying data in visual form. Used appropriately the charts and diagrams you will find here are very effective means of communicating the patterns and meaning contained in data, specifically the patterns and sequences in distributions. These are techniques that are very common in business documents so being able to understand what they mean is important.

In fact there are a variety of charts and diagrams which we can use to portray data; the key is to understand which ones are appropriate for the data we wish to present. The techniques we use depend on the type of data we want to present, in the same way as the suitability of the methods of arranging data featured in the last chapter depended on the type of data. Essentially, the simpler the data, the simpler the presentational tools that can be used to represent it; simple nominal data restricted to a few categories can be shown effectively in the form of a simple bar chart whereas ratio data requires the more rigorous scaling of something like a histogram.

5.2 Displaying qualitative data

Section 4.5.1 of Chapter 4 covered the arrangement of qualitative data, data which consists of categories of an attribute, in the form of a summary table. Such a table is not only a way of organising such data, it is also a useful basis for preparing a chart to present the data.

Charts and diagrams are much more effective ways of communicating data than tables because they are more readily appreciated visually. When you need to discuss data in a presentation or document this is very useful. It helps your audience concentrate on your argument because you will be presenting your data in a more accessible form; they won't have to focus on detailed lists of figures or tables.

Displaying qualitative data is fairly simple if there are few categories of the attribute or characteristic being investigated. With more categories, the task can be simplified by merging categories.

There are three widely used types of diagrams that we can use to present qualitative data: *pictographs, pie charts* and *bar charts*.

5.2.1 Pictographs

A pictograph is basically an extension of a simple summary table. The attribute categories are listed just as in a summary table, but we use pictures to show how many items are in each category. To emphasise what the data is about use pictures that have an obvious visual connection to the theme.

Pictographs like the one in Figure 5.1 are effective ways of displaying simple sets of qualitative data. The symbols used are simple devices that represent the number of items in each category. They also highlight the context of the data.

EXAMPLE 5.1

The table below lists four racehorse trainers and the number of horses they trained that won races at a horse race meeting.

Trainer	Number of winners
Nadia Amazonka	5
Freddie Conn	3
Lavinia Loshart	1
Victor Sedlow	2

Show this set of data in the form of a pictograph.

Solution

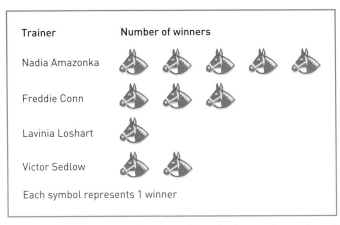

Figure 5.1 Pictograph of the number of winners by each trainer

Pictographs do have some shortcomings that may deter you from using them. If you are artistic you might be able to draw appropriate symbols but if not you will have to generate them using computer software. This can be difficult. Because the widely available spreadsheets and statistical packages cannot produce pictographs, you will probably have to graft pictures into a document using word processing software.

If you do use pictographs choose the pictures carefully. They need to be easy to connect with the theme and not too elaborate, otherwise the complexity of the images *per se* will be the centre of attention rather than the data you want them to illustrate.

Sometimes pictographs are used in academic and business work but they are much more common in the media. The main reason is that the computer graphics packages that reporters and editors have are more specialised than any of the software you will probably be using in your quantitative methods work.

5.2.2 Pie charts

The next method of illustrating qualitative data that we will look at is the pie chart. Pie charts are used much more than pictographs, in part because they can be produced using widely available computer software.

Like a pictograph a pie chart shows the number of items in the categories of an attribute but in a different way. It shows the complete set of data in the form of a circle or 'pie'. The pie is divided into a number of segments or 'slices'. The slices represent the categories, with the sizes of the slices in proportion to the composition of the data set. The bigger the slice the more items in the category.

Just about every spreadsheet or statistical package can produce a pie chart like Figure 5.2 either from the original data or from a summary table. These packages provide various ways of enhancing pie charts: colour and shading patterns, 3D effects, and detached or 'exploded' slices to emphasise a particular segment. With practice you will be able to use these tools to embellish pie charts, but avoid overdoing it. Bear in mind that it is the data that you should convey to your audience rather than your wizardry with the tricks in the software.

EXAMPLE 5.2

The Steeralny Appliance Repair Service has depots in Crewe, Doncaster, Exeter and Frome. The numbers of call-outs from each depot on one day are given in the following table:

Depot	Call-outs
Crewe	36 (26.1%)
Doncaster	57 (41.3%)
Exeter	28 (20.3%)
Frome	17 (12.3%)
Total	138 (100.0%)

Show this data in the form of a pie chart.

Solution

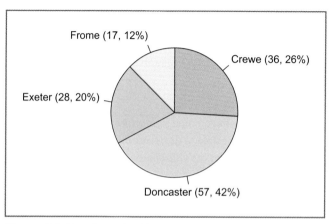

Figure 5.2 Number of call-outs by depot

Because pie charts are widely used and fairly straightforward to understand you may be tempted to treat them as your first choice method of illustrating qualitative data. Often they are appropriate, but there are situations where they are not.

As the role of a pie chart is to show how the parts comprise the whole, don't use one when you either can't show the whole or don't want to. This may be because there are some values missing from the data or perhaps there is an untidy 'Other' category for data that does not fit into the main categories. Leaving out any data, either for administrative or aesthetic reasons, means you won't be showing the whole, which is exactly what pie charts are designed to do.

One factor that makes pie charts accessible is that the basis of them is the rather obvious metaphor of slicing a pie. But this works so long as the pie chart actually resembles a pie. If a pie chart has so many slices that it resembles a bicycle wheel more than a pie, it can confuse rather than clarify the data. Should you have many categories in your data set, as a rough guide 10 or more, you can do one of two things. You can either merge some of the categories to reduce the number of slices in the chart or use an alternative device to illustrate the data.

5.2.3 Bar charts

Another method of portraying qualitative data is the bar chart. Like pie charts, bar charts are frequently used in business documents, are fairly simple to understand, and spreadsheet and statistical software will generate them. Their advantage over pie charts is that there are different types of bar charts, which makes them more flexible devices. We can use bar charts to illustrate not only simple categorisations but also two-way classifications.

Essentially a bar chart does the same job as a pie chart and a pictograph; it shows how many items are in each of a set of categories of an attribute. It represents the numbers of items, or frequencies, as a series of bars. The size of each bar is directly proportional to the frequency of items in the category; the longer the bar, the more items are in the category.

EXAMPLE 5.3 Produce a bar chart to display the data from Example 5.2.

Solution

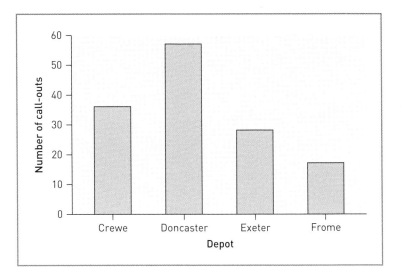

Figure 5.3 A bar chart of call-outs by depot

Figure 5.3 is a *simple* bar chart as it shows just one attribute, depot location. For data with two attributes we use a different type of bar chart, a *component* bar chart.

The call-outs data in Example 5.2 has been subdivided to show how many call-outs from each depot concerned washing machines and how many concerned other appliances. The numbers of the two call-out types from each depot are:

Depot	Washing machine call-outs	Other appliance call-outs
Crewe	21	15
Doncaster	44	13
Exeter	13	15
Frome	10	7

Display this data as a component bar chart.

Solution

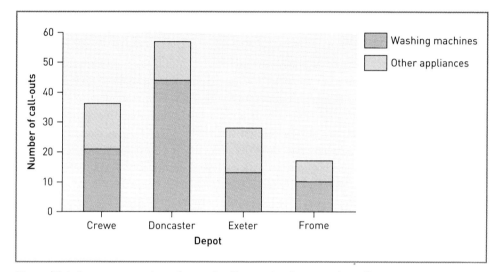

Figure 5.4 A component bar chart of call-outs by depot and appliance type

Figure 5.4 is a component bar chart. Each bar is divided into components, or parts. The other name for it, a *stacked* bar chart, reflects the way in which the components of each bar are stacked on top of one another.

A component bar chart is an effective way of giving focus to the subdivisions within the categories. It emphasises the balance *within* each category of one attribute (in Figure 5.3 the depot) and *between* the categories of the other (in Figure 5.4 the type of call-out).

If we want to focus on this balance exclusively and are not concerned about the absolute frequencies in each category we can use a component bar chart in which each bar is subdivided in percentage terms (such as Figure 5.5).

To emphasise the absolute differences *between* each category of one attribute (in Figure 5.3 the depots) and *within* each category of the other (in Figure 5.4 the types of call-out) a *clustered* bar chart is more useful.

Produce a component bar chart for the data in Example 5.4 in which the sections of the bars represent the percentages of call-outs by appliance type.

Solution

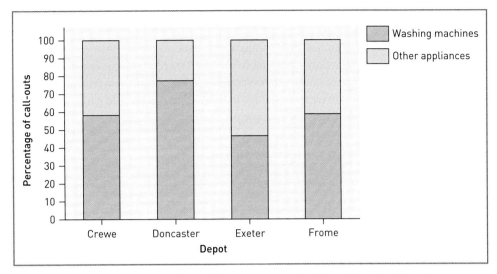

Figure 5.5 A component bar chart of percentages of call-outs by depot and appliance type

EXAMPLE
5.6

Produce a clustered bar chart to portray the data from Example 5.4.

Solution

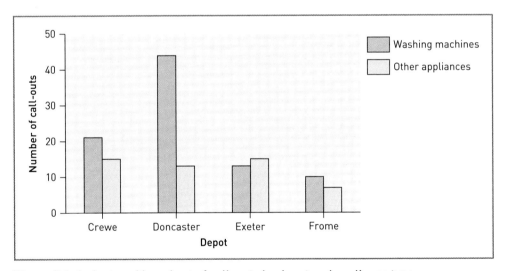

Figure 5.6 A clustered bar chart of call-outs by depot and appliance type

The type of bar chart shown in Figure 5.6 is called a clustered bar chart because it uses a group or cluster of bars to show the composition of each category of one attribute by categories of a second attribute. For instance in Figure 5.6 the bars for Crewe show how the call-outs from the Crewe depot are composed of call-outs for washing machines and call-outs for other appliances.

At this point you may find it useful to try **Review questions 5.1 and 5.7** at the end of the chapter.

5.3 Displaying quantitative data

Quantitative data is more sophisticated data than qualitative data so the diagrams used to portray it are generally more elaborate. The exception to this is where you want to represent the simplest type of quantitative data, discrete quantitative variables that have very few feasible values. You can treat the values in this data as you would categories in qualitative data, using them to construct a bar chart or pie chart.

EXAMPLE 5.7

In Example 4.6 the numbers of free refills taken by 20 customers visiting a department store café were tabulated as follows:

Number of refills	Number of customers
0	6
1	7
2	5
3	2

Figure 5.7 shows this data in the form of a bar chart.

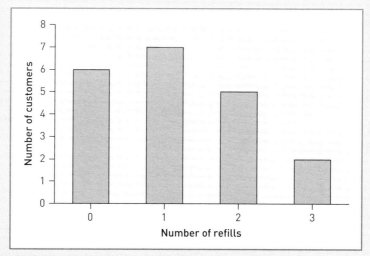

Figure 5.7 Number of customers by number of refills

5.3.1 Histograms

In general, quantitative data consists of a rather larger variety of values than the data portrayed in Figure 5.7. In section 4.5.2 of Chapter 4 we saw how grouped frequency distributions could be used to arrange quantitative data. Here we will look at what is probably the most widely used way of portraying data arranged in a grouped frequency distribution, the *histogram*. Essentially this is a more elaborate bar chart in which each of the bars or *blocks* represents the number of values in a class of values rather than the frequency with which each single value occurs. Because they are composed in this way histograms are sometimes called *block diagrams*.

EXAMPLE
5.8
In Example 4.7 the numbers of package holidays sold in one week by each of 27 independent travel agents were categorised in the following grouped frequency distribution.

Holidays sold	Frequency
0–19	12
20–39	7
40–59	4
60–79	3
80–99	1
Total frequency	27

Show this grouped frequency distribution as a histogram.

Solution

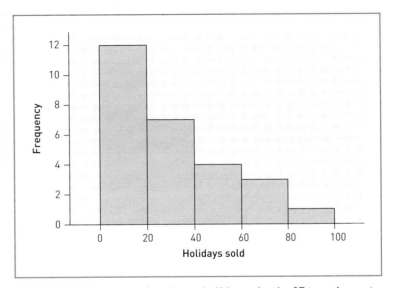

Figure 5.8 Histogram of package holiday sales by 27 travel agents

In Figure 5.8 there are no gaps between the blocks in the histogram. The classes on which
it is based start with '0–19' then '20–39' and so on. When plotting such classes you may be
tempted to leave gaps to reflect the fact that there is a numerical gap between the end of
the first class and the beginning of the next, but this would be wrong because the gap would be
meaningless as it is simply not possible to sell, say, 19.2 holidays.

A histogram illustrates the pattern of variation in, or distribution of, a set of observed values
of a variable. The key visual feature is the size of the blocks; the bigger the area of a block representing a class, the higher the number of values in the class. Because of this link between block
size and class frequency the vertical or 'Y'-axis scale should begin with zero, as in Figure 5.8.

If the classes in a grouped frequency distribution have the same width the *height* of each
block alone reflects the frequency of observed values in the class. Where the class widths are
not the same it is vital that the *areas* of the blocks are in proportion to the class frequencies.
The best way of ensuring this is to represent the *density* of values in the classes rather than the
frequency of each class. The density is the frequency of values in a class divided by the width
of the class times the number of values in the data set. It expresses how densely the values are
packed in the class to which they belong.

EXAMPLE 5.9

The grouped frequency distribution below shows the numbers of shares the 25 directors of a large company held in their company:

Number of shares (000s)	Frequency
0 and under 5	2
5 and under 10	5
10 and under 20	10
20 and under 30	7
30 and under 40	1

Calculate density figures for the classes in the distribution and use them to produce a histogram to portray the distribution.

Solution

The classes with their densities are:

Number of shares (000s)	Frequency	Density
0 and under 5	2	$2/(5*25) = 0.016$
5 and under 10	5	$5/(5*25) = 0.040$
10 and under 20	10	$10/(10*25) = 0.040$
20 and under 30	7	$7/(10*25) = 0.028$
30 and under 40	1	$1/(10*25) = 0.004$

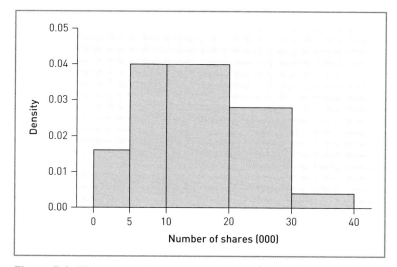

Figure 5.9 Histogram of numbers of shares (in 000s) held by company directors

Using densities to produce Figure 5.9 takes account of the varied class widths. There are only half the values in the '5 and under 10' class (5) as there are in the next class, '10 and under 20', which has 10. Although it has only *half* the frequency of the '10 and under 20' class the height of the block representing the '5 and under 10' class is the *same* as the height of the block representing the '10 and under 20' class. Because the '5 and under 10' class is only *half* the width of the class to the right of it, to keep the area in proportion to the frequency the height of the block is *doubled*.

SELF-ASSEMBLY GUIDE

How to calculate frequency densities

◆ In distributions like the one in Example 5.9 the class widths are inconsistent so frequency densities are needed to portray the distribution accurately.

◆ Divide the frequency of the class by the width of the class multiplied by the total number of values in the data set.

◆ In Example 5.9 divide the frequency of the first class (2) by the width of the class (5) times the total number of values (25) to give 0.016.

◆ Similarly the density of the second class is its frequency (5) divided by the class width (5) times the total number of values (25) giving 0.04.

◆ The density of the third class is its frequency (10) divided by the class width (10) times the total number of values (25) giving 0.04.

◆ In dividing by 25, the total number of values, as well as by the class width, the total area covered by all of the blocks combined is 1. We can check this by multiplying each density by the width of its class; the products should sum to 1.

$$(0.016 * 5) + (0.04 * 5) + (0.04 * 10) + (0.028 * 10) + (0.004 * 10)$$
$$= 0.08 + 0.2 + 0.4 + 0.28 + 0.04 = 1$$

◆ By having the total area add up to 1 we are representing the set of data as a probability distribution, which can be convenient for further analysis of the data.

Distributions differ in terms of their *symmetry* and *skew*. The distribution in Figure 5.9 has a pattern that is more balanced or *symmetrical* than the distribution in Figure 5.8. It has a concentration of values represented by the larger blocks flanked by smaller blocks on either side. In Figure 5.8, the pattern is *skewed*; the left-hand side block is largest and the blocks to its right diminish in size. It is an example of a *positively* skewed distribution. Studying Figure 5.8 we can deduce that most of the travel agents sold a small number of package holidays and only a few agents sold large numbers of holidays.

You may come across distributions that are *negatively* skewed. In these the classes on the left-hand side have smaller frequencies and those on the right-hand side have larger frequencies. Figure 5.10 illustrates an example of this type of distribution.

EXAMPLE 5.10

Raketa Airlines say they allow their passengers to take up to 5kg of baggage with them into the cabin. The weights of cabin baggage taken onto one flight by 62 passengers were recorded and the following grouped frequency distribution compiled from the data:

Weight of cabin baggage (kg)	Number of passengers
0 and under 1	2
1 and under 2	3
2 and under 3	8
3 and under 4	11
4 and under 5	20
5 and under 6	18

Portray this distribution in the form of a histogram.

Solution

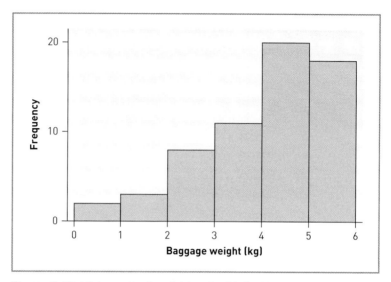

Figure 5.10 Histogram of weights of cabin baggage

5.3.2 Cumulative frequency graphs

Another way to display data that is categorised in a grouped frequency distribution is the *cumulative frequency graph*. This device shows how the data is *accumulated* across the grouped frequency distribution from the first to the last class. It is based on the same horizontal axis as we would use for a histogram of the same data, but it is important to ensure that the vertical axis, which must start at zero, goes up far enough to encompass the total frequency.

To construct a cumulative frequency graph we need to work out the cumulative frequency of every class in the distribution. This is the frequency of the class plus the combined frequencies, i.e. the cumulative frequency, of every one of the previous classes.

SELF-ASSEMBLY GUIDE

How to find cumulative frequencies

◆ The first cumulative frequency is easy; it is just the frequency of the first class since there are no previous classes.

◆ The second cumulative frequency is the frequency of the second class plus the frequency of the first one.

◆ The third cumulative frequency is the frequency of the third class plus the cumulative frequency of the second one, and so on.

If this is not clear try imagining that the individual values in the distribution are iron filings and you are travelling through the distribution with a powerful magnet. As you proceed from the start of the first class your magnet would pick up the iron filings as you go. The number of iron filings on your magnet by the time you reach the end of the first class is the cumulative frequency of values in the first class. As you travel through the second class your magnet picks up the iron filings there on top of those from the first class. When you reach the end of the second class your magnet will have accumulated the filings in the first *and* second class. The number of them is the cumulative frequency of the second class. If you continue, by the time you reach the end of the final class your magnet will have picked up all the filings.

**EXAMPLE
5.11**

Find the cumulative frequencies of each class in the grouped frequency distribution in Example 5.8.

Solution

Holidays sold	Frequency	Cumulative frequency
0–19	12	12
20–39	7	19
40–59	4	23
60–79	3	26
80–99	1	27

Note that in the case of the final class in Example 5.11, '80–99', the cumulative frequency is 27, which is the number of values in the data set, the total frequency of the distribution. This must be so. Once the values in the final class are added into the cumulative total we have accounted for all the values in the distribution.

In a cumulative frequency graph there is one point plotted for each class. This denotes the cumulative frequency of the class. It is positioned above the end of the class because it signifies the number of values accumulated in the distribution by the end of that class. To complete the diagram we connect all the points together using straight lines.

**EXAMPLE
5.12**

Plot a cumulative frequency graph for the data in Example 5.8.

Solution

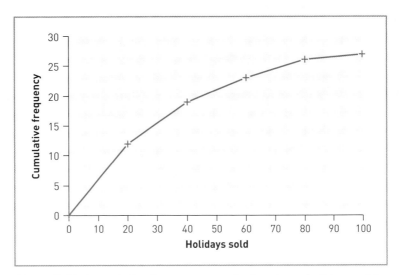

Figure 5.11 Cumulative frequency graph of package holidays sold by 27 travel agents

Notice that the plotted line in Figure 5.11 starts at zero on both the horizontal and vertical axes. This makes sense as in this case the first class starts at zero. The fact that it originates at zero on the vertical axis signifies that there are no values less than the beginning of the first class.

At first the line in Figure 5.11 climbs fairly steeply then it flattens out. The initial steep ascent reflects the relatively large number of values in the first class, nearly half the values in the distribution. The subsequent flatter parts of the line reflect the fact that as we proceed through the classes there are fewer and fewer values in them.

In Figure 5.12 the plotted line begins climbing gently and becomes steeper before levelling out gently to the right. This shows that there are relatively few values in the first classes with rather more in the classes in the middle and again fewer in the final classes. The distribution in Figure 5.12 is symmetrical in shape. In contrast, in Figure 5.11 we have a positively skewed distribution.

EXAMPLE 5.13

Plot a cumulative frequency graph for the distribution of contents of bottles of 'Meelar' shower gel in Example 4.8.

Shower gel (ml)	Frequency	Cumulative frequency
249.80–249.89	3	3
249.90–249.99	7	10
250.00–250.09	11	21
250.10–250.19	5	26
250.20–250.29	3	29
250.30–250.39	1	30

Solution

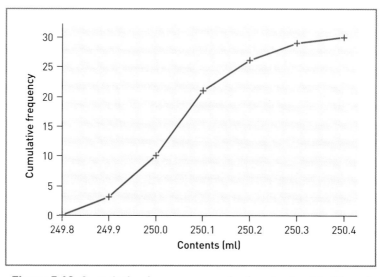

Figure 5.12 Cumulative frequency graph of contents of bottles of shower gel

A variation of the cumulative frequency graph is the cumulative *relative* frequency graph. In this, each plotted point symbolises the proportion of total values occurring in a class and in the classes that precede it. To put it another way, we plot the number of values accumulated *in relation* to the whole. This alternative is useful when the total number of values in the data set is an 'awkward' number, say 83 rather than a nice 'neat' 50.

<table>
<tr><td>EXAMPLE
5.14</td><td>The number of litres of fuel purchased by 73 customers at a petrol station is summarised in the following table. Plot a cumulative relative frequency graph to portray the distribution.</td></tr>
</table>

Litres	Frequency	Relative frequency	Cumulative relative frequency
0.00–9.99	5	5/73 = 0.068	0.126
10.00–19.99	17	17/73 = 0.233	0.437
20.00–29.99	31	31/73 = 0.425	0.781
30.00–39.99	16	16/73 = 0.219	0.966
40.00–49.99	4	4/73 = 0.055	1.000

Solution

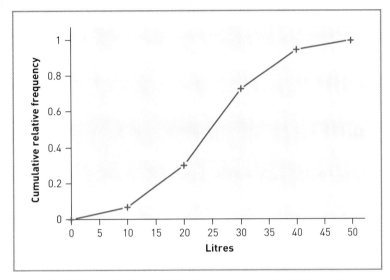

Figure 5.13 Cumulative relative frequency graph of litres of petrol purchased

At this point you may find it useful to try **Review questions 5.2, 5.3 and 5.8** at the end of the chapter.

5.3.3 Stem and leaf displays

Histograms and cumulative frequency graphs are commonly used means of illustrating quantitative data. For a long time they were the main techniques for doing this. However, 30 years or so ago an American statistician, John W. Tukey pioneered an innovative set of techniques he called Exploratory Data Analysis (EDA). This included a novel way of displaying quantitative data visually, the *stem and leaf display*. You can read more about EDA in Hoaglin, Mosteller and Tukey (2000).

Essentially stem and leaf displays do the same job as histograms; they show patterns of variation in distributions. But whereas a histogram is a set of blocks based on the grouping of data in a distribution, a stem and leaf display uses the data values themselves to portray the distribution. It is two things in one, both a list of the data and the shape of the distribution the data forms. This makes it very useful for investigating data. We can use it both to decide how best to describe the distribution and to identify interesting or unusual observations.

The way in which the numbers we use are structured is the basis of stem and leaf displays. It is the position of the digits in a number that dictate its value. We know that 24 and 42 are not the same although they both consist of a 2 and a 4. It is the fact that in 24 the 2 precedes the 4 that makes it 24. Because there are no other digits to the right of the 4 we naturally assume the 4 are the units and the 2 are the tens.

Why, you might ask, are they called stem and leaf displays? Stems and leaves are of course parts of plants. Typically a plant consists of a set of stems and on each stem there are a number of different leaves. The basis of stem and leaf displays is that we can think of the structure of numbers in the same way as we think of the structure of plants. Just as we can separate leaves from the stem of a plant we can separate the digits of a number. If we take the number 24 we treat the 2 as the stem and the 4 as the leaf. The number 27 has the same stem, 2 but a different leaf, 7. The number 42 has a different stem, 4 and a leaf digit of 2. In breaking up numbers in this way the larger denominations are the stems to which the smaller denominations, the leaves, are attached. In the case of 24, 27 and 42 the stems are the digits on the left, in what you might think of as the 'tens' column, and the leaves are the digits on the right, those in the 'units' column.

EXAMPLE 5.15

Musor Burgers operate fast-food restaurants. The seating capacities of the 27 restaurants they operate in East Anglia are:

53	38	59	62	51	51	28	45	61
39	59	50	48	74	52	41	73	68
47	48	52	56	52	55	47	52	41

Portray this data in a stem and leaf display.

SELF-ASSEMBLY GUIDE

How to construct a stem and leaf display

◆ Find the smallest and the largest observations in the data. In Example 5.15 the smallest value is 28 and the largest 74.

◆ List the stem digits that are spanned by the data down a column to the left of your page from the smallest to the largest. In Example 5.15 the list would start with 2, the stem digit of 28 and end with 7, the stem digit of 74.

◆ Take each observation in turn and record it in the display by putting its leaf digit to the right of its stem digit. In Example 5.15 the first value is 53. This has a stem of 5 and a leaf of 3 so to record it put 3 to the right of the stem digit 5:

Stem	Leaves
2	
3	
4	
5	3
6	
7	

◆ The next value in Example 5.15 is 38. This has a stem of 3 and a leaf of 8. Record it by putting 8 to the right of stem digit 3:

Stem	Leaves
2	
3	8
4	
5	3
6	
7	

◆ After doing this for every observed value the result is a set of stem lines with the stem digits on the left and leaf digits of each observation that shares the stem on the right.

Stem	Leaves
2	8
3	8 9
4	8 7 1 1 5 7 8
5	3 9 2 0 6 9 2 5 1 2 1 2
6	2 8 1
7	4 3

◆ The next stage is to rewrite the display with the leaf digits on each stem line arranged from smallest to largest:

Stem	Leaves
2	8
3	8 9
4	1 1 5 7 7 8 8
5	0 1 1 2 2 2 2 3 5 6 9 9
6	1 2 8
7	3 4

◆ Finally, bring in something to specify the scale of the observations. On the first stem line the stem (2) and leaf (8) can be rejoined to make the observation they represent, 28. To ensure that the observation really is understood to be 28 and not any other number that has a 2 followed by an 8, like 280 or 0.028, insert the note 'Leaf unit = 1'.

Stem	Leaves
2	8
3	8 9
4	1 1 5 7 7 8 8
5	0 1 1 2 2 2 2 3 5 6 9 9
6	1 2 8
7	3 4

Leaf unit = 1

◆ This final touch makes it clear that the leaves are in units or 'ones'. This implies that the stems must be in tens and hence 2 combined with 8 must be 28.

Stem and leaf displays can seem a little odd at first but they are worth knowing about because they have two advantages over histograms. First, we can use them to highlight specific values of interest. Histograms can't do this because they are made up of blocks not data. The second advantage is that we can contrast two distributions in one stem and leaf display. Technically we could plot two distributions in one histogram but one distribution would obscure at least part of the other. It would be better to have a separate histogram for each distribution.

EXAMPLE 5.16

Five of the Musor restaurants whose seating capacities are given in Example 5.15 are in city centre locations. The seating capacities for these restaurants are in bold type below:

53	38	**59**	**62**	51	51	28	45	61
39	59	**50**	48	74	52	41	**73**	68
47	48	52	56	52	55	47	52	41

We can embolden these values in the stem and leaf display.

Stem	Leaves
2	8
3	8 9
4	1 1 5 7 7 8 8
5	**0** 1 1 2 2 2 2 **3** 5 6 9 **9**
6	1 **2** 8
7	**3** 4

Leaf unit = 1

Based on this display it seems that the city centre restaurants are among those with larger seating capacities.

To construct a stem and leaf display for two distributions start by listing the stem digits down the middle. Enter the leaf digits of one distribution on the left of the stem digits and the leaf digits of the other distribution on the right. Because of the way the distributions

EXAMPLE 5.17

The seating capacities for the 24 Musor restaurants in the Bristol area are:

61	54	73	78	59	49	51	58	75	67	60
87	61	70	52	56	86	91	55	76	69	82	

Construct a stem and leaf display of this data alongside the seating capacity data from the Musor restaurants in East Anglia given in Example 5.15.

Solution

East Anglia	Stem	Bristol
8	2	
9 8	3	
8 7 7 5 1 1	4	9
9 9 6 5 3 2 2 2 2 1 1 0	5	1 2 4 5 6 8 9
8 2 1	6	0 1 1 7 9
4 3	7	0 3 5 6 8
	8	2 6 7
	9	1

Leaf unit = 1

are set out this type of stem and leaf display is sometimes referred to as a *back-to-back* stem and leaf.

The display in Example 5.17 shows that in general the restaurants in the Bristol area have larger seating capacities than those in East Anglia.

On the left-hand side of the stem and leaf display in Example 5.17 stem line 5 is heavily loaded with leaf digits. Stem and leaf displays can be customised to avoid having such lengthy sequences of leaf digits by stretching the stems. This means having more than one stem line for each stem digit. The result is a more detailed profile of the distribution.

EXAMPLE 5.18

Construct a stem and leaf display to show the seating capacities of the Musor restaurants in East Anglia in Example 5.15. Use two stems for each stem digit.

Solution

Stem	Leaves
2	8
3	
3	8 9
4	1 1
4	7 7 8
5	0 1 1 2 2 2 2 3
5	5 6 9 9
6	1 2
6	8
7	3 4

Leaf unit = 1

The stem and leaf display in Example 5.18 has two stem lines for the stem digits 3, 4, 5 and 6. In each case, the first of the two stem lines is for the leaf digits 0 to 4. The second of the two is for leaf digits 5 to 9. Note that we don't need two stem lines for stem digit 2 because there are no observations with a stem of 2 and a leaf digit less than 5. Similarly we don't need two stem lines for stem digit 7 as the there is no observation higher than 74.

Stem and leaf displays are based on splitting number into two types of digit, stems and leaves. This makes applying the two-digit observations fairly straightforward; the stem is on the left and the leaf is on the right. But suppose the observations have more than two digits. In this case we have to be a little inventive. We can round data, stretch stems as in Example 5.18, or try longer stems or longer leaves to construct the display so that it presents the data effectively.

EXAMPLE 5.19

The prices in £s of 15 different motor insurance quotations received by a motorist were:

473	443	355	327	479	385	318	367
547	522	383	476	601	558	377	

Present this data in the form of a stem and leaf display.

Solution

Stem	Leaves
3	18 27 55 67 77 83 85
4	43 73 76 79
5	22 47 58
6	01

Leaf unit = 1.0

SELF-ASSEMBLY GUIDE

Stem and leaf displays for three-digit data

◆ Data that consists of three-digit observations can be rounded to two significant figures. In Example 5.19 the first observation, 473, could be rounded to 470, the second, 443, to 440 and so on. Once this is done we could construct a stem and leaf display in the same way as in Example 5.16.

◆ Rounding the data means we lose definition. If we want to retain the detail and accommodate the three digits we can split the observations into stems and leaves either by using longer stems or longer leaves.

◆ With longer stems the two digits on the left of each observation are the stems and the digits on the right are the leaves. Using this approach for the data in Example 5.19 the observation 473 has a stem of 47 and a leaf of 3.

◆ The second possibility is to have longer leaves. The stems would be the digit on the left and the leaves would be the two digits on the right. In Example 5.19 the observation 473 has a stem of 4 and a leaf of 73.

◆ So, which is better? In this case longer stems result in too many stems. The smallest observation, 318, has a stem of 31 and the largest, 610, has a stem of 60. In the display the list of stem lines would have to go from 31 to 60. There would be 30 stem lines. There are only 15 observations so the data would be too widely scattered over so many stem lines to provide a useful profile of the distribution.

◆ The second approach is more viable. With one-digit stems and two-digit leaves, the observation 473 has a stem of 4 and a leaf of 73. The list of stems would be much shorter. The stem of the smallest observation, 318 is 3 and that for the largest, 602 is 6. This is how the display in Example 5.19 is structured.

The stem and leaf display in Example 5.19 portrays a positively skewed distribution. There are many smaller observations and fewer larger ones. Most of the quotations are at the cheaper end of the distribution.

A stem and leaf display presents data organised by stems in order of magnitude. Because of this they can be used as the basis for constructing a histogram. The stems are equivalent to the classes in a grouped frequency distribution.

EXAMPLE 5.20

Construct a histogram from the stem and leaf display in Example 5.19.

Solution

The stem lines in Example 5.19 are 3, 4, 5, 6. These are in hundreds, which even if we did not have the raw data we could deduce from the message 'Leaf unit = 1.0' in the display. The first stem line, the one for 3, is equivalent to a class of '300 and under 400', the second to '400 and under 500' and so on.

The histogram is shown in Figure 5.14.

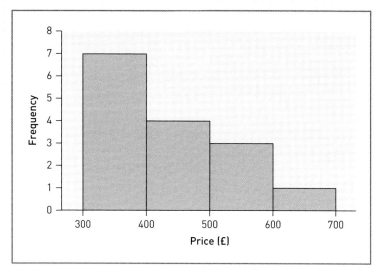

Figure 5.14 **Histogram of prices of motor insurance quotations**

At this point you may find it useful to try **Review questions 5.4, 5.9 and 5.11** at the end of the chapter.

5.4 Portraying bivariate quantitative data

So far in this chapter the techniques for presenting quantitative data have one thing in common; they are devices for showing the observations of a single variable. They are methods of *univariate* analysis.

But suppose we want to portray observations of two variables in a single diagram. We might want to do this to show a connection (or lack of one) between them. To do this we can use a *scatter diagram*. This is a method of *bivariate* analysis. As the name implies, bivariate analysis is about analysing values of two variables, which are bivariate data. Scatter diagrams are so-called because they portray the scatter or distribution of one variable in relation to the scatter of the other.

Bivariate data comprises two sets of observed values, one for each variable. Because they consist of one pair of values for every thing or person being measured or investigated they are also known as paired data. For convenience one variable is designated X and the other Y. Typically we are interested in whether one depends on the other, for instance how sales of products depend on their prices. To reflect this, Y is called the *dependent* variable and X the *independent* variable.

To produce a scatter diagram we start with a pair of axes on a graph. The horizontal one is for the values of X, so it is also called the *x-axis*. The vertical one is for the values of Y so it is the *y-axis*. The position of the point along the *x-axis* is determined by its x value. The position of the point along the vertical axis is determined by its y value. Once all points are plotted we have a *scatter* of points that should help us see how the variables are related to each other.

EXAMPLE
5.21

The maximum daytime temperatures (in degree Celsius) and the quantities of ice cream (in kg) sold at a supermarket on 12 summer days were:

Temperature (°C)	16	19	22	23	23	24	25	25	26	26	27	28
Ice cream sold (kg)	8	11	22	25	37	45	42	55	58	63	67	69

Specify which variable is the dependent (Y) one and which is the independent (X) one. Then construct a scatter diagram for these data.

Solution

Ice cream sold is the dependent (Y) variable because logically it depends on the temperature, which is the independent (X) variable.

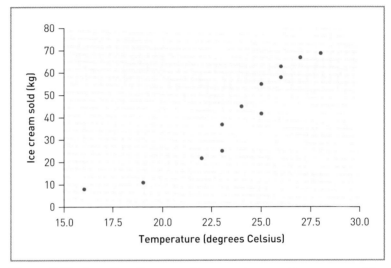

Figure 5.15   A scatter diagram of temperature and ice cream sold

In the scatter diagram in Figure 5.15 there are 12 points, one for each day. Every point represents both the temperature and the ice cream sold for one day. Where the point lies on the y-axis reflects the quantity sold that day; where it lies on the x-axis reflects the temperature that day. The day when the temperature was 16 degrees and the amount sold was 8kg is represented by the furthest left point in the diagram.

The scatter in Figure 5.15 suggests there is a clear connection between temperature and the amount of ice cream sold. The sales levels are generally higher when temperatures are higher. In this case we have a *direct* relationship, in which higher values of one variable coincide with higher values of the other. If higher values of one variable coincide with lower values of the other we have an *inverse* relationship.

At this point you may find it useful to try **Review questions 5.5 and 5.12** at the end of the chapter.

5.5 Portraying time series data

Time series data is made up of observations collected over time, typically at regular intervals. It is bivariate data where time is one of the variables. Most organisations gather time series data as a key way of monitoring performance. They will probably record things like daily sales, monthly stock levels, and quarterly profit. Time series data is important for businesses.

The best way of presenting time series data is a *time series plot*. It is like a scatter diagram because it is made up of points. Each point depicts a pair of values of two variables which are plotted against horizontal and vertical axes.

There are, however, two important differences between time series plots and scatter diagrams. The first of these is that a time series plot has a horizontal axis that represents the time variable. This is to reflect the passing of time. The scale of the axis starts with the earliest observation on the left and finishes with the latest observation on the right.

The second difference is that the points in a time series plot are always connected up with lines to stress the passage of time. In a scatter diagram the points should never be connected in this way.

The vertical axis of a time series plot should ideally start at zero to avoid over-emphasising any fluctuations over time. The exception to this is where the data values are so large that starting the scale at zero would make fluctuations too difficult to spot.

EXAMPLE 5.22

The numbers of employees of a biomedical company over nine years were:

Year	2003	2004	2005	2006	2007	2008	2009	2010	2011
Employees	16	26	47	103	118	132	141	141	145

Present this data in a time series plot.

Solution

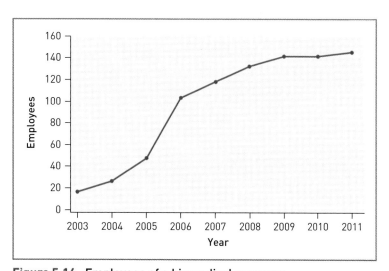

Figure 5.16 Employees of a biomedical company

Figure 5.16 illustrates that increasing numbers of employees have been hired during this time. The pattern shows a consistent upwards general movement or *trend*. Other time series might have broadly consistent fluctuations. These might be recurrent variations within the years, known as *seasonal* components, or recurrent patterns over periods of years, known as *cyclical* components.

EXAMPLE 5.23

The quarterly costs of energy supplied to the Komnata office building in London over two years were:

Year	Quarter			
	1	**2**	**3**	**4**
1	£5225	£1862	£2016	£6317
2	£5830	£1711	£2134	£6475

Present this data in a time series plot.

Solution

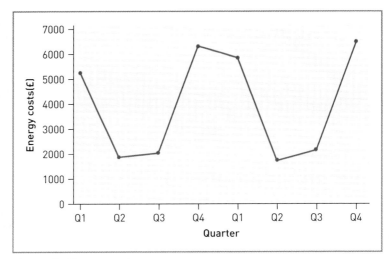

Figure 5.17 Quarterly energy costs

Figure 5.17 illustrates that the energy costs for this building are much higher in quarters 1 and 4 than in quarters 2 and 3. This is probably because heating costs are much higher in the autumn and winter (quarters 1 and 4) than in spring and summer (quarters 2 and 3). This is true for both years.

At this point you may find it useful to try **Review questions 5.6 and 5.10** at the end of the chapter.

REVIEW QUESTIONS

Answers to these questions are on page 446–7. There are tips and hints to help you with them on the supporting website at **www.pearsoned.co.uk/buglear**, where you will also find the fully worked solutions.

☆☆★ Basic questions

5.1 Vorovka Direct Marketing has offices in Liverpool, Motherwell and Newbury. The numbers of employees in each location are:

Office	Employees
Liverpool	20
Motherwell	24
Newbury	29

Plot a simple bar chart to show the total number of employees in each office.

5.2 The manager of the customer service department at Prastudar Promotions submits the following frequency distribution for the number of days in the previous week staff in the department were off sick:

Days off	Number of staff
0	17
1	4
2	2
3	1
4	0
5	2

Construct a bar chart to display this distribution.

5.3 A roadside breakdown assistance service answers 37 calls in Derbyshire on one day. The response times taken to deal with these calls were noted and have been arranged in the grouped frequency distribution below.

Response time (minutes)	Number of calls
20 and under 30	4
30 and under 40	8
40 and under 50	17
50 and under 60	6
60 and under 70	2

(a) Produce a histogram to portray this distribution.
(b) Describe the shape of the distribution.

5.4 The ages of 20 tourists on a cruise holiday are:

32	35	36	41	43	44	48	51	51	54
57	62	62	65	67	67	67	68	70	72

Construct a stem and leaf display for this data.

5.5 The Zakon law firm has eight lawyers. The numbers of years since qualification and the average monthly revenue they generate are:

Years since qualification	2	5	7	10	12	18	23	28
Monthly revenue (£000)	5	12	10	14	19	24	27	30

Plot this data on a scatter diagram and describe the relationship between the two variables.

5.6 The Miarky Software Solutions corporation was established in 2001 and ceased trading in 2010. Its annual profits over this period were:

Year	2001	2002	2003	2004	2005	2006	2007	2008	2009	2010
Profit ($m)	5	8	10	17	24	31	35	42	28	21

Portray this data in a time series plot.

☆★★ More testing questions

5.7 Tourists seeking holiday accommodation in a self-catering complex in the resort of Zidania can make either a one- or two-week booking. The manager of the complex has produced the following table to show the bookings she received last season:

Tourist's home country	Type of booking	
	One-week	Two-week
France	13	44
Germany	29	36
Holland	17	21
Ireland	8	5

(a) Produce a simple bar chart to show the total number of bookings by home country.
(b) Produce a component bar chart to show the number of bookings by home country and type of booking.
(c) Produce a clustered bar chart to show the number of bookings by home country and type of booking.

5.8 The company marketing the revolutionary 'Girth Control' diet have distributed a press release that includes a grouped frequency distribution showing the weight losses achieved by the 50 participants in the trial of the diet.

Weight lost (kg)	Number of participants
0 and under 2	3
2 and under 4	3
4 and under 6	4
6 and under 8	7
8 and under 10	24
10 and under 12	9

(a) Draw a histogram to portray this distribution and comment on the shape of the distribution.
(b) Calculate the cumulative frequency for each class.
(c) Draw a cumulative frequency graph of the distribution.

5.9 The ages of 22 tourists on an adventure holiday are:

21 22 24 24 27 28 29 30 32 32 32
34 35 36 37 39 40 42 45 46 51 53

(a)   Construct a back-to-back stem and leaf display to present both this data and the data in question 5.4.

(b)   Compare and contrast the two distributions.

5.10   Sales of cold and flu treatments (in £000) in a Manchester pharmacy during the last three years were:

	Quarter			
Year	1	2	3	4
1	11.3	5.1	3.9	9.5
2	12.6	7.9	3.7	8.8
3	10.9	6.2	4.7	9.3

Draw a time series plot for this data.

★★★   Challenging questions

5.11   The annual earnings (in £000s) of the Chief Executive Officers of 24 large companies are:

195   200   205   210   230   245   250   268   310   325   340   350
364   375   389   390   400   409   412   425   445   460   475   500

Present this data in a stem and leaf display.

5.12   The top speeds and engine sizes of 12 performance cars are:

Top speed (mph)	137	165	185	118	168	155	125	177	129	163	157	134
Engine size (litres)	2.0	5.9	3.6	1.7	3.2	4.2	1.8	4.2	1.8	5.5	2.7	2.2

(a)   Which variable is the independent (X) variable?

(b)   Draw a scatter diagram to represent this data.

(c)   Is there a direct or inverse relationship between the two variables?

THE DEBRIEF

Key things to remember from this chapter

→ There are a variety of diagrams that can portray data.

→ The diagram to use depends on the type of data.

→ Qualitative data, data that is based on categories, can be illustrated using pictograms, pie charts and bar charts.

→ Component and clustered bar charts present qualitative data divided into categories and subdivided into subcategories.

→ Quantitative data, data that is based on measurement against a scale, can be portrayed using histograms, cumulative frequency graphs, and stem and leaf displays.

THE DEBRIEF (Continued)

→ Stem and leaf displays use the data values themselves as building blocks; they list the data as well as portray it.

→ Bivariate quantitative data can be presented in scatter diagrams. These show whether the relationship between two variables is direct or inverse.

→ Time series data should be portrayed using time series plots. In these time is plotted along the horizontal axis.

References

Hoaglin, D.C., Mosteller, F. and Tukey, J.W. (eds) (2000) *Understanding Robust and Exploratory Data Analysis,* New York: Wiley-Blackwell.

Holmes, N. (1991) *Designers Guide to Creating Charts and Diagrams*, New York: Watson-Guptill.

Tata Motors Limited (2010) *65th Annual report 2009–2010,* Mumbai: Tata Motors. Available at: http://ir.tatamotors.com/performance/a_reports/pdf/2010/Annual-Report-2010.pdf

Tufte, E.R. (2001) *The Visual Display of Quantitative Information* (2nd edn), Cheshire, CT: Graphics Press.

Vodafone Group PLC (2010) *Annual report for the year ended 31 March 2010.* Newbury, Berkshire: Vodafone. Available at: http://www.vodafone.com/content/dam/vodafone/investors/annual_reports/annual_report_accounts_2010.pdf

CHAPTER 6

General directions – summarising data

CHAPTER OBJECTIVES

This chapter will help you to:

→ Understand and use summary measures of location: the mode, median and arithmetic mean

→ Understand and use summary measures of spread: the range, quartiles, semi-interquartile range, standard deviation and variance

→ Present order statistics using boxplots

→ Find summary measures from grouped data

THE BARE BONES

What you will find in this chapter . . .

- Using the mode, median and mean to describe central tendency
- How to choose which measures of location to use
- Finding measures of location and spread from frequency distributions and stem and leaf displays
- Approximating measures of location and standard deviations from grouped frequency distributions
- Using the range, semi-interquartile range and standard deviation to describe spread
- Approximating order statistics from cumulative relative frequency graphs
- How summary measures are used in quality management
- Review questions to test your understanding

. . . and on the supporting website (www.pearsoned.co.uk/buglear)

- How to use EXCEL, Minitab and SPSS to summarise data
- Fully worked solutions to the review questions
- More review questions

REALITY CHECK

Business use of summary measures

◆ The concept of summary measures stretches back centuries. The use of the arithmetic mean goes back to the ancient world. It was used in astronomy as a way of balancing out discrepancies in observations of the positions of stars. In the sixteenth, seventeenth and eighteenth centuries these were matters of considerable importance for navigation and therefore trade.

◆ The subject of errors in measurement was an important one for astronomers in those days. They were interested in the spread in their measurements, attempting to minimise what they called the probable error.

◆ In the 1920s summary measures were used to apply statistical quality control in manufacturing industry. A prominent pioneer in this field was Yasushi Ishida who worked for the Tokyo Shibaura Electric Company (which later became the Toshiba Corporation). Ishida used statistical methods to improve the quality of the light-bulbs the company produced. At the time these were among the company's most important products and the company wanted him to ensure that they lasted longer (for more about Ishida see Nonaka, 1995). At about the same time Walter Shewhart, an engineer who worked for the Bell System telephone combine in the USA, developed control charts that enabled managers to improve quality by using summary measures as benchmarks against which to judge the goods produced (Juran, 1995).

6.1 Introduction

The subject of this chapter is *summary measures*. These are ways of representing or *summarising* data that is quantitative, data produced by measuring against a scale. Since summary measures are used to *describe* data they are also known as *descriptive measures*.

The summary measures covered in this chapter are extremely useful ways of conveying the general nature of a set of data in single figures. This is especially useful when two distributions are to be compared. If you learn how to use and interpret summary measures you will be able to communicate quantitative information very effectively.

There are two ways in which data can be summarised. The first involves using a single figure to convey a general idea of the values in the set of data. This is what averages do. You have probably met them before; references to things like average height and average age are very common.

We use the term average in the sense of a 'typical' or 'middle' level. More precisely an average is a single figure used to represent all the observations in a distribution. Averages are also called *measures of location*, because they convey where the data is *located* on the scale of numbers. Another name for them is *measures of central tendency*, because averages suggest where the *centre* of a set of data lies.

The other way in which data is summarised is based on how widely it is dispersed or spread out. These summary measures are known as *measures of dispersion* or *measures of spread*. They are single figures that enable us to assess how widely data is dispersed.

These measures, of location and of spread, complement each other. Good practice is to use both a measure of location and a measure of spread to describe a set of data. Together they convey a general idea of a distribution; its centre and how broadly the data is scattered around the centre.

6.2 **Measures of location**

There are several measures of location, or averages, that can be used to summarise data. They are based on different notions of 'average'. We'll start with the one that is simplest to find and to interpret, the mode. Subsequently we'll consider the other two principal averages, the median and the mean.

6.2.1 **The mode**

The *modal value*, or simply the *mode*, is the value that occurs most often in a set of data. No calculation is necessary, finding the mode involves just looking carefully at the data.

EXAMPLE 6.1

There are 17 bar staff at a club. Their ages are:

19 20 23 20 18 21 19 30 18 22 20 19 19 21 19 24 22

Find the mode.

Solution

19 occurs 5 times, more often than any other value, so the mode is 19.

The mode is easy and quick to find. When dealing with data consisting of a small number of discrete values one of which occurs more often than any of the others the mode is an adequate way to summarise the data. In Example 6.1, by using the mode, describing the staff as on average 19 years old, we would give a reasonable idea of the distribution.

The mode is not so useful when the data consists of many different values. This is especially so if two or more values each occur as often as the other.

EXAMPLE 6.2

Eighteen sales staff work at a car showroom. Their ages are:

41 19 46 24 41 47 42 39 33
35 41 30 34 34 33 33 39 44

Find the mode.

Solution

33 and 41 both occur three times. The distribution has two modes.

In Example 6.2 the distribution is *bimodal* as there are two modes. Should another 34-year-old join the staff we would have a third mode. This is a problem. Because an average is supposed to be a *single* figure that summarises a distribution having more than one defeats the object of the exercise.

A second problem with the mode is that it is not useful for summarising continuous data. Such data usually consists of many differing values and very rarely contains the 'repeats' of a single value that constitutes the mode

6.2.2 **The median**

As averages go, the mode has a very limited role. In contrast the second of our measures of location, the *median*, is an average we can use with any set of data.

The median is the middle of a set of data. It is the point that divides a distribution in two; one half of the observations are below the median, the other half are above it. The median is an *order statistic* because it is chosen on the basis of its *order* or position within the data. Finding the median of a set of data involves first establishing *where* it is then *what* it is. To do this we start by arranging the data in order of magnitude, which means listing them from lowest to highest values in an *array*. We then find the position of the median by adding one to the number of observations, *n*, and dividing the result by two.

$$\text{The median position} = (n + 1)/2$$

EXAMPLE 6.3

What is the median of the data in Example 6.1?

Solution

Array:

18 18 19 19 19 19 19 20 **20** 20 21 21 22 22 23 24 30

There are 17 observations, i.e . $n = 17$, so the median position $= (17 + 1)/2 = 18/2 = 9$

The median is the 9th observation in the array and hence the 9th highest value. It is the second of the three values of 20 and is highlighted in bold type. As it is the middle value there are the same number of observations to the left of it in the array, eight, as there are to the right of it.

The staff members have a median age of 20.

In Example 6.3 there is an odd number of observations, 17, so there is one middle value. When the number of observations is even there can be no one middle value. In these circumstances, to get the median we find the middle pair of observations, add them together and divide the result by two.

EXAMPLE 6.4

What is the median of the data in Example 6.2?

Solution

Array:

19 24 30 33 33 33 34 34 **35**
39 39 41 41 41 42 44 46 47

Here we have 18 observations, $n = 18$, so the median position $= (18 + 1)/2 = 9.5$.

At first sight this seems odd as there is no such thing as the '9.5th' observation. This is the position of the median, and in this case it is positioned midway between two adjacent observations, the 9th and 10th ones. These are 35 and 39 respectively and are highlighted in bold in the array. To get the point midway between them, simply add them and divide by two.

$$\text{Median} = (35 + 39)/2 = 37$$

The staff members have a median age of 37.

SELF-ASSEMBLY GUIDE

How to find medians

♦ Arrange the data in an array, or to put it another way list it in order of size from lowest to highest.

♦ Take n, the number of observations, add 1 and divide by 2. The result is the median location. Sometimes people think that this is the median itself. It isn't. It is where the median is in the array.

♦ If n, the number of observations, is an odd number the result of adding 1 and dividing by 2 will be a whole number. Whatever that number is, count that far along the observations in the array and the one you reach is the median. For example, if the median location is 6, the median itself is the 6th value in the array.

♦ If n is an even number the result of adding 1 and dividing by 2 will not be a whole number but a number ending with a half, such as 6.5. Round the number down and count that far along the observations in the array. Take the observation you reach and add it to the next highest observation in the array. Divide the result by 2 to get the median. For example if the median location is 6.5 count to the 6th value, add it to the 7th value and divide by 2.

6.2.3 The arithmetic mean

You may well have met averages in your earlier studies. You may already know of the mode and the median but they may not be the averages you would think of first if you were asked to determine the average of a set of figures. The request might bring to mind a process of adding the figures together then dividing by the number of them.

This process is what people tend to associate with 'the average'. The proper name for this type of average is the *mean*, or to be more precise the *arithmetic mean*. This mean, like the median, is an average that we can use for any quantitative data.

The way to find the arithmetic mean does involve calculation. This makes it harder work than the mode, which is only a matter of examining the data, and the median, which is based on putting data in order. For the mean we need to add all the observations together then divide the sum by the number of them, n.

$$\text{The mean} = \sum x/n$$

In this expression x represents an observed value of X, a quantitative variable. $\sum x$ is the sum of the observed values of X. The symbol used to represent the mean is $\bar{x}$, or 'x-bar'. This is actually the symbol for the mean of a sample. The symbol for the population is the Greek letter μ, 'mu'. This is the Greek equivalent of m, which of course is the first letter of the word mean. Later on we will look at how sample means can be used to estimate population means, so it is important to recognise this difference.

The mean is not the only statistical term that is represented by two different symbols, one of which is Greek. The Greek symbol is always the one that represents the population measure. Since we seldom have the time or resources to work out something like the mean of an entire population we are usually calculating sample means.

EXAMPLE 6.5

In one month the total costs (to the nearest £) of the mobile phone calls made by 23 men were:

17 17 14 16 15 24 12 20 17 17 13 21
15 14 14 20 21 9 15 22 19 27 19

Find the mean monthly cost.

Solution

The sum of these costs: $\sum x = 17 + 17 + 14 + \cdots + 27 + 19 = 398$

The arithmetic mean: $\sum x / n = 398/23 = £17.30$ (to the nearest penny)

6.2.4 Choosing which measure of location to use

The job that measures of location do is to summarise a distribution of observations in one figure. The three averages we have looked at do this job in different ways. Each of them has strengths and weakness so it is important to know which one to use.

The main issues to consider are:

- the type of data;
- if the average must be easy to find;
- how the data is distributed;
- if the average will be used as the basis for more analysis of the data.

If the data we have is fairly simple discrete data then the mode is worth considering, especially if we want a measure of location that is a possible actual data value. An example is the number of children per family. We may want to use the mode, which is likely to be 2, rather than the mean, which may be something like 1.87 and as such not a feasible value of the variable. For more complex data the mode is very unlikely to be of any use.

EXAMPLE 6.6

The numbers of occupants in 12 vehicles embarking on a ferry were:

4 2 1 3 2 4 2 3 4 2 10 2

What are the mode, median and mean of these of data.

Solution

The mode is 2, a value which occurs more often than any other, five times.

Array: 1 2 2 2 2 2 3 3 4 4 4 10

The median position is: $(12 + 1)/2 = 6.5$th position

The median is: (6th value + 7th value)$/2 = (2 + 3)/2 = 2.5$

The mean $= (1 + 2 + 2 + 2 + 2 + 2 + 3 + 3 + 4 + 4 + 4 + 10)/12$
$= 39/12 = 3.25$

In Example 6.6 only the mode has a value (2) which is feasible. The median (2.5) is not feasible as half an occupant of a vehicle makes no sense. The mean (3.25) is also not a feasible value. With data such as those in Example 6.6 the mode is an appropriate measure to use; saying that the average number of passengers is 2 is a valid assertion.

Not only is the mode appropriate in this case but as Example 6.6 illustrates it is the most straightforward average to find. All we had to do was count the number of times each value occurred. This is typical; in the sort of simple data the mode suits it is usually clear which of the values is most frequent.

Aside from its suitability for simple data sets such as in Example 6.6 the mode is not very useful. There are three reasons for this:

- It is not appropriate for data where there are many different values.
- There may be more than one mode in a distribution. We usually want an average that sums up a distribution in a single figure not several.

- The mode is selective because the only observations that matter are those that have the modal value. The other observations in the distribution simply don't count. Compared to this the mean is an inclusive measure of location because all the observations are added together and none are excluded.

Unless the data is simple the choice of average is between median and mean. In deciding which of these to use we need to take into account the shape of the distribution that we want to study. If the distribution is skewed, as against being symmetrical, the median is the more reliable average to use.

EXAMPLE 6.7

Construct a bar chart to portray the data in Example 6.6. Describe the shape of the distribution.

Solution

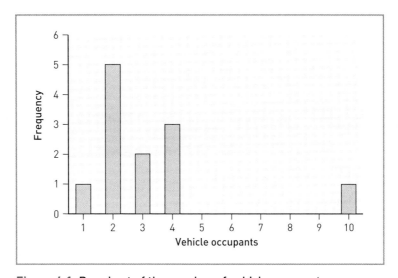

Figure 6.1 Bar chart of the number of vehicle occupants

The distribution is positively skewed. Most of the observations are on the left-hand side of the distribution.

In Example 6.6 the median is 2.5 and the mean 3.25. They are considerably different, particularly given that the smallest observation is 1 and the largest 10. The reason that the median and the mean differ is the skew of the distribution.

The median is the middle of a distribution. When we find a median we look for the middle observation or the middle pair of observations if n, the number of observations, is even. The rest of the observations on each side of the median really don't matter. However these observations are distributed has no impact on the value of the median. If the largest observation in Example 6.6 was 100 not 10 the median would remain 2.5. The median value depends on the number of observations either side of it, not what those values actually are.

In contrast, all of the observations impact on the value of the mean because they are all added together to calculate it. In Example 6.6, if the largest observation was 100 not 10 the value of the mean would be considerably higher, 10.75.

The way that the mean is calculated, by adding the observations together, makes it sensitive to *outliers*, unusually high or low observations. We represent the calculation of the mean as $\Sigma x/n$. Each observation contributes 1 towards n, the number of observations, and its value, *x*, towards Σx, the sum of the observations. An observation which is much less than the others will add very little to Σx and so lower the value of the mean. An observation that is much higher than the others will add considerably to Σx and so increase the value of the mean.

EXAMPLE 6.8

One observation in Example 6.6 was wrongly recorded. The '10' was in fact '4'. What are the mode, median and mean of the corrected data set?

Solution

The array is now: 1   2   2   2   2   2   3   3   4   4   4   4

The change has no effect on the mode; the most frequent value remains 2.

The change does not alter the median; the 6th and 7th observations in the array remain '2' and '3' so the median is still 2.5.

$$\text{The mean} = (1 + 2 + 2 + 2 + 2 + 2 + 3 + 3 + 4 + 4 + 4 + 4)/12$$
$$= 33/12 = 2.75$$

Changing the '10' to '4' has only affected the mean, which is now lower. The amended mean, 2.75 is much closer to the median, 2.5.

Skewed distributions will have extreme or unusual observations at one end. These observations will disproportionately influence, or to put it another way, distort the value of the mean. In Example 6.6 the highest value (10) was the reason why the mean (3.25) was so much higher than the median (2.5). We might describe it as dragging the mean above the median. When it was changed to 4 the mean became lower and much closer to the median.

The value of the mean in relation to the median depends on the skew in the distribution. In a positively skewed distribution like the one in Figure 6.1 the mean is higher than the median; the highest observations pull it above the median. In a negatively skewed distribution such as the one in Figure 5.10 the mean is lower than the median; the lowest observations pull it below the median.

This leads to the question of which is better to use to summarise a skewed distribution, the mean or the median? Out of the two the median is the more representative for skewed distributions. To illustrate this, look at the median and mean in Example 6.6. Because it is in the middle of the distribution there are six observations below the median (2.5) and six above it. In contrast there are eight observations below the mean (3.25) and just four above it. This imbalance suggests that the median has the better claim to represent the distribution.

One way of reducing the distortion that extreme observations exert on the mean it to 'top and tail' the distribution to produce what is known as a trimmed mean. This involves removing the lowest and highest observations and calculating the mean of the remaining ones.

EXAMPLE 6.9

Find a trimmed mean for the data in Example 6.6 by excluding the highest and lowest observations.

Solution

$$\text{The original mean} = (1 + 2 + 2 + 2 + 2 + 2 + 3 + 3 + 4 + 4 + 4 + 10)/12$$
$$= 39/12 = 3.25$$

$$\text{The trimmed mean} = (2 + 2 + 2 + 2 + 2 + 3 + 3 + 4 + 4 + 4)/10$$
$$= 28/10 = 2.80$$

Symmetrical distributions have a balance of observations. This means there are no extreme values on just one side to distort the mean. There is approximately the same weight of number on both sides. The upshot of this is that with symmetrical distributions the mean and median will be close, possibly the same.

EXAMPLE 6.10

Portray the data from Example 6.5 in a histogram. Find the median and mean of the distribution.

Solution

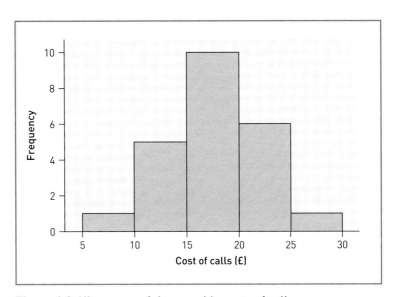

Figure 6.2 Histogram of the monthly costs of calls

With 23 observations the median is the $(23 + 1)/2 = 12$th observation. Array:

$$9 \quad 12 \quad 13 \quad 14 \quad 14 \quad 14 \quad 15 \quad 15 \quad 15 \quad 16 \quad 17 \quad \textbf{17}$$
$$17 \quad 17 \quad 19 \quad 19 \quad 20 \quad 20 \quad 21 \quad 21 \quad 22 \quad 24 \quad 27$$

The median is £17.

The mean $= (9 + 12 + \cdots + 24 + 27)/23 = 398/23 = $ £17.30 (to the nearest penny).

In Figure 6.2 the distribution is much more symmetrical than the one in Figure 6.1. The symmetry is the reason the mean (£17.30) is close to the median (£17).

There is another consideration that might determine our choice of average; whether it will be the basis for more quantitative analysis. If so we would use the mean as it is a more important representative measure than the median in statistical work.

Picking which type of average to use is not necessarily straightforward. To summarise the discussion in this section, the general guidelines are:

● to use the mode with data that is discrete and has a single mode;
● to use the median with skewed distributions;
● otherwise use the mean.

At this point you may find it useful to try **Review question 6.1** at the end of the chapter.

6.2.5 Measures of location from classified data

Sometimes we would like to use a measure of location to summarise a distribution but the data is only available in a classified form, such as a frequency distribution. In these situations the original data might have been deleted or the data may have been classified by someone else and we can't access it.

If we have the data in a stem and leaf display finding measures of location is not too difficult because the display is not only a picture of the distribution but also a list of the observations that are in it. The observations are listed, but each one is in a detached form, part stem and part leaf. To get the original data we have to reattach leaves to their stems.

It is possible to find all three main measures of location from a stem and leaf display. For the mode look for the leaf digit that occurs the most frequently. For the median count from one end of the distribution to the middle value, or pair of values if the number of observations, n, is even. For the mean, reassemble each observation then add them together and divide by n.

EXAMPLE 6.11

Use the following stem and leaf display of the data in Example 6.5 to obtain the mode, median and mean of the cost of calls.

Solution

Stem and leaf of cost of calls $n = 23$

```
0      9
1      2  3  4  4  4
1      5  5  5  6  7  7  7  7  8  9  9
2      0  0  1  1  2  4
2      7
```

Leaf unit = £1.00

The mode is £17 because there are four leaf digits '7' on second stem line for the stem digit '1'. No other leaf digit occurs as frequently.

The median position is $(23 + 1)/2 = 12$ so the median is the 12th observation. Find it by counting down the leaf digits from the top of the display.

The 1st observation is represented in the display by the leaf digit '9' on the '0' stem line. This observation is 09, i.e. £9, the smallest value in the distribution. The next stem line has five leaf digits, 2, 3, 4, 4, 4. These are on the first '1' stem line so these observations are £12, £13, £14, £14 and £14. They are the 2nd to 6th observations in order of size. The median is the 12th value so it can be none of these.

The next stem line has 11 leaf digits. These represent the 7th to 17th observations in order of size. The 12th observation, the median is among them. Starting from the first leaf digit on the stem line, which represents the 7th observation, we need to count a further six leaf digits along to reach the leaf digit that represents the 12th observation. This is the second of the four leaf digits '7' on this stem line, which is highlighted in bold in the display. The median is therefore £17.

For the mean we first need to reconstruct the observations from their stem and leaf components. When we add the observations (£9, £12, £13, £14, £14 etc.) the sum is £398. Dividing this by 23, the number of observations gives £17.30 (to the nearest penny), the same result as in Example 6.5.

In Example 6.11 we were able to obtain exactly the same results for the three measures of location as we did from the original data. This is because the stem and leaf display is built with the digits that make up the data. Even if we had rounded the observations to construct the stem and leaf display we would be able to obtain approximations of the mode, median and mean that are very close to the actual measures of location.

But suppose instead of a stem and leaf display we had a frequency distribution of the data or even just a bar chart? As long as we have the frequency of every value we can obtain the measures of location.

EXAMPLE 6.12

Using Figure 6.1, find the mode, median and mean of the distribution of vehicle occupants.

Solution

Figure 6.1 shows the frequency of each number of vehicle occupants in a bar chart. The height of each bar tells us how many vehicles have that number of occupants. We can derive the following frequency distribution from Figure 6.1:

Number of vehicle occupants	Frequency
1	1
2	5
3	2
4	3
5	0
6	0
7	0
8	0
9	0
10	1

The mode is '2' as this is the value that has occurred five times, more often than any other.

The median position is $(12 + 1)/2 = 6.5$th so the median is midway between the 6th and 7th observations. To find these observations we count down the lines of the frequency distribution in a similar way to how we counted down the leaf digits in the stem and leaf display in Example 6.11. The first line in the frequency distribution contains one '1', the smallest observation in the distribution. The second line has five '2's, the 2nd to 6th. One of these '2's is the first of the pair of observations we need to get the median. The third line has the two '3's, one of which is the 7th observation, the other one we need to get the median. So, the 6th observation is '2' and the 7th is '3'. The median is midway between these two, 2.5.

Since we know from the frequency distribution exactly how many times each value occurs we can add the individual observations before dividing by n, 12:

$$1 + 2 + 2 + 2 + 2 + 2 + 3 + 3 + 4 + 4 + 4 + 10 = 39/12 = 3.25.$$

Alternatively we can take a short cut. Multiply each value of the vehicle occupants that has occurred by its frequency then add up into the sum of these products. Formally if 'x' is the number of vehicle occupants and 'f' the frequency of each value, in other words the number of them that we have, this more direct way of getting the sum of the observations is Σfx. Since n, the number of observations, is the sum of the frequencies, Σf is an alternative

Solution cont expression to n. This shortcut method of getting the mean can be expressed as $\Sigma fx / \Sigma f$ and is illustrated in the following table:

Number of vehicle occupants	Frequency (f)	fx
1	1	1
2	5	10
3	2	6
4	3	12
5	0	0
6	0	0
7	0	0
8	0	0
9	0	0
10	1	10
	$\sum f = 12$	$\sum fx = 39$

$$\text{The mean} = \frac{\Sigma fx}{\Sigma f} = \frac{39}{12} = 3.25.$$

The mode, median and mean that we obtained in Example 6.12 are precisely the same as the results we produced in Example 6.6 from the raw data. This is because every value in the distribution is a category in its own right in the frequency distribution. In such cases we always know how many times each value occurs.

What if we want to find measures of location for a distribution but we only have the data in a grouped frequency distribution? In this situation the observations are grouped in classes not by individual value. This means we don't know how many times each value has occurred. We only know how many observations there are in each class, not the values of the observations. If this is the case we can't find the actual measures of location. The best we can do is to get approximations of them.

Grouped frequency distributions are generally used for data that takes many different values. The sheer variety of values is the reason for grouping them into classes. It is also the reason that the mode is unlikely to be our measure of location of choice. For some idea of the mode it is enough to find the *modal class*, the class that has the most observations.

EXAMPLE 6.13

What is the modal class of the distribution of the monthly costs of calls illustrated in Figure 6.2?

Solution

Figure 6.2 portrays the following grouped frequency distribution:

Cost (£)	Frequency
5 and under 10	1
10 and under 15	5
15 and under 20	10
20 and under 25	6
25 and under 30	1

The class with the most observations, i.e. the highest frequency, is '15 and under 20'. This is the modal class because it has 10 observations, more than in any other class.

Since a grouped frequency distribution does not show individual values we can't use it to find the exact value of the median, only an approximation of it. To do this we need to identify the median class, the class in which the median is located, but first we must find the median location. Once we have this we can use the fact that although the values are not listed in order of magnitude the classes that make up the grouped frequency distribution are. So it is a matter of looking for the class that contains the middle value of the distribution.

When we know which class the median is in we need to establish its likely position within that class. To do this we assume that all the values belonging to the median class are spread out evenly through the class.

How far we go through the median class to get an approximate value for the median depends on how many values in the distribution are in the classes before the median class. Subtracting this from the median position gives us the number of values we need to count into the median class to get our approximate median.

The distance we need to go into the median class is the median position less the number of values in the earlier classes divided by the number of values in the median class, which we then multiply by the width of the median class. We can express the procedure as follows:

$$\text{Approximate median} = \text{start of MC} + \frac{(\text{median position} - \text{number of observations to MC})}{\text{frequency of MC}} * \text{width of MC}$$

where MC stands for median class.

EXAMPLE 6.14 Find the approximate value of the median from the grouped frequency distribution in Example 6.13.

Solution With 23 observations in the distribution the median position $= (23 + 1)/2 = 12$ so the median is the 12th observation in the distribution.

The median value can't be in the first class, '5 and under 10'. This class has only one observation, the smallest in the distribution. Neither does it belong to the second class, which contains the 2nd to 6th observations. The median is actually in the third class. This one has the 7th to 16th observations, which includes the 12th one.

Where in the median class could the 12th observation be? The first value in the median class is the 7th value in the distribution. The 12th observation will be a further six values into the median class.

So what could the 12th observation be? It can't be less than £15 because it is in the median class and the median class, '£15 and under £20', begins with £15.

Assume that all 10 observations in the median class are distributed evenly through it. If that were the case the median would be 6/10ths of the way along the median class. Since the class width is £5 this means taking 6/10 of £5.

To sum up, to get an approximate value for the median,

Start where the median class begins	£15
Add to this 6/10ths of £5, the width of the median class	£3
Approximate value of the median	£18

The actual value of the median we found in Example 6.10 was £17 so this is a reasonable approximation.

SELF-ASSEMBLY GUIDE

Approximating a median from a grouped frequency distribution

◆ The general procedure is:

$$\text{Approximate median} = \text{start of MC} + \frac{(\text{median position} - \text{number of observations to MC})}{\text{frequency of MC}} * \text{width of MC}$$

◆ Find the median position $(n + 1)/2$. In Example 6.14 $n = 23$ so $(23 + 1)/2 = 12$.

◆ Find the median class (MC). This is the class that contains the observation in the median position. In Example 6.14 the median class is '£15 and under £20'.

◆ Find the total number of observations that are in the classes before the median class. In Example 6.14 this is the combined frequency of the first and second classes. The first has one observation and the second has five so there are six observations of less than £15.

◆ Find the frequency and width of the median class. In Example 6.14 these are 10 and £5 respectively.

◆ Enter the figures into the general procedure:

$$\text{Approximate median} = £15 + \frac{(12 - 6)}{10} * £5 = £15 + £3 = £18$$

Another way of approximating the median from a grouped frequency distribution is based on a cumulative frequency graph or a cumulative relative frequency graph of the distribution. These were introduced in section 5.3.2. The method works with either type of graph but is easier to apply with a cumulative relative frequency graph.

Plot the graph with the cumulative relative frequency scale on the vertical axis. Start from the point along this axis that represents exactly half the total cumulative relative frequency, 0.5. Draw a horizontal line across to the line depicting the cumulative relative frequency. At the point where these lines meet draw a vertical line down to the horizontal axis. The approximate value of the median is where this vertical line meets the horizontal axis.

EXAMPLE 6.15

Find the approximate value of the median monthly cost of calls data in Example 6.5 by constructing a cumulative relative frequency graph of the grouped frequency distribution in Example 6.13.

Solution

Cost (£)	Frequency	Cumulative frequency	Cumulative relative frequency
5 and under 10	1	1	0.04
10 and under 15	5	6	0.26
15 and under 20	10	16	0.70
20 and under 25	6	22	0.96
25 and under 30	1	23	1.00

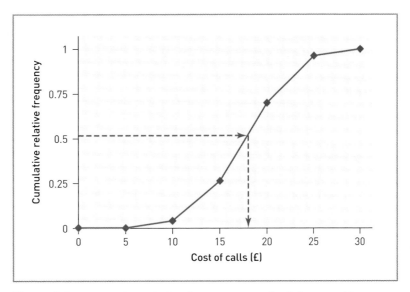

Figure 6.3 Cumulative relative frequency graph of the monthly costs of calls

The point where the vertical dotted line meets the horizontal axis is at approximately £18 on the horizontal scale (see Figure 6.3). This is the estimate of the median. From Example 6.9 we know that the actual median is £17 so our graphical approximation is quite close.

SELF-ASSEMBLY GUIDE

Approximating a median from a cumulative relative frequency graph

◆ Find 0.5 on the vertical axis.

◆ Draw a horizontal line from 0.5 on the vertical axis across to the cumulative relative frequency line.

◆ From the point where the two lines meet draw a vertical line down to the x-axis.

◆ The point where this vertical line meets the horizontal axis is the approximate value of the median.

To obtain an approximate value for the mean from a grouped frequency distribution we apply the same frequency-based approach as we used in Example 6.12. There we multiplied each value, x, by the number of times it occurred in the distribution, f, added up the products and divided by the total frequency of the distribution:

$$\bar{x} = \frac{\Sigma fx}{\Sigma f}$$

In Example 6.12 we worked from a frequency distribution which listed exactly how many times each value occurred. But what if we have data in a grouped frequency distribution? From this we know only the frequency of each class, not the frequency of each value. To get around this we assume that all the observations in a class take, on average, the value in the middle of the class, known as the class midpoint. The set of class midpoints is then used as the values of the variables, x, that make up the distribution. This is very unlikely to be true but the best we can do if we only have a grouped frequency distribution to work with.

Find the approximate value of the mean from the grouped frequency distribution in Example 6.13.

Solution

Cost of calls (£)	Midpoint (x)	Frequency (f)	fx
5 and under 10	7.5	1	7.5
10 and under 15	12.5	5	62.5
15 and under 20	17.5	10	175.0
20 and under 25	22.5	6	135.0
25 and under 30	27.5	1	27.5
		$\sum f = 23$	$\sum fx = 407.5$

The approximate value of the mean $= \sum fx / \sum f = 407.5/23 = £17.72$ (to the nearest penny), which is close to the actual value in Example 6.5, £17.30 (to the nearest penny).

At this point you may find it useful to try **Review questions 6.2 and 6.5** at the end of the chapter.

6.3 Measures of spread

In section 6.2 we looked at three measures of location that in different ways tell us about the central tendency of a distribution. Similarly, there are several measures of spread that can tell us how the observations in a distribution are dispersed. They measure spread in different ways. We'll start the simplest, the range, then look at using quartiles to measure spread and finally the most important measure of spread, the standard deviation.

Measures of spread are used with measures of location to convey two key features of a distribution; where the middle is and how the observations are scattered around the middle.

6.3.1 The range

The range is the most basic measure of spread. It is simply the difference between the lowest and highest observations in a distribution:

$$\text{Range} = \text{highest observation} - \text{lowest observation}$$

In some cases the range is a sufficient way of measuring spread, especially if we need only a general idea of the spread in a set of data. Its big drawback is that it is not always a reliable enough measure. This is because it is based on just two of the observations in a distribution. It is conceivable that two distributions have the same range but the observations are spread out in very different ways.

Two employment agencies, Rabota Recruitment and Slugar Selection, each have 9 employees. The length of service that their employees have (in years) is:

Rabota	1	5	5	7	8	9	11	12	15
Slugar	1	1	5	5	8	11	11	15	15

Calculate the range of each distribution.

$$\text{Range (Rabota)} = 15 - 1 = 14 \qquad \text{Range (Slugar)} = 15 - 1 = 14$$

Plot a histogram for each distribution and use them to compare the lengths of service of the employees of the agencies.

Solution

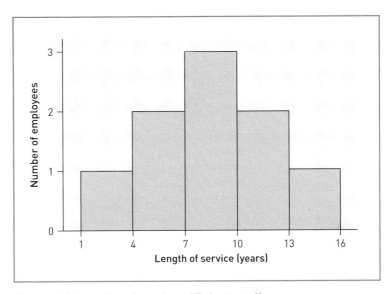

Figure 6.4 Lengths of service of Rabota staff

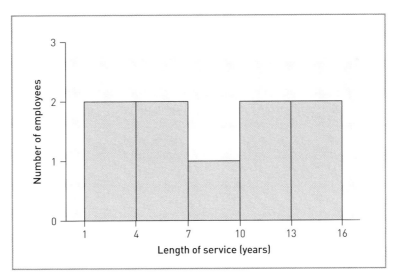

Figure 6.5 Lengths of service of Slugar staff

The ranges are exactly the same but, as Figures 6.4 and 6.5 show, the two distributions are different. The Rabota distribution has a central peak whereas the Slugar distribution dips in the centre with accumulations of observations at either end.

The ranges for the two distributions in Example 6.17 might be the same but the distributions are certainly not. The Rabota observations are more concentrated around the middle than the Slugar figures. There is more spread in the Slugar distribution but the range is not able to detect it. The range is therefore not a wholly reliable way of measuring the spread of data and this is because it is based only on the extreme observations.

6.3.2 Quartiles and the semi-interquartile range

The next measure of spread we will consider is the *semi-interquartile range*, which is often abbreviated to SIQR. We find this by using *quartiles*, which are order statistics like the median.

The median was the second measure of location we looked at in section 6.2. It is the middle point of a distribution that divides it in two. Half the observations are below the median and the other half are above it. The median cuts the distribution in half rather like a knife might cut a piece of cheese in half.

If we think of the median as cutting a distribution in two, the quartiles are the cuts that divide a distribution in four. The lower quartile cuts the lowest quarter of observations from the higher three-quarters. It is also known as the first quartile, or simply Q1. The median itself is the second of the quartiles as it cuts the lower half of the distribution (i.e. the lower two quarters of observations) away from the upper half (i.e. the upper two quarters of observations). The upper quartile cuts the highest quarter of observations from the lower three-quarters. It is also known as the third quartile, or simply Q3.

Quartiles are called *order statistics* as the values of them depend on sequence, or the order of observations in the distribution. There are other order statistics: *deciles* separate distributions into tenths, and *percentiles* separate distributions into hundredths.

Finding quartiles is similar to finding medians. We need the quartile position before we can get the quartile values.

The quartile position is midway between the median and the end of the distribution. We find it by starting with the median position, $(n + 1)/2$, in which n is the number of observations. The quartile position is the median position, which if not already a whole number must be rounded down to the nearest whole number, to which we add one then divide by two:

$$\text{Quartile position} = (\text{median position} + 1)/2$$

This is only where the quartiles are. Using an array, or a stem and leaf display, find the lower quartile by counting from the lowest observation to the quartile position. To get the upper quartile, count from the highest observation to the quartile position.

EXAMPLE 6.18

In one month the total costs (to the nearest £) of the mobile phone calls made by 23 women were:

14	5	15	6	17	10	26	10	12	17	13	29
7	27	33	16	30	9	15	7	33	28	21	

What are the median and upper and lower quartiles of this distribution?

Solution

Array:

5	6	7	7	9	10	10	12	13	14	15	15
16	17	17	21	26	27	28	29	30	33	33	

There are 23 observations so the median position $= (23 + 1)/2 = 12$th. The 12th value in the array is the second of the two 15s so the median is £15. The monthly cost of calls for half the women is less than £15, and the monthly cost for the other half is more than £15.

If the median position is 12 the quartile position $= (12 + 1)/2 = 6.5$th. The quartile position is therefore halfway between the 6th and 7th observations.

The lower quartile is midway between the 6th and 7th observations from the lowest. These are both 10, which means the lower quartile is £10. The monthly cost of calls for 25% of the women is less than £10.

The upper quartile is midway between the 6th and 7th observations from the highest. These are 27 and 26. The upper quartile is halfway between these, 26.5. The monthly cost of calls for 25% of the women is above £26.50.

SELF-ASSEMBLY GUIDE

Finding quartiles

◆ Start with the median position. This is $(n + 1)/2$, where n is however many observations there are in the distribution. In Example 6.18 there were 23 observations so the median position is $(23 + 1)/2 = 12$.

◆ Round down the median position to the nearest whole number. In Example 6.18 this is not necessary as the median location is already a whole number, 12.

◆ The quartile position is the median position plus 1 divided by 2. In Example 6.18 it is $(12 + 1)/2 = 6.5$, which puts it halfway between the 6th and 7th observations.

◆ This is the position of the lower and upper quartiles. The lower quartile is 6.5 observations from the lowest. The upper quartile is 6.5 observations from the highest.

◆ Using either an array or a stem and leaf display count along the observations to find the quartiles. In Example 6.18 the lower quartile is £10, midway between the 6th from lowest observation, 10, and the 7th from lowest, which is also 10. The lower quartile is therefore $(10 + 10)/2 = 10$.

◆ In Example 6.18 the upper quartile is £26.50, midway between the 6th from highest observation, 27, and the 7th from highest, 26. The upper quartile is therefore $(27 + 26)/2 = 26.5$.

The upper quartile, Q3, cuts the highest quarter of the distribution from the rest. The lower quartile, Q1, cuts off the lowest quarter from the rest. This means that between them the lower and upper quartiles span the middle half of the observations, in other words all the observations except for the lowest and highest quarters.

The difference between the lower and upper quartiles is the *interquartile range*. The semi-interquartile range (SIQR) is half the interquartile range:

$$SIQR = (Q3 - Q1)/2$$

EXAMPLE 6.19 What is the semi-interquartile range of the call costs data in Example 6.18?

Solution The lower quartile is £10 and the upper quartile is £26.50.

$$SIQR = (£26.50 - £10)/2 = £16.50/2 = £8.25$$

The semi-interquartile range measures spread. The bigger the SIQR is the more widely spread are the observations in the distribution.

EXAMPLE 6.20

What is the SIQR of the distribution in Example 6.5?

How does it compare to the SIQR in Example 6.19?

Solution

Array:

9	12	13	14	14	14	15	15	15	16	17	17
17	17	19	19	20	20	21	21	22	24	27	

Since we have 23 observations the median position is the $(23 + 1)/2 = 12$th.

The quartile position is $(12 + 1)/2 = 6.5$th.

$$Q1 = (£14 + £15)/2 = £14.50 \qquad Q3 = (£20 + £20)/2 = £20$$
$$SIQR = (£20 - £14.50)/2 = £2.75$$

The SIQR for the monthly call costs of the men (£2.75) is considerably less than the SIQR for the women (£8.25). This suggests that there is more spread in the women's call costs.

Order statistics are the basis of a type of diagram called a *box and whiskers plot*, often truncated to *boxplot*, which is a very useful way of comparing two or more distributions. The box is the heart of the plot. It has the lower and upper quartiles at either end. The median is represented by a line inside the box. The whiskers connect the ends of the box to the lowest and highest values.

EXAMPLE 6.21

Construct boxplots for the data in Examples 6.5 and 6.18, the monthly costs of calls data for men and women.

Solution

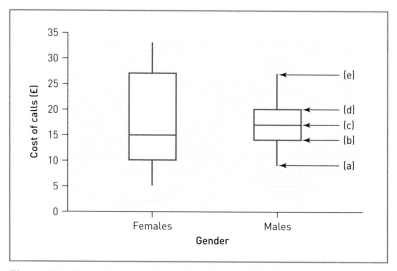

Figure 6.6 Monthly costs of mobile phone calls for men and women

Look at the right-hand side boxplot in Figure 6.6. This portrays the monthly costs of calls for the men. The letter labelling is as follows:

(a) is the lowest observation,

(b) is the lower quartile,

(c) is the median,

(d) is the upper quartile

(e) is the highest observation.

The boxplot on the left in Figure 6.6, the one representing the costs of the women's calls, is larger than the other one, which represents the costs of the men's calls. This reflects the greater variation in costs for females. Within the box for the distribution of women's calls the line that represents the median is quite low down. This suggests that the middle half of this distribution is skewed. There is more space in the box between the median line and the upper end of the box than there is between the median line and the lower end of the box. The same proportion of observations is represented by each part of the box, one quarter. The fact that the upper half of the box is more spacious means that the quarter of observations between the median and the upper quartile are more spread out than the quarter of observations between the median and the lower quartile.

Similarly the whisker above the left box extends further than the whisker below. This is further evidence of skew in the distribution. A longer whisker represents more spread, not more observations.

In the boxplot on the right, which represents the distribution of the costs of the men's calls, the median line is about midway between the top and the bottom of the box. This suggests that the spread of values in the middle half of the costs for males is symmetrical. The whiskers are, however, not the same length, which suggests some degree of skew between the outer quarters.

Boxplots, especially when produced using statistical software, are useful for spotting outliers. These are observations that are some way from the others. When they occur it is important to check that they have been measured and recorded accurately. If they have we would look for factors that make them unusual.

EXAMPLE 6.22

The lowest observation in the distribution of the costs of men's calls in Example 6.5 should be £4 not £9. Construct a boxplot to portray the distribution with this correction.

Solution

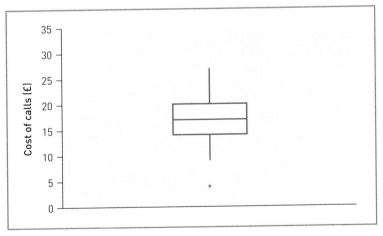

Figure 6.7 Monthly costs of calls for male mobile phone owners

In Figure 6.7 the amended smallest observation, 4, is represented as an asterisk. This is to emphasise its relative isolation from the rest of the observations.

The shape of a boxplot is a good guide to the shape of the distribution it represents. Figure 6.8 shows example boxplots for (a) symmetrical, (b) negative skewed and (c) positive skewed distributions, in each case compared to a histogram portraying the same distribution.

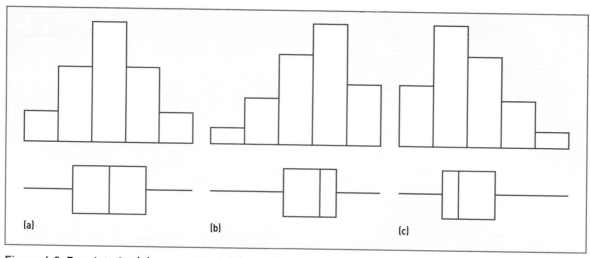

Figure 6.8 Boxplots for (a) symmetrical, (b) negative skewed and (c) positive skewed distributions compared to histograms

The semi-interquartile range (SIQR), based like boxplots on quartiles, is a useful way of measuring spread. Using it with the median is generally the most appropriate approach to summarising. Its shortcoming is that because it is based on selected observations in a distribution it won't always distinguish differences in spread between distributions.

EXAMPLE 6.23

What is the SIQR for each of the distributions of lengths of service of staff in the employment agencies in Example 6.17?

Solution

Each distribution has nine observations, which makes the median position $(9 + 1)/2 = $ 5th.

For each distribution the quartile position is $(5 + 1)/2 = $ 3rd.

Rabota	1	5	5	7	8	9	11	12	15
Slugar	1	1	5	5	8	11	11	15	15

Each distribution has a lower quartile of 5 and an upper quartile of 11. The SIQR in both cases is half the difference between the quartiles, 3 years' service. The fact that the SIQR is the same for both distributions is misleading; as Figures 6.4 and 6.5 showed, the spread of observations in these distributions is not the same.

At this point you may find it useful to try **Review questions 6.3, 6.6, 6.7 and 6.11** at the end of the chapter.

6.3.3 The standard deviation

The limitations of the both the range and the SIQR arise because they are based on only a few observations. An alternative measure of spread is the *standard deviation*. This is based on all the observations. It is the most important measure of spread in quantitative methods.

In the term 'standard deviation' the word 'standard' is synonymous with typical and 'deviation' means difference. The difference it refers to is the difference between an observation and the mean of the distribution to which it belongs. The standard deviation is therefore the typical difference between the observations in a distribution and the mean of the distribution.

Because the standard deviation is based on differences between the observations and the mean, to find it we start with the mean. Once we have this we can work out by how much each observation deviates from the mean.

EXAMPLE 6.24

Five fishing boats land the following numbers of kilograms of sprats on a particular day:

$$6 \quad 8 \quad 10 \quad 12 \quad 14$$

What is the deviation of this data from the mean in each case?

Solution

The mean, $\bar{x} = 50/5 = 10$

Observation (x)	Mean ($\bar{x}$)	Deviation ($x - \bar{x}$)
6	10	−4
8	10	−2
10	10	0
12	10	2
14	10	4

In Example 6.24 we have the deviations from the mean but how do we get the *standard* deviation? One way, perhaps the most obvious way, is to add them up and divide by the number of them. This would give us what we could call the *average* deviation. The problem with this is that when we add the deviations in the column on the right of the table in Example 6.24 we get zero:

$$(-4) + (-2) + 0 + 2 + 4 = 0$$

This is no fluke of this particular set of data. The sum of the deviations will always add up to zero because of the nature of the mean. It is rather like the centre of gravity of an object; there is as much numerical 'mass' to one side of it as there is to the other. The consequence is that the negative deviations, those between the mean and the observations below it will always cancel out the positive deviations, those between the mean and the observations above it.

For the standard deviation we solve this problem by squaring the deviations before adding them. This works because whether the deviation is negative or positive the square of it will always be positive. The standard deviation is based on the sum of the squared deviations, $\Sigma(x - \bar{x})^2$.

EXAMPLE 6.25

What is the sum of the squared deviations, $\Sigma(x - \bar{x})^2$, of the data in Example 6.24?

Solution

Observation (x)	Mean ($\bar{x}$)	Deviation ($x - \bar{x}$)	Squared deviation ($x - \bar{x}$)^2
6	10	−4	16
8	10	−2	4
10	10	0	0
12	10	2	4
14	10	4	16

$$\Sigma(x - \bar{x})^2 = 16 + 4 + 0 + 4 + 16 = 40$$

The sum of squared deviations is a reliable measure of total deviation. To get the standard deviation from it we need to involve the number of deviations. The obvious approach is to simply divide by the number of observations, n, since there is a deviation for each observation. This is not quite the case; we divide the sum of the squared deviations by $n - 1$, in other words one less than the number of observations.

The reason is to do with something called *degrees of freedom*. In a set of data there are as many degrees of freedom as there are observations, n. This means that if, for instance, we are told there are to be a certain number of observations we can choose all of them freely. On the other hand if we are told what the mean has to be we only have a free choice of one less than the number of observations. The final observation has to be the only figure that, in combination with the others, produces the mean. We will have lost one degree of freedom. To illustrate, if there are three observations and the mean must be 4, we could choose 2 and 3 as the first two observations but the third must be 7 so that the mean is 4, i.e. $2 + 3 + 7 = 12$ and $12/3 = 4$. If instead we had chosen 1 and 8 as the first two observations, the third would have to be 3.

In calculating the standard deviation we use the mean, which results in the loss of a degree of freedom. For this reason to calculate s, the standard deviation of a sample, we divide the sum of squared deviations by $(n - 1)$ not n.

It is only if we want to find σ, the standard deviation of a population, that we divide the sum of squared deviations by n. Since most investigations are based on sample data rather than populations it is very unlikely that you will need to find a population standard deviation.

Sample standard deviations are often used to estimate population standard deviations. This only works if the sample standard deviation is worked out appropriately, which means dividing the sum of squared deviations by $n - 1$.

Once we have divided the sum of squared deviations by $n - 1$ there is one last arithmetical task. This is to take the square root. We squared the deviations to start with so to make sure our standard deviation is in the same units as the observations we have in effect to reverse the process. Without doing this we would have a result for the data in Example 6.25 in 'kilograms squared'.

The process we use to find a sample standard deviation can be represented as:

$$s = \sqrt{\frac{\sum (x - \bar{x})^2}{(n - 1)}}$$

EXAMPLE 6.26   What is the standard deviation of the data in Example 6.24?

Solution   From Example 6.25 the sum of squared deviations is 40 and n, the number of observations, is 5. The standard deviation is:

$$s = \sqrt{\frac{40}{4}} = \sqrt{10} = 3.162$$

Calculating standard deviations as we have done it so far is cumbersome, especially for large sets of data, because it involves taking the mean away from every observation. A modified way to get a sample standard deviation is to square the observations and add them up to get the sum of the squared observations. Next take the sum of the observations and square that.

Divide it by the number of observations, n, and subtract the result from the sum of the squared observations. Finally, multiply by one divided by the number of degrees of freedom and take the square root. We can express the procedure as:

$$s = \sqrt{\frac{1}{n-1}\left(\sum x^2 - \frac{(\sum x)^2}{n}\right)}$$

EXAMPLE 6.27

Calculate the standard deviation for the data in Example 6.23 without subtracting each observation from the mean.

Solution

Observation (x)	x^2
6	36
8	64
10	100
12	144
14	196
$\sum x = 50$	$\sum x^2 = 540$

$$s = \sqrt{\frac{1}{5-1}\left(540 - \frac{(50)^2}{5}\right)} = \sqrt{\frac{1}{4}\left(540 - \frac{2500}{5}\right)} = \sqrt{\frac{1}{4}(540 - 500)}$$

$$= \sqrt{\frac{1}{4}(40)} = \sqrt{10} = 3.162$$

This is exactly the same as the result we obtained in Example 6.26 using the original approach.

SELF-ASSEMBLY GUIDE

Calculating the sample standard deviation

◆ Add up the observations to get $\sum x$. In Example 6.27 this came to 50.

◆ Add up the squared observations to get $\sum x^2$. In Example 6.27 this was 540.

◆ Square the sum of the observations to get $(\sum x)^2$, which was 2500 in Example 6.27.

◆ Divide the sum of the squared observations, $(\sum x)^2$, by n. In Example 6.27 this meant dividing 2500 by 5 to get 500.

◆ Take $(\sum x)^2/n$ away from the sum of the squared observations, $\sum x^2$. In Example 6.27 this meant taking 500 away from 540 to get 40.

◆ Divide the result by $n-1$, which in Example 6.27 meant dividing 40 by 4 to get 10.

◆ Take the square root of the result. In Example 6.27 this was 3.162.

If we have data for a whole population we don't need to worry about degrees of freedom. The procedure for working out the population standard deviation, sigma (σ), is:

$$\sigma = \sqrt{\frac{\sum(x - \mu)^2}{n}}$$

Note that to get the *population* standard deviation we subtract the *population* mean, μ, from every observation. The alternative approach, which does not involve subtracting every observation from the mean, is:

$$\sigma = \sqrt{\left(\sum x^2 - \frac{(\sum x)^2}{n}\right)}$$

Using these methods to find standard deviations is laborious, even with a small set of data. It is something best done using computer software or at least a scientific calculator.

The square of the standard deviation is the *variance*. This is an important measure in more advanced quantitative work. To find a variance we use the same procedure as for a standard deviation but we stop short before the final stage; we don't take the square root.

$$\text{The sample variance, } s^2 = \frac{\sum(x - \bar{x})^2}{n - 1}$$

$$\text{The population variance, } \sigma^2 = \frac{\sum(x - \mu)^2}{n}$$

When used with the mean the standard deviation gives an overall summary of a distribution. For some types of distribution the mean and the standard deviation are the *parameters* of the distribution. They are its defining characteristics.

The widespread use of the standard deviation is in part because it is a dependable way of measuring spread.

EXAMPLE 6.28

In Examples 6.17 and 6.23 the range and the SIQR were the same for the data from both employment agencies. What are the standard deviations of the distributions?

Solution

Rabota:

Length of service (x)	x^2
1	1
5	25
5	25
7	49
8	64
9	81
11	121
12	144
15	225
73	735

$$s = \sqrt{\frac{1}{8}\left(735 - \frac{(73)^2}{9}\right)} = \sqrt{\frac{1}{8}(735 - 592.111)} = \sqrt{\frac{1}{8}(142.889)}$$

$$= \sqrt{17.861} = 4.226$$

Slugar:

Length of service (x)	x^2
1	1
1	1
5	25
5	25
8	64
11	121
11	121
15	225
15	225
72	808

$$s = \sqrt{\frac{1}{8}\left(808 - \frac{(72)^2}{9}\right)} = \sqrt{\frac{1}{8}(808 - 576)} = \sqrt{\frac{1}{8}(232)}$$

$$= \sqrt{29} = 5.385$$

The Slugar standard deviation, 5.385, is higher than the Rabota standard deviation, 4.226. The difference between them reflects the contrast in the spread of the distributions as shown in Figures 6.4 and 6.5. The standard deviation has detected the differences where the range and the SIQR could not.

The standard deviation is used as a 'measuring rod' for distributions. In general almost all the observations in any distribution will be within three standard deviations either side of the mean. Similarly the interval within two standard deviations either side of the mean contains 90% or so of the observations in a distribution.

The standard deviation is used to mark out values in a distribution in relation to the mean. For instance, if the mean of a set of examination marks is 55 and the standard deviation is 10 a result of 75 marks could be described as being two standard deviations, i.e. two lots of 10 above the mean. A result of 40 could be described as being one and a half standard deviations below the mean.

You may meet the *coefficient of variation*, which is sometimes used to compare distributions, especially where the units of measurement differ. This is simply the standard deviation as a percentage of the mean:

$$\text{Coefficient of variation (CV)} = \frac{s}{\bar{x}} * 100$$

EXAMPLE 6.29

A transport consultant is asked to compare car use in the UK with that in the Netherlands. The mean annual mileage of a sample of motorists living in London was 12,466 with a standard deviation of 3281. The mean number of kilometres travelled by a sample of Amsterdam motorists was 15,170 with a standard deviation of 3594.

Calculate the coefficient of variation for each sample of motorists and use them to compare the annual distances travelled.

Solution

$$\text{London CV} = \frac{3281}{12,466} * 100 = 26.320\%$$

$$\text{Amsterdam CV} = \frac{3549}{15,170} * 100 = 23.395\%$$

The distances travelled by the Amsterdam motorists vary slightly less in relation to the mean.

At this point you may find it useful to try **Review questions 6.4 and 6.10** at the end of the chapter.

6.3.4 Measures of spread from classified data

We may want to find measures of spread for data that is only available to us in a classified form. The way we do this and how accurate the results will be depend on what type of data we are dealing with and how it is presented.

If the data consists of a limited number of discrete values whose frequencies are listed in a frequency distribution this is sufficient to allow us to work out the measures of spread we need in the same way as we would from the unclassified data.

If our data is in the form of a stem and leaf display we can reunite the leaves with their stems to get at least the approximate values of the original observations. From these we can get the same values of the measures of spread as we would from the raw data, or at least come very close to them.

Working out measures of spread is not so straightforward if the data is in a grouped frequency distribution. The observations are grouped in classes not listed individually so we can't get the actual measures of spread, only approximations. Below we will look at finding the semi-interquartile range from a cumulative relative frequency graph and approximating the standard deviation from a grouped frequency distribution.

Finding approximate values of quartiles using a cumulative relative frequency graph is similar to the way we approximated the median of the data from Example 6.5 in Example 6.15. To find the median, the halfway point in the distribution, we started halfway up the vertical axis. To find the lower quartile we start one quarter of the way up the vertical axis, and for the upper quartile, three-quarters of the way up.

EXAMPLE 6.30

Estimate lower and upper quartiles of the distribution of call costs in Example 6.5 using the cumulative relative frequency graph from Example 6.15, Figure 6.3. From these estimates produce an approximate value for the semi-interquartile range of the distribution.

Solution

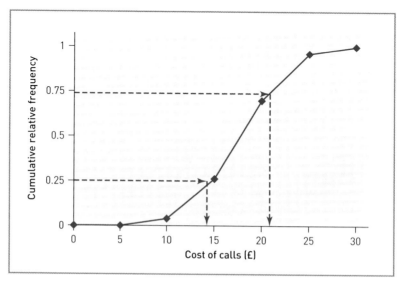

Figure 6.9 Cumulative relative frequency graph of the monthly costs of calls

From Figure 6.9 the estimate of the lower quartile is where the vertical dashed line on the left reaches the horizontal axis, at roughly £14. The estimate of the upper quartile is where the vertical dashed line on the right reaches the horizontal axis, at roughly £21. The difference between these estimates is £7. The semi-interquartile range is half this, £3.50.

In Example 6.20 the actual lower and upper quartiles were £14.50 and £20, making the actual semi-interquartile range £2.75 so the estimate is reasonably close.

We only know from a grouped frequency distribution how many observations are in each class. We can't get the observations themselves from it. Working out a standard deviation as we have done in section 6.3.3 requires the actual observations. If these are not available we need a way of representing the observations using their classes. We use the class midpoints to approximate the observations in the class. We used the same method to determine the mean using a grouped frequency distribution in section 6.2.5.

The approximate value of the standard deviation is:

$$s = \sqrt{\frac{1}{\sum f - 1}\left[\sum fx^2 - \frac{(\sum fx)^2}{\sum f}\right]}$$

In this expression f is the frequency of a class and x is the midpoint of a class.

EXAMPLE 6.31

Use the grouped frequency distributions from Example 6.13 to estimate the standard deviation of the costs of calls.

Solution

Cost of calls	Midpoint (x)	Frequency (f)	fx	x²	fx²
5 and under 10	7.5	1	7.5	56.25	56.25
10 and under 15	12.5	5	62.5	156.25	781.25
15 and under 20	17.5	10	175.0	306.25	3062.50
20 and under 25	22.5	6	135.0	506.25	3037.50
25 and under 30	27.5	1	27.5	756.25	756.25
		$\sum f = 23$	$\sum fx = 407.5$		$\sum fx^2 = 7693.75$

$$s = \sqrt{\frac{1}{23 - 1}\left[7693.75 - \frac{(407.5)^2}{23}\right]} = \sqrt{\frac{1}{22}\left[769.75 - \frac{166,056.25}{23}\right]}$$

$$= \sqrt{\frac{1}{22}[7693.75 - 7219.837]} = \sqrt{21.5415} = 4.641$$

The original data is in Example 6.5. From this we can work out the actual standard deviation, 4.128.

At this point you may find it useful to try **Review questions 6.8 and 6.9** at the end of the chapter.

6.4 Summary measures in quality management

In many fields of business the quality of the product or service is paramount. To improve quality organisations strive to increase the consistency of their output. This means reducing the extent to which key aspects of their products or services vary. These might be variables such as the product weight or service delivery time. Because the standard deviation measures spread, i.e. how extensively observations vary, it is a key tool in controlling quality.

One widely used quality management technique is the *control chart*. The central feature of this is a horizontal line that represents the performance target, the desired mean of the variable. There are parallel lines one of which is three standard deviations below the mean; this is the *lower control limit (LCL)*. The other is three standard deviations above the mean, which is the *upper control limit (UCL)*. When each product is produced or service delivered the performance variable is measured and the resulting observation is plotted on the chart. Whenever a point is below the LCL or above the UCL, the operation is deemed out of control. The cause of this should be investigated and some sort of remedial action taken.

EXAMPLE 6.32

The Speedy ReTyre company promises customers it will fit car tyres in half an hour. The mean and standard deviation of the tyre fitting times are 22 minutes and 3 minutes respectively. As a result of installing new equipment the layout of the fitting bay has been changed. The fitting times for the first ten customers after the reorganisation are:

32.5   28.3   30.7   27.9   26.9   25.2   23.1   32.6   25.0   32.7

Produce a control chart and plot the data on it. Comment on the performance after the reorganisation.

Solution

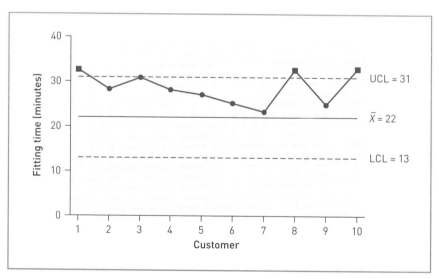

Figure 6.10 Control chart for tyre fitting times

In Figure 6.10, the first fitting time is too high, then the times improve so that they are within the control limits until the erratic pattern in the last three observations. These suggest the process may be going out of control. Note that in this chart the points outside the control limits are plotted as squares to distinguish them from the 'in control' points plotted as circles.

Example 6.32 illustrates a relatively simple control chart. Typically samples of products or services are taken and the means of these samples used to track consistency, but the standard deviation is used in the same way. To find out more about statistical quality control see Montgomery (2004).

At this point you may find it useful to try **Review question 6.12** at the end of the chapter.

REVIEW QUESTIONS

Answers to these questions are on page 448. There are tips and hints to help you with them on the supporting website at **www.pearsoned.co.uk/buglear**, where you will also find the fully worked solutions.

☆☆★ Basic questions

6.1 The numbers of credit cards carried by 25 shoppers are:

2 5 2 0 4 3 0 1 2 7 2 4 1
3 9 4 1 4 1 5 5 2 3 1 2

(a) Determine the mode and median of this distribution.
(b) Calculate the mean of the distribution and compare it to the mode and median. What can you conclude about the shape of the distribution?
(c) Draw a bar chart to represent the distribution and confirm your conclusions in (b).

6.2 The numbers of driving tests taken to pass by 28 clients of a driving school are given in the following table:

Tests taken	Number of clients
1	10
2	8
3	4
4	3
5	3

(a) Obtain the mode, median and mean from this frequency distribution and compare their values.
(b) Plot a simple bar chart of the distribution.

6.3 Find the lower and upper quartiles of the data in question 6.1, and use them to work out the semi-interquartile range.

6.4 Voditel International owns a large fleet of company cars. The mileages, in thousands of miles, of a sample of 17 of its cars over the last financial year were:

11 31 27 26 27 35 23 19 28 25 15 36 29 27 26 22 20

Calculate the mean and standard deviation of these mileage figures.

☆★★ More testing questions

6.5 Spina Software Solutions operate an online help and advice service for PC owners. The numbers of calls made to them by subscribers in a month are tabulated below:

Calls made	Number of subscribers	
	Female	Male
1	31	47
2	44	42
3	19	24
4	6	15
5	1	4

Find the mode, median and mean for both distributions and use them to compare the two distributions.

6.6 Toofley the Chemists own 29 pharmacies. The stem and leaf display below shows the numbers of packets of a new skin medication sold in each of their shops in a week.

Stem	Leaves
0	5 6 7 8 8 9 9
1	0 1 2 2 2 3 3 3 3
1	5 7 8 8 9 9
2	0 0 1 2 2 2
2	
3	3

Leaf unit $= 1.0$

(a) Find the mode and range of this data.
(b) Identify the median of the data.
(c) Find the lower and upper quartiles.
(d) Determine the semi-interquartile range.

6.7 Construct a boxplot to represent the data in question 6.6 using your answers to parts (b) and (c) of the question. Does the boxplot suggest the distribution is skewed, and if so is the skew negative or positive?

6.8 Farmer Fred has a dairy herd of 100 cattle. The annual milk yields of the cows in the herd are given in the following table:

Annual yield (litres)	Number of cows	Cumulative relative frequency
4500 and under 5000	5	0.05
5000 and under 5500	13	0.18
5500 and under 6000	24	0.42
6000 and under 6500	28	0.70
6500 and under 7000	21	0.91
7000 and under 7500	9	1.00

Construct a cumulative relative frequency graph of the distribution and use it to find approximate values of the median and semi-interquartile range.

★★★ Challenging questions

6.9 Zilliony plc likes its workers to cycle to work rather than travel by car. The company commissioned a study of commuting habits among the staff at its Gazonville office. This found that 33 workers cycle to work and 61 travel by car. The distances these workers travel to work are given in the following grouped frequency distributions:

Distance travelled (km)	Cyclists	Motorists
0 and under 5	13	3
5 and under 10	10	8
10 and under 15	9	22
15 and under 20	1	18
20 and under 25	0	10

(a) Find approximate values for the mean and median of the distributions.
(b) Find approximate values for the standard deviation of each distribution.
(c) Use the figures you obtain for (a) and (b) to compare the two distributions.

6.10 Three credit card companies each produced an analysis of their customers' bills over the last month. The following results have been published:

Company	Mean bill size	Standard deviation of bill sizes
Akula	£761	£241
Bremia	£925	£135
Dolg	£679	£196

Are the following statements true or false?

(a) Dolg bills are on average the lowest and vary more than those of the other two companies.
true/false

(b) Bremia bills are on average the highest and vary more than those of the other two companies.
true/false

(c) Akula bills are on average higher than those from Dolg and vary more than those of Bremia.
true/false

(d) Akula bills are on average lower than those from Bremia and vary less than those of Dolg.
true/false

(e) Bremia bills are on average higher than those from Akula and vary more than those of Dolg.
true/false

(f) Dolg bills vary less than those from Akula and are on average lower than those of Bremia.
true/false

6.11 The ages of holidaymakers staying at two Adriatic resorts were taken and the boxplots below were produced.

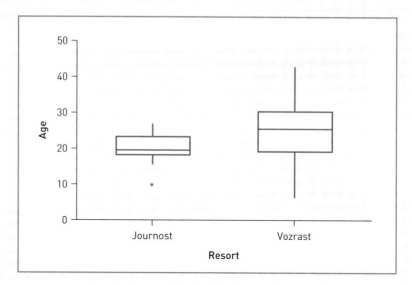

Study the diagram and say whether each of the following is true or false.

(a) The youngest holidaymaker is in Journost.
(b) The SIQR for Vozrast is larger.
(c) There is one outlier, the youngest holidaymaker in Journost.
(d) The middle half of the ages of holidaymakers in Vozrast is more symmetrically distributed.
(e) The upper quartile of ages in Vozrast is about 25.
(f) The median age in Journost is about 19.
(g) The median age in Vozrast is higher than the upper quartile age in Journost.

6.12 A 'while-you-wait' shoe repair service offers to replace certain types of heels on ladies' shoes in three minutes. Long experience has shown that the mean replacement time for these heels is 2.8 minutes and the standard deviation is 0.15 minutes. A trainee achieves the following times on her first day:

$$2.5 \quad 3.2 \quad 2.9 \quad 3.0 \quad 2.7 \quad 3.1 \quad 2.4 \quad 3.2$$
$$2.7 \quad 3.2 \quad 2.6 \quad 3.0 \quad 3.1 \quad 3.2 \quad 3.5$$

Construct a control chart using these figures and use it to assess the performance of the new trainee.

THE DEBRIEF

Key things to remember from this chapter

→ The difference between location and spread. Location is about where the centre of a distribution is located on the numerical scale. Spread is about how widely the observations in the distribution are spread around its centre.

→ Measures of location, generally known as averages, are used with measures of spread to present an overall impression of distributions.

→ There are three main measures of location: the mode, median and mean. These are respectively the most frequent value, the middle value and $\sum x / n$.

THE DEBRIEF (Continued)

→ There are three main measures of spread; the range, the semi-interquartile range (SIQR) and the standard deviation.

→ The SIQR is half the distance between the lower and upper quartiles. These quartiles are order statistics like the median and the SIQR is used in combination with the median.

→ Boxplots are diagrams based on order statistics. They are useful for comparing distributions.

→ The standard deviation is based on differences between the observations and the mean. It is used in combination with the mean.

→ Summary measures are important in quality management.

References

Juran, J.M. (1995) 'The history of managing for quality in the United States', in J.M. Juran (ed.), *A History of Managing for Quality*, Milwaukee: ASQC Quality Press, pp. 553–602.

Montgomery, D.C. (2004) *Introduction to statistical quality control* (5th edn), Chichester: Wiley.

Nonaka, I. (1995) 'The recent history of managing for quality in Japan', in J.M. Juran (ed.), *A History of Managing for Quality*, Milwaukee: ASQC Quality Press, pp. 517–52.

CHAPTER 7

Two-way traffic – investigating relationships between two variables using correlation and regression

Business use of quantitative bivariate analysis

◆ In Human Resources Management (HRM) correlation analysis has been used to assess the relationship between the performances applicants achieve in selection tests and how well they perform as employees following appointment. Simpson (2002) presents correlation analysis for various selection methods from interview performance to handwriting.

◆ Health and safety is an area of business where correlation and regression are used extensively. In industries where employees are exposed to hazards the effects on health may well depend on the extent of exposure to those hazards. An example is in mining. Kuempel *et al.* (2003) report the results of a study of the relationship between exposure to coal mine dust and lung disorders in coal miners.

◆ In product testing it is often important to investigate relationships between the lifetime of the product and its operating characteristics. In the offshore oil industry the durability of ropes for long-term mooring of floating structures is important. Ming-Yao *et al.* (2000) use regression analysis to relate the minimum break strength to the duration of use.

7.1 Introduction

This chapter introduces techniques used to investigate relationships between two variables. They analyse data that is referred to as *bivariate* data since it is made up of observations of two variables. They constitute an important part of what is called bivariate analysis. The two aspects of bivariate analysis we will look at are *correlation* and *regression*.

Bivariate data consists of observations of two variables, generally symbolised by *X* and *Y*. Each observation consists of a value of *X*, and the associated value of *Y*; these are paired data because they consist of pairs of values. To find out if there is a relationship between *X* and *Y* we use correlation. This measures the strength and direction of any relationship, in other words the degree of association or connection between the variables. Regression enables us to find what form that relationship takes. Knowing this enables us to make predictions of one variable using the other.

Suppose we operate an ice cream van and want to understand the link between sales and temperature. People tend to buy more ice cream in hot weather but how exactly are the two variables related?

Before embarking on bivariate analysis we need a theory about the direction of the link between the variables. One of the variables is the *dependent* variable because we believe its values depend on the values of the other variable. The dependent variable is denoted by the letter *Y* and so is known as the *Y* variable. Another name for it is the *response* because it is assumed to respond to the other variable.

The other variable is the *independent* variable. It is also called the *X* variable because it is represented by the letter *X*. Another name for it is the *predictor* because potentially we can use it to predict values of *Y*.

In the case of the ice cream van it makes sense to define sales as the *Y* variable as logically sales depend on temperature, which is therefore the *X* variable. It just doesn't make sense the other way round; the temperature doesn't depend on how much ice cream people buy.

When you use bivariate analysis it is very important to be clear about dependency. In most cases it is fairly obvious. If it isn't, try thinking it through both ways round and pick the one that makes more sense.

7.2 Correlation

Correlation tells us if two variables are correlated, that is connected or associated with one another. The scatter diagrams that depict quantitative bivariate data can shed some light on this. Plotting a scatter diagram should be the first stage in investigating a bivariate relationship. It provides visual evidence of correlation but it doesn't provide a measure of the strength of the correlation. For this we need the *correlation coefficient*.

Here we'll look at two types of correlation coefficient. They both measure the linear or straight-line association between two variables. The first and more important is *Pearson's correlation coefficient*. Karl Pearson (1857–1936) made pioneering contributions in many fields, including statistics. See Aldrich (1995) for an insight into Pearson's thinking on correlation. Another important measure, the coefficient of determination, is based on the Pearson coefficient.

The second measure is *Spearman's rank correlation coefficient*. Charles Spearman (1863–1945) was a psychologist who pioneered a number of statistical innovations. For the context of Spearman's work on correlation see Lovie and Lovie (2010).

Pearson's coefficient is suitable for measuring the strength of the connection between quantitative variables. These are variables whose values are measured in fixed units, they are interval or ratio data (see section 4.4). Spearman's coefficient is a more flexible tool. It measures the correlation between two variables, one or both of which have ordinal values, values that can be ranked in order.

7.2.1 Pearson's correlation coefficient

Like the standard deviation the Pearson correlation coefficient is about the spread of data. The difference is that the spread that correlation coefficients measure is in two dimensions. When bivariate data is plotted in a scatter diagram the points that represent the data are spread out, or scattered, vertically and horizontally.

The Pearson correlation coefficient of sample data is represented by the lower case r. The symbol used for the population correlation coefficient is the Greek equivalent of r, ρ ('rho'). In practical work it is generally sample data that we have so working out population correlation coefficients from raw data is quite rare.

The coefficient is the ratio between the coordinated scatter in the data to the total scatter in the data. The first of these, the coordinated scatter, is how much the variation in one variable is matched by the variation in the other. This is measured by the *covariance* of the data.

To get the covariance we take each x value and work out how far it is from $\bar{x}$, the mean of the sample of X values. We multiply each of these by the distance between the corresponding y value and $\bar{y}$, the mean of the sample of Y values. For each observation, i.e. each pair of x and y values that we have, we work out:

$$(x - \bar{x})\ (y - \bar{y})$$

This will produce a positive result when the x value is more than $\bar{x}$ and its associated y value is more than $\bar{y}$. In this case both $(x - \bar{x})$ and $(y - \bar{y})$ will be positive so multiplying them gives a positive product. If the x value is less than $\bar{x}$ and the y value is less than $\bar{y}$ both $(x - \bar{x})$ and $(y - \bar{y})$ will be negative. Again multiplication will give a positive product. It is only when the x value is less than $\bar{x}$ and the y value is more than $\bar{y}$ or the x value is more than $\bar{x}$ and the y value is less than $\bar{y}$ that multiplying $(x - \bar{x})$ and $(y - \bar{y})$ will give a negative product. These are the only cases where one distance is positive and the other negative.

For the covariance we take the sum of these $(x - \bar{x})(y - \bar{y})$ products and divide it by one fewer than the number of pairs of values, n. We reduce n by one as we used the sample means in working out the distances for the covariance. The consequence is that we lose one degree of freedom (see section 6.3). The expression for the covariance is:

$$\text{Cov}_{XY} = \frac{\sum (x - \bar{x})(y - \bar{y})}{n - 1}$$

If values of X higher than $\bar{x}$ tend to occur with values of Y higher than $\bar{y}$ and values of X lower than $\bar{x}$ with values of Y lower than $\bar{y}$, the covariance will be positive. To put it another way, a positive covariance means large x values are associated with large y values and small x values are associated with small y values. This would imply that there is a positive or *direct* relationship between the two variables; the higher the value of X the higher the value of Y.

EXAMPLE 7.1

The volumes of ice cream sold from an ice cream van and the maximum temperature on a random sample of six days were:

Sales volume (litres) (Y)	3	7	8	10	14	18
Temperature (°C) (X)	14	18	20	22	21	25

Find the covariance of this data and show it on a scatter diagram.

Solution

The X and Y variables are temperature and sales respectively. For the covariance we need the distances the x and y values are from their means. To start with we need the means:

$$\bar{y} = (3 + 7 + 8 + 10 + 14 + 18)/6 = 60/6 = 10 = \text{mean sales}$$
$$\bar{x} = (14 + 18 + 20 + 22 + 21 + 25)/6 = 120/6 = 20 = \text{mean temperature}$$

x	$\bar{x}$	$x - \bar{x}$	y	$\bar{y}$	$y - \bar{y}$	$(x - \bar{x})(y - \bar{y})$
14	20	−6	3	10	−7	42
18	20	−2	7	10	−3	6
20	20	0	8	10	−2	0
22	20	2	10	10	0	0
21	20	1	14	10	4	4
25	20	5	18	10	8	40

$$\sum (x - \bar{x})(y - \bar{y}) = 92$$

n, the number of observations = 6, so

$$\text{Cov}_{XY} = \frac{\sum (x - \bar{x})(y - \bar{y})}{n - 1} = \frac{92}{5} = 18.4$$

See Figure 7.1.

Solution
cont

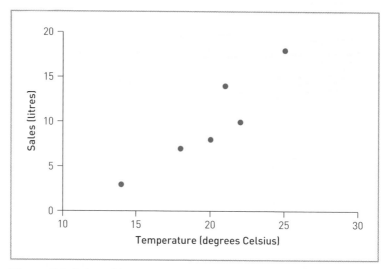

Figure 7.1 Sales of ice cream and temperature

When X values below $\bar{x}$ occur with values of Y above $\bar{y}$ and values of X above $\bar{x}$ with values of Y below $\bar{y}$, the covariance is negative. In other words a negative covariance means large x values are associated with small y values and small x values are associated with large y values. This implies a negative or *inverse* relationship between the two variables; the higher the value of X the lower the value of Y.

EXAMPLE 7.2

Noggar Footwear stocks six brands of rigger boots. The numbers of each brand sold in one months and their prices (in £) are as follows:

Number sold (Y)	25	18	18	13	12	4
Price (£) (X)	15	20	25	30	40	50

Find the covariance of this data and show it on a scatter diagram.

Solution

In this case the Y variable is numbers sold and the X variable price. The numbers sold are assumed to depend on the price.

$$\bar{y} = (25 + 18 + 18 + 13 + 12 + 4)/6 = 90/6 = 15 = \text{mean number sold}$$

$$\bar{x} = (15 + 20 + 25 + 30 + 40 + 50)/6 = 180/6 = 30 = \text{mean price}$$

x	$\bar{x}$	$x - \bar{x}$	y	$\bar{y}$	$y - \bar{y}$	$(x - \bar{x})(y - \bar{y})$
15	30	−15	25	15	10	−150
20	30	−10	18	15	3	−30
25	30	−5	18	15	3	−15
30	30	0	13	15	−2	0
40	30	10	12	15	−3	−30
50	30	20	4	15	−11	−220

$$\sum (x - \bar{x})(y - \bar{y}) = -445$$

n, the number of observations = 6, so $\text{Cov}_{XY} = \dfrac{\sum (x - \bar{x})(y - \bar{y})}{n - 1} = \dfrac{-445}{5} = -89$

See Figure 7.2.

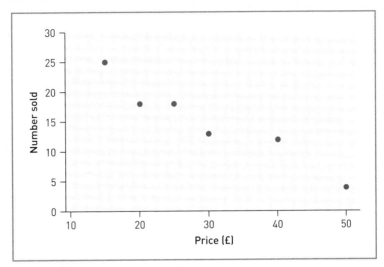

Figure 7.2 Sales of rigger boots and price

The covariance measures the coordinated scatter in the data but for the Pearson correlation coefficient we also need to consider the total scatter. This is the horizontal and vertical scatter or spread. We measure it using standard deviations. The standard deviation of the x values, s_x is a measure of horizontal spread and the standard deviation of the y values, s_y is a measure of vertical spread. Multiplying them together provides a measure of total scatter.

To get the Pearson correlation coefficient, r, we divide the covariance of X and Y by the product of the two standard deviations:

$$r = \frac{\text{Cov}_{XY}}{(s_x * s_y)}$$

Standard deviations are always positive. This means that if the covariance is positive, r will be positive. Conversely if the covariance is negative, r will be negative. The other thing to note is that it is impossible for the coordinated scatter to be more than the total scatter; after all the total scatter is *all* the scatter in the data. This means that r cannot be more than 1 or -1.

EXAMPLE 7.3

What is the Pearson correlation coefficient for the ice cream sales data in Example 7.1?

Solution

To start with we need the sample standard deviations of X and Y.

Temperature				Sales			
(x)	$\bar{x}$	$x - \bar{x}$	$(x - \bar{x})^2$	(y)	$\bar{y}$	$y - \bar{y}$	$(y - \bar{y})^2$
14	20	-6	36	3	10	-7	49
18	20	-2	4	7	10	-3	9
20	20	0	0	8	10	-2	4
22	20	2	4	10	10	0	0
21	20	1	1	14	10	4	16
25	20	5	25	18	10	8	64
			70				142

$\rightarrow$

Solution cont

The sample standard deviation of the temperatures,

$$s_x = \sqrt{\sum (x - \bar{x})^2/(n-1)} = \sqrt{70/5} = 3.742$$

The sample standard deviation of the sales,

$$s_y = \sqrt{\sum (y - \bar{y})^2/(n-1)} = \sqrt{142/5} = 5.329$$

In Example 7.1 we found the covariance for this data was 18.4, so the Pearson correlation coefficient,

$$r = (18.4)/(3.742 * 5.329)$$
$$= 18.4/19.940 = 0.923$$

Because r is positive there is positive correlation between these variables. As it is close to the maximum positive value of r, which is 1, the correlation seems to be strong. This confirms the linear association between temperature and sales that is evident in Figure 7.1.

A more direct way of finding the Pearson correlation coefficient, based on rearranging the expressions for the standard deviation and the covariance is:

$$r = \frac{n \sum xy - \left(\sum x * \sum y\right)}{\sqrt{\left(n \sum x^2 - \left(\sum x\right)^2\right) * \left(n \sum y^2 - \left(\sum y\right)^2\right)}}$$

This procedure is simpler because it involves addition rather than finding means and conducting a series of subtractions. Our shopping list of the five summations for this consists of the sum of the x values, the sum of the squared x values, the sum of the y values, the sum of the squared y values, and the sum of the products of the x and y values. The only other ingredient we need is n, the number of pairs of values.

EXAMPLE 7.4

Find the Pearson correlation coefficient for the ice cream data in Example 7.1 using the direct approach.

Solution

Temperature (x)	x^2	Sales (y)	y^2	xy
14	196	3	9	42
18	324	7	49	126
20	400	8	64	160
22	484	10	100	220
21	441	14	196	294
25	625	18	324	450
$\sum x = 120$	$\sum x^2 = 2470$	$\sum y = 60$	$\sum y^2 = 742$	$\sum xy = 1292$ $n = 6$

The Pearson correlation coefficient, $r = \dfrac{6 * 1292 - 120 * 60}{\sqrt{(6 * 2470 - 120^2) * (6 * 742 - 60^2)}}$

$$= \frac{7752 - 7200}{\sqrt{(14{,}820 - 14{,}400) * (4452 - 3600)}}$$

$$= \frac{552}{\sqrt{420 * 852}} = \frac{552}{\sqrt{357{,}840}}$$

$$= \frac{552}{598.173} = 0.923$$

This is the same result as we got via the covariance and standard deviations in Example 7.3.

The value of r in Example 7.4 is positive and close to $+1$, the largest possible positive value of r. This is entirely in keeping with the picture of the data we have in Figure 7.1. In this we can see that the points are scattered from the bottom left of the diagram to the top right. Although they do not lie in a neat straight line, they are not far off it. This is strong positive correlation; the low x values are associated with low y values and the high x values with high y values. There appears to be a direct relationship between sales volume and temperature.

EXAMPLE 7.5

Find the Pearson correlation coefficient for the rigger boots data in Example 7.2 using the direct approach.

Solution

Price (x)	x^2	Number sold (y)	y^2	xy
15	225	25	625	375
20	400	18	324	360
25	625	18	324	450
30	900	13	169	390
40	1600	12	144	480
50	2500	4	16	200
$\sum x = 180$	$\sum x^2 = 6250$	$\sum y = 90$	$\sum y^2 = 1602$	$\sum xy = 2255$ $n = 6$

The Pearson correlation coefficient,

$$r = \frac{6 * 2255 - 180 * 90}{\sqrt{(6 * 6250 - 180^2) * (6 * 1602 - 90^2)}}$$

$$= \frac{13{,}530 - 16{,}200}{\sqrt{(37{,}500 - 32{,}400) * (9612 - 8100)}}$$

$$= \frac{-2670}{\sqrt{5100 * 1512}} = \frac{-2670}{\sqrt{77{,}1200}}$$

$$= \frac{-2670}{2776.905} = -0.962$$

The value of r in Example 7.5 is negative and close to -1, the largest possible negative value of r. This is consistent with the scatter diagram in Figure 7.2. The points are scattered from the top left of the diagram to the bottom right. Although they are not perfectly in line, they are not far off it. This is strong negative correlation; the low x values are associated with high y values and the high x values with low y values. There appears to be an inverse relationship between number sold and price.

Examples 7.4 and 7.5 show that calculating a correlation coefficient, even for a limited amount of data, is hard work. In practice, Pearson correlation coefficients are seldom calculated in this way because just about all spreadsheet and statistical packages have functions to produce them.

The Pearson correlation coefficient is a measure of linear correlation. It helps us answer the question; 'Is there a straight-line relationship between the two variables?' As long as the arithmetic has been done properly the coefficient we calculate will always be between -1 and $+1$ inclusive. These are the extremes of the scale.

If we have a correlation coefficient of $+1$ it indicates that there is *perfect positive correlation* between the two variables. The scatter diagram will have all the points lying along the path of an upward-sloping straight line. You can see this sort of pattern in Figure 7.3.

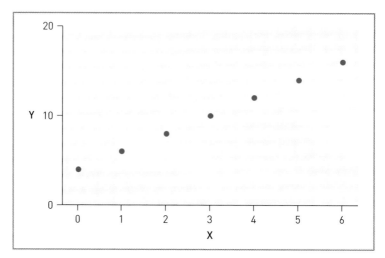

Figure 7.3 Perfect positive correlation ($r = +1$)

At the other end of the scale of Pearson correlation coefficient values is -1. This indicates that there is *perfect negative correlation*, between the two variables. The scatter diagram will show the points lying in a downward-sloping straight line. This is shown in Figure 7.4.

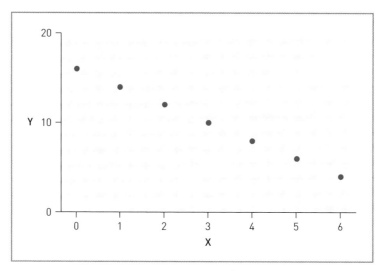

Figure 7.4 Perfect negative correlation ($r = -1$)

Relationships that give rise to correlation coefficients of exactly $+1$ or -1 do crop up in science but are extremely unlikely with business data. You are more likely to find relationships that generate coefficients near $+1$ or -1. These values indicate strong positive and strong negative correlation.

The data depicted in Figure 7.5 has a correlation coefficient of $+0.9$. The points are not perfectly in line as in Figure 7.3 but there is a clear upward-sloping linear pattern in the scatter.

The data portrayed in Figure 7.6 has a Pearson correlation coefficient of -0.9. Although the points are not in a perfect line like Figure 7.4 there is a distinct downward-sloping pattern.

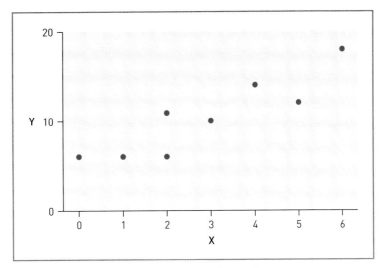

Figure 7.5 Good positive correlation ($r = +0.9$)

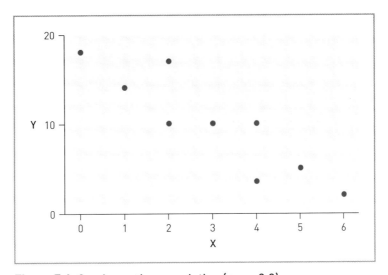

Figure 7.6 Good negative correlation ($r = -0.9$)

The nearer the coefficient is to $+1$ the stronger the positive correlation. The nearer it is to -1 the stronger the negative correlation. Midway between the extremes of $+1$ and -1 is zero. A correlation coefficient of zero indicates there is no linear correlation in the data. A coefficient close to zero suggests there is little or no linear association between the variables. The data portrayed in Figure 7.7 has a coefficient near zero.

The data in Figure 7.8 has a correlation coefficient of $+0.5$ which suggests weak positive correlation. It is not immediately clear from the diagram that there is rather more correlation than in Figure 7.7. The Pearson correlation coefficient enables us to assess the degree of linear association between two variables more robustly than just looking at scatter diagrams.

It is important to use both scatter diagrams and correlation coefficients when you analyse bivariate data. If you only use a scatter diagram you may miss evidence of modest correlation. If you only use a correlation coefficient you may draw the same conclusions about data sets that have the same values of the correlation coefficient but very different scatters. The data portrayed in Figure 7.9 has exactly the same correlation coefficient, $+0.5$ as the data in Figure 7.8, but as you can see the pattern of scatter differs considerably. In the case of Figure 7.9 there is one outlying point in an otherwise perfect positive scatter. In Figure 7.8 the relationship itself seems weak.

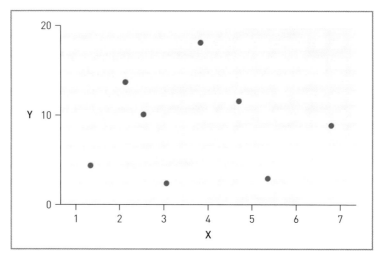

Figure 7.7 Near zero correlation ($r \approx 0$)

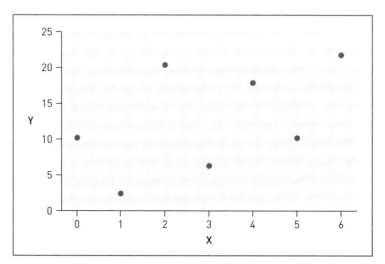

Figure 7.8 Weak positive correlation ($r = +0.5$)

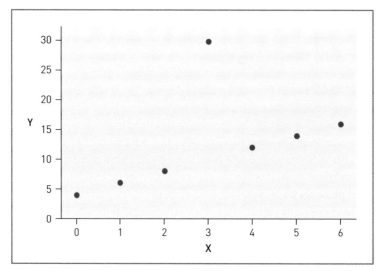

Figure 7.9 Strong positive correlation with prominent outlier ($r = +0.5$)

Remember that the Pearson correlation coefficients assess the strengths of *linear* relationships. If the relationship between two variables is *not* linear then we are likely to get a low or even zero correlation coefficient. This is another reason why you should look at scatter diagrams and correlation coefficients together. The data in Figure 7.10 indicates there is distinct non-linear association between X and Y but the Pearson correlation coefficient is zero.

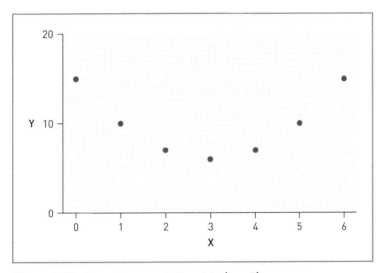

Figure 7.10 A non-linear relationship (*r* = 0)

If you have to write about correlation analysis results you may find the following descriptions useful:

Values of *r*	Suitable adjectives
+0.9 to +1.0	Strong, positive
+0.6 to +0.89	Fair/moderate, positive
+0.3 to +0.59	Weak, positive
0.0 to +0.29	Negligible/scant positive
0.0 to −0.29	Negligible/scant negative
−0.3 to −0.59	Weak, negative
−0.6 to −0.89	Fair/moderate, negative
−0.9 to −1.0	Strong, negative

SELF-ASSEMBLY GUIDE

How to interpret the Pearson correlation coefficient

◆ The coefficient measures the strength of the correlation between two variables. This is how closely they are linked or connected or associated.

◆ It can have any value from −1 to +1 inclusive.

◆ A positive value means there is a direct or upward-sloping relationship.

◆ A negative value means there is an inverse or downward-sloping relationship.

◆ The nearer the coefficient value is to +1 or −1 (and therefore the further away from zero) the stronger the association.

◆ It can only measure the strength of linear relationships.

◆ The golden rule: look at the scatter diagram when you assess the correlation coefficient.

At this point you may find it useful to try **Review questions 7.1, 7.2, 7.5 and 7.9** at the end of the chapter.

7.2.2 The coefficient of determination

The *coefficient of determination* is another tool that we can use to measure connections in bivariate data. It is based on the Pearson correlation coefficient, r. In fact it is the square of r, usually written in the upper case, R^2. Although related to r, the coefficient of determination is interpreted in a different way. The reason for calling it the coefficient of determination is because it enables us to gauge the extent to which the values of one variable are *determined* or shaped by the values of the other.

The Pearson correlation coefficient is based on using standard deviations to measure total scatter. Being the square of the Pearson correlation coefficient the coefficient of determination is derived from the standard deviation squared, which is the variance.

The coefficient of determination, like the Pearson coefficient, is a ratio. It is the ratio between how much of the variance in the data the relationship between X and Y can explain, and the total variance. As it is a ratio it can't be bigger than one. As it is a square it will always be positive. It is usually stated as a percentage.

EXAMPLE 7.6

What is the coefficient of determination, R^2, for the sales and temperature data in Example 7.1?

Solution

From Example 7.3, $r = 0.923$.

The coefficient of determination, $R^2 = (0.923)^2 = 0.852$.

This suggests 85.2% of the variation in ice cream sales can be explained by the variation in the temperature.

In Example 7.6 the phrase 'can be explained' is important. Evidence of association is not proof of causality. In other words, if we do have a high coefficient it does not mean that one variable does actually explain the other. It could be that the connection is coincidental, or perhaps a third variable is influencing the two that we are analysing. The only way of establishing whether one variable does actually explain the other is to consider the context of the data. In the case of Example 7.6 it is reasonable that the variation in the temperature explains the variation in sales.

Using R^2 can be a more convenient way of expressing the strength of the link between variables. The only drawback is that, unlike the Pearson coefficient, it does not tell us if the association is positive or negative. This is not insurmountable; we can show this in a scatter diagram.

7.2.3 Spearman's rank correlation coefficient

If you want to investigate links involving ordinal or ranked data (see section 4.4) you should not use the Pearson correlation coefficient as it is based on the arithmetic measures of location and spread, the mean and the standard deviation. Fortunately there is an alternative, the Spearman rank correlation coefficient.

It is possible to use the Spearman coefficient with interval and ratio data provided the data is ranked. You find the value of the coefficient from the ranked data rather than the original observations you would use to get the Pearson coefficient. This may be a preferable alternative as you may find calculating the Spearman coefficient easier. If your original observations contain extreme values the Pearson coefficient may be distorted by them, just as the mean is sensitive to extreme values, in which case the Spearman coefficient may be more reliable.

To calculate the Spearman coefficient, usually represented by the symbol r_s, subtract the ranks of your y values from the ranks of their corresponding x values to give a difference in rank, d, for each pair of observations. Next square the differences and add them up to get $\sum d^2$. Multiply the sum of the squared differences by 6 then divide the result by n, the number of pairs of observations, multiplied by the square of n minus 1. Finally subtract the result from 1 to arrive at the coefficient. The procedure can be expressed as follows:

$$r_s = 1 - \frac{6\sum d^2}{n(n^2 - 1)}$$

EXAMPLE 7.7

The total annual cost of players' wages for eight football clubs and their final league positions are as follows:

Wages bill (£m)	Final league position
45	1
32	2
41	3
13	4
27	5
15	6
18	7
22	8

Work out the Spearman coefficient for the correlation between the league positions and wages bills of these clubs.

Solution

One variable, league position, is already ranked, but before we can calculate the coefficient we have to rank the values of the other variable, the wage bill.

Rank of wages bill	League position	d	d^2
1	1	0	0
3	2	+1	1
2	3	+1	1
8	4	+4	16
4	5	−1	1
7	6	+1	1
6	7	−1	1
5	8	−3	9
		$\sum d^2 = 30$	$n = 8$

$$r_s = 1 - \frac{6 * 30}{8(8^2 - 1)} = 1 - \frac{180}{8(64 - 1)} = 1 - \frac{180}{8 * 63}$$

$$= 1 - \frac{180}{504} = 1 - 0.357 = 0.643$$

The interpretation of the Spearman coefficient is the same as we use for the Pearson coefficient. In Example 7.7 the coefficient is positive, indicating positive correlation and rather less than $+1$ suggesting the degree of correlation is modest.

Using the Spearman coefficient with ranked data that contains ties is not quite as straightforward. The ranks for the tied elements need to be adjusted so that they share the ranks they would have had if they were not equal. For instance if two elements are ranked second equal, in effect they share the second and third positions. To reflect this we would give them a rank of 2.5 each.

EXAMPLE 7.8

Rank the data in Example 7.2 from lowest to highest and find the Spearman rank correlation coefficient for the prices of the boots and the numbers sold.

Solution

Price (x)	Rank (x)	Number sold (y)	Rank (y)	d	d^2
15	1	25	6	$1 - 6 = -5$	25
20	2	18	4.5	$2 - 4.5 = -2.5$	6.25
25	3	18	4.5	$3 - 4.5 = -1.5$	2.25
30	4	13	3	$4 - 3 = 1$	1
40	5	12	2	$5 - 2 = 3$	9
50	6	4	1	$6 - 1 = 5$	25
				$\sum d^2 =$	68.5 $\quad n = 6$

$$r_s = 1 - \frac{6 * 68.5}{6(6^2 - 1)} = 1 - \frac{411}{6(36 - 1)} = 1 - \frac{411}{6 * 35}$$

$$= 1 - \frac{411}{210} = 1 - 1.957 = -0.957$$

In Example 7.8 the Spearman coefficient for the ranked data is very similar to the value of the Pearson coefficient we obtained in Example 7.5 for the original observations, -0.962. Both results show that the correlation between numbers sold and prices is strong and negative.

At this point you may find it useful to try **Review questions 7.3, 7.6 and 7.10** at the end of the chapter.

7.3 Simple linear regression

Although correlation gets us some way to understanding the linear relationship between two variables it doesn't tell us the whole story. A correlation coefficient tells us about the strength and direction of the connection but not the exact form of the relationship. If we want to know precisely how the two are associated we have to turn to the other component of basic bivariate analysis, *regression*.

Regression analysis is an umbrella term for a set of techniques that are used to fit models to data. This modelling consists of finding the best general representation of relationships between two or more variables. They vary in complexity. The simplest, *simple linear regression*, is a tool for finding the most appropriate, or 'fitting', straight line to embody the connection between two variables. This line is based on observations of the two variables. Since it describes the relationship it is akin to a measure of location but in two dimensions.

It summarises the connection between the variables in the same way as an average encapsulates a distribution.

The reason simple linear regression is *simple* is because it analyses just two variables. The *linear* part of the name is because it is designed to find straight lines that are most suited to sets of bivariate data. The third part of the name, *regression*, seems odd. It means reverting or going back to. The reason for this peculiar name lies in the origin of the technique. It was developed by Sir Francis Galton (1822–1911), who was an eminent statistician. As part of his work on genetics he wanted to show how the diameters of sweet pea seeds were constrained to mediocrity or 'regressed' compared to the diameters of their parent seeds. Stanton (2003) provides a good introduction to Galton's work on regression.

Simple linear regression fits straight lines to data. But do we need it? After all if the data is plotted in a scatter diagram we could make do with a ruler. We could simply take a scatter diagram like Figure 7.1 and draw a line through the points. If we can't get a line actually through the points, then we can draw one as close as possible to them. This is fitting a line 'by eye'. It can be a good enough way of finding a quick approximation to the best line for the data. However, unless we have data like those in Figure 7.1 where the few points lie in an obvious linear pattern it is fairly arbitrary.

The two critical drawbacks of line fitting by eye are its inconsistency and unreliability. The inconsistency arises because the exact position of the line will depend on the visual judgement of the line drawer. Because judgement varies from one person to the next we will get different lines from different people for precisely the same data. What is more, we can have a variety of lines from these different people yet none of them may be the line that really is the best fit of the data. This makes visual line fitting unreliable; we simply can't depend on it producing the best result.

Simple linear regression is both reliable and consistent. It is a method of finding the best line for the data, the so-called line of best fit. This is the line that takes the path that is as close as possible to all the points in a scatter diagram of the data. The way simple linear regression does this is to find the two key features that define the line, the *intercept*, which is where it begins, and the *slope*, which is how it travels. Figure 7.11 illustrates the two of them.

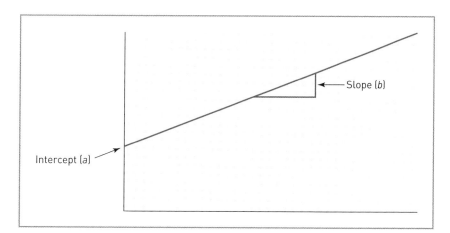

Figure 7.11 The intercept and slope of a line

The intercept in Figure 7.11 is the point where the line begins its journey from the vertical axis. The slope is the amount by which it climbs for each step it progresses to the right. These features define the equation of the line, which in simple linear regression has the style:

$$Y = a + bX$$

As before, Y is the dependent variable or response, and X is the independent variable or predictor. When we specify values for a and b we define the equation that represents the line. Knowing the equation we can plot the line.

All we have to do then is to find the pair of a and b values that define the line that best fits the data we want to model. The purpose of simple linear regression is to find those values for us.

How does it do it? Let's start with the idea that the best fit line for a set of data is the line that comes closest to the points when the data is plotted in a scatter diagram. Two things follow from this. First, all the points count; regression is inclusive in that it draws on every observation in the data set. Secondly, the distance between each point and the line is important.

The distance between a point and a line is the difference between the y value that does actually occur with an x value and the y value that the line suggests should occur with the x value. This is referred to as the 'fit' as it is the y value that fits with the x value according to the line. It is represented by the symbol $\hat{y}$, 'y-hat'.

EXAMPLE 7.9

Find a line to fit the sales volume and temperature data from Example 7.1.

Solution

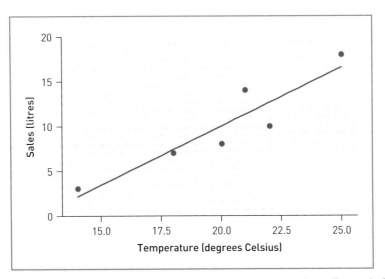

Figure 7.12 A fitted line for the ice cream sales data from Example 7.1

The line in Figure 7.12 is the best-fit line for the ice cream sales data. It was produced by simple linear regression, but more about exactly how later. For now let's concentrate on the line. The equation of the line is:

$$\text{Sales} = -16.286 + 1.314 \text{ Temperature}$$

We can interpret this as meaning that according to the line the sales are expected to be -16.286 plus 1.314 times whatever the temperature is. If we specify a temperature, say 14 degrees, then the sales that the line suggests should occur are:

$$\text{Sales} = -16.286 + 1.314 * 14 = -16.286 + 18.396 = 2.110$$

This figure, 2.11 litres, is the 'fit' for the temperature of 14 degrees. If the temperature is 18 degrees the expected sales are:

$$\text{Sales} = -16.286 + 1.314 * 18 = -16.286 + 23.652 = 7.366$$

If we check the original data we find that on the day that the temperature was 18 degrees the sales were actually 7 litres, rather less than the line predicts. Similarly, when it was 14 degrees the actual sales were 3 litres, more than the 2.11 litres the line predicted.

The differences between the actual y values and the fits, the $\hat{y}$ values, are fundamental to the way that simple linear regression works. It takes account of the differences between every y value and its fitted equivalent.

EXAMPLE 7.10

Find the differences between the actual sales in the data from Example 7.1 and the predicted sales from the line in Example 7.9.

Solution

Temperature (x)	Sales (y)	Predicted sales ($\hat{y}$)	Difference ($y - \hat{y}$)
14	3	2.110	0.890
18	7	7.366	−0.366
20	8	9.994	−1.994
22	10	12.622	−2.622
21	14	11.308	2.692
25	18	16.564	1.436
			$\sum (y - \hat{y}) = 0.036$

How well a line fits a set of points depends on these differences. The smaller they are, the better the line fits the data. We have to take account of all of them. The easiest way to do this is to add them up to get the sum of the differences. Unfortunately, because some points are above the line and some below, we have both positive and negative differences. If we simply add them together the sum of the differences will be reduced as a result of positives and negatives cancelling each other out. In Example 7.10 the sum of the differences is almost zero.

To get around this problem, instead of adding the differences we add the squared differences. Whether a number is positive or negative the square of it is always positive.

EXAMPLE 7.11

Find the sum of the squared differences between the actual and predicted values of y in Example 7.10.

Solution

Temperature (x)	Sales (y)	Predicted sales ($\hat{y}$)	Difference ($y - \hat{y}$)	$(y - \hat{y})^2$
14	3	2.110	0.890	0.792
18	7	7.366	−0.366	0.134
20	8	9.994	−1.994	3.976
22	10	12.622	−2.622	6.875
21	14	11.308	2.692	7.247
25	18	16.564	1.436	2.062
				$\sum (y - \hat{y})^2 = 21.086$

The sum of squared differences is the criterion at the heart of simple linear regression. The lower it is the better the line fits the data. We can judge one line against another using this as a measure.

EXAMPLE 7.12

Figure 7.13 shows another line fitted to the ice cream sales data from Example 7.1. The equation of this line is:

$$\text{Sales} = -16.075 + 1.387 \text{ Temperature}$$

Work out the sum of the squared differences for this line.

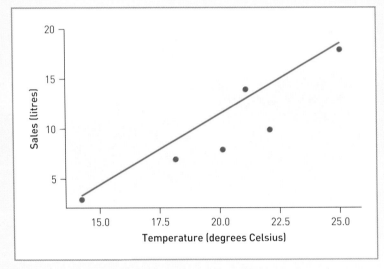

Figure 7.13 An alternative line for the data from Example 7.1

Solution

The predicted sales for a day when the temperature is 14 degrees are:

$$\text{Sales} = -16.075 + 1.387 * 14 = -16.075 + 19.418 = 3.343$$

This and the other $\hat{y}$ values are in the third column of the following table:

Temperature (x)	Sales (y)	Predicted sales ($\hat{y}$)	Difference ($y - \hat{y}$)	$(y - \hat{y})^2$
14	3	3.343	-0.343	0.118
18	7	8.891	-1.891	3.576
20	8	11.665	-3.665	13.432
22	10	14.439	-4.439	19.705
21	14	13.052	0.948	0.899
25	18	18.600	-0.600	0.360
			$\sum (y - \hat{y})^2 =$	38.090

The sum of the squared differences in Example 7.12 (38.09) is considerably larger than the equivalent figure in Example 7.11 (21.086). This demonstrates that the line in Example 7.11 is the better fit and confirms what we might suspect from comparing Figure 7.12 with Figure 7.13. The line in Figure 7.12 is closer overall to the points.

By taking the sum of the squared differences we can tell whether one line is better than another, but how do we get the *best* line? We could try every conceivable line and work out the sum of the squared differences. Fortunately we don't have to; simple linear regression offers us a direct route to the line of best fit. It finds the line that has the lowest sum of squared differences between the points and the line. Because of this it is also known as *least squares regression*.

So, how does simple linear regression find the best-fit line? It certainly doesn't require us to plot lines to find the best one; as long as we have the data we can get the line of best fit. The method boils down to using two expressions, one for the slope of the line of best fit, b, and the other one for its intercept, a. These expressions are:

For the slope:
$$b = \frac{\sum xy - \left(\sum x * \sum y\right)/n}{\sum x^2 - \left(\sum x\right)^2/n}$$

For the intercept:
$$a = \left(\sum y - b * \sum x\right)/n$$

These expressions were derived using calculus. This branch of mathematics is concerned, among other things, with finding maximum and minimum values. The pair of a and b values that we get from these expressions is the one for the equation of the line that minimises the sum of squared differences. This is the best-fit line.

EXAMPLE 7.13

What is the equation of the line of best fit for the ice cream sales data in Example 7.1?

Solution

There are five ingredients we need for the simple linear regression expressions: the sum of the x values, the sum of the y values, the sum of the squared x values, the sum of the products of every pair of x and y values and the number of observations, n.

Temperature (x)	x^2	Sales (y)	xy
14	196	3	42
18	324	7	126
20	400	8	160
22	484	10	220
21	441	14	294
25	625	18	450
$\sum x = 120$	$\sum x^2 = 2470$	$\sum y = 60$	$\sum xy = 1292$

The slope of the line of best fit, $b = \dfrac{\sum xy - \left(\sum x * \sum y\right)/n}{\sum x^2 - \left(\sum x\right)^2/n} = \dfrac{1292 - (120 * 60)/6}{2470 - 120^2/6}$

$$= \frac{1292 - 7200/6}{2470 - 14{,}400/6} = \frac{1290 - 1200}{2470 - 2400} = \frac{92}{70} = 1.3143$$

The intercept of the line of best fit, $a = \left(\sum y - b * \sum x\right)/n = (60 - 1.3143 * 120)/6$

$$= (60 - 157.68)/6 = (-93.68)/6 = -16.286$$

The equation of the line is in the form $Y = a + bX$

Inserting the values of a and b from above gives us the following equation for the ice cream sales data from Example 7.1:

$$\text{Sales} = -16.286 + 1.3143 \text{ Temperature}$$

This equation is the one for the line used in Example 7.9 and plotted in Figure 7.12. It is the line with the least sum of squared differences between it and the plotted points.

The equation we get from simple linear regression is called the *regression* equation. It is also known as the *regression model* as it models or represents the relationship between X and Y.

Using simple linear regression and plotting the best-fit line

◆ Set out your data in a table with columns for the x values, the y values, the squared x values and the $x \times y$ products.

◆ Find the sum of the values in the columns.

◆ Work out the slope of the line of best fit first; you need this to work out the intercept.

◆ Work out the intercept.

◆ Write down the equation of the line of best fit, $Y = a + bX$.

◆ To plot the line you will need to find two points that are on the line. You may be inclined to work out more but you only need two.

◆ For the first point, choose an x value to the left of the horizontal axis of the graph. To plot the best-fit line in Figure 7.13 we could choose 15. Try to pick round numbers to make the arithmetic easier.

◆ Put your chosen x value in the equation of the line of best fit and work out the y value that fits the line. In Example 7.13 this would be: Sales $= -16.286 + 1.3143 * 15 = 3.4285$. This gives us the fix or coordinates of our first point; it will be at 15 along the x-axis and 3.4285 up the y-axis. This is the point on the left in Figure 7.14.

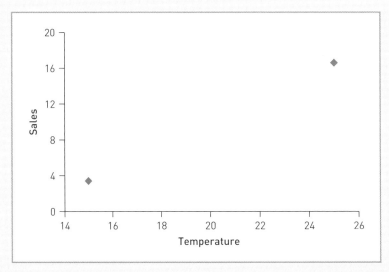

Figure 7.14 Two points along the regression line from Example 7.13

◆ For the second point choose an x value that is on the right of the horizontal axis. The reason for choosing one at the other end is to be able to draw the line more precisely; two points close together give too much leeway. In Example 7.12 we could choose 25 as the second x value. If the temperature is 25 then: Sales $= -16.286 + 1.3143 * 25 = 16.5715$. This is the point on the right in Figure 7.14.

◆ Finally draw a straight line between the two points. All the points along this line represent pairs of x and y values that fit the regression line. Figure 7.15 shows the line of the regression equation from Example 7.13.

→

SELF-ASSEMBLY GUIDE (Continued)

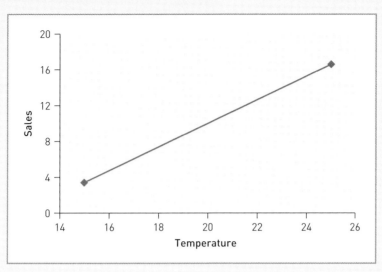

Figure 7.15 The regression line from Example 7.13

The two components of the regression equation, the intercept and slope, can give us a better understanding of the relationship between X and Y. In Example 7.13, the value of the slope implies that for every one degree rise in the temperature the sales of ice cream will increase by 1.3143 litres. This works the other way as well; for every drop of one degree in the temperature ice cream sales are expected to fall by 1.3143 litres. The slope tells us the *rate of change* in ice cream sales relative to temperature.

The intercept of the regression equation is the value of Y we expect when X is zero. It is the starting point of the line and is not always meaningful in its own right. This is especially true when the lowest x value is some way above zero as in Example 7.13. The intercept of the regression equation in Example 7.13 is -16.286. This implies that when the temperature is zero ice cream sales are -16.286 litres. This is absurd both practically and theoretically. Ice cream vans are not usually out in freezing weather, and it is impossible to have a negative quantity of ice cream.

Regression lines like the one plotted in Figure 7.12 can be used to assess performance. The line itself represents the general level of performance. In Figure 7.12 it represents the general levels of sales across a range of temperatures. We can use the line to benchmark actual performance. Points that are above the line reflect better than expected performance. In Figure 7.12 the fact that the fourth point from the left is above the line shows that on the day when the temperature was 21 degrees there were better than expected sales. Conversely the fifth point from the left being below the line suggests sales were lower than expected on the day when it was 22 degrees Celsius.

Sometimes there are points so far away from the line that they stand out as real oddities. These are outliers, such as the highest point in Figure 7.9. When they do occur they raise questions; is the data recorded correctly, and if so what makes the observation so unusual? These must be addressed.

Regression equations can be used to make predictions, indeed this is often the main reason for finding them. They enable us to find the values of Y that are likely to be associated with specific values of X. Because such y values are what the line expects to occur they are called *expected values* of Y. To distinguish them from the y values that have actually occurred we use the symbol $\hat{y}$, 'y-hat', to represent them. The regression equation, $Y = a + bX$ is a general statement of how Y is related to X. For predictions we insert an x value and work out the expected y value:

$$\hat{y} = a + bx$$

EXAMPLE 7.14

According to the regression equation in Example 7.13 what are the expected ice cream sales values when the temperature is 16, 24 and 60 degrees?

Solution

The regression equation is: Sales $= -16.286 + 1.3143$ * Temperature

When the temperature is 16   Sales $= -16.286 + 1.3143$ * $16 = 4.743$ litres
When the temperature is 24   Sales $= -16.286 + 1.3143$ * $24 = 15.257$ litres
When the temperature is 60   Sales $= -16.286 + 1.3143$ * $60 = 62.572$ litres

There is an important limitation to bear in mind when you use regression equations to make predictions. If the predictions are based on x values that are outside the range of x values in the data then they are unreliable. The further the x values are outside this range the more unreliable the predictions will be. In Example 7.14 the first two predictions are OK because the x values used to calculate them, 16 and 24, are within the range of x values in the data, which was from 14 to 25 degrees. The third prediction is decidedly dodgy. The x value, 60 degrees, is way beyond the highest x value in the data set, 25. Not only that, it is probably higher than the highest temperature recorded anywhere on earth.

Using simple linear regression with anything other than a small set of data is onerous. Fortunately statistical and spreadsheet packages have regression analysis tools that will save you the trouble. You can leave the hard work to the software but of course you still need to know how to interpret the results.

At this point you may find it useful to try **Review questions 7.4, 7.7, 7.8, 7.11 and 7.12.**

REVIEW QUESTIONS

Answers to these questions are on pages 448–9. There are tips and hints to help you with them on the supporting website at **www.pearsoned.co.uk/buglear**, where you will also find the fully worked solutions.

☆☆★ Basic questions

7.1 Consider which of the relationships below are likely to have a positive and which are likely to have a negative correlation coefficient.

(a) The distance a vehicle travels and the fuel consumed
(b) The demand for laptop computers and their price
(c) The average temperature of countries and the sales of warm clothing
(d) The amount consumers spend on motor insurance and their age

(e) The population of countries and the amount of electricity used

(f) The income of people and the amount of income tax they pay

(g) The fuel efficiency of cars and their engine size

7.2 A leak of a hazardous substance at a chemical plant means that all employees working in the area of the plant affected have been tested for contamination. The following figures are the hours worked in the affected area since the leak and the contamination levels (in micrograms per litre of blood) of the first six workers to be tested:

Hours worked	2	3	4	6	8	8
Contamination level	18	29	38	58	75	82

(a) Plot this data on a scatter diagram taking the Contamination level as the dependent variable (Y).

(b) Find the Pearson correlation coefficient and interpret it.

7.3 A panel of film critics ranked what they consider the six best new films. Their rankings and the box office takings of the films to date are:

Critics' rank	Takings ($m)
1	2.2
2	0.8
3	7.3
4	1.6
5	1.0
6	0.5

Calculate the Spearman correlation coefficient for this data and comment on its value.

7.4 Work out the equation of the line of best fit for the chemical plant data in question 7.2 and plot it on a scatter diagram of the data.

☆★★ More testing questions

7.5 The cost of placing a full-page colour advertisement and the circulation figures of nine magazines are:

Cost (£000)	9	43	16	17	19	13	20	44	35
Circulation (000)	135	2100	680	470	450	105	275	2250	695

(a) Which of these variables should be the dependent variable (Y), and why?

(b) Plot a scatter diagram to portray the data.

(c) Determine the Pearson correlation coefficient and assess its value.

7.6 There are eight electoral wards in a town. The crime levels in these wards have been ranked by the local police, with the lowest crime area ranked 1, and the level of house prices ranked by a local estate agent, with the lowest price level ranked 1. The results are:

Crime level	1	2	3	4	5	6	7	8
House price level	7	6	8	3	5	1	4	2

Find the value of the Spearman correlation coefficient for these figures and assess its meaning.

7.7 The mid-season league positions and numbers of goals scored by nine top division football clubs are given in the table below.

Team	League position	Goals scored
Sporting Salford	1	43
Athletico Woolwich	3	42
AFC Wonderland	6	25
Tynecastle Rovers	8	34
Burslem United	10	26
Hammersmith City	14	22
Perry Barr	15	25
Womborne Wanderers	17	21
East Mallet United	20	22

(a) Which variable is the response (Y)?
(b) Plot the data on a scatter diagram.
(c) Find the regression line and plot this on your scatter diagram.
(d) Comment on any unusual observations.

7.8 An economist studying the market for designer watches has produced a regression model to describe the relationship between sales of the different brands of watch (in thousands of units) and the advertising expenditure used to promote them (in £m).

$$\text{Sales} = 4.32 + 6.69 \text{ Advertising expenditure}$$
$$R^2 = 64.8\%$$

(a) If there was no advertising expenditure to promote a brand of watch, what sales could be expected?
(b) By how many units would sales be expected to increase for every extra £1m spent on advertising?
(c) What sales could be expected if advertising expenditure was £8m?
(d) What is the value of the Pearson correlation coefficient?

★★★ Challenging questions

7.9 Eight companies dominate a particular industry. The annual revenue and annual gross profit for these companies are as follows:

Company	Revenue (£m)	Gross profit (£m)
Mirovoy	2815	322
Materique	1139	198
Strannar	626	73
Malenky	557	41
Ribar	291	47
Krevetka	172	25
Meesh	144	33
Blochar	85	9

(a) Calculate the Pearson correlation coefficient.
(b) What does the value of the coefficient suggest about the association between revenue and profit?

7.10 Ten popular cars were studied by a team of designers who ranked them for design and style. The same cars were studied by a team of road accident investigators who ranked them for safety. The results are set out below:

Design ranking	1	2	3	4	5	6	7	8	9	10
Safety ranking	4	6	1	5	2	3	10	7	9	8

Work out the value of Spearman's rank correlation coefficient and explain how it should be interpreted.

7.11 The percentages of workers in trade unions and the mean hourly wage in nine US states are:

Union membership (%)	7.5	17.2	9.1	16.1	25.4	16.9	23.7	19.5	9.2
Mean hourly wage ($)	13.80	16.81	13.40	18.00	20.00	15.60	16.63	16.07	11.51

(a) Which one of these should be the dependent variable (Y)?
(b) Plot the data on a scatter diagram.
(c) Determine the equation of the line of best fit and plot it on your diagram.
(d) Find the coefficient of determination and assess its value.

7.12 An international road transport consultant wants to see if the extent of a country's motorway network (in kilometres) depends on its land area (in thousands of square kilometres). She has collected figures for a selection of European countries:

Land area	84	31	43	337	544	357	132	41	69	301
Motorway network	1596	1666	930	394	9140	11,200	420	2300	70	8860

(a) Plot the data on a scatter diagram.
(b) Ascertain the line of best fit and plot it on your scatter diagram.
(c) Find the coefficient of determination and use it to advise the consultant.
(d) Identify any possible outliers.

THE DEBRIEF

Key things to remember from this chapter

→ Correlation and regression are often used together but they have different roles. They are methods of analysing connections between two variables, one of which is the dependent one, Y, and the other the independent one, X.

→ Correlation is about measuring the strength of the connection between two variables and whether they are directly or inversely related, in other words whether the correlation is positive or negative.

→ The Pearson correlation coefficient is used with quantitative variables, Spearman's rank correlation coefficient with ordinal, or ranked data.

→ The coefficients can take values between −1 and +1. A negative value means an inverse relationship, a positive one a direct relationship. The closer the value is to either extreme the stronger the correlation. Values close to zero indicate a lack of relationship.

THE DEBRIEF (Continued)

→ Correlation coefficients measure linear association. If there is a non-linear relationship between the variables they will not recognise it.

→ Regression is about finding the best model to represent the relationship between the variables. Simple linear regression is used to get the best straight line fit between two variables.

→ Simple linear regression finds the intercept and slope of the line of best fit from the data values.

→ The regression model can be used to predict values of *Y* for specified values of *X*. If the values of *X* are outside the range of *x* values that occur in the data the predictions are less reliable. The further outside they are, the more unreliable the predictions.

References

J. Aldrich (1995) 'Correlations Genuine and Spurious in Pearson and Yule', *Statistical Science*, 10(4), pp. 364–76.

Lovie, S. and Lovie, P. (2010) 'Charles Spearman and correlation: a commentary on "The proof and measurement of association between two things"', *International Journal of Epidemiology*, 39(5), pp. 1151–3. Available at: http://ije.oxfordjournals.org/content/39/5/1151.full

Kuempel, E.D., Attfield, M.D., Vallyathan, V., Lapp, N.L., Hale, J.M., Smith, R.J. and Castranova, V. (2003) 'Pulmonary inflammation and crystalline silica in respirable coal mine dust: dose-response', *Journal of Biosciences*, 28(1), pp. 61–9.

Ming-Yao, L., Devlin, P. and Chi-Tat, T.K. (2000) 'Development of API RP 2SM for synthetic fiber rope moorings', Offshore Technology Conference, Houston, Texas, 1–4 May 2000. Available at: http://www.offshoreengineering.org/moorings/PDF/OTC12178.pdf

Simpson, S. (2002) 'Selection', in J. Leopold (ed.), *Human resources in organisations*, Harlow: Pearson Education.

Stanton, J.M. (2003) 'Galton, Pearson and the Peas: A Brief History of Linear Regression for Statistics Instructors', *Journal of Statistics Education*, 9(3). Available at: http://www.amstat.org/publications/jse/v9n3/stanton.html

CHAPTER 8

Counting the cost – summarising money variables over time

CHAPTER OBJECTIVES

This chapter will help you to:
- → Understand simple and aggregate index numbers
- → Use weighted aggregate price indices
- → Adjust figures for the effects of inflation using price indices
- → Apply methods of investment appraisal

THE BARE BONES

What you will find in this chapter . . .

- Using simple price indices to measure price changes of single commodities
- Applying aggregate price indices to gauge price changes in several items
- Measuring price changes in sets of commodities with the Laspeyre base-weighted index
- Measuring price changes in sets of commodities with the Paasche current-weighted index
- Using price indices to change money amounts so they are expressed at constant prices
- Evaluating investment projects using the accounting rate of return, payback, net present value and internal rate of return methods

. . . and on the supporting website (www.pearsoned.co.uk/buglear)

- How to use EXCEL for investment appraisal
- Fully worked solutions to the review questions
- More review questions

Business use of price indices and investment appraisal

◆ Price indices are widely used by accountants and other business professionals who analyse costs and prices. A leading accounting publication, *Accountancy Age,* shows how they are used. Examples are in the valuation of pensions (Collins, 2010) and the measurement of environmental impact (Singh, 2010).

◆ The origins of assessing projects using investment appraisal go back over three centuries. Parker (1968) shows that the concept of present value underpinned interest tables published by the Dutch mathematician Simon Stevin (1548–1620) in 1582. Tables like these were used extensively by the banking and insurance companies of the time.

◆ Discounting in the assessment of industrial as against financial investments started rather later, featuring in the early history of the UK railway industry. Many pioneers, such as Brunel, assumed that railways would last so long that there was no need to worry about replacing and upgrading the track. Twenty or so years after the first railway journeys Captain Mark Huish, General Manager of the London and North Western Railway, realised that as locomotives and wagons became heavier, trains longer and journeys more frequent the original track was wearing out faster than anticipated. In 1853 Huish and two colleagues investigated the problem. They argued that an annual reserve invested at a certain level of interest would be needed to generate enough funds to restore the track (Huish *et al.*, 1853: 273).

◆ Rail companies made large investments that paid off over long periods. Weighing up the returns against the original investment was no simple matter. Similar concerns arose in the South African gold mining industry in the early twentieth century. Frankel found present value was used in the first attempt to measure return on capital in Witwatersrand (1967: 10).

◆ Later in the twentieth century engineers in capital-intensive industries, primarily oil and chemicals used discounting approaches to investment decisions. Johnson and Kaplan (1991) list three major US oil companies (ARCO, Mobil and Standard Oil of Indiana) where this occurred. Weaver and Reilly (1956) of the Atlas Powder Company of Delaware advocated discounting in the chemical industry.

◆ Surveys of company practice suggest that both net present value and internal rate of return are widely used. In his 1992 survey of UK companies Pike (1996) found that 81% used internal rate of return and 74% used net present value. In a study of large US industrial companies Klammer *et al.* (1991) discovered that approximately 80% used discounting in appraising investment in the expansion of existing operations and in the setting up of new operations.

8.1 Introduction

In the last two chapters we have looked at ways of summarising data. In Chapter 6 we concentrated on measuring the location and spread in univariate (single variable) data, in Chapter 7 we focused on measuring the strength and direction in bivariate data. In both chapters the data concerned was cross-sectional data, data relating to the same point or period of time. In this chapter and the next we will consider ways of summarising data relating to different periods of time.

Time-based data consists of numerical observations that can be measured and summarised using the techniques you met in the previous two chapters. We could, for instance, collect the price of gold at various points in time and calculate the mean price of gold over the period, or use correlation analysis to measure the association between the price of gold and the price of silver at various points in time. However, often the most important aspect of time-based data is the time factor and the techniques in the previous two chapters would not allow us to bring that out of the data.

In this chapter we will look at techniques to summarise money variables that relate to different time periods. We will start by exploring index numbers and how they can be used to summarise movements in prices over time. Then we will look at how such price indices can be used to adjust money amounts for the effects of inflation. Later in the chapter we will consider summarising amounts of interest accumulated over time and how this approach is used to assess the worth of investment projects.

8.2 Index numbers

For businesses probably the most significant index numbers are those that track changes in costs and prices. One example is the way indices of general price levels such as the UK Consumer Price Index (CPI) are used as the basis of pay negotiations.

Compiling an index like the CPI, which encapsulates the changes in the prices of a large range of goods and services, is a sophisticated process. To appreciate how index numbers work we'll start with the most basic form of price index, the *simple price index*. This can only be used for comparing prices of a single commodity, for instance oil or cement, over time. To produce a simple price index to measure the change in price between the current period and a reference period in the past, usually referred to as the base period, take the current price (represented as p_c) and divide by the base period price, p_0. Since the base period is the basis or origin we treat it as 'period zero'. The final stage is to multiply the result by 100. This makes it easier to use the index number to talk about percentage changes in the price, although the % sign is generally not written beside the index number. The process can be represented as:

$$\text{Simple price index} = \frac{\text{current price}}{\text{base period price}} * 100 = \frac{p_c}{p_0} * 100$$

EXAMPLE 8.1

Antonia Gate makes silver rings. The cost of the ring shanks she uses was £4.50 in 2008. This had risen to £6.25 in 2011. Use a simple price index to measure this price change.

Solution

$$\text{Simple price index} = \frac{\text{current price}}{\text{base period price}} * 100 = \frac{p_c}{p_0} * 100$$

$$\frac{6.25}{4.50} * 100 = 138.9 \text{ to 1 decimal place}$$

This shows us that the price of the shanks rose by 38.9% between 2008 and 2011.

At this point you may find it useful to try **Review question 8.1** at the end of the chapter.

Typically, businesses deal in more than one commodity so the simple price index is an inadequate way of reflecting the price changes they face. There are *aggregate* indices that summarise price changes of more than one commodity. These are of much greater use.

The most basic aggregate index is the simple aggregate price index. Calculating this for a mix of commodities involves dividing the sum of their prices in the current period by the sum of the prices of the same commodities in the base period. We then multiply the result by 100.

$$\text{Simple aggregate price index} = \frac{\sum p_c}{\sum p_0} * 100$$

EXAMPLE
8.2

Antonia Gate purchases ring shanks, large Slatkirite gemstones and small Tyeplochite gem-stones to use in making her rings. The costs of these items per unit in 2008 and 2011 are:

Item	2008	2011
Ring shank	£4.50	£6.25
Slatkirite gemstone	£1.65	£1.95
Tyeplochite gemstone	£0.41	£0.75

The simple aggregate price index for comparing these figures:

$$\frac{\sum p_c}{\sum p_0} * 100 = \frac{6.25 + 1.95 + 0.75}{4.50 + 1.65 + 0.41} * 100 = \frac{8.95}{6.56} * 100 = 136.4 \text{ to 1 decimal place}$$

This suggests that the prices Antonia Gate paid rose by 36.4% between 2008 and 2011.

At this point you may find it useful to try **Review question 8.2** at the end of the chapter.

The price index in Example 8.2 is a more useful guide to the general rise in prices faced by the ring-maker as it includes all of the items she buys. Its limitation is that it cannot reflect a situation where some prices are more significant than others simply because more of these commodities are bought. The prices of these are more important than the prices of other com-modities of which less is purchased.

The simple aggregate price index treats each price as equally important so they are all included. Actually the significance of one price in a simple aggregate price index depends purely on its size. In Example 8.2, the index value, 136.4, is near the simple price index figure for the ring shank in Example 8.1, 138.9. This is largely due to the ring shank price being the highest of the three prices in Example 8.2.

The significance of the price of a commodity is not only its price but also how much of it is purchased. To reflect this we need to weight the prices of the commodities by the quantities that are bought. These enable us to calculate weighted aggregate price indices.

There are two basic approaches to weighting the prices. One involves using the quantities purchased in the base year. The amount of a commodity bought in the base period is symbol-ised by q_0. This index is called the *Laspeyre* or *base-weighted price index*. Calculating it involves working out the combined cost of the quantities purchased in the base period if they were bought at current period prices (p_c), dividing this by the combined cost of the quantities pur-chased in the base period at the prices in the base period (p_0), and finally multiplying by 100:

$$\text{Laspeyre (base-weighted) price index} = \frac{\sum q_0 p_c}{\sum q_0 p_0} * 100$$

EXAMPLE
8.3

In 2008 Antonia Gate bought 100 ring shanks, 150 Slatkirite stones and 400 Tyeplochite stones. Using these and the prices from Example 8.2 produce a Laspeyre index of the prices of 2011 compared to the prices of 2008.

Solution

$$\frac{\sum q_0 p_c}{\sum q_0 p_0} * 100 = \frac{(100 * 6.25) + (150 * 1.95) + (400 * 0.75)}{(100 * 4.50) + (150 * 1.65) + (400 * 0.41)} * 100$$

$$= \frac{1217.5}{861.5} * 100$$

$$= 141.3 \text{ to 1 decimal place}$$

This indicates that the prices Antonia Gate paid rose by 41.3% between 2008 and 2011, which is higher than the figure in Example 8.2, 36.4%. This is largely due to fact that the price of the Tyeplochite stones, which increased proportionately more than the other two prices, has the biggest weight.

The Laspeyre index uses quantities from the past as weights. This is an advantage because usually such figures are easy to obtain. Its disadvantage is that being historical the base period quantities may differ considerably from quantities purchased in the current period.

The second method, which is particularly useful if the quantities purchased have changed markedly, is based on using the current period quantity for each commodity, q_c to weight its price. This is the Paasche, or current-weighted price index. Calculating it involves working out the combined cost of the quantities purchased in the current period bought at current period prices (p_c), dividing this by the combined cost of the quantities if they were purchased at the prices in the base period (p_0), and finally multiplying by 100:

$$\text{Paasche (current-weighted) price index} = \frac{\sum q_c p_c}{\sum q_c p_0} * 100$$

EXAMPLE 8.4

In 2011 Antonia Gate bought 120 ring shanks, 200 Slatkirite stones and 800 Tyeplochite stones. Using these and the prices from Example 8.2 produce a Paasche index of the prices of 2011 compared with the prices of 2008.

Solution

$$\frac{\sum q_c p_c}{\sum q_c p_0} * 100 = \frac{(120 * 6.25) + (200 * 1.95) + (800 * 0.75)}{(120 * 4.50) + (200 * 1.65) + (800 * 0.41)} * 100$$

$$= \frac{1740}{1198} * 100$$

$$= 145.2 \text{ to 1 decimal place}$$

This indicates that the prices Antonia Gate paid rose by 45.2% between 2008 and 2011, which is higher than the 41.3% in Example 8.3. The amount of Tyeplochite stones purchased in 2011 compared to 2008 is much higher than the increases in the quantities of other commodities. This means the weighting of the Tyeplochite price is much greater in the Paasche index than in the Laspeyre index.

Because the quantity figures used in the Paasche price index are from the current period the index is based on up-to-date rather than historical data. The difficulty is that current consumption figures may not be readily available, especially if a large range of commodities are to be included in the index.

A further difficulty with the Paasche index is that current quantity figures are needed for every period we want to compare to the base period. For every new period we need new quantity data. Should the ring-maker in Example 8.4 require a Paasche figure to compare the prices in 2012 to those from 2008 she would need to have the quantity data for 2012. These would not be necessary to get a Laspeyre figure for 2012; she would only need to know the prices in 2012 as she would use the 2008 quantities.

An important feature of the Laspeyre and Paasche methods is that although they compare prices from *different* periods, the quantities used to weight the prices are from the *same* period. In the Laspeyre index it is the base period quantities that are used to weight *both* the current period and base period prices. In the Paasche index it is the current period quantities that are used to weight *both* the current period and base period prices. It is important to remember that they are *price* indices that compare *prices* over time, not *quantities*.

SELF-ASSEMBLY GUIDE

Using Laspeyre and Paasche price indices

◆ To compare the prices of a set of items in one period (the current period) to those of an earlier period (the base period) you need the price of each item in the current period (p_c) and the base period (p_0).

◆ For a Laspeyre index, as well as the prices you need the amount of each item purchased in the base period (q_0).

◆ For each item multiply the q_0 figure by the p_c figure.

◆ Add the $q_0 p_c$ products up to get the total cost of the quantities from the base period if they had been bought at current period prices, $\sum q_0 p_c$.

◆ For each item multiply the q_0 figure by the p_0 figure.

◆ Add the $q_0 p_0$ products together to get the total cost of the base period quantities at the base period prices, $\sum q_0 p_0$.

◆ Divide the total cost at current prices, $\sum q_0 p_c$, by the total cost at base period prices, $\sum q_0 p_0$, and multiply by 100.

◆ For a Paasche index you need the quantity of each item bought in the current period (q_c).

◆ For each item multiply q_c by p_c, the current period price.

◆ Add the $q_c p_c$ products up to get the total cost of the current period quantities at current period prices, $\sum q_c p_c$.

◆ For each item multiply q_c by p_0, the base period price.

◆ Add the $q_c p_0$ products together to get the total cost of the current period quantities if they had been bought at the base period prices, $\sum q_0 p_0$.

◆ Divide the total cost at current prices, $\sum q_c p_c$, by the total cost at base period prices, $\sum q_c p_0$, and multiply by 100.

At this point you may find it useful to try **Review question 8.5** at the end of the chapter.

Organisations use index numbers to adjust financial figures to reflect general price changes, in other words to adjust for the effects of inflation. They do this because an amount of money in one period is not equivalent to the same money amount in another period if prices have changed between the two periods. These price changes mean that the amount of goods and services that can be purchased also changes. To compare amounts from different periods meaningfully we need to alter them to take account of the changes in price levels. The usual method is to use general price indices produced by government statistical services to measure changes in the cost of living such as the UK Retail Price Index (RPI) and the Consumer Price Index (CPI). This is known as *deflating* because it reverses the effects of *inflation*. It is also known as expressing figures *at constant prices* or *in real terms*.

**EXAMPLE
8.5**

The following table shows the annual salary of the Operations Manager at Leetso Cosmetics in the years 2007 to 2010 and the RPI figures for those years. How has the real value of her pay changed?

	2007	**2008**	**2009**	**2010**
Annual salary (£000)	35	37	39	40
RPI (1987 = 100)	206.6	214.8	213.7	223.6

Source: Office for National Statistics.

Solution

To deflate the 2008, 2009 and 2010 figures so that they are all in '2007 pounds' multiply each of them by the 2007 RPI figure then divide by the RPI figure for the year when the salary was paid.

$$\text{The adjusted 2008 salary} = 37 * \frac{206.6}{214.8} = 35.588 \text{ or } £35,588$$

$$\text{The adjusted 2009 salary} = 39 * \frac{206.6}{213.7} = 37.704 \text{ or } £37,704$$

$$\text{The adjusted 2010 salary} = 40 * \frac{206.6}{223.6} = 36.959 \text{ or } £36,959$$

Over the entire period the Operations Manager's salary increased in real terms although it did fall between 2009 and 2010.

Note that there is no need to adjust the 2007 salary as it is already in 2007 pounds.

SELF-ASSEMBLY GUIDE

Adjusting for inflation

◆ Find appropriate price index values such as CPI or RPI for each of the periods covered by the figures you want to adjust.

◆ Taking each money amount, except the first, multiply by the price index figure for the first year and divide by the price index figure for the year in which the money amount occurred, e.g. to adjust a 2010 figure so it is expressed at 2007 prices multiply by the 2007 price index value and divide by the 2010 price index value.

◆ In periods of inflation the results will be less than the original money amounts.

◆ If the results go up over time then the real value of the amounts has increased; if they go down the real value has decreased.

At this point you may find it useful to try **Review questions 8.3, 8.6 and 8.10** at the end of the chapter.

8.3 Investment appraisal

Almost every organisation at one time or another has to take decisions about making investments. These decisions may involve something as big as the construction of a new plant or something more mundane like the purchase of a new piece of machinery. One of the main difficulties that managers face when taking these sorts of decisions is that the cost of making the investment is incurred when the plant is built or the machine is purchased, yet the income which it is intended to help generate arises in the future, perhaps over many years.

In this section we will look at techniques that enable managers to appraise, or weigh up, investment in long-lasting assets by relating the initial outlay to the future revenue. These techniques are used by businesses both to assess specific investments and to decide between alternative investments. Companies take these decisions very seriously because they involve large amounts of resources and once made they cannot be reversed.

We will begin with the accounting rate of return method then we will consider the payback period approach, and finally the more sophisticated discounting techniques. Despite the differences between them they all involve determining single figures that summarise the likely financial outcome of an investment project.

8.3.1 The accounting rate of return

Generally, a rate of return expresses the *return* or profit resulting from the use of assets such as machinery or equipment in terms of the expenditure involved in purchasing them, usually in percentage terms. You will find that accountants make extensive use of these types of summary measure; look at a business newspaper or a company report and you will probably find reference to measures like the ROCE (Return on Capital Employed). These measures are used by companies to indicate how effectively they have managed the assets under their control.

The accounting rate of return (ARR) is the use of this approach to weigh up the attraction of an investment proposal. To apply it we need to establish the average (mean) profit per year and divide that by the average (mean) level of investment per year.

To calculate the average profit per year we add up the annual profits and divide by the number of years over which the investment will help generate these revenues. Having said that, the profit figures we use must be profits after allowing for *depreciation*. Depreciation is the spreading of the cost of an asset over its useful life. The simplest way of doing this is to subtract the *residual value* of the asset, which is the amount that the company expects to get from the sale of the asset when it is no longer of use, from the purchase cost of the asset and divide by the number of years of useful life the asset is expected to have. This approach is known as *straight-line depreciation* and it assumes that the usefulness of the asset, in terms of helping to generate profits, is reasonably consistent over its useful life.

To work out the average level of investment, we need to know the cost of the asset and the residual value of the asset. The average investment value is the difference between the initial cost and the residual value divided by two, in other words we split the difference between the highest and lowest values of the asset while it is in use. After dividing the average return by the average investment we multiply by 100 to give a percentage result. The procedure can be represented as:

$$\text{Average annual return} = \frac{\text{average annual return}}{\text{average annual investment}} * 100$$

where

$$\text{Average annual investment} = (\text{purchase cost} - \text{residual value})/2$$

Should the company in Example 8.6 regard the accounting rate of return for this project as high enough to make the investment worth its while? In practice it would compare this

EXAMPLE 8.6

The Budisha Bus Company is thinking of purchasing a new luxury coach to sustain its prestige client business. The purchase cost of the vehicle, including licence plates and delivery, is £120,000. The company anticipates that it will use the vehicle for five years and be able to sell it at the end of that period for £40,000. The revenue the company expects to generate using the coach is as follows:

By the end of year	Net profit before depreciation (£)
1	30,000
2	30,000
3	30,000
4	25,000
5	20,000

What is the accounting rate of return for this investment?

Solution

The average annual profit before depreciation is:

$$\frac{(30{,}000 + 30{,}000 + 30{,}000 + 25{,}000 + 20{,}000)}{5} = \frac{135{,}000}{5} = £27{,}000$$

From this amount we must subtract the annual cost of depreciation, which is:

$$\frac{120{,}000 - 40{,}000}{5} = \frac{85{,}000}{5} = £16{,}000$$

The annual average profit after depreciation is: $27{,}000 - 16{,}000 = £11{,}000$

The average annual investment is:

$$\frac{120{,}000 - 40{,}000}{2} = \frac{80{,}000}{2} = £40{,}000$$

The accounting rate of return is:

$$\frac{11{,}000}{40{,}000} * 100 = 27.5\%$$

figure to accounting rates of return for alternative investments that it could make with the same money, or perhaps it has a company minimum rate that any project has to exceed to be approved.

The accounting rate of return is widely used to evaluate investment projects. It produces a percentage figure which managers can easily compare to interest rates and it is essentially the same approach to future investment as accountants take when working out the ROCE to evaluate a company's past performance.

The critical weakness in using the accounting rate of return to appraise investments is that it is completely blind to the timing of the initial expenditure and future income. It ignores what is called the *time value of money*.

The value that an individual or business puts on a sum of money is related to when the money is received; for example, if you were offered the choice of a gift of £1000 now or £1000 in two years' time you would most likely prefer the cash now. This may be because you need cash now rather than then, but even if you have sufficient funds now you would still be better off having the money now because you could invest the money in a savings account and receive interest on it.

The other investment appraisal techniques we shall examine have the advantage of bringing the time element into consideration. The other difference between them and the accounting rate of return approach is that they are based on net cash flows into the company, which are essentially net profits before depreciation.

8.3.2 Payback period

The payback period approach to investment appraisal does take the timing of cash flows into account and is based on a straightforward concept – the time it will take for the net profits earned using the asset to cover the purchase cost of the asset. We need only accumulate the negative (expenditure) and positive (net profits before depreciation) cash flows relating to the investment over time and ascertain when the cumulative cash flow reaches zero. At this point the initial outlay on the asset will have been paid back.

EXAMPLE 8.7

Work out the payback period for the investment proposal being considered by the Budisha Bus Company in Example 8.6.

Solution

The net cash flows associated with the acquisition of the luxury coach can be summarised as follows:

End of year	Cost/receipt	Net cash flow (£)	Cumulative cash flow (£)
0	Cost of coach	−120 000	−120 000
1	Net profit before depreciation	30 000	−90 000
2	Net profit before depreciation	30 000	−60 000
3	Net profit before depreciation	30 000	−30 000
4	Net profit before depreciation	25 000	−5 000
5	Net profit before depreciation	20 000	+15 000
5	Sale of coach	40 000	+55 000

Payback is achieved in year 5. We can be more precise by adding the extra cash flow required after the end of year 4 to reach zero cumulative cash flow (£5000) divided by the net cash flow received by the end of the fifth year (£20,000):

$$\text{Payback period} = 4 + \frac{5000}{20,000} = 4.25 \text{ years}$$

Note that in the net cash flow column of the table in Example 8.7 the initial outlay for the coach has a negative sign to indicate that it is a flow of cash out of the business. You will find that accountants use round brackets to indicate an outflow of cash, so where we have written −120,000 for the outgoing cash to buy the coach an accountant would represent it as (120,000).

The payback period we found in Example 8.7 might be compared with a minimum payback period the company required for any investment or with alternative investments that could be made with the same resources.

At this point you may find it useful to try **Review question 8.4** at the end of the chapter.

The payback period is a simple concept for managers to apply and it is particularly appropriate when firms are very sensitive to risk because it indicates the time during which they are exposed to the risk of not recouping their initial outlay A cautious manager would probably be comfortable with the idea of preferring investment opportunities that have shorter payback periods. Because of its simplicity it is used for the first stage of project selection to filter out less attractive investments leaving the remainder to be scrutinised with more sophisticated methods.

The weakness of the payback approach is that it ignores cash flows that arise in periods beyond the payback period. Where there are two alternative projects it may not suggest the one that performs better overall.

EXAMPLE 8.8

Gravura Print specialises in precision graphics for the art poster market. To expand their business they want to purchase a flying-arm stamper. There are two manufacturers that produce such machines: Smeshnoy and Pazorna. The cash flows arising from the two ventures are expected to be as follows:

Smeshnoy Machine

End of year	Cost/receipt	Net cash flow (£)	Cumulative cash flow (£)
0	Cost of machine	−30000	−30000
1	Net profit before depreciation	7000	−23000
2	Net profit before depreciation	8000	−15000
3	Net profit before depreciation	8000	−7000
4	Net profit before depreciation	7000	0
5	Net profit before depreciation	7000	+7000
5	Sale of machine	5000	+12000

Pazorna Machine

End of year	Cost/receipt	Net cash flow (£)	Cumulative cash flow (£)
0	Cost of machine	−30000	−30000
1	Net profit before depreciation	12000	−18000
2	Net profit before depreciation	12000	−6000
3	Net profit before depreciation	6000	0
4	Net profit before depreciation	2000	+2000
5	Net profit before depreciation	1000	+3000
5	Sale of machine	2000	+5000

In Example 8.8 the payback period for the Smeshnoy machine is four years and for the Pazorna machine three years. Applying the payback period criterion we should choose the Pazorna machine, but in doing so we would be passing up the opportunity of achieving the higher overall return, £12,000, from investing in the Smeshnoy machine.

A better approach would be to base our assessment of investments on all of the cash flows involved rather than just the earlier ones, and to bring into our calculations the time value of money. Techniques that allow us to do this adjust or *discount* cash flows to compensate for the time that passes before they arrive. The first of these techniques that we shall consider is the net present value.

8.3.3 **Net present value**

The net present value (NPV) of an investment is a single figure that summarises all the cash flows arising from an investment, both expenditure and receipts, each of which have been adjusted so that whenever they arise in the future it is their current or *present* value that is used in the calculation. Adjusting, or *discounting*, them to get their present value means working out how much money would have to be invested now in order to generate that specific amount at that time in the future.

To do this we use the same approach as we would to calculate the amount of money accumulating in a savings account. We need to know the rate of interest and the amount of money initially deposited. The amount in the account at the end of one year is the original amount deposited plus the rate of interest, r, applied to the original amount:

$$\text{Amount at the end of the year} = \text{Deposit} + (\text{Deposit} * r)$$

We can express this as:

$$\text{Amount at the end of the year} = \text{Deposit} * (1 + r)$$

If the money stays in the account for a second year:

$$\text{Amount at the end of the second year} = \text{Deposit} * (1 + r) * (1 + r)$$

$$= \text{Deposit} * (1 + r)^2$$

EXAMPLE 8.9

If you invested £1000 in a savings account paying 5% interest per annum, how much money would you have in the account after two years?

Solution

$$\text{Amount at the end of the first year} = 1000 * (1 + 0.05) = £1050$$

If we invested £1050 for a year at 5%, at the end of one year it would be worth:

$$1050 * (1 + 0.05) = £1102.5$$

We can combine these calculations:

$$\text{Amount at the end of the second year} = 1000 * (1 + 0.05)^2$$

$$= 1000 * 1.05^2 = 1000 * 1.1025 = £1102.5$$

In general if we deposit an amount in an account paying an annual interest rate r for n years, the amount accumulated in the account at the end of the period will be:

$$\text{Deposit} * (1 + r)^n$$

The deposit is, of course, the sum of money we start with, it is the *present value* (PV) of our investment, so we can express this procedure as:

$$\text{Amount at the end of year } n = \text{PV} * (1 + r)^n$$

This expression enables us to work out the future value of a known present value, like the amount we deposit in an account. When we assess investment projects we want to know how much a known (or at least expected) amount to be received in the future is worth now. Instead of knowing the present value and wanting to work out the future, we need to reverse the process and determine the present value of a known future amount. To obtain this we can rearrange the expression we used to work out the amount accumulated at the end of a period:

$$\text{Present value (PV)} = \frac{\text{Amount at the end of year } n}{(1 + r)^n}$$

EXAMPLE 8.10

You are offered £1000 to be paid to you in two years' time. What is the present value of this sum if you can invest cash in a savings account paying 5% interest per annum?

Solution

$$\text{Present value} = \frac{1000}{(1 + 0.05)^2} = \frac{1000}{1.05^2} = \frac{1000}{1.1025} = 907.029$$

The present value of £1000 received in two years' time is £907.03, to the nearest penny. In other words, if you invested £907.03 at 5% now in two years' time the amount would be worth:

$$\text{Amount at the end of year two} = 907.03 * (1 + 0.05)^2$$
$$= 907.03 * 1.1025$$
$$= £1000.00 \text{ to the nearest penny}$$

When companies use NPV to assess investments they discount future cash flows in the same way as we did in Example 8.10, but before they can do so they need to identify the appropriate rate of interest to use. In Example 8.10 we used 5% as it might reflect the *opportunity cost* of not receiving the money for two years, that is, the amount you have had to forgo by having to wait.

The interest, or *discount*, rate a company uses is likely to reflect the opportunity cost, which may be the interest it could earn by investing the money in a bank. It may also reflect the prevailing rate of inflation and the risk of the investment project not working out as planned.

EXAMPLE 8.11

What is the net present value of the proposed investment in a luxury coach by the Budisha Bus Company in Example 8.6? Use a 10% interest rate.

Solution

The cash flows involved in the project, including the sale of the coach at the end of year 5, were:

End of year	Cash flow (£)	Calculation for PV	PV (to the nearest £)
0	−120000	$−120000/(1 + 0.1)^0$	−120000
1	30000	$30000/(1 + 0.1)^1$	27273
2	30000	$30000/(1 + 0.1)^2$	24794
3	30000	$30000/(1 + 0.1)^3$	22539
4	25000	$25000/(1 + 0.1)^4$	17075
5	20000	$20000/(1 + 0.1)^5$	12418
5	40000	$40000/(1 + 0.1)^5$	24837
		Net present value =	£8936

The net present value of the project in Example 8.11 is £8936. The initial outlay of £120,000 in effect purchases future returns that are worth £128,936. Because the discount rate used is in effect a threshold of acceptable returns from a project, any opportunity that results in a positive NPV such as in Example 8.11 should be approved and any opportunity producing a negative NPV should be declined.

The calculation of present values of a series of cash flows is an arduous process, so it is easier to use *discount tables*, tables that give values of the discount factor, $1/(1 + r)^n$ for different values of r and n. You can find discount tables in Table 1 of Appendix 1 at the end of the book.

EXAMPLE 8.12

Use Table 1 in Appendix 1 to find the net present values for the company in Example 8.8. Apply a discount rate of 8%.

Solution

Gravura Print can purchase two makes of flying-arm stamper. The cash flows involved and their present values are:

Smeshnoy Machine

End of year	Cash flow (£)	Discount factor	PV (Cash flow * discount factor)
0	−30 000	1.000[†]	−30 000
1	7 000	0.926	6 482
2	8 000	0.857	6 856
3	8 000	0.794	6 352
4	7 000	0.735	5 145
5	6 000	0.681	4 086
5	5 000	0.681	3 405
		Net present value =	£2 326

[†]*Note*: these figures occur in the present so they do not need to be adjusted.

Pazorna Machine

End of year	Cash flow (£)	Discount factor	PV (Cash flow * discount factor)
0	−30 000	1.000[†]	−30 000
1	12 000	0.926	11 112
2	12 000	0.857	10 284
3	6 000	0.794	4 764
4	2 000	0.735	1 470
5	1 000	0.681	681
5	2 000	0.681	1 362
		Net present value =	−£327

[†]*Note*: these figures occur in the present so they do not need to be adjusted.

The company should choose the Smeshnoy machine as it will deliver not only a better NPV than the other machine, but an NPV that is positive.

SELF-ASSEMBLY GUIDE

Net present value

◆ Decide the discount rate to be used.

◆ Find the discount values for the periods in which future cash flows occur.

◆ Multiply each future cash inflow by the discount factor for the period.

◆ Add up the discounted cash flows and subtract from this total the initial expenditure to give the net present value of the project.

◆ If there is a choice of projects choose the one with the higher/highest net present value.

8.3.4 The internal rate of return

A fourth investment appraisal method widely used by businesses is the internal rate of return (IRR). It is closely related to the net present value approach; in fact the IRR is the discount rate at which the total present value of the cash flows into a business arising from an investment precisely equals the initial outlay. To put it another way, the internal rate of return is the discount rate that would result in a net present value of zero for the investment. Because the concept of discounting is at the heart of both NPV and IRR they are known as *discounted cash flow* (DCF) methods.

Finding the internal rate of return for a project is a rather hit-and-miss affair. Start by trying one discount rate and if the result is a positive NPV try a higher discount rate. If the result is negative, try a lower discount rate.

EXAMPLE 8.13

Find the internal rate of return for the proposed luxury coach purchase by the Budisha Bus Company in Example 8.6.

Solution

We know from Example 8.11 that if we apply a discount rate of 10% the net present value of the project is £8936. Since this is positive the internal rate of return will be higher, so we might try 15%:

End of year	Cash flow (£)	Discount factor	PV (Cash flow * discount factor)
0	−120 000	1.000	−120 000
1	30 000	0.870	26 100
2	30 000	0.756	22 680
3	30 000	0.658	19 740
4	25 000	0.572	14 300
5	20 000	0.497	9 940
5	40 000	0.497	19 880
		Net present value =	−£7 360

This negative NPV suggests that the internal rate of return is not as high as 15%. We could try a lower discount rate such as 12% or 13%, but it is easier to use the NPV figures we have for the discount rates of 10% and 15% to approximate the internal rate of return.

Using the discount rate of 10% in Example 8.11 the NPV for the project was £8936 and using the discount rate of 15% the NPV is −£7360. The difference between these two figures is:

$$8936 - (-7360) = 8936 + 7360 = £16,296$$

This difference arises when we change the discount rate by 5%. The change in NPV per 1% change in discount rate is £16,296 divided by five, roughly £3260. We can conclude from this that for every 1% increase in the discount rate there will be a drop of roughly £3000 in the NPV of the project. The NPV at the discount rate of 10% was just under £9000 so the discount rate that will yield an NPV of zero is about 13%.

Often it is sufficient to find an approximate value of the IRR, as we have done in Example 8.13. If you need a precise value you can try several discount rates and plot them against the resulting NPV figures for the project.

EXAMPLE 8.14

The net present values for the coach purchase by the Budisha Bus Company were calculated using different discount rates. The results are:

Discount rate	Net present value (£)
10%	8936
12%	1980
13%	−1265
15%	−7360

Plot these and use the graph to estimate the internal rate of return for the project.

Solution

Look carefully at Figure 8.1 and you will see that the plotted line crosses the horizontal axis about midway between 10 and 15. This suggests that the internal rate of return for the project, the discount rate that produces a zero net present value, is about 12.5%.

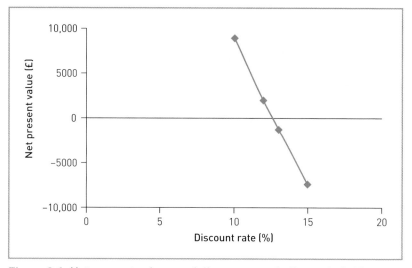

Figure 8.1 Net present values and discount rate in Example 8.14

The result we obtained in Example 8.14 could be used to compare the coach purchase to other investment opportunities open to the company, or perhaps the cost of borrowing the money to make the investment, if it needed to do so. In general, the higher the internal rate of return, the more attractive the project.

The internal rate of return and the net present value methods of investment appraisal are similar in that they summarise all the cash flows associated with a venture and are therefore superior to the payback method. They also take the time value of money into account and are therefore superior to the accounting rate of return approach.

The drawback of the internal rate of return technique compared to the net present value method is that the IRR is an interest rate, a relative amount, which unlike the NPV gives no idea of the scale of the cash flows involved. Both IRR and NPV are rather laborious to calculate. Companies may well use the fairly basic approach of the payback period as the threshold that any proposed investment must meet, and then use either NPV or IRR to select from those that do.

At this point you may find it useful to try **Review questions 8.7, 8.8, 8.11 and 8.12** at the end of the chapter.

If you want to find out more about investment appraisal, you will probably find Drury (2007) helpful.

REVIEW QUESTIONS

Answers to these questions are on page 449–50. There are tips and hints to help you with them on the supporting website at **www.pearsoned.co.uk/buglear**, where you will also find the fully worked solutions.

☆☆★ Basic questions

8.1 A confectioner buys cocoa to use in manufacturing its products. The price it has paid per kilogram has been:

Year	2005	2007	2009	2011
Cost ($)	230	290	310	330

(a) Calculate a simple price index for

(i) the price in 2011 relative to 2005
(ii) the price in 2009 relative to 2005
(iii) the price in 2011 relative to 2007
(iv) the price in 2009 relative to 2007

(b) Compare your answers to (a) (i) and (ii) with your answers to (a) (iii) and (iv).

8.2 An office manager purchases paper and ink cartridges for printers. The prices of these items over the years 2009 to 2011 were:

	2009	**2010**	**2011**
Paper (per ream)	£7.99	£9.99	£10.99
Cartridge	£10.99	£13.49	£14.49

Calculate a simple aggregate price index for the prices in 2010 and 2011 using 2009 as the base period.

8.3 Anne Teak purchased a Georgian commode for £400 in 2000. Since then she has had it valued every two years. These valuations were:

Year	2002	2004	2006	2008	2010
Valuation (£)	£430	£480	£490	£500	£525

The values of the Retail Price Index (RPI) for these years are:

Year	2002	2004	2006	2008	2010
RPI	176.2	186.7	198.1	214.8	223.6

Source: Office for National Statistics

The RPI figure for 2000 is 170.3.

Use the RPI figures to adjust the valuations so they are all expressed in 2000 pounds. How has the value of the commode changed in real terms since 2000?

8.4 A young aspiring DJ has saved up £4000 to buy the equipment she needs. She anticipates that the equipment will last for five years, after which it will be obsolete and have no disposal value. During these five years she believes she can use it to earn the following amounts, after allowing for her own wages and costs of travelling to clubs and events:

End of year	Net cash flow (£)
1	1200
2	1800
3	2000
4	2000
5	2000

(a) Work out the accounting rate of return for the investment, allowing for depreciation of one-fifth of the cost of the equipment per year.

(b) Find the payback period for the investment.

☆★★ More testing questions

8.5 Meg Tort makes cakes on a commercial basis for local cafés and shops. The main ingredients she buys are dried fruit, eggs and flour. The prices of these in 2007 and 2011 were:

	2007	2011
Dried fruit (kg)	£1.50	£2.50
Eggs (10 pack)	£0.95	£1.40
Flour (kg)	£0.40	£0.50

(a) In 2007 Meg purchased 200kg of dried fruit, 100 packs of eggs and 500kg of flour. Calculate the weighted aggregate price index for the prices in 2011 based on the prices in 2007 using the Laspeyre method.

(b) In 2011 Meg purchased 150kg of dried fruit, 120 packs of eggs and 700kg of flour. Calculate the weighted aggregate price index for the prices in 2011 based on the prices in 2007 using the Paasche method. How does this compare to your answer to (a)?

8.6 A media and entertainments company operates two theme parks in two different countries: Dorrogoy and Stoymost. The annual profits of each theme park over the first five years of operations, in millions of units of local currency (the Lukar in Dorrogoy and the Dyengi in Stoymost) were:

	2005	2010
Dorrogoy (m Lukars)	46.1	182.2
Stoymost (m Dyengi)	15.2	51.4

The governments of the two countries each monitor the general level of prices using a weighted aggregate price index. Values of these indices for the years 2005 and 2010 are:

	2005	2010
Dorrogoy	112.7	281.4
Stoymost	103.4	192.3

(a) Deflate the profits for Dorrogoy so that the profit figures are expressed in 2005 Lukars.

(b) Deflate the profits for Stoymost so that the profit figures are expressed in 2005 Dyengi.

(c) Compare the results you obtain for (a) and (b), and comment on the relative success of the two theme parks over the period 2005 to 2010.

8.7 An advertisement offers a time share investment in a luxury apartment in the Algarve region of Portugal. Investors can purchase the use of the apartment for an eight-week period each year to rent out to tourists. The cost of the time share is £15,000 for five years and it is claimed that the net rental income will be £4000 per year.

(a) What is the payback period for the investment?

(b) What is the net present value of the investment to an investor who would otherwise be able to earn 5% on their money?

(c) In the small print of the advertisement it says 'a service charge of £1000 per annum is charged for the cleaning and general maintenance of the property'. Work out how this will alter the net present value of the investment.

8.8 Ricky Sadovnik, a geologist, discovered a deposit of decorative stone during a holiday in Scotland. He wants to establish a quarry to extract the stone and sell it to gardeners. The owner of the land is prepared to allow him to open and operate a quarry on the site for five years for a fee of £150,000. In addition he must landscape the site at the end of the period, at a cost of £50,000. Ricky intends to hire the digging equipment for the quarry. The net cash flows from the sale of the stone are predicted to be:

End of year	Net cash flow (£)
1	30,000
2	50,000
3	60,000
4	60,000
5	60,000

(a) Determine the net present value for this project based on a discount rate of 15%.

(b) Find the net present value using a discount rate of 10% and by comparing this figure to your answer to (a) estimate the internal rate of return for the project.

★★★ Challenging questions

8.9 Perry Stroiker, the builder, specialises in small-scale domestic building work, especially house extensions. He buys considerable quantities of bricks, cement mix, plasterboard and timber. The prices he paid for these commodities in 2005, 2008 and 2011 are as follows:

	2005	2008	2011
Bricks (per 500 pack)	£220	£275	£300
Cement mix (25kg bag)	£7.25	£8.60	£9.90
Plasterboard (sheet)	£4.50	£4.75	£5.40
Timber (2.4m length)	£2.80	£2.90	£3.00

(a) Perry bought 25 packs of bricks, 200 bags of cement mix, 100 sheets of plasterboard and 400 lengths of timber in 2005. Calculate Laspeyre price indices for 2008 and 2011 using 2005 as the base year.

(b) In 2008 Perry bought 35 packs of bricks, 250 bags of cement mix, 120 sheets of plasterboard and 500 lengths of timber. Calculate a Paasche price index for 2008 using 2005 as the base year.

(c) In 2011 Perry bought 22 packs of bricks, 180 bags of cement mix, 75 sheets of plasterboard and 350 lengths of timber. Calculate a Paasche price index for 2011 using 2005 as the base year.

8.10 The annual revenue figures for two large UK-based corporations over the six years from 2005 to 2010 were:

	2005	2006	2007	2008	2009	2010
Le Kartsvo (£bn)	21.7	23.2	22.7	24.4	28.4	28.4
Z-Vonia (£bn)	18.4	19.5	20.2	20.7	21.4	20.9

The values of the retail price index (RPI) for these years are:

	2005	2006	2007	2008	2009	2010
RPI	192.0	198.1	206.6	214.8	213.7	223.6

Source: Office for National Statistics

Deflate the revenue figures using the RPI values so that they are all expressed in 2005 pounds. How have these companies fared in real terms between 2005 and 2010?

8.11 A Russian businessman offers a Korean car manufacturer an eight-year lease on a disused tank factory in Southern Russia. The company could refit the factory and use it to manufacture low-cost recreational off-road vehicles for the holiday car-hire market in Southern Europe. The total cost of the investment, including the lease and the installation of equipment is $55m. Once the plant is operational the following net cash flows are expected:

End of year	Net cash flow ($m)
1	8
2	12
3	15
4	20
5	20
6	10
7	10
8	5

At the end of the eighth year the lease would expire. The disposal value of the equipment is likely to be $5m.

(a) Using a discount rate of 20%, work out the net present value for this proposal.

(b) Work out the net present value applying a discount rate of 15% and estimate the internal rate of return by comparing this to your answer to (a).

8.12 Otto Carr owns a chain of car parks in small towns. He wants to expand his business by leasing a suitable site in a city centre. There are two sites that would be appropriate. There is a six-year lease available on the Markets site for £200,000 and a seven-year lease available on the Riverside site for £300,000. The cost of clearing, marking out and equipping Markets is £120,000.

The equivalent figure for Riverside is £100,000. The cash flows (in £000s) arising from these projects are:

End of year	Net cash flow (Markets)	Net cash flow (Riverside)
1	60	120
2	80	120
3	80	80
4	90	80
5	90	40
6	80	40
6	10[†]	
7		40
7		10[†]

[†]disposal value of equipment

(a) Determine the payback period for each site.
(b) Using a discount rate of 8% calculate the net present value for each site.
(c) Which site should Otto acquire and why?

THE DEBRIEF

Key things to remember from this chapter

→ Price indices are used to measure price changes over time relative to a base period. They range from the simple price index, which gauges the change in the price of only one commodity, to aggregate price indices which cover the price changes in several commodities.

→ The simple aggregate price index measure changes in the sum of the prices of a set of commodities. Weighted aggregate price indices attach quantity figures to each price to reflect the amounts actually purchased.

→ The two classic types of weighted aggregate are the Laspeyre and Paasche indices. The Laspeyre index uses quantity data from the base period; the Paasche index uses quantity data from the period being compared to the base period.

→ The Laspeyre index is easier to calculate as the quantity figures remain the same. The Paasche index is more appropriate when quantities purchased change considerably.

→ Price indices such as the RPI are used to deflate money amounts so that they are expressed at constant prices. This makes financial data from different time periods easier to compare as it removes the effects of inflation.

→ Investment appraisal is used to select projects where the returns accrue over time. The methods of doing this include the accounting rate of return, the payback period, NPV and IRR.

→ The accounting rate of return and the payback technique do not take account of the time value of money.

→ NPV and IRR are based on discounting, adjusting future income streams to reflect the time value of money.

→ NPV involves identifying the appropriate discount rate to use then balancing the discounted future cash inflows against the initial outlay. The result is the net present value. If there is a choice of projects the one with the highest NPV should be selected.

→ IRR is the discount rate at which the discounted future cash inflows match the initial outlay. If there is a choice of projects the one with the highest IRR should be chosen.

References

Collins, A. (2010) 'Shifting pensions valuation to CPI is costly', *Accountancy Age,* December. Available at: http://www.accountancyage.com/aa/opinion/1933170/shifting-pensions-valuation-cpi-costly

Drury, C. (2007) *Management and Cost Accounting* (7th edn), London: Business Press.

Frankel, S.H. (1967) *Investment and the Return to Equity Capital in the South African Gold Mining Industry, 1887–1965*, Oxford: Basil Blackwell.

Huish, M., Woodhouse, H. and Watkin, E. (1853) 'Report to the Permanent Way Committee on the Renewal Fund', in J.R. Edwards (ed.), *Reporting Fixed Assets in Nineteenth-Century Company Accounts*, New York: Garland Publishing, 1986, pp. 269–86.

Johnson, H.T. and Kaplan, R.S. (1991) *Relevance Lost – The Rise and Fall of Management Accounting*, Boston: Harvard Business School Press.

Klammer, T., Koch, B. and Wilner, N. (1991) 'Capital budgeting practices – a survey of corporate use', *Journal of Management Accounting Research*, 3, pp. 113–30.

Parker, R.H. (1968) 'Discounted cash flow in historical perspective', *Journal of Accounting Research*, Spring, pp. 58–71.

Pike, R. (1996) 'A longitudinal survey on capital budgeting practices', *Journal of Business Finance and Accounting*, 23(1), pp. 79–92.

Singh, R. (2010) 'Index compares share price with emissions', *Accountancy Age,* March. Available at: http://www.accountancyage.com/aa/analysis/1808706/index-compares-share-price-emissions

Weaver, J.B. and Reilly, R.J. (1956) 'Interest rate of return for capital expenditure evaluation', *Chemical Engineering Progress*, 52(10), pp. 405–12.

CHAPTER 7

Long distance – analysing time series data

This chapter will help you to:

→ Identify the components of time series

→ Employ classical decomposition to analyse time series data

→ Produce forecasts of future values of time series variables

→ Apply exponential smoothing to analyse time series data

What you will find in this chapter . . .

- Using the additive decomposition model to identify the trend and seasonal components of time series data
- Employing the multiplicative decomposition model to identify the trend and seasonal factors of time series data
- Finding the error components in time series using decomposition and using these to review performance
- Producing measures of accuracy using error components and using them to select appropriate time series models
- Forecasting using the decomposition and exponential smoothing models

. . . and on the supporting website (www.pearsoned.co.uk/buglear)

- How to use Minitab and SPSS to analyse time series data
- Fully worked solutions to the review questions
- More review questions

Business use of time series analysis and forecasting

◆ For most businesses time series data, and forecasting future values from them, is immensely important. If sales for the next period can be forecast then managers can order the necessary stock. If future profits can be forecast, investment plans can be made. It is therefore not surprising that in Kathawala's study of the use of quantitative techniques by American companies 92% of respondents reported that they made moderate, frequent or extensive use of forecasting (Kathawala, 1988).

◆ In a more specific study, Sparkes and McHugh (1984) surveyed members of the Institute of Cost and Management Accountants in key posts in UK manufacturing. They found that 98% of respondents had an awareness or working knowledge of moving averages, and 58% of these used the technique. Also, 92% of their respondents had an awareness or working knowledge of trend analysis, 63% of whom used it. Respondents reported that they used these time series analysis techniques to forecast market share, production and stock control, and to make financial projections.

◆ Forecasting is particularly important in industries where large-scale investment decisions depend on demand many years into the future. An example is electricity generation where constructing new capacity may take 10 years or so, and minimising costs depends on forecasting peak demand in the future. In a survey of US electricity supply companies Huss (1987) found that nearly 98% of managers saw forecasting as either very important or critical for electricity generation planning and 93% regarded it as very important or critical for financial planning.

◆ According to a manager at the Thames Water Authority in the UK, the water industry had similar concerns. Million (1980) explained that justification of investment in new reservoirs depended on forecast water demand 20 years or so into the future.

◆ The Corporate Planning Director of the French paper company Aussedat-Rey described decomposition as 'the oldest and most commonly used approach to forecasting' (Majani, 1987: 219). He shows how decomposition was used to analyse the changes in the consumption of newsprint in France (Ibid.: 224–8).

◆ The role of forecasting is not restricted to strategic planning. Zhongjie (1993) outlines the problems of overloading on the Chinese rail network and demonstrates how time series analysis was used to forecast freight traffic at a railway station in southern China in order to promote better utilisation rates of freight cars. Sutlieff (1982) illustrates how forecasting emergency jobs at North Thames Gas in the UK enabled the company to plan the workload of its fitters more effectively.

◆ A consistent feature of time series data is seasonal variation. Consumer purchasing patterns are highly seasonal, as are levels of activity in the construction business. There is a rich variety of examples of seasonal fluctuation in both business and other spheres in Thorneycroft (1987).

9.1 Introduction

Businesses gather time series data, data that consists of observations recorded at regular intervals, on a routine basis. An organisation might compile data about daily takings, weekly wages and monthly employee absences. Its annual report will probably present time series data like its quarterly revenue and annual profits.

The value of time series data to managers is that unlike a single figure relating to one period a time series shows changes over time; maybe increases in the sales of some products and decreases in the sales of others. The single figure is like a photograph that captures a single moment, a time series is like a video that shows events unfolding. This sort of record assists managers in reviewing the company performance over time and is a basis for predicting future performance.

By portraying time series data in the form of a time series chart it is possible to use the series to both review performance and anticipate future direction. If you look back at the time series charts in Figures 5.16 and 5.17 you will see they show how the series changes over time. You can inspect such diagrams for evidence of the general movement in the series, the *trend*, and regular movements above and below the trend.

When you look at a plotted time series the points representing the observations may form a straight line pattern. If this is the case you can use the regression analysis that we looked at in section 7.3, taking time as the independent variable, to model the series and predict future values. Typically time series data that businesses need to analyse is seldom this straightforward so we need to consider different methods.

9.2 Components of time series

Whilst plotting a time series graphically gives a general idea of the patterns in the series, to investigate it fully we have to probe it more systematically. One approach is the *decomposition* method, which entails separating or *decomposing* the observations into distinct *components*. This is an appropriate method for time series that have recurring patterns, which is often the case with time series data that businesses use.

In the decomposition model time series data is assumed to consist of the following components:

- The *trend* (T): the basic long-term movement. This might be upward, downward or constant.
- The *seasonal* elements (S): short-term recurrent components. Although the name implies they repeat on a seasonal basis they could be daily, weekly or monthly fluctuations depending on the time periods used in the series.
- The *cyclical* elements (C): long-term recurrent components that repeat over several years.
- The *error* or *random* or *residual* elements (E): these are the 'leftovers', which are not part of the trend, seasonal or cyclical components.

The nature of the 'seasonal' component in a time series depends on the timeframe of the series. If data is collected daily we look for components for the different periods of the day. If it is collected weekly we look for components for different days. We look for seasonal components in data that is collected quarterly. To find cyclical components, which reflect patterns repeating over several years, we need data for a considerable number of years.

Although it is conceivable that there may be more than one 'seasonal' component in a series, perhaps data collected daily may show regular variations from month to month and from week to week, typically time series analysis consists of finding the trend and only one repeating component.

EXAMPLE 9.1

A 'DIY' superstore is open seven days every week. The following numbers of customers (to the nearest thousand) visited the store each day over a three-week period:

Week	Day	Number of customers (000s)
1	Monday	4
	Tuesday	6
	Wednesday	6
	Thursday	9
	Friday	15
	Saturday	28
	Sunday	30
2	Monday	3
	Tuesday	5
	Wednesday	7
	Thursday	11
	Friday	14
	Saturday	26
	Sunday	34
3	Monday	5
	Tuesday	8
	Wednesday	7
	Thursday	8
	Friday	17
	Saturday	32
	Sunday	35

Construct a time series chart for the data and examine it for evidence of a trend and seasonal components for days of the week.

Solution

Figure 9.1 shows a general upward movement in the series over the three weeks. This is evidence of the trend in the numbers of customers increasing. There is also a substantial variation in the numbers of customers between the different days of the week. The week-day observations are consistently lower than those for the weekend days.

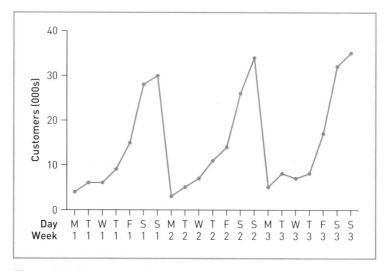

Figure 9.1 Customers visiting the DIY store in Example 9.1

Note that in Example 9.1 it is not possible to look for cyclical components as the data covers only three weeks. Neither is it possible to identify error components as these 'leftover' components can only be discerned when the trend and seasonal components have been 'sifted out'. We can do this using classical decomposition analysis.

9.3   Classical decomposition of time series data

Classical decomposition involves taking apart a time series so that we can identify the components that make it up. The first step is to identify the trend components. To estimate these we find *moving averages* of the observations. As the name implies, moving averages are based on sequences of observations in the time series.

A moving average (MA) is the mean of a run of observations comprising one from each of the different time periods in the series. For the Example 9.1 data each MA is the mean of a sequence of observations that consists of one figure from each of the seven days in a week. As the moving average will be based on seven observations, in other words seven points of data, it is termed a *seven-point* MA.

The first MA is the mean of the observations from the Monday to the Sunday of the first week. The second is the mean of the figures from the Tuesday to the Sunday of the first week and the Monday of the second week. In both cases the mean is based on seven figures, one from each of the different days of the week. To calculate the second MA we do not include the observation from the Monday of the first week, instead we include the observation from the Monday of the second week, but we still have one Monday figure, one Tuesday figure and so on. We carry on like this through the series, dropping the earliest observation in the set and replacing it with the next one after the end of the set, rather like the way the caterpillar tracks on a bulldozer work; as one plate lifts from the ground, another one sets down in its place.

EXAMPLE 9.2

Find moving averages for the time series in Example 9.1 and plot them graphically.

Solution

Day	M T W T F S S M T
The first MA	$= (4 + 6 + 6 + 9 + 15 + 28 + 30)/7 \qquad = 98/7 = 14.000$
The second MA	$= \qquad (6 + 6 + 9 + 15 + 28 + 30 + 3)/7 \quad = 97/7 = 13.857$
The third MA	$= \qquad (6 + 9 + 15 + 28 + 30 + 3 + 5)/7 = 96/7 = 13.714$ etc.

Week	Day	Number of customers (000s)	7-point MA
1	Monday	4	
	Tuesday	6	
	Wednesday	6	
	Thursday	9	14.000
	Friday	15	13.857
	Saturday	28	13.714
	Sunday	30	13.857
2	Monday	3	14.143
	Tuesday	5	14.000
	Wednesday	7	13.714
	Thursday	11	14.286
	Friday	14	14.571
	Saturday	26	15.000
	Sunday	34	15.000

**Solution
cont**

Week	Day	Number of customers (000s)	7-point MA
3	Monday	5	14.571
	Tuesday	8	15.000
	Wednesday	7	15.857
	Thursday	8	16.000
	Friday	17	
	Saturday	32	
	Sunday	35	

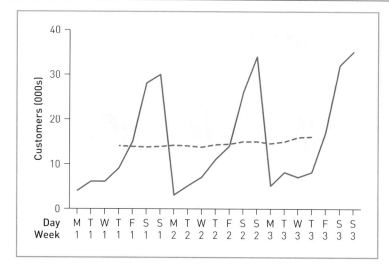

Figure 9.2 The moving averages and series values in Example 9.2

In Figure 9.2 the solid line represents the original time series observations and the dashed line represents the moving average estimates of the trend.

There are three points to note about the moving averages in Example 9.2. The first is that whilst the series values vary from 3 to 35 the moving averages vary only from 13.714 to 16.000. The moving averages are estimates of the trend at different stages of the series. The trend is in effect the backbone of the series and underpins the fluctuations around it. When we find the trend using moving averages we are 'averaging out' these fluctuations to leave a relatively smooth trend.

The second point is that, like any other average, we can think of a moving average as being in the middle of the set of data from which it has been calculated. In the case of a moving average we associate it with the middle of the period covered by the observations that we used to calculate it. The first moving average is therefore associated with Thursday of Week 1 because that is the middle day of the first seven days, the days whose observations were used to calculate it, the second is associated with Friday of Week 1 and so on. This positioning of the moving averages alongside the middle period of the periods the observations are from is termed *centring*.

The third point is that there are fewer moving averages (15) than observations (21). This is inevitable since every moving average is based on seven observations, one from each of the different days. The first three of the observations are from days before the middle day of the seven and the last three are from days after the middle day. There is no moving average to associate with the Monday of Week 1 because we do not have observations for three days before then. There is no moving average to associate with the Sunday of Week 3 because there are no observations after that. Compared with the list of customer numbers the list of moving averages is 'topped and tailed'.

In Example 9.1 there were seven daily values for each week; the series has a *periodicity* of seven. Centring is more complicated if the time series has an even number of smaller time periods within each larger time period. In quarterly time series data the periodicity is four because there are observations for each of four quarters in every year. For such data you have to use four-point moving averages and to centre them we have to work down the list of them taking the mean of adjacent moving averages. This brings them 'in phase' with observations of the series.

EXAMPLE 9.3

The numbers of raincoats sold in a UK department store over a three-year period were:

Year	Winter	Spring	Summer	Autumn
1	248	88	20	364
2	272	96	28	380
3	304	104	36	396

This data is plotted in Figure 9.3.

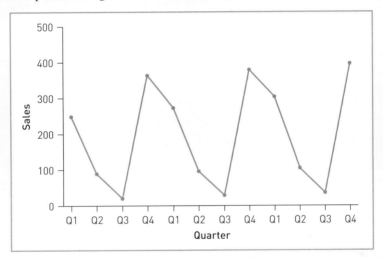

Figure 9.3 Sales of raincoats in Example 9.3

Estimate the trend by calculating four-point MAs and centring them.

Solution

First MA $= (248 + 88 + 20 + 364)/4 = 720/4 = 180$
Second MA $= (88 + 20 + 364 + 272)/4 = 744/4 = 186$ etc.

Year	Quarter	Sales	4-point MA
1	Winter	248	
1	Spring	88	
			180
1	Summer	20	
			186
1	Autumn	364	
			188
2	Winter	272	
			190
2	Spring	96	
			194

Solution cont

Year	Quarter	Sales	4-point MA
2	Summer	28	
			202
2	Autumn	380	
			204
3	Winter	304	
			206
3	Spring	104	
			210
3	Summer	36	
3	Autumn	396	

These moving averages are 'out of phase' with the observations as the middle of the four periods is midway between the middle pair of them. For instance the first MA, 180, is based on observations from the four quarters of Year 1. The middle of this period is between the Spring and Summer of Year 1. To align them with observations we need to centre them.

The centred four-point MA for Summer Year 1 = (180 + 186)/2 = 183
The centred four-point MA for Autumn Year 1 = (186 + 188)/2 = 187

and so on.

Year	Quarter	Sales	4-point MA	Centred 4-point MA
1	Winter	248		
1	Spring	88		
			180	
1	Summer	20		183
			186	
1	Autumn	364		187
			188	
2	Winter	272		189
			190	
2	Spring	96		192
			194	
2	Summer	28		198
			202	
2	Autumn	380		203
			204	
3	Winter	304		205
			206	
3	Spring	104		208
			210	
3	Summer	36		
3	Autumn	396		

At this point you may find it useful to try **Review questions 9.1 and 9.2** at the end of the chapter.

Centred moving averages are the estimates of the trend components for specific periods in the series. It is important that we can compare them directly to observations so that we can sift out the other components.

Calculating moving averages to estimate the trend of a time series

◆ Identify the periodicity of the series, which is the number of each of the shorter time periods that are in each of the longer time periods.

◆ The periodicity determines the number of observations, or points of data, to use to calculate each moving average. If a series has a periodicity of three, use three-point moving averages, if it is four use four-point moving averages and so on.

◆ Work through the series from the first observation to the last taking the appropriate number of observations to work out the moving averages.

◆ The first moving average is the mean of the first observation and as many of the subsequent ones as are necessary, e.g. for the first of a set of three-point moving averages take the first observation and the next two.

◆ The second moving average is the mean of the second observation and as many of the next ones as are necessary, e.g. for the second of a set of three-point moving averages take the third and fourth observations as well as the second one.

◆ Continue until the last observation has been included in the calculation of a moving average.

◆ If the periodicity is even, such as four quarters per year, the moving averages need to be centred. Take the mean of the first and second moving averages, then the mean of the second and third, and so on.

The way we separate out the components depends on how we assume they combine together to make up the observations. We might assume that each observation is the sum of the components, in other words the observations (Y) consist of components added together:

$$Y = T \text{ (Trend component)} + S \text{ (Seasonal component)}$$
$$+ C \text{ (Cyclical component)} + E \text{ (Error component)}$$

Unless the time series covers many years the cyclical component is impossible to distinguish from the trend as both are long-term movements. We can therefore simplify the model to:

$$Y = T \text{ (Trend component)} + S \text{ (Seasonal component)}$$
$$+ E \text{ (Error component)}$$

This is the *additive* model of decomposition. To analyse a time series that is assumed to be additive, we decompose the series by subtracting out the components, since subtraction is the reverse of addition. Start by taking the centred moving averages, the trend estimates (T), away from the observations (Y) from the same time period. The results are the deviations from the trend and these contain just the seasonal (S) and error (E) components:

$$Y - T = S + E$$

EXAMPLE 9.4

Find the deviations from the trend ($Y - T$) for the data in Example 9.3.

Solution

Year	Quarter	Sales (Y)	Centred 4-point MA (T)	$Y - T$
1	Winter	248		
1	Spring	88		
1	Summer	20	183	−163
1	Autumn	364	187	177

Solution cont

Year	Quarter	Sales (Y)	Centred 4-point MA (T)	Y − T
2	Winter	272	189	83
2	Spring	96	192	−96
2	Summer	28	198	−170
2	Autumn	380	203	177
3	Winter	304	205	99
3	Spring	104	208	−104
3	Summer	36		
3	Autumn	396		

To estimate the seasonal components (S) set out the $Y - T$ results by the quarters of the year and find the mean deviations from the trend for each quarter.

EXAMPLE 9.5

Estimate the seasonal components (S) from the $Y - T$ values in Example 9.4. What is the seasonal variation in raincoat sales?

Solution

	Winter	Spring	Summer	Autumn
Year 1			−163	177
Year 2	83	−96	−170	177
Year 3	99	−104		
Total seasonal deviation	182	−200	−333	354
Mean seasonal deviation	91	−100	−166.5	177

The sum of these four mean seasonal deviations (91, −100, −166.5 and 177) is 1.5. They should sum to zero as they are variations about the trend. If they don't they amount to a deviation from the trend. To solve the problem, divide the total by 4, as there are four mean seasonal deviations and take this amount (1.5/4 = 0.375) away from each of them. They will then sum to zero:

$$\begin{aligned}
\text{Adjusted mean winter deviation} &= 91 - 0.375 & &= 90.625 \\
\text{Adjusted mean spring deviation} &= -100 - 0.375 & &= -100.375 \\
\text{Adjusted mean summer deviation} &= -166.5 - 0.375 & &= -166.875 \\
\text{Adjusted mean autumn deviation} &= 177 - 0.375 & &= \underline{176.625} \\
& & & 0.000
\end{aligned}$$

These adjusted mean seasonal deviations are the estimated seasonal components (S) for the four quarters. They suggest that raincoat sales are on average 90.625 units above the trend in winter quarters, 100.375 units below the trend in spring quarters, 166.875 units below the trend in summer quarters and 176.625 units above the trend in autumn quarters.

The final stage of the decomposition is to sift out the error components (E). To do this we take the seasonal components (S) away from the $Y - T$ figures:

$$E = Y - T - S$$

The T components are what the model suggests the trend should be at a particular time and the S components are the deviations from the trend that the model suggests occur in the different

---

SELF-ASSEMBLY GUIDE

Finding the seasonal components of a time series using the additive decomposition model

◆ Set out the trend estimates, the centred moving averages alongside the observations of the series with which they align, i.e. in each case the middle period of the set of observations used to calculate the moving average.

◆ Subtract the trend estimates from the observations.

◆ Work out the mean deviation between the trend estimates and the observations for each type of time period, e.g. Quarter 1, Quarter 2 and so on.

◆ Add the mean deviation together. If they do not add up to zero adjust them so that they do. If they add up to more than zero an amount will need to be subtracted from each of them. The amount to subtract is the total of the mean deviations divided by the periodicity. If the mean deviations add up to less than zero the sum of the mean deviations divided by the periodicity will have to be added to each.

◆ The mean deviations, adjusted if necessary, are the seasonal components.

---

quarters; the T and S values combined are the predicted values for the series. The error components are the differences between the actual values (Y) and the predicted values ($T + S$):

$$E = \text{Actual sales} - \text{Predicted sales} = Y - (T + S)$$

EXAMPLE 9.6

Find the error components for the data in Example 9.3 using the table produced in Example 9.4 and the seasonal components from Example 9.5.

Solution

Year	Quarter	Actual sales (Y)	T	S	Predicted sales ($T + S$)	Error = Actual − Predicted
1	Winter	248				
1	Spring	88				
1	Summer	20	183	−166.875	16.125	3.875
1	Autumn	364	187	176.625	363.625	0.375
2	Winter	272	189	90.625	279.625	−7.625
2	Spring	96	192	−100.375	91.625	4.375
2	Summer	28	198	−166.875	31.125	−3.125
2	Autumn	380	203	176.625	379.625	0.375
3	Winter	304	205	90.625	295.625	8.375
3	Spring	104	208	−100.375	107.625	−3.625
3	Summer	36				
3	Autumn	396				

We can use error components to review past performance. In Example 9.6 a negative error such as in the winter quarter of year 2 indicates that the sales were less than expected. A positive error such as in the spring quarter of year 2 indicates that sales were more than expected. Identifying unusually poor and unusually good performances in this way could help the store managers improve sales; they can address the factors that resulted in poor performances and consolidate the factors that contributed to good performances.

Sometimes a particularly large error component is revealed by the decomposition method. This would probably have arisen as a result of unexpected factors like a sudden increase in oil prices. Generally any prominent peaks or dips, known as spikes, that show up when the time series is plotted reflect the presence of a large error component.

The error components have another role in time series analysis; they are used to judge how well a time series model fits the data. If the model is appropriate the errors will be small and show no pattern of variation. You can investigate this by plotting them over time.

EXAMPLE 9.7

Plot the errors in Example 9.6 and comment on the result.

Solution

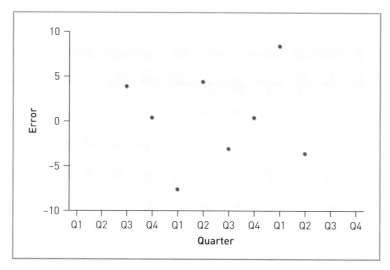

Figure 9.4 The error components of the raincoat sales

The errors in Figure 9.4 show no systematic pattern and are broadly scattered.

There are statistical measures that are used to summarise the errors; they are called *measures of accuracy* because they assess how accurately a time series model fits a set of time series data. The most useful is the Mean Squared Deviation (MSD). It is similar in concept to the standard deviation that we met in section 6.3.3, but instead of measuring deviation from the mean of a distribution it measures deviation between actual and predicted values of a time series.

The standard deviation is based on the squared differences between observations and their mean because deviations from the mean can be positive or negative, and can therefore cancel each other out. In the same way deviations between actual and predicted time series values can be negative and positive, so in calculating the MSD we square the deviations. The MSD is the sum of the squared deviations divided by the number of deviations (n):

$$\text{MSD} = \frac{\sum (\text{Error})^2}{n}$$

EXAMPLE 9.8

Calculate the MSD of the decomposition model of the raincoat sales data from Example 9.3.

Solution

Year	Quarter	Actual sales (Y)	Predicted	Error = Actual sales − Predicted	Squared error
1	Winter	248			
1	Spring	88			
1	Summer	20	16.125	3.875	15.016
1	Autumn	364	363.625	0.375	0.141
2	Winter	272	279.625	−7.625	58.141
2	Spring	96	91.625	4.375	19.141
2	Summer	28	31.125	−3.125	9.766
2	Autumn	380	379.625	0.375	0.141
3	Winter	304	295.625	8.375	70.141
3	Spring	104	107.625	−3.625	13.141
3	Summer	36			
3	Autumn	396			
				Total squared deviation	185.628
				Mean squared deviation (MSD)	23.203

At this point you may find it useful to try **Review questions 9.4 and 9.6** at the end of the chapter.

There are other measures of accuracy. The Mean Absolute Deviation (MAD) is the mean of the absolute values of the errors, which means ignoring any negative signs when you add them up. There is also the Mean Absolute Percentage Error (MAPE) which is the mean of the errors as percentages of the actual values they are part of. As with the MSD, the lower the values of these measures, the better the model fits the data.

The MSD result in Example 9.8 is a figure that we can compare to the MSD figures we get when other models are applied to the time series. The best model is the one that produces the smallest MSD.

The model we have applied so far is the additive decomposition model that assumes the components of a time series are added together. This model is appropriate for series that have regular and constant fluctuations around a trend. The alternative form of the decomposition model is the multiplicative model in which we assume that the components of the series are multiplied together. This is appropriate for series that have regular but increasing or decreasing fluctuations around a trend such as in Figure 9.5(a) or Figure 9.5(b). If the fluctuations are consistent, such as in Figure 9.5(c), the additive model is more appropriate.

To apply the multiplicative model we need exactly the same centred moving averages as we need for the additive model, but instead of subtracting them from the actual series values to help us get to the seasonal components we divide the observations (Y) by their corresponding centred moving averages (T) to get *seasonal factors*. We then find the average seasonal factor for each quarter (S), adjusting as necessary. Once we have the set of seasonal factors we multiply them by the trend estimates to get the predicted series values, which we can subtract from the actual values to get the errors.

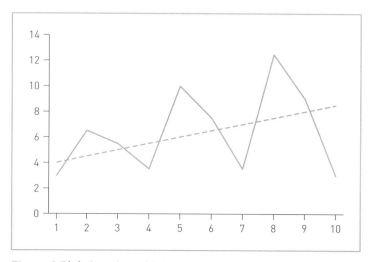

Figure 9.5(a) A series with increasing fluctuations around the trend

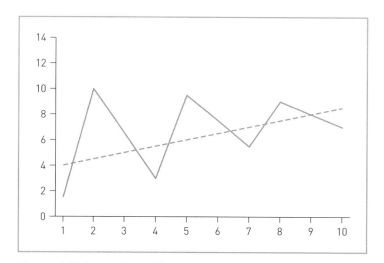

Figure 9.5(b) A series with decreasing fluctuations around the trend

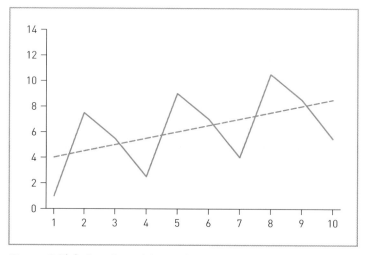

Figure 9.5(c) A series with consistent fluctuations around the trend

EXAMPLE 9.9

Apply the multiplicative model to the raincoat sales data from Example 9.3. Obtain the errors, plot them and use them to calculate the MSD for the model.

Solution

The first stage is to calculate the seasonal factors:

Year	Quarter	Sales (Y)	Centred 4-point MA (T)	Y/T
1	Winter	248		
1	Spring	88		
1	Summer	20	183	0.109
1	Autumn	364	187	1.947
2	Winter	272	189	1.439
2	Spring	96	192	0.500
2	Summer	28	198	0.141
2	Autumn	380	203	1.872
3	Winter	304	205	1.483
3	Spring	104	208	0.500
3	Summer	36		
3	Autumn	96		

The next stage is to find the mean seasonal factor for each quarter and adjust them so that they add up to 4, since the average should be one, the only factor that makes no difference to the trend when applied to it.

	Winter	Spring	Summer	Autumn
Year 1			0.109	1.947
Year 2	1.439	0.500	0.141	1.872
Year 3	1.483	0.500		
Total	2.922	1.000	0.250	3.819
Mean	1.461	0.500	0.125	1.910

Sum of the means $= 1.461 + 0.500 + 0.125 + 1.910 = 3.996$

To ensure they add up to 4, add one-fourth of the difference between 3.996 and 4, 0.001, to each mean:

$$\text{Adjusted winter factor} = 1.461 + 0.001 = 1.462$$
$$\text{Adjusted spring factor} = 0.500 + 0.001 = 0.501$$
$$\text{Adjusted summer factor} = 0.125 + 0.001 = 0.126$$
$$\underline{\text{Adjusted autumn factor} = 1.910 + 0.001 = 1.911}$$
$$4.000$$

We can now use these adjusted factors to work out the predicted values and hence find the error terms:

Year	Quarter	Actual sales (Y)	T	S	Predicted sales ($T * S$)	Error = Actual − Predicted
1	Winter	248				
1	Spring	88				
1	Summer	20	183	0.126	23.058	−3.058
1	Autumn	364	187	1.911	357.357	6.643

Year	Quarter	Actual sales (Y)	T	S	Predicted sales ($T * S$)	Error = Actual − Predicted
2	Winter	272	189	1.462	276.318	−4.318
2	Spring	96	192	0.501	96.192	−0.192
2	Summer	28	198	0.126	24.948	3.052
2	Autumn	380	203	1.911	387.933	−7.933
3	Winter	304	205	1.462	299.710	4.390
3	Spring	104	208	0.501	104.208	−0.208
3	Summer	36				
3	Autumn	396				

The error terms are plotted in Figure 9.6. The absence of a systematic pattern and lesser scatter than in Figure 9.4 indicates that the multiplicative model is more appropriate for this set of data than the additive model.

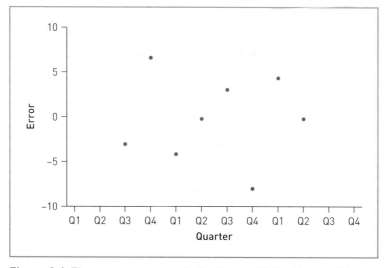

Figure 9.6 The error components for the multiplicative model

Year	Quarter	Actual sales (Y)	Predicted	Error = Actual − Predicted	Squared error
1	Winter	248			
1	Spring	88			
1	Summer	20	23.058	−3.058	9.351
1	Autumn	364	357.357	6.643	44.129
2	Winter	272	276.318	−4.318	18.645
2	Spring	96	96.192	−0.192	0.037
2	Summer	28	24.948	3.052	9.315
2	Autumn	380	387.933	−7.933	62.932
3	Winter	304	299.710	4.390	19.272
3	Spring	104	104.208	−0.208	0.043
3	Summer	36			
3	Autumn	396			
				Total squared deviation	163.724
				(MSD)	20.466

This MSD is smaller than the MSD for the additive model from Example 9.8, 23.203, suggesting that the multiplicative model is the more appropriate one for this data.

At this point you may find it useful to try **Review questions 9.5 and 9.7** at the end of the chapter.

Decomposition models can be used to produce forecasts of future observations. This involves firstly projecting the trend into future periods for which we want predictions then applying the appropriate seasonal component or factor. With the additive model this means a forecast ($\hat{y}$) is the trend projection (T) plus the seasonal component (S):

$$\hat{y} = T + S$$

If we are using the multiplicative model we multiply the trend projection by the appropriate seasonal factor:

$$\hat{y} = T * S$$

Note that these expressions for $\hat{y}$ do not include error components, which are unpredictable by definition.

The simplest approach to projecting the trend is to plot the centred moving averages and extend the line by eye. If the trend is smooth this is straightforward but otherwise can be erratic. An alternative approach that does not involve graphical work is to take the difference between the first and last trend estimates for your series and divide by the number of periods between them; if you have n trend estimates you divide the difference between the first and last of them by $n - 1$. The result is the mean change in the trend per period. To forecast a value three periods ahead you add three times this amount to the last trend estimate, four periods ahead, add four times this to the last trend estimate, and so on.

EXAMPLE 9.10

Use the additive and multiplicative decomposition models to forecast the raincoat sales at the department store in Example 9.3 for the four quarters of year 4.

Solution

The first trend estimate was for the summer quarter of year 1, 183. The last trend estimate was for the spring quarter of year 3, 208. The difference between these figures, 15, is the increase in the trend over the seven quarters between the summer of year 1 and the spring of year 3. The mean change per quarter in the trend is one-seventh of this amount, 2.143.

To forecast the winter quarter sales in year 4 using the additive model we must add three times the trend change per quarter, since the winter of year 4 is three quarters later than the spring quarter of year 3, the last quarter for which we have a trend estimate. Having done this we add the seasonal component for the winter quarter, 90.625:

Forecast for the winter quarter of year 4 = 208 + (3 * 2.143) + 90.625 = 305.054

Forecasting the three other quarters of year 4 involves adding more trend change and the appropriate seasonal component:

Forecast for the spring quarter of year 4 = 208 + (4 * 2.143) + (−100.375) = 116.197

Forecast for the summer quarter of year 4 = 208 + (5 * 2.143) + (−166.875) = 51.840

Forecast for the autumn quarter of year 4 = 208 + (6 * 2.143) + 176.625 = 397.483

To obtain forecasts using the multiplicative model we project the trend as we have done for the additive model, but multiply by the seasonal factors:

Forecast for the winter quarter of year 4 = $[208 + (3 * 2.143)] * 1.462 = 313.495$

Forecast for the spring quarter of year 4 = $[208 + (4 * 2.143)] * 0.501 = 108.503$

Forecast for the summer quarter of year 4 = $[208 + (5 * 2.143)] * 0.126 = 27.558$

Forecast for the autumn quarter of year 4 = $[208 + (6 * 2.143)] * 1.911 = 422.060$

At this point you may find it useful to try **Review questions 9.9 and 9.10** at the end of the chapter.

Another method of projecting the trend is to apply the simple regression analysis covered in section 7.3. To do this make the centred moving averages the values of the dependent variable and the time periods the values of the independent variable. The regression equation that this produces is known as the *trend line equation*.

In business, forecasts produced using time series analysis are used to set budgets, to determine future order levels and so on.

9.4 Exponential smoothing of time series data

The decomposition models we considered in the last section are called static models because in using them we assume that the components of the model are fixed over time. They are appropriate for series that have a clear structure. They are not appropriate for series that are more erratic. To produce forecasts for these types of series we can turn to dynamic models such as *exponential smoothing* which use recent observations in the series to predict the next one.

In exponential smoothing we create a forecast for the next period by taking the forecast we generated for the previous period and adding a proportion of the error in the previous forecast. The error is the difference between the actual and forecast values for the previous period. We can represent this as:

$$\text{New forecast} = \text{previous forecast} + \alpha * (\text{previous actual} - \text{previous forecast})$$

The symbol α represents the *smoothing constant*, the proportion of the error we add to the previous forecast to adjust for the error in the previous forecast. Being a proportion, α must be between 0 and 1 inclusive. If it is zero then no proportion of the previous error is added to the previous forecast to get the new forecast, so the forecast for the new period is always the same as the forecast for the previous period. If α is one, the entire previous error is added to the previous forecast so the new forecast is always the same as the previous actual value.

When we forecast using exponential smoothing every new forecast depends on the previous one, which in turn depends on the one before that and so on. The influence of past forecasts diminishes with time; mathematically the further back the forecast the greater the power or exponent of an expression involving α that is applied to it: hence the term exponential in the name of the technique.

The lower the value of α we use the less the weight we attach to the previous forecast and the greater the weight we give to forecasts before it. The higher the value of α, the greater the weight we attach to the previous forecast relative to forecasts before it. This contrast means that lower values of α produce smoother sequences of forecasts compared to those we get with higher values of α. On the other hand, higher values of α result in forecasts that are more responsive to sudden changes in the time series.

Selecting the appropriate α value for a particular time series is a matter of trial and error. The best α value is the one that results in the lowest values of measures of accuracy like the mean squared deviation (MSD).

Before we can use exponential smoothing we need a forecast for the previous period. The easiest way of doing this is to take the actual value for the first period as the forecast for the second period.

<table>
<tr><td>EXAMPLE
9.11</td><td>The numbers of customers paying home contents insurance premiums to the Domashny Insurance Company by telephone over the past 10 weeks are:</td></tr>
</table>

Week	1	2	3	4	5	6	7	8	9	10
Customers	360	410	440	390	450	380	350	400	360	420

Using a smoothing constant of 0.2, produce forecasts for the series to week 11, calculate the mean squared deviation for this model, and plot the forecasts against the actual values.

Solution

If we take the actual value for week 1, 360, as the forecast for week 2, the error for week 2 is:

Error (week 2) = actual (week 2) − forecast (week 2) = 410 − 360 = 50

The forecast for week 3 will be:

Forecast (week 3) = forecast (week 2) + 0.2 * error (week 2) = 360 + 0.2 * 50 = 370

Continuing this process we can obtain forecasts to week 11:

Week	Actual	Forecast	Error (Actual − Forecast)	0.2 * Error	Error^2
1	360	—	—	—	—
2	410	360.000	50.000	10.000	2500.000
3	440	370.000	70.000	14.000	4900.000
4	390	384.000	6.000	1.200	36.000
5	450	385.200	64.800	12.960	4199.040
6	380	398.160	−18.160	−3.632	329.786
7	350	394.528	−44.528	−8.906	1982.743
8	400	385.622	14.378	2.876	206.727
9	360	388.498	−28.498	−5.700	812.136
10	420	382.798	37.202	7.440	1383.989
11		390.238			
					16350.408

The mean squared deviation (MSD) = 16350.408/9 = 1816.712

Figure 9.7 shows the forecasts (broken line) against the actual values (solid line):

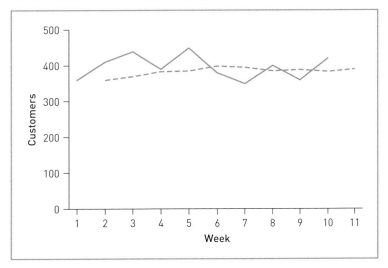

Figure 9.7 Actual values and forecasts of the customer calls data in Example 9.11

We could try other smoothing constants for the series in Example 9.11 to see if we could improve on the accuracy of the forecasts. If you try a constant of 0.3 you should obtain an MSD of around 1613, which is about the best; a higher constant for this series results in a higher MSD, for instance a constant of 0.5 gives an MSD of around 1674.

At this point you may find it useful to try **Review questions 9.3, 9.8, 9.11 and 9.12** at the end of the chapter.

In this chapter we have concentrated on relatively simple methods of analysing time series data. The field of time series analysis is substantial and contains a variety of techniques. If you would like to read more about it, try Chatfield (2003) or Cryer and Chan (2008).

REVIEW QUESTIONS

Answers to these questions are on page 450. There are tips and hints to help you with them on the supporting website at **www.pearsoned.co.uk/buglear**, where you will also find the fully worked solutions.

☆☆★ **Basic questions**

9.1 A garage starts a breakdown service that offers assistance in mornings, afternoons and evenings. The numbers of call-outs during the first three days of this service were:

	Morning	Afternoon	Evening
Day 1	12	6	9
Day 2	15	9	12
Day 3	18	9	15

(a) Plot the data over time.
(b) Work out three-point moving averages for the series and plot them on your graph.

9.2 The quarterly sales (in £000) of greeting cards in a supermarket were:

	Quarter			
	1	2	3	4
Year 1	12.0	14.8	9.6	19.2
Year 2	13.1	16.3	8.2	22.8
Year 3	14.8	18.9	6.9	25.1

(a) Produce a time series plot of these figures.
(b) Work out centred four-point moving averages for this series and plot them on your graph.

9.3 A new security system was installed at the Platia Clothing Store eight weeks ago. The numbers of items stolen from the store in the period since are:

Week	1	2	3	4	5	6	7	8
Items stolen	63	56	49	45	51	36	42	37

(a) Use the exponential smoothing model with a smoothing constant of 0.8 to predict values of the series to week 9.

(b) Plot the series and the forecasts on the same graph.

☆★★ More testing questions

9.4 Using the results from Review question 9.1 and applying the additive decomposition model:

(a) Determine the recurring components for each part of the day.

(b) Calculate the MSD for the model.

9.5 Using the multiplicative model and your answers to Review question 9.1:

(a) Evaluate the recurring factors for the parts of the day.

(b) Calculate the MSD for the model.

(c) Compare the MSD for this model with your answer to Review question 9.4 part (b) and say which model is more appropriate for the service call-outs data.

9.6 Draw on your answers to Review question 9.2 and apply the additive decomposition model to:

(a) Identify the seasonal components for each quarter.

(b) Work out the MSD for the model.

9.7 Building on your answers to Review question 9.2 use the multiplicative decomposition model to:

(a) Find the seasonal factors for each quarter.

(b) Calculate the MSD for the model.

(c) By contrasting your answer to part (b) with the MSD for the additive model you obtained for Review question 9.6 part (b) state which is the better model for the greeting card sales series.

9.8 In the nine months since new parking regulations were introduced the numbers of vehicles impounded by a city highways department were:

Month	1	2	3	4	5	6	7	8	9
Vehicles	207	246	195	233	218	289	248	292	276

(a) Apply the exponential smoothing model with an α value of 0.5 to predict values of the series to the tenth month.

(b) Portray the actual values and the forecasts on the same graph.

★★★ Challenging questions

9.9 Basing your work on the answers you obtained to Review questions 9.1, 9.4 and 9.5, use the more appropriate decomposition model to produce forecasts for the breakdown service call-outs in the morning, afternoon and evening of day 4.

9.10 Referring to your answers to Review questions 9.2, 9.6 and 9.7, generate forecasts for the greeting card sales in the quarters of year 4 using the more appropriate decomposition model.

9.11 The bookings taken by a cruise company on the first eight days after a well-publicised outbreak of food poisoning on one of its ships were:

Day	1	2	3	4	5	6	7	8
Bookings	78	33	41	86	102	133	150	210

(a) Produce predictions up to and including day 9 using the exponential smoothing model with a smoothing constant of 0.3 and calculate the MSD of the errors.

(b) Construct predictions to day 9 using a smoothing constant of 0.6 and compute the MSD of the errors. Is this a better model?

9.12 To minimise the risk of accidents from their activities pigeons nesting in the tunnels of an underground railway system are culled every night. The numbers of birds shot over recent weeks have been:

Week	1	2	3	4	5	6	7	8	9
Birds shot	260	340	190	410	370	280	330	400	450

(a) Generate predictions for weeks 2 to 10 by means of an exponential smoothing model with a smoothing constant of 0.5 and compute the MSD of the errors.

(b) Using a smoothing constant of 0.2, calculate the MSD for this model and comment on whether it is more suitable than the model in (a).

THE DEBRIEF

Key things to remember from this chapter

→ Time series data consists of values collected at regular intervals over time.

→ Analysis of time series is used to review performance in the past and produce forecasts for the future.

→ The decomposition model is used to separate out the components of a time series, specifically the trend, seasonal and error components.

→ There are two variants of the decomposition model, the additive and the multiplicative. The additive model assumes the components are added together, the multiplicative assumes they are multiplied together.

→ The error components are used to find the measures of accuracy. These help us decide which model is most appropriate.

→ To forecast with the decomposition model, project the trend then apply the seasonal components or factors.

→ The exponential smoothing model uses weighted past values to predict future ones.

References

Chatfield, C. (2003) *The Analysis of Time Series: An Introduction* (6th edn), London: Chapman and Hall.

Cryer, J.D. and Chan, K. (2008) *Time Series Analysis: With Applications in R*, (2nd edn), New York: Springer.

Huss, W.R. (1987). 'Forecasting in the electric utility supply industry', in S. Makridakis and S.C. Wheelwright (eds), *The Handbook of Forecasting: A Manager's Guide*, New York: Wiley, pp. 87–117.

Kathawala, Y. (1988) 'Applications of quantitative techniques in large and small organisations in the United States: an empirical analysis', *Journal of the Operational Research Society*, 39(11), pp. 981–9.

Majani, B. (1987) 'Decomposition methods for medium-term planning and budgeting', in S. Makridakis and S.C. Wheelwright (eds), *The Handbook of Forecasting: A Manager's Guide*, New York: Wiley, pp. 219–37.

Million, G. (1980) 'Some problems in forecasting the demand for water in England and Wales', in O.D. Anderson (ed.), *Forecasting Public Utilities: Proceedings of the International Conference held at Nottingham University*, March 1980, Amsterdam: North-Holland Publishing, pp. 9–15.

Sparkes, J.R. and McHugh, A.K. (1984) 'Awareness and use of forecasting techniques in British Industry', *Journal of Forecasting*, 3(1), pp. 37–42.

Sutlieff, H. (1982) 'Forecasting emergency workload for day ahead', *Journal of the Operational Research Society*, 33(2), pp. 129–36.

Thorneycroft, W.T. (1987) *Seasonal Patterns in Business and Everyday Life,* Aldershot: Gower.

Zhongjie, X. (1993) *Case Studies in Time Series Analysis*, Singapore: World Scientific.

CHAPTER 10

Is it worth the risk? – introducing probability

CHAPTER OBJECTIVES

This chapter will help you to:

→ Measure risk and chance using probability

→ Recognise the types of probability

→ Apply the addition rule of probability

→ Apply the multiplication rule of probability

→ Deal with conditional probabilities and apply Bayes' rule

THE BARE BONES

What you will find in this chapter . . .

- Understanding how probabilities are determined
- Using Venn diagrams to represent alternatives and combinations
- Finding chances of alternative outcomes using the addition rule of probability
- Finding chances of combination of outcomes using the multiplication rule of probability
- Calculating conditional probabilities and using Bayes' rule to find prior probabilities
- Constructing and using tree diagrams to map sequences of outcomes

. . . and on the supporting website (www.pearsoned.co.uk/buglear)

- Fully worked solutions to the review questions
- More review questions

Business use of probability

◆ There is one business where the very definition of the products is probability; the betting industry. Whether it is horse racing, football or even the weather, placing a bet is buying a chance, a chance measured in terms of probability, known as 'the odds'.

◆ Another industry based on probability is insurance. Buying insurance means paying an insurer to meet the financial consequences of any calamity that occurs. For instances motor insurance covers the costs arising from road accidents. Companies selling motor insurance base the price they charge for it on the chances of the motorist having an accident, which is why when you apply for motor insurance you have to provide so much information about yourself and your vehicle. If the motorist doesn't have an accident the company makes a profit; if they do it loses money. Insurance companies study records of motor accidents. They reference the motorist's information – age, gender, type of vehicle and so on – against these records to assess the probability of the motorist having an accident and base the price of the insurance on this probability.

◆ The legal context within which businesses operate obliges them to protect the health and safety of their workers, and to ensure that their products are not harmful to their customers or the environment. This is why they undertake risk assessments. These may involve using probability to define the risks that their activities may pose. Boghani (1990) describes how probability was used in assessing the risks of transporting hazardous materials on special trains. North (1990) explains how judgemental evaluation was used to ascertain probabilities of potential damage to forestry production and fish stocks in the lakes of Wisconsin from sulphur dioxide emissions. In the same paper North shows how experimental data was used to assess the health risks arising from the use of a particular solvent in dry-cleaning.

10.1 Introduction

The purpose of this chapter is to introduce the subject of probability. This is a field within mathematics that is about the chances of things happening. These things may be actual events or theoretical possibilities. The origins of probability were in gambling, and specifically the attempts by the French mathematicians, Fermat and Pascal, to find the chances of getting particular results in games of dice.

The reason that probability is much more than a historical footnote is that it became an essential tool of analysis in a wide variety of spheres including business and economics as well as the sciences. It became so important because it offers a systematic approach to weighing up chances and risks. By using probability to do this, analysing a problem or taking a decision can become much more effective.

With probability we can deal with risk rather than face uncertainty. Uncertainty is when it is possible that different outcomes can occur but we don't know how likely each one is. Risk is when there are different outcomes but we do know, or at least have a good idea, how likely each one is.

The conditions in which business organisations operate are frequently uncertain. There may be changes in economic prospects, consumer preferences and currency values. Launching new products or services and investing in new facilities are typically risky ventures. Alongside these commercial risks, there may other more unforeseeable risks such as bad weather disrupting supplies, earthquakes destroying factories etc.

The subject matter of this chapter is intended to provide you with an understanding of how businesses assess the risks they face. But this is not the only reason why probability is a key part of studying business. It also has a vital role in statistical investigation.

Many of the statistical results that you will meet during your studies and beyond, for instance market research findings, will be based on sample data. Generally the researchers would like to learn something about the whole population, perhaps consumer expenditure on certain types of goods or TV viewing habits, but to study every element of the population would cost too much and take too long. The best they can do is to focus on a sample of elements from the population and get some understanding of the population from analysing the sample results. As long as the sample is random and the risks involved are taken into account this can be very effective.

A sample is only random if the chance of selecting that sample from the population is precisely the same as the chance of selecting any other sample of the same size. A sample that is not random is of less use in understanding the population.

Since we can take different samples of the same size from a population, the process of sampling involves risk. The samples are not clones; they will be made up of different elements from the population and so give different results. Some might produce results close to the ones that we would get if we could study the entire population. Others will yield results that are not such an accurate reflection of the whole population.

Using sample results to gain insights about the population it is drawn from means having some idea of the chances of them being close to the population results despite not knowing what those population results are. To do this we use probability.

10.2 **Measuring probability**

A *probability* is a measure of the chance of a specific outcome happening and is represented by the capital letter *P*. It is a number on a scale from zero to one inclusive. Probabilities are often expressed as percentages.

At one end of this scale, a probability of zero means there is no chance of the outcome occurring. At the other end, a probability of one means the outcome will definitely occur. Midway between the extremes, a probability of a half means the outcome is as likely to happen as not to happen, in other words a 50/50 chance.

So how is the probability of an outcome occurring decided? There are three ways of attaching a probability to an outcome: the *judgemental, experimental* and *theoretical* methods.

The judgemental method is to assess the chance of an outcome purely on the basis of expert, or at least informed, judgement. Typically the judgemental approach is used for outcomes that are infrequent or complex such as election results and currency fluctuations. Sometimes people use the judgemental method to arrive at a probability when more sophisticated approaches are possible, for example assessing the chance of a horse winning a race on the basis of its name rather than its track record or 'form'.

Using the horse's form to assess the probability that it wins a race is the experimental method. It involves inspecting the results of previous 'experiments', which would be the number of races the horse entered. The number of races the horse won as a proportion of the number of races it entered, in other words the *relative frequency* of wins, constitutes an estimate of the probability of the horse winning the next race it enters. Such a relative frequency, being based on a finite number of experiments, can only be an estimate of the real probability, which is the relative frequency of the outcomes of an infinite number of experiments.

EXAMPLE 10.1

Malodiets, a promising colt, has entered 20 races and won 8 of them. Find the probability he will win his next race.

Solution

Using the experimental approach the estimated probability of the horse winning the next race is the relative frequency of the wins in his previous races, 8, divided 20, the total number of races he entered:

$$\text{Relative frequency} = \frac{8}{20} = 0.4 \text{ or } 40\%$$

The probability of the horse winning next time is:

$$P(\text{Malodiets wins}) = 0.4$$

Example 10.1 is much simpler than how racing pundits would really do this sort of thing. They would take account of the condition of the track, the other horses competing etc., but nevertheless the basis of their evaluation of a horse's prospects is the experimental method of measuring probabilities.

The experimental method is appropriate for other cases where estimating the probability of a particular outcome of a process is important. If we wanted to advise a car manufacturer whether it should offer a three-year warranty on its cars we might visit its dealers and find out the relative frequency of the cars that needed major repairs before they were three years old. This relative frequency would be an estimate of the probability of a car needing major repair before it is three years old, which the manufacturer would have to pay for under a three-year warranty.

In some situations it is not necessary to use the experimental method and the data gathering and analysis it involves. This is when we can deduce the probability of a particular outcome if the process that produces it has a finite, known number of possible results and one of them occurs every time the process takes place. This is the theoretical method of determining probabilities. Examples are common in gambling, even if there is a large number of possible results, such as in a lottery. Every time the lottery is run there may be many potential outcomes, but they remain the same outcomes and it is possible to identify them all, although doing so would be time-consuming.

We can work out the chances of particular outcomes in a lottery because the process involves the same number of balls and machines. We can't use the same approach for working out the chances of a horse winning a race as factors like the length of the race and the other horses in the field vary.

EXAMPLE 10.2

There are 1728 possible outcomes on a simple gaming machine in a bar. Fifty of these result in the £25 cash prize. Find the probability of winning £25.

Solution

One approach is to buy a similar machine, run it over and over again and note down the number of times the cash prize combinations occur. Another way would be to ask people who have used the machine before and ascertain how many won the cash prize. These are experimental approaches to estimating the probability.

Since we know how many outcomes win cash we don't need to do this, we can use the theoretical approach. Fifty of the 1728 outcomes give cash prizes so:

$$P(\text{cash prize}) = \frac{50}{1728} = 0.029 \text{ or } 2.9\%$$

The gambling business is full of examples of applied probability since it involves games of chance but it is not the only business that uses probability. If you purchase insurance the price of it is based on the experimental method of assigning probabilities.

At this point you may find it useful to try **Review questions 10.1, 10.2 and 10.12** at the end of the chapter.

10.3 The types of probability

The probabilities in the previous section are examples of *simple* probabilities. A simple probability is the chance of a single outcome occurring, such as the probability of the horse winning in Example 10.1. The chance of the horse winning his next two races is an example of a *compound* probability.

A compound probability is the chance of a combination of outcomes. The gaming machine in Example 10.2 might also have non-cash prizes such as a snack or a meal. The chance of winning £25 is a simple probability, but the chance of winning £25 or a non-cash prize is a compound probability.

There are several types of compound probability. We can demonstrate them by using the experimental method with bivariate data: data that consists of observations of two variables. Estimating compound probabilities involves working out relative frequencies from tabulated data.

EXAMPLE 10.3

The Shirokoy Balota shopping mall has a food hall with three fast-food restaurants; Bolshoyburger, Gatovielle and Kuriatina. A survey of transactions in these establishments produced the following results.

Customer profile	Bolshoyburger	Gatovielle	Kuriatina	Total
Lone	170	360	10	540
Couple	20	10	50	80
Family	10	30	340	380
Total	200	400	400	1000

What is the probability that the customer profile is Family?
What is the probability that a transaction is in Kuriatina?

Solution

Both of these are simple probabilities. In each case they are about only one of the variables; in the first case customer profile, in the second, the restaurant.

The totals column shows that in 380 of the 1000 transactions the customer profile was Family, so:

$$P(\text{Family}) = \frac{380}{1000} = 0.38 \text{ or } 38\%$$

This is the relative frequency of Family customer profiles.

According to the totals row at the bottom of the table, 400 transactions were in Kuriatina, so:

$$P(\text{Kuriatina}) = \frac{400}{1000} = 0.4 \text{ or } 40\%$$

This is the relative frequency of transactions in Kuriatina.

Obtaining compound probabilities from tables like the one in Example 10.3 involves using figures from the cells of the table to work out relative frequencies.

EXAMPLE 10.4

Find the probability that the profile of a customer in Example 10.3 is Lone and their purchase is from Bolshoyburger.

Solution

There were 170 Lone customers in the survey who made a purchase from Bolshoyburger so:

$$P(\text{Lone customer and Bolshoyburger purchase}) = \frac{170}{1000} = 0.17 \text{ or } 17\%$$

Writing full descriptions of the outcomes such as the one in Example 10.4 is tedious; it is easier to abbreviate them. We can use '*L*' to represent Lone customers, '*C*' for Couple customers and '*F*' for Family customers. Similarly, we can use '*B*' for Bolshoyburger, '*G*' for Gatovielle and '*K*' for Kuriatina. This means we can put the probability in Example 10.4 more succinctly.

$$P(\text{Lone customer and Bolshoyburger purchase}) = P(L \text{ and } B) = 0.17$$

The description of the compound probability in Example 10.4 contains the word 'and'. It is the probability that two outcomes jointly occur, their *joint* probability; to put it another way, it is the *intersection* of the two outcomes. The relative frequency used to estimate the probability is the proportion of the number of people in one of the customer profile categories and one of the restaurant categories. It is the proportion of people at the intersection or 'crossroads' of the 'Lone' and 'Bolshoyburger' categories.

Obtaining the probability of an intersection between two outcomes is fairly simple if we have tabulated bivariate data. In other cases, for example if only simple probabilities are available, we have to apply the *multiplication rule* of probability, which we will deal with in section 10.4.

Another type of compound probability is one that assesses the chance that one of two or more alternative things happen. The definition of this type of compound probability will contain the word 'or'.

EXAMPLE 10.5

Using the data in Example 10.3 find the probability of a transaction involving a Couple or being at the Kuriatina restaurant.

Solution

The chance that one (and implicitly both) of these things are true depends on the proportion of the transactions in one or other category. Since they are alternatives the implication is that to get the probability we need to add the number of transactions at Kuriatina to the number of transactions involving customers profiled as Couple then divide by the number of transactions in the survey.

$$\text{Number of transactions at Kuriatina} = 10 + 50 + 340 = 400$$

$$\text{Number of transactions involving Couples} = 20 + 10 + 50 = 80$$

The number 50 is part of both of these totals. This means that when we add the number of transactions at Kuriatina to the number of transactions involving Couples we will

→

Solution cont
double-count the 50 transactions involving both Kuriatina and Couples. This will mean that the probability we obtain will be too large.

This has happened because we added the 50 transactions by Couples at Kuriatina in twice. To amend this and get the correct probability we need to subtract the 50 *once*.

$$P(K \text{ or } C) = \frac{(10 + 50 + 340) + (20 + 10 + 50) - 50}{1000} = \frac{400 + 80 - 50}{1000}$$

$$= \frac{430}{1000} = 0.43 \text{ or } 43\%$$

In Example 10.5, the compound probability, we combined or 'united' the chances of the outcomes occurring, in other words it is the *union* of the outcomes. The proportion used as the estimated probability is derived from the combined number of transactions in the categories of the 'customer profile' and 'restaurant' characteristics. It is the relative frequency of transactions in the union or 'merger' of the 'Couple' and 'Kuriatina' categories.

If we need the probability of a union of outcomes but do not have tabulated bivariate data we can apply the *addition rule* of probability. We will cover this in section 10.4.

The third category of compound probability is *conditional* probability. A conditional probability assesses the chance that one thing happens if, or on *condition* that, another thing has already happened.

EXAMPLE 10.6
Using the data in Example 10.3 obtain the probability that a transaction in Gatovielle involves a Lone customer.

Solution
Another way of putting this is that given (or on condition) that the transaction is in Gatovielle, what is the probability that a Lone customer has made the purchase. We represent this as:

$$P(L|G)$$

Here '|' is shorthand for 'if' or 'given that'.

Find this by taking the transactions involving Lone customers as a proportion of the total number of transactions at Gatovielle.

$$P(L|G) = \frac{360}{400} = 0.9 \text{ or } 90\%$$

This is the relative frequency of a subset of the 1000 transactions in the survey. We exclude the majority of them, the 600 transactions that were not at Gatovielle, as they don't fit the condition of the probability, i.e. being transactions at Gatovielle.

At this point you may find it useful to try **Review questions 10.4 to 10.6** at the end of the chapter.

We can always find compound probabilities directly from bivariate data such as the data in Example 10.3 using the experimental method. But sometimes this sort of data is not available.

Maybe all that we have are probabilities established judgementally or theoretically, or the original data that was used to estimate probabilities experimentally is not accessible. In such circumstances we can turn to the rules of probability.

10.4 The rules of probability

When experimental data is not available and we want to find compound probabilities we need to adopt alternative approaches. We use the two rules of probability: the addition rule and the multiplication rule.

10.4.1 The addition rule

The addition rule of probability is used to obtain probabilities of unions of outcomes, probabilities where the definition includes the word 'or'.

The addition rule states that the compound probability of one or both of two outcomes, say outcome A and outcome B, happening is the simple probability of A occurring added to the simple probability of B occurring. From this sum we take away the compound probability of both A and B occurring jointly:

$$P(A \text{ or } B) = P(A) + P(B) - P(A \text{ and } B)$$

EXAMPLE 10.7

Using the addition rule find the probability of a transaction in the food hall in Example 10.3 being at Kuriatina or involving a Couple.

Solution

$$P(K \text{ or } C) = P(K) + P(C) - P(K \text{ and } C)$$

The simple probability that a transaction is at Kuriatina: $P(K) = \dfrac{400}{1000}$

The simple probability that a transaction involves a Couple: $P(C) = \dfrac{80}{1000}$

The probability that a transaction is at Kuriatina and involves a Couple:

$$P(K \text{ and } C) = \frac{50}{1000}$$

$$P(K \text{ or } C) = \frac{400}{1000} + \frac{80}{1000} - \frac{50}{1000}$$

So:

$$= \frac{400 + 80 - 50}{1000} = \frac{430}{1000} = 0.43 \text{ or } 43\%$$

The answer in Example 10.7 is exactly the same as the answer in Example 10.5. Here the addition rule is just another way of getting the same result. It is a little more straightforward since it uses row and column totals from the table in Example 10.3 rather than figures from several different cells.

The addition rule can look more complicated than it actually is as despite being called the addition rule it contains a subtraction. To understand why this is we can illustrate the situation with a *Venn* diagram, a type of diagram used in a field within mathematics known as *set theory*.

A Venn diagram portrays the entire set of possible outcomes, called the *sample space*, as a rectangle. Circles within the rectangle represent the outcomes.

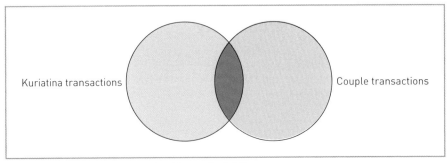

Figure 10.1 Venn diagram for Example 10.7

The circle on the left in Figure 10.1 represents the Kuriatina transactions and the one on the right the Couple transactions. The total area of both circles represents the probability of a transaction being at Kuriatina or involving a Couple. The overlap between the circles represents the probability that a transaction is both at Kuriatina and involves a Couple. The area outside the circles contains transactions that are not at Kuriatina and do not involve Couples.

The area of the overlap or intersection belongs to both circles. If we just add the areas of the two circles together to get the area covered by both circles, we include the intersection twice. By subtracting it once from the combined area of the two circles we only count it once.

Without the sort of overlap that we have in Figure 10.1 the addition rule would be more straightforward. If it is impossible for the two outcomes to occur jointly there would be no overlap. This is means the outcomes are *mutually exclusive*. The probability that they both occur is zero. In such cases the addition rule changes from:

$$P(A \text{ or } B) = P(A) + P(B) - P(A \text{ and } B)$$

to $$P(A \text{ or } B) = P(A) + P(B)$$

since $$P(A \text{ and } B) = 0$$

EXAMPLE 10.8

During a special promotion event 150 people visit a car showroom. They are given the opportunity to test drive one of three vehicles: the off-road 'Almiak', the 'Balanda' hatchback or the 'Caverza' sports car. Of the 150, 36 tested the 'Almiak', 59 the 'Balanda' and 25 the 'Caverza'.

Find the probability that a visitor tested the 'Balanda' or the 'Caverza'.

Solution

Since each visitor can only test drive one car the choices are mutually exclusive and the simpler form of the addition rule is appropriate.

Using the letter A for 'Almiak', B for 'Balanda' and C for 'Caverza',

$$P(B \text{ or } C) = P(B) + P(C) = \frac{59}{150} + \frac{25}{150} = \frac{84}{150} = 0.56 \text{ or } 56\%$$

In Example 10.8 the three choices of car are mutually exclusive but they do not constitute all of the alternative outcomes. Since they do not cover all the possible outcomes they are not *collectively exhaustive*. The missing outcome is that some visitors have chosen not to take a test drive. By taking the number of visitors taking a test drive, 120, away from the total number of visitors, 150, we find that 30 visitors declined the offer of a test drive.

An implication of the addition rule is that when there is a set of mutually exclusive and collectively exhaustive outcomes their probabilities add up to one. Since a probability of one means certainty, if the outcomes are mutually exclusive and collectively exhaustive, one and only one of them must occur.

EXAMPLE 10.9

Find the probability that one of the visitors in Example 10.8 chose the 'Almiak' or the 'Balanda' or the 'Caverza' or declined a test drive.

Solution

We will use the letter N to denote No test drive.

$$\text{The simple probability that a visitor test drives the 'Almiak'} = P(A) = \frac{36}{150}$$

$$\text{The simple probability that a visitor test drives the 'Balanda'} = P(B) = \frac{59}{150}$$

$$\text{The simple probability that a visitor test drives the 'Caverza'} = P(C) = \frac{25}{150}$$

$$\text{The simple probability that a visitor declines a test drive} = P(N) = \frac{30}{150}$$

$$P(A \text{ or } B \text{ or } C \text{ or } N) \frac{36 + 59 + 25 + 30}{150} = \frac{150}{150} = 1 \text{ or } 100\%$$

It follows from Example 10.9 that we can use the addition rule to find probabilities of any one of a set of mutually exclusive and collectively exhaustive outcomes as long as we have the probabilities of the others.

EXAMPLE 10.10

Find the probability that a visitor in Example 10.8 declined a test drive using the probabilities of the other outcomes.

Solution

$$P(\text{Visitor declined a test drive}) = 1 - P(A) - P(B) - P(C)$$

$$= 1 - \frac{36}{150} - \frac{59}{150} - \frac{25}{150}$$

$$= 1 - 0.240 - 0.393 - 0.167$$

$$= 1 - 0.8 = 0.2 \text{ or } 20\%$$

The result in Example 10.10, 0.2, is the decimal equivalent of the 30/150 we had for $P(N)$ in Example 10.9.

SELF-ASSEMBLY GUIDE

Using the addition rule of probability

◆ To find the probability of either one outcome **or** another happening decide whether the two outcomes are mutually exclusive or not.

◆ Mutually exclusive outcomes cannot both occur; it must be one or the other.

◆ If the outcomes are mutually exclusive, to find the probability that one or the other occurs add the simple probability of the first to the simple probability of the second:

$$P(A \text{ or } B) = P(A) + P(B)$$

◆ If the outcomes are not mutually exclusive you will need the probability that both occur, $P(A \text{ and } B)$.

◆ For the probability that one or the other, or both of two outcomes occur add the simple probabilities and take away the probability that they both occur:

$$P(A \text{ or } B) = P(A) + P(B) - P(A \text{ and } B)$$

10.4.2 The multiplication rule

The multiplication rule of probability is used to find compound probabilities that have the word 'and' in their description, probabilities of intersections of outcomes.

The multiplication rule states that the compound probability of two outcomes both occurring is the simple probability of the first occurring multiplied by the *conditional* probability of the second occurring, if the first outcome has already occurred:

$$P(A \text{ and } B) = P(A) * P(B|A)$$

In gambling, accumulator bets are worked out using the multiplication rule. These are bets on a sequence of outcomes, like a series of selected horses winning different races. To win the bet all the horses have to win their races. The chances of this sort of thing happening are usually something like a thousand to one. The numbers involved, like a thousand, are so large because multiplication is used to work them out.

EXAMPLE 10.11

Find the probability that a transaction at the food hall in Example 10.3 involved a Lone customer and was at Bolshoyburger using the multiplication rule.

$$P(L \text{ and } B) = P(L) * P(B|L)$$

Solution

Using the data in Example 10.3:

$$P(L) = \frac{540}{1000}$$

This is the relative frequency of transactions involving a Lone customer

and

$$P(B|L) = \frac{170}{540}$$

This is the relative frequency of transactions involving Lone customers that were at Bolshoyburger.

Applying the multiplication rule,

$$P(L \text{ and } B) = \frac{540}{1000} * \frac{170}{540} = \frac{170}{1000} = 0.17 \text{ or } 17\%$$

The result in Example 10.11 is exactly the same as the answer in Example 10.4 which was obtained directly from the tabulated data in Example 10.3.

The multiplication rule may seem a little complicated because it contains a conditional probability. The conditional probability for the second outcome is necessary because the chance that it happens may be affected by whether or not the first outcome has happened. This is referred to as *dependency*, or to put it another way one outcome depends on the other.

How do we know if two outcomes are dependent? We compare the *conditional* probability of one outcome occurring if the other has occurred with the *simple* probability that it occurs. If they differ it means the outcomes are dependent. If they do not the outcomes are independent; the chances of one happening are not influenced by whether the other has happened.

EXAMPLE 10.12

At the car showroom in Example 10.8, 25 visitors test drove the Caverza car. Of these, 10 said they intended to buy one. Overall 30 of the 150 visitors said they intended to buy a Caverza.

Are test driving the Caverza and intending to buy one dependent?

Solution

The simple probability that a visitor intends to buy a Caverza is 30/150 or 20%.

The conditional probability of a visitor intending to buy a Caverza given that they test drove one is 10/25 or 40%.

There is a difference between these two figures, which suggests that intending to buy a Caverza is dependent on test driving one.

By rearranging the multiplication rule we can use it to find conditional probabilities:

The multiplication rule is $\qquad P(A \text{ and } B) = P(A) * P(B|A)$

Dividing both sides by $P(A)$ we get

$$P(A \text{ and } B)/P(A) = P(B|A)$$

Swapping this around, $\qquad P(B|A) = P(A \text{ and } B)/P(A)$

EXAMPLE 10.13

Find the probability that a transaction at Gatovielle in the food hall in Example 10.3 involves a Lone customer.

Solution

$$P(L|G) = \frac{P(L \text{ and } G)}{P(G)}$$

From Example 10.3

$$P(L \text{ and } G) = \frac{360}{1000} = 0.36$$

and

$$P(G) = \frac{400}{1000} = 0.40$$

so

$$P(L|G) = \frac{0.36}{0.40} = 0.9 \text{ or } 90\%$$

The result in Example 10.13 is exactly the same as the answer in Example 10.6 which was obtained directly from the tabulated data in Example 10.3.

The multiplication rule can be simplified if the outcomes are *independent*, in other words when the probability of one outcome occurring is the same whether or not the other outcomes have occurred. In such cases the conditional probability of the outcome is the same as its simple probability so we don't need to use the conditional probability, the simple probability will suffice.

The multiplication rule, becomes because

$$P(A \text{ and } B) = P(A)*P(B|A)$$
$$P(A \text{ and } B) = P(A)*P(B)$$
$$P(B) = P(B|A).$$

EXAMPLE 10.14

Find the probability that someone who plays the gaming machine in Example 10.2 twice, wins £25 both times.

Solution

Fifty of the 1728 possible outcomes result in the £25 prize, so the probability of a cash prize in any one game is 50/1728.

If we assume that the machine is fair the conditional probability of a player winning £25 in their second game given that they have won £25 in their first game is also 50/1728. The outcomes of the two games are independent; that is to say the outcome of the second game is not affected by, or conditional on, the result of the first.

If C represents the winning of a £25 prize, then we will use C_1, to represent the winning of £25 in the first game and C_2 the winning of £25 in the second.

$$P(C_1 \text{ and } C_2) = P(C)*P(C) = \frac{50}{1728} * \frac{50}{1728} = 0.000837 \text{ or less than } 0.1\%$$

Conditional probabilities are particularly important if you want to work out the chance of a sequence of outcomes involving a limited number of elements. In these cases the selection of one of the elements alters the probabilities of further selections.

EXAMPLE 10.15

Bella is taking her friend out for the evening but has forgotten to take some cash out of her bank account. She reaches the cash machine, but can't remember the exact sequence of her PIN number. She knows that the digits in her PIN number are 2, 7, 8 and 9. What is the probability that Bella enters the correct PIN number?

Solution

There are four digits in Bella's PIN number so the chance that she keys in the correct first digit is one chance in four. The conditional probability that assuming she has keyed in the correct first digit she then keys in the correct second digit is one in three as there are three possible digits remaining and only one of them is the correct one. The conditional probability that given she gets the first two right she then keys in the correct third digit is one in two as she is left with two digits, one of which is the correct one. The conditional probability that she gets the last one right, assuming that she has keyed in the first correctly, is one since there is only one digit left and it must be the correct fourth digit.

$$P(\text{PIN number correct}) = \frac{1}{4} * \frac{1}{3} * \frac{1}{2} * 1 = 0.042$$

Using the multiplication rule of probability

◆ To find the probability of one outcome **and** another happening decide whether the two outcomes are independent.

◆ The outcomes are independent if the probability of one of the outcomes happening is the same whether or not the other outcome has happened.

◆ If the outcomes are independent, to find the probability that one or the other occurs multiply the simple probability of the first by the simple probability of the second:

$$P(A \text{ and } B) = P(A) * P(B)$$

◆ If the outcomes are not independent you will need the conditional probability that the second outcome occurs given that the first has happened, $P(A|B)$.

◆ For the probability that both occur multiply the simple probability of the first by the conditional probability of the second:

$$P(A \text{ and } B) = P(A) * P(B|A)$$

At this point you may find it useful to try **Review questions 10.3, 10.7, 10.8 and 10.11** at the end of the chapter.

10.4.3 Bayes' rule

In section 10.4.2 we saw how the multiplication rule, which is used to work out the compound probability of two outcomes both occurring, can be changed around to give a formula for the conditional probability of the second outcome occurring given that the first outcome had occurred. That is if

$$P(A \text{ and } B) = P(A) * P(B|A)$$

then

$$P(B|A) = P(A \text{ and } B)/P(A)$$

Generally we assume that A happens before B, for instance the probability that a person buys a car (B) given that they have test driven it (A).

The eighteenth-century clergyman and mathematician Thomas Bayes developed this further. He argued that if:

$$P(B \text{ and } A) = P(B) * P(A|B)$$

then
$$P(A|B) = P(B \text{ and } A)/P(B)$$

This allows us to find the probability that A occurred given that B subsequently occurred. This is as an 'after-the-event' or *posterior* probability. Using this terminology, the simple probability of A occurring is a 'before-the event' or *prior* probability.

Key to Bayes' rule is the fact that the compound probability of both A and B occurring is the same if we describe it as the probability of A and B or the probability of B and A:

$$P(A \text{ and } B) = P(B \text{ and } A)$$

According to the multiplication rule then:

$$P(A \text{ and } B) = P(A)*P(B|A) = P(B \text{ and } A)$$

So in the expression $\qquad P(A|B) = P(B \text{ and } A)/P(B)$

we can replace $\qquad\qquad\quad P(B \text{ and } A)$

with $\qquad\qquad\qquad\quad P(A)*P(B|A)$

This allows us to define the conditional probability that A occurred given that we know B subsequently occurred as:

$$P(A|B) = \frac{P(A)*P(B|A)}{P(B)}$$

This is Bayes' rule, which is also called Bayes' theorem.

EXAMPLE 10.16

The manager of the car showroom in Example 10.8 wants to know the probability that buyers of the Balanda car took a test drive in the car before buying. The showroom staff log the details of 'prospects', people visiting the showroom who they feel are potential buyers of particular models of car. Based on these records the probability that a Balanda prospect takes a test drive is 0.4. Of those who take a test drive 30% buy a Balanda. One in 10 prospects who do not take a test drive buys a Balanda.

What is the probability that a customer took a test drive given that they bought a Balanda?

Solution

Using T to represent a test drive and B to represent buying a Balanda, the probability the manager wants is the conditional probability that a customer took a test drive given that they bought a Balanda, $P(T|B)$.

Applying Bayes' rule:

$$P(T|B) = \frac{P(T)*P(B|T)}{P(B)}$$

The probability that a Balanda prospect took a test drive, $P(T)$, is 0.4. We also know the probability of a prospect buying a Balanda given that they took a test drive, $P(B|T)$, is 0.3. The other probability we need for using Bayes' rule is $P(B)$, the probability that a prospect bought a Balanda.

A prospect who bought a Balanda must have either taken or not taken a test drive. The simple probability of a prospect buying a Balanda is the sum of the probability that a prospect took a test drive and bought a Balanda, and the probability that a prospect did not take a test drive and bought a Balanda:

$$P(B) = P(T \text{ and } B) + P(NT \text{ and } B)$$

In this expression NT represents no test drive.

We don't have these compound probabilities but we can find them using the multiplication rule:

$$P(T \text{ and } B) = P(T) * P(B|T) = 0.4*0.3 = 0.12$$

The probability of a prospect not taking a test drive (NT) is 0.6, and the probability of a prospect buying a Balanda given they didn't take a test drive, $P(B|NT)$, is 0.1, so:

$$P(NT \text{ and } B) = P(NT)*P(B|NT) = 0.6*0.1 = 0.06$$

So
$$P(B) = 0.12 + 0.06 = 0.18$$

We now have the probabilities to apply Bayes' rule to find the probability that a Balanda buyer took a test drive, $P(T|B)$:

$$P(T|B) = \frac{P(T) * P(B|T)}{P(B)} = \frac{0.4 * 0.3}{0.18} = \frac{0.12}{0.18} = 0.667$$

Based on this we can advise the manager that two-thirds of Balanda buyers took a test drive.

At this point you may find it useful to try **Review question 10.13** at the end of the chapter.

10.4.4 Applying the rules of probability

In the sections above we introduced the various types of probability and the rules associated with them. Although we dealt with them separately they are used together when it comes to investigating situations where there are sequences of outcomes. Example 10.17 demonstrates how the topics covered in this chapter can be used to address a deceptively simple problem.

EXAMPLE 10.17

Substantial sections of the personal details of customers on the sales database at the car showroom in Example 10.8 have been lost following a systems failure. A salesperson has a credit card payment query about a customer called Mr Smith. The database only has family names and the days and months – but not the years – of the dates of birth of customers.

On checking the database the salesperson finds there are 25 males with the family name Smith. If she can find the birthday of her Mr Smith what is the probability that this will be enough to identify the customer on the database?

Solution

This is the probability that no two or more of the 25 Mr Smiths share the same birthday. To find this we'll start with one Mr Smith. His birthday could be on any day as there are no other Mr Smiths to consider. Out of the 365 days in the year one of them is 'occupied' by Mr Smith's birthday, the other 364 are 'unoccupied'.

Suppose we have two Mr Smiths. The probability that our second Mr Smith has his birthday on the same day as the first Mr Smith is one chance in 365. The probability that it is on a different day is 364 chances in 365, i.e. 364/365.

Now we'll introduce a third Mr Smith. If the first two Mr Smiths have birthdays on different days, in other words we have two 'occupied' days and 363 'unoccupied days', the probability that the third Mr Smith's birthday does not clash with the birthday of the first Mr Smith or the birthday of the second Mr Smith is 363/365. This is actually a conditional probability: the probability of the third Mr Smith's birthday being on a different day than the birthdays of the other two, given that the birthdays of the other two don't clash.

If the first, second and third Mr Smiths have birthdays on different days the probability that a fourth Mr Smith has a birthday that does not clash with the birthdays of the first three Mr Smiths is 362/365. If all four have birthdays on different days the probability that a fifth Mr Smith's birthday doesn't clash with those of the first four is 361/365 etc.

→

Solution cont

Finally, when we introduce the 25th Mr Smith, the probability that his birthday does not coincide with those of the other 24, assuming that they all have birthdays on different days, is 341/365. This and the other probabilities above represent the chances of the birthdays of specific Mr Smiths being on different days from those of other specific Mr Smiths. We need something more general; the probability that there are no clashes whatsoever. To find this we must combine these probabilities. But how should we do it; adding or multiplying?

Since we want the probability that the second Mr Smith's birthday doesn't clash with that of the first Mr Smith and the third Mr Smith's birthday doesn't clash those of the first two Mr Smiths etc. we have to multiply them.

So
$$P(\text{no clashes}) = \frac{364}{365} * \frac{363}{365} * \frac{362}{365} * \ldots * \frac{342}{365} * \frac{341}{365}$$
$$= 0.4252 \text{ or } 42.52\%$$

This is the probability that there are no clashes and hence the salesperson can identify her Mr Smith.

What is the chance that two or more Mr Smiths do share the same birthday, in which case the salesperson cannot solve her problem so easily? There are many ways this could happen. There might be a clash on 1st January or the 2nd January and so on. There might be clashes on two days. Three birthdays might coincide.

It would be far too laborious to work out the chances of all of these different possibilities, especially as we can use the addition rule. Since having a clash of birthdays and not having a clash of birthdays are mutually exclusive and collectively exhaustive events:

$$P(\text{no clash}) + P(\text{one or more clashes}) = 1$$

So

$$P(\text{one or more clashes}) = 1 - P(\text{no clash})$$

$$= 1 - 0.4252 = 0.5748 \text{ or } 57.48\%$$

This, the chance of two or more people sharing a birthday in a group of 25, is possibly rather higher than you might have thought; it is more likely to occur than not occur. Next time you are with 25 or so people you might like to find out it there is a clash of birthdays.

10.5 Tree diagrams

There are situations when it is difficult to ensure that all the different combinations of outcomes that could happen are included in the analysis of a problem. Writing them all down helps, as do Venn diagrams, but probably the best method is a *tree diagram*.

A tree diagram, also referred to as a *probability tree*, portrays the possible sequences of outcomes in the form of a tree branching out from left to right. Every branch represents an outcome and each sequence of branches represents a combination of outcomes. To work out the probability that these sequences of outcomes occur we apply the multiplication rule.

EXAMPLE
10.18

The Alpha Business Corporation has summoned three senior staff to an important meeting at company headquarters in London. Ali has to fly in from Alma-Ata, Banita from Bangui and Chuck from Chicago. Extreme weather conditions are affecting flights on the routes they have to travel. The probability that Ali will make the meeting is 0.6, the probability that Banita will make it is 0.7 and the probability of Chuck making it is 0.9. Using a tree diagram find:

● The probability of all three attending the meeting.

● The probability of two of them attending the meeting.

● The probability of only one of them attending the meeting.

Solution

To simplify the notation on the diagram we'll use A for Ali, B for Banita and C for Chuck. To distinguish between someone attending or not attending we can use their letter to represent attendance and their letter with a single quotation mark to represent non-attendance. For instance A represents Ali attending and A' represents Ali not attending.

A' is what is known as the *complement* of A. An outcome and its complement are mutually exclusive and collectively exhaustive. The probability of the complement of an outcome is always one minus the probability of the outcome. In this case the probability that Ali attends the meeting, $P(A)$, is 0.6 so the probability of the complement of A, Ali not making the meeting, $P(A')$, is 0.4.

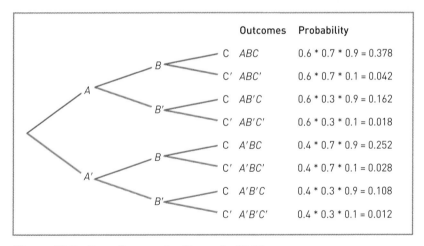

Figure 10.2 Tree diagram for Example 10.18

In Figure 10.2 the probability of all three attending, $P(ABC)$, is the first probability on the right, 0.378.

The probability of two of them attending is the probability that either only Chuck misses the meeting, sequence ABC' or only Banita misses it, $AB'C$, or only Ali misses it, $A'BC$. These sequences are mutually exclusive so the simpler form of the addition rule applies:

$$P(ABC' \text{ or } AB'C \text{ or } A'BC) = P(ABC') + P(AB'C) + P(A'BC)$$

$$= 0.042 + 0.162 + 0.252 = 0.456$$

The probability of only one of them attending is the probability that either Ali is the only one there, sequence $AB'C'$ or that it is only Banita, $A'BC'$ or that it is only Chuck, $A'B'C$.

Solution cont

These sequences are mutually exclusive too, so again the simpler form of the addition rule applies:

$$P(AB'C' \text{ or } A'BC' \text{ or } A'B'C) = P(AB'C') + P(A'BC') + P(A'B'C)$$
$$= 0.018 + 0.028 + 0.108 = 0.174$$

The branches in a tree diagram must cover all the possibilities. To check this we can add up the probabilities. Since the outcomes are mutually exclusive and collectively exhaustive they should come to one. In Example 10.18:

$$0.378 + 0.042 + 0.162 + 0.252 + 0.018 + 0.028 + 0.108 + 0.012 = 1$$

At this point you may find it useful to try **Review questions 10.9, 10.10, 10.14 and 10.15** at the end of the chapter.

REVIEW QUESTIONS

Answers to these questions are on pages 450–1. There are tips and hints to help you with them on the supporting website at **www.pearsoned.co.uk/buglear**, where you will also find the fully worked solutions.

☆☆★ Basic questions

10.1   Visitors to the CentreLarks holiday village can choose between three types of chalet; the Hick, the Chic and the Luxe. Out of the 1640 bookings received 905 are for the Hick and 483 for the Chic. All of these bookings are for a single chalet only. If one of these bookings is selected at random,

(a)   What is the probability it is for a Hick chalet?
(b)   What is the probability it is for a Chic chalet?
(c)   What is the probability it is for a Luxe chalet?
(d)   What is the probability it is for either a Chic or a Luxe chalet?

10.2   The Botinky store sells cosmetics and medicine. One day 276 customers made a purchase from the store: 152 bought cosmetics and of these 29 bought both cosmetics and medicine. If one of the 276 customers is chosen at random,

(a)   What is the probability they have bought only cosmetics?
(b)   What is the probability they have bought both cosmetics and medicine?
(c)   What is the probability they have bought only medicine?

10.3   Riadom Fashions recently had a sale. In the week before the sale there were 591 transactions and in 37 cases the goods were subsequently returned. In the sale there were 1278 transactions and in 352 cases the goods were subsequently returned.

(a)   From this data estimate:

(i)   the simple probability that goods are returned
(ii)   the probability that goods purchased are returned if they are not bought in a sale.
(iii) the probability that goods purchased are returned if they are bought in a sale.

(b)   Are the returning of goods and whether or not there is a sale independent?

10.4 In a survey of internet shopping, respondents were asked whether or not they had made a purchase via the internet during the previous month. They were also asked their age. The table below summarises the results.

Age category	Internet purchase	No internet purchase	Total
Under 30	48	12	60
30 and under 50	30	25	55
50 and over	15	40	55
Total	93	77	170

(a) If one of these respondents is chosen at random what is the probability that:

   (i)   they are under 30?
   (ii) they have made an internet purchase?
   (iii) they are 30 and under 50 and have not made an internet purchase?
   (iv) they have made an internet purchase if they are 50 and over?

(b) Based on your answers to (a) (ii) and (a) (iv), are age category and making an internet purchase independent?

☆★★ More testing questions

10.5 A soft drinks company has commissioned an investigation of the level of recognition of one of its brands in various countries that are considered important markets. Random samples of respondents in each country were asked to identify the product from the brand image. The results are:

Country	Brand recognition	
	Yes	No
Czech Republic	115	29
Estonia	66	35
Hungary	87	61
Poland	131	20

(a) What is the probability that a respondent recognises the brand?
(b) What is the probability that a respondent is from Hungary?
(c) What is the probability that a respondent recognises the brand and is from Estonia?
(d) If a respondent is from Poland, what is the probability that he or she recognises the brand?
(e) Compare your answers to (a) and (d), and comment on whether the country of residence of a respondent and brand recognition are independent.

10.6 The Human Resources Director of Shass-Levy plc has conducted an employee satisfaction survey. The results are summarised in the following table:

Employee grade	Satisfaction level		
	High	Medium	Low
Management	15	6	2
Senior	34	27	17
Junior	29	11	45

(a) What is the probability that an employee expresses Low satisfaction?
(b) What is the probability that an employee is Management and expresses Medium satisfaction?

(c) What is the probability that an employee is Senior or expresses High satisfaction?

(d) If an employee is Junior what is the probability they express Low satisfaction?

(e) If an employee is Management what is the probability they express Low satisfaction?

(f) Comparing your answers to (a), (d) and (e), comment on whether Employee grade and Satisfaction level are independent.

10.7 LyokiJet offers its passengers the opportunity to check in online instead of at the airport. Based on its check-in data the probability that a customer will check in online is 0.7. The probability that a customer only has hand luggage given that they check in online is 0.8. What is the probability that:

(a) a customer checks in online and only has hand luggage?

(b) a customer checks in online and has hold luggage?

(c) a customer checks in at the airport and has hold luggage if the conditional probability that a customer who checked in at the airport has hold luggage is 0.6?

(d) a customer checks in at the airport and only has hand luggage?

10.8 A first-year fashion student wants to be a designer at a fashion house. The probability he reaches his final year is 0.85. If he does the probability that he will be chosen to exhibit his work at the student fashion show is 0.12. The show is visited by professionals from the industry looking for talent. The probability that he is offered a designer post based on his work at the exhibition is 0.4. What is the probability that the student will become a designer in a fashion house?

10.9 Athletico Carlton is in the quarter-finals of a football competition. The manager reckons there is a 60% chance the team will win their quarter-final. If they do he rates their chances of winning their semi-final at 40%. If they win this he estimates they have a 30% chance of winning the final.

(a) What is the probability the team reach the final?

(b) What is the probability that the team win the competition?

10.10 Bash, Di and Rich are presenters on the popular TV car show *Priamaya Perrydacha*. For one programme they each have to drive an old vehicle from Plymouth to Inverness. Bash estimates that the probability that his car completes the journey is 0.75. Di assesses the probability of completing the journey in her car to be 0.7. Rich puts the probability of him finishing at 0.9. What is the probability that:

(a) all of them finish the journey?

(b) two of them finish the journey?

(c) none of them finish the journey?

10.11 Sian goes to a business meeting where the chair hands round a plate of biscuits. There are six biscuits on the plate; three are milk chocolate and three are plain chocolate. Sian likes plain chocolate biscuits. All of the biscuits have the same wrapper. There are three people who will take a biscuit before the plate reaches Sian. Assuming that none of the three people taking their biscuits before Sian take them out of the wrapper before the plate reaches Sian what is the probability that there is a plain chocolate biscuit left for her?

★★★ Challenging questions

10.12 Harvey the milkman delivers milk to houses on a large estate. The orders on the estate are:

Number of pints of milk	0	1	2	3	4
Number of households	49	13	35	57	22

If one of these households is chosen at random what is the probability that:

   (a) they have ordered two pints?
   (b) they have ordered two or fewer pints?
   (c) they have ordered one or more pints?
   (d) they have ordered less than four pints?
   (e) they have ordered more than two pints?

10.13 Florrie's Fashion Store and Mary's market stall both sell a particular style of sweatshirt. They are the only outlets for the garment in the area, with Florrie's accounting for 70% of the total number sold and Mary's accounting for the remainder. Unfortunately colour dye that faded prematurely was used to manufacture the first batches of the product. The supplier estimates that 15% of the stock supplied to Florrie and 25% of the stock supplied to Mary have this problem. Use Bayes' rule to find the probability that if a sweatshirt is defective it was sold by Mary.

10.14 Thursday, Friday and Saturday are the busiest nights at the Jopper bar. Police records show that on 12 of the last 50 Thursdays, 15 of the last 50 Fridays, and 16 of the last 50 Saturdays they were summoned to deal with a disturbance at the bar. Construct a tree diagram and use it to find the probability that over the next Thursday, Friday and Saturday nights there will be:

   (a) no trouble
   (b) trouble on Thursday only
   (c) trouble on one night only
   (d) trouble on Friday and Saturday only
   (e) trouble on two nights only

Assume that events on any one night are independent of events on any other night.

10.15 You win a prize in a raffle. The prize, donated by an airline, consists of three return tickets to a destination in Africa; Cairo, Dar-es-salaam and Entebbe. The seats you are allocated on the journeys will be either Business or Economy, the only seat types the airline offers, and will be picked at random by the airline. The flight to Cairo has 200 seats, 50 of which are Business. The flight to Dar-es-salaam has 300 seats, 90 of which are Business. The flight to Entebbe has 150 seats, of which 60 are Business. Assuming that if you are allocated a Business seat it is for both the outward and return parts of the journey:

   (a) What is the probability that you are allocated a Business seat on none of the journeys?
   (b) What is the probability that you are allocated a Business seat on one of the journeys?
   (c) What is the probability that you are allocated a Business seat on two or more of the journeys?

THE DEBRIEF

Key things to remember from this chapter

→ Probability is a measure of risk. The scale of measurement goes from 0 to 1.

→ A probability of zero means no chance and a probability of one means certainty.

→ A simple probability is the chance of one outcome occurring. A compound probability involves more than one outcome.

→ A compound probability might be a joint probability that two outcomes both occur or a conditional probability that one outcome occurs given that another has occurred.

→ Mutually exclusive items cannot both occur. Collectively exhaustive outcomes constitute the entire set of possible outcomes.

THE DEBRIEF (Continued)

→ The addition rule is used to work out the probability that either or both of two outcomes occur. If the outcomes are mutually exclusive this is the sum of the simple probabilities of the outcomes. If the outcomes are not mutually exclusive it is the sum of their simple probabilities minus the joint probability that they both occur.

→ The multiplication rule is used to work out the probability of outcomes jointly occurring. If the outcomes are independent this is the simple probability of one times the simple probability of the other. If they are not it is the simple probability of the first times the conditional probability of the second given that the first occurred.

→ Bayes' rule is used to work out prior probabilities of outcomes, which means the sequence of outcomes in conditional probabilities can be reversed.

→ Probability trees are devices for mapping out complex sets of related outcomes.

References

Boghani, A.B. (1990) 'Are special trains really safer?', in L.A. Cox, Jr. and P.F. Ricci (eds), *New Risks: Issues and Management*, New York: Plenum Press, pp. 681–92.

North, D.W. (1990) 'Decision analysis in environmental risk management: applications to acid deposition and air toxins', in L.A. Cox, Jr. and P.F. Ricci (eds), *New Risks: Issues and Management*, New York: Plenum Press, pp. 33–43.

CHAPTER 11

Finding the right way – analysing decisions

CHAPTER OBJECTIVES

This chapter will help you to:

→ Understand the concept of expectation

→ Appreciate attitudes to risk and apply decision rules

→ Construct and use decision trees

→ Use sensitivity analysis to explore findings from decision trees

→ Apply Bayes' rule to decision tree analysis

THE BARE BONES

What you will find in this chapter . . .

- Working out expected values using probabilities, including expected monetary values (EMVs)

- Applying decision rules to make choices between alternative strategies in situations of uncertainty

- Using decision trees to inform decision-making under conditions of risk

- Applying 'what if' questions to conclusions from decision trees

- Using posterior probabilities in decision trees

. . . and on the supporting website (www.pearsoned.co.uk/buglear)

- Fully worked solutions to the review questions

- More review questions

REALITY CHECK

Business use of decision analysis

◆ Brown, Kahr and Peterson (1974) describe the use of decision analysis in several major US corporations; deciding the scale of pilot production of a new product at Du Pont, which type of packaging was more appropriate for grocery products at Pillsbury, finding the optimal pricing and production strategy for a maturing product at General Electric, and identifying a product policy to deal with increasing competition at the Tractor Division of the Ford Motor Company.

◆ The confectionery company Cadbury is a good example of a company that launches new products on a regular basis. The decision whether to launch a new product might begin with small-scale consumer testing using samples of the product from a pilot production run. Beattie (1969) explains how decision tree analysis was applied to the next stage in the product launch, deciding whether to proceed directly to a full national launch of the product or to test market the product in a UK region and decide whether or not to go for a full launch on the basis of the performance of the product in the test market. If they went directly to a full launch then, assuming it proved a success, they would earn profits on the product earlier, but they would risk a large financial outlay on full-scale production and promoting the product on a national basis. According to Beattie the main advantage that Cadbury staff gained from using decision tree analysis was that the framework offered a systematic way of examining the problem and investigating it from different perspectives.

◆ Phillips (1982) describes how a company producing outboard motors for boats earned most of their revenue from sales of a particular engine, which sold well across the world. When it was banned in the USA as it failed to meet federal emission constraints, the company had to decide whether to continue producing the engine or to replace it with a new and technologically superior product that had already been designed. Customers valued the reliable old product and might be unwilling to accept a new product that was yet to prove as robust. A further complication was that they thought a rival company was about to launch a product with similar specifications but more advanced technology. There were limited resources available for the company to invest in equipment for making the new product. The company used decision tree analysis to model the situation and sensitivity analysis to explore the results.

◆ The oil and gas industry, especially the exploration and production arm of it, has used decision analysis extensively. Their decisions involve bidding procedures, drilling decisions, when to increase capacity and the length of supply contracts. These decisions are taken against a background of fluctuating oil and gas prices and uncertainty about the scale of reserves in new fields. Coopersmith *et al.* (2000) give an overview of these applications and illustrate how Aker Maritime Inc., who make offshore platforms, used decision tree analysis to advise a customer on the selection of the most appropriate deepwater oil production system for a new oilfield off the West African coast. The customer, the operating company, had to decide whether to purchase an adaptable system that could be installed relatively quickly and would enable production to be increased if the reserves were larger than anticipated. If they did this they would produce oil and earn revenue earlier than if they adopted the alternative strategy of drilling more wells to get a better idea of the size of the reservoir of oil in the field and then purchase a production system that would be optimal for the scale of reserves they could tap.

11.1 Introduction

In the previous chapter we looked at how probability can be used to assess risk. In this chapter we will consider how probability is used in the analysis of decisions. We will begin with *expectation*, the process of multiplying probabilities by the tangible results of the outcomes whose chances they measure to obtain *expected values* of the process or situation under investigation. We will move on to examine various quantitative approaches to making decisions, including decision trees.

11.2 **Expectation**

Probability is about evaluating the chance that a certain outcome occurs. Expectation, which is based on probability, is about assessing the predicted or expected value of an outcome.

Producing an expected value involves applying probability to something finite. If the process that we want to investigate is something that is repeated, we can use expectation to predict how often a particular outcome occurs if we know how many times the process will happen. To do this we multiply the probability of the outcome by the number of times the process is repeated.

EXAMPLE 11.1

The probability that a customer visiting the Kenigar Bookshop makes a purchase is 0.35. If 500 customers visit the shop one day, how many should be expected to make a purchase?

Solution

Expected number of customers making a purchase = 0.35 * 500 = 175

The result in Example 11.1 is a prediction. As with any prediction it won't always turn out to be true. The result doesn't mean that for every 500 customers that visit the store exactly 175 will make a purchase. What it does mean is that we would expect that *on average* the number of customers making a purchase is 175 in every 500 that visit the store. It is a general long-run prediction.

Sometimes it is the financial consequences of outcomes that are important. In cases like this probabilities are applied to the monetary results of the outcomes to give a predicted average amount of money income or expenditure. Such predictions are *expected monetary values (EMVs)*.

EXAMPLE 11.2

Nebo Airlines operates flights in the European Union. Under EU regulations it is obliged to compensate passengers for late departures. If one of its flights is more than two hours late passengers are entitled to meals and phone calls. The cost of this is €20 per passenger. If the flight is more than three hours late passengers are entitled to compensation of €250 as well as meals and phones calls. The total cost of compensation for a flight delayed by over two hours, based on the average occupancy of 100 passengers, is €2000, and for a flight delayed by more than three hours it is €27,000.

The probability of a flight being more than two hours late is 0.05 and the probability of it being more than three hours late is 0.01. Find the expected monetary value (EMV) of the compensation per flight.

Solution

There are three possible outcomes; a flight is less than two hours late, two and up to three hours late, and over three hours late. We take the probability of each of these outcomes (0.94, 0.05 and 0.01) and multiply them by the respective compensation costs of €0, €2000, and €27,000. Adding the products of the probabilities times the costs gives us the EMV.

$$EMV = (0.94 * 0) + (0.05 * 2000) + (0.01 * 27,000) = 0 + 100 + 270 = 370$$

The airline can expect that on average late flight compensation costs will be €370 per flight.

Calculating EMVs

◆ Make sure you have the probability of every possible outcome of the process. Check by making sure that the probabilities add up to one.

◆ Make sure you have a figure for the monetary results of each outcome, including any that have a zero result.

◆ For each outcome multiply the probability by the monetary result.

◆ The EMV is the sum of these products.

At this point you may find it useful to try **Review questions 11.1, 11.2 and 11.5** at the end of the chapter.

11.3 Decision rules

From time to time companies are faced with decisions that are pivotal to their future. These involve developing new products, building new facilities, introducing new working practices and so on. In most cases the managers who take these decisions will not know whether they have chosen the correct strategies for months or years to come. They have to take these decisions against a background of either uncertainty, where they cannot attach a probability to each of the outcomes, or risk, where they can put a probability to each of the outcomes.

In this section we will look at decision rules, techniques available to managers taking decisions under conditions of uncertainty. All of these techniques assist managers by helping them analyse the decisions and the possible outcomes in a systematic way. The starting point is the *pay-off table* in which the results or pay-offs of the different possibilities or *strategies* that could be chosen are arranged according to the conditions or *states of nature* affecting the pay-off that might prevail.

EXAMPLE 11.3

Following the success of their CeeZee Seafood fast-food restaurant in London, the proprietors, Soll and Perretts, are thinking of expanding the business. They could do this by investing in new sites or by franchising the operation to aspiring fast-food entrepreneurs who would pay a fee to Soll and Perretts. The estimated profits for each strategy depend on the future demand for healthy fast-food, which could increase, remain stable, or decline. Another possibility for Soll and Perretts is to accept the offer of £20m that a major international fast-food company has made for their business. The expected profits are shown in Table 11.1.

Table 11.1 Expected profits (in £m) for Soll and Perretts

| Strategy | State of future demand | | |
	Increasing	Steady	Decreasing
Invest	100	40	−30
Franchise	60	50	0
Sell	20	20	20

The pay-off table in Example 11.3 does not in itself indicate what strategy would be best. This is where decision rules can help. When you apply them remember that the decision you are analysing involves choosing between the available strategies not between the states of nature, which are by definition beyond the control of the decision-maker.

11.3.1 The maximax rule

According to the maximax rule the best strategy is the one that offers the highest pay-off irrespective of other possibilities. We apply the maximax rule by identifying the best pay-off for each strategy and choosing the strategy that has the best among the best, or *maxi*mum among the *maxi*mum, pay-offs.

EXAMPLE 11.4	Which strategy should be selected in Example 11.3 according to the maximax decision rule?

Solution

The best pay-off available from investing is £100m, from franchising, £50m, and from selling, £20m, so according to the maximax rule they should invest.

The attitude of the decision-maker has a bearing on the suitability of decision rules. The maximax rule is appropriate for decision-makers who are risk-seekers; those who are prepared to accept the chance of losing money in gambling on the biggest possible pay-off. However, we should add that the attitude of the decision-maker may well be influenced by the financial state of the business. If it is cash-rich, the maximax approach would make more sense than if it were strapped for cash. In the former case it would have the resources to cushion the losses that may result in choosing the strategy with the highest pay-off.

11.3.2 The maximin rule

If maximax is the rule for the optimists and the gamblers, maximin is for the pessimists and the risk-avoiders. The maximin rule is to pick the strategy that offers the best of the worst returns for each strategy, the *maxi*mum of the *mini*mum pay-offs.

EXAMPLE 11.5	Which strategy should be selected in Example 11.3 according to the maximin decision rule?

Solution

The worst pay-off available from investing is −£30m, from franchising, £0m, and from selling, £20m, so according to the maximin rule they should sell.

This approach would be appropriate for a business that does not have large cash resources and would therefore be especially vulnerable to taking a loss. It would therefore make sense to pass up the opportunity to gain a large pay-off if it carries with it a risk of a loss and settle for more modest prospects without the chance of losses.

11.3.3 The minimax regret rule

This rule is a compromise between the optimistic maximax and the pessimistic maximin. It involves working out the opportunity loss or *regret* you would incur if you selected any but the best strategy for the conditions that come about. To apply it you have to identify the best strategy for each state of nature. You then allocate a regret of zero to each of these strategies, as you would have no regret if you had picked them and it turned out to be the best thing for that state of nature, and work out how much worse off you would be under that state of nature had you chosen another strategy. Finally look for the largest regret figure for each strategy and choose the strategy with the lowest of these figures: in doing so you are selecting the strategy with the *mini*mum of the *max*imum *regrets*.

EXAMPLE 11.6

Which strategy should be selected in Example 11.3 according to the minimax regret decision rule?

Solution

If the proprietors knew that demand would increase in the future they should choose to invest, but if instead they had chosen to franchise they would be £40m worse off (£100m − £60m), and if they had chosen to sell they would be £80m (£100m − £20m) worse off.

These figures are the opportunity losses for the strategies under the increasing demand state of nature.

The complete set of opportunity loss figures are given in Table 11.2.

Table 11.2 Opportunity loss figures (in £m) for Example 11.3

	State of future demand		
Strategy	**Increasing**	**Steady**	**Decreasing**
Invest	0	10	50
Franchise	40	0	20
Sell	80	30	0

From Table 11.2 the maximum opportunity loss from investing is £50m, from franchising, £40m, and from selling, £80m. These are the largest regret figures in each of the rows for the three strategies. The minimum of these is the £40m from franchising, so according to the minimax regret decision rule this is the strategy they should adopt.

11.3.4 The equal likelihood decision rule

In decision-making under uncertainty there is insufficient information available to assign probabilities to the different states of nature. The equal likelihood approach involves assigning probabilities to the states of nature on the basis that, in the absence of any evidence to the contrary, each state of nature is as likely to prevail as any other state of nature; for instance, if there are two possible states of nature we give each of them a probability of 0.5. We then use these probabilities to work out the expected monetary value (EMV) of each strategy and select the strategy with the highest EMV.

EXAMPLE 11.7

Which strategy should be selected in Example 11.3 according to the equal likelihood decision rule?

Solution   In this case there are three possible states of nature – increasing, steady and decreasing future demand – so we assign each one a probability of one-third. The investing strategy represents a one-third chance of a £100m pay-off, a one-third chance of a £60m pay-off and a one-third chance of a −£30m pay-off. To get the EMV of the strategy we multiply the pay-offs by the probabilities assigned to them:

$$\text{EMV(Invest)} = 1/3 * 100 + 1/3 * 60 + 1/3 * (-30) = 33.333 + 20 + (-10) = 43.333$$

Similarly the EMVs for the other strategies are:

$$\text{EMV(Franchise)} = 1/3 * 40 + 1/3 * 50 + 1/3 * 0 = 13.333 + 16.667 + 0 = 30$$

$$\text{EMV(Sell)} = 1/3 * 20 + 1/3 * 20 + 1/3 * 20 = 20$$

According to the equal likelihood approach they should choose to invest, since it has the highest EMV.

At this point you may find it useful to try **Review questions 11.3 and 11.6** at the end of the chapter.

11.4 Decision trees

The decision rules we examined in the previous section help to deal with situations where there is uncertainty about the states of nature and no probabilities are available to represent the chances of their happening. If we are dealing with conditions of risk, situations where we do have probabilities for the different states of nature, we can use these probabilities to determine expected monetary values (EMVs) for each strategy. This approach is at the heart of decision trees.

Decision trees portray sequences of strategies that can be selected and outcomes in the form of a tree. Every one of the branches, which extend from left to right, represents either a decision or an outcome. The places where branches separate out are the *nodes*. The branches that grow out of the nodes represent either outcomes, in which case the node is a *chance node*, or decisions, in which case the node is a *decision node*. Chance nodes are shown as circles and decision nodes as squares.

Every path in a decision tree ends up with a particular monetary result. This could be either positive, such as income or profit, or negative, such as cost or loss. The probability of an outcome occurring appears next to the branch that represents it. By combining the probabilities and the monetary results we can ascertain the expected monetary values (EMVs) of the decisions. The last stage is to pick which decision, or sequence of decisions if there are several decision nodes, has the best EMV. If the monetary results are values of something that we want to maximise, such as income, we look for the largest EMV. If they are values of something we want to minimise, such as cost, we look for the smallest EMV.

EXAMPLE 11.8   The proprietors of the business in Example 11.3 estimate that the probability that demand increases in the future is 0.4, the probability that it remains stable is 0.5 and the probability that it decreases is 0.1. Using this information construct a decision tree to represent the situation and use it to advise Soll and Perretts.

Solution

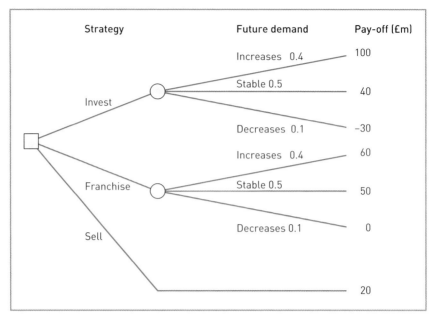

| Strategy | Future demand | Pay-off (£m) |

Increases 0.4 — 100

Stable 0.5 — 40

Invest

Decreases 0.1 — -30

Increases 0.4 — 60

Franchise — Stable 0.5 — 50

Decreases 0.1 — 0

Sell

— 20

Figure 11.1   Decision tree for Example 11.8

The decision tree is shown in Figure 11.1.

EMV for the Invest strategy $= 0.4 * 100 + 0.5 * 40 + 0.1 * (-30) = £57m$

EMV for the Franchise strategy $= 0.4 * 60 + 0.5 * 50 + 0.1 * 0 = £49m$

EMV for the Sell strategy $= £20m$

The proprietors should choose to invest.

The probabilities of the states of nature in Example 11.8 were provided by the decision-makers themselves, but what if they could commission an infallible forecast of future demand? How much would this be worth to them? This is the value of perfect information, and we can put a figure on it by working out the difference between the EMV of the best strategy and the expected value with perfect information. This latter amount is the sum of the best pay-off under each state of nature multiplied by the probability of that state of nature.

EXAMPLE 11.9

Work out the expected value of perfect information for the proprietors of the fast-food business in Example 11.3.

Solution

We will assume that the proprietors' probability assessments of future demand are accurate; the chance of increasing demand is 0.4 and so on. If they knew for certain that future demand would increase they would choose to invest, if they knew demand was definitely going to remain stable they would franchise, and if they knew demand would decrease they would sell. The expected value with perfect information is:

$$0.4 * 100 + 0.5 * 50 + 0.1 * 20 = £67m$$

From Example 11.8 the best EMV was £57m, for investing. The difference between this and the expected value with perfect information, £10m, is the value to the proprietors of perfect information.

The decision tree we used in Example 11.8 is a fairly basic one, representing just one point at which a decision has to be made and the ensuing three possible states of nature. Decision trees really come into their own when there are a number of stages of outcomes and decisions; when there is a multi-stage decision process.

Sam 'the Chemise' has a market stall in a small town where she sells budget clothing. Unexpectedly the local football team have reached the semi-finals of a major tournament. A few hours before the semi-final is to be played a supplier offers her a consignment of the team's shirts at a good price but says she can have either 500 or 1000 and has to agree to the deal right away.

If the team reach the final, the chance of which a TV commentator puts at 0.6, and Sam has ordered 1000 shirts she will be able to sell all of them at a profit of £10 each. If the team do not reach the final and she has ordered 1000 she will not sell any this season but could store them and sell them at a profit of £5 each next season, unless the team change their strip in which case she will only make a profit of £2 per shirt. The probability of the team changing their strip for next season is 0.75. Rather than store the shirts she could sell them to a discount chain at a profit of £2.50 per shirt before next season.

If Sam orders 500 shirts and the team reaches the final she will be able to sell all the shirts at a profit of £10 each. If they do not make the final and she has ordered 500 she will not have the option of selling to the discount chain as the quantity would be too small for them. She could only sell them next season at a profit of £5 each if the team strip is not changed and at a profit of £2 each if it is. Sam could of course decline the offer of the shirts. Draw a decision tree to represent the situation Sam faces.

Solution

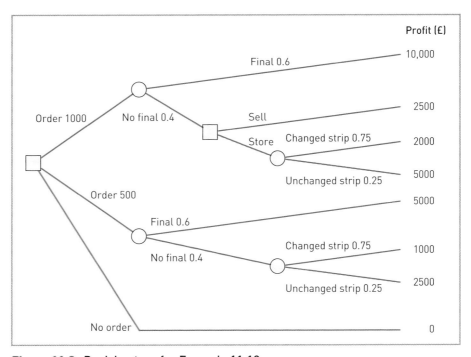

Figure 11.2 Decision tree for Example 11.10

A decision tree like the one in Figure 11.2 only represents the situation; the real point is to come to some recommendation. This is a little more complex when, as in Figure 11.2, there is more than one point at which a decision has to be made. Since the consequences for the first decision, on the left-hand side of the diagram, are influenced by the later decision we have to work back through the diagram using what is called *backward induction* or the *roll back* method to make a recommendation about the later decision before we can analyse the earlier one. We assess each strategy by determining its EMV and select the one with the highest EMV, just as we did in Example 11.8.

EXAMPLE 11.11

Find the EMV for each decision that Sam, the market trader in Example 11.10, could make if she had ordered 1000 shirts and the team did not make it to the final.

Solution

$$EMV(Store) = 0.75 * 2000 + 0.25 * 5000 = £2750$$

Since this figure is higher than the value of selling the shirts to the discount chain, £2500, Sam should store rather than sell the shirts at this stage.

Once we have come to a recommendation for the later course of action we assume that the decision-maker would follow our advice at that stage and hence we need only incorporate the preferred strategy in the subsequent analysis. We work out the EMV of each decision open to the decision-maker at the earlier stage and recommend the one with the highest EMV.

EXAMPLE 11.12

Find the EMV for each decision that Sam, the market trader in Example 11.10, could take concerning the offer made to her by the supplier.

Solution

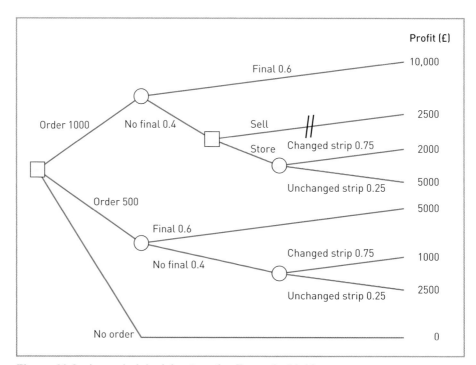

Figure 11.3 Amended decision tree for Example 11.10

We can indicate as shown in Figure 11.3 that the option of selling the stock if she were to order 1000 and the team do not reach the final should be excluded. This makes the EMV of the decision to order 1000 shirts much easier to ascertain. In working it out we use the

EMV of the preferred strategy at the later stage, storing the shirts, as the pay-off if the team were not to make the final.

$$\text{EMV(Order 1000)} = 0.6 * 10000 + 0.4 * 2750 = £7100$$

In identifying the EMV of the decision to order 500 shirts we have to take account of the chance of the team strip being changed as well as the chance of the team reaching the final. This involves applying the multiplication rule of probability; the probability that Sam makes a profit of £2500 is the chance that the team fail to reach the final *and* don't change their strip next season.

$$\text{EMV(Order 500)} = 0.6 * 5000 + 0.4 * 0.75 * 1000 + 0.4 * 0.25 * 2500 = £3550$$

We would recommend that Sam orders 1000 as the EMV for that strategy is higher, £7100, than the EMV for ordering 500, £3550, and the EMV of not making an order, £0.

SELF-ASSEMBLY GUIDE

Constructing a decision tree

◆ Distinguish between the strategies, the possible decisions and the outcomes. The strategies can be chosen; the outcomes cannot be chosen, they are beyond the control of the decision-maker.

◆ Map out the diagram from the initial strategies to the final outcomes.

◆ Use a square to represent points when a decision has to be made and a circle to represent points where different outcomes can occur.

◆ Write in the probabilities of each outcome alongside the branch that represents it.

◆ The probabilities of all the outcomes coming out from each circle should add up to one.

◆ Write the monetary result of each sequence of strategies and outcomes to the right of the final branch in the sequence.

◆ Work out the EMV for each strategy. This is the sum of the products of the probabilities and monetary results of each outcome that can arise after taking the strategy.

◆ Select the strategy with the best EMV.

At this point you may find it useful to try **Review questions 11.4 and 11.7 to 11.10** at the end of the chapter.

11.4.1 Sensitivity analysis

The probabilities used in decision trees are often little more than educated guesses, yet they are an integral part of the analysis. It is therefore useful to see how the recommendation might change if the probabilities of the relevant outcomes are altered, in other words to see how sensitive the recommendation is to changes in these probabilities. *Sensitivity analysis* involves finding out by how much the probabilities would have to change for a different decision to be recommended.

EXAMPLE 11.13

In Example 11.11 we recommended that Sam, the market trader in Example 11.10, should store rather than sell the shirts if she had ordered 1000 shirts and the team did not make it to the final. We worked out the EMV that led to this conclusion using the probability that the team would change its strip, 0.75. But what if it changed? At what point would we alter our advice and say she should sell the shirts to the discount chain instead?

Solution

If we use p to represent the probability the team strip changes and $1 - p$ to represent the probability it doesn't, then the point at which the sell and store strategies have equal value is when:

$$p * 2000 + (1 - p) * 5000 = 2500$$
$$2000p + 5000 - 5000p = 2500$$
$$-3000p = -2500$$
$$p = \frac{2500}{3000} = 0.833$$

This result suggests that if the probability of the team changing its strip is more than 0.833, then Sam should sell the shirts to the discount chain rather than store them. We can check this by taking a higher figure:

$$\text{EMV(Store)} = 0.9 * 2000 + 0.1 * 5000 = £2300$$

This is lower than the value of selling the shirts to the discount chain, £2500, so if the probability of the team changing its strip were 0.9, Sam should sell the shirts.

The probability in Example 11.13 would not have to change by very much, from 0.75 to 0.833, for our advice to change; the decision is *sensitive* to the value of the probability. If it needed a substantial shift in the value of the probability we would consider the decision to be *robust*.

At this point you may find it useful to try **Review questions 11.11 and 11.12** at the end of the chapter.

11.4.2 Using Bayes' rule in decision trees

The probabilities that we have used in the decision trees we have studied so far have been prior, or before-the-event, probabilities, and conditional probabilities. There are situations where we need to include posterior, or after-the-event probabilities, which we can work out using the Bayes' rule that we looked at in section 10.4.3.

EXAMPLE 11.14

Karovnick Construction has acquired a piece of land where a disused warehouse currently stands. It plans to build apartments in the shell of the warehouse building. It is a speculative venture which depends on the existing building being sound enough to support the new work. Karovnick's own staff put the probability of the building being sound at 0.5. The company can sell the building for £4m without doing any work on the site or it could go ahead and build.

If the building proves to be sound it will make a profit of £15m, but if it is not sound the extra costs of extensive structural work will result in a profit of only £1m. It could decide at the outset to commission a full structural survey. The firm it would hire to carry this out have a good record, but they are not infallible; they were correct 80% of the time when a building they surveyed turned out to be sound and 90% of the time when a building they surveyed turned out to be unsound. The surveyor's report would only be available to Karovnick, so whatever the conclusions it contains the company could still sell the site for £4m.

Solution   We can draw a decision tree to represent this situation:

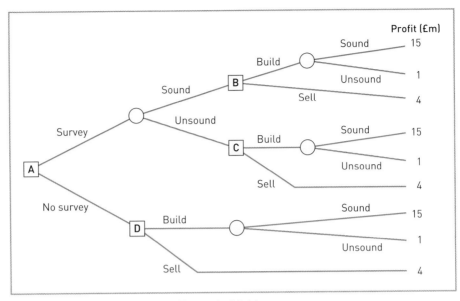

Figure 11.4   **Decision tree for Example 11.14**

The decision nodes in Figure 11.4 have been labelled A, B, C and D to make it easier to illustrate the subsequent analysis. Note that although we have included all the pay-offs in this decision tree, the majority of outcomes do not have probabilities. This is because we do not know for instance the probability that the building turns out to be sound, given that the surveyor's report predicts the building is sound. This probability depends on the probability that the surveyor predicts the building is sound, which is either accurate or inaccurate. To help us sort out the probabilities we need we can construct a probability tree:

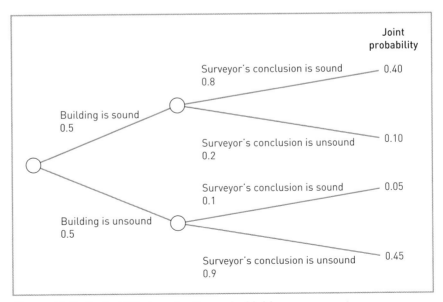

Figure 11.5   **Probability tree for Example 11.14**

Solution cont

Using the joint probabilities on the right-hand side of Figure 11.5 we can work out:

$$P(\text{Surveyor's conclusion is sound}) = 0.40 + 0.05 = 0.45$$

$$P(\text{Surveyor's conclusion is unsound}) = 0.10 + 0.45 = 0.55$$

Using Bayes' rule:

$$P(A|B) = \frac{P(B \text{ and } A)}{P(B)}$$

we can work out:

$$P(\text{Building is sound}\,|\,\text{Surveyor's conclusion is sound}) = 0.40/0.45 = 0.889$$

$$P(\text{Building is unsound}\,|\,\text{Surveyor's conclusion is sound}) = 0.05/0.45 = 0.111$$

$$P(\text{Building is sound}\,|\,\text{Surveyor's conclusion is unsound}) = 0.10/0.55 = 0.182$$

$$P(\text{Building is unsound}\,|\,\text{Surveyor's conclusion is unsound}) = 0.45/0.55 = 0.818$$

We now have the probabilities we need to complete the decision tree as in Figure 11.6.

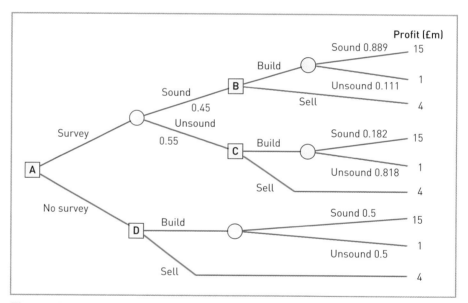

Figure 11.6 Amended decision tree for Example 11.14

We are now in a position to work out the expected monetary values for the decisions represented in the upper part of the diagram by nodes *B* and *C*.

At node *B*:

$$\text{EMV(Build)} = 0.889 * 15 + 0.111 * 1 = £13.446\text{m}$$

This is much higher than the value of the alternative Sell strategy, £4m, so if the surveyor finds the building sound, the company should Build.

At node *C*:

$$\text{EMV(Build)} = 0.182 * 15 + 0.818 * 1 = £3.548\text{m}$$

This is lower than the value of the Sell strategy, £4m, so should the surveyor find the building unsound, it should Sell.

We now need to use the EMVs of the preferred strategies at nodes *B* and *C*, Build and Sell respectively, as the pay-offs to work out the EMV for the Survey strategy at node *A*:

$$EMV(Survey) = 0.45 * 13.446 + 0.55 * 4 = £8.251m$$

We need to compare this to the EMV of the alternative strategy at node *A*, No survey. (At node *D* the Sell strategy will only yield £4m, so the preferred strategy is to Build.)

$$EMV(No\ survey) = 0.5 * 15 + 0.5 * 1 = £8m$$

Since this is lower than the EMV for the Survey strategy we would advise the company to commission a survey. In the event that the surveyor finds the building sound, it should Build; if the surveyor finds the building unsound, it should Sell.

As a footnote to Example 11.14, you may notice that the EMV figures for the two possible decisions at node A are very close (£8.251m and £8m), suggesting that the conclusion is highly sensitive to changes in the probability values. We can interpret the difference between the two figures, £0.251m or £251,000, as the most it is worth the company paying for the surveyor's report.

11.4.3 The limitations of decision trees

Decision trees are a valid way of analysing decisions but they do have shortcomings.

First, their usefulness depends on the reliability of the data on which they are based. Should the probability and money figures be unreliable then so will the conclusions. This is a key consideration if like the situation in Example 11.8 the data is highly speculative and relates to outcomes occurring well into the future.

Secondly, they ignore the attitudes that decision-makers have about risk. For example, if Soll and Perretts in Example 11.8 had substantial cash resources they would probably be more disposed to risk a loss than if they had a cash-flow problem.

Thirdly, it is not easy to accommodate factors that are either difficult or impossible to quantify. For example, the area where the site is located where the construction company in Example 11.14 wants to build may be one in which skilled building workers are in short supply.

Fourthly, the types of decisions that decision trees are intended to help resolve are typically key decisions that affect the future of the organisation facing them. These decisions are often contentious and involve a variety of staff with different expertise and perspectives. The way the decision is taken, and indeed the definition of what information is relevant, reflects the balance of power and influence within the organisation. For a useful insight into these issues, try Jennings and Wattam (1998).

Although they have these limitations decision trees can assist in the analysis of decisions, particularly if we want to consider the impact of changing some of the data to ascertain how the conclusions might be affected.

At this point you may find it useful to try **Review question 11.13** at the end of the chapter.

REVIEW QUESTIONS

Answers to these questions are on pages 451–2. There are tips and hints to help you with them on the supporting website at **www.pearsoned.co.uk/buglear**, where you will also find the fully worked solutions.

☆☆★ Basic questions

11.1 A tennis player reaches the quarter finals of a major US tournament. Three more wins and he will win the $1m top prize. If he is the defeated finalist he will get $0.5m prize money. If he reaches the semi-final and loses it he will get $200,000. If he loses his quarter-final he will get $100,000. He estimates the probability of winning his quarter-final to be 0.4. If he wins his quarter-final he puts the probability that he wins his semi-final at 0.3. If he wins his semi-final he estimates the probability of winning the final to be 0.2. What is the expected value of his prize money?

11.2 Grabby Tyell plc sells health insurance. Claims made by policyholders are either for minor or major treatment. On average minor treatment costs the company £1,000 and major treatment costs it £10,000. The probability that a policyholder claims for minor treatment over the course of a year is 0.08. The probability that a policyholder claims for major treatment during a year is 0.02. Assuming that no policymaker makes more than one claim a year what is the expected cost of treatment per policyholder?

11.3 Zaq 'the Snack' rents a pitch for his stall at a music festival. The night before the festival he has to decide whether to load his van with ice-cream products, or burgers, or a mix of burgers and ice-cream products. The takings he can expect (in £) depend on the weather, as shown in the following table:

Load	Weather	
	Sun	Showers
Ice cream	2800	1300
Mix	2100	2200
Burgers	1500	2500

Recommend which load Zaq should take using:

(a) the maximax decision rule
(b) the maximin decision rule
(c) the minimax regret decision rule
(d) the equal likelihood decision rule

11.4 Jem O'Dann is booking flights to Heraklion for a short holiday. She is not sure whether all her luggage will fit in one bag that she can take as cabin baggage. If she takes hold baggage she will have to pay an extra £10. If she doesn't do this there is a probability of 0.4 that the airline will consider the bag to be oversize. If they do she will have to pay a surcharge of £30.

(a) What should Jem do?
(b) If the surcharge is £50 what should she do?
(c) If the surcharge is £50 and the extra cost for hold baggage is £25 what should she do?

☆★★ More testing questions

11.5 Ackney Windows plc makes and installs conservatories for £8000. The sales per week for the 50 weeks they were open for business last year were distributed as follows:

Weekly sales	0	1	2	3	4
Number of weeks	5	22	14	6	3

What is their expected sales revenue per week?

11.6 Ivana Loyer claims she has been unfairly dismissed by her employers. She consults the law firm of Zackon and Vorovat, who agree to take up her case. They advise her that if she wins her case she can expect compensation of £15,000, but if she loses she will receive nothing. They estimate that their fee will be £1500, which she will have to pay whether she wins or loses. Under the rules of the relevant tribunal she cannot be asked to pay her employer's costs. As an alternative they offer her a 'no win no fee' deal under which she pays no fee but if she wins her case Zackon and Vorovat take one-third of the compensation she receives. She could decide against bringing the case, which would incur no cost and result in no compensation. Advise Ivana what to do:

(a) using the maximax decision rule
(b) using the maximin decision rule
(c) using the minimax regret decision rule
(d) using the equal likelihood decision rule

11.7 V. Nimania plc builds water treatment facilities throughout the world. One contract it has concerns an installation in an area prone to outbreaks of a dangerous disease. The company has to decide whether or not to vaccinate the employees who will be working there. Vaccination will cost £200,000, which will be deducted from the profit it makes from the venture. The company expects a profit of £1.2m from the contract but if there is an outbreak of the disease and the workforce has not been vaccinated, delays will result in the profit being reduced to £0.4m. If the workforce has been vaccinated and there is an outbreak of the disease, the work will progress as planned but disruption to infrastructure will result in their profit being reduced by £0.2m. The public health authorities estimate the probability of an outbreak to be 50%. Advise the company using a decision tree.

(a) Construct a decision tree to portray the situation.
(b) Calculate the EMV of vaccinating and not vaccinating. What do these figures suggest the company should do?
(c) If the probability of an outbreak is revised downwards to 20% should the company change their decision?

11.8 Cloppock Cotton is an agricultural collective in a central Asian republic. Their operations have been reliant on a government subsidy paid out to cotton farmers to support the production since cotton is a key export commodity. There are rumours that the government will reduce the subsidy for the next crop. The Cloppock farmers have to decide whether to increase or decrease the number of hectares they farm, or to keep it the same. The pay-offs (in Soom, the national currency) for these strategies with the same subsidy and with the reduced subsidy are:

Area	Same subsidy	Reduced subsidy
Increased	80,000	− 40,000
The same	40,000	10,000
Decreased	20,000	16,000

(a) Illustrate the situation with a decision tree.
(b) Which strategy should the farmers take if the probability of the subsidy being reduced is
(i) 0.4; (ii) 0.6; (iii) 0.8?

★★★ Challenging questions

11.9 A freight company has to transport a container by road from Amsterdam to Tabriz. There are two routes that are viable. Route A is longer but less dangerous than Route B. If the container reaches its destination successfully the company will receive a fee of €15,000. Fuel and other direct costs incurred amount to €6000 on Route A and €4500 on Route B. The probability that the container is hijacked on Route A is put at 0.2; on Route B it is estimated to be 0.5. If the container is hijacked the company will receive no fee but anticipates it will only have to meet two-thirds of the fuel and other direct costs. The company will not be insuring the container because of the prohibitive cost of cargo insurance for such a journey.

(a) Draw a decision tree to represent the situation the company faces.
(b) Calculate the EMV for each route and use these to advise the company which route it should take.
(c) There are reports of armed incursions across a border at a critical point on Route A. As a result, the probability of the container being hijacked on Route A must be revised to 0.4. Explain what effect, if any, this has on the advice you gave in your answer to (b).

11.10 Kholodny plc installs ventilation systems. At present its order book is rather thin and it has no work for the forthcoming period. It has been offered two contracts abroad, of which it can take only one. The first contract is to install a ventilation system in the Presidential Palace of the republic of Sloochai. The contract should earn the company a profit of £8m but the country is unstable and there is a 70% probability that the president will be overthrown before the work is finished. If the president is overthrown his opponents are not expected to pay for the work and the company would face a loss of £0.5m.The second contract is to install a ventilation system in an administration building in the republic of Parooka. The company can expect a profit of £6m from this contract unless the local currency is devalued during the completion of the project in which case the profit will fall to £3m. Financial experts put the probability of devaluation at 0.5.

(a) Construct a decision tree to portray the situation the company faces.
(b) Calculate the EMV for each project and use them to suggest which project the company should take.
(c) The President of Sloochai gives a key opponent a prominent post in his government. As a result the probability of the president being overthrown is revised to 40%. Does this new information alter the advice you gave in your answer to (b) and if so why?

11.11 Kenny Videnia, a film producer, has to decide whether to bid for the film rights of a modestly successful novel. He believes that there is a 0.9 chance that he will be successful. If the bid is unsuccessful he will have to meet legal and administrative costs of $0.5m. If he is successful he has to decide whether to engage a big star for the main role. If he hires a big star the probability that the movie will be successful and make a profit of $50m is 0.3 and the chance that it fails and makes a loss of $20m is 0.7. If he doesn't hire a big star there is a 0.2 chance of the film making a profit of $30m and a 0.8 chance that it makes a loss of $10m.

(a) Suggest what Kenny should do using a decision tree.
(b) How sensitive is your advice to changes in the probability of the film making a profit if Kenny does not hire a big star?

11.12 Scientists at the Medicament Drug Company have synthesised a new drug which they believe will be an effective treatment for stress and anxiety. The company must decide whether to proceed with the commercial development of the new drug or not. If it decides not to develop it, no further costs will be incurred. If it decides to develop it, it has to submit it for clinical testing before it can be sold. The probability that it will pass the tests is estimated to be 0.75. If it fails the tests the costs incurred will be £2m. If it passes the test the company has to decide whether to set up a small-scale or a large-scale production facility. The money it will make from the drug depends on whether it is approved for National Health Service use. If it is approved and it has set up large-scale production it will make a profit of £60m, compared with the £20m it will make if it has only small-scale production. If the drug is not approved it will make a loss of £40m if it has large-scale production and a profit of £5m if it has small-scale production. The probability of getting approval for NHS use is 0.4.

(a) Advise the company using a decision tree.
(b) How sensitive is the choice of large- or small-scale production to a change in the probability of the drug being approved for NHS use?

11.13 Lord Du Raq owns a crumbling castle in Scotland. The revenue from visitors is no longer sufficient to cover the upkeep of the property and he must decide what to do. A national heritage organisation has offered to buy the property for £8m. Alternatively he could have a theme park constructed in the grounds. If this proves to be a success he will make a profit of £25m, but if it is not he will incur a loss of £5m. He estimates that the chance of success in the venture will be 0.6. He could start building the theme park right away, but a tourist authority contact has suggested that before he decides whether or not to build the park he should hire Baz Umney, an expert on leisure developments, to assess the prospects of the venture. Baz has a distinguished record, accurately predicting the success of similar ventures 70% of the time and accurately predicting the failure 80% of the time. Create a decision tree to model the situation Lord Du Raq faces and, using Bayes' rule, suggest what he should do.

THE DEBRIEF

Key things to remember from this chapter

→ Expectation involves multiplying the results of outcomes by the probabilities that they occur.

→ An expected monetary value (EMV) is expectation involving monetary results of outcomes.

→ Decision-making involves choosing between different strategies. If there is more than one possible outcome of a strategy decision analysis can be useful.

→ If probabilities cannot be assigned to the outcomes it is a situation of uncertainty and decision rules can be used to select the best strategy.

→ The equal likelihood decision rule assumes each outcome has the same probability and is based on EMVs calculated using these probabilities.

→ If probabilities can be assigned to the outcomes it is a situation of risk and decision trees can be used to select the best strategy.

→ Decision trees are used to portray sequences of strategies and related outcomes. The preferred strategy is the one with the best EMV.

References

Beattie, D.W. (1969) 'Marketing a new product', *Operational Research Quarterly*, 20, pp. 429–35. Also in S. French (ed.)(1989) *Readings in Decision Analysis*, London: Chapman and Hall, pp. 64–70.

Brown, R.V., Kahr, A.S. and Peterson, C.R. (1974) *Decision Analysis for the Manager*, New York: Holt Rinehart and Winston.

Coopersmith, E., Dean, G., McVean, J. and Storaune, E. (2000) 'Making decisions in the oil and gas industry', *Oilfield Review*, Winter 2000/2001 pp. 2–9.

Jennings, D.R. and Wattam, S. (1998) *Decision Making: An Integrated Approach* (2nd edn), London: Pitman Publishing.

Phillips, L.D. (1982) 'Requisite decision modelling: a case study', *Journal of the Operational Research Society*, 33, pp. 303–11. Also in S. French (ed.) (1989), *Readings in Decision Analysis*, London: Chapman and Hall, pp. 110–22.

CHAPTER 12

Accidents and incidence – discrete probability distributions and simulation

CHAPTER OBJECTIVES

This chapter will help you to:

→ Understand discrete probability distributions

→ Model business processes with the binomial distribution

→ Model business processes with the Poisson distribution

→ Simulate simple random business processes

THE BARE BONES

What you will find in this chapter . . .

- Working out probabilities for simple probability distributions
- Using the binomial distribution to find probabilities of the number of successes in a given number of trials
- Applying the Poisson distribution to find probabilities of numbers of random events occurring over a period of time
- Using probability distributions and random numbers to simulate random processes

. . . and on the supporting website (www.pearsoned.co.uk/buglear)

- How to use EXCEL, Minitab and SPSS to produce probabilities of the binomial and Poisson distributions
- Fully worked solutions to the review questions
- More review questions

Business use of discrete probability distributions and simulation

◆ Risk is very important in the insurance industry. The analysis of it involves discrete probability distributions. The binomial distribution can be used to model claims that policy-holders make, since if there are a fixed number of policy-holders ('trials') then any one of them can either not make a claim ('success', from the insurer's point of view) or make a claim ('failure'). However, since the insurer is likely to be interested in the number of claims in a given period the Poisson distribution is of greater importance. Daykin, Pentikäinen and Pesonen (1994) produced an authoritative work in this field.

◆ Tippett (1935) applied statistical techniques in his work on the manufacture of cotton. The quality of yarn varied as a result of a number of factors, including changing humidity and differences in the tension of the yarn during the production process. He studied yarn production in Lancashire mills that spun American and Egyptian cotton in order to analyse quality variation. In part of his work he applied the Poisson distribution to the incidence of faults in cloth arising from deficiencies in cotton yarn.

◆ The large increase in UK demand for lager in the 1980s presented problems for brewers in terms of building new capacity or switching capacity from the production of ale, a product that was experiencing declining demand. Mackenzie (1988) describes how simulation was used to address this dilemma at the Edinburgh brewing complex of Scottish and Newcastle Breweries. The company was looking at a variety of proposals for expanding the tank capacity for the fermentation and maturation of its lager products. The simulation had to take into account factors that included the number of different products made at the plant, variation in the processing time, maintenance breaks and the finite number of pipe routes through the plant. The problem was made more complex by other factors, including the introduction of new filtration facilities, longer processing times to enhance product quality and a new packaging facility that required different supply arrangements. The results of the analysis enabled the company to meet demand even during a period when lager production at another plant suffered a short-term halt.

◆ Gorman (1988) explains how simulation was used to resolve the design of a production unit for the engineering firm Mather and Platt. The unit was to consist of a suite of new technology machines, including a laser cutter and robots, for the production of parts of electric motors. The simulation was used to model two possible scenarios, one based on the existing arrangements and the other with the new equipment. The aim was to investigate the efficiency of the systems and to identify potential bottlenecks. Running simulations of various scenarios enabled the company to find the best way to set up the unit and the optimal level of staffing support for it.

12.1 **Introduction**

In this chapter we bring together two key concepts from earlier chapters. The first of these is the idea of a frequency distribution, which shows the frequency or regularity with which the values of a variable occur, in other words how they are distributed across their range. The second key concept is that of probability, which we considered in Chapter 10. Here we will be looking at *probability distributions* which portray not the frequency with which values of a distribution actually occur but the probability with which we predict they will occur.

Probability distributions are very important tools for modelling or representing processes that occur at random, such as customers visiting a website or accidents on a building site. These are examples of *discrete random variables* as they vary in a random fashion and can have only certain values, whole numbers in both cases; we cannot conceive of half a customer visiting a website or 0.3 of an accident happening. We use *discrete probability distributions* to model these sorts of variables.

In studying probability distributions we will look at how they can be derived and how we can *model* or represent the chances of different combinations of outcomes using the same sort of approach as we use to arrange data into frequency distributions. Following that we will examine two standard discrete probability distributions, the binomial and the Poisson. Lastly we will look at how random numbers and discrete probability distributions can be used to simulate the operation of random business processes.

12.2 Simple probability distributions

In section 4.5.2 we considered how data could be presented in a frequency distribution. To do this we defined categories or classes and counted how many observations were in each one. These were the class frequencies. The table of the class frequencies showed how the observations were distributed across the range of the data, which is why it is called a frequency distribution.

A *probability distribution* is very like a frequency distribution. It has a set of categories, but rather than classes of values there are types of outcomes. The other key difference is that instead of a frequency for each category there is a probability of the outcome or outcomes occurring. In a similar way as a frequency distribution shows how often each type of value occurs, a probability distribution shows us how likely each type of outcome is to occur.

In section 5.3.1 we saw how histograms present a frequency distribution. We can use the same type of diagram to present a probability distribution.

In Chapter 6 we used the mean and the standard deviation to summarise distributions of observations. In the same way we use the mean and the standard deviation to summarise distributions of probabilities.

A frequency distribution is based on a set of data. A probability distribution is based on a set of compound outcomes but to start with we need the simple probabilities of the individual outcomes that constitute the combinations of outcomes.

EXAMPLE 12.1

Imported Loobov condoms are sold in packets of three. Following customer complaints the importer commissioned product testing which showed that due to a randomly occurring manufacturing fault 10% of the condoms tear in use. What are the chances that a packet of three includes zero, one, two and three defective condoms?

Solution

The probability that a condom is defective (D) is 0.1 and the probability it is good (G) is 0.9.

The probability that a packet of three contains no defectives is the probability that a sequence of three good condoms were put in the packet.

$$P(GGG) = 0.9 * 0.9 * 0.9 = 0.729$$

The probability that a packet contains one defective is a little more complicated because we have to take into account the fact that the defective one could be the first or the second or the third condom to be put in the packet, so

$$P(1 \text{ Defective}) = P(DGG \text{ or } GDG \text{ or } GGD)$$

Because these three sequences are mutually exclusive, according to the addition rule of probability (you may like to refer back to section 10.4.1):

$$P(1 \text{ Defective}) = P(DGG) + P(GDG) + P(GGD)$$

The probability that the first of these sequences occurs is:

$$P(DGG) = 0.1 * 0.9 * 0.9 = 0.081$$

The probability of the second: $P(GDG) = 0.9 * 0.1 * 0.9 = 0.081$

It is no accident that the probabilities of these sequences are the same. Although the exact sequence is different the elements that make up both are the same. To work out the compound probabilities that they occur we use the same simple probabilities but in a different order, and the order does not affect the result when we multiply them together. If you work out $P(GGD)$ you should find that it also is 0.081.

The probability of getting one defective is therefore:

$$P(1\ \text{Defective}) = 0.081 + 0.081 + 0.081 = 3 * 0.081 = 0.243$$

We find the same sort of thing when we work out the probability that there are two defectives in a packet.

$$P(2\ \text{Defectives}) = P(DDG\ \text{or}\ DGD\ \text{or}\ GDD)$$

$$P(DDG) = 0.1 * 0.1 * 0.9 = 0.009$$

$$P(DGD) = 0.1 * 0.9 * 0.1 = 0.009$$

$$P(GDD) = 0.9 * 0.1 * 0.1 = 0.009$$

$$\text{So}\ P(2\ \text{Defectives}) = 3 * 0.009 = 0.027$$

$$\text{Finally}\ P(3\ \text{Defectives}) = 0.1 * 0.1 * 0.1 = 0.001$$

We can consolidate these results in the following probability distribution.

Number of defectives (x)	$P(x)$
0	0.729
1	0.243
2	0.027
3	0.001
	1.000

Note that the sum of these probabilities is 1 because they are mutually exclusive (we cannot have both one defective and two defectives in a single packet of three) and collectively exhaustive (there can be only none, one, two or three defectives in a packet of three).

The probability distribution in Example 12.1 shows the number of defectives as a variable, X, with individual values x. X is a *discrete random variable*. The reason it is discrete is that it can only have a finite number of values: 0, 1, 2 or 3. The reason it is random is that the values of X arise from a random process.

$P(x)$ represents the probability that X takes a specific value, x. For instance, we can represent the probability that the number of defectives is 1, as:

$$P(X = 1) = 0.243$$

Figure 12.1 shows the probability distribution from Example 12.1 in graphical form.

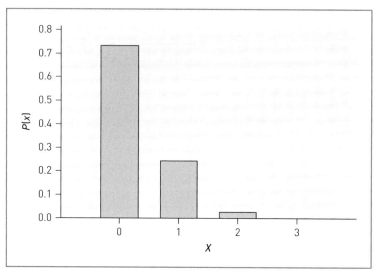

Figure 12.1 The probability distribution of *X*, the number of defectives

We can use summary measures to represent the probability distribution in Example 12.1 in the same way as we use them to represent frequency distributions. The only difference in that instead of using the frequencies of observations to work out the summary measures we weight each value of *X* using the probability that it occurs. The mean of a probability distribution is the sum of each value of *x* multiplied by its probability:

$$\mu = \sum xP(x)$$

We have used the Greek equivalent of m, μ, 'mu', to represent the mean in this case because the mean of a probability distribution is a population mean; the distribution consists of the probabilities of every possible value of the variable.

Having worked out the mean we can determine the variance and standard deviation. The variance, σ^2, is the sum of the squares of the *x* values multiplied by their corresponding probabilities minus the square of the mean:

$$\sigma^2 = \sum x^2 P(x) - \mu^2$$

The square root of the variance is the standard deviation, σ. Once again we use a Greek letter for the variance and the standard deviation because they are population measures.

EXAMPLE 12.2

Work out the mean and the standard deviation for the probability distribution in Example 12.1.

Solution

x	*P(x)*	*x P(x)*	x^2	$x^2 P(x)$
0	0.729	0.000	0	0.000
1	0.243	0.243	1	0.243
2	0.027	0.054	4	0.108
3	0.001	0.003	9	0.009
		0.300		0.360

The mean, μ, is the *x P(x)* column total, 0.300.

The variance, σ^2, is the $x^2 P(x)$ column total, 0.360, minus the mean squared, μ^2:

$$\sigma^2 = 0.360 - 0.300^2 = 0.360 - 0.090 = 0.270$$

The standard deviation, $\sigma = \sqrt{\sigma^2} = \sqrt{0.270} = 0.520$

The mean of a probability distribution is also called the *expected value* of the distribution. This is because it tells us what, on average, the values of the variable are likely, or *expected,* to be.

Sometimes we need to find the probability of a discrete random variable taking a specific value or a lower one. This is a *cumulative* probability; to get it we have to add up or *accumulate* other probabilities. We can work out cumulative probabilities from a probability distribution.

EXAMPLE 12.3

Compile cumulative probabilities using the probability distribution in Example 12.1.

Solution

What if we need the probability that X, the number of defectives, is either two or less than two?

We can express this as the probability of X being less than or equal to two, $P(X \leq 2)$. ('$\leq$' means 'less than or equal to'; X is at the small end of the '$\leq$', and 2 is at the large end, so X is smaller than 2.)

To get cumulative probabilities for each x value we start with the probability of X having that value then add the probability that X is less than x. The resulting cumulative probabilities are in the column on the right in the following table:

Number of defectives (x)	$P(x)$	$P(X \leq x)$
0	0.729	0.729
1	0.243	0.972
2	0.027	0.999
3	0.001	1.000

The cumulative probability of X being zero or less, $P(X \leq 0)$, is simply the probability that X is zero, 0.729, because X cannot be less than zero so there is nothing to add to 0.729.

The second cumulative probability is the probability of X being 1 or less, $P(X \leq 1)$. This is the probability of X being 1, 0.243, plus the probability of X being less than 1, i.e. the probability that X is zero, 0.729. The sum of these two probabilities is $P(X \leq 1)$, 0.972.

The third cumulative probability is the probability of X being 2 or less, $P(X \leq 2)$. For this we add the probability of X being 2, 0.027, to the probability of X being less than 2, or to put it another way the probability that X is 1 or less, $P(X \leq 1)$. This is the last cumulative probability we worked out, 0.972. Adding this to $P(X = 2)$, 0.027, we get 0.999.

The fourth and final cumulative probability of the set is the probability of X being 3 or less, $P(X \leq 3)$. X simply can't be more than 3 as there are only three condoms in a packet, so we can be certain X is 3 or less. This means the cumulative probability, $P(X \leq 3)$ must be 1, the probability that represents certainty. We can check by adding the probability of X being 3, 0.001, to the cumulative probability of X being less than 3, i.e. the probability that it is 2 or less, $P(X \leq 2)$ which was 0.999.

Cumulative probabilities like those in Example 12.3 tell us the probability of a variable taking a specific value or a smaller one, but suppose we want the probability of a variable being larger than a specific value?

We can use the addition rule of probability to find these sorts of probability from cumulative probabilities. For example, suppose we need the probability of a variable, X, being more than 2. To get this we take the probability of X being 2 or less from 1.

$$P(X > 2) = 1 - P(X \leq 2)$$

This works because the two outcomes, that X is more than 2 and that X is less than or equal to 2, are mutually exclusive and collectively exhaustive. Only one of them can occur and one of them must occur. There is simply no other possibility.

In $P(X > 2)$, the probability of X being more than 2, the symbol '>' means 'greater than'. In this case it is the 2 that is at the small end of $>$ and X at the large end so X is bigger than 2.

In Example 12.1 the situation was relatively simple as there were only three condoms per packet. Even so the procedure we used to find the probabilities was quite laborious. If there were six condoms per pack rather than just three this approach would be more arduous. Establishing the three different ways of there being two defectives in a packet of three was fairly tricky but checking how many different ways there are of getting two defectives in a packet of six would be far worse.

Luckily there is a way of exploring more complex probability distributions that does not depend on such onerous mental exertions. This is to use a type of probability distribution called the *binomial* distribution.

At this point you may find it useful to try **Review question 12.1** at the end of the chapter.

12.3 The binomial distribution

The binomial distribution was developed by the Swiss mathematician James Bernoulli (1654–1705) and has many practical applications. It is especially useful as it enables us to not only answer a particular question but also investigate the repercussions of changing the situation without actually doing so.

The binomial distribution is used to solve problems that have a *binomial structure*. These arise in situations when there is a set number of 'experiments', or 'trials', that recur. Every trial has two mutually exclusive and collectively exhaustive outcomes, which is reflected by the *bi* part of the word binomial. Conventionally one outcome is referred to as 'success' and the other as 'failure'.

To apply the binomial distribution we need to have the probability of each outcome and it must stay the same for each trial. To put it another way, the trial results have to be independent of one another.

The use of 'experiment' and 'trial' in describing binomial situations came about because the binomial distribution was, and continues to be, widely used in science. Despite being used extensively in many other fields, these scientific expressions have stuck.

The process in Example 12.1 has a binomial structure. Taking each of the three condoms out of a packet is effectively a series of three trials. In every trial, that is, each time a condom is taken out of a packet, there must be one of the only two possible outcomes: it is either defective or it is not.

Generally we use tables such as Table 2 of Appendix 1 to use the binomial distribution. These have been created with an equation known as the binomial equation. Almost certainly you won't have to remember it, and seldom should you need to use it, but we will consider it here just to illustrate how it works.

We'll use X to denote the number of 'successes' in a specific number of trials, n. X is what is referred to as a binomial random variable and takes individual values, x. We'll use p to represent the probability of success in a trial.

The binomial equation states that the probability of x successes in n trials is:

$$P(X = x) = \frac{n!}{x!(n - x!)} * p(1 - p)^{n-x}$$

In this expression there are three exclamation marks. In mathematics an exclamation mark denotes a *factorial*. This is a number which is multiplied by one less than itself then multiplied by two less than itself and so on until we end up multiplying by 1. For example, five factorial, 5!, is five times four times three times two times one, i.e. 5 * 4 * 3 * 2 * 1, which is 120.

EXAMPLE 12.4

Find the first two probabilities in the probability distribution in Example 12.1 using the binomial equation.

Solution

Start with the number of trials to insert in the binomial equation. Taking three condoms out of a packet means conducting three 'trials', so $n = 3$.

X is the number of defectives in a packet of three. We need to find the probabilities that X is 0 and the probability that X is 1; these are the x values.

10% of all of the condoms are defective so if we define 'success' as a defective condom, then p, the probability of 'success' in any one trial, in other words getting a defective condom, is 0.1.

Next we can put these numbers into the binomial equation. The probability that there are no defectives in a packet of three, in other words that $X = 0$, is:

$$P(X = 0) = \frac{3!}{0!(3 - 0)!} * 0.1^0 (1 - 0.1)^{3-0}$$

We can tidy this up considerably. A number raised to the power zero is 1 so $0.1^0 = 1$. Zero factorial, 0!, is 1 as well. We can also do the subtractions.

$$P(X = 0) = \frac{3!}{1(3)!} * 1(0.9)^3$$

$$= \frac{3 * 2 * 1}{3 * 2 * 1} * (0.9 * 0.9 * 0.9)$$

$$= 1 * 0.729 = 0.729$$

If you check in Example 12.1, you will see that this is exactly the same as the first figure in the probability distribution. The figure beneath it, 0.243, is the probability of one defective in a packet of three, in other words that $X = 1$. We can use the binomial equation to get this as well:

$$P(X = 1) = \frac{3!}{1!(3 - 1)!} * 0.1^1 (1 - 0.1)^{3-1}$$

$$= \frac{3 * 2 * 1}{1(2!)} * 0.1(0.9)^2$$

$$= \frac{6}{1(2 * 1)} * 0.1(0.81) = 3 * 0.081 = 0.243$$

Look carefully at this expression. You can see that the first part of it, which involves the factorials, is there to reflect the number of ways there are of getting a packet with one defective, 3(DGG, GDG and GGD). In the earlier expression, for $P(X = 0)$, the first part of the expression came to 1, since there is only one way of getting a packet with no defectives (GGG).

Try using the binomial equation to work out $P(X = 2)$ and $P(X = 3)$.

Binomial distribution tables mean we can avoid extensive calculations to get the figures we need for problems like the one in Example 12.1. In fact we can use them to analyse much more complex problems such as the one in Example 12.5.

EXAMPLE 12.5

Vodalas Marine salvages sunken vessels and equipment. On one project it sends 10 divers down to an area of ocean floor inhabited by the poisonous Yadovity fish. Unless an antidote is taken quickly the victim will become paralysed. The probability of a diver getting bitten is estimated to be 0.1.

The antidote is in short supply and the project leader has been able to acquire only two doses. What is the probability that there will not be enough doses of antidote?

Solution

There is a binomial structure to this problem. We'll use X to represent the number of divers who are bitten. The dive that each diver takes is a 'trial' that can result in 'success', being bitten, or 'failure', not being bitten. The probability of 'success', p, is in this case the probability that a diver is bitten, 0.1. There are 10 divers so the number of trials, n, is 10.

The probability distribution for this problem is the binomial distribution with $n = 10$ and $p = 0.1$.

Table 2 in Appendix 1 has the following information about the distribution:

For 10 trials $(n = 10); p = 0.1$

	$P(x)$	$P(X \leq x)$
$x = 0$	0.349	0.349
$x = 1$	0.387	0.736
$x = 2$	0.194	0.930
$x = 3$	0.057	0.987
$x = 4$	0.011	0.998
$x = 5$	0.001	1.000
$x = 6$	0.000	1.000
$x = 7$	0.000	1.000
$x = 8$	0.000	1.000
$x = 9$	0.000	1.000
$x = 10$	0.000	1.000

The $P(x)$ column lists the probabilities that a particular number of 'successes', x, occurs. For instance the probability of 2 'successes' in 10 trials, $P(2)$, is 0.194. The column headed $P(X \leq x)$ lists the probability of x or fewer 'successes', for example the probability of 2 or fewer 'successes', $P(X \leq 2)$, is 0.930.

If only one or two divers are bitten there are enough antidotes to treat them. Only if three or more divers are bitten will there be insufficient doses of antidote. We need the probability of more than two divers being bitten, which is the probability that X is greater than 2, $P(X > 2)$.

One way of getting this is to add up all the probabilities in the $P(x)$ column except the first three; the probability that X is zero, $P(0)$, the probability that X is 1, $P(1)$ and $P(2)$. An easier way is to take the probability of 2 or fewer, $P(X \leq 2)$, away from 1:

$$P(X > 1) = 1 - P(X \leq 2) = 1 - 0.930 = 0.070 \text{ or } 7.0\%$$

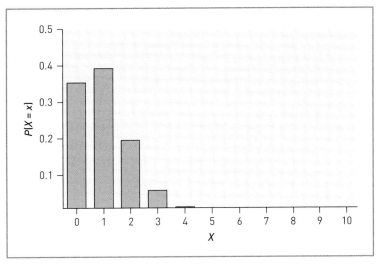

Figure 12.2 The binomial distribution for $n = 10$ and $p = 0.1$

Figure 12.2 shows the binomial distribution from Example 12.5 graphically.

The block for 0 in Figure 12.2 represents the probability of X being 0, $P(0)$, which is 0.349. All the other blocks together represent the probability of X being more than 0, $P(X > 0)$, which is 0.651.

SELF-ASSEMBLY GUIDE

Using the binomial distribution

◆ You will need to have the number of trials, n, and the probability of success in any one trial, p. With these you can find probabilities of different numbers of successes, X.

◆ You will also need to clarify precisely what type of probability you are looking for. This might be the probability of a specific number of successes, x, which is $P(x)$, or the probability that there are x or fewer successes, $P(X \leq x)$, or the probability that there are more than x successes, $P(X > x)$.

◆ Table 2 in Appendix 1 will give you $P(x)$ and $P(X \leq x)$ directly. If you need $P(X > x)$ then take $P(X \leq x)$ away from one, e.g. for $P(X > 2)$ take $P(X \leq x)$ away from 1.

◆ Table 2 in Appendix 1 provides probabilities for the binomial distribution for some combinations of n and p. If the combination you need to apply is not in Table 2 use the probability distributions tools of a computer package such as Excel, Minitab or SPSS. Details of how to use them are available on the website that supports this book, **www.pearsoned.co.uk/buglear**.

The mean of a binomial distribution, μ, is the number of trials, n, times the probability of success, p:

$$\mu = n * p$$

The variance, σ^2, is the number of trials times the probability of success times 1 minus the probability of success:

$$\sigma^2 = n * p * (1 - p)$$

The standard deviation, σ, is the square root of the variance.

EXAMPLE
12.6

Work out the mean, variance and standard deviation of the binomial distribution in Example 12.5.

Solution

The number of trials, n, is 10 and the probability of success, p, is 0.1, so the mean number of bitten divers is:

$$\mu = n * p = 10 * 0.1 = 1.0$$

The variance, $\sigma^2 = n * p(1 - p) = 10 * 0.1(1 - 0.1) = 1.0 * 0.9 = 0.9$

The standard deviation, $\sigma = \sqrt{\sigma^2} = \sqrt{0.9} = 0.949$

The binomial distribution is known as a *discrete probability distribution* because it demonstrates the variation of certain types of discrete random variables, binomial variables. Such variables have to do with the number of times specific outcomes happen over a certain number of trials.

But suppose we want to investigate how many times an outcome happens during a period of time? For this we use another type of discrete probability distribution, the *Poisson* distribution.

At this point you may find it useful to try **Review questions 12.2, 12.5 and 12.6** at the end of the chapter.

12.4 The Poisson distribution

Some business problems concern incidents that are inherently unpredictable. Typically they are incidents that occur over a period of time, such as the number of goals in a football match. It could also be how many features there are within an area, like the number of potholes in a road.

The Poisson distribution models the behaviour of variables like the number of goals per game or the number of potholes in a given area of road. We can use it to establish the probability of a certain number of incidents arising over a specific period or area. The distribution is named after the French mathematician Simeon Poisson (1781–1840), who outlined the idea in 1837, but the credit for demonstrating its usefulness belongs to the Russian statistician Vladislav Bortkiewicz (1868–1931), who applied it to a variety of situations including famously the incidence of deaths by horse kicks amongst soldiers of the Prussian army.

The Poisson distribution is fairly straightforward to use, indeed you will probably find it easier to use than the binomial distribution. This is because we don't need to know as much about the situation. To use the binomial distribution we have to know the number of trials and the probability of success in each trial. These are the two defining features, or *parameters*, of the binomial distribution. The Poisson distribution has only one parameter, the mean.

As long as we know the mean of the variable we want to analyse we can get the probabilities of the Poisson distribution from Table 3 in Appendix 1.

EXAMPLE
12.7

Fasterdale Fisheries catch salmon from a small boat off the west coast of Scotland. At the end of each day during the fishing season they put the catch in their cold storage area and it is sent to the wholesaler the following day. The storage area has enough capacity to keep three fish. If the mean number of fish they catch per day is two, what is the probability they will not have enough storage capacity for their catch?

Solution   The variable, X, is the number of salmon caught in a day. Since this is discrete, in other words they only catch whole fish, we can use the Poisson distribution to analyse the situation. The mean of X is 2.

The storage area can accommodate three fish, so the probability that there are more fish than they can store is the probability of X being more than 3, $P(X > 3)$.

We need to use the Poisson distribution with a mean of 2. Table 3 in Appendix 1 has the following figures for this distribution:

$\mu = 2.0$	$P(x)$	$P(X \le x)$
$x = 0$	0.135	0.135
$x = 1$	0.271	0.406
$x = 2$	0.271	0.677
$x = 3$	0.180	0.857
$x = 4$	0.090	0.947
$x = 5$	0.036	0.983
$x = 6$	0.012	0.995
$x = 7$	0.003	0.999
$x = 8$	0.001	1.000

The column below $P(x)$ contains the probabilities of a specific number of incidents, x, happening. From this column we can establish, for instance that the probability of 0 incidents, $P(0)$, is 0.135. The column below $P(X \le x)$ contains the probabilities that x or fewer incidents happen, for example the probability of 2 or fewer incidents, $P(X \le 2)$, is 0.677.

The probability we need, the probability of catching more than 3 fish, $P(X > 3)$, is not listed in the table but we can get it by taking the probability that X is 3 or less, $P(X \le 3)$, which is the probability of catching up to 3 fish, from 1:

$$P(X > 3) = 1 - P(X \le 3) = 1 - 0.857 = 0.143 \text{ or } 14.3\%$$

We can find the Poisson probabilities in Example 12.7 without a table by using the formula for the distribution. You don't need to remember it, and will seldom if ever need to use it, but if we look at how the probabilities are produced it may assist your understanding of the distribution.

The probability of the number of incidents, X, having a specific value, x, is:

$$P(X = x) = \frac{e^{-\mu} * \mu^x}{x!}$$

In this expression e is a mathematical constant called Euler's number. This is 2.7183 to 4 decimal places, so we insert this into the expression:

$$P(X) = x = \frac{2.7183^{-\mu!} * \mu^x}{x!}$$

The other symbols are more familiar; μ is the mean of the distribution and x is the value of X for which we want a probability. The mean in Example 12.7 is 2, so the probability of catching no fish, $P(X = 0)$ is:

$$P(X = 0) = \frac{2.7183^{-\mu} * \mu^0}{0!} = \frac{2.7183^{-2} * 2^0}{1}$$

Any number raised to the power zero is 1, so μ to the power zero is 1, so,

$$P(X = 0) = \frac{2.7183^{-2} * 2^0}{1} = \frac{2.7183^{-2} * 1}{1}$$

The 2.7183^{-2} in this expression is $1/2.7183^2$ because a number raised to a negative power is the reciprocal of the number raised to the positive power so, to 3 decimal places,

$$P(X = 0) = \frac{1}{2.7183^2} = 0.135$$

If you are not sure about the arithmetic we have used here you may find it helpful to refer back to section 1.4.3.

The extract from Table 3 in Example 12.7 has the same value for $P(0)$. The figure under $P(0)$, 0.135, is the probability that X is 1, $P(1)$, 0.271. We can also calculate this.

$$P(X = 1) = \frac{2.7183^{-\mu} * \mu^1}{1!} = \frac{2.7183^{-2} * 2}{1}$$

$$= \frac{2}{2.7183^2} = 0.271$$

Figure 12.3 shows the shape of the Poisson distribution with a mean of 2 that we used in Example 12.7.

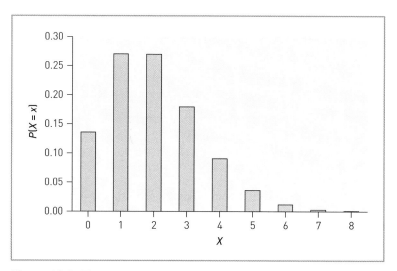

Figure 12.3 The Poisson distribution with a mean of 2

At this point you may find it useful to try **Review questions 12.3, 12.4 and 12.7** at the end of the chapter.

12.5 Simulating business processes

Most businesses conduct operations that involve random variables; the numbers of customers booking a vehicle service at a garage, the number of products damaged in transit, the number of workers off sick etc. The managers of these businesses can use probability distributions to represent and analyse these variables. They can take this approach a stage further and use the probability distributions that best represent the random processes in their operations to *simulate* the effects of the variation on those operations.

Simulation is particularly useful where a major investment such as a garage building another service bay is under consideration. It is possible to simulate the operations of the vehicle servicing operation with another service bay so that the benefits of building the extra bay in terms of increased customer satisfaction and higher turnover can be explored before the resources are committed to the investment.

There are two stages in simulating a business process; the first is setting up the structure or framework of the process, the second is using random numbers to simulate the operation of the process. The first stage involves identifying the possible outcomes of the process, finding the probabilities for these outcomes and then allocating bands of random numbers to each of the outcomes in keeping with their probabilities. In making such allocations we are saying that whenever a random number used in the simulation falls within the allocation for a certain outcome, for the purposes of the simulation that outcome is deemed to have occurred.

**EXAMPLE
12.8**

The Munich company AT-Dalenni Travel organises adventure holidays for serious travellers. It runs 'Explorer' trips to the Tien Shan mountain range in Central Asia. Each trip has 10 places and it runs 12 trips a year. The business is not seasonal, as customers regard the experience as the trip of a lifetime and demand is steady. The number of customers wanting to purchase a place on a trip varies according to the following probability distribution:

Number of customers	Probability
8	0.15
9	0.25
10	0.20
11	0.20
12	0.20

Use this probability distribution to set up random number allocations to simulate the operation.

Solution

The probabilities in these distributions are specified to two places of decimals so we need to show how the range of two-digit random numbers from 00 to 99 should be allocated to the different outcomes. It is easier to do this if we list the cumulative probabilities for the distribution:

Number of customers	Probability	Cumulative probability	Random number allocation
8	0.15	0.15	00–14
9	0.25	0.40	15–39
10	0.20	0.60	40–59
11	0.20	0.80	60–79
12	0.20	1.00	80–99

Notice how the random number allocations match the probabilities; we allocate one of the hundred possible two-digit random variables for every one-hundredth (0.01) measure of probability. The probability of eight customers is 0.15 or 15 hundredths so the random number allocation is 15 random numbers, 00 to 14 inclusive. The probability of nine customers is 0.25 or 25 hundredths so the allocation is 25 random numbers, 15 to 39 inclusive, and so on.

In Example 12.8 we have set up the simulation, but what we actually need to run it are random numbers. We could generate some random numbers using a truly random process such as a lottery machine or a roulette wheel. Since we are unlikely to have such equipment to hand it is easier to use tables of them such as Table 4 in Appendix 1, which are generated using computer software.

EXAMPLE 12.9

Use the following random numbers to simulate the numbers of customers on 12 trips undertaken by AT-Dalenni.

06 18 15 50 06 46 63 92 67 12 91 70

Solution

We will take each random number in turn and use it to simulate the number of customers on one trip. Since it is possible for there to be more customers wanting to take a trip than there are places on it we will include a column for the number of disappointed customers. To keep things simple we will assume that customers who do not get on the trip are not prepared to wait for the next one. The results are tabulated below.

Trip number	Random number	Number of customers	Disappointed customers
1	06	8	0
2	18	9	0
3	15	9	0
4	50	10	0
5	06	8	0
6	46	10	0
7	63	11	1
8	92	12	2
9	67	11	1
10	12	8	0
11	91	12	2
12	70	11	1

The results of this simulation suggest that there are few disappointed customers, only seven in 12 trips, or on average 0.583 per trip.

The simulation in Example 12.9 is relatively simple, so instead of simulating the process we could work out the mean of the probability distribution and subtract 10 from it to find the average number of disappointed customers per trip. (If you want to try it you should get an answer of 0.05.) Simulation really comes into its own when there is an interaction of random variables.

EXAMPLE 12.10

The profit AT-Dalenni makes each trip varies; weather conditions, availability of local drivers and guides, and currency fluctuations all have an effect. The profit per customer varies according to the following probability distribution:

Profit per customer (€)	Probability
400	0.25
500	0.35
600	0.30
700	0.10

Make random number allocations for this distribution and use the following random numbers to extend the simulation in Example 12.9 and work out the simulated profit from the 12 trips.

$$85 \quad 25 \quad 63 \quad 11 \quad 35 \quad 12 \quad 63 \quad 00 \quad 38 \quad 80 \quad 26 \quad 67$$

Solution

Profit per customer	Probability	Cumulative probability	Random numbers
400	0.25	0.25	00–24
500	0.35	0.60	25–59
600	0.30	0.90	60–89
700	0.10	1.00	90–99

Trip	Random number (1)	Customers	Random number (2)	Profit (€)
1	06	8	85	600 * 8 = 4 800
2	18	9	25	500 * 9 = 4 500
3	15	9	63	600 * 9 = 5 400
4	50	10	11	400 * 10 = 4 000
5	06	8	35	500 * 8 = 4 000
6	46	10	12	400 * 10 = 4 000
7	63	11	63	600 * 10 = 6 000
8	92	12	00	400 * 10 = 4 000
9	67	11	38	500 * 10 = 5 000
10	12	8	80	600 * 8 = 4 800
11	91	12	26	500 * 10 = 5 000
12	70	11	67	600 * 10 = 6 000
				57 500

The simulated total profit is €57,500.

Note: in working out the profit for trips 7, 8, 9, 11 and 12 we have multiplied the simulated profit per customer by 10 customers rather than the simulated number of customers. This is because the company can only take 10 customers per trip.

Simulation allows us to investigate the consequences of making changes. The company in Example 12.10 might, for instance, want to consider acquiring vehicles that would allow it to take up to 12 customers per trip.

EXAMPLE 12.11

How much extra profit would AT-Dalenni have made, according to the simulation in Example 12.10, if it had the capacity to take 12 customers on each trip?

Solution

In Example 12.10 there are five trips that had more customers interested than places available. The simulated numbers of customers and profit per customer for these trips were:

Trip	Number of customers	Profit per customer	Extra profit
7	11	600	600
8	12	400	800
9	11	500	500
11	12	500	1000
12	11	600	600
			3500

The extra profit they could have made is €3,500.

In practice, simulations are performed on computers and the runs are much longer than the ones we have conducted in this section, and in practice there would be many runs carried out. Much of the work in using simulation involves testing the appropriateness or *validity* of the model. Only when the model is demonstrated to be reasonably close to the real process can it be of any use. For more on simulation try Brooks and Robinson (2001) and Oakshott (1997).

At this point you may find it useful to try **Review questions 12.8 to 12.12** at the end of the chapter.

REVIEW QUESTIONS

Answers to these questions are on page 452. There are tips and hints to help you with them on the supporting website at **www.pearsoned.co.uk/buglear**, where you will also find the fully worked solutions.

☆☆★ Basic questions

12.1   There are three very old X-ray security machines in the departure complex of an airport. All three machines are exactly the same. The probability that a machine breaks down in the course of a day is 0.2. If they are all in working order at the beginning of a day, and breakdowns are independent of each other, find the probability that during the day:

(a) there are no breakdowns
(b) one machine breaks down
(c) two machines break down
(d) all three machines break down

12.2   If 30% of the adult population has made an airline booking through the internet work out the probability that out of four adults:

(a) none has made an internet booking
(b) one has made an internet booking
(c) two have made an internet booking
(d) three have made an internet booking
(e) all four have made an internet booking

12.3   Wasim's word processing skills are good. On average he only makes 0.5 mistakes on each page he types. What is the probability that in a document 10 pages long he makes:

(a) no mistakes?
(b) less than four mistakes?
(c) no more than six mistakes?
(d) at least eight mistakes?

12.4   On average Nadia receives four texts an hour. What is the probability that in one hour she receives

(a) no texts
(b) one text
(c) no more than two texts
(d) more than four texts?

☆★★ More testing questions

12.5 Two in five people can associate a particular piece of music with the product it is used to promote in an advertising campaign. Identify the probability that in a group of 10 people:

(a) none will recognise it
(b) less than half will recognise it
(c) exactly six will recognise it
(d) more than six will recognise it

12.6 A holiday park offers pony trips to children. There are 10 ponies, only two of which are suitable for children under 5 years of age. Ten per cent of children at the park are under 5.

(a) If children turn up at random for these trips what is the probability that there will be more than two children under five in a group of 10 children wanting to take the pony trip?
(b) As a result of a special promotion the proportion of children under five is 20%. Will the probability of more than two children in a group of 10 change, and if so to what?
(c) Work out the mean and standard deviation of the distributions in (a) and (b).

12.7 The mean number of assaults per week on students in a university with a city centre campus is four.

(a) What is the probability that at least one student is assaulted in a week?
(b) The outside lighting at the campus is upgraded and the mean number of assaults per week drops to three. Will the probability of at least one student being assaulted in a week change, and if so to what?

12.8 Furgon Van Hire rents out trucks and vans. One service it offers is a same-day rental deal under which account customers can call in the morning to hire a van for the day. Five vehicles are available for hire on these terms. The demand for the service varies according to the following distribution:

Demand (vans)	0	1	2	3	4	5	6	7	8
Probability	0.05	0.05	0.10	0.15	0.20	0.20	0.15	0.05	0.05

Simulate the demand for this service over a period of 10 days and using your results work out the average number of disappointed customers per day. Use random numbers from Table 4 in Appendix 1, starting at the top of column 10 and working down.

★★★ Challenging questions

12.9 Orders for the Potchtar Mail Order Company are sent in batches of 50 by the Post Office. The number of orders arriving each working day varies according to the following probability distribution:

Number of orders	Probability
150	0.05
200	0.15
250	0.30
300	0.30
350	0.15
400	0.05

These orders are opened and keyed into the company's system by a data entry assistant. The rate per day at which he processes orders varies as follows:

Orders processed	Probability
100	0.1
150	0.2
200	0.4
250	0.2
300	0.1

Any orders that are not processed by the end of one day are held over and dealt with first the following day.

(a) Simulate the operation of this system for 10 working days using two streams of random numbers from Table 4 in Appendix 1. Start at the top of column 2 and go down the column for the orders received and start at the top of column 5 and go down the column for the orders processed. From your results work out the average number of orders held over per day.

(b) Another assistant may be appointed to help out. If this happens the distribution of processing times is expected to be:

Orders processed	Probability
200	0.15
250	0.15
300	0.40
350	0.20
400	0.10

Simulate the operation of the new arrangement for 10 days using the same sets of random numbers you used in part (a). Work out the average number of orders held over per day and compare your result to those you obtained for part (a).

12.10 A restaurant serves fresh locally grown strawberries as part of its 'Wimbledon working lunch' menu for 10 working days in the early summer. The supplier provides 100kg per day and sells to the hotel at a price that varies according to the probability distribution:

Price per kg (£)	1.00	1.10	1.20	1.30	1.40
Probability	0.10	0.25	0.35	0.20	0.10

The number of portions sold per day at £3 per 250g per portion varies according to the probability distribution:

Portions ordered	200	240	280	320	400
Probability	0.30	0.20	0.20	0.20	0.10

Any strawberries not sold during the lunch are sold to a jam-maker the same day for £0.50 per kilogram.

Using simulation, estimate the profit that the restaurant can expect to make over the 10 days. (The answer to this question in Appendix 2 is based on using random numbers from Table 4 in

Appendix 1, starting with row 3 column 1 and moving right for the price and row 9 column 2 and moving right for the portions ordered.)

12.11 A book trader has taken out a 13-week lease on a small unit in a shopping mall prior to it being fitted out as a new outlet by a major retailer. The trader intends to sell remaindered books, 'coffee table classics' selling for £3 each and children's books selling at £1 each. She has a stock consisting of 2000 of the former and 5000 of the latter. The demand for the books per week is expected to vary as follows:

Demand (£3 books)	Probability	Demand (£1 books)	Probability
100	0.10	300	0.20
120	0.10	325	0.20
140	0.20	350	0.30
160	0.30	375	0.10
180	0.15	400	0.12
200	0.15	425	0.08

Simulate the sales and use them to estimate the total revenue over the 13 weeks the shop will be open. (The answer to this question in Appendix 2 is based on using random numbers from Table 4 in Appendix 1, starting with column 1 row 2 and going to the right for the £3 books, and starting with column 1 row 7 and going to the right for the £1 books.)

12.12 A builder completes a large project for a property company who, due to cash flow problems, offer him a small seaside hotel in lieu of payment. The builder, who has no desire to enter the hotel business, has found a buyer for the hotel, but this deal will not be completed until 12 weeks after the hotel is due to open for the summer season. The builder has decided to operate the hotel himself for these 12 weeks. To keep this simple he has decided to accept only one-week bookings. There are eight double rooms and three single rooms in the hotel. The cost of a double room for one week will be £300, and the cost of a single room for one week, £200. The numbers of rooms of each type booked per week varies according to the following distributions:

Double rooms	Probability	Single rooms	Probability
1	0.05	0	0.10
2	0.10	1	0.40
3	0.10	2	0.30
4	0.15	3	0.20
5	0.25		
6	0.20		
7	0.10		
8	0.05		

Simulate the operation of the hotel for these 12 weeks and work out the total revenue. (The answer to this question in Appendix 2 was obtained using random numbers from Table 4 in Appendix 1, starting at the top of column 8 and going down for the double rooms and starting at the top of column 11 and going down for the single rooms.)

THE DEBRIEF

Key things to remember from this chapter

→ The probability distributions we have looked at in this chapter are discrete distributions; they are tools that are used to analyse variables that can only have whole-number values.

→ The binomial distribution applies to situations where there is a series of episodes, known as trials, that occur. In each trial there are two possible results, success or failure.

→ To use the binomial distribution we have to know how many trials take place and what the probability is of success in any one trial. The probability of success must be the same for every trial.

→ Binomial tables provide the probability of a number of successes in the set of trials. They also provide cumulative probabilities associated with different numbers of successes.

→ The Poisson distribution applies to situations where a number of events take place over a specified time period. To use it we have to know the mean number of events per period of time.

→ We can simulate the operation of business processes that involve random events if we can express the variation involved in the form of a probability distribution. We use the distribution to produce allocations of possible values of random numbers and then use random numbers to simulate the process.

→ Simulation is particularly useful for exploring the effects of changes in the process such as installing extra facilities.

References

Brooks, R. and Robinson, S. (2001) *Simulation*, Basingstoke: Palgrave.

Daykin, C.D., Pentikäinen, T. and Pesonen, M. (1994) *Practical Risk Theory for Actuaries*, London: Chapman and Hall.

Gorman, J. (1988) 'Manufacturing with robots', in J. Szymankiewicz, J. McDonald and K. Turner (eds), *Solving Business Problems by Simulation* (2nd edn), London: McGraw–Hill, pp. 353–60.

Mackenzie, R. (1988) 'More lager, please', in J. Szymankiewicz, J. McDonald and K. Turner (eds), *Solving Business Problems by Simulation* (2nd edn), London: McGraw–Hill, pp. 369–75.

Oakshott, L. (1997) *Business Modelling and Simulation*, London: Pitman.

Tippett, L.H.C. (1935) 'Some applications of statistical methods to the study of variation of quality in the production of cotton yarn', *Journal of the Royal Statistical Society*, Supplement 2, 27–55.

Smooth running – continuous probability distributions and basic queuing theory

CHAPTER 13

CHAPTER OBJECTIVES

This chapter will help you to:

→ Make use of the normal distribution and appreciate its importance

→ Employ the standard normal distribution in the analysis of normal distribution problems

→ Apply the exponential distribution and be aware of its usefulness in analysing queues

THE BARE BONES

What you will find in this chapter . . .

- The key features of the normal distribution
- Finding areas of the standard normal distribution using Table 5 in Appendix 1
- Identifying points in the standard normal distribution that cut off areas in the tails of the distribution
- Analysing populations that are normally distributed by finding z-equivalents and using the standard normal distribution
- Finding areas of the exponential distribution
- Modelling simple queuing systems using the exponential distribution

. . . and on the supporting website (**www.pearsoned.co.uk/buglear**)

- How to use EXCEL, Minitab and SPSS to analyse the normal distribution
- Fully worked solutions to the review questions
- More review questions

Business use of the normal distribution

◆ Most successful businesses pay considerable attention to the quality of their products, services and procedures. This involves managers analysing the variation in the quality of what they produce. In many cases this variation follows a normal distribution and quality objectives are therefore based on it. An example is a supermarket that wants to keep the proportion of customers waiting more than a certain time at a checkout within a defined limit. It might aim to ensure that no more than 1% of customers have to wait more than five minutes. Using the normal distribution the waiting time of five minutes must be 2.33 standard deviations more than the mean waiting time. It would need to know the mean and standard deviation of the distribution of waiting times and what they would have to be in order to meet its objective and how these parameters compare with current performance. This would tell the supermarket by how much it would have to improve one or both. In this illustration 1% sounds an acceptably small proportion of customers, but if the store has on average 20,000 shoppers each day we would expect 200 of them to have to wait more than five minutes. For the store manager this may well be an unacceptably high number of shoppers to alienate and potentially lose.

◆ This focus on the absolute numbers rather than the proportion resulted in quality experts developing an approach called *six sigma*. The Greek letter sigma, σ, represents the standard deviation of the normal distribution. The pioneers of six sigma argued that unacceptable performance should be restricted not to the proportion of the distribution beyond two or even three sigma, i.e. two or three standard deviations beyond the mean, but to six standard deviations beyond the mean. By doing this, unacceptable performance should only occur in a very small part of 1% of cases.

◆ Eckes (2001) describes the application of the six sigma strategy in one of the hotels in the Westin Hotels chain in the USA. The hotel offered delivery of room service meals to guests' rooms. The manager found from customer feedback that guests considered an interval of more than 30 minutes between phoning in their order and the meal being delivered unacceptable. Room service meal delivery times at the hotel were thought to be normally distributed with a mean of 26 minutes, which meant that the threshold of unacceptable service, 30 minutes, was roughly three sigmas (standard deviations) above the mean. Introducing improvements in communicating and processing customer orders cut the mean to 23 minutes and meant that the unacceptable service threshold was more than four sigmas above the mean. The six sigma target could be met either by reducing the mean further, which would probably prove difficult, or by reducing the value of sigma, the standard deviation, by making the delivery times more consistent (perhaps by rationalising the room service menu), or by a combination of both.

◆ In a later work Eckes (2005) explains how six sigma is used by major companies such as Honeywell and Motorola.

13.1 Introduction

In section 4.4 we distinguished between discrete and continuous data. The observations of discrete random variables have a finite number of feasible values such as the number of employees absent through illness or the number of defects in a product. The observations of continuous random variables can have values anywhere on a continuous scale of measurement such as distance or time.

Theoretical probability distributions, distributions derived mathematically, can be used to model the patterns of variation of random variables. In cases where these variables take discrete values we use discrete probability distributions, primarily the binomial and Poisson distributions, as models to analyse the behaviour of the variables. For continuous random variables we use continuous probability distributions. Such distributions are also used with discrete random variables that can take many different values.

In quantitative methods the main continuous probability distribution is the normal distribution. As you might imagine from the name the distribution is used to model the distributions of numerous 'normal' or 'typical' variables. You may find the distribution referred to as the Gaussian distribution after the German mathematician Carl Friedrich Gauss (1777–1855) who developed it to model observation errors that arose in surveying and astronomy measurements. Like other probability distributions its main use is to model variation in population data rather than sample data.

The normal distribution is particularly important in quantitative work as it has two roles. The first is enabling us to analyse variables which have observations that vary in keeping with the normal distribution. The second is that under certain circumstances the normal distribution accurately represents the variation in results from samples. This is essential for predicting population parameters from sample data, such as estimating the population mean using a sample mean.

13.2 The normal distribution

There are different versions of each type of probability distribution. This is true for the normal distribution. A normal variable, one in which the observations in the population form a normal distribution, will have its specific version of the normal distribution. Each version is defined by two statistical measures or parameters: the mean and the standard deviation.

There are three distinct characteristics of the normal distribution:

- A single peak; it is what is known as *unimodal*, i.e. it has a single mode.
- One side is the exact mirror image of the other; it is *symmetrical about its centre.*
- The sides tail off gradually on each side but despite getting closer and closer to it the further it is from the centre, the line depicting the shape of the distribution never meets the horizontal axis; it is what is known as *asymptotic.*

The other key feature of the normal distribution is that, like other probability distributions, the total area of the distribution is one. In probability a value of one means certainty; every observation is represented so each one is certain to be there.

Since it is a symmetrical distribution and has a single peak, the mean, median and mode all occur together in the middle. This is very convenient because the mean is the only measure of location we need to use when analysing the normal distribution. Because we use the mean as the measure of location, we use the standard deviation, which is based on the mean, as the measure of spread.

The normal distribution is also called the *bell curve* as it is bell-shaped. Figure 13.1 shows the distribution's shape. It is portrayed as a smooth curve. This reflects the fact that it depicts the probabilities of a continuous variable having values across the entire range of the distribution.

Using any probability distribution to analyse a population involves dealing with areas. For instance, to find the probability that an observation exceeds a particular value means finding the area under the curve to the right of where the value is located along the horizontal axis. This is tricky with a continuous probability distribution like the normal distribution.

For one thing we have to specify a range of values – not a single value – as we have continuous values. For example, referring to the probability of a variable, X, being 10 is inadequate as in a continuous distribution this implies the probability that X is precisely 10.000000 etc. Instead we would have to specify the probability that X is between 9.500

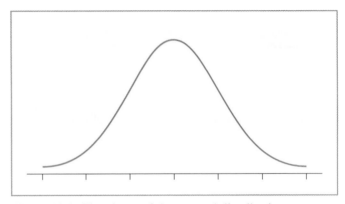

Figure 13.1 **The shape of the normal distribution**

and 10.499 to three decimal places. This probability would be represented in a diagram by the area below the curve between the points 9.500 and 10.499 on the horizontal axis as a proportion of the total area below the curve. The probability that a continuous variable takes a precise value is, in effect, zero. This means that in practice there is no difference between, say, the probability that X is less than 10, $P(X < 10.000)$ and the probability that X is less than or equal to 10, $P(X \leq 10.000)$. Similarly, the probability that X is more than 10, $P(X > 10.000)$, is essentially indistinguishable from the probability that X is more than or equal to 10, $P(X \geq 10.000)$. For convenience the equalities are left out of the probability statements in what follows.

Although we can portray the area that represents such probabilities in a diagram, calculating the size of an area of the distribution is not easy because the shapes are complex. It would be straightforward if we were dealing with rectangles or triangles but we are not. The shape of the distribution, the normal curve, changes in slope and direction which makes the mathematics involved difficult and probably beyond most people.

The difficulty of calculating the areas that represent normal distribution probabilities meant that the only realistic way was to use tables that mapped out the areas of the distribution. The trouble was that since there could be different versions of the normal distribution having a table for every conceivable one was simply not practicable.

This difficulty was overcome by producing a table that detailed the areas of a benchmark normal distribution, the *standard normal distribution*. This made it possible to analyse any version of the distribution by comparing positions in it with their equivalents in the standard normal distribution. With these equivalent points the standard normal distribution could be used to analyse any version of the normal distribution.

The statistical software available today means the standard normal distribution is no longer the only viable tool to investigate different versions of the normal distribution. Despite this it is worth knowing about it. It is not only useful should you be unable to access statistical software, but also important for further quantitative analysis.

13.3 The standard normal distribution

The standard normal distribution depicts the pattern of variation of an invented variable known as Z, and the individual values of it are z values. This variable is normally distributed. It has a mean of zero and a standard deviation of one. Z is also known as the *standard normal variable* so the standard normal distribution is often called the *Z distribution*. Figure 13.2 shows the standard normal, or Z, distribution.

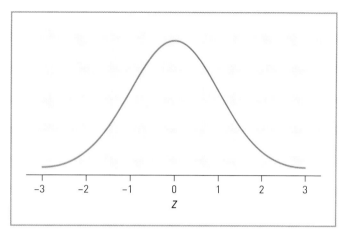

Figure 13.2 **The standard normal distribution**

In Figure 13.2 the greater part of the distribution is fairly close to the centre, where the mean, 0, is located. The tails either side of the mean are asymptotic. Both on the left and right the further the line is away from the centre the closer to the horizontal axis it becomes but it never actually touches the horizontal axis. This means that the z values range from minus infinity on the left to plus infinity on the right.

The distribution in Figure 13.2 is symmetrical so half of the standard normal distribution is on the left of zero, the centre of the distribution, and half on the right. The implication of this is that half of the possible z values, the ones to the left of the centre, are negative, and half are positive, those to the right of the centre.

Table 5 of Appendix 1, on pages 438–9, gives a comprehensive classification of the areas under the curve of the standard normal distribution. These areas represent probabilities. The table can be used to obtain the probability that Z, the standard normal variable, is more than a particular value, z, or less than z. To illustrate how to do this, an extract from Table 5 is reproduced in Table 13.1.

To show you how to use the table, suppose we want the probability that Z is more than 0.63, $P(Z > 0.63)$. We start by locating the value of z, 0.63, to the first decimal place, i.e. 0.6, down the column headed Z on the far left of Table 13.1. This is shown in blue. From there we search along the row to the right until we reach the figure in the column headed 0.03, which

Table 13.1 **Extract from Table 5 of Appendix 1**

Z	0.00	0.01	0.02	0.03	0.04	0.05	0.06	0.07	0.08	0.09
0.0	0.5000	0.4960	0.4920	0.4880	0.4840	0.4801	0.4761	0.4721	0.4681	0.4641
0.1	0.4602	0.4562	0.4522	0.4483	0.4443	0.4404	0.4364	0.4325	0.4286	0.4247
0.2	0.4207	0.4168	0.4129	0.4090	0.4052	0.4013	0.3974	0.3936	0.3897	0.3859
0.3	0.3821	0.3783	0.3745	0.3707	0.3669	0.3632	0.3594	0.3557	0.3520	0.3483
0.4	0.3446	0.3409	0.3372	0.3336	0.3300	0.3264	0.3228	0.3192	0.3156	0.3121
0.5	0.3085	0.3050	0.3015	0.2981	0.2946	0.2912	0.2877	0.2843	0.2810	0.2776
0.6	0.2743	0.2709	0.2676	0.2643	0.2611	0.2578	0.2546	0.2514	0.2483	0.2451
0.7	0.2420	0.2389	0.2358	0.2327	0.2297	0.2266	0.2236	0.2206	0.2177	0.2148
0.8	0.2119	0.2090	0.2061	0.2033	0.2005	0.1977	0.1949	0.1922	0.1894	0.1867
0.9	0.1841	0.1814	0.1788	0.1762	0.1736	0.1711	0.1685	0.1660	0.1635	0.1611
1.0	0.1587	0.1562	0.1539	0.1515	0.1492	0.1469	0.1446	0.1423	0.1401	0.1379

is shown in blue. The number that is in both the 0.6 row and the 0.03 column is the area of the distribution on the right of 0.63, 0.2643, also shown in blue. It is this area that represents the probability of Z being more than 0.63, so $P(Z > 0.63)$ is 0.2643 or 26.43%.

To find the probability that Z is less than a specific value we need to use the fact that the total area under the curve is one. To illustrate this, suppose we want the probability that Z is less than 1.05, $P(Z < 1.05)$. We look first for 1.0 in the Z column on the left then look along to the right of this as far as the number in the column headed 0.05, 0.1469. This, the area on the right of 1.05, represents the probability of Z being greater than 1.05. For the probability of Z being less than 1.05 we have to take this away from 1, the total area under the curve:

$$P(Z < 1.05) = 1 - P(Z > 1.05) = 1 - 0.1469 = 0.8531 \text{ or } 85.31\%$$

Example 13.1 provides more illustrations of using Table 5, including diagrams showing the relevant areas of the distribution. While you are learning how to use the standard normal distribution it is a good idea to sketch the distribution and mark out the areas you need to find.

EXAMPLE 13.1

From Table 5 of Appendix 1 find:

(a) The probability that Z is more than 1.0, $P(Z > 1.0)$.

(b) The probability that Z is less than 1.0, $P(Z < 1.0)$.

(c) The probability that Z is more than 2.11, $P(Z > 2.11)$.

(d) The probability that Z is more than -1.62, $P(Z > -1.62)$.

(e) The probability that Z is less than -1.62, $P(Z < -1.62)$.

(f) The probability that Z is more than 0.38 and less than 2.43, $P(0.38 < Z < 2.43)$.

(g) The probability that Z is more than -1.77 and less than -0.64, $P(-1.77 < Z < -0.64)$.

(h) The probability that Z is more than -0.45 and less than 1.29, $P(-0.45 < Z < 1.29)$.

Solution

(a) The probability that Z is more than 1.0, $P(Z > 1.0)$.
The value of Z here is only specified to one place of decimals, so the figure we need is the first one to the right of 1.0 in Table 5, under the column headed 0.00, 0.1587. This represents the probability of Z being more than 1.0 and is the shaded area in Figure 13.3. We can also interpret this as meaning that 15.87% of z values are more than 1.0.

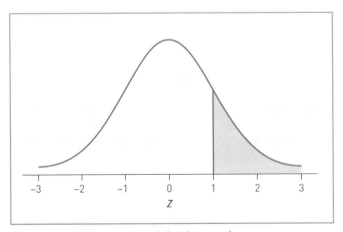

Figure 13.3 Example 13.1 (a): $P(Z > 1.0)$

(b) The probability that Z is less than 1.0, $P(Z < 1.0)$.

From (a) we ascertained that the probability that Z is more than 1.0 is 0.1587. We can assume that the probability of Z being exactly 1.0, i.e. 1.000000 etc., is infinitely small so if the proportion of the distribution to the right of 1.0 is 0.1587, the proportion to the left of 1.0 is $1 - 0.1587$ which is 0.8413. This is shown as the unshaded area in Figure 13.3 and is the probability that Z is less than 1.0.

(c) The probability that Z is more than 2.11, $P(Z > 2.11)$.

In Table 5 the number in the row for 2.1 and in the column headed 0.01 is 0.0174. This is the area to the right of 2.11, represented by the shaded area in Figure 13.4. This means that the probability of Z being more than 2.11 is 0.0174.

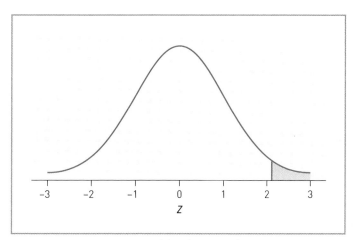

Figure 13.4 Example 13.1 (c): $P(Z > 2.11)$

(d) The probability that Z is more than -1.62, $P(Z > -1.62)$.

In Table 5 the number in the row for -1.6 and the column headed 0.02 is 0.9474. This is the area to the right of -1.62, represented by the shaded area in Figure 13.5. This means that the probability of Z being more than -1.62 is 0.9474.

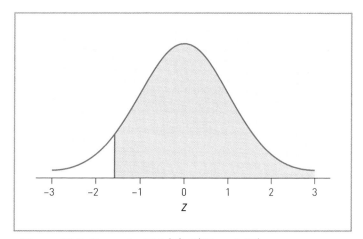

Figure 13.5 Example 13.1 (d): $P(Z > -1.62)$

When you deal with negative z values remember that a phrase like 'more than -1.62' means a negative number smaller than -1.62 such as -1.2 as well as all the positive numbers, whereas 'less than -1.62' means a larger negative number such as -1.8.

(e) The probability that Z is less than -1.62, $P(Z < -1.62)$.
In part (d) we found that the probability Z is more than -1.62 is 0.9474. We can assume that the probability of Z being exactly -1.62, i.e. -1.6200000 etc., is infinitely small, so if the proportion of the distribution to the right of -1.62 is 0.9474, the proportion to the left of -1.62 is $1 - 0.9474$ which is 0.0526. This is the unshaded area in Figure 13.5 and represents the probability that Z is less than -1.62.

(f) The probability that Z is more than 0.38 and less than 2.43, $P(0.38 < Z < 2.43)$.
From Table 5 the probability of Z being more than 0.38, $P(Z > 0.38)$, is in the row for 0.3 and the column headed 0.08, 0.3520. Similarly, the probability of Z being more than 2.43 is in the row for 2.4 and the column headed 0.03, 0.0075. To get the probability of Z being both more than 0.38 and less than 2.43 subtract the probability of Z being more than 2.43 from the probability of Z being more than 0.38:

$$P(0.38 < Z < 2.43) = P(Z > 0.38) - P(Z > 2.43) = 0.3520 - 0.0075$$
$$= 0.3445$$

This is the shaded area in Figure 13.6.

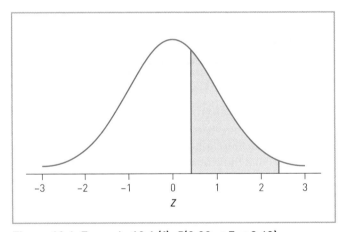

Figure 13.6 Example 13.1 (f): $P(0.38 < Z < 2.43)$

An alternative approach is to think that if 35.20% of the total area under the curve is on the right of 0.38 and 0.75% of the area is on the right of 2.43, the difference between these two percentages, 34.45%, must be the area that lies between 0.38 and 2.43.

(g) The probability that Z is more than -1.77 and less than -0.64, $P(-1.77 < Z < -0.64)$.
From Table 5 the probability of Z being more than -1.77, $P(Z > -1.77)$, is in the row for -1.7 and the column headed 0.07, 0.9616. The probability of Z being more than -0.64 is in the row for -0.6 and the column headed 0.04, 0.7389. To get the probability of Z being both more than -1.77 and less than -0.64 take the

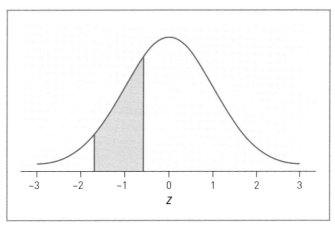

Figure 13.7 Example 13.1 (g): $P(-1.77 < Z < -0.64)$

probability of Z being more than -0.64 away from the probability of Z being more than -1.77:

$$P(-1.77 < Z < -0.64) = P(Z > -1.77) - P(Z > -0.64) = 0.9616 - 0.7389$$
$$= 0.2227$$

This is the shaded area in Figure 13.7.

(h) The probability that Z is greater than -0.45 and less than 1.29, $P(-0.45 < Z < 1.29)$. From Table 5 the probability of Z being more than -0.45, $P(Z > -0.45)$, is in the row for -0.4 and the column headed 0.05, 0.6736. The probability of Z being more than 1.29 is in the row for 1.2 and the column headed 0.09, 0.0985. For the probability of Z being both more than -0.45 and less than 1.29 take the probability of Z being more than 1.29 away from the probability of Z being more than -0.45:

$$P(-0.45 < Z < 1.29) = P(Z > -0.45) - P(Z > 1.29) = 0.6736 - 0.0985$$
$$= 0.5751$$

This is the shaded area in Figure 13.8.

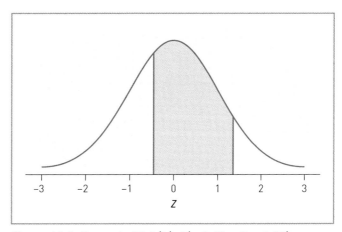

Figure 13.8 Example 13.1 (h): $P(-0.45 < Z < 1.29)$

In some situations, especially when we want to estimate population parameters from sample data, we use the standard normal distribution rather differently. Rather than using a z value to find a probability, we start with a probability and want to find the z value that isolates or 'cuts off' the area representing the probability from the rest of the distribution. The area is denoted by the symbol α and the z value associated with it is denoted as z_α.

EXAMPLE 13.2

Using Table 5 of Appendix 1 find the value of Z, z_α, so that the area to the right of it, the probability of Z being more than z_α, $P(Z > z_\alpha)$, is:

(a) 0.4602

(b) 0.0250

(c) 0.0099

Solution

(a) Scan down the probabilities listed in Table 5 and just over half way down the page you should see 0.4602 immediately to the right of 0.1 in the z column: so if α is 0.4602, z_α is 0.1. This is the probability of Z being more than 0.1, so $P(Z > 0.1) = 0.4602$. This is the shaded area in Figure 13.9.

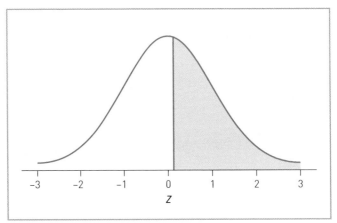

Figure 13.9 Example 13.2 (a): $0.4602 = P(Z > 0.1)$

(b) The further down the list of probabilities in Table 5 we go the smaller they become and 0.0250 is towards the bottom of the page. It is in the row for 1.9 and the column headed 0.06, so 0.0250 is the probability of Z being more than 1.96, i.e. $P(Z > 1.96) = 0.0250$. This is the shaded area in Figure 13.10.

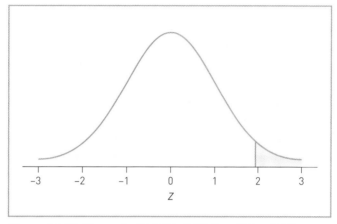

Figure 13.10 Example 13.2 (b): $0.0250 = P(Z > 1.96)$

(c) The z value with an area of 0.0099 to its right is in the row for 2.3 and the column headed 0.03. This means 0.0099 is the probability of Z being more than 2.33, i.e. $P(Z > 2.33) = 0.0099$. This is the shaded area in Figure 13.11.

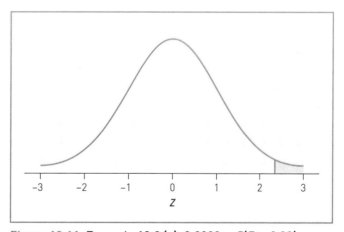

Figure 13.11 Example 13.2 (c): $0.0099 = P(Z > 2.33)$

The notation in Example 13.2 involves using z_α for the value of Z that has the area α beyond it, in other words,

$$P(Z > z_\alpha) = \alpha$$

For Example 13.2(c) z_α is 1.96 and α is the area to the right of 1.96 which represents the probability of Z being more than 1.960, i.e. $P(Z > 1.96) = 0.0250$. As Figure 13.11 shows, it is actually quite a small area out along the tail of the distribution on the right. Usually such an area is referred to as a *tail area*.

For convenience a specific value of Z is denoted by the letter z with the tail area beyond, α, written alongside as a suffix. For example, 1.96 can be described as $z_{0.0250}$ because it has a tail area of 0.0250 beyond it. We can also describe 1.96 as the z value that cuts off a tail area of 0.0250.

Later on you will find specific z values are referred to in this way because the z value we need to use is based on the tail area. The values of Z that cut off tails of 5%, 2.5%, 1% and 0.5% are particularly important for the topics covered in Chapter 16. The z values that cut off these specific tail areas are, to two decimal places, 1.64, 1.96, 2.33 and 2.58, and they are generally denoted as $z_{0.05}$, $z_{0.025}$, $z_{0.01}$ and $z_{0.005}$ respectively.

At this point you may find it useful to try **Review question 13.1** at the end of the chapter.

13.3.1 Using the standard normal distribution

The standard normal distribution is not a real distribution. Its sole purpose is to help us analyse versions of the normal distribution that are real. To do this we convert the value in the real distribution into a value of Z in much the same way as we might convert pounds or dollars into euros. This process is called finding the *z-equivalent* or Z *score* of the value.

Suppose we have a distribution for X, a variable with observations that form a normal distribution with a mean μ and a standard deviation σ. Working out the z-equivalent, z of a particular value, x, of X is a two-stage process; first we subtract the mean, μ, from x then we divide the result by the standard deviation, σ:

$$z = \frac{x - \mu}{\sigma}$$

All we are doing here is dividing the difference between the value, x, and the mean of the distribution, μ, by the standard deviation of the distribution, σ. Actually the z-equivalent is nothing more than how many standard deviations the value is away from the mean of the distribution. Note that we are using Greek letters here and these represent the *population* mean (μ) and the *population* standard deviation (σ). This is because we use probability distributions to model populations.

Armed with the z-equivalent of our x value we simply go to the standard normal distribution table, Table 5 in Appendix 1, for the probabilities related to it.

EXAMPLE 13.3

CookNear plc supplies the contract catering trade with sealed individual portions of instant coffee powder. The labels say that each portion consists of 10 grams of coffee but there are inconsistencies so the contents vary. The actual amounts are normally distributed with a mean of 10.2 grams and a standard deviation of 0.25 grams. Find the probability that a portion will contain:

(a) more than 10.5 grams.

(b) more than 10 grams.

(c) less than 9.6 grams.

Solution

(a) Using X to represent the amounts of coffee in the portions, we want to find $P(X > 10.5)$. This is represented by the shaded area on the right of the distribution in Figure 13.12.

The z-equivalent of $x = 10.5$ is

$$z = \frac{10.5 - 10.2}{0.25} = 1.2$$

This tells us that 10.5 grams in the coffee portions distribution is equivalent to 1.2 in the Z distribution. The probability of X being more than 10.5 is therefore equivalent to the probability of Z being more than 1.2. According to Table 5 in Appendix 1:

$$P(Z > 1.2) = 0.1151$$

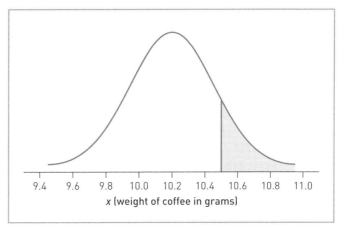

Figure 13.12 Example 13.3 (a): $P(X > 10.5)$

(b) The z-equivalent of 10 is

$$z = \frac{10 - 10.2}{0.25} = -0.6$$

We can conclude that 10 grams in the coffee portions distribution is equivalent to -0.6 in the Z distribution. The probability of X being more than 10 is therefore equivalent to the probability of Z being greater than -0.6. From Table 5:

$$P(Z > -0.6) = 0.7257 \text{ or } 72.57\%$$

(c) The z-equivalent of 9.6 is

$$z = \frac{9.6 - 10.2}{0.25} = -2.2$$

In this case the probability of X being less than 9.6 is the same as the probability of Z being less than -2.2. According to Table 5 the probability of Z being greater than -2.2 is 0.9861, so the probability of Z being less than -2.2 is $1 - 0.9861$ which is 0.0139, or 1.39%.

Since probabilities reflect relative frequencies an alternative way of expressing a result like the one in Example 13.3(c) is to say that 1.39% of the coffee portions contain less than 9.6 grams.

SELF-ASSEMBLY GUIDE

Finding z-equivalents

◆ You need to know the mean, μ, and the standard deviation, σ, of the distribution you want to investigate, the distribution of the variable X.

◆ To find the z-equivalent of a specific value in the distribution, x, take the mean, μ away from x. This is the difference between the two *but* it is in the same units as the values of the distribution, e.g. if X is measured in centimetres this difference will be in centimetres.

◆ Remember that when x is less than μ the difference between x and μ can be negative. This is not a problem.

◆ Divide the difference between x and μ by the standard deviation of the X distribution, σ. This is the z-equivalent.

◆ Because both the difference between x and μ, and σ are expressed in the same units of measurement, the units of measurement are cancelled when we divide one by the other. What you have is the difference between x and the mean of the distribution measured in standard deviations, i.e. the z-equivalent.

Sometimes it is necessary to identify a point in the normal distribution that cuts off a tail area of a certain size. For this we first find the z value that cuts off that area in the standard normal distribution. Once we have this z value, we work out the point that is that number of standard deviations away from the mean. If it is a positive value of z, add that number of standard deviations to the mean; if it is negative, subtract that number of standard deviations from the mean.

EXAMPLE 13.4

In the population of coffee portion weights in Example 13.3, what is:

(a) The minimum weight of coffee in the heaviest 10% of portions?

(b) The maximum weight of coffee in the lightest 20% of portions?

Solution

For **(a)**, look down the probabilities in Table 5 in Appendix 1 until you reach the figure nearest to 0.1, 0.1003. This figure is in the 1.2 row and the 0.08 column. This means that the z value of Z that cuts off a 10% tail to the right of the distribution is 1.28. In other words $P(Z > 1.28)$ is 0.1003.

Since 10% of the standard normal distribution is to the right of 1.28, 10% of any version of the normal distribution, including the distribution of weights of coffee portions in Example 13.3, is to the right of the point 1.28 standard deviations above the mean. The mean of the distribution is 10.2 grams and the standard deviation is 0.25 grams, so 10% of portions weigh more than:

$$10.2 + (1.28 * 0.25) = 10.52 \text{ grams}$$

The heaviest 10% of the portions weigh more than 10.52 grams.

For **(b)**, the maximum weight of the lightest 20% of coffee portions is also the minimum weight of the heaviest 80% of portions. From Table 5 the z value that cuts off 80% of the area to the right of it is -0.84. If 80% of the standard normal distribution is above -0.84 then 20% is below it. This means that the lowest 20% of any version of the normal distribution is 0.84 standard deviations below the mean, so the lightest 20% of coffee portions will weigh less than:

$$10.2 - (0.84 * 0.25) = 9.99 \text{ grams}$$

The normal distribution is such an important distribution because it enables us to analyse the many continuous variables in business and other fields that have values which are distributed in a normal pattern. What makes it particularly important, indeed probably the most important distribution in Statistics, is that we can use it to understand how sample results vary. To take one example, means of samples taken from a population will vary. Their values form what is called a *sampling distribution* and this may well have a normal pattern.

At this point you may find it useful to try **Review questions 13.2, 13.3, 13.6, 13.7, 13.8, 13.10 and 13.11** at the end of the chapter.

13.4 The exponential distribution

The importance of the normal distribution and the attention rightly devoted to it in quantitative methods programmes often obscures the fact that it is not the only continuous probability distribution. The normal distribution is a symmetrical distribution and is therefore an entirely appropriate model for continuous random variables that vary in a symmetrical pattern. But not all continuous random variables that crop up in business analysis exhibit this characteristic.

Many business operations involve queues or waiting-lines; you have probably waited in a queue to pay for groceries, you may have waited in a queue for access to a telephone help-line. These are fairly obvious examples, but there are many others; you may have taken a flight in an aircraft that has had to wait in a queue in the airspace above an airport before it can land, and when you post a letter in effect it joins a queue to be sorted by the postal service.

In the next section we shall consider a basic queuing model, but before we do so we will look at the exponential distribution. This is a continuous probability distribution that is important for analysing, among other things, service times in queuing processes.

The exponential distribution differs from the normal distribution in two respects; it describes variables whose values can only be positive, and it is not symmetrical around the mean. The probability that an exponential random variable takes a particular value can be worked out using the formula:

$$P(X = x) = \frac{e^{-x/\mu}}{\mu}$$

where μ is the mean of the distribution and x is the value of interest. The letter e represents Euler's number, 2.7183 to four decimal places. Because the exponential distribution is a continuous probability distribution we are almost always interested in a cumulative probability such as the probability that the variable is greater than a particular value, which we can find using:

$$P(X > x) = e^{-x/\mu}$$

Or the probability that the variable is less than a particular value, which is:

$$P(X < x) = 1 - e^{-x/\mu}$$

To use these expressions for any specific distribution you need to know only the mean of the distribution and the specific value of interest.

EXAMPLE 13.5

The times taken to serve customers visiting a bus company office to renew their bus passes are exponentially distributed with a mean of 2 minutes. What is the probability that a customer has to wait more than 5 minutes?

Solution

If X represents the service times,

$$P(X > 5) = e^{-5/2} = e^{-2.5} = 2.7183^{-2.5} = 1/2.7183^{2.5} = 1/12.182 = 0.082$$

The calculation of the cumulative probability in Example 13.5 is shown in full, but you should be able to work out an expression like $e^{-2.5}$ on your calculator. Look for a key with e^x on or above it. It is unlikely to be the first function of the key so you may have to use a sequence like **SHIFT** then e^x then key in 2.5 then press $+/-$ then $=$. Your calculator may require a sequence that begins with the exponent, so you will have to key in 2.5 then press $+/-$ then **SHIFT** (or possibly **2nd** for second function) then e^x.

The exponential distribution for the service times in Example 13.5 is shown in Figure 13.13. The shaded area represents the probability that the service time exceeds 5 minutes.

You may recall that e, Euler's number, appeared in the expression for the Poisson distribution that we looked at in section 12.4. The similarity is no accident; the two distributions are connected. The Poisson distribution is used to model incidents occurring over a period of time.

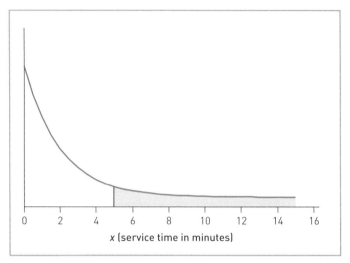

Figure 13.13 The distribution of service times in Example 13.5

If the number of accidents at a factory follows a Poisson distribution then the time interval between accidents will follow an exponential distribution with a mean that is the reciprocal of the mean of the Poisson distribution.

**EXAMPLE
13.6**

The number of serious injuries occurring per month at the Appasney Engineering plant behaves according to the Poisson distribution with a mean of 2. What is the probability that the time between successive serious injuries exceeds a month?

Solution

If the mean number of serious injuries is 2, then the mean time interval between injuries is 1/2, 0.5. This is the mean of the exponential distribution of the times between serious injuries, X. The probability that the time between serious injuries is more than a month is:

$$P(X > 1) = e^{-1/0.5} = e^{-2} = 2.7183^{-2} = 1/2.7183^2 = 1/7.389 = 0.135$$

At this point you may find it useful to try **Review questions 13.4 and 13.5** at the end of the chapter.

13.5 A simple queuing model

Queues are quite complex processes because they usually depend on the behaviour of random variables – the number of arrivals per unit of time and the time taken to deal with the people or things concerned. They can be difficult to manage because if, for instance, customers wait too long they may take their business elsewhere, yet devoting too many staff to provide the service may result in their being unoccupied for significant periods of time.

Because of the importance of queuing systems in business operations, queuing theory is a substantial subject. Here we will look at one of the simpler models.

The point of any queuing theory model is to provide us with information about the operation of the queuing system it represents, specifically the average waiting time and the average length of the queue. If we make certain assumptions about the behaviour of individuals in the queue and know the patterns of arrivals and service times we can do this.

The behaviour assumptions underlying the model we will consider are that having joined the queue an individual will stay in it until they have been served and that individuals in the queue are served on a FIFO (First In First Out) basis, in other words, first come first served. We will further assume that individuals join the queue according to the Poisson distribution with a mean of λ and that service times are exponentially distributed according to the exponential distribution with a mean of μ.

The symbol λ, lambda, is the Greek letter l, which we will use to distinguish the mean of the Poisson arrivals distribution from the mean of the exponential service times distribution in keeping with the conventions of notation in queuing theory. Both means need to be expressed in the same style so we define λ, the mean of the arrivals distribution, as the mean arrival rate, and μ, the mean of the service times, as the mean service rate.

In queuing theory, models are identified by the distributions of arrivals and service times, with M used to represent the Poisson and exponential distributions. In the simple model we shall study we assume there is just one service point. This model is known as the M/M/1, indicating Poisson arrivals, exponential service times and one server.

The ratio between the mean arrival rate and the mean service rate, λ/μ, is the *traffic intensity* in the queuing system, represented by the Greek letter rho, ρ, the Greek r. For a queuing system to be viable the traffic intensity must be less than 1, in other words the mean arrival rate must be less than the mean service rate, otherwise the queue would simply continue to grow and the system would 'explode'.

By means of mathematical derivations involving probability and differentiation it is possible to determine a number of operating measures of an M/M/1 queuing system including:

The probability that the server is idle $= 1 - \rho$
The probability that there are more than r individuals in the queue $= \rho^{r+2}$
The mean number in the queue, $L_q = \rho^2/(1 - \rho)$
The mean waiting time in the queue, $W_q = \rho/(\mu - \lambda)$

EXAMPLE 13.7

Between midnight and 6am there is one cashier on duty at a 24-hour service station. During this time customers arrive at the cash desk to pay for their fuel and other goods according to a Poisson distribution with a mean of 12 per hour, and service times are exponentially distributed with a mean of three minutes.

The mean arrival rate, λ, is 12 per hour, the mean service rate, μ, is 20 per hour so ρ the traffic intensity, is 12/20, 0.6.

The probability that the cashier is idle $= 1 - \rho = 1 - 0.6 = 0.4$

The probability that there is more than one person in the queue $= \rho^{2+1} = 0.6^3 = 0.216$

The mean number in the queue $= \rho^2/(1 - \rho) = 0.6^2/(1 - 0.6) = 0.36/0.4 = 0.9$

The mean waiting time in the queue $= \rho/(\mu - \lambda) = 0.6/(20 - 12)$

$$= 0.6/8 = 0.075 \text{ hours or 4 minutes}$$

At this point you may find it useful to try **Review questions 13.9 to 13.12** at the end of the chapter.

This queuing model is only one of many models that constitute queuing theory. For more about the topic try Taha (2006) or Hillier and Lieberman (2009).

REVIEW QUESTIONS

Answers to these questions are on pages 452–3. There are tips and hints to help you with them on the supporting website at **www.pearsoned.co.uk/buglear**, where you will also find the fully worked solutions.

☆☆★ Basic questions

13.1 Use Table 5 of Appendix 1 to identify the areas of the standard normal distribution that represent the following probabilities:

(a) $P(Z > 1.67)$
(b) $P(Z > -0.18)$
(c) $P(Z < 2.21)$
(d) $P(Z < -1.52)$
(e) $P(0.75 < Z < 1.86)$
(f) $P(-2.03 < Z < -0.24)$
(g) $P(-0.49 < Z < 0.68)$

13.2 The lengths of classes at Umney University are normally distributed with a mean of 55 minutes and a standard deviation of 3.4 minutes. What is the probability of a class lasting:

(a) more than an hour?
(b) more than 45 minutes?
(c) less than 55 minutes?
(d) less than 50 minutes?
(e) between 53 and 59 minutes?

13.3 The playing times, after a full battery charge, of the new MP-Z players form a normal distribution that has a mean of 25 hours and a standard deviation of 0.73 hours. Find the probability that following a full charge a player will operate for:

(a) more than 27 hours?
(b) more than 26 hours?
(c) less than 24 hours?
(d) less than 26 hours?
(e) between 24 and 26 hours?
(f) between 23 and 27 hours?

13.4 The delays in the departures of flights operated by Flotair follow an exponential distribution with a mean of 13 minutes. Find the probability that one of its flights:

(a) departs less than 10 minutes late
(b) departs more than 30 minutes late
(c) departs between 5 and 15 minutes late

13.5 The times that elapse between the announcements of the winning numbers in a lottery and winners claiming their prizes are exponentially distributed with a mean of 20 hours. Work out the probability that the length of time a winner takes to claim their prize is:

(a) more than 24 hours
(b) less than 12 hours
(c) between 36 and 48 hours.

☆★★ More testing questions

13.6 The Doroga Motor Company offers a warranty of 60,000 miles on the cars it produces. Any part that fails before the car has attained that mileage is supplied and fitted at the company's expense. The lifetimes of the bearings it currently fits in its vehicles are normally distributed with a mean of 73,200 miles and a standard deviation of 7155 miles.

(a) What proportion of bearings will fail before the warranty mileage is reached?

(b) An alternative supplier offers the company bearings with a mean lifetime of 69,230 miles and a standard deviation of 4620 miles. What proportion of these bearings can be expected to fail before the warranty mileage is reached?

(c) Should the company change suppliers, and if so, why?

13.7 The manager of the Burger-Off restaurant likes customers to finish their meals as quickly as possible so he can maximise the turnaround of diners. The times that diners take follows a normal distribution with a mean of 14 minutes and a standard deviation of 2.1 minutes.

(a) What is the probability that a diner will finish their meal in:
(i)   more than 15 minutes?
(ii)   less than 10 minutes?
(iii) between 12 and 16 minutes?

(b) If the manager replaces the chairs in the restaurant with stools he believes that the times that diners will take to finish their meals will still be normally distributed but with a mean of 13 minutes and a standard deviation of 2.6 minutes. If he is right, what would be the probability that a diner will finish their meal in:
(i)   more than 15 minutes?
(ii)   less than 10 minutes?
(iii) between 12 and 16 minutes?

13.8 According to an agricultural expert the milk yield of cows per year is normally distributed with a mean of 6200 litres and a standard deviation of 430 litres.

(a) What is the probability of the milk yield of a cow being:
(i)   more than 7000 litres?
(ii)   less than 5000 litres?
(iii) less than 6500 litres?
(iv)   between 6000 and 6700 litres?

(b) What is the minimum milk yield of the 10% most efficient cows?

(c) What is the maximum milk yield of the 5% least efficient cows?

13.9 A large clothing store offers a 'no quibble' returns policy under which shoppers can return unwanted goods to the store and receive their money back. They have to take their unwanted goods to a returns desk where there is one server. Customers arrive at the desk according to a Poisson distribution with a mean of 24 per hour and service times at the desk are exponentially distributed with a mean of two minutes.

(a) What is the traffic intensity in the returns system?

(b) What is the probability that there are more than three customers queuing?

(c) What is the mean waiting time?

(d) What is the mean queue length?

★★★ Challenging questions

13.10 A DIY store stocks 2.4-metre lengths of planed timber. There are three sawmills who can supply them. The suppliers and the means and standard deviations of their output are as follows:

Supplier	Mean	Standard deviation
Beamer	2.404 metres	0.008 metres
Knowknots	2.402 metres	0.011 metres
Plankston	2.397 metres	0.006 metres

Assuming that the lengths of timber produced by each of these suppliers are normally distributed, which supplier would be best if:

(a) The store wanted the proportion of lengths above 2.4 metres to be as low as possible?
(b) The store wanted the proportion of lengths below 2.4 metres to be as low as possible?
(c) The store wanted the proportion of lengths between 2.395 and 2.405 to be as high as possible?

13.11 In the Republic of Staria the ages to which people live are normally distributed with a mean of 79 years and a standard deviation of 7.6 years. The state pays citizens a pension from the age of 66. Those of 85 years and older are entitled to free heating in their homes. The president sends those reaching 100 years of age a congratulatory message.

(a) What proportion of the population will live to receive (i) a pension, (ii) free heating, and (iii) a message from the president?
(b) The ages to which the men of Staria live are normally distributed with a mean of 75 years and a standard deviation of 8.8 years. What proportion of them will live to receive (i) a pension, (ii) free heating, and (iii) a message from the president?
(c) The women of Staria tend to live longer than the men. The ages to which they live are normally distributed with a mean of 82 years and a standard deviation of 6.8 years. What proportion of them will live to receive (i) a pension, (ii) free heating, and (iii) a message from the president?

13.12 There is only one pharmacist dispensing prescribed medicines in a small pharmacy. The pattern of customers arriving to obtain a prescription follows a Poisson distribution with a mean of six per hour. The times taken for the pharmacist to dispense the drugs are exponentially distributed with a mean of 7.5 minutes.

(a) (i)   What is the traffic intensity of the system?
     (ii) What is the mean queue length?
     (iii) What is the mean waiting time in the queue?
(b) If increasing the proportion of generic drugs in the pharmacy can reduce the mean service time to six minutes,
     (i)   What is the traffic intensity of the system?
     (ii) What is the mean queue length?
     (iii) What is the mean waiting time in the queue?

THE DEBRIEF

Key things to remember from this chapter

→ The normal distribution is a continuous probability distribution and is an important model for analysing many real-life variables.

→ The shape of the distribution, the normal curve, is symmetrical, has a central peak and sides that taper off at each end.

→ The two defining characteristics of the normal distribution are the mean and the standard deviation.

→ It is a probability distribution so the total area under the curve is one. An area under the curve to the right of a point represents the probability that the variable takes a value above that point. The area to the left of it represents the probability the variable takes a value below that point. The area between two points represents the probability that the variable takes a value between the two points.

→ The standard normal distribution (SND), also called the Z distribution is a special case of the normal distribution. It has a mean of zero and a standard deviation of one.

→ The SND is used to analyse other versions of the normal distribution. Doing this involves finding the z-equivalent of points in the distribution. The z-equivalent is the difference between the point and the mean of the distribution divided by the standard deviation of the distribution.

→ The exponential distribution is a continuous probability distribution which is asymmetrical. Its single defining characteristic is the mean.

→ Probability distributions are used in modelling queuing systems. The exponential distribution is used to model the distribution of service times in queues.

References

Eckes, G. (2001) *The Six Sigma Revolution: How General Electric and Others Turned Process into Profits*, New York: Wiley.

Eckes, G. (2005) *Six Sigma Execution: How the World's Greatest Companies Live and Breathe Six Sigma*, New York: McGraw-Hill.

Hillier, F.S. and Lieberman, G.J. (2009) *Introduction to Operations Research*, New York: McGraw-Hill.

Taha, H.A. (2006) *Operations Research* (8th edn), New York: Prentice-Hall.

CHAPTER 14

Getting from A to B – project planning using networks

This chapter will help you to:

→ Plan projects using network diagrams and critical path analysis (CPA)

→ Use the programme evaluation and review technique (PERT)

→ Conduct cost analysis of projects

THE BARE BONES

What you will find in this chapter . . .

- Constructing network diagrams to represent projects that involve many connected activities
- Identifying the earliest and latest event times for project activities and establishing the critical path of a project
- Incorporating variable activity durations in project planning using PERT
- Exploring the cost implications of reducing project duration
- Choosing optimal strategies of reducing project duration

. . . and on the supporting website (www.pearsoned.co.uk/buglear)

- Fully worked solutions to the review questions
- More review questions

Business use of critical path analysis and PERT

◆ Critical path analysis and PERT were both developed around the middle of the twentieth century. Although they are similar the contexts in which they were developed were very different. Critical path analysis was originally known as the Kelly–Walker method after the two pioneers of the technique: J.E. Kelly of the Remington Rand Company and M.R. Walker of the Du Pont Company, the giant US chemicals corporation that developed Dynamite, Nylon, Teflon and Lycra as well as many other technological innovations. At the time, Remington Rand was the computer systems subsidiary of Du Pont. The initial application of the technique was in the construction of a major new chemical plant at Louisville, Kentucky.

◆ While the origins of critical path analysis were civilian, the roots of PERT lie in the military. In the early phase of the Cold War the US military authorities were desperate to develop intercontinental ballistic missiles. They were concerned about the projections for the completion time of key projects: first the Atlas missile, then more prominently the Polaris system. To expedite matters a central coordinator was appointed to oversee the Polaris project. He assumed control of the entire project and under him PERT evolved as the means by which the myriad of activities involving hundreds of subcontractors were planned so that the Polaris programme was completed much sooner than the 10 years that was initially anticipated.

◆ The success of the Polaris project meant that PERT became widely publicised. In telling the story of its development, Morris (1994: 31) notes that by 1964 there were almost 1000 overwhelmingly enthusiastic articles and books published about PERT. Whilst in retrospect this amounted to overselling the technique, like its close relation critical path analysis it has become widely accepted as a key tool in successful project management.

◆ In his study of the use made of quantitative methods in US businesses, Kathawala (1988) found that 54% of companies in his survey reported that they made moderate, frequent or extensive use of critical path analysis and PERT. Planning tools like these are used in projects like the expansion of the King's Cross underground station in London (Lane, 2003). Klein (2001) discusses the general capabilities of the methods.

14.1 Introduction

Many business operations involve planning and coordinating a project – a series of inter-linked tasks or activities all of which have to be performed in the correct sequence and within the least amount of time in order to achieve a successful conclusion to the venture. This is not only typical of large-scale projects such as you would find in industries like construction and shipbuilding, but also occurs on a more modest basis in administrative processes such as organising events like conferences and concerts.

To help plan and execute projects successfully managers can turn to *network analysis*, a system of representing and linking the activities involved in a project. Once they have designed a network they can use *critical path analysis (CPA)* to establish the minimum duration of the project by identifying those tasks whose completion on time is essential, the *critical* activities. Beyond this they can bring into consideration the probability distributions that reflect the chances of the activities being completed by specific times using the *programme evaluation and review technique (PERT)*. In this chapter we will look at these techniques.

14.2 Network analysis

We can apply network analysis to any project that consists of a series of distinct activities provided that we know which activities must be completed before other activities can commence. This is called the precedence of the activities because it involves identifying the activities that must *precede* each activity. These are crucial because the point of a network diagram is to show how the activities in a project are linked.

The diagrams used for network analysis are built up using a single arrow for each activity. The arrow begins at a circle representing the point in time at which the activity begins and finishes at another circle that represents the completion of the activity. These circles are known as *event nodes*. We would represent a single activity as shown in Figure 14.1.

Figure 14.1 A single activity

In Figure 14.1 the direction of the arrow tells us that the event node on the right marks the completion of the activity. The activity is labelled using a letter and the events nodes are numbered. Network diagrams consist of many arrows and many event nodes, so logical layout and labelling is important.

Networks should be set out so that the beginning of the project is represented by the event node on the extreme left of the diagram and the completion by the event node on the extreme right. In compiling them you should try to ensure that the event nodes are labelled sequentially from left to right from event number 1, the start of the project.

All the arrows should point from left to right either directly or at angle and certainly not from right to left. This is usually straightforward because the purpose of an arrow in a network is to represent the *position* of the activity in relation to other activities and not its *duration*. A network diagram is not intended to be to scale.

EXAMPLE 14.1

Avia Petitza is an independent airline flying short-haul routes in South America. The new general manager is keen to improve efficiency and believes that one aspect of its operations that can be improved is the time it takes to service planes between flights. She has identified the activities involved and their preceding activities and compiled the following table:

Activity	Description	Precedence
A	Drive service vehicles to plane	None
B	Attach stairway	A
C	Unload baggage	A
D	Refuel	A
E	Passengers disembark	B
F	Clean cabin	E
G	Load baggage	C
H	Load food and beverages	E
I	Stock up water tanks	A
J	Service toilets	I
K	Passengers embark	F, H
L	Detach stairway	K
M	Drive service vehicles from plane	D, G, J, L

Produce a network diagram to portray this project.

Solution   Activity A has no preceding activities so we can start the network with this as shown in Figure 14.2(a). Four subsequent activities, B, C, D and I depend on activity A being completed so we can extend the network as shown in Figure 14.2(b). Activity G must follow activity C and activity J follows activity I as depicted in Figure 14.2(c). Activity E follows activity B and activity F follows activity E as shown in Figure 14.2(d).

Before activity K can take place activity H must also have finished. This presents a problem because we cannot have two or more activities starting at the same event node and finishing at the same event node. If we did we would not be able to use the diagram for the sort of scheduling analysis you will meet in the next section of this chapter. To avoid activities F and H having the same event node marking their start and the same event node marking their completion we can introduce a *dummy activity*, an activity that takes no time or uses any resources. Its role is merely to help us distinguish two activities that might otherwise be confused in later analysis. To distinguish between a dummy activity and real activities it is portrayed as a dotted line. You can see a dummy activity in Figure 14.2(e) used to ensure that the event node that marks the conclusion of activity H is not the same as that marking the end of activity F.

The final diagram, Figure 14.2(f), incorporates activities K, L and M. Activities K and L share the same finishing event as activities D and J. This event represents the beginning of activity M, whose closing event marks the conclusion of the project. We can also number the events now the diagram is complete.

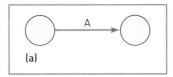

(a)

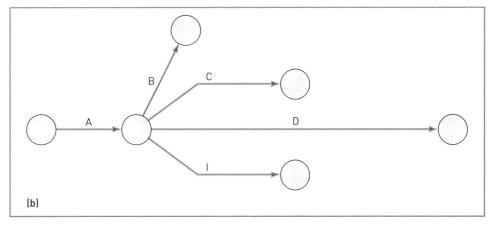

(b)

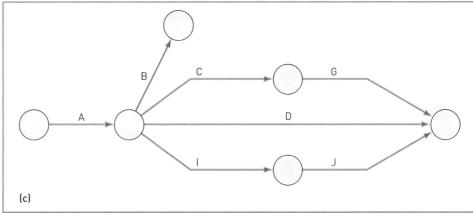

(c)

**Solution
cont**

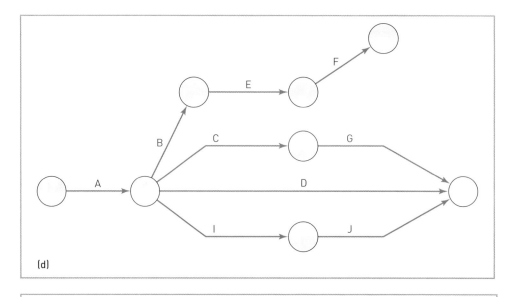

(d)

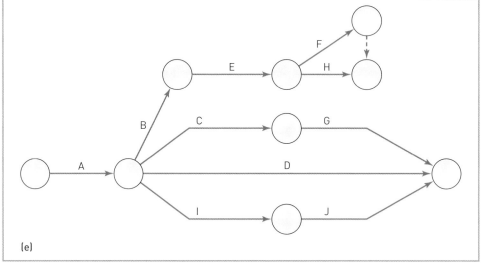

(e)

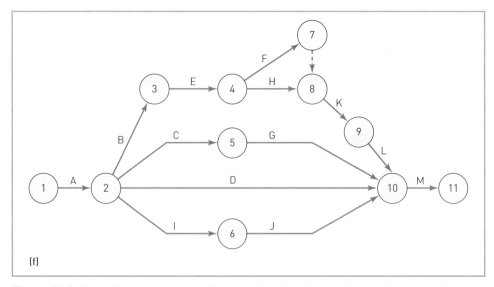

(f)

Figure 14.2 Compiling the network diagram for aircraft servicing in Example 14.1

The dummy activity in Figure 14.2(e) helps us to identify two separate activities. A dummy activity used in this way is an *identity dummy*. Dummy activities are also used to resolve logical difficulties that arise in some networks. A dummy activity used to do this is a *logical dummy*. Both types of dummy activity serve only to clarify the network and avoid ambiguity. The important distinction between real and dummy activities is that the latter do not take time or use resources.

EXAMPLE 14.2

Two building workers, Bru and Chai, like a mug of black tea in their morning break at work. Bru takes sugar, Chai does not. Making their tea involves four activities:

Activity	Description	Precedence
A	Put tea bags in the mugs	None
B	Put sugar in Bru's mug	None
C	Pour hot water in Chai's mug	A
D	Pour hot water in Bru's mug	A, B

Solution

It is tempting to represent these activities in the form of the network in Figure 14.3(a), but this implies that activity C, putting hot water in Chai's mug, depends on activity B, putting sugar in Bru's mug, which is not the case. To get around this we can include a dummy activity as shown in Figure 14.3(b).

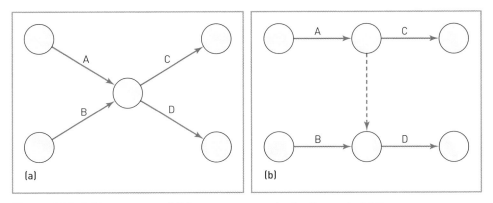

Figure 14.3 (a) Incorrect and (b) correct networks for Example 14.2

Compiling network diagrams often brings an understanding of the way in which activities that make up a project fit together. It enables you to clarify uncertainties about the planning of the project. This is something usually achieved by constructing drafts of the network before producing the final version.

Whilst an understanding of the sequence is important, there is much more to successful project planning. Ascertaining the minimum time in which the project can be completed and scheduling the activities over time are typically the central issues. The technique that enables us to do this is critical path analysis.

Compiling a network diagram

◆ You will need a list of the project activities, how long they are expected to take, and their precedence: in other words, what if any activities must be completed before they can be started.

◆ Don't expect to produce the complete diagram in one go. Be prepared to make at least one rough draft.

◆ Start by drawing the initial event node on the left. Every activity that has no precedent activity starts from this node. Draw a line from the event node for each starting activity.

◆ Deal with each of the remaining activities one at a time. Each one will start at the point where one of the preceding activities finishes. Draw an event node at the point where the preceding activity finishes and a line from it to represent the activity.

◆ If two or more activities start at the same event node and finish at the same event node use dummy activities to distinguish them.

◆ In your first draft the activities that have no activities depending on them, the finishing activities, probably finish at different points. In drawing your final version ensure that they all end in an event that marks the end of the project.

14.3 Critical path analysis

If we know the duration of each activity we can use a network diagram to find out the least amount of time it will take to finish the project.

A network diagram shows the way that activities are linked; in effect it portrays the project as a series of paths of activities. Since every activity must be finished for the project to be completed, the minimum duration of the project is the length of time required to carry out the most time-consuming path of activities. This path is known as the *critical path* since any delay in the completion of activities along it will prolong the entire project. Finishing those activities on the critical path on time is therefore *critical* for the project; they are known as *critical* activities.

Critical path analysis involves increasing the amount of information in the network by enhancing the role of the event nodes. In drawing a network diagram the event nodes are in effect the punctuation marks in the diagram; they bring order to the sequence of arrows. In critical path analysis they become distinct points in time. For each event node we assign an *earliest event time (EET)* and a *latest event time (LET)*. These are written in the circle that represents the event node beneath the event number, as illustrated in Figure 14.4.

The circle on the left in Figure 14.4 is the event node that marks the point in time when activity X begins. The number in the upper part of the circle is the event number, 20. The number below it to the left is the earliest event time and the number below it on the right is the latest event time. These numbers tell us that the earliest time that activity X can start is time period 9 and the latest time it can start is time period 11. From the equivalent figures in the event node

Figure 14.4 Earliest and latest event times for a single activity

to the right of activity X you can tell that the earliest time the activity can be completed is time period 13 and the latest time it can be completed is time period 15.

To work out the earliest and latest times for the events in a network we use the activity durations. Starting with the event node at the beginning of the network and working through the network from left to right we write in the earliest time that each event node in the network can occur. This is referred to as making a *forward pass* through the network. When doing this you need to remember that where there are two or more activities leading to the same event node it is the duration of the longest of the activities that determines the earliest time for the event since all the activities must be completed before the event is reached. We write the earliest event times in the lower left-hand side of the event nodes.

EXAMPLE 14.3

The durations of the activities undertaken during the ground servicing operation in Example 14.1 are given in the following table:

Activity	Description	Duration (minutes)
A	Drive service vehicles to plane	2
B	Attach stairway	3
C	Unload baggage	25
D	Refuel	15
E	Passengers disembark	8
F	Clean cabin	20
G	Load baggage	30
H	Load food and beverages	10
I	Stock up water tanks	5
J	Service toilets	5
K	Passengers embark	15
L	Detach stairway	3
M	Drive service vehicles from plane	2

Using these figures we can enter the earliest event times in the network. These are included in Figure 14.5.

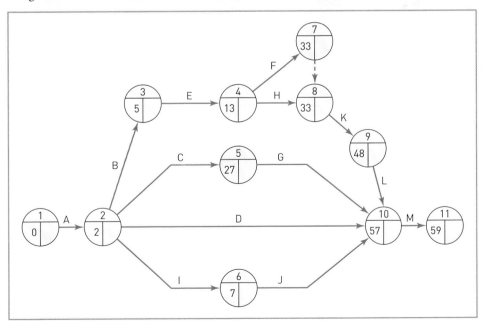

Figure 14.5 Network for ground servicing with earliest event times

If you look carefully at Figure 14.5 you will see that the earliest event time for event 1 is 0 reflecting the fact that 0 minutes of project time have elapsed at the beginning of the project. The earliest event time for event 2 is 2, reflecting the 2 minutes needed for the completion of the only activity between event node 1 and event node 2, activity B, driving the service vehicles to the plane.

The earliest event time for event 8 is perhaps less obvious. The figure entered, 33, has been worked out based on the longest route to it. The activities leading to event node 8 are activity F, with its associated dummy activity between events 7 and 8, and activity H. The earliest time that activity F can start is the earliest event time on the event marking its beginning; the 13 in event 4. If we add the 20 minutes that activity F, cleaning the cabin, takes to the earliest event time for event 4 we get 33 minutes as the earliest time activity F can be completed. Event 4 also marks the beginning of activity H, loading the food and beverages. If we add the time this activity takes, 10 minutes, to the earliest event time of activity 4 we get 23 minutes. This would be the earliest event time for event 8 if we did not need to complete activity F, but since both activity F and activity H have to be completed before event 8 can occur, the earliest time we can get there must allow for the longer activity, activity F, to be concluded, hence the earliest event time for event 8 is 33 and not 23.

The event node indicating the completion of the project on the extreme right of the network has an earliest event time of 59 minutes. This is the minimum duration of the entire project; given the activity durations it cannot be completed in a lesser amount of time. We now need to turn our attention to the latest event times, as comparing these with the earliest event times will enable us to identify the critical path for the project.

Once we have established the minimum project duration, in the case of Example 14.3, 59 minutes, we assume that the project manager will want to complete it in that time. We now undertake the same sort of task to find the latest event times as we used to find the earliest event times, but this time we start on the right-hand side and work back through the network ascertaining the latest time each event can occur if the project is to be finished in the minimum time. This is referred to as making a *backward pass* through the network.

The latest event times for Example 14.3 are included in Figure 14.6. Each event now has a number entered in the lower right-hand side of its node.

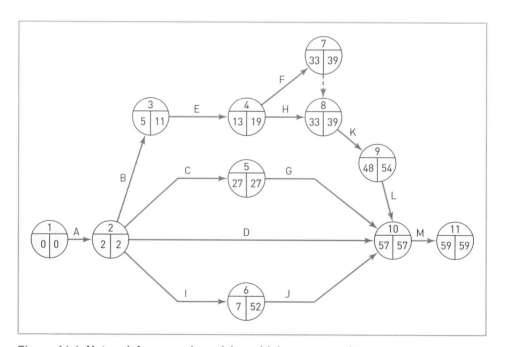

Figure 14.6 Network for ground servicing with latest event times

Looking at Figure 14.6 you can see that the latest event time for the last event, event 11, is 59 minutes. If the project is to be completed in 59 minutes then the latest time we must reach this point is 59 minutes. The latest event time of event 10 is 57 minutes, 59 minutes less the 2 minutes we must allow for activity M to be completed.

Several activities conclude at event 10, including activities G and L. Activity G begins at event 5. The latest event time of event 5 is 27 minutes, sufficient to allow the 30 minutes necessary for the completion of activity G in time for event 10 to be reached in 57 minutes, which in turn allows for the 2 minutes to complete activity M and thus conclude the project in 59 minutes. Activity L begins at event 9. Since activity L, detaching the stairway, takes 3 minutes, the latest event time for event 9 is 54 minutes, sufficient to allow the 3 minutes for the completion of activity L so that event 10 can be reached in 57 minutes and thus leave 2 minutes for activity M to finish in time for completing the project in 59 minutes.

If you study Figure 14.6 carefully you will see that some events, such as event 5, have the same earliest and latest event times while other events, such as event 6, have different ones. In the case of event 6 the earliest event time is 7 minutes whereas the latest event time is 52 minutes. This implies that activity I can be completed by 7 minutes but it doesn't have to be finished until 52 minutes have elapsed. In other words, there is time to spare for the completion of activities I and J; they have what is called *slack* or *float*.

In contrast, the latest event time for event 5 is the same as its earliest event time, 27 minutes. In this case the earliest time event 5 can be reached is the same as the latest time it has to be reached if the project is to be completed in 59 minutes. This implies there is no slack or float for activities C and G; they must be undertaken at the earliest feasible opportunity as their completion on time is *critical* for the conclusion of the project, they are *critical activities*. If you look at the event nodes that have the same earliest and latest event times you will see that they connect activities A, C, G and M. These activities are driving service vehicles to the plane, unloading and loading baggage, and driving service vehicles from the plane. They form the longest or *critical* path through the network; a delay in the execution of any of them will result in the project being prolonged beyond 59 minutes. On the other hand, any reduction in the duration of any of them will reduce the duration of the project, but only up to a point; at some point another path will become critical.

At this point you may find it useful to try **Review questions 14.1 to 14.5** at the end of the chapter.

By definition the critical activities in a network have no slack or float, but other activities will. A project manager is likely to be very interested in the float available for these activities, as it indicates the degree of latitude available in scheduling them.

To work out the total float for an activity we need to know the latest event time for the event that marks its completion, its *finishing event*, and the earliest event time for the event that represents its beginning, its *starting event*. If we subtract the duration of the activity from the difference between these times what is left over is the total float for the activity. We can summarise this procedure as:

$$\text{Total float} = \text{Latest event time (finishing event)}$$
$$- \text{earliest event time (starting event)}$$
$$- \text{activity duration}$$

Using abbreviations:

$$\text{TF} = \text{LET (F)} - \text{EET (S)} - \text{AD}$$

Look carefully at Table 14.1 in Example 14.4 and you will see that some activities have a zero float. These are the activities on the critical path A–C–G–M. In contrast there is a float of 6 minutes in the path B–E–F–K–L, which is the uppermost path in Figure 14.6. This is the float associated with the path rather than an individual activity; once used up by, say, taking 9 minutes rather than 3 minutes for activity B, attaching the stairway, it would not be available for the subsequent activities E, F, K and L, which as a consequence would become as critical as the activities on the critical path.

EXAMPLE 14.4

Find the total floats for the ground servicing activities in Example 14.1.

Solution

Table 14.1 Total floats for activities in Example 14.1

Activity	LET (F) (1)	EET (S) (2)	AD(3)	TF–(1)–(2)–(3)
A	2	0	2	0
B	11	2	3	6
C	27	2	25	0
D	57	2	15	40
E	19	5	8	6
F	39	13	20	6
G	57	27	30	0
H	39	13	10	16
I	52	2	5	45
J	57	7	5	45
K	54	33	15	6
L	57	48	3	6
M	59	57	2	0

Activity H, loading the food and beverages, has a total float of 16 minutes, 6 of which are shared with the other activities along its path: B, E, K and L. The remaining 10 minutes are specific to activity H; it must be completed by the same time as activity F, cleaning the cabin, if the project is to be finished in the minimum time, yet it takes 10 minutes less to perform.

Activity D, refuelling, has a float of 40 minutes, which cannot be shared with the other activities along its path, A and M, as they are both critical. The relatively large amount of float for this activity allows the project manager considerable flexibility in scheduling this activity. Similar flexibility exists for activities I and J, the water operations, which share a total float of 45 minutes.

At this point you may find it useful to try **Review questions 14.1 to 14.5** at the end of the chapter.

SELF-ASSEMBLY GUIDE

Event times, the critical path and floats

◆ Starting from the event that marks the beginning of the project, which should be on the left of your diagram, work out the earliest time that the next event can be reached. If there is more that one activity between the two events this is the duration of activity that takes longest.

◆ Work out the earliest event time for every event. Be especially careful where there are different sequences of activities meeting at a single event.

◆ The earliest event time of the event that marks the end of the project is the minimum project time. It is also the starting point for working out the latest event times for the events.

◆ The latest event time for the final event is the same as its earliest event time. Beginning from this event work out the latest time that the preceding events must have been reached in order to finish the project in the minimum project time. Be careful to take the longest path if there is more than one between events.

◆ Having worked back to the event that marks the beginning of the project you should find that its latest event time is 0, the same as its earliest event time.

◆ There should be a sequence of activities that are linked by event nodes that have the same latest event times as earliest event times. This sequence is the critical path.

◆ The activities on the critical path have no slack, or float; they have to be finished on schedule otherwise the whole project is delayed.

◆ All other activities have some float. To work out how much take the earliest event time of the event node that precedes the activity plus its duration away from the latest event time of the event that follows the activity.

14.4 The programme evaluation and review technique (PERT)

So far we have assumed that the activities making up a project each have fixed durations. In reality this is unlikely to be the case. In the ground servicing project introduced in Example 14.1 factors such as the state of equipment, the time of the day or night, and weather conditions will influence the time it takes to complete the activities. Rather than being fixed, activity durations are more likely to be variable. PERT allows us to take this into account.

In using PERT we assume that the duration of an activity is a continuous variable that follows a continuous probability distribution. We looked at continuous probability distributions like the normal distribution in Chapter 13. The distribution used in PERT as the model for activity durations is the *beta distribution*. Like the normal distribution it is continuous, but unlike the normal distribution it can be skewed or symmetrical and it has a minimum and a maximum value. The key characteristics or parameters of the beta distribution are the minimum or *optimistic* duration, a, the maximum or *pessimistic* duration, b, and the *most likely* duration, m.

You can see two types of beta distribution in Figure 14.7. The diagram on the left portrays a symmetrical distribution with a minimum of 0 and a maximum of 10. The most likely value of

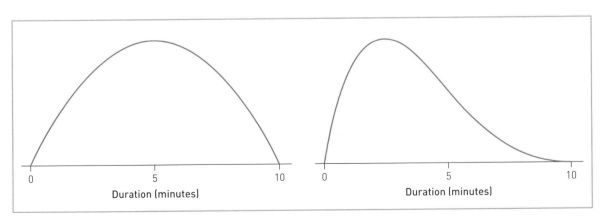

Figure 14.7 Examples of the beta distribution

this distribution is 5 minutes, midway between the extremes. In the asymmetrical beta distribution in the diagram on the right the minimum and maximum durations are the same as in the other diagram but the most likely value is rather lower.

If you know the optimistic (a), most likely (m) and pessimistic (b) durations of an activity you can work out its mean duration using the expression:

$$\mu = \frac{a + 4m + b}{6}$$

The standard deviation of the activity duration is:

$$\sigma = \frac{(b - a)}{6}$$

The variance of the activity duration is the square of its standard deviation:

$$\sigma^2 = \frac{(b - a)}{6^2}$$

The mean duration of an entire project is the sum of the mean durations of the activities that are on the critical path, the critical activities. The variance of the project duration is the sum of the variances of the critical activities and the standard deviation of the project duration is the square root of its variance. Note that you cannot get the standard deviation of the project duration by adding together the standard deviations of the durations of the critical activities; it is the variances that sum, not the standard deviations.

EXAMPLE 14.5

Using time sheets and airport records, the general manager in Example 14.1 has established the optimistic, most likely and pessimistic durations of the activities involved in the ground servicing of aircraft. They are set out in Table 14.2. Using appropriate figures from this table, work out the mean and standard deviation of the project duration.

Table 14.2 Optimistic, most likely and pessimistic durations of ground operations

Activity	Description	Duration (minutes) Optimistic (a)	Most likely (m)	Pessimistic (b)
A	Drive vehicles to plane	1	2	3
B	Attach stairway	2	3	5
C	Unload baggage	22	25	30
D	Refuel	14	15	17
E	Passengers disembark	6	8	12
F	Clean cabin	15	20	25
G	Load baggage	25	30	32
H	Load food and beverages	8	10	12
I	Stock up water tanks	4	5	7
J	Service toilets	3	5	10
K	Passengers embark	8	15	20
L	Detach stairway	2	3	4
M	Drive vehicles from plane	1	2	3

Solution

The mean project duration is the sum of the mean durations of the critical activities. In this project the critical activities are A, C, G and M. The means of these activities are:

$$\mu_A = \frac{1 + (4 * 2) + 3}{6} = 2$$

$$\mu_C = \frac{22 + (4 * 25) + 31}{6} = 25.5$$

$$\mu_G = \frac{25 + (4 * 30) + 32}{6} = 29$$

$$\mu_M = \frac{1 + (4 * 2) + 3}{6} = 2$$

The mean duration of the critical path is the sum of these means:

$$\mu_{CP} = \mu_A + \mu_C + \mu_G + \mu_M = 2 + 25.5 + 29 + 2 = 58.5 \text{ minutes}$$

The standard deviation of the critical path is the square root of the variance of the critical path, which is the sum of the variances of the critical activities, A, C, G and M. The variances of these activities are:

$$\sigma_A^2 = ((3 - 1)/6)^2 = 4/36 = 1/9$$

$$\sigma_C^2 = ((31 - 22)/6)^2 = 81/36 = 9/4$$

$$\sigma_G^2 = ((32 - 25)/6)^2 = 49/36$$

$$\sigma_M^2 = ((3 - 1)/6)^2 = 4/36$$

The variance of the duration of the critical path is:

$$\sigma_{CP}^2 = \sigma_A^2 + \sigma_C^2 + \sigma_G^2 + \sigma_M^2 = \frac{4 + 81 + 49 + 4}{36} = \frac{138}{36} = 3.833$$

The standard deviation of the duration of the critical path is:

$$\sigma_{CP} = \sqrt{\sigma_{CP}^2} = \sqrt{3.833} = 1.958 \text{ minutes}$$

Unless there is clear evidence that the distributions of the durations of the individual activities are consistently skewed, we can assume that the distribution of the project duration is approximately normal. This means we can use the standard normal distribution to work out the probability that the project is completed within a certain timescale or beyond a certain timescale.

EXAMPLE 14.6

What is the probability that the ground servicing operation whose activity durations were detailed in Example 14.5 can be completed in one hour?

Solution

If X is the project duration, we want:

$$P(X < 60) = P\left(Z < \frac{60 - 58.5}{1.958}\right) = P(Z < 0.766)$$

If you check Table 5 in Appendix 1 you will find that the probability that Z is more than 0.77 is 0.2206. The probability that Z is less than 0.77 is 1 less 0.2206, 0.7794, which is the probability that the ground servicing operation is completed within an hour.

We can also work out the timescale within which a certain proportion of ground operations should be completed using the Z distribution.

EXAMPLE
14.7

What is the timescale within which 90% of ground servicing operations should be completed?

Solution

For this you will need the z value that cuts off a tail of 10%, $z_{0.10}$. You can find it by looking down the probabilities in Table 5 until you reach the figure closest to 10%, the 0.1003 in the row for 1.2 and the column headed 0.08, so $z_{0.10}$ is approximately 1.28. For a more precise figure for $z_{0.10}$ use the bottom row of the related Table 6 in Appendix 1. The figure in this row and in the column headed 0.10 is 1.282 so 90% of the normal distribution is to the left of, or less than, 1.282 standard deviations above the mean. We can apply this to the distribution of the duration of the ground servicing operation; 90% of the operation will be completed in a time less than 1.282 standard deviations above the mean:

$$\mu_{CP} + 1.282\,\sigma_{CP} = 58.5 + 1.282 * 1.958 = 61.010 \text{ minutes}$$

At this point you may find it useful to try **Review questions 14.6 to 14.8 and 14.12** at the end of the chapter.

14.5 Cost analysis: crashing the project duration

PERT is designed to allow for random fluctuations in the duration of activities. These are by definition in large part difficult or impossible to anticipate, yet they can have a substantial impact on the duration of a project.

In contrast, it may be possible to reduce the project duration by cutting activity durations by intent. Typically this involves incurring extra cost, defined as the cost of *crashing* the duration of an activity below its anticipated duration.

In most projects there are at least some activities that can be performed more quickly, perhaps by providing more or better equipment, perhaps by allocating more staff, perhaps by hiring a subcontractor. These contingencies will come at an additional cost, the *crash cost*, the cost of carrying out the activity in its *crash duration* rather than its normal duration.

Although there may be several activities in a project that can be crashed, it may not be worthwhile crashing all of them. The project duration is the critical path, the path of critical activities, whose completion on schedule is crucial for the minimum duration of the project to be achieved. If an activity is not on the critical path it is not worth crashing, or at least not until it might have become critical following the crashing of one or more critical activities. Crashing a non-critical activity will not reduce the duration of the critical path, but crashing a critical activity will always reduce the duration of the critical path. Having said that, there is a limit. Once the critical path activities have been crashed to the point that another path loses its float and becomes critical, it is not worth crashing critical activities any further. Any further project reduction has to involve further crashing of the activities on the original critical path as well as crashing activities that have become critical after the initial crashing of the critical path activities.

There may be several critical activities than can be crashed. If this is the case the activities to be crashed should be selected on the basis of cost, with the cheapest options implemented first.

EXAMPLE 14.8

The general manager in Example 14.1 has found that three of the activities that make up the ground servicing operation can be crashed; activities C, unloading the baggage, F, cleaning the cabin, and G, loading the baggage. The crash durations and crash costs of these activities are set out in Table 14.3.

Table 14.3 **Crash durations and crash costs of operations C, F and G**

Activity	Normal duration (minutes)	Crash duration (minutes)	Crash cost ($)	Crash cost per minute ($)
C	25	20	200	40
F	15	8	140	20
G	30	26	200	50

Although the cheapest activity to crash is activity F, cleaning the cabin, if you look back at Figure 14.6 you will see that it is not on the critical path; indeed if you check Example 14.4 you will find that there are 6 minutes of float available for activity F. Cutting its duration will merely add to its float and not reduce the minimum duration of the project.

Activities C and G are both on the critical path, so it is worth considering crashing them. The cheaper to crash is activity C, at $40 per minute compared to $50 per minute for crashing activity G.

To what extent should activity C be crashed?

Solution

The answer is up to the point when the path with the least float becomes critical. The path B–E–F–K–L has 6 minutes of float, so it would be worth reducing the duration of activity C by 6 minutes. Since the crash duration of activity C is only 5 minutes, to achieve a reduction of 6 minutes in the project duration we would have to reduce the duration of activity G by 1 minute as well.

A greater reduction in the project duration would involve further crashing of activity G and crashing activity F. The possible stages in reducing the project duration and their associated costs are:

Stage 1: Crash activity C by 5 minutes at a cost of $200 and reduce the project duration to 54 minutes.

Stage 2: Crash activity G by 1 minute at a cost of $50 and reduce the project duration to 53 minutes. Total crashing cost $250.

Stage 3: Crash activity G by a further 3 minutes and crash activity F by 3 minutes at a combined cost of $210 and reduce the project duration to 50 minutes. Total crashing cost $460.

Would it be worth incurring the extra costs of crashing in a case like Example 14.8? It depends on the circumstances. It may be that the normal duration of the ground servicing operation is longer than the allotted time slot at the airport and as a result the airline has to pay penalty costs to the airport authority. Alternatively, reducing the ground servicing time may enable the airline to schedule more flights and thus increase revenue. In either case, deciding how far to go in crashing the project will rest on balancing the costs of crashing and the financial, and possibly other, benefits of doing so.

At this point you may find it useful to try **Review questions 14.9 to 14.11** at the end of the chapter.

REVIEW QUESTIONS

Answers to these questions are on page 453. There are tips and hints to help you with them on the supporting website at **www.pearsoned.co.uk/buglear**, where you will also find the fully worked solutions.

☆☆★ Basic questions

14.1 Bibb and Tukka own and operate a successful chain of clothing stores. They plan to open a new outlet. The activities involved are listed below with the activities that must precede them and their durations.

Activity	Description	Precedence	Duration (days)
A	Negotiate the lease	–	10
B	Install the fixtures	A	8
C	Install the furnishings	B	3
D	Appoint the staff	A	2
E	Train the staff	D	10
F	Arrange the opening ceremony	D	7
G	Opening ceremony	C, E, F	1

(a) Compile a network diagram to represent this venture.
(b) Find the earliest and latest event times for the events in your network, and use them to identify the minimum duration of the project and the activities that are on its critical path.

14.2 Nat Chelnick has to go on an unexpected but urgent business trip to a city in Central Asia. The arrangements he has to make are:

Activity	Description	Precedence	Duration (days)
A	Renew his passport	–	8
B	Obtain a visa	A	10
C	Go for vaccination shots†	–	6
D	Order and receive currency	–	4
E	Order and receive tickets	B	1
F	Book accommodation	E	3
G	Book airport parking	E	2

† Includes time to allow for side-effects of vaccine

Compile a network for this venture and, using it, find how long Nat will have to wait before he can make the trip, and state which activities are critical.

14.3 The renowned rock band Kamien has just completed a highly successful national tour. Tickets have sold so well that they would like to put on an extra concert. The tasks involved in organising this, together with their preceding activities and expected durations, are:

Activity	Description	Precedence	Duration (days)
A	Agree the leasing of the hall	–	10
B	Engage the support acts	A	6
C	Hire security staff	A	8
D	Order and receive merchandising	B	14
E	Organise ticket sales	B	2
F	Early promotional work	E	4
G	Book hotels and transport	B	2
H	Final promotional work	F	5
I	Stage rehearsal/sound checks	G	1

(a) Create a network for this project.
(b) Find the minimum duration of the project and indicate the activities on the critical path.

14.4 The Raketa Racing Team are a new entrant to motor racing. They have been practising their pit stop procedures and their performance is detailed below:

Activity	Description	Precedence	Duration (seconds)
A	Guide driver to pit	–	3
B	Jack up the car	A	2
C	Remove the old wheels	B	5
D	Fit the new wheels	C	5
E	Refuel the car	B	16
F	Wipe driver's visor	B	2
G	Release and clear jacks	D, F	2
H	Check all clear	E, G	2
I	Signal GO	H	1

(a) Draw a network for the pit stop procedure.
(b) Using your diagram work out the earliest and latest time for each event, find the minimum duration for the pit stop and identify the critical path.

☆★★ More testing questions

14.5 Members of the Keeshka Dining Club meet once a month to enjoy a meal with a set two-course menu at the club premises while listening to a string quartet. Planning the meal entails scheduling the activities listed below:

Activity	Description	Precedence	Duration (minutes)
A	Lay table covers	–	10
B	Set out condiments and cutlery	A	5
C	Set out glasses	A	10
D	Set up musicians' equipment	–	40
E	Greet guests with aperitif	B, C	10
F	Seat guests	D, E	4

(Continued)

Activity	Description	Precedence	Duration (minutes)
G	Take wine orders	F	6
H	Serve wine	G	8
I	Serve main course	H	5
J	Guests eat main course	I	30
K	Clear main course	J	5
L	Serve dessert	K	4
M	Guests eat dessert	L	15
N	Clear dessert	M	3
O	Serve coffee	M	6

(a) Prepare a network diagram for this procedure and from it ascertain the earliest time that the serving of coffee will be completed if the laying of the table covers begins at 11.30am.

(b) Identify the critical activities.

14.6 Nat Chelnick, the business traveller in Question 14.2, has found out more about how long his preparations for the trip will take:

Activity	Description	Duration (days)		
		Optimistic	Most likely	Pessimistic
A	Renew his passport	5	8	12
B	Obtain a visa	6	10	20
C	Go for vaccination shots	6	6	8
D	Order and receive currency	3	4	6
E	Order and receive tickets	1	1	3
F	Book accommodation	1	3	4
G	Book airport parking	1	2	2

(a) Work out the mean and the standard deviation for these preparations.

(b) Nat would like to make the trip within the next 30 days. What are the chances of his doing so?

(c) Within what timescale does he have an 80% chance of making the trip?

14.7 The head of the Raketa Racing Team from Question 14.4 monitors the pit stop performances and presents the figures below:

Activity	Description	Duration (seconds)		
		Optimistic	Most likely	Pessimistic
A	Guide driver to pit	2	3	5
B	Jack up the car	1	2	4
C	Remove the old wheels	4	5	6
D	Fit the new wheels	5	5	7
E	Refuel the car	13	16	20
F	Wipe driver's visor	2	2	2
G	Release and clear jacks	2	2	4
H	Check all clear	2	2	3
I	Signal GO	1	1	2

(a) Calculate the mean and the standard deviation of the pit stop duration.

(b) The performance target for the team is 22 seconds. What is the probability that they will make it?

14.8 Slattkey Sweets proposes to re-launch one of its mature brands, the Zubirot Bar. The brand manager has identified the tasks involved and produced the following information about them:

Activity	Description	Precedence	Duration (weeks)
A	Redesign the bar	–	8
B	Redesign the packaging	–	4
C	Build pilot production line	A, B	13
D	Trial production run	C	1
E	Consumer panel tests	D	1
F	Main pilot production	E	6
G	Design promotional material	E	4
H	Test market redesigned product	F, G	10
I	Produce report for the Board	H	2

(a) Draw a network to portray this enterprise and use it to find the minimum duration of the project and those activities that are on the critical path.

(b) The brand manager obtains more details of the re-launch tasks:

Activity	Description	Duration (weeks)		
		Optimistic	Most likely	Pessimistic
A	Redesign the bar	5	8	10
B	Redesign the packaging	3	4	5
C	Build pilot production line	10	13	16
D	Trial production run	1	1	2
E	Consumer panel tests	1	1	1
F	Main pilot production	4	6	9
G	Design promotional material	2	4	5
H	Test market redesigned product	8	10	15
I	Produce report for the Board	2	2	3

(i) Determine the mean and the standard deviation for the product re-launch.
(ii) Ascertain the probability that the project will be finished in 40 weeks.
(iii) Within what number of weeks is there a 99% chance of completion?

14.9 Marsh and Root Construction have won the contract to widen and resurface a section of road. The site manager has identified the following tasks together with the tasks that must precede them and their anticipated durations:

Activity	Description	Precedence	Duration (days)
A	Relocate bus stop	–	2
B	Install temporary traffic lights	–	1
C	Install safety barriers	A, B	1
D	Plane road	C	2
E	Lift kerbstones	C	3
F	Replace ironworks	D	3
G	Lay and roll tarmac	F	1
H	Replace kerbstones	E	4
I	Road painting	G	2
J	Remove safety barriers	I	1
K	Remove temporary traffic lights	J	1
L	Restore bus stop	H	2

(a) Construct a network to portray the project.
(b) Identify the critical path and hence ascertain the minimum duration for these roadworks.
(c) Marsh and Root Construction can earn a bonus of £1000 for every day less than 13 days the completion of the roadworks takes. They can crash the tasks listed below:

Activity	Normal duration (days)	Crash duration (days)	Crash cost (£)
D	2	1	600
E	3	2	200
F	3	2	300
H	4	2	500

Identify the activities that should be crashed and calculate the extra money they can make as a result.

★★★ Challenging questions

14.10 Bibb and Tukka from Question 14.1 have assembled further information about the completion times of the activities involved in their opening the new outlet:

Activity	Description	Duration (days)		
		Optimistic	Most likely	Pessimistic
A	Negotiate the lease	6	10	12
B	Install the fixtures	5	8	15
C	Install the furnishings	2	3	6
D	Appoint the staff	1	2	4
E	Train the staff	8	10	14
F	Arrange the opening ceremony	4	7	8
G	Opening ceremony	1	1	1

(a) Calculate the mean and the standard deviation of the project duration.
(b) The original plan was to complete everything, including the opening ceremony, in 22 days. What is the probability that this will be achieved?
(c) Within what time will there be a 95% chance of completing everything?
(d) Bibb and Tukka have identified the potential for crashing some of the tasks involved in opening their new outlet. The details are:

Activity	Normal duration (days)	Crash duration (days)	Crash cost (£)
B	8	4	800
C	3	1	300
E	10	8	600
F	7	5	400

(i) Use your network diagram for the project to work out the total float for each activity.
(ii) Work out the crash cost per day for each activity that can be crashed. Outline what activities Bibb and Tukka should crash and in which order. Identify for each stage of crashing the reduction in the project duration and the total cost involved.
(iii) If Bibb and Tukka make a net loss of £400 a day from lost business for every day the outlet is not open, what is their optimal crashing strategy?

14.11 The Dom Stila fashion house intends to stage a fashion show to promote its autumn collection. Three designers, Mallover, Millisha and Mockry, have been commissioned to produce designs for the show. The tasks entailed in completing the project, together with their durations and the tasks that must precede them, are:

Activity	Description	Precedence	Duration (days)
A	Mallover prepares designs	–	8
B	Millisha prepares designs	–	16
C	Mockry prepares designs	–	14
D	Select models	A, B, C	1
E	Make up Mallover designs	D	5
F	Make up Millisha designs	D	10
G	Make up Mockry designs	D	12
H	Design show (music, chore-ography and lighting etc.)	A, B, C	6
I	Construct the set	H	12
J	Obtain props and accessories	I	1
K	Design and print publicity	H	9
L	Distribute publicity	K	3
M	Rehearse show	E, F, G, J	2

(a) Produce a network for this project, list the critical activities and ascertain the minimum duration of the project.

(b) In the light of information about a competitor's fashion show Dom Stila wants to reduce the time it takes to stage its show by three days, but at the least cost. A number of activities can be crashed:

Activity	Normal duration (days)	Crash duration (days)	Crash cost (£)
B	16	13	900
C	14	12	800
F	10	8	500
I	12	9	1500

Which activities should be crashed, by how much and at what total cost?

14.12 The Easkritsy Car Valet Service defines the standard car clean it offers as consisting of the following operations:

Activity	Description	Precedence	Duration (minutes)
A	External pre-wash	–	5
B	External main wash	A	8
C	External rinse	B	2
D	External wax and polish	C	12
E	Polish external windows	D	1
F	Enhance tyre wall black	D	4
G	Remove floor mats	–	2
H	Vacuum seats	G	4
I	Vacuum floor	H	6
J	Polish fascia and door panels	I	6
K	Apply air freshener	J	1

(a) Draw a network to portray this enterprise and use it to find the minimum duration of the project and those activities that are on the critical path.

(b) The company promotes its standard car clean as its '30-minute valet'. Using the information below find the proportion of standard car cleans that are completed within 30 minutes:

Activity	Description	Duration (minutes)		
		Optimistic	Most likely	Pessimistic
A	External pre-wash	4	5	6
B	External main wash	5	8	12
C	External rinse	2	2	3
D	External wax and polish	9	12	15
E	Polish external windows	1	1	2
F	Enhance tyre wall black	3	4	5
G	Remove floor mats	1	2	3
H	Vacuum seats	3	4	6
I	Vacuum floor	5	6	7
J	Polish fascia and door panels	3	6	8
K	Apply air freshener	1	1	1

THE DEBRIEF

Key things to remember from this chapter

→ Network diagrams are devices to show how the activities that make up a project are connected. They are composed of lines that represent activities and circles that represent points in time at which activities start or finish.

→ The critical path of a project is the sequence of activities within the project that takes longer to complete than the other paths through the network.

→ Any delay in completing an activity on the critical path will delay the project.

→ The float or slack of an activity is how much it can be delayed without delaying the project. All activities on the critical path have zero float.

→ The programme evaluation and review technique (PERT) enables the variation in activity completion times to be taken into account in project planning. Doing this means that the probability of completing a project within a specific period can be assessed.

→ The project completion time can be cut by 'crashing', reducing activity durations. Usually this involves extra cost. Deciding which activities to crash depends on knowing which activities are on the critical path and how much float the other activities have.

References

Kathawala, Y. (1988) 'Applications of quantitative techniques in large and small organisations in the United States: an empirical analysis', *Journal of the Operational Research Society*, 39(11), pp. 981–9.

Klien, J.H. (2001) *Critical Path Analysis*, Basingstoke: Palgrave.

Lane, K. (2003) 'Making connections at King's Cross', *Project Manager Today*, May 2003, pp. 8–12.

Morris, P.W.G. (1994) *The Management of Projects*, London: Thomas Telford.

CHAPTER 15

Taking short cuts – sampling methods

CHAPTER OBJECTIVES

This chapter will help you to:

→ Appreciate the reasons for sampling

→ Understand sampling bias and how to avoid it

→ Employ probabilistic sampling methods and be aware of their limitations

THE BARE BONES

What you will find in this chapter . . .

- Understanding the consequences of bias in the process of taking samples
- Using random numbers to select simple random samples
- Applying other probabilistic sampling methods: systematic, stratified and cluster sampling
- Applying non-probabilistic sampling methods: quota, judgemental, snowball, convenience and self-selection sampling

. . . and on the supporting website (www.pearsoned.co.uk/buglear)

- Simple random sampling using Minitab and SPSS

Business use of sampling

◆ In his survey of US corporations' use of quantitative methods Kathawala (1988) found that 69% of companies made moderate, frequent or extensive use of statistical sampling. The heaviest users included life insurance companies and electrical utilities.

◆ In their history of market research McDonald and King (1996) explain the importance of sampling for many large companies, including Barclaycard, Gillette and Unilever.

◆ The MTV television channel undertook sample investigations of the tastes, preferences and lifestyles of its subscribers. Wilson (2006) describes one of their surveys in which passages of music were played over the phone to a random sample of the MTV target audience who were then asked whether or not they considered it suitable for the channel.

◆ Wilson (2006) also outlines the use of multi-stage sampling in the UK National Readership survey, a key source of information for advertisers who want to know about the readership of publications in which they might place advertisements, as well as for the publishers, who use the same information to set prices for the advertisements.

◆ Kinnear and Taylor describe how Black and Decker used sample research in developing their Quantum range of equipment (1996: 6–8). Their premium DeWalt range of power tools was aimed at professionals and considered too expensive by DIY enthusiasts. Quantum was developed as a quality brand but with a price strategy attuned to DIY customers.

15.1 Introduction

A *population* is the entire set of items or people that form the subjects of study in an investigation and a *sample* is a subset of a population. Companies need to know about the populations they deal with: populations of customers, employees, suppliers, products and so on. Typically these populations are very large, so large that they are to all intents and purposes infinite.

Gathering data about such large populations is likely to be very expensive, time-consuming and to a certain extent impractical. The scale of expense can be immense; even governments of large countries only commit resources to survey their entire populations, that is, to conduct a census, about every 10 years.

The amount of time involved in surveying the whole population means that it may be so long before the results are available that they are completely out of date. There may be some elements within the population that simply cannot be included in a survey of it; for instance, a car manufacturer may want to conduct a survey of all customers buying a certain model three years before in order to gauge customer satisfaction. Inevitably a number of those customers will have died in the period since buying their car and thus cannot be included in the survey.

To satisfy their need for data about the populations that matter to them without having to incur great expense or wait a long time for results companies turn to sampling, the process of taking a sample from a population in order to use the sample data to gain insight into the entire population. Although not as accurate as the results of a population survey, sample results can be precise enough to serve the purposes of the investigation.

The downside of sampling is that many different samples can be taken from the same population, even if the samples are the same size. You can work out the number of samples of n items that could be selected from a population of N items:

$$\text{Number of samples size } n = \frac{N!}{n!(N-n)!}$$

EXAMPLE 15.1

Work out the number of samples of size six that could be selected from a very small population of just 20 items.

Solution

$$\text{Number of samples size } 6 = \frac{20!}{6!\ 14!} = 38,760$$

Given how small the population is in Example 15.1, as you might imagine the number of samples that could be selected from a much larger population will be so very large as to border on the infinite.

Each of the samples you could select from a population inevitably excludes much of the population, so sample results will not be precisely the same as those from the entire population. There will be differences known as *sampling errors* between sample results and the results of a population survey and furthermore different samples will yield different results and hence different sampling errors.

In this chapter you will find details of a variety of sampling methods, but before we look at them we need to consider what companies might look for in sampling, and what they would prefer to avoid.

15.2 Bias in sampling

The point of selecting a sample from a population is to study it and use the results to understand the population. To be effective a sample should therefore reflect the population as a whole. However, there is no guarantee that the elements of the population that are chosen for the sample will collectively reflect the population. Even if the population is quite small there will be an enormous number of combinations of elements that you could select in a sample. Inevitably some of these samples will represent the entire population better than others.

Although it is impossible to avoid the possibility of getting an unrepresentative sample, it is important to avoid using a sampling method that will almost invariably lead to your getting an unrepresentative sample. This means avoiding bias in selecting your sample.

Effective methods of sampling are those that minimise the chances of getting unrepresentative samples and allow you to anticipate the degree of sampling error using appropriate probability distributions. Such methods should give every element of the population the same chance of being selected in a sample as any other element of the population, and consequently every possible sample of a certain size the same chance of selection as every other sample of the same size.

If some elements of the population have a greater chance of being selected in a sample than others, then we have bias in our sampling method. Bias has to be avoided as the samples that can result will be extremely unlikely to reflect the population as a whole and such misleading results may have disastrous consequences.

<table>
<tr><td>

EXAMPLE 15.2

</td><td>

Packaged potato crisps are sold by the million every day of the week; it is a huge market. You might think that the company that pioneered the product would by now be a very large and successful one, but you would be wrong; after its initial success it ran into problems that eventually led to its being taken over. Occasionally the company that now owns the brand re-launches it as a retro product, with the distinctive small blue paper twist of salt in the crisp packet.

A key factor in the decline of the potato crisp pioneer was product quality. The company received a consistent stream of complaints from customers about the number of charred and green-tinged crisps. The company directors knew of these complaints but were baffled by them; they knew their product was good because they tasted a sample taken from the production line every day with their morning coffee.

The problem for the directors was the method used to take the samples from the production line. The sample was selected by the shop floor staff, who knew they were destined for the boardroom and quite understandably ensured that only the best were selected. The samples provided for the directors were therefore biased; the charred and green crisps that their customers wrote about had no chance of being selected in the samples taken for the directors.

The directors were reluctant to take action to deal with a problem they were convinced did not exist. This made it easier for competitors to enter the market and the initial advantage the pioneer enjoyed was lost.

</td></tr>
</table>

In Example 15.2 the company directors were completely misled by the bias in the selection of their samples of potato crisps. Biased samples will mislead, no matter how large the samples are; in fact, the larger such samples are, the greater the danger of misrepresentation since it is always tempting to attach more credibility to a large sample.

<table>
<tr><td>

EXAMPLE 15.3

</td><td>

In the 1936 presidential election in the USA the incumbent Democrat, Franklin Roosevelt, faced the Republican governor of Kansas, Alfred Landon. Roosevelt was associated with the New Deal programme of large-scale public expenditure to alleviate the high level of unemployment in the depression of the time. Landon on the other hand wanted to end what he considered government profligacy.

The prominent US weekly magazine of the time, *The Literary Digest*, conducted one of the largest polls ever undertaken to predict the result of the election. After analysing the returns from over 2 million respondents, the *Digest* confidently predicted that Landon would win by a large margin, 56% to 44%. The actual result was that Roosevelt won by a large margin, obtaining 60% of the vote. How could the *Digest* poll have been so wrong?

The answer lay in the sampling method they used. They sent postcards to millions of people listed in telephone directories, car registration files and magazine subscription lists. The trouble was that in the USA of 1936 those who had telephones and cars and subscribed to magazines were the better-off citizens. In restricting the poll to such people, who largely supported Landon, the poll was biased against the poor and unemployed, who largely voted for Roosevelt.

</td></tr>
</table>

The most effective way of avoiding bias in sample selection is to use probabilistic methods, which ensure that every element in the population has the same chance of being included in the sample. In the next section we will look at sampling methods that yield samples from which you can produce *unbiased estimators* of population measures, or *parameters* such as a mean or a proportion.

15.3 Probabilistic sampling methods

Perhaps the obvious way of giving every element in a population the same chance of being selected in a sample is to use a random process such as those used to select winning numbers in lottery competitions. Lotteries are usually regarded as fair because every number in the population of lottery numbers has an equal chance of being picked as a winning number.

15.3.1 Simple random sampling

Selecting a set of winning numbers in a lottery is an example of simple random sampling, whether the process involves elaborate machines or simply picking the numbers from the proverbial hat. You can use the same approach in drawing samples from a population.

Before you can undertake simple random sampling you need to establish a clear definition of the population and compile a list of the elements in it. In the same way as all the numbers in a lottery must be included if the draw is to be fair, all the items in the population must be included for the sample we take to be random. The population list is the basis or framework of our sample selection so it is known as the *sampling frame*.

Once you have the sampling frame you need to number each element in it and then you can use random numbers to select your sample. If you have 100 elements in the population and you need a sample of 15 from it you can take a sequence of 15 two-digit random numbers from Table 4 in Appendix 1 and select the elements for the sample accordingly; for instance, if the first random number is 71 you take the 71st element on the sampling frame, if the second random number is 09 you take the ninth element and so on. If the random number 00 occurs in the sequence you take the 100th element.

| EXAMPLE 15.4 | Strani Systems have 2000 employees in the UK. The HR director of the company wants to select a sample of 400 employees to answer questions about their experience of working for the company. How should she go about using simple random sampling? |

Solution

The population in this case consists of all the Strani employees in the UK. The sampling frame would be a list of employees, perhaps the company payroll, with each employee numbered from 1 to 2000. The HR director should then take a sequence of four-digit random numbers such as those listed along row 7 of Table 4 in Appendix 1:

$$1426 \quad 7156 \quad 7651 \quad 0042 \quad 9537 \quad 2573 \quad \text{and so on}$$

She does face a problem in that only two of the random numbers, 1426 and 0042, will enable her to select an employee from the list as the others are well above 2000. To get round this she could simply ignore the ones that are too high and continue until she has 400 random numbers that are in the appropriate range. This may take considerable time and she may prefer to replace the first digit in each number so that in every case they are either 0 or 1, making all the four-digit numbers in the range 0000 to 1999 (0000 would be used for the 2000th employee):

$$\text{Change } 0, 2, 4, 6, 8 \text{ to } 0$$
$$\text{Change } 1, 3, 5, 7, 9 \text{ to } 1$$

By applying this to the figures from row 7 of Table 4 she would get:

$$1426 \quad 1156 \quad 1651 \quad 0042 \quad 1537 \quad 0573$$

Now she can use every number in the sequence to select for the sample.

Simple random sampling has several advantages; it is straightforward and inexpensive. Because the probability of selection is known it is possible to assess the sampling error involved and ensure that estimates of population parameters based on the sample are unbiased.

A potential disadvantage of simple random sampling is that in a case such as Example 15.3 the sample may consist of elements all over the country, which will make data collection expensive. Another is that whilst it is an appropriate method for largely homogenous populations, if a population is subdivided by, for instance, gender and gender is an important aspect of the analysis, using simple random sampling will not ensure suitable representation of both genders.

15.3.2 Systematic random sampling

A faster alternative to simple random sampling is systematic sampling. This involves selecting a proportion of elements from the sampling frame by choosing elements at regular intervals through the list. The first element is selected using a random number.

EXAMPLE 15.5

How can the HR director in Example 15.4 use systematic sampling to select her sample of 400 employees?

Solution

Since there are 2000 employees she needs to select every fifth employee in the list that constitutes the sampling frame. To decide whether she should start with the first, second, third, fourth or fifth employee on the list she could take a two-digit random number and if it is between 00 and 19 start with the first employee, between 20 and 39 the second, between 40 and 59 the third, between 60 and 79 the fourth, and between 80 and 99 the fifth. The first two-digit number at the top of column 9 of Table 4 of Appendix 1 is 47, so using this she should start with the third employee and proceed to take every fifth name after that.

As well as being cheap and simple, systematic sampling does yield samples with a definable sampling error and is therefore able to produce unbiased estimates. This is true as long as the population list used to select the sample is not drawn up in such a way as to give rise to bias. In Example 15.4 a list of employees in alphabetical order should not result in bias but if most employees worked in teams of five, one of whom was the team leader and the list of employees was set out by teams rather than surnames, then the systematic sampling of every fifth employee would generate a sample with either all or none of the employees selected being team leaders.

Systematic sampling has the same disadvantages as simple random sampling; expensive data collection if the sample members are widely dispersed, and the possibility of subsections of the population being under-represented.

15.3.3 Stratified random sampling

One problem with both sampling methods we have looked at so far is that the samples they produce may not adequately reflect the balance of different constituencies within the population. In the long run this unevenness will be balanced out by other samples selected using the same methods, but this is little comfort if you only have the time or resources to take one sample.

To avoid sections of a population being under-, or for that matter over-represented you can use stratified random sampling. As the name implies, the sample selection is random, but it is structured using the sections or *strata* in the population. The starting point is to define the size of the sample and then decide what proportion of each section of the population needs to be selected for the sample. Once you have decided how many elements you need from each section, then use simple random sampling to choose them. This ensures that all the sections of the population are represented in the sample yet preserves the random nature of the selection and thus your ability to produce unbiased estimators of the population parameters from your sample data.

**EXAMPLE
15.6**

The 2000 UK employees of Strani Systems are based at six locations; 400 work in Leeds, 800 in Manchester, 200 in Norwich, 300 in Oxford, 100 in Plymouth, and 200 in Reading. How can the HR director in Example 15.4 use stratified random sampling to choose her sample of 400 employees?

Solution

A sample of 400 constitutes 20% of the workforce of 2000. To stratify the sample in the same way as the population she should select 20% of the employees from each site; 80 from Leeds, 160 from Manchester, 40 from Norwich, 60 from Oxford, 20 from Plymouth and 40 from Reading. She should then use simple random sampling to choose the sample members from each site. For this she would need a sampling frame for each location.

The advantage of stratified random sampling is that it produces samples that yield unbiased estimators of population parameters whilst ensuring that the different sectors of the population are represented. The disadvantage in a case like Example 15.6 is that the sample consists of widely dispersed members and collecting data from them may be expensive, especially if face-to-face interviews are involved.

15.3.4 Cluster sampling

If the investigation for which you require a sample is based on a population that is widely scattered you may prefer to use cluster sampling. This method is appropriate if the population you wish to sample is composed of geographically distinct units or *clusters*. You simply take a complete list of the clusters that make up your population and take a random sample of clusters from it. The elements in your sample are *all* the individuals in each selected cluster.

**EXAMPLE
15.7**

How can the HR director from Example 15.4 use cluster sampling to select a sample of employees?

Solution

She can make a random selection of two or maybe three locations by simply putting the names of the location in a hat and drawing two out. All the employees at these locations constitute her sample.

A rather more sophisticated approach would be to make the probability that a location is selected proportionate to its size by putting one ticket in the hat for every 100 employees at a location – four tickets for Leeds, eight for Manchester and so on.

As an alternative to drawing tickets from a hat, she could follow the approach we used in section 12.5 to simulate business processes and employ random numbers to make the selections in accordance with the following allocations:

Solution
cont

Location	Random number allocation
Leeds	00–19
Manchester	20–59
Norwich	60–69
Oxford	70–84
Plymouth	85–89
Reading	90–99

The advantages of cluster sampling are that it is cheap, especially if the investigation involves face-to-face interviews, because the number of locations to visit is small and you only need sampling frames for the selected clusters rather than the entire population.

The disadvantages are that you may well end up with a larger sample than you need and there is a risk that some sections of the population may be under-represented. If Leeds and Manchester were the chosen clusters in Example 15.6, the sample size would be 1200 (the 400 employees at Leeds and the 800 at Manchester), a far larger sample than the HR director requires. If the overall gender balance of the company employees in Example 15.6 is 40% male and 60% female yet this balance was 90% male and 10% female at the Norwich and Reading sites there would be a serious imbalance in the sample if it consisted of employees at those two sites.

15.3.5 Multi-stage sampling

Multi-stage is a generic term for any combination of probabilistic sampling methods. It can be particularly useful for selecting samples from populations that are divided or layered in more than one way.

EXAMPLE 15.8

The HR director from Example 15.4 likes the idea of cluster sampling as it will result in cost savings for her investigation, but she wants to avoid having a sample of more than 400 employees. How can she use multi-stage sampling to achieve this?

Solution

She can use cluster sampling to select her locations and then, rather than contact all the employees at each site, she could use stratified sampling to ensure that the sample size is 400. For instance, if Leeds and Manchester were selected the 1200 employees at those sites constitute three times as many as the HR director requires in her sample so she should select one-third of the employees at each site; 133 at Leeds and 267 at Manchester. She could use either systematic or simple random sampling to choose the sample members.

The advantage of multi-stage sampling is that you can customise your approach to selecting your sample; it enables you to benefit from the advantages of a particular method and use others alongside it to overcome its disadvantages. In Example 15.8 the HR director is able to preserve the cost advantage of cluster sampling and use the other methods to keep to her target sample size. Like other probabilistic methods it produces results that can be used as unbiased estimators of population parameters.

15.4 Non-probabilistic sampling methods

Wherever possible you should use probabilistic sampling methods, not because they are more likely to produce a representative sample (which is not always true) but because they allow you to make a statistical evaluation of the sampling error and hence you can use the results to make predictions about the population the sample comes from that are statistically valid. Doing this with samples obtained by other methods does not have the same validity.

Why then is it worth looking at other methods at all? There are several reasons: some populations that you might wish to investigate simply cannot be listed, such as the potential customers of a business, so it is impossible to draw up a sampling frame; secondly, some of these methods are attractive because they are convenient; and thirdly, they are used by companies and therefore it is a good idea to be aware of them and their limitations. They are often used at the initial, exploratory stage of research, and followed up with the use of probabilistic sampling.

15.4.1 Quota sampling

In one respect quota sampling is similar to stratified random sampling: you start by working out what proportion of the population you want to include in your sample and then apply that proportion to the sections of the population to work out the *quota* of respondents needed from each section of the population. You then fill each quota by finding enough elements from each section of the population.

EXAMPLE 15.9

How can the HR director from Example 15.4 use quota sampling to obtain a sample of 400 Strani employees?

Solution

Since she requires a sample that amounts to 20% of the workforce of 2000, she can set a quota of 20% of the employees at each location; 80 of the 400 at Leeds, 160 of the 800 at Manchester, 40 of the 200 at Norwich, 60 of the 300 at Oxford, 20 of the 100 at Plymouth and 40 of the 200 at Reading. She could then despatch her researchers to each site and they could approach employees as they were leaving the staff restaurant after their lunch. When the quota is filled they have completed the task; for instance, once the researchers at Leeds have data from 80 employees at the site they have finished.

The advantages of quota sampling are that the resulting sample should be representative, and that the process is cheaper and easier than using stratified sampling. In addition, there is no need to find named individuals, who may, once found, decline to participate. Quota sampling is particularly useful for sampling from large populations for which an accurate sampling frame is unavailable, a situation that polling organisations typically face.

The disadvantages are that it is susceptible to bias and the results from quota samples are not unbiased estimators of population parameters as the sample selection process is not based on probability. The bias might arise inadvertently from the researcher; for instance in Example 15.9 a young male researcher may well be disposed to approach young female employees rather more than others.

15.4.2 Judgemental sampling

In judgemental sampling the selection of the sample is based entirely on the expertise of the investigator, who uses their judgement to select a sample they consider representative.

EXAMPLE 15.10

The HR director from Example 15.4 knows that the Reading workforce consists almost entirely of younger women who have young children, whereas at other locations the workforce is largely composed of older males with grown-up families. Given this, she may judge that an appropriate sample would consist of all the employees at Reading and samples of the workforce at other locations.

The advantage of judgemental sampling is that it does allow you to customise your approach to sample selection. The disadvantage is that it is entirely subjective and non-random and as such does not yield results that can be used to predict the features of the population with any statistical rigour.

15.4.3 Snowball sampling

This method involves starting by finding a relatively few respondents who have a particular feature of interest to the investigator and using them to identify others who share the same feature. The sample 'snowballs' to include these others and perhaps yet more potential respondents whom they identify.

EXAMPLE 15.11

The HR director from Example 15.4 is interested in promoting the health of employees by opening gyms on the company's premises. She may wish to ascertain the interest in such a venture by obtaining a sample of employees who already use gyms. She could simply ask around her contacts to identify a 'starter' group of respondents and through them build up a sample.

Snowballing is a useful means of obtaining a sample of a population that may be difficult to access by other means, such as small-scale building contractors. It is open to bias because the initial respondents or contacts decide whose names to pass on to you and there is no valid way of assessing the sampling error so any generalisation from the results is not statistically valid.

15.4.4 Convenience sampling

This method is very simple: samples are chosen purely on the basis of accessibility.

EXAMPLE 15.12

The HR director from Example 15.4 is based at Strani's Manchester site. To select her sample she sends an email to all the employees in the building where her office is situated and invites them to a meeting where she asks them to complete a questionnaire.

Convenience sampling, as the name suggests, is easy and cheap. It can be a useful means of conducting an initial exploratory investigation but the sample is unlikely to be representative of the whole population and results from it should certainly not be used for estimating population parameters as they lack statistical validity.

15.4.5 Self-selection

This is sample selection by invitation; you might send an email or display a notice asking for people to participate in an interview or complete a questionnaire. The advantages are that it is cheap and easy, and what is more you are guaranteed to get willing respondents. Unfortunately this approach to sampling is almost invariably prone to bias; usually it is the people who have stronger feelings on the issues under investigation who put themselves forward and the sample composition is therefore biased against those with more neutral views.

THE DEBRIEF

Key things to remember from this chapter

→ The purpose of sampling is to understand a population by analysing data from a sample selected from the population.

→ It is important to avoid bias in selecting samples.

→ There are probabilistic and non-probabilistic methods of sampling.

→ In probabilistic sampling a random process is used to select the sample from a list of the elements in the population, a sampling frame.

→ Non-probabilistic sampling does not require a sampling frame and is often used for speed and convenience.

→ For analytical purposes probabilistic sampling is better because the sampling error can be assessed. This is not possible with non-probabilistic sampling.

References

Kathawala, Y. (1988) 'Applications of quantitative techniques in large and small organisations in the United States: an empirical analysis', *Journal of the Operational Research Society*, 39(11), pp. 981–9.

Kinnear, T.C. and Taylor, J.R. (1996) *Marketing Research: An Applied Approach* (5th edn), New York: McGraw-Hill.

McDonald, C. and King, S. (1996) *Sampling the Universe: The growth, development and influence of market research in Britain since 1945*, Henley-on-Thames: NTC Publications.

Wilson, A. (2006) *Marketing Research: An Integrated Approach* (2nd edn), Harlow: Prentice Hall.

CHAPTER 16

Test driving – sampling theory, estimation and hypothesis testing

This chapter will help you to:

→ Appreciate the concept of sampling distributions

→ Understand how confidence intervals work

→ Appreciate the connection between precision, confidence and sample size

→ Assess hypotheses about population means, proportions and medians, and draw appropriate conclusions

What you will find in this chapter . . .

- Using the standard normal (Z) and t distributions to model sampling distributions

- Producing confidence intervals for population means using sample means

- Producing confidence intervals for population proportions using sample proportions

- Working out required sample sizes for interval estimation

- Testing hypotheses about the population mean, population proportion and population median

. . . and on the supporting website (www.pearsoned.co.uk/buglear)

- How to use EXCEL, Minitab and SPSS to estimate population parameters and test hypotheses

- Fully worked solutions to the review questions

- More review questions

Business use of small sample inference, the origins of the *t* distribution and testing population proportions

◆ When you first meet theories and models like the sampling distributions in this chapter it is easy to assume that they are all abstract and were invented by professors pursuing purely academic interests. In the case of what is arguably the most important development in statistical inference, the *t* distribution, this is far from the case.

◆ The *t* distribution was a key step forward because it offered a way of using results from small samples to make predictions and assessments of populations with a known probability of error. Small samples are cheaper to collect and quicker to process than large ones, so the *t* distribution is invaluable for companies looking for economy and speed in their quantitative analysis.

◆ The original name of the *t* distribution was 'Student's *t* distribution'. 'Student' was the pseudonym of William Sealy Gosset (1876–1937), an Oxford science graduate, who worked for Guinness from 1899 until his death. He was employed by Guinness initially as a brewer and later became the manager of the Guinness brewery in London.

◆ Guinness was a long-established company even in Gosset's day. By the late nineteenth century its demand for barley dominated the Irish economy and the beer it produced was successful both in Ireland and abroad. Guinness specialised in a type of dark beer known as porter. Like any producer of a generic product the company wanted to establish the distinctiveness of its own beer and cement the brand loyalty of its customers. One way it did this was to name its product 'stout' rather than porter. Another was to recruit scientists like Gosset to help it manage the production process more effectively and hence make the quality of the product more consistent.

◆ The problem for Gosset was that brewing beer was a very erratic affair; the quality of key ingredients like barley and yeast varied, and the process was notoriously susceptible to temperature changes. Brewers took samples to try to monitor and control the process and the quality of the ingredients, but given the number of changing factors such samples were inevitably small and it was impossible to calculate the likely error in using the results from them to draw general conclusions.

◆ In the late nineteenth century the subject of Statistics in the British Isles was dominated by the biometric school. Biometry was the study of human measurements and characteristics, a field developed in the wake of Charles Darwin's work on heredity. The biometricians dealt with large samples, typically running to thousands of elements, and assumed that sample statistics from such large samples differed little from the parameters of the populations from which they were drawn. They found it difficult to conceive that anyone would want to draw conclusions with a known probable error about populations using small samples. Indeed, the contrast between their practice and Gosset's objectives meant that in one work on the period he is referred to as 'The Outsider' (MacKenzie, 1981: 111).

◆ Gosset created an approach, encapsulated in the *t* distribution, which enabled him to use small samples to make inferences about populations with known levels of probable error, or confidence. He took great interest in applying his work to the improvement of the yield from barley crops in Ireland as well as in the growth of yeast. You can read more about Gosset in McMullen (1970) and the development of his ideas in Pearson (1970).

◆ Testing hypotheses is often about assessing the effects of a change. An example of this is the Nottingham City Homes investigation of the drop in the proportion of their properties that were burgled after double glazing was installed (Nottingham City Homes, 2010). This work featured in a Parliamentary debate on housing (HC Deb 27 January 2011).

16.1 **Introduction**

In Chapter 15 we considered the ways of taking samples from populations in order to gain some understanding of those populations. In this chapter we look at how to use sample results to obtain estimates of key features, or parameters, of the populations from which they were selected. It is important to note that the techniques described in this chapter, and the theory on which they are based, can only reliably be used with results of samples selected using probabilistic, or random sampling methods. The techniques are based on knowing, or at least having a reliable estimate of, the sampling error and this is not possible with non-random sampling methods.

In Chapter 13 we looked at the normal distribution, an important statistical distribution that enables you to investigate the very many continuous variables that occur in business and many other fields, whose values are distributed in a normal pattern. What makes the normal distribution especially important is that it enables us to anticipate how sample results vary. This is because many *sampling distributions* have a normal pattern.

16.2 **Sampling distributions**

Sampling distributions are distributions that portray the variation in sample results. They are the 'population distributions' of sample results and are very important in quantitative work as they make it possible to use sample data to make statistically valid estimates or conclusions about a population. The advantages in using sample results like this are considerable, particularly when the population is so large that accessing all of it is impossible, or when surveying the whole population is too costly or would take too much time.

A sample contains observations taken from a population, in other words it is a subset of a population. If it is a random sample it consists of observations drawn from the population by means of a random process.

It is possible to take very many different random samples of the same size from a population. The number of samples that we could take from it is effectively infinite unless the population is very small. Even when, as in Example 15.1 the population contains only 20 elements, we could draw over 38,000 different samples of size six from it. If we think of the population as the 'parent' there are to all intents and purposes an infinite number of 'offspring' samples of a certain size that could be taken from it.

These samples will have the same number of elements but their means, standard deviations and other summary measures will not be the same. The consequence of this is that if we want to predict a population mean using a sample mean we would be using something that varies from one sample to another, i.e. the mean of the sample ($\bar{x}$), to predict something that is fixed, i.e. the mean of the population (μ).

A sample mean is a good basis for estimating a population mean but it is only a start; we also need to take account of how sample means vary. We have to treat them as observations, $\bar{x}$s, of the variable $\bar{X}$ and factor in exactly how they vary. Furthermore, we need to be able to link the parameters of the distribution of $\bar{X}$ to the parameters of the population from which the samples were taken. The $\bar{X}$ distribution is known as the *sampling distribution* of the sample mean.

To start with we will consider the simplest case, which is when the parent population is normally distributed, in other words the population is normal. If this is true, what can we say about the sampling distribution of the sample mean?

Suppose you take every possible random sample of n observations from a normal population that has a mean of μ and a standard deviation of σ. If you plot them all the resulting distribution, the sampling distribution of the sample mean, would also be normal. In addition, if you worked out the mean of the sampling distribution you would find that it is precisely the same as the mean of the population, μ. If you worked out the standard deviation of all the sample means you would find it is the population standard deviation divided by the square root of the sample size, $\sigma/\sqrt{n}$.

In short, the sample means of all the samples size n that it is possible to take from a normal population with a mean μ and a standard deviation σ form a normal distribution that has a mean of μ and a standard deviation of $\sigma/\sqrt{n}$. The sample means are distributed around the population mean but they have less spread than the population because n is always more than one and hence $\sigma/\sqrt{n}$ is always less than σ. For example, if the sample size is four, $\sigma/\sqrt{n}$ is $\sigma/2$; compared to the population distribution the distribution of the means of samples that each contains four observations has half the spread.

The bigger the samples, the less will be the spread of their means. If the sample size is 100 the standard deviation of the sampling distribution is $\sigma/10$, just a tenth of the standard deviation of the population.

This is a key issue. When we take samples we 'average out' differences between the observations and the larger our samples, the greater the extent of this 'averaging out'. This is why in general using bigger samples to predict population parameters is better than using smaller ones.

If you look at the results of an opinion poll see how many people have been asked for their opinion. Typically it is a thousand or more. Such results are products that the pollsters sell to newspapers and TV companies. To be successful they need to persuade their buyers that the poll results are reliable. This would be very difficult if their poll results were based on responses from a small number of people.

The standard deviation of the sampling distribution, $\sigma/\sqrt{n}$, is usually called the *standard error* as it reflects the error involved in using sample means to estimate the population mean. Because samples are not the same, and hence their means vary, there is always an element of error in using sample statistics to predict population parameters.

The upshot of the above is that as long as we have the mean and the standard deviation of the parent population we can ascertain the probabilities of means of samples from the population falling within certain ranges. If the population is normally distributed the sampling distribution is also normally distributed and we can use the standard normal distribution to do this.

EXAMPLE 16.1

Reebar Frozen Foods produces packs of four fish portions. On the packaging they claim that the average weight of the portions is 120 grams. If the mean weight of the fish portions they buy is 124 grams with a standard deviation of 4 grams, what is the probability that the mean weight of a pack of four portions will be less than 120 grams?

Solution

We will assume that the selection of the four portions to put in a pack is random. Imagine we took every possible sample of four portions from the population of fish portions purchased by Reebar (which we will assume for practical purposes to be infinite) and calculated the mean weight of each sample. We would find that the sampling distribution of all these means has a mean of 124 grams and a standard error of $4/\sqrt{4}$, which is 2 grams.

Solution cont

The probability that a sample of four portions has a mean of less than 120 grams is the probability that a normal variable with a mean of 124 grams and a standard deviation of 2 grams is less than 120 grams.

The z-equivalent of 120 grams in the sampling distribution is

$$z = \frac{\bar{x} - \mu}{\sigma/\sqrt{n}} = \frac{120 - 124}{4/\sqrt{4}} = -2.00$$

In Table 5 in Appendix 1 the probability of Z being less than −2.00 is 0.0228 or 2.28%. From this it seems there is less than a one in 40 chance that four portions in a pack chosen at random have a mean weight of less than 120 grams. We can compare this with the probability of one fish portion selected at random weighing less than 120 grams:

$$z = \frac{\bar{x} - \mu}{\sigma} = \frac{120 - 124}{4} = -1.00$$

In Table 5 the probability that Z is less than −1.00 is 0.1587 or 15.87%, approximately a one in six chance. This is rather greater than the chance of getting a pack of four whose mean weight is less than 120 grams (2.28%). This is typical; there is always less variation among sample means than there is among single points of data.

SELF-ASSEMBLY GUIDE

Using the Z distribution to analyse sampling distributions

◆ You need to know the mean, μ, and the standard deviation, σ, of the parent population distribution and the sample size, n. You will also need to work out the standard error of the sampling distribution, $\sigma/\sqrt{n}$.

◆ To find the z-equivalent of a specific value in the sampling distribution, $\bar{x}$, take the population mean, μ, away from $\bar{x}$.

◆ Divide the difference between $\bar{x}$ and μ by the standard error of the sampling distribution deviation of the X distribution, $\sigma/\sqrt{n}$. This is the z-equivalent.

The procedure in Example 16.1 can be used whether we have small or large samples. If the population from which the samples are taken is normal the sampling distribution will form a normal distribution with a mean of μ and a standard deviation of $\sigma/\sqrt{n}$.

So far we have assumed that the parent population is normally distributed, but suppose it isn't. Many real-life variables are not normally distributed, including distributions of household incomes and distributions of annual revenues of businesses.

For these situations there is something called the central limit theorem that allows us to use sample data to produce predictions and judgements about populations. According to this theorem if the sample size, *n,* is large enough, which is generally interpreted as meaning at least 30, the sample means are normally distributed with a mean of μ and a standard deviation of $\sigma/\sqrt{n}$. This applies *whatever* shape the population distribution has. In practice it means that as long as the samples we use are sufficiently large we can use the same approach as we would if the parent population were normal.

**EXAMPLE
16.2**

Suppose the ages at which people pass the driving test form a skewed distribution with a mean of 20 years and a standard deviation of 3.5 years. Find the probability that a random sample of 50 drivers will, on average, have passed the test at 21 or more years of age.

Solution

The sample size, 50, is higher than 30 so the sampling distribution of the sample means will be normally distributed. It has the same mean as the population, 20 years, and a standard error of $3.5/\sqrt{50}$ years.

The z-equivalent of 21 years in the sampling distribution is

$$z = \frac{\bar{x} - \mu}{\sigma/\sqrt{n}} = \frac{21 - 20}{3.5/\sqrt{50}} = 2.02$$

In Table 5 of Appendix 1 the probability of Z being more than 2.02 is 0.0217. So the probability of a random sample of 50 drivers passing their test at 21 or more years of age is also 0.0217 or 2.17%, which is slightly more than a one in 50 chance.

The central limit theorem does not apply when the samples taken from a non-normal population have less than 30 observations in them. The sample means of small samples taken from populations that are not normally distributed do not form normal distributions. Having said that, if sample sizes are nearly 30, such as 28, the sample means will be approximately normally distributed so using the central limit theorem is possible although not strictly legitimate.

At this point you may find it useful to try **Review questions 16.1 to 16.3, 16.8 and 16.9** at the end of the chapter.

16.2.1 When σ is unknown: estimating the standard error with large samples

Sampling distributions are important because they enable us to use samples to estimate and assess population parameters when studying the entire population is either not feasible or impracticable. Generally we use a sample that we can access to investigate a population that we can't access. For instance, we will have the mean of a sample and want to use it to estimate the mean of the population.

In the previous section we were able to describe sampling distributions of sample means by using parameters of the population; the mean and the standard deviation, μ and σ. We have assumed that we know both of these but if we can't access the whole population, how do we know what μ and σ are? In practice the answer is that we don't. As far as the population mean, μ, is concerned this is not an issue since it is the very thing we want to estimate or assess. But in the absence of the population standard deviation, σ, we have to find another way of measuring the spread of the sampling distribution.

Since we will have the sample data, the obvious way to proceed is to use the sample standard deviation, s, which we can calculate from the sample data, as a substitute for the population standard deviation, σ. Instead of using the actual standard error, $\sigma/\sqrt{n}$, we can estimate the standard error of the sampling distribution with $s/\sqrt{n}$.

Using the estimated standard error, $s/\sqrt{n}$, is all right if the sample size, n, is large (in practice 30 or more). If we do have a large sample we can simply use $s/\sqrt{n}$ to approximate $\sigma/\sqrt{n}$. As long as n is at least 30 the sampling distribution will be normally distributed with a mean of μ and an estimated standard error of $s/\sqrt{n}$. This will be the case even if the parent population is not normally distributed thanks to the central limit theorem.

EXAMPLE 16.3

The mean volume of liquid soap in the dispensers produced by Meelo plc is known to be 502 millilitres. A hotel manager buys 36 dispensers. The standard deviation of this sample is 8 millilitres. If the hotel manager's sample was chosen at random find the probability that the mean volume of the sample is less than 500 millilitres.

Solution

The population mean, μ, is 502 millilitres and the sample standard deviation, s, is 8 millilitres. We need the probability of $\bar{x}$ being less than 500 millilitres, i.e. $P(\bar{X} < 500)$. The z-equivalent of 500 millilitres is:

$$z = \frac{\bar{x} - \mu}{s/\sqrt{n}} = \frac{500 - 502}{8/\sqrt{36}}$$

$$= -1.5$$

$$\text{So } P(\bar{X} < 500) = P(Z < -1.5)$$

According to Table 5 the probability of Z being less than -1.5 is 0.0668, so the probability that the sample mean is less than 500 millilitres is 0.0668 or 6.68%.

It is important to remember that $s/\sqrt{n}$ is not the actual standard error but the *estimated* standard error. Because it is based on the sample standard deviation, s, and the composition of samples varies, $s/\sqrt{n}$ will vary. Provided that the standard deviation is from a large sample it will be sufficiently close to the population standard deviation and the estimated standard error, $s/\sqrt{n}$, will therefore be close enough to the real standard error, $\sigma/\sqrt{n}$.

16.2.2 When σ is unknown: estimating the standard error with small samples and the t distribution

Section 16.2.1 showed how we can describe sampling distributions with the sample standard deviation, s, when we don't have the population standard deviation, σ. Without σ we cannot obtain the standard error, $\sigma/\sqrt{n}$, but if the sample size, n, is 30 or more the estimated standard error, $s/\sqrt{n}$, is consistent enough to measure the spread of the sampling distribution.

When the sample size, n, is below 30 the standard deviations from different samples vary so much that estimated standard error, $s/\sqrt{n}$, is not consistently close enough to the actual standard error, $\sigma/\sqrt{n}$. The smaller the sample size, the more the sample standard deviations will vary and consequently the estimated standard errors will vary more. It is possible to describe the sampling distribution using the estimated standard error, but only if the parent population is normal. If this is the case we can model the sampling distribution using a modified normal distribution.

This modified normal distribution is called the t *distribution*. The development of this was an important advance as it meant populations could be investigated using small sample data. Since taking small samples is usually cheaper and quicker than large samples the t distribution broadened the scope for analysis based on sample data considerably.

The t distribution is a more spread-out version of the standard normal, or Z distribution. Figure 16.1 illustrates the difference between them.

Notice that the mean and standard deviation of what we might call the 'standard' t distribution are 0 and 1 respectively. Essentially it is the equivalent of the standard normal distribution and is used in the same way but it has a lower peak and fatter tails. This reflects the larger

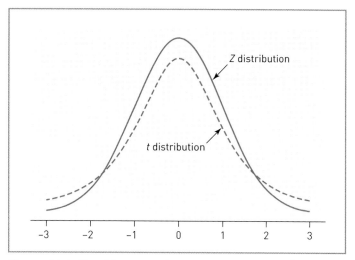

Figure 16.1 The *Z* (solid line) and the *t* distribution (dotted line)

spread in the *t* distribution, which takes account of the greater variation among small sample standard deviations compared to the variation among large sample standard deviations.

The smaller the size of the sample, the more we need to compensate for the variation in sample standard deviations. This means that unlike the *Z* distribution, which is a 'one-size-fits-all' distribution, there are different versions of the *t* distribution. What distinguishes them is the number of degrees of freedom, denoted by the Greek letter ν (nu, the Greek equivalent of the letter n), which is the sample size less one, $n - 1$. This is how we use sample size to select the appropriate version of the *t* distribution. For a reminder of what degrees of freedom are all about look back at section 6.3.3.

Finding the probability of the mean of a small sample from a normal population being greater than or less than a specific value involves finding the *t*-equivalent, or *t* value. This is just the same as the procedure we used to get the *z*-equivalent. We still work out how many standard errors there are between the sample mean and the population mean, but we are using a different model for the sampling distribution, the *t* distribution. The procedure is:

$$t = \frac{\bar{x} - \mu}{s/\sqrt{n}}$$

**EXAMPLE
16.4**

The hotel manager in Example 16.3 decides to buy only 16 liquid soap dispensers from Meelo. The volumes of soap in the dispensers are normally distributed with a mean of 502 millilitres. The standard deviation of the volumes of the 16 dispensers purchased by the hotel manager is 6.2 millilitres. What is the probability that the mean volume of 16 dispensers is more than 504 millilitres?

Solution

The population mean, μ, is 502 millilitres and the sample standard deviation, s, is 4.56 millilitres. We need the probability that $\bar{X}$ is more than 504 millilitres, $P(\bar{X} < 504)$. The *t* value for 500 millilitres is:

$$t = \frac{\bar{x} - \mu}{s/\sqrt{n}} = \frac{504 - 502}{4.56/\sqrt{16}} = 1.754$$

So $P(\bar{X} > 504) = P(t > 1.754)$

$\rightarrow$

Solution cont

Table 6 in Appendix 1 contains some details, 'edited highlights' so to speak, of the t distribution. Look down the column headed v on the left until you reach 15, the number of degrees of freedom in this case (the sample size, n, is 16 so $n - 1 = 15$). Scan along the row to the right where there are five figures relating to the t distribution with 15 degrees of freedom. The nearest we can get to 1.754 is the figure in the second column along, 1.753. This is in the column headed 0.05 which means that 5% of the t distribution with 15 degrees of freedom is above 1.753. To put it another way, this is the probability of t being more than 1.753, 0.05. Since 1.753 is approximately equal to the t value for 504 millilitres, 1.754, the probability of the mean volume of 16 dispensers being more than 504 millilitres is approximately 0.05 or 5%.

We could write the t value in Example 16.4 as $t_{0.05,15}$ as it is the value of t that cuts off the tail area of 5% in the t distribution with 15 degrees of freedom. Similarly, $t_{0.01,20}$ denotes the t value that cuts off the 1% tail area in the t distribution with 20 degrees of freedom. Note that the tail area is the first suffix and the degrees of freedom the second.

The way the t distribution is generally used is in relation to tail areas. Because of this and the fact that the t distribution varies depending on the number of degrees of freedom, printed tables are not as comprehensive as standard normal distribution tables. Table 6 in Appendix 1 therefore provides only selected values of t for the tail areas used most often, which are 10%, 5%, 2.5%, 1% and 0.5%. If you need t distribution values that are not in Table 6 you can obtain them using computer software. The way to do this is described on the supporting website.

EXAMPLE 16.5

Using Table 6, find:

(a) t with 6 degrees of freedom that cuts off a tail area of 0.10, $t_{0.10,6}$

(b) t with 6 degrees of freedom that cuts off a tail area of 0.05, $t_{0.05,6}$

(c) t with 18 degrees of freedom that cuts off a tail area of 0.05, $t_{0.05,18}$

(d) t with 25 degrees of freedom that cuts off a tail area of 0.01, $t_{0.01,25}$

(e) t with 100 degrees of freedom that cuts off a tail area of 0.005, $t_{0.005,100}$.

Solution

From Table 6:

(a) $t_{0.10,6}$ is in the row for 6 degrees of freedom and the column headed 0.10, 1.440. This means that the probability that t, with 6 degrees of freedom, is greater than 1.440 is 0.10 or 10%.

(b) $t_{0.05,6}$ is in the row for 6 degrees of freedom and the column headed 0.05, 1.943. This is larger than the figure in (a), 1.440, although there are the same number of degrees of freedom. The tail area, 5%, is smaller so we have to go further along the axis to cut it off.

(c) $t_{0.05,18}$ is in the row for 18 degrees of freedom and the column headed 0.05, 1.734. This is smaller than the figure in (b), 1.943, although the tail area is the same. The larger number of degrees of freedom, 18 compared to the 6 in (b), means the distribution is not as widely spread and we don't have to go as far along the axis to cut off a 5% tail.

(d) $t_{0.01,25}$ is in the row for 25 degrees of freedom and the column headed 0.01, 2.485.

(e) $t_{0.005,100}$ is in the row for 100 degrees of freedom and the column headed 0.005, 2.626.

Have a careful look at the bottom row of Table 6, the row for an infinite (∞) number of degrees of freedom. The figure in the column headed 0.025, $t_{0.025,\infty}$ is 1.96. Now look at Table 5 and find the probability of 0.0250 to the lower right of the table. This is in the row for 1.9 and the column for 0.06. This is $z_{0.025}$. It is no accident that it is the same as $t_{0.025,\infty}$. The more degrees of freedom there are the more the t distribution 'morphs' into the Z distribution until with an infinite number of degrees of freedom they are the same distribution. The bottom row of Table 6 is an easier way of finding $z_{0.01}$, $z_{0.05}$, $z_{0.025}$, $z_{0.01}$ and $z_{0.005}$ than Table 5. This is very convenient for the topics in the rest of the chapter.

SELF-ASSEMBLY GUIDE

Choosing the right model for a sampling distribution

◆ Both the Z and t distributions can be used to model sampling distributions, but how do you choose which one to use?

◆ The first issue is whether the samples come from a population that is distributed normally. If it is then it is possible to model the sampling distribution.

◆ If the parent population is not normal it is possible to model the sampling distribution as long as the sample size, n, is at least 30.

◆ The second issue is whether you know the population standard deviation, σ. If you do then provided that the parent population is normal you can use the Z distribution whatever the sample size.

◆ If you don't know σ you can use the Z distribution only when the sample size is at least 30. Without σ you won't be able to obtain the standard error, $\sigma/\sqrt{n}$, so you'll have to use the sample standard deviation, s, and the estimated standard error based on it, $s/\sqrt{n}$.

◆ If the parent population is normal, you don't know σ and the sample size is under 30 you should use the t distribution and the estimated standard error based on the sample standard deviation.

◆ If the parent population is not normal and the sample size is under 30 you can't use either the Z distribution or the t distribution to model the sampling distribution. This is true even if you know σ.

16.3 Statistical inference: estimation

In business, statistical analysis helps managers understand situations and solve problems. Generally the data used in their analysis will be from a sample. Typically it is too costly or time-consuming to gather data from the entire population. In some cases this is not even possible. In view of this, if managers are encountering customer dissatisfaction they will look for data from a sample of customers, not all of them. If there are product quality difficulties they will look at a sample of products rather than all of them. If staff training is a problem they will investigate the feedback from a sample of staff rather than the entire staff.

In each case the reason for looking at sample data is to draw conclusions about the whole population. Provided that the sample data they gather is from random samples, in other words they are observed values taken by some random process from the population, they can generalise from their sample results in a statistically sound way.

The process of using sample data to draw conclusions, or make deductions, about populations is called *statistical inference*. This comes from the word *infer*, which means conclude or deduce. The part of statistical inference that deals with testing assumptions about population parameters is called *statistical decision-making* as it is used to assist organisations and individuals to make decisions.

In the previous section we considered sampling distributions. These are the theoretical fundamentals that are the basis of statistical inference. They link the patterns of variation in sample results to the distribution of the population the samples are from.

We will look at two types of statistical inference technique in this chapter. The first one we will consider is *estimation*, which is the use of sample data to predict the values of population measures such as means and proportions. The second is *hypothesis testing*, which is the use of sample data to support or refute assumptions about the values of population measures. This will be covered in section 16.4.

Although typically gathering data from a sample is easier than collecting data from a population it is often a costly and lengthy business. In practice therefore organisations avoid gathering more data than they need, but they have to balance this against the risk of having insufficient data to obtain the conclusive results they would like. This issue, deciding how large samples need to be, is also covered in this section.

16.3.1 Statistical estimation

Statistical estimation involves using sample measures like the sample mean or sample proportion to predict the values of their population equivalents. The obvious way of doing this is to use the sample measure to predict its population counterpart. For instance, taking a sample mean and using it to estimate the population mean. This is called *point estimation*. It is often used as a quick and simple way of getting some idea of a population value and is a perfectly acceptable use of the sample measure.

The key drawback of point estimation is in the name; it is only a single value, one shot at predicting the population measure. It is a very basic approach to estimating a population measure. Because we don't know what the population measure actually is we can't tell whether or not it is a good estimate, i.e. one that is close to the measure we want to predict. We can't even tell how likely it is to be a good estimate.

We can improve on point estimates by using a more sophisticated approach. The most effective way of using sample measures to estimate population parameters is *interval estimation*. In this the estimate takes the form of a range or *interval*. This enables us to specify the likelihood of the interval being accurate; to put it another way, how *confident* we are that the population measures lies somewhere within the interval. Since the confidence that we have in the interval estimate being accurate is important, interval estimates are also known as *confidence intervals*. For now we will focus on sample means, although interval estimation is used for other population parameters.

Before considering how to construct interval estimates, it is useful to review the key points about sampling distributions.

- We can obtain many different samples of the same size from a population.
- The sampling distribution of sample means shows how the means of all the different samples of the same size, n, are distributed.
- If the sample size is 30 or more the sampling distribution that describes the variation in the sample means is approximately normal.
- The sampling distribution of sample means has the same mean as the population, μ.
- The standard deviation of the sampling distribution of sample means is the standard error, $\sigma/\sqrt{n}$. The distribution of sample means is always less dispersed than the population.

Sampling distributions that are normally distributed, the ones depicting the variation between sample means from large samples, have all the characteristics of the normal distribution. One of these is that the area between a point two standard deviations to the left of the mean and another point two standard deviations to the right of the mean is roughly 95% of the area of the distribution.

More precisely, 95% of the normal distribution is between the points 1.96 standard deviations either side of the mean. To put it another way, 95% of the observations are within 1.96 standard deviations of the mean.

This applies to normal sampling distributions; 95% of sample means in a sampling distribution that is normally distributed are between the points 1.96 standard errors below and 1.96 standard errors above the mean. This is shown in Figure 16.2.

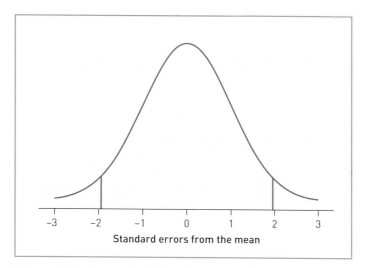

Figure 16.2 The central 95% of the area of a sampling distribution

The area within 1.96 standard errors of the mean is contained within two points:

- $\mu - 1.96\,\sigma/\sqrt{n}$ on the left, and
- $\mu + 1.96\,\sigma/\sqrt{n}$ on the right.

This means that the biggest possible difference between any of the sample means in the middle 95% of the sampling distribution and the population mean, μ, is just 1.96 standard errors, $1.96\,\sigma/\sqrt{n}$. Every one of the sample means in the central 95% will be no more than 1.96 standard errors away from the population mean. We can put this another way; the probability that any one of them is within 1.96 standard errors of the population mean is:

$$P(\mu - 1.96\,\sigma/\sqrt{n} < \bar{X} < \mu + 1.96\,\sigma/\sqrt{n}) = 0.95$$

Applying the sampling distribution in this way we could estimate sample means using the population mean. In practice this is of little interest as we won't know the population mean. Usually the population mean is the very thing we want to estimate using a sample mean not the other way round. The value of sampling distributions is that they do enable us to do this.

From what we have said so far, if we add 1.96 standard errors to the population mean and subtract 1.96 standard errors from the population mean we define an interval containing 95% of the sample means in the sampling distribution. But suppose instead of doing this we add 1.96 standard errors to and subtract 1.96 standard errors from every sample mean in the distribution?

In doing this we would have an interval around each sample mean. Ninety-five per cent of these intervals, those constructed around the 95% of sample means in the middle of the distributions and hence closest to the population, will include the population mean. The other 5% of the intervals, those constructed around the 5% of sample means in the tails of the distribution and thus furthest away from the population, won't include the population mean.

The implication of this is that in taking the means of large samples and constructing ranges around them by adding 1.96 standard errors for the upper figure, and subtracting 1.96 standard errors for the lower figure, 95% of the time the interval will contain somewhere within it the population mean. Each range is a *95% interval estimate* or a *95% confidence interval* because, although we are not absolutely certain that the interval contains the population mean, we can say we are 95% confident that it does.

**EXAMPLE
16.6**

According to the Ministry of Tourism on the holiday island of Ostrov the ages of tourists visiting the island have a mean of 30 years and a standard deviation of eight years. A researcher, who does not know that the population mean is 30 years, asks the ages of a random sample of 49 visitors in order to use the sample mean to estimate the population mean.

Solution

The sampling distribution that the mean of this sample belongs to is shown in Figure 16.3. The standard error of the distribution is $8/\sqrt{49} = 1.143$.

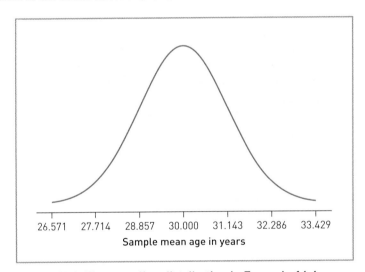

Figure 16.3 The sampling distribution in Example 16.6

Of the sample means in this distribution, 95% are between 1.96 standard errors below the mean, which is:

$$30 - (1.96 * 1.143) = 30 - 2.24 = 27.76$$

and 1.96 standard errors above the mean, which is:

$$30 + (1.96 * 1.143) = 30 + 2.24 = 32.24$$

So, 95% of the sample means will be between 27.76 and 32.24. This is shown in Figure 16.4.

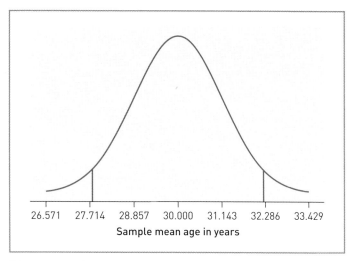

Figure 16.4 The central 95% of the sampling distribution in Example 16.6

Suppose the mean of the researcher's sample is 29 years. This is within the interval 27.76 to 32.24. By adding and subtracting 1.96 standard errors to and from the researcher's sample mean we get:

$$29 \pm (1.96 * 1.143) = 29 \pm 2.24 = 26.76 \text{ to } 31.24$$

This interval does cover the population mean, 30.

This expression includes the symbol '$\pm$'. This is shorthand for both adding *and* subtracting the amount after it, in this case 1.96 * 1.143. Adding gives us the higher figure, 31.24, and subtracting gives us the lower figure, 26.76.

Imagine the researcher takes another random sample of 49 visitors and the mean age of this second sample is 32 years. This is higher than the first sample mean but it is within the central 95% of the sampling distribution. By adding and subtracting 1.96 standard errors to and from this second mean we get:

$$32 \pm (1.96 * 1.143) = 32 \pm 2.24 = 29.76 \text{ to } 34.24$$

Like the interval around the researcher's first sample mean this interval contains the population mean of 30.

Suppose the researcher in Example 16.6 took very many samples and constructed an interval around each one by adding and subtracting 1.96 standard errors. Some intervals would not contain the population mean.

EXAMPLE 16.7

The researcher in Example 16.6 takes a random sample of 49 visitors that produces a mean of 27.3 years (to one decimal place). Construct a 95% confidence interval around this sample mean.

Solution

$$27.3 \pm (1.96 * 1.143) = 27.3 \pm 2.24 = 25.06 \text{ to } 29.54$$

This interval does not contain the population mean of 30, which is higher than the upper end of the interval.

When will the researcher in Example 16.6 get an interval that does not contain the population mean? Every time the sample mean is among the 5% of sample means furthest from the centre of the sampling distribution; either one of the smallest 2.5% or the largest 2.5% of sample means. When the sample mean is one of the smallest 2.5% the interval around it will be so low, the population mean will be above the upper end, which is the case in Example 16.7. When the sample mean is one of the largest 2.5% the interval around it will be so high, the population mean will be below the lower end.

Provided that the sample mean is one of the 95% between the smallest 2.5% and the largest 2.5%, the interval created around it by adding and subtracting 1.96 standard errors will contain the population mean. It will accurately estimate the population mean.

We use interval estimates to predict the population mean. If we know the population mean we wouldn't need an interval estimate. Generally it is when we don't know the population mean that we need to estimate it.

If we don't know the population mean we cannot know if the sample mean we have is one of the 95% that will produce accurate interval estimates or whether it is one of the 5% that will produce inaccurate interval estimates. You might thus be tempted to think that interval estimates are no more than blind guesses of the value of the population mean, but they are not. The critical issue is that if we take sample means and create intervals around them by adding and subtracting 1.96 standard errors 95% of the time we will get an accurate interval, one that does contain the population mean. Putting it another way, on average 19 in every 20 samples will yield an accurate estimate, and 1 out of 20 won't. That's why we call them 95% interval estimates or 95% confidence intervals.

Often the process of finding an interval estimate for a population measure is described as adding and subtracting an *error* to and from the sample statistic:

$$\text{Estimate of the population measure} = \text{sample statistic} \pm \text{error}$$

The error takes account of two factors. The first is the level of confidence we want, in other words the proportion of estimates that will be accurate. The second is the uncertainty inherent in using sample data to predict a population measure, in other words the fact that samples are not all the same.

The error consists of two components, the standard error and the number of standard errors. The number of standard errors is based on how confident we want to be that the estimate is accurate and the standard error reflects the variation in sample results.

Assume you need to estimate μ, the population mean, using the mean of a large sample (a sample that contains at least 30 observations). You know σ, the standard deviation of the population, and you would like to be $(100 - \alpha)\%$ confident of getting an accurate interval estimate. To get your interval estimate of μ, add and subtract the error from $\bar{x}$, the sample mean:

$$\bar{x} \pm (z_{\alpha/2} * \sigma/\sqrt{n})$$

The two parts of the error are $z_{\alpha/2}$ and $\sigma/\sqrt{n}$. The job of the standard error, $\sigma/\sqrt{n}$, is to factor in the spread in the sampling distribution. The reason for the z is that the sample mean belongs to a sampling distribution that is normal, and hence we can use the Z distribution to model it. Which specific z value you use depends on how confident you want to be that the estimate is accurate.

Suppose we want to be 95% confident in the estimate. This means that $(100 - \alpha)\%$ is 95%, α is 5% and $\alpha/2$ is 2.5% or 0.025. The z value we need is $z_{0.025}$, 1.96. This is the z value that cuts off a 2.5% tail in the Z distribution. The point 1.96 standard errors from the mean of a normal sampling distribution, which is the same as the population mean, μ, cuts off a tail area of 2.5%. So a 95% confidence interval for μ is:

$$\bar{x} \pm (1.96 * \sigma/\sqrt{n})$$

This is how we produced the estimates in Example 16.6.

Probably 95% is the most frequently used level of confidence interval but other levels are quite common. Suppose we needed a higher level of confidence, for instance 99%? For this level of confidence mean we need 99% of sample means to produce accurate estimates.

For a 99% confidence interval the only thing we need to change is the z value. When $(100 - \alpha)$% is 99%, α is 1% and $\alpha/2$ is 0.5% or 0.005. The z value we need is $z_{0.005}$, which according to the bottom row in Table 6 of Appendix 1 is 2.576. This is the z value that cuts off a 0.5 tail in the Z distribution. So a 99% interval estimate for μ is:

$$\bar{x} \pm (2.576 * \sigma/\sqrt{n})$$

The most frequently used confidence levels and the z values on which they are based are shown in Table 16.1.

Table 16.1 Selected levels of confidence and the z values to use

Level of confidence $(100 - \alpha)$%	$\alpha/2$	$z_{\alpha/2}$
90%	0.050	1.645
95%	0.025	1.960
99%	0.005	2.576

EXAMPLE 16.8

Using the sample mean from Example 16.7, 27.3 years, construct a 99% confidence interval for the population mean age of visitors to Ostrov.

Solution

According to Table 16.1 the z value to use for a 99% confidence interval is 2.576, so the interval is:

$$27.3 \pm (2.576 * 1.143) = 27.3 \pm 2.944 = 24.356 \text{ to } 30.244$$

The 95% interval estimate in Example 16.7 did not include the population mean age, 30, whereas the confidence interval in Example 16.8 does. This is despite the fact that they are both based on the same sample mean, 27.3. The reason for this is that the sample mean, 27.3, is not in the middle 95% of the sampling distribution, but it is in the middle 99% of the sampling distribution.

By increasing the confidence level to 99% we produced an accurate interval, although it is wider. The 95% confidence interval estimate was 25.06 to 29.54 years. The difference between the lower and upper bounds of the interval is 4.48 years. The 99% confidence interval is 24.356 to 30.244 years. The difference between these is 5.888 years.

At this point you may find it useful to try **Review question 16.4** at the end of the chapter.

16.3.2 What sample size should we use for estimating μ?

The fact that the 99% confidence interval in Example 16.8 was wider than the 95% confidence interval in Example 16.7 illustrates that using a higher level of confidence means accepting that the confidence interval will be wider. We lose precision. This is unfortunate because in general it is better to have more precise estimates than less precise ones. Narrower estimates are better than wider ones. To be more confident in our estimation and avoid losing precision, we can increase the sample size.

In the examples of estimation in the previous section we were given the sample size and worked out the error to use in constructing the confidence interval. But suppose you wanted to make sure that the sample size, n, is large enough to enable you to construct a sufficiently precise estimate with a specific level of confidence. To show how we can work out the necessary sample size we'll start from the expression we used to calculate the error of a confidence interval if we know the population standard deviation, σ:

$$error = z_{\alpha/2} * \sigma / \sqrt{n}$$

When we used this in the last section we started with σ, n and looked up $z_{\alpha/2}$ in Table 6 of Appendix 1. We used these three things to work out the error. Suppose we turn this round and start by deciding the size of the error. If we know σ and the level of confidence so that we can look up $z_{\alpha/2}$ we would have three things and use them to work out the other one, the sample size, n. This involves changing round the expression for the error to define the sample size:

$$error = z_{\alpha/2} * \sigma / \sqrt{n}$$

Swap error and $\sqrt{n}$: $\qquad\qquad \sqrt{n} = z_{\alpha/2} * \sigma / error$

Square both sides: $\qquad\qquad n = (z_{\alpha/2} * \sigma / error)^2$

So, if you specify the precision you want, i.e. the error, and the confidence level, to select the appropriate $z_{\alpha/2}$, and you know the population standard deviation, σ, you can work out the size of the sample.

EXAMPLE 16.9

Suppose the researcher in Example 16.6 wants a 95% confidence interval for the population mean age of the visitors to Ostrov that has a width of just three years. What sample size is necessary to achieve this?

Solution

If the width of the estimate is 3 then the amount to add and subtract to and from the sample mean is 1.5. This is the size of the error for the precision the researcher wants. If the level of confidence is 95% then $z_{\alpha/2}$ is 1.96. The population standard deviation, σ, is 8.

$$\text{The required sample size, } n = (z_{\alpha/2} * \sigma / error)^2$$
$$= (1.96 * 8 / 1.5)^2$$
$$= (10.453)^2 = 109.272$$

The sample size has to be a whole number. In this case the idea of 0.272 of a visitor makes no sense. Usually if the figure after the decimal point is less than 5 we would round down but when we are working out sample sizes to use in estimation we *always* round up. This is to avoid exceeding the specified error:

If $n = 109$, the error will be $\qquad 1.96 * 8 / \sqrt{109} = 1.502$, which is more than 1.5

If $n = 110$, the error will be $\qquad 1.96 * 8 / \sqrt{110} = 1.495$, which is less than 1.5

We should therefore conclude that for a 95% confidence interval with a width of three years the researcher needs to take a sample of 110 visitors.

16.3.3 Estimating the population mean without σ

So far, in estimating μ, the population mean, we have assumed we know σ, the population standard deviation. In practice we are unlikely to know σ. After all, if we could access the population to calculate σ how come we didn't calculate μ at the same time and save ourselves the trouble of estimating it?

Almost invariably we will only have sample results for interval estimation. This means that in the absence of σ we have to use a sample standard deviation, s, to estimate the standard error of the sampling distribution that the sample mean is from. Provided that the sample is quite large, consisting of at least 30, the procedure we use to produce a confidence interval is the same as the one we used in the last section.

So if $n \geq 30$ and σ is not known, instead of

$$\text{Confidence interval for } \mu = \bar{x} \pm (z_{\alpha/2} * \boldsymbol{\sigma}/\sqrt{n})$$

use

$$\text{Confidence interval for } \mu = \bar{x} \pm (z_{\alpha/2} * \boldsymbol{s}/\sqrt{n}).$$

EXAMPLE 16.10

The mean fare paid by a random sample of 50 rail passengers for the train journey between Falking and Stirlirk was £7.65. The sample standard deviation was £2.31. Construct a 90% confidence interval for the mean fare paid by all passengers on the route.

Solution

Here $(100 - \alpha)\% = 90\%$ so α is 10% or 0.1 and $\alpha/2$ is 5% or 0.05. According to Table 16.1 $z_{0.05}$ is 1.645.

$$\begin{aligned}
90\% \text{ confidence interval for } \mu &= \bar{x} \pm (1.645 * s/\sqrt{n}) \\
&= 7.65 \pm (1.645 * 2.31/\sqrt{50}) \\
&= 7.65 \pm 0.573 \\
&= £7.113 \text{ to } £8.187
\end{aligned}$$

We don't actually know from Example 16.10 if the parent population from which the sample was taken is normal or not. Thanks to the central limit theorem, which says that if the sample size is 30 the sampling distribution of sample means is normal whatever the shape of the parent population, this doesn't matter. The sample size, 50, is clearly more than the threshold of 30 at which the central limit theorem applies. In Example 16.10 the population distribution is likely to be skewed because generally in the rail industry commuters travelling during peak times are not only the largest group of customers but also those that pay the most.

16.3.4 Estimating the population mean with small samples

In the previous section we said that assuming we don't know σ, the population standard deviation, we can produce confidence intervals using s, the sample standard deviation, as long as the sample size is at least 30. But what if it isn't? There are many situations where a sample as large as 30 would be difficult to obtain, for instance a pharmaceutical company wanting to test a new treatment may find it difficult to obtain a sample of 30 people suffering from a rare medical condition.

Constructing confidence intervals using results from samples with fewer than 30 observations is not as straightforward as when the sample size is 30 or more. To start with, the parent population must be normal. Secondly, we cannot simply use the estimated standard error, $s/\sqrt{n}$, instead of $\sigma/\sqrt{n}$ and use the Z distribution as we did in the last section because when the sample size is less than 30, the sample standard deviation of a small sample is not a sufficiently reliable estimate of σ, the population standard deviation. Instead we have to use the t distribution for the number of estimated standard errors to add and subtract for a specific level of confidence.

So if $n < 30$ and σ is not known, instead of

$$\text{Confidence interval for } \mu = x \pm (z_{\alpha/2} * \sigma/\sqrt{n})$$

we have to use

$$\text{Confidence interval for } \mu = x \pm (t_{\alpha/2,v} * s/\sqrt{n}).$$

The t value we use depends on the number of degrees of freedom, v. This is the sample size minus one $(n - 1)$. For the most common levels of confidence the t values you will need are listed in Table 6 of Appendix 1.

EXAMPLE 16.11	The mean muzzle velocity of a random sample of 12 Pushka rifles is 736.4 metres per second with a standard deviation of 4.7 metres per second. Assuming muzzle velocities are normally distributed produce a 95% confidence interval for the mean muzzle velocity of Pushka rifles.
Solution	Here $(100 - \alpha)\% = 95\%$ so α is 5% or 0.05 and $\alpha/2$ is 2.5% or 0.025. The number of degrees of freedom, v, is $n - 1$, 11, so:

$$95\% \text{ confidence interval for } \mu = \bar{x} \pm (t_{0.025,11} * s/\sqrt{n})$$

According to Table 6, $t_{0.025,11}$ is 2.201, so:

$$95\% \text{ confidence interval for } \mu = 736.4 \pm (2.201 * 4.7/\sqrt{12})$$

$$= 736.4 \pm 2.986$$

$$= 733.414 \text{ to } 739.386 \text{ metres per second}$$

At this point you may find it useful to try **Review questions 16.10 to 16.12** at the end of the chapter.

16.3.5 Estimating π, the population proportion

Population means are not the only population parameters that can be estimated using their sample counterparts. You have almost certainly at some stage seen sample proportions used as estimates of population proportions. Perhaps the most obvious examples are opinion polls. An opinion poll is an estimate of the proportion of the population, in this case the electorate that will vote for a particular party or candidate. The source of the estimate is a sample of citizens that the pollsters will have selected from the electorate.

Estimating the proportion of a population, represented by π (the Greek equivalent of p), using a sample proportion, represented by the letter p, is similar to the way we estimated the population mean using a sample mean. The process involves taking a random sample, calculating a sample result and constructing an interval around it by adding and subtracting an error. The error is based on the standard error of the sampling distribution to which the sample result belongs, and the level of confidence we need to have that the estimate is accurate.

Having said that there are important differences in the method we use to estimate population proportions compared to the way we estimate population means. This is because the type of data is different. Proportions are used to summarise qualitative data, data that is based on putting observations into categories. The observations are characteristics such as gender or voting for a particular party in an election. When there are just two alternative characteristics, or if we choose to collate our data into only two categories, the variable will be binomially distributed.

This is convenient because the only sample result we have to use is p, the sample proportion. Unfortunately this means it is not possible to produce reliable estimates based on small sample proportions, those from samples containing fewer than 30 observations. We used the t distribution to construct confidence intervals with small sample means and we can only do this if the parent population is normal. We cannot do this with sample proportions from a small sample, those containing less than 30 observations, because the sampling distributions of small sample proportions are not normally distributed.

Sampling distributions of sample proportions are approximately normal when the samples are large, i.e. at least 30, and the sample proportion is reasonably close to 0.5. Of course in practice we can't know the sample proportion before we take the sample so generally we play safe and uses sample sizes of 100 or more.

As long as we have a large sample, we can produce a confidence interval for π, the population proportion, by starting with p, the sample proportion, then adding and subtracting the appropriate error. To calculate the sample proportion divide the number of elements in the sample that have the specific characteristic of interest, x, by the number of elements in the sample, n.

$$\text{Sample proportion}, p = x/n$$

The error to add to and subtract from the sample proportion is the z value for the level of confidence we require multiplied by the estimated standard error of the sampling distribution of the sample proportions. The estimated standard error is derived from the sample proportion:

$$\text{Estimated standard error} = \sqrt{\frac{p(1-p)}{n}}$$

The confidence interval for π is

$$p \pm z_{\alpha/2} * \sqrt{\frac{p(1-p)}{n}}$$

EXAMPLE 16.12

The Pushka rifles in Example 16.11 are difficult for left-handed people to use because of the way that they jettison spent bullet cases. In a random sample of 150 soldiers there are 18 who are left-handed. Produce a 95% confidence interval of the proportion of all soldiers who are left-handed.

Solution

$$p = 18/150 = 0.12$$

$(100 - \alpha)\% = 95\%$, so α is 5% or 0.05 and $\alpha/2$ is 0.025. The z value we need to use is $z_{0.025} = 1.96$

$$\text{Confidence interval for } \pi = 0.12 \pm 1.96 * \sqrt{\frac{0.12 (1 - 0.12)}{150}}$$

$$= 0.12 \pm 1.96 * 0.0265 = 0.12 \pm 0.052$$

$$= 0.068 \text{ to } 0.172$$

We can be 95% confident that the proportion of soldiers who are left-handed is between 6.8% and 17.2%.

At this point you may find it useful to try **Review question 16.5** at the end of the chapter.

16.3.6 What sample size should we use for estimating π?

If we have a required level of confidence, in other words the likelihood that our confidence interval is accurate, and a specified degree of precision, i.e. a maximum figure for the error, we can determine the necessary sample size to use.

The precision, or width of the interval depends in part on the estimated standard error of the sample proportions, $\sqrt{p(1-p)/n}$. The bigger this is, the wider the interval will be. The value of the estimated standard error is based on p, the sample proportion, which is used to find $p(1-p)$. The problem is that we cannot know the sample proportion before we collect the sample data and we can't collect the sample data until we know what sample size to use. To get around this dilemma we have to make an assumption about the sample proportion.

The value of $p(1-p)$ varies with p. We need to be cautious and assume that the value of p is the one that gives the highest possible value of $p(1-p)$. Unless we do this we could end up by having an interval that is narrower than it should be and overstating the actual level of confidence.

We need to establish what value of the sample proportion, p, will produce the highest value of $p(1-p)$. Suppose we start with a low value of p and see what happens to $p(1-p)$ as we increase p:

$$\text{If } p \text{ is } 0.1, p(1-p) = 0.1(1-0.1) = 0.1(0.9) = 0.09$$

$$\text{If } p \text{ is } 0.2, p(1-p) = 0.2(1-0.8) = 0.2(0.8) = 0.16$$

$$\text{If } p \text{ is } 0.3, p(1-p) = 0.3(1-0.7) = 0.3(0.7) = 0.21$$

$$\text{If } p \text{ is } 0.4, p(1-p) = 0.4(1-0.6) = 0.4(0.6) = 0.24$$

$$\text{If } p \text{ is } 0.5, p(1-p) = 0.5(1-0.5) = 0.5(0.5) = 0.25$$

$$\text{If } p \text{ is } 0.6, p(1-p) = 0.6(1-0.4) = 0.6(0.4) = 0.24$$

Notice that when p is 0.6 we get the same result for $p(1-p)$ as when p is 0.4. Arithmetically the process is the same. Similarly $p(1-p)$ for $p = 0.7$ is the same as when $p = 0.3$ and so on, so actually we didn't need to continue beyond $p = 0.5$. At this value of p, $p(1-p)$ reaches the maximum value, 0.25. Therefore to avoid the possibility of having an unduly narrow interval we assume that p, the sample proportion, is 0.5. This is the 'worst-case' scenario.

The error in a confidence interval for the population proportion is:

$$z_{\alpha/2} * \sqrt{\frac{p(1-p)}{n}}$$

If we set p at 0.5, and factor in the largest possible value of $p(1-p)$:

$$\text{The error} = z_{\alpha/2} * \sqrt{\frac{0.5(1-0.5)}{n}}$$

$$= z_{\alpha/2} * \sqrt{\frac{0.5 * 0.5}{n}}$$

$$= z_{\alpha/2} * \frac{0.5}{\sqrt{n}}$$

We can turn this around and get an expression for n:

$$\text{The error} = z_{\alpha/2} * \frac{0.5}{\sqrt{n}}$$

$$\text{so} \quad \sqrt{n} = \frac{z_{\alpha/2} * 0.5}{\text{error}} \quad \text{and}$$

$$n = \left[\frac{z_{\alpha/2}}{2 * \text{error}} \right]^2$$

EXAMPLE 16.13

How many soldiers would we need to have in the sample in Example 16.12 if we required a confidence interval for the proportion of left-handed soldiers that was within 5% of the actual population proportion, π, with a 95% degree of confidence?

Solution

For the error to be 5%, or 0.05:

$$n = \left[\frac{1.96}{2 * 0.05} \right]^2 = 19.6^2 = 384.16$$

Since we always have to have a whole number for the sample size we need to round this up to 385. Even though the actual result, 384.16, is nearer to 384 we round up as otherwise the error would be too large.

At this point you may find it useful to try **Review question 16.13** at the end of the chapter.

16.4 Statistical inference: hypothesis testing

We produce confidence intervals to get some idea of the likely value of the population parameter we would like to know. Hypothesis testing is the other side of the coin. Rather than starting with sample data and producing an estimate of a population parameter, we start with an assumption about the population parameter and use sample data to assess the validity of the assumption.

The assumption, or claim about the population parameter, typically that it has a specific value or range of values, is the *hypothesis*, and using sample results to investigate whether or not it is valid is known as *hypothesis testing*. To start with we will focus on how to test hypotheses about population means using sample means. Later on we will cover testing hypotheses about population proportions and population medians.

The first stage in hypothesis testing involves writing the assumption about the population parameter formally as what is called the *null hypothesis*. This is the start of the process and is denoted using the symbol H_0, 'H-nought'. The '0' reflects the notion of the origin or beginning.

It is possible that the null hypothesis is wrong. If so, we reject it in favour of an *alternative hypothesis*, denoted by H_1, 'H-one'. This alternative hypothesis must include all possible values of the population parameter except the one or ones specified in the null hypothesis. The '0' and '1' designations in the symbols for the hypotheses are binary; if '0' is not true, '1' must be, and *vice versa*. Generally the situations described by H_0 and H_1 are mutually exclusive and collectively exhaustive. H_0 and H_1 are complements of each other.

There are different types of null hypothesis. There are those that specify only a single value for the population parameter. The alternative hypothesis for such a null hypothesis must cover all other values of the parameter, both below and above the one specified in the null hypothesis. Since the alternative hypothesis contains *both* higher and lower values, the process used to investigate a null hypothesis that specifies a single value is known as a *two-sided test*.

Other null hypotheses specify either a minimum or a maximum value. If H_0 specifies a minimum value, in the style 'greater than or equal to', H_1 contains all lower values. If H_0 specifies a maximum value, in the style 'less than or equal to', H_1 contains all higher values. Either way the alternative hypothesis consists of values either lower or higher but not both and the process used to investigate the null hypothesis is known as a *one-sided test*. The three possible combinations of null and alternative hypotheses are listed in Table 16.2.

Table 16.2 Combinations of null and alternative hypotheses

Null hypothesis	Alternative hypothesis	Type of test
$H_0: \mu = \mu_0$	$H_1: \mu \neq \mu_0$ (not equal)	Two-sided
$H_0: \mu \leq \mu_0$	$H_1: \mu > \mu_0$ (greater than)	One-sided
$H_0: \mu \geq \mu_0$	$H_1: \mu < \mu_0$ (less than)	One-sided

The symbol μ_0 in Table 16.2 represents the value of μ, the population mean that we want to test.

The type of null hypothesis to use depends on the context and the point of view of the investigator.

EXAMPLE 16.14

The Harry Key Nut Company claims that the mean weight of the bags of pine nuts they produce is 100 grams. What forms of null and alternative hypotheses are appropriate for research by

(a) a student who wants to analyse the weight of the bags for a project?

(b) the company accountant who is worried about usage variance and wants to control costs by ensuring that the bags of nuts are not overweight?

(c) the company marketing manager who wants to avoid customers complaining that the bags of nuts are underweight?

Solution

(a) The student is only interested in whether or not the mean weight is 100 grams so appropriate hypotheses would be that the population mean weight is either equal to 100 grams or it isn't.

$$H_0: \mu = 100 \text{ grams} \qquad H_1: \mu \neq 100 \text{ grams}$$

(b) The accountant has a more focused perspective and is concerned that the mean weight is no more than 100 grams. Their null hypothesis is that the population mean weight is less than or equal to 100 grams and the alternative hypothesis is that it is more.

$$H_0: \mu \leq 100 \text{ grams} \qquad H_1: \mu > 100 \text{ grams}$$

(c) The marketing manager also has 'an agenda' and is worried that the mean weight is at least 100 grams. Their null hypothesis is that the population mean weight is greater than or equal to 100 grams and the alternative hypothesis is that it is less.

$$H_0: \mu \geq 100 \text{ grams} \qquad H_1: \mu < 100 \text{ grams}$$

After establishing the hypotheses they can be tested with sample evidence. This means ascertaining if the sample evidence is consistent with the null hypothesis. If so, we should not reject it. If on the other hand the sample evidence is not consistent with the null hypothesis we should reject it in favour of the alternative hypothesis.

How do we decide if the sample evidence supports the null hypothesis or not? To make this judgement we need a *decision rule* that we can apply to the sample evidence. In drawing up the decision rule we assume that the null hypothesis is true. We treat the null hypothesis as credible until the sample evidence suggests otherwise.

We start by assuming that μ, the population mean, is the value specified in the null hypothesis, μ_0. Provided that we know σ, the population standard deviation, and n, the size of the sample we are going to use as evidence to test the null hypothesis, we can describe the sampling distribution of sample means that contains the mean of our sample.

EXAMPLE 16.15

The population standard deviation of the pine nut bags in Example 16.14 is 2.7 grams. Suppose we intend to measure the weight of a random sample of 50 bags to test the company's claim that the mean weight of the bags is 100 grams. What can we say about the distribution the sample means of samples of 50 bags form?

Solution

In all three parts of Example 16.14 the null hypothesis specified a population mean, μ, of 100 grams. If true the implication of this is that the mean of the sampling distribution of the means of all samples with 50 observations is 100 grams. Since the population standard deviation, σ, is 2.7 grams the standard error of the sampling distribution, $\sigma/\sqrt{n}$, is $2.7/\sqrt{50}$ which is 0.382 grams.

The mean weight of a random sample of 50 bags will belong to a sampling distribution which has a mean of 100 grams and a standard error of 0.352 grams, assuming that H_0 is true. We can add that since the sample size is more than 30 this sampling distribution will be normal.

Next we need to compare the sample mean we get from our sample to the sampling distribution it comes from if H_0 is true. If it is not all that far away from the middle of the distribution H_0 is credible; the sample mean could well come from the sampling distribution. On the other hand, if the sample mean is far from the middle of the sampling distribution H_0 is not credible.

To assess how likely it is that the sample mean belongs to the sampling distribution we need to find the z-equivalent of the sample mean. We can use this to find out the probability that a sample mean like the one we have belongs to the sampling distribution that is based on H_0 being true. Since it involves a z-equivalent such an hypothesis test is called a z *test*.

EXAMPLE 16.16

The mean weight of a random sample of 50 bags of Harry Key pine nuts is 100.76 grams. Find the z-equivalent of this sample mean, based on the assumption that H_0 is true and the mean weight of all the bags of nuts really is 100 grams.

Solution

If H_0 is true the sample mean, 100.76, belongs to a sampling distribution that has a mean of 100 and a standard error of 0.352. The z-equivalent is:

$$z = \frac{\bar{x} - \mu}{\sigma/\sqrt{n}} = \frac{100.76 - 100}{0.352} = 2.159$$

Solution cont

From this z-equivalent we can find the probability of a sample mean of 100.76 (or more) which comes from a sampling distribution with a mean of 100 and a standard error of 0.352. From Table 5 of Appendix 1 and rounding the z-equivalent to 2.16:

$$P(z > 2.16) = 0.0154$$

This means $P(X > 100) = 0.0154$ or 1.54%

This is illustrated in Figure 16.5. The shaded area represents the probability of a sample mean of being 100.76 or more, based of course on H_0 being true.

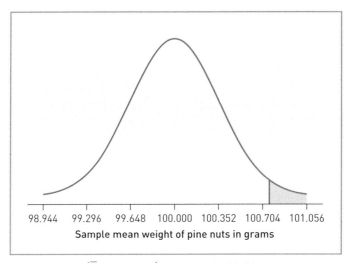

Figure 16.5 $P(\bar{X} > 100.76)$ in Example 16.16

If we know the probability that a sample mean like the one we have belongs to the sampling distribution that is based on the null hypothesis being true, we can assess the null hypothesis. We need to distinguish sample means that are consistent with the null hypothesis, which we will call 'acceptable' sample results, from those that are inconsistent with the null hypothesis, which we will call 'unacceptable' sample results.

If the probability of the sample mean belonging to the sampling distribution is quite high then the sample result is 'acceptable'. If it is quite low it is 'unacceptable'. In Example 16.16 the probability of the sample mean (or a larger one) belonging to the sampling distribution based on H_0 being true is just 1.54%, or about one chance in 65. This is so low we can regard it as 'unacceptable'.

But where do we draw the line? What precisely are 'quite high' and 'quite low' probabilities? This depends on our decision rule.

Hypothesis testing is used to confirm that goods or services meet the standards agreed between a supplier and a customer. In these cases the parties involved agree a decision rule that defines what sample results are acceptable. If a sample result is unacceptable the goods would be rejected.

A decision rule needs to specify how low the probability has to be that a sample mean, or a more extreme one, occurs before it is deemed 'unacceptable'. 'Unacceptable' sample means are what are called *significant*; they differ significantly from the sort of sample means we would expect if the null hypothesis were true. How low the probability has to be for the sample mean to be significant is the *level of significance* and is represented by the symbol α.

A 5% level of significance says that if the chance that a sample mean (or a more extreme one) belongs to the sampling distribution based on H_0 is less than 5% or 0.05 we will regard it as 'unacceptable'. Because the null hypothesis is 'on trial' here not the sample result we should swap this round and say that if our sample result is 'unacceptable' we will consider that the null hypothesis is not credible and reject it. It is the null hypothesis that is 'unacceptable' given the sample results.

This level of significance, 5%, tells us that if the probability of a sample mean (or a more extreme one) coming from the sampling distribution based on H_0 is less than one in 20, it is such an unlikely result that we believe it refutes the null hypothesis. To put it another way, if a sample mean is one of the 5% least likely to come from the sampling distribution based on H_0 being true, we should reject H_0.

If the sample mean leads us to reject H_0 it belongs to a different sampling distribution, since it is so unlikely to belong to the one based on H_0. It might be very unlikely, but it is not impossible. A sample mean, which according to our decision rule, is significant or 'unacceptable', might possibly belong to the sampling distribution based on H_0. If this were true then we would wrongly reject H_0. This is a Type I error, rejecting H_0 when we shouldn't. (There is also a Type II error which is to fail to reject H_0 when we should.) The level of significance is the risk of wrongly rejecting H_0 that we are prepared to take.

The decision rule we draw up must reflect the type of null hypothesis we want to test. If it says that the population mean takes one specific value we should assess it using a two-sided test. This means that if the sample mean we have is *either* too high *or* too low, we will reject H_0.

In a two-sided test there can be two types of 'unacceptable' or significant sample results and the decision rule has to take this into account. In using a 5% level of significance for a two-sided test, the 5% of sample means least likely to occur if H_0 is true, those sample means that would result in our rejecting the null hypothesis must include *both* the very lowest 2.5% of sample means *and* the very highest 2.5% of sample means. It follows that should the probability of our sample mean (or a more extreme one) belonging to the sampling distribution based on H_0 be less than 2.5%, or 0.025, we should reject H_0. As the test is two-sided and the two 2.5% of sample means leading to the rejection of H_0 amount to 5% of the sampling distribution we can describe our decision as rejecting H_0 *at the 5% level*.

These two extremes of the sampling distribution are referred to as the *rejection regions*, because we reject H_0 when a sample mean falls in either one of the tails of the distribution. An alternative approach involves using the z values that cut off tails of the Z distribution of the same size as the rejection regions. These z values are benchmarks against which we can assess the z-equivalent of a sample mean. The z-equivalent of the sample mean is the *test statistic* and the z values that cut off the tails that constitute the rejection regions are referred to as the *critical values* of z. Since two-sided tests involve tails at both ends of the Z distributions they are also known as *two-tail* tests.

For a two-tail test with a 5% level of significance the rejection regions are the 2.5% tails on the left and right of the sampling distribution. The critical z values are -1.96 and $+1.96$. These cut off 2.5% of the Z distribution on the left- and right-hand side respectively. Should the test statistic, the z-equivalent of a sample mean, be either less than -1.96 or greater than $+1.96$, we reject H_0. Figure 16.6 shows these rejection regions. If the test statistic is in the area between -1.96 and $+1.96$ we can't reject H_0.

EXAMPLE 16.17

Test the hypothesis that the population mean weight of the bags of nuts in Example 16.14 is 100 grams, $H_0: \mu = 100$, against the alternative hypothesis that it is not 100 grams.

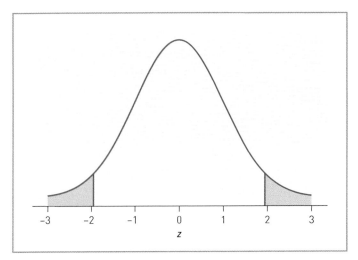

Figure 16.6 Rejection regions for a two-tail test at the 5% level of significance

Solution Use the sample mean from Example 16.16, 100.76 grams, and a 5% level of significance.

$$H_0: \mu = 100 \text{ grams} \quad H_1: \mu \neq 100 \text{ grams}$$

The level of significance, $\alpha = 0.05$

From Example 16.16 the probability of a sample mean being 100.76 grams or more belonging to a sampling distribution with a mean of 100 and a standard error of 0.352 is 0.0154, or 1.54%. This is below 2.5% so we should reject the null hypothesis at the 5% level.

Alternatively, compare the test statistic, the z-equivalent of the sample mean, 2.159, to the critical values of z that cut off 2.5% tails in the Z distribution, -1.96 and $+1.96$. Since 2.159 is more than $+1.96$, the null hypothesis should be rejected. The sample evidence suggests that the mean weight of the bags is not 100 grams and seems to be higher than 100 grams.

When H_0 says that the population mean is *less than or equal to* a specific value we use a one-sided, or *one-tail* test. With a 5% level of significance we would reject H_0 should the sample mean be one of the highest 5% of samples in the sampling distribution based on H_0.

In this case the null hypothesis allows for the population mean to be lower than the specified value. Because of this, however low the sample mean is, it is consistent with H_0. We would reject H_0 only if the sample mean is significantly higher than the population mean value stated in H_0.

The decision rule is that should the probability of the sample mean, or a higher one belonging to the sampling distribution based on H_0, be below 5% or 0.05 then reject H_0 as long as the sample mean is higher than the population mean stated in H_0. Using the alternative approach, if the test statistic is more than 1.645, which is the z value that cuts off a tail of 5% on the right of the Z distribution, reject H_0. This tail area is the rejection region and is depicted in Figure 16.7.

EXAMPLE 16.18 Using the sample mean in Example 16.16 test the hypothesis that the mean weight of the bags of nuts is less than or equal to 100 grams using the 5% level of significance.

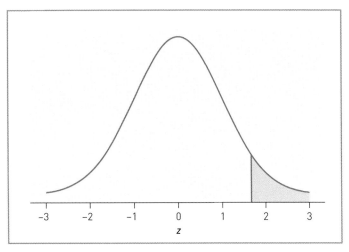

Figure 16.7 Rejection region for a one-tail test of a 'less than or equal' null hypothesis at the 5% level of significance

Solution This is the null hypothesis that fits the perspective of the company accountant in Example 16.14 who wanted to avoid the weight of the bags being too high. The appropriate pair of hypotheses is:

$$H_0: \mu \leq 100 \text{ grams} \qquad H_1: \mu > 100 \text{ grams}$$

$$\text{The level of significance, } \alpha = 0.05$$

The sample mean in Example 16.16 was 100.76. The probability that a sample mean this high or higher belonging to a sampling distribution with a mean of 100 and a standard error of 0.352 was 0.0154 or 1.54%. This is less than the level of significance so we should reject H_0. The mean weight of the bags seems to be more than 100 grams, so the accountant will not be happy.

The alternative approach is to compare the z-equivalent of 100.76 grams, 2.159, the test statistic, with the z value that cuts off the 5% tail on the right of the Z distribution, $+1.645$. We find that 2.159 is in the rejection region shown in Figure 16.7.

When H_0 says that the population mean is *greater than or equal to* a specific value, we also use a one-tail test. But the difference is that we reject H_0 if the sample mean is one of the lowest 5% of samples in the sampling distribution based on H_0.

Here the null hypothesis allows for the population mean to be higher than the specified value. Because of this, however high the sample mean is, it is consistent with H_0. We would reject H_0 only if the sample mean is significantly lower than the population mean value stated in H_0.

The decision rule is that should the probability of the sample mean, or a lower one belonging to the sampling distribution based on H_0, be below 5% or 0.05 then reject H_0 as long as the sample mean is higher than the population mean stated in H_0. Applying the alternative approach, if the test statistic is less than -1.645, which is the z value that cuts off a tail of 5% on the left of the Z distribution, then reject H_0. This tail area is the rejection region and is depicted in Figure 16.8.

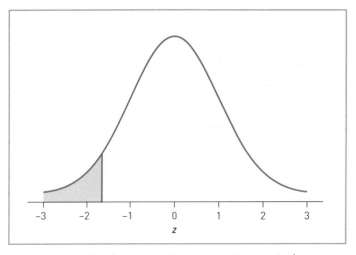

Figure 16.8 Rejection region for a one-tail test of a 'greater than or equal' null hypothesis at the 5% level of significance

The hypotheses that fit the perspective of the marketing manager in Example 16.14 are:

$$H_0: \mu \geq 100 \text{ grams} \qquad H_1: \mu < 100 \text{ grams}$$

The level of significance, $\alpha = 0.05$

If we test this null hypothesis using the sample mean from Example 16.16 we would not reject it. Although the probability that a sample mean of 100.76 or more belongs to a sampling distribution with a mean of 100 and a standard error of 0.352 is 0.0154, the null hypothesis allows for the population mean to be more than 100 grams so we cannot reject H_0 and the marketing manager will be happy.

Using the alternative approach, the test statistic, 2.159, is not less than -1.64 and is therefore not in the rejection region shown in Figure 16.8.

What if there was a mistake in recording the weights of the sample of bags and the actual sample mean is 99.24 grams? The z-equivalent of this is $(99.24 - 100)/\sqrt{50}$, which is -2.159. This is in the rejection region and we would reject H_0. The marketing manager would not be happy but the accountant would be; the null hypothesis that the mean is less than or equal to 100 grams would not now be rejected.

Just as there are different levels of confidence in estimation, there are different levels of significance in hypothesis testing. The common levels of significance are 10%, 5%, 1% and 0.1%. The lower the level of significance we use, the more stringent the test. When it is vital that hypothesis testing is rigorous, as in medicine, a 0.1% level of significance would be appropriate.

The level of significance used sets the size of the rejection region and the critical value or values of z. Once we decide on the level of significance we can then find the critical value(s) by scanning Table 5 of Appendix 1 for the appropriate values of either α (for a one-tail test) or $\alpha/2$ (for a two-tail test) and identifying the associated z values. Alternatively, we can ascertain the probability that the sample result (or one beyond it in the tail of the distribution) occurs if H_0 is true by working out its z-equivalent and then using Table 5 to obtain the critical value.

EXAMPLE 16.20

From Example 16.19 the mean weight of the sample of 50 bags of nuts was 99.24 grams. Use this to test the marketing manager's null hypothesis that the population mean weight is greater than or equal to 100 grams using a 1% level of confidence.

$$H_0: \mu \geq 100 \text{ grams} \qquad H_1: \mu < 100 \text{ grams}$$

The level of significance, $\alpha = 0.01$

Solution

According to Table 5 the probability that Z is less than -2.16, the approximate z-equivalent of a sample mean of 99.24 grams in a sampling distribution with a mean of 100 grams and a standard error of 0.352 grams, is 0.0154 or 1.54%. This is not less than the level of significance of 0.01 so we should not reject H_0.

Using the alternative approach, from Table 5 the value of z that cuts off a tail area of 0.01, $z_{0.001}$, on the left of the distribution is approximately -2.33, which is the appropriate critical value for this test. Since the test statistic, -2.159, is not beyond -2.33 it does not fall in the rejection region and so we should not reject H_0 at the 1% level of significance.

A sample mean that leads us to reject a null hypothesis is termed *significant*. When, as in Example 16.20 the sample result means rejecting the null hypothesis at a rigorous level of significance like 1%, the sample result is consider *highly significant*.

SELF-ASSEMBLY GUIDE

Drawing up decision rules and finding critical values

♦ The trickiest part of hypothesis can be the decision rule. This is important because it determines which critical value or values to use.

♦ When testing $H_0: \mu = \mu_0$, reject if the test statistic is either below $-z_{\alpha/2}$ or above $z_{\alpha/2}$.

♦ When testing $H_0: \mu \leq \mu_0$, reject if the test statistic is above z_α.

♦ If you are testing $H_0: \mu \geq \mu_0$, reject if the test statistic is below $-z_\alpha$.

16.4.1 Hypothesis testing without σ

So far in discussing hypothesis testing we have assumed that we know σ, the population standard deviation. This is possible, especially when we want to assess the consequences of a change in the situation we are investigating by comparing sample data from after the change and there is population data from before the change. This could be a confectionery company that rebrands a product and would like to find out whether there has been a significant effect on sales. The sales database may well be sufficiently comprehensive to generate the population standard deviation of the sales before the rebranding. From this they could determine the standard error of the sampling distribution for the test.

Typically though, we won't have σ, the population standard deviation. If this is the case the sample size is a key factor. If the sample evidence is from a sample of 30 or more observations, the sample standard deviation, s, will be close enough to σ for us to use a z test; our decision rule can be based on the Z distribution. All we have to do is use s instead of σ and work out the estimated standard error. In other words, without σ we use $s/\sqrt{n}$ instead of the actual standard error, $\sigma/\sqrt{n}$.

<table>
<tr><td>**EXAMPLE**
16.21</td><td>The manufacturer of the 'Geroy' light van claims that the population mean fuel efficiency of the vehicles is 35 miles per gallon (mpg). A dispatch company purchased 40 vehicles and found that their mean fuel efficiency was 34.2 mpg with a standard deviation of 3.9 mpg. Do these results support the manufacturer's claimed fuel efficiency? Use a 10% level of significance.</td></tr>
</table>

Solution

Assuming that the dispatch company is only concerned that the actual fuel efficiency is less than the claimed figure as this would adversely affect its fuel costs the appropriate hypotheses are:

$$H_0: \mu \geq 35 \qquad H_1: \mu < 35$$

$$\text{Level of significance, } \alpha = 0.1$$

If the population mean is 35, the means of samples size 40 have a sampling distribution with a mean of 35 and an estimated standard error of $3.9/\sqrt{40}$. The test statistic is:

$$z = \frac{34.2 - 35}{3.9/\sqrt{40}} = -1.297$$

From Table 5, the probability that a z value is less than -1.30 (-1.297 rounded to 2 decimal places) is 0.0968, or 9.68%. This is less than 10%, the level of significance, so we should reject H_0. Note that because 0.0968 is not less than 0.05 we would not reject H_0 at the 5% level of significance.

Using the alternative approach, the z value that cuts off a 10% tail on the left of the Z distribution is -1.28. Since the test statistic, -1.297, is less than -1.28, H_0 should be rejected at the 10% level.

16.4.2 Hypothesis testing with small samples

We can use the mean of a sample with less than 30 observations to test a hypothesis if we don't know σ, the population standard deviation. The proviso is that we have to be fairly sure that the parent population the sample comes from is normally distributed.

With samples of 30 or more observations the sample standard deviation, s, is close enough to the population standard deviation, σ, for us to use a z test. Unfortunately this is not the case with a sample standard deviation from small samples. They vary too much to allow us to use s instead of σ as we can do with larger samples so we cannot use a z test. To get around this we must use the t distribution not the Z distribution as the benchmark for comparing sample results to sampling distributions based on null hypotheses being true. Hypothesis tests based on the t distribution are called t *tests*.

<table>
<tr><td>**EXAMPLE**
16.22</td><td>Suppose the dispatch company in Example 16.21 had purchased only 20 Geroy vans. If the sample mean and standard deviation are 34.2 and 4.9 mpg respectively, test the hypothesis that the population mean fuel efficiency of the vans is 35 mpg. Use a 10% level of significance.

The appropriate hypotheses remain:</td></tr>
</table>

$$H_0: \mu \geq 35 \qquad H_1: \mu > 35$$

$$\text{Level of significance, } \alpha = 0.10$$

Solution   The test statistic is

$$t = \frac{(\bar{x} - \mu)}{\sigma/\sqrt{n}} = \frac{34.2 - 35}{3.9/\sqrt{20}} = -0.917$$

The critical value we need to compare to this test statistic is the t value that cuts off the 10% tail on the left of the distribution with 19 degrees of freedom, one less than the sample size, 20. According to Table 6 in Appendix 1, $t_{0.10,19}$ is 1.328. This is the t value that cuts off the 10% tail on the right. We need the value that cuts off the 10% tail on the left, $-t_{0.10,19}$ which is -1.328. Since the test statistic, -0.917, is not less than -1.328, we cannot reject H_0.

Although we used the same hypotheses, level of significance, sample mean and sample standard deviation as in Example 16.21 the result is different. In that case we rejected H_0 but here we did not. The reason is that the estimated standard error is larger ($3.9/\sqrt{20}$ compared to $3.9/\sqrt{40}$). We also have a lower critical value, -1.328, compared to -1.28.

At this point you may find it useful to try **Review questions 16.6 and 16.14** at the end of the chapter.

16.4.3 Testing hypotheses about π, the population proportion

The way we test hypotheses about population proportions is very similar to how we test hypotheses about population means. We start with a null hypothesis that specifies the value of π (the Greek equivalent of p), the population proportion we want to test, π_0. If H_0, the null hypothesis, is the 'equal to' type we perform a two-tail test. With 'less than or equal to' and 'greater than or equal to' null hypotheses, we perform a one-tail test. Table 16.3 lists the three possible combinations of hypotheses.

Table 16.3 Types of hypotheses for the population proportion

Null hypothesis	Alternative hypothesis	Type of test
$H_0: \pi = \pi_0$	$H_1: \pi \neq \pi_0$ ('not equal')	Two-sided
$H_0: \pi \leq \pi_0$	$H_1: \pi > \pi_0$ ('greater than')	One-sided
$H_0: \pi \geq \pi_0$	$H_1: \pi < \pi_0$ ('less than')	One-sided

In this table π_0 represents the value of the population proportion that is to be tested.

The test statistic is derived from p, the sample proportion from the sample we intend to use to test H_0. The sample proportion is assumed at the outset to belong to the sampling distribution with a mean of π_0 and a standard error of:

$$\sqrt{\frac{\pi_0(1 - \pi_0)}{n}}$$

When we estimated π in section 16.3.5 we used the estimated standard error based on p, the sample proportion. Here we use π_0 the population specified in H_0, the null hypothesis, which is presumed to be true until we have reason to believe otherwise.

The sampling distribution of sample proportions is distributed normally if the samples are large, over 100. This means we can use the Z distribution for the test; it is a z test.

The test statistic is:

$$z = \frac{p - \pi_0}{\sqrt{\pi_0(1 - \pi_0)/n}}$$

Testing a population proportion involves drawing up a decision rule just as we do when testing population means. The decision rule specifies the level of significance we want to use to assess the null hypothesis.

EXAMPLE 16.23

According to *Obasher* magazine one in eight adults is vegetarian. In a random sample of 165 adults, 18 are vegetarians. Does this sample evidence support the assertion made in the magazine? Use a 5% level of significance.

Solution

We can use a two-tail test here because we are asked to assess whether or not the population proportion is one in eight, 12.5%. The appropriate hypotheses are:

$$\text{H}_0\text{: } \pi_0 = 0.125 \qquad \text{H}_1\text{: } \pi_0 \neq 0.125$$

$$\text{Level of significance, } \alpha = 0.05$$

The sample proportion, $p = 18/165 = 0.109$

$$\text{The test statistic, } z = \frac{p - \pi_0}{\sqrt{\pi_0(1 - \pi_0)/n}}$$

$$= \frac{0.109 - 0.125}{\sqrt{0.125(1 - 0.125)/165}}$$

$$= -0.621$$

According to Table 5, the probability that z is -0.62 (-0.621 rounded to two decimal places) or less is 0.2676, or 26.76%. Since this is more than $\alpha/2$, 2.5%, we should not reject H_0. The magazine's claim seems reasonable.

Using the alternative approach, the critical z values for a two-tail test at a 5% level of confidence are -1.96 and $+1.96$. The test statistic, -0.621, is within these figures so the sample result is not significant. The sample proportion is lower than π_0, 0.125, but not significantly so.

At this point you may find it useful to try **Review question 16.15** at the end of the chapter.

16.4.4 A hypothesis test for the population median

In the sections above we concentrated on testing hypotheses about population means. As long as sample sizes are large, at least 30, this is generally a viable approach to assessing the central tendency of a population. If, however, the samples are small, consisting of less than 30 observations, testing hypotheses about population means is not as straightforward.

To use small sample results to test a hypothesis about a population mean using a small sample we have to assume that the parent population is normally distributed. In some cases this is simply not so. Variables such as household income and car journey durations are not usually normal in shape.

If a distribution is skewed the sampling distributions for means of small samples taken from it is also skewed. In section 6.2, the part of Chapter 6 that deals with averages, we noted that the median was a better measure of location for skewed distributions. In this section we will consider how to test hypotheses about the population median using the *sign* test. We can use this to run tests based on small sample data from populations that are not normally distributed.

The basis of the sign test is quite straightforward. When the population observations are arranged in order of magnitude, the population median is the value in the middle of them. Half of the observations are above the median and half below it. If we select an observation at random the probability that it is lower than the median is 0.5 and the probability it is higher than the median is 0.5. When we take a random sample, the observations in it will be either more than or less than the median. We can model the number of observations in the sample that are above and below the median with the binomial distribution, defining 'success' as an observation being above the median. The probability of 'success' is 0.5. The number of trials is the number of observations.

The null and alternative hypotheses we use are just like the ones we would use in testing a population mean or a population proportion; the only difference is that they are about the population median. The null hypothesis should specify the particular value of the population median we want to test.

The next step is to allot a '+' sign to every observation in the sample higher than the median and a '−' to every observation that is less than the median. Should an observation have exactly the same value as the population median specified in the null hypothesis, which is unlikely, allot a sign on the basis of a random process, like tossing a coin, or just ignore it.

After assigning the observations plusses and minuses, count the number of plus signs and the number of minus signs. The last stage is to define the rejection region based on the binomial distribution that is appropriate for the required level of significance.

EXAMPLE 16.24

One printer is shared by a large number of office workers. The numbers of pages of output per job sent to the printer form a skewed distribution. The number of pages in a random sample of 10 jobs were:

1   12   1   2   4   7   1   3   2   1

Test the hypothesis that the population median number of pages per job is 2.5. Use a 5% level of significance.

Solution

$$H_0: \text{median} = 2.5 \qquad H_1: \text{median} \neq 2.5$$

Allocate a sign to each observation, minus if it is below 2.5 and plus if it is above 2.5.

1   12   1   2   4   7   1   3   2   1

−   +   −   −   +   +   −   +   −   −

There are four plusses and six minuses. The number of trials, n, is 10, and p, the probability of a 'success', which we will define as an observation being allocated a '+', is 0.5. To conduct the test we need to use the binomial distribution for $n = 10$ and $p = 0.5$. The probabilities for this distribution are listed in Table 2 in Appendix 1.

The level of significance is 5%, so α is 0.05. We need to perform a two-tail test so the two parts of the rejection are the two tails of the distribution, each of which has an area of $\alpha/2$, 0.025. We reject H_0 if there are too many plus signs, i.e. too many values above the population median specified in H_0, or too few of them. But exactly how many are too many and how many are too few?

The number of plusses will form a discrete distribution. This means that the tail areas will have to be approximate. According to Table 2 the probability of 0 or 1 successes in the

Solution cont
binomial distribution for $n = 10$ and $p = 0.5$ is 0.011. Since p is 0.5 the distribution is symmetrical so the probability of 9 or 10 successes is also 0.011.

Applying this distribution, if the population median is 2.5, the probability of getting 0, 1, 9 or 10 plusses, i.e. observations above 2.5, will be twice 0.011, i.e. 0.022 or 2.2%. The rejection region is made up of the probabilities of these numbers of plusses. If the number of plusses is between 2 and 8 inclusive, we shouldn't reject H_0.

Here we have 4 plusses so we can't reject H_0. The population median could be 2.5.

We have actually used a 2.2% level of significance for this test. This is as close as we can get to 5%. To increase the level of significance we would have to include 2 and 8 in the rejection region. According to Table 2 the probability of 0, 1 or 2 successes is 0.055 so the probability of getting 0, 1, 2, 8, 9, or 10 successes is 0.11, or 11%. This is far higher than the 5% level of significance we require.

The sign test is one of a number of tests that can be used more generally than the so-called 'classical' methods we covered earlier. These are referred to as *nonparametric* tests since they are not based on the parameters used in the classical methods, such as the mean and standard deviation. They are also called *distribution-free* methods since they do not involve making assumptions about parent population distributions.

In general, nonparametric tests are easier to use and more broadly applicable than the classical methods although they aren't as efficient. Usually to perform a nonparametric test we need more data than we would for a classical test for a given degree of rigour. Sprent and Smeeton (2007) provide a thorough coverage of nonparametric methods.

At this point you may find it useful to try **Review question 16.7** at the end of the chapter.

REVIEW QUESTIONS

Answers to these questions are on page 454. There are tips and hints to help you with them on the supporting website at **www.pearsoned.co.uk/buglear**, where you will also find the fully worked solutions.

☆☆★ Basic questions

16.1 Beer Necessities sells its ale in 330 millilitre (ml) bottles. The mean contents of these bottles are normally distributed with a mean of 333 millilitres and a standard deviation of 5ml. The ale is sold in packs of six bottles in supermarkets.

(a) What is the probability that the mean content per bottle of a pack of six bottles is (i) more than 330ml, (ii) more than 335ml, (iii) less than 330ml, (iv) less than 328ml, (v) between 332 and 336ml, (vi) between 330 and 339ml?

(b) Compare your results for (a) to the probabilities that the content of a single bottle is (i) more than 330ml, (ii) more than 335ml, (iii) less than 330ml, (iv) less than 328ml, (v) between 332 and 336ml, (vi) between 330 and 339ml.

16.2 The lifetimes of Voltair AA batteries are normally distributed with a mean of 5.9 hours and a standard deviation of 0.4 hours. They are sold in packs of 12.

(a) Find the probability that the mean lifetime of a pack of 12 batteries is (i) more than 6 hours, (ii) less than 5.75 hours, (iii) between 5.8 and 6.1 hours.

(b) A battery-operated toy requires four batteries. What is the probability that four batteries will last on average (i) more than 6 hours, (ii) less than 5.75 hours, (iii) between 5.7 and 6.2 hours?

16.3 The balances in savings accounts at the Vorovaty Bank form a skewed distribution with a mean of £3800 and a standard deviation of £1200.

(a) Work out the probability that the mean balance of a random sample of 50 accounts is (i) more than £4000, (ii) more than £4200, (iii) less than £3500, (iv) less than £4100, (v) between £3400 and £4000, (vi) between £3300 and £3600.

(b) Should you use the same method as you used in (a) to work out the probabilities about a sample mean if the sample size were 20? Explain your answer.

16.4 Vint Engineering produces brass screws. The lengths of its two-inch screws are normally distributed with a population standard deviation of 0.05 inches. The sample mean of a random sample of 35 screws is 1.97 inches.

(a) Construct confidence intervals for the population mean length of the screws using (i) a 90% level of confidence, (ii) a 95% level of confidence, and (iii) a 99% level of confidence.

(b) It emerges that the sample consisted of only 25 screws. Produce confidence intervals for the population mean length of the screws at the same three levels of confidence as in (a) and compare your results to the ones you have for (a).

16.5 A large trade union plans to ballot the membership about strike action. In consultations with a random sample of 100 members 73 of them said they would vote for the strike.

(a) Using this sample result construct interval estimates for the population proportion that will vote to strike using (i) a 95% level of confidence, and (ii) a 99% level of confidence.

(b) Assuming all members vote, do the confidence intervals in (a) suggest that a majority will vote for strike action?

16.6 Letchen Healthfoods claims that the mean volume of its cod liver oil capsules is 410 milligrams (mg). The mean and standard deviation volumes of a random sample of 40 capsules are 407mg and 15mg respectively. Test the null hypothesis that the population mean volume is 410mg using (i) a 5% level of significance, and (ii) a 1% level of significance.

16.7 The household incomes in the city of Seredina are believed to have a skewed distribution. The monthly incomes of a random sample of 10 households (in £000s) were:

1.2   3.5   2.9   1.5   4.2   6.8   1.9   0.8   2.6   2.0

Use this data to test the null hypothesis that the median household income in Seredina is £3000 using a 5% level of significance.

☆★★ More testing questions

16.8 Sacker Supplies sells catering packs of sugar sachets. The weights of sugar in the sachets are normally distributed with a mean of 3.1 grams and a standard deviation of 0.4 grams. The sachets are sold in packs of 100 and 25.

(a) Find the probability that the mean weight of sugar per sachet in a pack of 100 sachets is (i) more than 3.2 grams, (ii) less than 3.02 grams, (iii) between 2.99 and 3.05 grams.

(b) Find the probability that the mean weight of sugar per sachet in a pack of 25 sachets is (i) more than 3.2 grams, (ii) less than 3.02 grams, (iii) between 2.99 and 3.05 grams.

(c) Compare your answers to parts (a) and (b). Why are they different?

16.9 An 'extreme' ride at a theme park takes groups of 20 riders at a time in a capsule and drops them over a sheer incline. The load limit for the ride is 1600 kilograms (kg), so if the mean weight of the riders is more than 80kg the ride is unsafe.

(a) If the weights of the population are normally distributed with a mean of 75kg and a standard deviation of 14kg what is the probability that the load limit will be exceeded?

(b) What is the probability that the ride will be overloaded if the number of riders is reduced to 19?

(c) The owners of the theme park intend to include the ride at a new park they are opening in another country. The distribution of weights of the population there are normal with a mean of 78kg and a standard deviation of 12kg. What is the probability that the load limit for the ride will be exceeded at the new location if (i) there are 20 riders, and (ii) there are 19 riders?

16.10 The Careers Service at Chicarny University wants to estimate the mean salary of Chicarny graduates five years after their graduation. The annual salaries of a random sample of 46 graduates had a mean of £35,000 and a standard deviation of £4000.

(a) Estimate the population mean graduate salary using (i) a 90% level of confidence, (ii) a 95% level of confidence, and (iii) a 99% level of confidence.

(b) It transpires that half of the graduates in this sample had graduated more than five years ago and the Careers Service removes their figures from the sample data. The sample mean of the remaining salaries is £32,000 and the standard deviation is £2400. Assuming that Chicarny graduate salaries are approximately normally distributed, use these figures to construct confidence intervals for the population mean at (i) 90%, (ii) 95%, and (iii) 99% levels of confidence.

(c) If the population standard deviation of Chicarny graduate salaries five years after graduation is £1500, what sample size would the Careers Service need to use to estimate the population mean salary so that the confidence interval is no wider than £200 with (i) a 90% level of confidence, (ii) a 95% level of confidence, and (iii) a 99% level of confidence?

16.11 The View4U bookings agency rents out self-catering holiday accommodation. Out of a random sample of 379 recent bookings 101 were made through the company internet pages.

(a) Estimate the population proportion of bookings using confidence levels of (i) 90%, (ii) 95%, and (iii) 99%.

(b) What sample size would be required to estimate the population proportion so that the confidence interval is no wider than 0.04 with (i) a 90% level of confidence, (ii) a 95% level of confidence, and (iii) a 99% level of confidence?

★★★ Challenging questions

16.12 The temperatures of a random sample of 32 hot beverages delivered by a drinks machine were measured. The mean temperature of these was 78.9° Celsius and the standard deviation was 1.6° Celsius.

(a) Estimate the population mean temperature of the hot beverages from the machine using (i) a 90% level of confidence, (ii) a 95% level of confidence, and (iii) a 99% level of confidence.

(b) Unfortunately eight of the drinks in the sample of 32 were left to stand for some minutes at room temperature so that they cannot be included in the analysis. The mean and standard deviation of the other drinks were 80.4° and 2.2° respectively. Produce confidence intervals for the population mean at the (i) 90%, (ii) 95%, and (iii) 99% levels of confidence.

(c) What do you need to assume about the population for the analysis in (b) to be valid?

(d) If the population standard deviation of the hot drinks temperatures is known to be 1.4° what sample size would need to be used to estimate the population mean temperature so that the confidence interval is no wider than (i) 1° at the 95% level of confidence, (ii) 2° at the 99% level of confidence?

16.13 The times taken for the room service staff at a hotel to deliver drinks and snacks are normally distributed. The mean and standard deviation of the times taken to deliver a random sample of 30 room service orders were 14.2 minutes and 2.7 minutes.

(a) Construct confidence intervals for the population mean delivery time using (i) 90%, (ii) 95%, and (iii) 99% levels of confidence.

(b) Five of the room service orders in the sample included hot meals and should not have been included in the sample. The mean and standard deviations of the remaining delivery times were 11.3 minutes and 1.8 minutes respectively. Find (i) a 90% confidence interval, (ii) a 95% confidence interval, and (iii) a 99% confidence interval for the population mean delivery time.

(c) If the population standard delivery time is 1.5 minutes what sample sizes are required for the following interval estimates of the population mean delivery time?

   (i)   An estimate 1 minute wide with a 95% level of confidence.
   (ii) An estimate 1 minute wide with a 99% level of confidence.
   (iii) An estimate 0.5 minutes wide with a 90% level of confidence.
   (iv) An estimate 0.5 minutes wide with a 95% level of confidence.

16.14 A high street chemist has installed a new stock control system to expedite the delivery of prescription medicines to its customers. Prior to the installation of this system the mean time interval between customers presenting prescriptions and the medicines being dispensed to them was 10.8 minutes. Since the introduction of the new system the manager measured the time taken to dispense prescriptions to a random sample of 41 customers. The mean time taken to dispense prescriptions to this sample of customers was 9.6 minutes with a standard deviation of 5.3 minutes.

(a) Test the hypothesis that the new stock control system has resulted in a faster average dispensing time using a 5% level of significance.

(b) Later it emerges that 25 of the prescriptions out of the sample of 41 were dispensed by an employee who had received no training in the use of the system. If these results are removed the mean and standard deviation of the dispensing times of the remaining prescriptions were 8.1 and 4.6 respectively. Test the hypothesis that the new stock control system has yielded a faster average dispensing time using these sample results and a 5% level of significance.

(c) Contrast the results of the two tests and identify the assumption that must be made for the second test to be valid.

16.15 According to police records 8% of houses in the Bedniarky estate were burgled in the year before last. None of the houses on the estate had double glazing. At the end of that year the housing authority that owned all the houses on the estate installed double glazing in 530 properties. 28 of these were burgled during the following year. By testing an appropriate hypothesis ascertain whether this evidence suggests the proportion of double glazed houses that were burgled is significantly lower. Use (i) 10%, (ii) 5%, and (iii) 1% levels of significance.

THE DEBRIEF

Key things to remember from this chapter

→ Different samples of the same size can be taken from a population. They will have different sample statistics (sample means, sample standard deviations and sample proportions).

→ Sampling distributions describe the pattern of variation of sample statistics.

→ The sampling distribution of the sample mean has the same mean as the population and a standard deviation, known as the standard error, which is the population standard deviation divided by the square root of the sample size. Sample means are located around the same mean as the population but with a smaller spread. Sample statistics always vary less than individual points of data.

→ Interval estimation, the construction of confidence intervals, involves adding and subtracting an error to and from a sample statistic. The error takes account of the spread of sample results and the level of confidence.

→ Hypothesis testing begins with a pair of mutually exclusive statements about the value of a population parameter. The null hypothesis, a statement of what is assumed to be true, is tested using a sample statistic.

References

HC Deb 27 January 2011 vol 552 c147WH [online]. Available at http://www.publications.parliament.uk/pa/cm201011/cmhansrd/cm110127/halltext/110127h0001.htm#11012769000001

MacKenzie, D.A. (1981) *Statistics in Britain, 1865–1930*, Edinburgh: Edinburgh University Press.

McMullen, L. (1970) '"Student" as a man', in E.S. Pearson and M.G. Kendall (eds), *Studies in the History of Statistics and Probability*, London: Griffin, pp. 355–60.

Nottingham City Homes (2010) The 'Secure Warm Modern' programme in Nottingham – Decent Homes impact study: Crime report [online]. Available at http://www.nottinghamcityhomes.org.uk/documents/modern_warm_secure/impact_studies/Decent_homes_impact_study_crime_report.pdf

Pearson, E.S. (1970) '"Student" as a statistician', in E.S. Pearson and M.G. Kendall (eds), *Studies in the History of Statistics and Probability*, London: Griffin, pp. 360–403.

Sprent, P. and Smeeton, N.C. (2007) *Applied Nonparametric Statistical Methods* (7th edn), London: Chapman and Hall.

CHAPTER 17

High performance – statistical inference for comparing population means and bivariate data

CHAPTER OBJECTIVES

This chapter will help you to:

→ Test the difference between population means

→ Test the significance of correlation and regression model coefficients

→ Produce interval estimates using regression equations

→ Perform contingency analysis

THE BARE BONES

What you will find in this chapter . . .

- Using two independent samples to test hypotheses about the difference between the means of the populations they come from
- Testing differences between two population means using dependent samples; the paired *t* test
- Applying analysis of variance (ANOVA) to test differences between more than two population means
- Constructing confidence intervals and prediction intervals using simple linear regression models
- Testing for association between category variables using the chi-square distribution

. . . and on the supporting website (www.pearsoned.co.uk/buglear)

- How to use EXCEL, Minitab and SPSS to test differences between population means, apply correlation and regression inference, and contingency analysis
- Fully worked solutions to the review questions
- More review questions

Business use of contingency analysis and ANOVA

◆ Contingency analysis is widely used in questionnaire research. This type of research is very common in investigations of consumer preferences and behaviour.

◆ Schimmel and Nicholls (2003) report the findings of a survey of internet users undertaken for an internet retailer to assess the influence of gender on inclination to shop on the internet. They applied contingency analysis to assess the association between gender and the frequency with which respondents made purchases, and between gender and the amounts respondents spent on internet shopping. They found no significant associations between gender and the number of purchases or the amount spent in internet transactions.

◆ Retailers are interested in how intangible factors, or 'atmospherics', influence the behaviour of customers visiting their stores. Areni and Kim (1993) studied the effect that different types of background music had on the inclination of visitors to browse and make purchases in a US wine store. They observed the behaviour of customers and analysed till records over a three-month period. On some evenings 'classical' background music was played, on others 'Top-Forty' top-selling music was played. They used ANOVA and contingency analysis to investigate association between age group and influence of music type, and customer type (gender, single or couple or group) and influence of music type. They found that classical music influenced customers to spend more, but by buying more expensive wines rather than greater quantities.

◆ Baysan (2001) surveyed attitudes of tourists towards environmental issues related to tourism to find out if attitude was associated with the nationality of tourists, their levels of education and their occupations. The respondents were German, Russian and Turkish holiday-makers staying at a resort in the Antalya region of Turkey. Using chi-square analysis he found that there was a stronger association between nationality and attitudes than between either education level or occupation and attitudes. German tourists were distinctly more sensitive towards environmental issues than their Russian and Turkish counterparts when asked, among other things, about their inclination to engage in motorboat sports or use oil-based sun-creams.

◆ In US employment law there are landmark cases in which statistical evidence was of central importance. Meier, Sacks and Zabell (1994) discuss a number of cases in which statistical analysis, including contingency analysis, was used as evidence of racial discrimination in employment. This analysis was used in cases involving the fairness of written tests in recruitment and promotion procedures.

17.1 Introduction

In the previous chapter we looked at statistical inference in relation to univariate data, estimating and testing single population parameters like the mean using single sample results. Here we will consider statistical inference methods that enable us to compare the means of two or more populations, to test population correlation coefficients, to make predictions from simple linear regression models and to test for association in qualitative data.

17.2 Testing hypotheses about two population means

In section 16.4 we looked at tests of the population mean based on a single sample mean. In this section we will consider tests designed to assess the difference between two population means. In businesses these tests are used to investigate whether, for instance, the introduction of a new logo improves sales.

To use these tests you need to have a sample from each of the two populations. For the tests to be valid the samples must be random, but they can be *independent* or *dependent*.

Independent samples are selected from each population separately. Suppose a domestic gas supplier wanted to assess the impact of a new charging system on customers' bills. The company could take a random sample of customers and record the size of their bills under the existing charging system then, after the new system is introduced, take another random sample of customers and record the size of their bills. These samples would be independent.

Dependent samples consist of matched or paired values. If the gas supplier took a random sample of customers and recorded the size of their bills both before and after the introduction of the new charging system it would be using a paired or dependent sample.

The choice of independent or dependent samples depends on the context of the test. Unless there is a good reason for using paired data it is better to use independent samples. We will begin by looking at tests for use with independent samples and deal with paired samples later in this section.

As with single sample tests the size of the samples is important because it determines the nature of the sampling distribution. In this section we will assume that the population standard deviations are not known.

17.2.1 Large independent samples

The null hypothesis we use in comparing population means is based on the difference between the means of the two populations, $\mu_1 - \mu_2$. The possible combinations of null and alternative hypotheses are shown in Table 17.1.

Table 17.1 Types of hypotheses for comparing population means

Null hypothesis	Alternative hypothesis	Type of test
$H_0: \mu_1 - \mu_2 = 0$	$H_1: \mu_1 - \mu_2 \neq 0$	Two-sided
$H_0: \mu_1 - \mu_2 \leq 0$	$H_1: \mu_1 - \mu_2 > 0$	One-sided
$H_0: \mu_1 - \mu_2 \geq 0$	$H_1: \mu_1 - \mu_2 < 0$	One-sided

The hypotheses listed in Table 17.1 all assume that the focus of the test is that there is no difference between the population means. This is typical but the same formats can be used to test whether the difference between two population means is a non-zero constant, e.g. $H_0: \mu_1 - \mu_2 = 6$.

If both of the samples contain 30 or more items the difference between their means, $\bar{x}_1 - \bar{x}_2$, belongs to the sampling distribution of $\bar{X}_1 - \bar{X}_2$. This sampling distribution is normally distributed with a mean of $\mu_1 - \mu_2$, and a standard error of:

$$\sqrt{\frac{\sigma_1^2}{n_1} + \frac{\sigma_2^2}{n_2}}$$

σ_1 and σ_2 are the standard deviations of the first and second populations, and n_1 and n_2 are the sizes of the samples from the first and second populations.

We will assume that the population standard deviations are not known, in which case the estimated standard error of the sampling distribution is:

$$\sqrt{\frac{s_1^2}{n_1} + \frac{s_2^2}{n_2}}$$

The test statistic is:

$$z = \frac{(\bar{x}_1 - \bar{x}_2) - (\mu_1 - \mu_2)}{\sqrt{\dfrac{s_1^2}{n_1} + \dfrac{s_2^2}{n_2}}}$$

If the null hypothesis suggests that the difference between the population means is zero, we can simplify this to:

$$z = \frac{(\bar{x}_1 - \bar{x}_2)}{\sqrt{\dfrac{s_1^2}{n_1} + \dfrac{s_2^2}{n_2}}}$$

Once we have calculated the test statistic we need to compare it to the appropriate critical value from the standard normal distribution.

EXAMPLE 17.1

A national breakdown recovery service has depots at Oxford and Portsmouth. The mean and standard deviation of the times that it took for the staff at the Oxford depot to assist each of a random sample of 47 motorists were 51 minutes and seven minutes respectively. The mean and standard deviation of the response times recorded by the staff at the Portsmouth depot in assisting a random sample of 39 customers were 49 minutes and five minutes respectively. Test the hypothesis that there is no difference between the mean response times of the two depots. Use a 5% level of significance.

Solution

$$H_0: \mu_1 - \mu_2 = 0 \qquad H_1: \mu_1 - \mu_2 \neq 0$$

$$\text{Test statistic, } z = \frac{51 - 49}{\sqrt{\dfrac{7^2}{47} + \dfrac{5^2}{39}}}$$

$$= 2/1.298 = 1.541$$

This is a two-tail test using a 5% level of confidence so the critical values are $\pm z_{0.025}$. Unless the test statistic is below -1.96 or above $+1.96$ the null hypothesis cannot be rejected. The test statistic, 1.541, is within ± 1.96 so we cannot reject H_0. The population mean response times of the two breakdown services could be equal.

Notice that in Example 17.1 we have not said anything about the distributions of response times. The central limit theorem allows us to use the same two-sample z test whatever the shape of the populations from which the samples were drawn as long as the size of both samples is 30 or more.

At this point you may find it useful to try **Review question 17.1** at the end of the chapter.

17.2.2 Small independent samples

If the size of the samples you want to use to compare population means is small, less than 30, you can only follow the procedure outlined in the previous section if both populations are normal and both population standard deviations known. In the absence of the latter it is possible to test the difference between two population means using small independent samples but only under certain circumstances.

If both populations are normal and their standard deviations can be assumed to be the same, that is $\sigma_1 = \sigma_2$, we can conduct a two-sample t test. We use the sample standard deviations to produce a pooled estimate of the standard error of the sampling distribution of $\bar{X}_1 - \bar{X}_2$, s_p.

$$s_p = \sqrt{\frac{(n_1 - 1)s_1^2 + (n_2 - 1)s_2^2}{n_1 + n_2 - 2}}$$

The test statistic is

$$t = \frac{(\bar{x}_1 - \bar{x}_2)}{s_p * \sqrt{\dfrac{1}{n_1} + \dfrac{1}{n_2}}}$$

We then compare the test statistic to the appropriate critical value from the t distribution. The number of degrees of freedom for this test is $n_1 + n_2 - 2$, one degree of freedom is lost for each of the sample means.

EXAMPLE 17.2

A cereal manufacturer claims to use no more oats, the cheapest ingredient, in producing packets of 'own-brand' muesli for a supermarket chain than they use to produce their own premium brand. The mean and standard deviation of the oat content by weight of a random sample of 14 'own-brand' packets are 34.9% and 1.4% respectively. The mean and standard deviation of the oat content of a random sample of 17 premium brand packets are 33.4% and 1.1% respectively. Test the hypothesis that the mean oat content of the premium brand is no greater than the mean oat content of the 'own-brand' muesli using a 1% level of significance.

Solution

We will define μ_1 as the population mean of the 'own-brand' and μ_2 as the population mean of the premium product.

$$H_0: \mu_1 - \mu_2 \leq 0 \qquad H_1: \mu_1 - \mu_2 > 0$$

First we need the pooled estimate of the standard error:

$$s_p = \sqrt{\frac{(14 - 1)1.4^2 + (17 - 1)1.1^2}{14 + 17 - 2}}$$

$$= 1.243$$

Now we can calculate the test statistic:

$$t = \frac{34.9 - 33.4}{1.243 * \sqrt{\dfrac{1}{14} + \dfrac{1}{17}}}$$

$$= 3.344$$

This is a one-tail test so the null hypothesis will only be rejected if the test statistic exceeds the critical value. From Table 6 of Appendix 1, $t_{0.01,29}$ is 2.462. Since the test statistic is greater than the critical value we can reject the null hypothesis at the 1% level. The difference between the sample means is very significant.

At this point you may find it useful to try **Review question 17.6** at the end of the chapter.

17.2.3 Paired samples

If you want to test the difference between population means using dependent or paired samples the nature of the data enables you to test the mean of the differences between all the paired values in the population, μ_d. This approach contrasts with the methods described in the earlier parts of this section where we tested the difference between population means, $\mu_1 - \mu_2$.

The procedure involved in testing hypotheses using paired samples is very similar to the one-sample hypothesis testing we discussed in section 16.4. We have to assume that the differences between the paired values are normally distributed with a mean of μ_d, and a standard deviation of σ_d. The sampling distribution of sample mean differences will also be normally distributed with a mean of μ_d and a standard error of $\sigma_d/\sqrt{n}$, where n is the number of differences in the sample. Since we assume that σ_d is unknown we have to use the estimated standard error $s_d/\sqrt{n}$, where s_d is the standard deviation of the sample differences.

Typically, samples of paired data tend to be small so the benchmark distribution for the test is the t distribution. The test is therefore called the *paired t test*. Table 17.2 lists the three possible combinations of hypotheses.

Table 17.2 Types of hypotheses for the mean of the population of differences

Null hypothesis	Alternative hypothesis	Type of test
$H_0: \mu_d = \mu_{d0}$	$H_1: \mu_d \neq \mu_{d0}$ (not equal)	Two-sided
$H_0: \mu_d \leq \mu_{d0}$	$H_1: \mu_d > \mu_{d0}$ (greater than)	One-sided
$H_0: \mu_d \geq \mu_{d0}$	$H_1: \mu_d < \mu_{d0}$ (less than)	One-sided

In this table μ_{d0} represents the value of the population mean that is to be tested.

The test statistic is:

$$t = \frac{\bar{x}_d - \mu_{d0}}{s_d/\sqrt{n}}$$

where $\bar{x}_d$ is the mean of the sample differences.

We then compare the test statistic to the appropriate critical value from the t distribution with $n - 1$ degrees of freedom.

EXAMPLE 17.3

A business school claims that, on average, people who take its MBA programme will enhance their annual salary by at least £8000. Each of a random sample of 12 graduates of the programme was asked for their annual salary prior to beginning the programme and their current annual salary. Use the sample data to test whether the mean difference in annual earnings is £8000 or more using a 10% level of significance.

$$H_0: \mu_d \geq 8.00 \qquad H_1: \mu_d < 8.00$$

Solution

To conduct the test we first need to find the mean and standard deviation of the salary differences in the sample.

Graduate	1	2	3	4	5	6	7	8	9	10	11	12
Prior salary (£000)	22	29	29	23	33	20	26	21	25	27	27	29
Current salary (£000)	31	38	40	29	41	25	29	26	31	37	41	36
Salary difference (£000)	9	9	11	6	8	5	3	5	6	10	14	7

The mean and standard deviation of the sample differences are 7.75 and 3.05, to two decimal places. The test statistic is:

$$t = \frac{7.75 - 8.00}{3.05/\sqrt{12}} = \frac{-0.25}{0.88} = -0.284$$

From Table 6 in Appendix 1, $t_{0.10,11}$ is 1.363. The alternative hypothesis is that the population mean salary difference is less than £8000 so the critical value is -1.363. A sample mean that produces a test statistic this low or lower would lead us to reject the null hypothesis. In this case, although the sample mean is less than £8000, the test statistic, -0.284, is not less than the critical value and the null hypothesis cannot be rejected. The population mean of the salary differences could well be £8000.

At this point you may find it useful to try **Review question 17.2** at the end of the chapter.

17.3 Testing hypotheses about more than two population means – one-way ANOVA

In some investigations it is important to establish whether two random samples come from a single population or from two populations with different means. The techniques we looked at in the previous section enable us to do just that. But what if we have three or more random samples and we need to establish whether they come from populations with different means?

You might think that the obvious answer is to run t tests using each pair of random samples to establish whether the first sample came from the same population as the second, the first sample came from the same population as the third and the second sample came from the same population as the third and so on. In doing this you would be testing the hypotheses:

$$H_0: \mu_1 = \mu_2 \quad H_0: \mu_1 = \mu_3 \quad H_0: \mu_2 = \mu_3 \text{ etc.}$$

Although feasible, this is not the best way to approach the investigation. For one thing the more random samples that are involved the greater the chance that you miss out one or more possible pairings. For another, each test you conduct carries a risk of making a Type I error, wrongly rejecting a null hypothesis because you happen to have a sample result from an extreme end of its sampling distribution. The chance of this occurring is the level of significance you use in conducting the test. The problem when you conduct a series of related tests is that the probability of making a Type I error increases; if you use a 5% level of significance then the probability of not making a Type I error in a sequence of three tests is, using the multiplication rule of probability, 0.95 * 0.95 * 0.95 or 0.857. This means the effective level of significance is 14.3%, considerably greater than you might have assumed.

To establish whether more than two samples come from populations with different means we use an alternative approach, *analysis of variance*, usually abbreviated to *ANOVA*. At first sight it seems rather odd to be using a technique based on variance, a measure of *spread*, to assess hypotheses about means, which are measures of *location*. The reason for doing this is that it enables us to focus on the spread of the sample means; after all, the greater the differences between the sample means the greater the chance that they come from populations with different means. However, we have to be careful to put these differences into context because, after all, we can get different samples from the *same* population. Using ANOVA involves looking at the balance between the variance of the sample means and the variance in the sample data overall. Example 17.4 illustrates why this is important.

**EXAMPLE
17.4**
The Kranilisha Bank operates cash dispensing machines in Gloucester, Huddersfield and Ipswich. The amounts of cash dispensed (in £000s) at a random sample of machines during a specific period were:

Gloucester	25	30	32	39	44
Huddersfield	17	25	27	31	–
Ipswich	29	34	44	47	51

These are independent samples and so the fact that one sample (Huddersfield) contains fewer values does not matter. The sample data are shown in the form of boxplots in Figure 17.1.

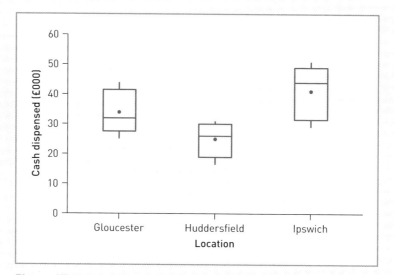

Figure 17.1 Cash dispensed at machines in Gloucester, Huddersfield and Ipswich

The distributions in Figure 17.1 suggest that there are differences between the amounts of cash dispensed at the machines, with those in Ipswich having the largest turnover and those in Huddersfield having the smallest. The sample means, which are represented by the dots, bear out this impression: 34 for Gloucester, 25 for Huddersfield and 41 for Ipswich.

In Example 17.4 the sample means are diverse enough and the distributions shown in Figure 17.1 distinct enough to indicate differences between the locations, but is it enough to merely compare the sample means?

**EXAMPLE
17.5**
Many of the figures for the cash dispensing machines in Example 17.4 were recorded incorrectly, although the means are correct. The amended figures are:

Gloucester	14	21	32	49	54
Huddersfield	15	18	27	40	–
Ipswich	19	29	44	49	64

These revised figures are depicted in Figure 17.2.

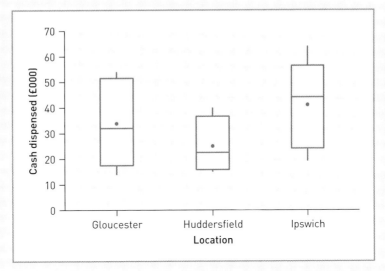

Figure 17.2 Revised amounts of cash dispensed at machines in Gloucester, Huddersfield and Ipswich

In Figure 17.2 the considerable overlaps between the data from the three locations suggest that despite the contrasts in the means it is more likely that the three samples come from the same population. Concentrating on the means alone in this case would have led us to the wrong conclusion.

So how we can test whether the three samples all come from the same population, in other words that there is no difference between the population mean amounts of cash dispensed per period in the three towns? For convenience we will use μ_G, μ_H and μ_I to represent the population means for Gloucester, Huddersfield and Ipswich respectively. The hypothesis we need to test is:

$$H_0: \mu_G = \mu_H = \mu_I$$

The alternative hypothesis is that there is a difference between at least two of the population means for the three towns.

If the null hypothesis is true and the three samples all come from a single population, the best estimate of the mean of that population is the mean of the values in all three samples, the *overall mean*. Since we already know the three sample means we can work this out by taking the mean of the sample means, being careful to weight each mean by the number of observations in the sample. In the first instance we will use the original data from Example 17.4:

$$\bar{x} = \frac{(5 * 34) + (4 * 25) + (5 * 41)}{14} = \frac{475}{14} = 33.929$$

The test statistic we will use is based on comparing the variation between the sample means with the variation within the samples. One of the measures of variation or spread that we looked at in Chapter 6 was the sample variance, the square of the sample standard deviation:

$$s^2 = \frac{\sum_{i=1}^{n} (x_i - \bar{x})^2}{n - 1}$$

The basis of the variance is the sum of the squared deviations between each observation and the sample mean. This amount, which is usually abbreviated to the *sum of squares*, is used to measure variation in analysis of variance. The sum of squares for the Gloucester sample, which we will denote as SS_G, is:

$$SS_G = \sum_{i=1}^{n}(x_i - \bar{x}_G)^2 = (25 - 34)^2 + (30 - 34)^2$$
$$+ (32 - 34)^2 + (39 - 34)^2 + (44 - 34)^2$$
$$= 81 + 16 + 4 + 25 + 100 = 226$$

We can work out the equivalent figures for the Huddersfield and Ipswich samples:

$$SS_H = \sum_{i=1}^{n}(x_i - \bar{x}_H)^2 = (17 - 25)^2 + (25 - 25)^2$$
$$+ (27 - 25)^2 + (31 - 25)^2 = 104$$

$$SS_I = \sum_{i=1}^{n}(x_i - \bar{x}_I)^2 = (29 - 41)^2 + (34 - 41)^2$$
$$+ (44 - 41)^2 + (47 - 41)^2 + (51 - 41)^2 = 338$$

The sum of these three sums of squares is the sum of the squares *within* the samples, *SSW*:

$$SSW = SS_G + SS_H + SS_I = 226 + 104 + 338 = 668$$

The measure we need for the variation between the sample means is the sum of the squared deviations between the sample means and the mean of all the observations in the three samples. This is the sum of the squares *between* the samples, *SSB*. In calculating it we have to weight each squared deviation by the sample size:

$$SSB = (n_G) * (\bar{x}_G - \bar{x})^2 + (\bar{x}_H) * (\bar{x}_H - \bar{x})^2 + (n_I) * (\bar{x}_I - \bar{x}_I)^2$$
$$= 5 * (34 - 33.929)^2 + 4 * (25 - 33.929)^2 + 5 * (41 - 33.929)^2$$
$$= 568.929$$

If we add the sum of squares within the samples, *SSW*, to the sum of squares between the samples, *SSB*, the result is the total sum of squares in the data, denoted by *SST*. The total sum of squares is also the sum of the squared deviations between each observation in the set of three samples and the mean of the combined data:

$$SST = (25 - 33.929)^2 + (30 - 33.929)^2 + (32 - 33.929)^2 + (39 - 33.929)^2$$
$$+ (44 - 33.929)^2 + (17 - 33.929)^2 + (25 - 33.929)^2 + (27 - 33.929)^2$$
$$+ (31 - 33.929)^2 + (29 - 33.929)^2 + (34 - 33.929)^2 + (44 - 33.929)^2$$
$$+ (47 - 33.929)^2 + (51 - 33.929)^2$$

$$= 79.719 + 15.434 + 3.719 + 25.719 + 101.434 + 286.577 + 79.719$$
$$+ 48.005 + 8.577 + 24.291 + 0.005 + 101.434 + 170.862 + 291.434$$

$$= 1236.929$$

$$= SSW + SSB = 668 + 568.929 = 1236.929$$

When you calculate a sample variance you have to divide the sum of squared deviations by the sample size less one, $n - 1$. This is the number of degrees of freedom left in the data; we lose one degree of freedom because we use the mean in working out the deviations from it. Before we can use the sums of squares we have determined above to test the hypothesis of no difference between the population means we need to incorporate the degrees of freedom associated with each sum of squares by working out the mean sum of squares. This makes the variation within the samples directly comparable to the variation between samples.

The mean sum of squares within the samples, MSW, is the sum of squares within the samples divided by the number of observations in all three samples, in this case 14, less the number of samples we have, three. You may like to think of subtracting three as reflecting our using the three sample means in working out the sum of squares within the samples. If we use k to represent the number of samples we have:

$$MSW = \frac{SSW}{n-k} = \frac{668}{14-3} = 60.727$$

The mean sum of squares between the samples, MSB, is the sum of squares between the samples divided by the number of samples, k minus one. We lose one degree of freedom because we have used the overall mean to find the sum of squares between the samples.

$$MSB = \frac{SSB}{k-1} = \frac{568.929}{3-1} = 284.465$$

The test statistic used to decide the validity of the null hypothesis is the ratio of the mean sum of squares between samples to the mean sum of squares within the sample. Because the benchmark distribution we shall use to assess it is the F distribution, after its inventor, R. A. Fisher, the test statistic is represented by the letter F:

$$F = \frac{MSB}{MSW} = \frac{284.465}{60.727} = 4.684$$

Before comparing this to the F distribution it is worth pausing to consider the meaning of the test statistic. If the three samples came from a single population, in other words the null hypothesis is true, both the MSB above the line, the numerator, and the MSW below the line, the denominator, would be unbiased estimators of the variance of that population. If this were the case, the test statistic would be close to one.

If on the other hand the samples do come from populations with different means, in other words the null hypothesis is not true, we would expect the MSB, the numerator, to be much larger than the denominator. Under these circumstances the test statistic would be greater than one.

In order to gauge how large the test statistic would have to be to lead us to reject the null hypothesis we have to look at it in the context of the F distribution. This distribution portrays the variety of test statistics we would get if we compared all conceivable sets of samples from a single population and worked out the ratio of MSB to MSW. Since neither the MSB nor the MSW can be negative, as they are derived from *squared* deviations, the F distribution consists of entirely positive values.

The version of the F distribution you use depends on the numbers of degrees of freedom you use to work out the MSB and the MSW, respectively the nominator and denominator of the test statistic. The F distribution with two degrees of freedom in the numerator and 11 degrees of freedom in the denominator, which is the appropriate version for the bank data from Example 17.4, is shown in Figure 17.3.

We can assess the value of the test statistic for the data from Example 17.4 by comparing it with a benchmark figure or *critical value* from the distribution shown in Figure 17.3. The critical value you use depends on the level of significance you require. Typically this is 5% or 0.05. The shaded area in Figure 17.3 is the 5% of the distribution beyond 3.98. If the null hypothesis really were true we would only expect to have test statistics greater than 3.98 in 5% of cases. In the case of Example 17.4 the test statistic is rather higher, 4.684, so the null hypothesis should be rejected at the 5% level. At least two of the means are different.

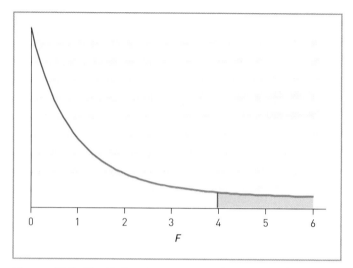

Figure 17.3 The F distribution with 2 (numerator) and 11 (denominator) degrees of freedom

In general, reject the null hypothesis if the test statistic is greater than $F_{k-1,\,n-k,\,\alpha}$, where k is the number of samples, n is the number of values in the samples overall and α is the level of significance. Note that this is a one-tail test; it is only possible to reject the hypothesis if the test statistic is larger than the critical value you use. Values of the test statistic from the left-hand side of the distribution are consistent with the null hypothesis.

Table 7 in Appendix 1 contains details of the F distribution. You may like to check it to locate $F_{2,\,11,\,0.01}$ which is the value of F with two numerator degrees of freedom and 11 denominator degrees of freedom that cuts off a right-hand tail area of 1%, 7.21. This value is greater than the test statistic for the data from Example 17.4 so we cannot reject the null hypothesis at the 1% level of significance.

EXAMPLE 17.6

Use the revised bank data from Example 17.5 to test whether there are differences between the population means of the amounts of cash dispensed in Gloucester, Huddersfield and Ipswich.

Solution

The overall mean and the three sample means are exactly the same as those derived from the data in Example 17.4 so the mean sum of squares between the samples is unchanged, 284.465.

We need to calculate the sum of squares within the samples for the amended data:

$$SS_G = \sum_{i=1}^{n} (x_i - \bar{x}_G)^2$$

$$= (14 - 34)^2 + (21 - 34)^2 + (32 - 34)^2 + (49 - 34)^2 + (54 - 34)^2 = 1198$$

$$SS_H = \sum_{i=1}^{n} (x_i - \bar{x}_H)^2$$

$$= (15 - 25.0)^2 + (18 - 25.0)^2 + (27 - 25.0)^2 + (40 - 25.0)^2 = 378$$

$$SS_I = \sum_{i=1}^{n} (x_i - \bar{x}_I)^2$$

$$= (19 - 41)^2 + (29 - 41)^2 + (44 - 41)^2 + (49 - 41)^2 + (64 - 41)^2 = 1230$$

$$SSW = SS_G + SS_H + SS_I = 1198 + 378 + 1230 = 2806$$

$$MSW = \frac{2806}{11} = 255.091$$

$$\text{The test statistic, } F = \frac{284.465}{255.091} = 1.115$$

In this case the test statistic is much lower than the critical value for a 5% level of significance, 3.98, and the null hypothesis should not be rejected; it is a reasonable assumption that these three samples come from a single population, confirming the impression obtained from Figure 17.2.

There are several assumptions that apply when we use analysis of variance to test differences between population means. To begin with the populations from which the samples are drawn should be normal and the populations should have the same variance. Furthermore, the samples must be random and independent.

In this section we have used *one-way* analysis of variance; one-way because we have only considered one factor, geographical location, in our investigation. There may be other factors that may be pertinent to our analysis, such as the type of location of the cash dispensers in Example 17.4, i.e. town centre, supermarket or garage. ANOVA is a flexible technique that can be used to take more than one factor into account. For more on its capabilities and applications see Roberts and Russo (1999).

At this point you may find it useful to try **Review questions 17.11 to 17.13** at the end of the chapter.

17.4 Testing hypotheses and producing interval estimates for quantitative bivariate data

In this section we will look at statistical inference techniques that enable you to estimate and test relationships between variables in populations using sample data. The sample data we use to do this is called *bivariate* data because it consists of observations of *two* variables. The reason for collecting such data is usually to ascertain if there is a relationship between the two variables, and in the event that there is, to determine what type of relationship exists.

Businesses use this analysis to investigate many facets of their operations including consumer behaviour, revenue and cost, product characteristics and service delivery. The results can have a dramatic impact. One example is what happened to the tobacco industry. The reason tobacco products carry health warnings is because some time ago researchers using this type of analysis established a relationship between tobacco use and serious medical conditions.

The quantitative bivariate analysis that we considered in Chapter 7 involved two related methods; correlation and regression. Correlation analysis, which is based on correlation coefficients, tells us the strength and direction of any relationship that exists between the values of two variables. Regression analysis is used to identify the equation of the line that best fits the data, the *regression model*.

Here we will look at how to use correlation and regression results from sample data for testing and estimating population correlation and regression model coefficients.

17.4.1 Testing the population correlation coefficient

The sample correlation coefficient, r, measures the linear association in a sample of observations of two variables, X and Y. The formula for the sample correlation coefficient is:

$$r = \frac{\text{Cov}_{XY}}{(s_x * s_y)}$$

The covariance,
$$\text{Cov}_{XY} = \frac{\sum (x - \bar{x})(y - \bar{y})}{(n - 1)}$$

and s_x and s_y are the sample standard deviations of the x and y values.

Assuming we have a random sample and the populations of X and Y are *both* normal, the sample correlation coefficient, r, is an unbiased estimate of the population coefficient, denoted by ρ (rho, the Greek r). Generally the purpose of the sample correlation coefficient is to provide an assessment of any linear association between the X and Y populations.

The sample correlation coefficient is of some use in assessing correlation between the two populations, but testing that the population correlation coefficient is zero is a more robust approach. The appropriate null hypothesis is:

$$H_0: \rho = 0$$

We can use one of three alternative hypotheses depending on our purpose. If we would like to demonstrate significant correlation in the population, then we would use:

$$H_1: \rho \neq 0$$

If we are interested in testing for significant positive correlation in the population we would use:

$$H_1: \rho > 0$$

If we want to test for significant negative correlation we would use:

$$H_1: \rho < 0$$

If we decide on $H_1: \rho \neq 0$ we need to use a two-tail test. With either of the others we use a one-tail test. Typically we test for a positive or negative correlation rather than both.

After deciding the type of alternative hypothesis we need to work out the test statistic from the sample data. This is:

$$t = \frac{r\sqrt{n - 2}}{\sqrt{1 - r^2}}$$

In this expression r represents the sample correlation coefficient and n the number of *pairs* of observations in the sample.

EXAMPLE 17.7

The ages and number of friends of a random sample of eight social network users are:

Age in years	Friends
15	151
19	211
23	83
29	153
36	106
45	14
53	5
60	77

This data is plotted in Figure 17.4.

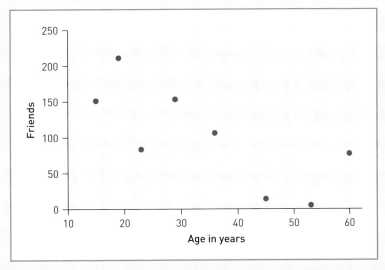

Figure 17.4 The data in Example 17.7

The sample correlation coefficient, r, for this data is -0.744. Using a 5% level of confidence, test the hypothesis of zero correlation between Age and Friends against the alternative of negative correlation using a 5% level of significance.

Solution

The appropriate hypotheses are:

$$H_0: \rho = 0 \text{ and } H_1: \rho < 0$$

$$\text{The test statistic, } t = r\frac{\sqrt{n-2}}{\sqrt{1-r^2}} = \frac{-0.744 * \sqrt{8-2}}{\sqrt{1-0.744^2}}$$

$$= -2.727$$

We need to benchmark this against the t distribution with $n - 2$, in this case six, degrees of freedom. From Table 6 of Appendix 1 the value of t with six degrees of freedom that cuts off a 5% tail on the right of the distribution, $t_{0.05,6}$, is 1.943 so the value that cuts off a 5% tail on the left, $-t_{0.05,6}$, is -1.943, which is the critical value for the test. As the test statistic is less than -1.943 the null hypothesis should be rejected at the 5% level of significance. The sample evidence indicates that there is negative correlation between Age and Friends; older people tend to have fewer social network friends.

If the populations of both X and Y are normally distributed and H_0 is true, in other words there is no association between the X and Y populations, the test statistic belongs to the t distribution with $n - 2$ degrees of freedom and a mean of zero.

At this point you may find it useful to try **Review question 17.3** at the end of the chapter.

17.4.2 Testing regression models

The other bivariate quantitative technique we looked at in Chapter 7 was simple linear regression analysis. This allows us to establish the equation of the line of best fit for two variables, X and Y, which is known as the regression equation. Such an equation has two defining features or coefficients, the *intercept* and the *slope*. In the generic formula a represents the intercept and b represents the slope:

$$Y = a + bX$$

The regression equation line is the best way to represent the relationship between the dependent variable, Y, and the independent variable, X. Generally it is based on the analysis of sample data and suggests the likely relationship between the populations of X and Y. Because it is derived from a sample we have used Roman rather than Greek letters in the regression equation.

The sample regression equation gives us some understanding of the relationship between the populations. The coefficients are point estimates for the intercept and slope of the population regression equation. These are represented by α and β, the Greek equivalents of a and b. The population regression equation is:

$$Y = \alpha + \beta X$$

In much the same way as we used sample means to test hypotheses about population means in section 16.4 we can use the intercept and slope of the sample regression equation to test hypotheses about the population intercept and slope. To do this we generally use null hypotheses that state that the population values are zero:

$$H_0: \alpha = 0 \text{ for the population intercept}$$

$$H_0: \beta = 0 \text{ for the population slope}$$

If the population intercept is zero, the population regression equation will be $Y = 0 + \beta X$. This means the regression line will begin at the origin as shown in Figure 17.5.

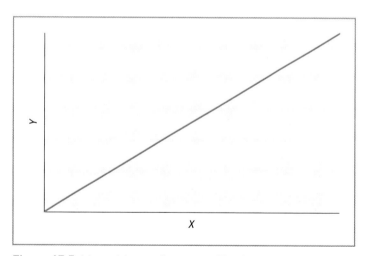

Figure 17.5 Line with zero intercept, $Y = 0 + \beta X$

To find out if the population intercept could be zero, we test the null hypothesis $H_0: \alpha = 0$ against the alternative hypothesis that it is not zero: $H_1: \alpha \neq 0$.

In regression analysis testing the intercept value is not usually important. In some contexts it is of interest, such as investigating the relationship between the output and costs of a business in different time periods. In this case the intercept would represent the fixed costs.

Generally the slope of the regression line is of much more interest. It is the key component of the model as it indicates how the dependent variable reacts to changes in the independent variable. To reflect this, the slope is referred to as the *coefficient* of the independent variable.

If the population slope is zero the dependent variable does not respond to the independent variable at all. The implication is that the independent variable cannot explain how the dependent variable behaves and that it is of no use for predicting values of the dependent variable for specific values of the independent variable.

If the slope of the population regressions line is zero, the equation of the line will be $Y = \alpha + 0X$. The regression line will be perfectly horizontal as shown in Figure 17.6.

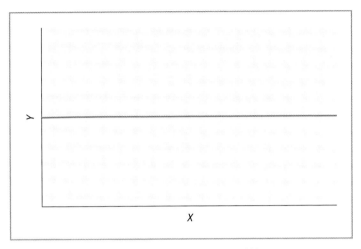

Figure 17.6 Line with zero slope, $Y = \alpha + 0X$

As Figure 17.6 shows, whether the value of X is among the small ones on the left of the horizontal axis or the large ones on the right of it, the value of Y is the same. The size of X has no bearing on Y, and the regression model is of no consequence.

In general we want to produce useful results from regression analysis; models that help us represent and predict the behaviour of dependent variables. To establish the usefulness of a model we can test the null hypothesis that the slope is zero using sample data. In doing this we hope that the sample results enable us to reject the null hypothesis in favour of the alternative, that the slope is not zero. The test statistic for the test is:

$$t = \frac{b - 0}{s_b}$$

In this expression b is the sample slope and 0 is the population slope stated in the null hypothesis. The third component, s_b is the estimated standard error of the sampling distribution of b, the sample slope.

The estimated standard error, s_b, is based on s, the standard deviation of the sample residuals. These are the parts of the sample values of Y that the regression line does not explain. To get s_b we divide s by the square root of the sum of the squared deviations between sample values of X and their mean, $\bar{x}$.

$$s_b = \frac{s}{\sqrt{\sum (x - \bar{x})^2}}$$

We compare the test statistic, t, to the t distribution with $n - 2$ degrees of freedom. There are two fewer degrees of freedom than the number of pairs of x and y values in the sample.

**EXAMPLE
17.8**

The regression equation for the sample data in Example 17.7 is:

$$\text{Friends} = 212.256 - 3.207\,\text{Age}$$

Test the hypothesis that the population slope is zero. Use a 5% level of significance.

$$H_0: \beta = 0 \qquad H_1: \beta \neq 0$$

Solution

The first step is to work out the standard deviation of the residuals. To get the residuals we put each x value into the regression equation and work out the value of Y that the model predicts, $\hat{y}$. The residual is the difference between $\hat{y}$, and the y value that actually occurs with the x value.

To show how this works we'll consider the first pair of values in the sample, the 15-year-old with 151 friends. If we put the number of friends into the regression equation we get the predicted number of friends that the 15 year old 'should' have:

$$\text{Friends} = 212.256 - 3.207 * 15 = 164.151$$

The residual is the difference between the actual number of friends, 151, and the predicted number of friends:

$$\text{Residual} = 151 - 164.151 = -13.151$$

The standard deviation of the residuals is derived from the squares of the residuals. The residuals and their squares are:

Age	Friends	Residuals	Squared residuals
15	151	−13.151	172.949
19	211	59.677	3561.344
23	83	−55.495	3079.695
29	153	33.747	1138.860
36	106	9.196	84.566
45	14	−53.941	2909.631
53	5	−37.285	1390.171
60	77	57.164	3267.723
			15604.939

The standard deviation of the residuals is the square root of the sum of the squared residuals divided by n, the number of residuals: in this case 8, minus 2. (We subtract 2 from n because we 'lose' two degrees of freedom by using the intercept and slope in working out the residuals.)

$$s = \sqrt{15604.939/(8 - 2)} = \sqrt{15604.939/6} = 50.998$$

To get the estimated standard error we divide this by the sum of squared differences between the age figures and their mean.

Age (x)	$\bar{x}$	$x - \bar{x}$	$(x - \bar{x})^2$
15	35	−20	400
19	35	−16	256
23	35	−12	144
29	35	−6	36
36	35	1	1
45	35	10	100
53	35	18	324
60	35	25	625
			1886

The estimated standard error is:

$$s_b = s/\sqrt{\sum (x - \bar{x})^2}/ = 50.998/\sqrt{1886} = 50.998/43.428 = 1.174$$

The test statistic, $t = (b - 0)/s_b = -3.207/1.174 = -2.732$

According to Table 6 of Appendix 1, the t value with six degrees of freedom that cuts off a tail area of 2.5% on the right of the distribution, $t_{6,0.025}$, is 2.447. If H_0 is true and the population slope really is zero then 2.5% of test statistics will be more than 2.447 and 2.5% will be less than -2.447. The significance level is 5% so the decision rule is to reject H_0 if the test statistic is outside the range ± 2.447. In this case the test statistic is -2.732 so we should reject H_0. The evidence indicates that the population slope is not zero.

The sort of result we arrived at in Example 17.8 suggests the regression equation is a sound enough basis for predicting the number of social network friends using age.

The test statistic in Example 17.8, -2.732, is very similar to the test statistic derived from the sample correlation coefficient in Example 17.7, -2.727. In calculating them a certain amount of rounding has been used. If we calculated them without rounding we would get exactly the same figure for each test statistic. This is no accident as the two tests are equivalent. The slope is the form of the association between the variables whereas the correlation coefficient assesses the strength of that association. We have used the same data in the same sort of way to test both slope and correlation coefficient.

17.4.3 Constructing interval predictions

If we use a regression equation for prediction, as we did in Example 17.8, to work out the residuals, the result is a single figure, $\hat{y}$, which is the y value associated with the x value we specify.

EXAMPLE 17.9

Using the regression equation in Example 17.8 predict the number of social network friends that a 22-year-old will have.

Solution

If Age = 22, according to the regression equation:

$$\text{Friends} = 212.256 - 3.207\,(22) = 141.702$$

Since the number of friends must be discrete we should round this to 142 friends.

Single-figure predictions like the one in Example 17.9 are of limited use because we have no idea how likely they are to be accurate. It would be better to have an interval which we can anticipate, with a specific level of confidence, that will be accurate.

Before we consider how to do this, it is useful to clarify the difference between predicting and estimating. Although we might think of them as synonymous, in regression analysis there is a difference. The figure in Example 17.9 can be used as a *prediction* of the number of social network friends a 22-year-old will have. We could also use it to *estimate* the mean number of social network friends that all 22-year-olds have, in other words it is a point estimate of the mean number of friends of 22-year-old social network users.

We can produce an interval estimate, or confidence interval, of the mean number of friends of all social network users of 22 years old by starting from the point estimate and adding and subtracting an error in the same way as we constructed confidence intervals for the population mean in section 16.3. The error is the standard error of the sampling distribution of the point estimates multiplied by a figure from the t distribution with $n - 2$ degrees of freedom. The t value we use is based on the level of confidence we require.

We can express this procedure using the formula:

$$\text{Confidence interval} = \hat{y} \pm t_{\alpha/2,n-2} * s \sqrt{\frac{1}{n} + \frac{(x_0 - \bar{x})^2}{\sum (x - \bar{x})^2}}$$

In this expression $\hat{y}$ is the point estimate of the mean of the y values associated with the x value of interest, x_0, s is the standard deviation of the sample residuals and $\bar{x}$ is the sample mean of the x values.

EXAMPLE 17.10

Produce a 95% confidence interval for the mean number of social network friends 22-year-old social network users will have.

Solution

From Example 17.9 the point estimate for the mean Friends when Age is 22, $\hat{y}$, is 141.702. We can use the precise value of $\hat{y}$ because the mean number of friends, unlike the number of friends for one 22-year-old, doesn't have to be discrete. In Example 17.8 we worked out s, the standard deviation of the sample residuals, 50.998, and $\sum (x - \bar{x})^2$, 1886. The sample mean of the x values, $\bar{x}$, is 35.

The t value for a 95% level of confidence is 2.447. This is the value that cuts off a tail of 2.5% in the t distribution with $8 - 2 = 6$ degrees of freedom. The value of x_0, the Age for which we want to estimate Friends, is 22.

$$\text{Confidence interval} = \hat{y} \pm t_{\alpha/2,n-2} * s \sqrt{\frac{1}{n} + \frac{(x_0 - \bar{x})^2}{\sum (x - \bar{x})^2}}$$

$$= 141.702 \pm 2.447 * 50.998 \sqrt{[1/8 + (22 - 35)^2/1886]}$$

$$= 141.702 \pm 57.811 = 83.891 \text{ to } 199.513$$

The confidence interval in Example 17.10 is a reliable estimate of the mean value for Friends when Age is 22 because, although there was no one actually aged 22 in the sample, the range of ages was 15 to 60, which includes 22.

If we produce a confidence interval for the mean of the y values associated with an x value outside the range of x values in the sample it will be unreliable and wider.

EXAMPLE 17.11

Produce a 95% confidence interval for the mean number of social network friends 5-year-old social network users will have.

Solution

The point estimate for the mean, $\hat{y} = 212.256 - 3.207 (5) = 196.221$

$$\text{Confidence interval} = \hat{y} \pm t_{\alpha/2,n-2} * s \sqrt{\frac{1}{n} + \frac{(x_0 - \bar{x})^2}{\sum (x - \bar{x})^2}}$$

$$= 196.221 \pm 2.447 * 50.998 \sqrt{[1/8 + (5 - 35)^2/1886]}$$

$$= 196.221 \pm 96.841 = 99.380 \text{ to } 293.062$$

The confidence interval in Example 17.11 is of no real use because the age on which it is based, 5, is outside the range of ages in the sample. The further the x value is away from the mean of the x values the wider the confidence interval will be as shown in Figure 17.7.

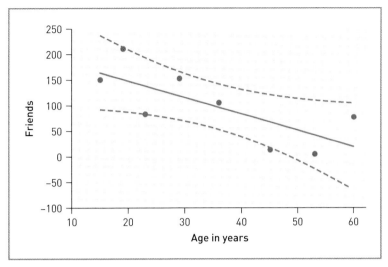

Figure 17.7   95% confidence intervals based on the regression line in Example 17.8

If we need to predict individual y values associated with particular x values rather than estimate mean y values associated with x values, with a specific level of confidence, we use what are known as a *prediction intervals*. This term is used to distinguish them from confidence intervals, which is the name used for interval estimates of population measures such as means.

The method of producing prediction intervals is like the one used to construct confidence intervals for means of values of the Y variable.

$$\text{Prediction interval } = \hat{y} \pm t_{\alpha/2, n-2} * s\sqrt{1 + \frac{1}{n} + \frac{(x_0 - \bar{x})^2}{\Sigma(x - \bar{x})^2}}$$

The only difference between this and the method of obtaining a confidence interval is the addition of one to the expression under the square root sign. The effect of this is to widen the interval substantially. This reflects the greater variation in individual values than in summary measures like means, which come from sets of values.

EXAMPLE 17.12

Produce a 95% prediction interval for the number of social network friends of a social network user aged 22.

Solution

$$\text{Prediction interval } = \hat{y} \pm t_{\alpha/2, n-2} * s\sqrt{1 + \frac{1}{n} + \frac{(x_0 - \bar{x})^2}{\Sigma(x - \bar{x})^2}}$$

$$= 141.702 \pm 2.447 * 50.998\sqrt{[1 + 1/8 + (22 - 35)^2/1886]}$$

$$= 141.702 \pm 137.532 = 4.170 \text{ to } 279.234$$

The prediction interval in Example 17.12 is much wider than the confidence interval in Example 17.10 although the level of confidence, 95%, is the same.

Like confidence intervals generated from regression equations, the nearer the *x* value is to the mean of the *x* values the more dependable they are. Prediction intervals based on *x* values beyond the range of the *x* values in the sample data are seldom of any value.

The usefulness of estimates produced using regression equations depends largely on the sample size. The bigger the sample that is used to create the regression equation, the more precise and confident the predictions and estimates are.

Because the width of interval estimates is greater the further the *x* value is from the sample mean of the *x* values, if you need to produce intervals based on certain values of *x* try to make sure that the range of *x* values in your sample is large enough to cover them when you gather your data.

At this point you may find it useful to try **Review question 17.17** at the end of the chapter.

17.4.4 When simple linear models won't do the job

Until now we have only considered the simple linear regression model. This is used extensively and, in many cases, is the most appropriate model. However some quantitative bivariate data have patterns that cannot adequately be modelled with simple linear regression. It is possible to test hypotheses about the slopes in simple linear regression equations and conclude that the slopes are not significant yet some relationship between the variables exists. This occurs when the relationship is non-linear and hence the best fit model is some form of curve rather than a straight line.

EXAMPLE 17.13

An HR consultant is investigating the relationship between job satisfaction and the size of organisations. She took a random sample of 20 employees and measured their job satisfaction on a scale of 0 to 100. The scores and the number of employees in their organisations are plotted in Figure 17.8.

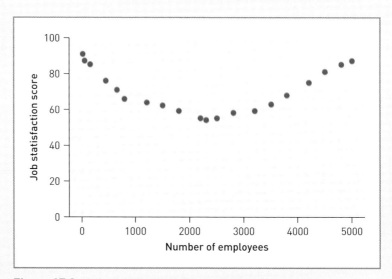

Figure 17.8 Job satisfaction score and number of employees

Figure 17.8 shows that the relationship between the job satisfaction score and the number of employees doesn't seem to be linear. In this case, to find an appropriate model you would have to use methods of non-linear regression not simple linear regression. There are many different non-linear models and it is not possible to deal with them here, but they are covered in Bates and Watts (2007) and Seber and Wild (2003). Non-linear models might seem daunting at first but often what is involved is adjusting the data and applying the simple linear model, effectively 'straightening' the data and using the straight-line model.

Another reason why the simple linear model may not be effective is because the two variables that we are investigating may not be 'the whole story'. There could be other variables that have influence. A good way of exploring this is to use residual plots.

One type of *residual plot* is a plot of the residuals against the fits (the values of the Y variable that should, according to the model, have occurred, i.e. the $\hat{y}$ values). It can be particularly useful in revealing systematic variation in the data that is not explained by the model.

EXAMPLE 17.14

Plot the residuals against the fits for the simple linear regression model from Example 17.8.

Solution

The regression equation in Example 17.8 was:

$$\text{Friends} = 212.256 - 3.207\,\text{Age}$$

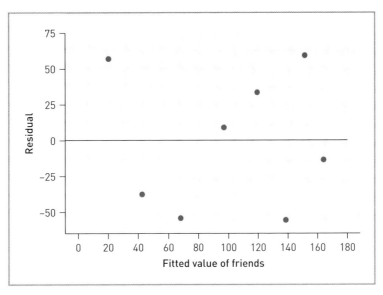

Figure 17.9 A residual plot for the model in Example 17.8

The absence of a systematic pattern in the scatter of points in Figure 17.9 suggests that there is no point searching for another variable. In this case the simple linear model seems to be appropriate.

EXAMPLE 17.15

Plot the residuals against the fits for the job satisfaction and number of employees data shown in Figure 17.8.

Solution

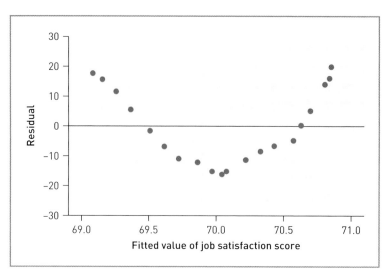

Figure 17.10 A residual plot for the data in Figure 17.8

In contrast to Figure 17.9, where there was no obvious pattern in the residuals plot, in Figure 17.10 there is a clear pattern. It seems that job satisfaction scores are higher for those working in small or large organisations and lower for those working in medium-sized organisations. This might reflect friendlier working environments in small organisations and better rewards in large organisations, whereas medium-sized organisations might be lacking in both friendliness and rewards. There might be variables we could include in the model, such as wage levels, to improve it. The method used to do this is multiple regression analysis. It is outside the scope of this book but covered well by Dielman (2005) and Hair *et al.* (2009).

17.5 Contingency analysis

To investigate association between qualitative variables, where the observations are divided into categories of attributes or characteristics, we use contingency analysis. This tests if one variable is associated with, or *contingent* upon, the other. Sometimes it is used with quantitative data that either is discrete with just a few possible values or is sorted into categories.

Contingency analysis is frequently used to analyse questionnaire research results, for instance to establish connections between gender and voting intention or socio-economic class and leisure spending. Contingency tests enable us to see if the link between variables that might exist in sample data is strong enough to conclude that there is an association between the variables in the population, in other words to ascertain whether the sample results are *significant*.

The procedure for contingency testing begins with the two mutually exclusive and collectively exhaustive hypotheses testings we considered previously. The initial premise, the null hypothesis, H_0, is always that there is no association between the variables. The alternative hypothesis, H_1, is that there is some association between them.

Once we have established the hypotheses we produce a test statistic from sample results and, using a decision rule, compare it to a critical value to decide which hypothesis is the more plausible at a given level of significance. The first stage in analysing the sample data is to set them out in a *contingency table*.

As part of a research project about gender and career aspirations a random sample of 100 business students were each asked which of three careers they would prefer to enter after graduation; Accountancy, Human Resource Management (HRM) or Marketing. The researcher wants to test the following hypotheses:

H_0: There is no association between gender and career

H_1: There is some association between gender and career

The responses of the students and their genders are in the following contingency table:

	Females	Males	Total
Accountancy	10	14	24
HRM	20	16	36
Marketing	20	20	40
Total	50	50	100

The contingency table in Example 17.16 demonstrates that the male students are more inclined to select Accountancy than the female students and less inclined to select HRM. This is evidence of association in the sample, but it is only a sample and there are a very large number of samples we could have chosen from the population. The key question is whether the association in the sample is strong enough to suggest that there is association between gender and career in the population. In other words, is it significant? Alternatively, is it a relatively modest level of association that we might expect in sample results even if in the population they come from there is no association? To answer these questions we need to test H_0, the null hypothesis of no association.

The test statistic that we use to do this is based on all of the sample results. We consolidate them into a single test statistic that measures the contingency, or association, in the sample data. This test statistic is called *chi-square* (after another Greek letter, chi, χ) and the benchmark distribution we use to assess its value is the chi–square (χ^2) distribution.

We work out chi-square by comparing the actual sample results, called the *observed* frequencies and denoted by the letter O, to the results that we would expect if the null hypothesis, H_0 were true. These values, which we need to calculate, are called the *expected* frequencies and are denoted by the letter E.

Work out the results we should expect to see in the contingency table in Example 17.16 if H_0 is true and there is no association between gender and career field in the population.

Solution

From the contingency table in Example 17.16 we know that 24 respondents are interested in Accountancy, 36 in HRM and 40 in Marketing. There are the same numbers of Females, 50 as there are Males. If there is no association between career field and gender we would expect the numbers preferring each career to be split evenly by gender. In other words, if gender makes no difference to career preference, we would expect the same proportion of Females as Males in each career category and the contingency

Solution cont table would look like this:

	Females	Males	Total
Accountancy	12	12	24
HRM	18	18	36
Marketing	20	20	40
Total	50	50	100

In this table the Females and Males have been divided equally between career fields. These are the expected figures we need for the test statistic.

Note: the figures in the table have been changed but the row and column totals are the same.

There is a more formal way of working out expected frequencies. This involves working through the contingency table a cell at a time and multiplying the row total by the column total then dividing the results by the overall total. To establish how many Females in Example 17.17 we would expect to prefer Accountancy, assuming H_0 is true and there is no association, multiply the number of students preferring Accountancy (the row total, 24) by the total number of Females (the column total, 50) and divide the result by 100, the total number in the sample:

$$\text{Expected frequency} \;=\; \frac{\text{row total} * \text{column total}}{\text{overall total}} = \frac{24 * 50}{100} = 12$$

To get some idea of the overall association in the sample we can put the expected frequencies alongside the corresponding observed frequencies, which are the actual results, in one table.

EXAMPLE 17.18

Produce a contingency table containing the observed frequencies from Example 17.16 and the expected frequencies from Example 17.17. Compare the observed and expected frequencies.

Solution

In the following table the expected frequencies are shown in brackets:

	Females	Males	Total
Accountancy	10 (12)	14 (12)	24
HRM	20 (18)	16 (18)	36
Marketing	20 (20)	20 (20)	40
Total	50	50	100

The observed and expected frequencies for Marketing are the same but the observed number of Females preferring Accountancy, 10, is lower than number we would expect if there was no association. There are similar discrepancies in Males preferring Accountancy, and both females and males preferring HRM.

The results in Example 17.18 indicate there is some association in the sample data, but is it enough to be significant? To put it another way, does the sample evidence suggest there is association in the entire population? To find out we need the test statistic, χ^2.

The test statistic is based on the differences between the observed values and the expected values. The larger these differences, the bigger the test statistic. To get the test statistic we take each expected frequency away from its corresponding observed frequency and square the result. The reason for squaring the differences between observed and expected frequencies is that we will be adding them together and we need to avoid them cancelling each other out in which case the test statistic will be useless. Before adding the differences we divide each one by its expected frequency. This is known as standardising and enables us to compare the test statistic to the χ^2 distribution. The last stage is to add the standardised squared differences. The sum of the standardised squared differences is the test statistic, χ^2, for the sample data.

The following formula summarises the procedure:

$$\chi^2 = \sum [(O - E)^2 / E]$$

EXAMPLE 17.19

Work out the test statistic, χ^2, for the sample data in Example 17.16.

Solution

We will start with the contingency table in Example 17.18.

	Females	Males
Accountancy	10 (12)	14 (12)
HRM	20 (18)	16 (18)
Marketing	20 (20)	20 (20)

Let's begin with the Females who prefer Accountancy. The observed frequency, O, is 10 and the expected frequency, E, is 12.

$$(O - E)^2/E = (10 - 12)^2/12 = 4/12 = 0.333$$

Next, the Females who prefer HRM.

$$(O - E)^2/E = (20 - 18)^2/18 = 4/18 = 0.222$$

The Females who prefer Marketing.

$$(O - E)^2/E = (20 - 20)^2/20 = 0/20 = 0$$

The Males who prefer Accountancy.

$$(O - E)^2/E = (14 - 12)^2/12 = 4/12 = 0.333$$

The Males who prefer HRM.

$$(O - E)^2/E = (16 - 18)^2/18 = 4/18 = 0.222$$

The Males who prefer Marketing.

$$(O - E)^2/E = (20 - 20)^2/20 = 0/20 = 0$$

The test statistic, χ^2, is the sum of these six figures:

$$\chi^2 = 0.333 + 0.222 + 0 + 0.333 + 0.222 + 0 = 1.110$$

The key question is whether the test statistic, χ^2 in Example 17.19, suggests there is association between gender and career preference in the population. To establish this we need to compare the test statistic to the benchmark distribution.

The distribution used in contingency analysis to assess the test statistic is the chi-square distribution. The procedure is known as a *chi-square test*. The chi-square distribution describes the variation in chi-square that we would expect if there is no association in the population. This variation arises because we can take different samples from the same

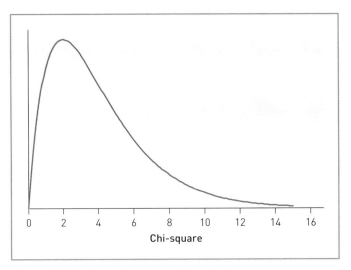

Figure 17.11 **The chi-squared distribution**

population and they will not produce the same test statistic. The chi-square distribution is portrayed in Figure 17.11.

The chi-square distribution has different forms depending on the number of degrees of freedom in the sample data. Figure 17.11 shows the chi-square distribution with four degrees of freedom. The degrees of freedom are the number of rows in the contingency table (r) minus one multiplied by the number of columns in the table (c) minus one.

$$\text{Degrees of freedom} = (r - 1) * (c - 1)$$

In Example 17.19 the contingency table has three rows and two columns. This means there are $(2 - 1)$ times $(3 - 1)$, two degrees of freedom. The chi-square distribution with two degrees of freedom shows the pattern of chi-square values we would get if we took all possible samples from a population in which there is no association between two variables, one of which had two categories and the other had three categories, worked out the chi-square value for each sample and plotted them.

Once we have established the degrees of freedom in the sample data we can specify the decision rule for the test. This is based on the level of significance required, α, and together with the degrees of freedom enables us to identify the critical value of χ^2 to test H_0, the null hypothesis of no association. The test is always one-tailed simply because the test statistic is based on squared differences and so can never be negative. The decision rule is to reject H_0 if the test statistic is larger than the critical value. If this is the case the likelihood that the sample comes from a population with no association is less than the level of significance.

Table 8 in Appendix 1 gives tail areas of the chi-square distribution with up to 10 degrees of freedom. Each row of the table contains figures for a specific number of degrees of freedom, ν (nu, the Greek equivalent of n). The second row has tail areas of the χ^2 distribution with two degrees of freedom. The figure that is in this row and the column headed 0.10 is 4.605. This is the value of χ^2 with two degrees of freedom that cuts off a tail area of 10% on the right of the distributions, $\chi^2_{0.10, 2}$. It tells us that the proportion of the area to the right of 4.605 is 10%. The implication is that if we use a 10% level of significance to test H_0, then the test statistic from the sample data would have to be greater than 4.605 for us to reject H_0 at the 10% level of significance and conclude that there is evidence of association in the population. The area to the right of 4.605, shown in Figure 17.12, is the rejection region for the test.

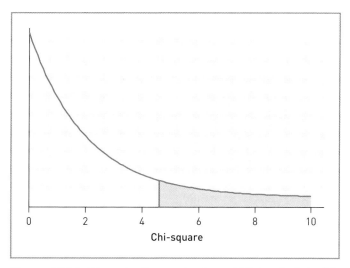

Figure 17.12 The rejection region for a 10% level of significance and 2 degrees of freedom

The next figure along the second row in Table 8 is the 5.991 in the column headed 0.05. This is the figure that cuts off 5% of the distribution on the right-hand side. If our test statistic is greater than 5.991 we could reject H_0 at the 5% level of significance. To reject H_0 at the 1% level the test statistic would have to be greater than the figure in the second row in the column headed 0.01, 9.210.

It is important to remember that the bigger the test statistic, the stronger the evidence of association. If it is big enough to reject the null hypothesis at 1% the result is much more conclusive than if we can only reject at 10%. This is logical because the test statistic, χ^2, is based on the differences between the observed frequencies in the contingency table and those we would expect to get if there was no association. Association in the population will usually result in large differences between the observed and expected frequencies. If there is no association in the population the differences between the observed and expected frequencies will usually be small.

In Example 17.19 the test statistic was 1.110, which is too small to allow us to reject H_0, the null hypothesis of no association at even the 10% level of significance. The sample evidence suggests that there is no association between gender and career preference.

EXAMPLE 17.20

There was an error in some of the data in Example 17.16. Four students who expressed a preference for Accountancy were wrongly recorded as Females whereas they were actually Males. Work out the test statistic, χ^2, for the amended data and use it to test H_0, the null hypothesis that there is no association between gender and career preference.

The contingency table is now:

	Females	Males
Accountancy	6 (12)	18 (12)
HRM	20 (18)	16 (18)
Marketing	20 (20)	20 (20)

Solution   The contributions from each cell to the test statistic are:

Females who prefer Accountancy: $(O - E)^2/E = (6 - 12)^2/12 = 36/12 = 3.000$

Females who prefer HRM: $(O - E)^2/E = (20 - 18)^2/18 = 4/18 = 0.222$

Females who prefer Marketing: $(O - E)^2/E = (20 - 20)^2/20 = 0/20 = 0$

Males who prefer Accountancy: $(O - E)^2/E = (18 - 12)^2/12 = 36/12 = 3.000$

Males who prefer HRM: $(O - E)^2/E = (16 - 18)^2/18 = 4/18 = 0.222$

Males who prefer Marketing: $(O - E)^2/E = (20 - 20)^2/20 = 0/20 = 0$

The test statistic, $\chi^2 = 3.000 + 0.222 + 0 + 3.000 + 0.222 + 0 = 6.444$

This is larger than the value of χ^2 that cuts off the tail of 5% on the right of the χ^2 distribution with two degrees of freedom, $\chi^2_{0.05,2}$, which is 5.991. This means we can reject the null hypothesis of no association at the 5% level of significance. There does seem to be association between gender and career preference in the population.

Since the test statistic is not greater than $\chi^2_{0.01,2}$, 9.210, we cannot reject H_0 at the more stringent 1% level of significance.

The contingency table in Example 17.20 is a fairly simple one with just three rows and two columns. Typically contingency analysis involves larger tables with more rows and/or columns. No matter how large the table, the process of testing for contingency is essentially the same. However, there are two key issues to consider.

First, the more rows and columns you have the greater the number of degrees of freedom. It is important to use the appropriate form of the χ^2 distribution.

Secondly, the viability of contingency analysis depends on the amount of data. In all statistical testing, basically the more data you have the more robust your conclusions will be. In contingency testing the results are unreliable if any of the expected frequencies are below five. If any are below one the results are of no use.

If there are expected frequencies that are so low they invalidate the test there are two ways of getting round the problem; either collect more data, or merge categories to reduce the number of rows or columns. Bear in mind that it is possible to minimise the chances of getting expected frequencies that are too low by planning the data collection carefully at the outset.

EXAMPLE 17.21   The following contingency table contains the results achieved by a random sample of 200 honours graduates and which type of course they completed, Full-time or Sandwich:

		Degree classification			
Course	First	Upper second	Lower second	Third	Total
Full-time	7	35	34	4	80
Sandwich	13	65	41	1	120
Total	20	100	75	5	200

Test for association between degree classification and course using a 10% level of significance.

H_0: There is no association between degree classification and type of course.

H_1: There is some association between degree classification and type of course.

Solution   The expected frequencies for the graduates of each course with Thirds is less than five:

Expected number of Full-time students with Thirds
$$= \text{(row total * column total)/overall total} = (80 * 5)/200 = 2$$

Expected number of Sandwich course graduates with Thirds $= (120 * 5)/200 = 3$

This weakens the test. We can resolve this by merging the Lower second and Third categories:

	First	Upper second	Lower second/Third	Total
Full-time	7	35	38	80
Sandwich	13	65	42	120
Total	20	100	80	200

The expected values are now:

Full-time and First $= (80 * 20)/200 = 8$

Full-time and Upper second $= (80 * 100)/200 = 40$

Full-time and Lower second/Third $= (80 * 80)/200 = 32$

Sandwich and First $= (120 * 20)/200 = 12$

Sandwich and Upper second $= (120 * 100)/200 = 60$

Sandwich and Lower second/Third $= (120 * 80)/200 = 48$

These are the figures in brackets in the contingency table below.

	First	Upper second	Lower second/Third	Total
Full-time	7 (8)	35 (40)	38 (32)	80
Sandwich	13 (12)	65 (60)	42 (48)	120
Total	20	100	80	200

The test statistic is:

$$\chi^2 = [(7 - 8)^2/8] + [(35 - 40)^2/40] + [(38 - 32)^2/32]$$
$$+ [(13 - 12)^2/12] + [(65 - 60)^2/60] + [(42 - 48)^2/48]$$
$$= 0.125 + 0.625 + 1.125 + 0.083 + 0.417 + 0.750$$
$$= 3.125$$

The number of degrees of freedom $= \text{(rows} - 1) * \text{(columns} - 1)$
$$= (2 - 1) * (3 - 1) = 2.$$

From Table 8 of Appendix 1, $\chi^2_{0.10,2}$, the value of χ^2 that cuts off a 10% area in the right-hand side of the χ^2 distribution with two degrees of freedom, is 4.605. This is the critical value of χ^2 at the 10% level. The test statistic, 3.125, is less than the critical value so we can't reject the null hypothesis. The sample evidence indicates that there is no significant association between type of course and degree classification.

Although the conclusion is no association it is worth noting that of the six contributions to the test statistic the two largest, 1.125 and 0.750, relate to the Lower second/Third category. More Full-time and less Sandwich students gain these classifications than we would expect.

SELF-ASSEMBLY GUIDE

Using chi-square to test for association

◆ The null hypothesis, H_0 is always that there is no association between the variables.

◆ The data must be collated in a contingency table. Calculate the row, column and overall totals.

◆ Work out the expected value for each cell. Check which row and column the cell is in then multiply the row total by the column total and divide the product by the overall total.

◆ For each cell subtract the expected value from the observed (i.e. actual) value, square the result and divide by the expected value. This is the cell's contribution to the test statistic.

◆ Add the contributions from the cells together to get the test statistic, χ^2.

◆ Work out the degrees of freedom, ν, which is the number of rows minus one times the number of columns minus one.

◆ Find the critical value for the degrees of freedom, ν, and the level of significance required, α, $\chi^2_{\alpha,\nu}$. If the test statistic is more than $\chi^2_{\alpha,\nu}$ reject H_0, otherwise do not reject it.

At this point you may find it useful to try **Review questions 17.4, 17.5, 17.8–17.10, 17.14 and 17.15** at the end of the chapter.

REVIEW QUESTIONS

Answers to these questions are on page 455. There are tips and hints to help you with them on the supporting website at **www.pearsoned.co.uk/buglear**, where you will also find the fully worked solutions.

☆☆★ **Basic questions**

17.1 Professor Soyuz, adviser to a trade union, has been asked to ascertain whether the mean hours worked per week are higher in the Deshovy region than in the Bugatty region. The mean and standard deviation of hours worked per week by a random sample of 62 workers in Deshovy are 43.7 and 4.1 respectively. The mean and standard deviation of hours worked by a random sample of 55 workers in Bugatty are 41.9 and 3.2 respectively. Test the hypothesis that on average workers in Deshovy work no more hours per week than workers in Bugatty. Use a 5% level of significance.

17.2 The Zilioni-Meer garage offers a 'clean and green engine makeover', which it promises will reduce the amount of CO_2 emissions from cars. A random sample of 10 cars was tested for CO_2 emissions before and after the service. The emission figures (in grams of CO_2 per kilometre travelled) were:

Car	1	2	3	4	5	6	7	8	9	10
Before	174	160	196	214	219	149	292	158	186	200
After	169	158	183	210	204	148	285	155	179	183

Test the hypothesis that after the service emission levels are at least as high as before against the alternative that emission levels are lower. Use a 1% level of significance.

17.3 An HR consultant undertook a survey of a random sample of 52 employees of the D.N. Ghee International Bank. She found a correlation coefficient of −0.377 between the satisfaction levels reported by employees and the length of service they had achieved. Test the hypothesis that there is significant negative correlation at the 1% level.

17.4 A leak of a hazardous substance at the Apassney Engineering factory threatens the health of the workforce. A random sample of 60 employees had their contamination levels checked. The results were:

	Department	
Level of contamination	Production	Administration
High	25	5
Medium	10	5
Low	5	10

Test the hypothesis that there is no association between department and contamination level. Use a 5% level of significance.

17.5 In a poll about changes to pension entitlements a random sample of 160 workers were asked if they would prefer to retire at 65 years of age or work beyond 65. Their responses, and the nature of their work is summarised in the following contingency table:

Nature of work	Retire at 65	Work beyond 65
Professional/managerial	12	18
Administrative/clerical	47	33
Craft/manual	34	16

Test the null hypothesis of no association between retirement preference and nature of work department using (i) a 5% level of significance, and (ii) a 1% level of significance.

☆★★ More testing questions

17.6 The speeds of a random sample of 28 cars travelling through a residential area were recorded. The mean speed of these cars was 31.7 mph with a standard deviation of 4.1 mph. After a major poster campaign urging motorists to reduce speed when driving through the area the speeds travelled by a random sample of 24 cars were recorded. The mean speed of this second sample was 29.5 mph with a standard deviation of 3.2 mph. Test the hypothesis that the poster campaign resulted in no reduction of speed in the area using a 5% level of significance and a pooled estimate of the standard error.

17.7 The engine capacity (in litres) and the fuel efficiency (in miles per gallon) of a random sample of 10 petrol-driven cars are:

Capacity	1.0	1.2	1.4	1.6	2.0	2.4	2.5	2.8	3.2	4.0
Fuel efficiency	44	47	41	37	33	30	25	26	23	21

(a) Determine the regression equation and test the hypothesis that the population slope is zero using a 1% level of significance.

(b) Construct a 99% confidence interval for the mean fuel efficiency of cars with an engine capacity of 1.8 litres.

(c) Construct a 99% prediction interval for the fuel efficiency of a single car with an engine capacity of 1.8 litres.

17.8 A travel company wants to investigate the relationship between socio-economic class and the number of vacations people take. In a survey a random sample of 140 adults were each asked how many holidays they had taken the previous year. The results were as follows:

Socio-economic class	Number of holidays		
	None	1 or 2	3 or more
A/B (Professional/managerial)	6	25	9
C1/C2 (Clerical/skilled)	6	47	7
D/E (Unskilled/other)	12	25	3

(a) Test the null hypothesis that there is no association between socio-economic class and number of holidays using (i) a 5% level of significance, and (ii) a 1% level of significance.
(b) Identify the two cells that provide the largest contributions to the test statistic, χ^2, and explain why they are so large.

17.9 A convenience store is thinking of introducing supplementary charges for customers who pay transactions of less than £10 by credit card. Before doing this it undertook a survey of a random sample of 210 transactions of less than £10 and recorded the payment method and age category of the customer. The results are summarised below:

Age category	Payment method		
	Credit card	Debit card	Cash
Under 25	42	9	49
25 and under 50	21	6	13
50 and over	17	16	37

(a) Test the null hypothesis that there is no association between age category and payment method using (i) a 5% level of significance, and (ii) a 1% level of significance.
(b) Which two cells make the largest contributions to the test statistic, and why are their contributions so large?

17.10 In a national survey of eating habits a random sample of 250 young adults in four UK cities were each asked whether or not they were vegetarian. The following results were obtained:

	Lincoln	Manchester	Nottingham	Oxford
Vegetarian	11	15	9	20
Non-vegetarian	39	65	51	40

(a) Test the null hypothesis of no association between city and whether or not young adults are vegetarian at the (i) 10% level of significance, and (ii) 5% level of significance.
(b) There is one error in the figures for Oxford. A Non-vegetarian was wrongly recorded as being a Vegetarian. Amend the data and repeat the test at (i) 10% level of significance, and (ii) 5% level of significance.

★★★ Challenging questions

17.11 Truba Construction has a major contract to lay pipelines for the oil industry in the Caucasus. The necessary steel pipes are unavailable locally and must be transported from a railhead in the Ukraine. There are three ways the company can get these supplies from there to their destination: on barges through the canals, by rail and using convoys of trucks. All of these take considerable time, and whilst in transit the cargo is subject to loss through accidental damage and theft. The company has tried all three modes of transport a number of times and recorded the percentage of the cargo lost each time:

Canal	17%	1%	10%	19%	4%	18%
Rail	0%	20%	25%	15%	2%	–
Truck	19%	15%	12%	15%	10%	–

Use one-way ANOVA and a 5% level of significance to test for differences between the population mean percentage losses for the three modes of transport.

17.12 Book-Galtier-Ritzar (BGR) is a large international accounting firm that recruits graduate trainees. Recently the firm recruited 15 graduates who have now taken their professional examinations. Their overall mark in these examinations by the universities from which they graduated are:

Neesky University graduates	38	33	58	51	50	–
Seredina University graduates	62	48	59	44	63	58
Visocky University graduates	52	84	77	77	–	–

Test the hypothesis that there is no difference between the mean professional examination marks achieved by graduates of these universities using a 1% level of significance.

17.13 A water company supplies the city of Sukoy from three reservoirs, all of which are prone to low level pollution from the local metal-processing industry. The company takes samples from each reservoir in order to monitor levels of pollution. Chemical analysis of the most recent samples has yielded the following results:

Reservoir	Pollution level (parts per million)				
Cheesty	5.2	10.6	7.0	10.4	3.9
Griazny	12.7	21.2	17.8	8.0	15.0
Mussor	9.0	8.0	10.8	12.4	10.9

The company believes that there is no difference between the pollution levels of the three reservoirs. Test this hypothesis at both the 5% and 1% levels of significance.

17.14 As part of a project on 'Green Consumerism' a random sample of 300 adults were each asked the question 'Do you take account of environmental factors when buying groceries?' Their responses and where they reside in the UK are summarised in the following table:

Take account of environmental issues?	England	Northern Ireland	Scotland	Wales
Always	14	7	12	9
Sometimes	68	26	51	43
Seldom	38	7	17	8

(a) Test the null hypothesis that there is no association between the responses and area of residence using a 10% level of significance.

(b) What is the largest contribution to test statistic, χ^2, and why is it so large?

(c) It emerges that one of the respondents from England was wrongly entered as 'Always' taking into account environmental issues and two more were wrongly recorded as 'Sometimes' taking into account environmental issues. All three reported that they 'Seldom' took account of environmental issues. Amend the data and test the null hypothesis of no association at (i) the 10% level of significance and (ii) the 5% level of significance.

17.15 Accident reporting data at two large building sites was analysed. The data is summarised in the following table:

Site	Result of accident			
	No injury	Minor injury	Major injury	Death
Apassno	24	36	13	2
Zdarova	31	21	8	0

(a) Is the chi-square test of association appropriate for the data in this form? Explain your answer.

(b) Merge the 'Major injury' and 'Death' figures and test the null hypothesis of no association between accident result and site at (i) the 10% level of significance, and (ii) the 5% level of significance.

THE DEBRIEF

Key things to remember from this chapter

→ We can use independent or dependent samples to test differences between population means. Independent samples are separately taken from each population. Dependent samples consist of matched pairs of values.

→ With large independent samples the test is based on the Z distribution, with small independent samples it is based on the t distribution and is only valid if both populations are normal.

→ With dependent samples use the paired t test which is based on the differences between the pairs of values.

→ To test the differences between more than two population means use ANOVA and the F distribution.

→ Test the value of the population correlation coefficient using the sample correlation coefficient. The null hypothesis is always that the population correlation coefficient is zero.

→ Test the population regression intercept and slope using the sample intercept and slope. The null hypothesis in each case is that the population coefficient is zero. In most cases testing the slope is of more interest than testing the intercept.

→ Regression equations can be used to estimate the mean value of the dependent variable, Y, when the independent variable, X, has a specific value, x. This is a confidence interval.

→ Regression equations can also be used to estimate a single y value when X has a specific value, x. This is a prediction interval.

→ Test the association between qualitative or category variables using chi-square. The null hypothesis is always no association. The test statistic is based on the differences between observed and expected values. The larger the differences, the larger the test statistic and the more likely the null hypothesis of no association will be rejected.

→ The chi-square test of association requires every expected value to be more than one and preferably all of them to be more than five.

References

Areni, C.S. and Kim, D. (1993) 'The influence of background music on shopping behaviour: classical versus top-forty music in a wine store', *Advances in Consumer Research*, 20, pp. 336–40.

Bates, D.M. and Watts, D.G. (2007) *Nonlinear Regression Analysis and its Applications*, New York: Wiley-Blackwell.

Baysan, S. (2001) 'Perceptions of the environmental impacts of tourism: a comparative study of the attitudes of German, Russian and Turkish tourists in Kemer, Antalya', *Tourism Geographies*, 3(2), pp. 218–35.

Dielman, T.E. (2005) *Applied Regression Analysis: A Second Course in Business and Economic Statistics* (4th edn), Pacific Grove, California: Brooks/Cole.

Hair, J.F., Black, W.C., Babin, B.J. and Anderson, R.E. (2009) *Multivariate Data Analysis: A Global Perspective* (7th edn), Harlow: Pearson Education.

Meier, P., Sacks, J. and Zabell, S.L. (1994) 'What happened in Hazelwood: statistics, employment discrimination and the 80% rule', in M.H. Degroot and S.E. Fienberg (eds), *Statistics and the Law*, New York: Wiley, pp. 1–48.

Roberts, M.J. and Russo, R. (1999) *A Student's Guide to Analysis of Variance*, London: Routledge.

Schimmel, K. and Nicholls, J. (2003) 'Gender differences and e-commerce behavior and perceptions', *Journal of Internet Banking and Commerce* [online], 8(1). Available at, http://www.arraydev.com/commerce/jibc/0306-01.htm

Seber, G.A.F. and Wild, C.J. (2003) *Nonlinear Regression*, New York: Wiley-Blackwell.

CHAPTER 18

Going off-road – managing quantitative research for projects and dissertations

CHAPTER OBJECTIVES

This chapter will help you to:

→ Plan quantitative research work

→ Use secondary data

→ Undertake questionnaire research

THE BARE BONES

What you will find in this chapter . . .

- Finding a topic and identifying data requirements
- The pros and cons of using secondary data
- Sampling and sample size issues in collecting primary data
- Designing, testing and using questionnaires
- Presenting quantitative analysis effectively in dissertations and projects

. . . and on the supporting website (www.pearsoned.co.uk/buglear)

- Coding data using Minitab

18.1   **Introduction**

As you approach your final year you will probably find out that you will have to do a final year project or dissertation. Generally this involves identifying a project topic, writing a project proposal, undertaking research on your project topic, and producing a lengthy document to deliver your findings.

This may seem a daunting prospect, especially at the beginning, but be positive, manage it well and you will achieve a great deal from it. In many cases a good final year project improves the grade of qualification students attain. It is also something to use to showcase your talents to potential employers. Since it is yours and yours alone it gives them a good idea of what you can do.

The project is possibly the first, perhaps the only, time that you get to choose what to study. Every other module had a menu of topics that the tutors considered you ought to study. The project is a different matter; it is very much your gig.

It is difficult to do a good project unless you are committed to it, so at the outset it really is worth investing some time in identifying several potential topics.

After finding a feasible project topic you'll probably be asked to describe your topic in a formal proposal and conduct a literature survey. Good proposals typically have defined research questions, in other words questions that the research is intended to answer, and specific propositions or hypotheses to be tested. Good literature surveys explore the published material as it relates to the topic. This helps to shape the direction and scope of the proposed research.

This is the stage at which you should think about your data requirements. Maybe the data you need is already available from published or organisational sources. If not, you need to

---

SELF-ASSEMBLY GUIDE

Thinking up ideas for project topics

◆ Set aside some time in a quiet place with pen and paper to make some lists.

◆ Write down the parts of your course you have enjoyed most. These might be entire modules or specific topics within modules.

◆ Note down what you consider to be your academic strengths.

◆ List the interests you have outside your studies.

◆ Write down any especially interesting aspects of any work experience you have. This might be a placement, a part-time job or work before you began your course.

◆ Write down any contacts and/or resources that you can access.

◆ Look over what you have written for connections. Suppose you have listed Marketing as a favourite subject, you like football and you have worked part-time as a programme-seller for a football club. This might lead you to consider a topic like football clubs' marketing of season tickets. This has the 'holy trinity' of strands; relevance (it is based on the content of your course), interest and feasibility (knowledge of and contacts in a football club).

◆ If no topics come to mind, discuss your lists with someone else, maybe a friend or a tutor. They need not be involved with your course; just going through it all with someone may spark some good ideas.

◆ If you are still stuck for ideas look at news websites, especially business news areas of them. Look for stories that interest you but avoid the ones that are likely to be ephemeral.

decide how you can get it yourself. It is possible that some of your data requirements can be met from published sources and some will entail collecting data yourself.

The published data that you use will have been collected and analysed by somebody else. It is what is called secondary data, 'second-hand' so to speak. Whoever collected the data did so to meet their own requirements not yours, so assess the value of the data for your project carefully.

If you collect data yourself it is you who decides the key issues, including what questions to ask, who to approach and so on. These require careful consideration because getting them wrong can be very frustrating and time-consuming. The data you gather is called primary data.

Once you have decided how your data requirements will be met you will also need to think about how to analyse and present the data in the final document. We will consider this later.

In this chapter we concentrate on the data gathering and analysis aspects of final year projects. There are excellent texts that offer good advice on the broad span of issues involved in business research projects (Bryman and Bell, 2010; Collis and Hussey, 2009; Fisher, 2010; Jankowicz, 2007; Saunders, Lewis and Thornhill, 2009).

18.2 Using secondary data

Whoever compiled the secondary data chose the data collection method. You had no say in the matter or in how the data is presented. You may be lucky; the secondary data may be precisely what you need for your project. It may even be presented in a form that is appropriate for you. But be careful; you need to consider issues carefully.

There are questions you should ask about how the data was collected. Precisely when was it collected? All published results are inevitably historic since the very process of publishing them takes time. Data published in a journal or on a website may be relatively recent but data published in a book is likely to be older.

If your topic is in a field that has not changed all that much since the secondary data was published it may well be of use. On the other hand, if your topic is in a field that has changed considerably, secondary data is unlikely to be as useful. If you do use it you need to alert your audience to the limited validity it may have for the present and explain why the changes in the field have reduced the usefulness of the data. An example of this is UK unemployment figures. The way in which these are defined has changed considerably and current figures are not directly comparable with those of a generation ago.

If you intend to use the secondary data to compare situations over time it is the age of the data that makes it of use. You need to ensure that any data you collect about the current situation can be compared directly to the secondary data. This will entail asking the same or similar questions or measuring the same things, possibly also taking the same sort of sample.

The second consideration is the process of data collection. Unless there are observations from every element in the population, they are sample data. If so, what was the size of the sample? How was the sample selected? Was it a random sample? If the population was inanimate, in other words made up of objects or episodes, precisely what was measured or counted, and how was this done? If the population was human, how and when was the data elicited from the respondents?

To answer these questions look at the source of the secondary data carefully. There may be a section with a title like 'Methods' or 'Methodology' which discusses the data-collection methods. There may also be footnotes or notes at the end of the document that explain how the data was collected, problems that the researchers encountered and caveats about the validity of their findings.

The next thing to address is how the secondary data is presented. The author or authors may include the raw data in the publication, maybe attached as an appendix. If the data is there you can choose how to present it in your project, and use presentation techniques that will best assist your discussion of the data.

Generally though, the researchers who collected the data do not include it in their published work. If the study was large this is inevitably for reasons of space alone. You will probably find that diagrams and statistical measures are used to present the data. Although the techniques the researchers have used to present their data may not have been your choices, they may suit your purposes.

If this is not the case and data is presented in a form that is not suitable for your work, is there an alternative way to present it based on the form in which it is presented in the sources? For instance, if the source provides a grouped frequency distribution of the data, it is possible to produce a histogram from it, or approximate the mean and standard deviation. Alternatively, if there is a contingency table, it is possible to create a bar chart to depict the data.

If you just cannot present the data as you would wish to in the form in which it is published, consider contacting the authors of the work and asking if you can have access to the raw data. This may seem obtrusive but bear in mind that they have probably devoted much time and effort to conducting their study and are probably very proud of it. Any enquiry about it, especially from someone such as yourself who is researching the same area and is likely to introduce their work to a new audience, is welcome. Authors generally provide an email address on their work so that anyone interested in the work can get in touch with them. The worst that can happen is that they decline to help or ignore your request.

Think about contacting the authors of secondary sources with any questions you may have about their research, such as whether they, or anyone else, have developed the work since they published their study. Allow some time for them to reply. They may have moved to another post or just be too busy to get back to you right away. Contact them a month or so before the time you need their reply so that you have it in time to use it.

When writing your final document it is essential to acknowledge the sources of the secondary data you use, even if you have presented it in a different form from that in which it was originally published. By all means quote data or text from the work of others but cite the reference, which means identifying where it came from using an appropriate style of academic referencing like the Harvard system.

18.3   **Collecting primary data**

The main problem with secondary data is that it may not meet your data requirements. If it is simply not the sort of data that you need to support the argument you want to develop you will need to consider collecting primary data. The upside of doing this is that not only will the data be up to date but it will also be precisely what you need. The downside is that gathering primary data involves careful planning and is time-consuming.

Because of the time it takes to collect you need to decide if you will be collecting primary data as early as possible. Identify your data requirements about the same time as you do the literature survey. Collecting primary data successfully is very difficult to do quickly.

When you have your data requirements there are two questions to address: who can give you the data, and how can you get it from them?

If you can get the data you need by conducting experiments in somewhere like a laboratory, or by direct observation, the first questions is answered; you will be getting the data yourself. The next question is what experiment or method of observation to use? You will also need to define the population, determine the sample size and sample selection method.

Although some business research, such as in ergonomics and health and safety, does involve experiment and observation much of it entails obtaining data from individuals or organisations. If this is what you will be doing then you must define the types of people or organisations as precisely as possible. Those that fit your definition make up your target population. If only a modest number of people or organisations fit your definition you can survey the entire population. If there are a large number of potential targets you will need to draw a sample from the population.

The choice of sample selection methods you have depends on whether or not you can draw up a *sampling frame*. This is a list of all the elements, whether people or organisations, in the population that you intend to research. If it is possible to compile a sampling frame, for instance if your population consists of the English league football clubs, then depending on the structure of the population you can use the random selection procedures described in section 15.3. The advantage of these methods is that you can produce statistically sound estimates about the population from them. If you cannot draw up a sampling frame, which may well be the case if you want to investigate, for instance, small-scale building contractors, then you will have to consider the alternative selection methods outlined in section 15.4.

18.3.1 Choosing the right sample size

In addition to choosing how to select your sample you will have to determine the size of your sample. In general, bigger samples are better, but they are also more time-consuming. You need to consider two issues: firstly, how much data is required for the analytical techniques you would like to use, and secondly what *response rate*, in other words what proportion of targets that you approach actually respond to your request for data, will you achieve.

Although larger samples are generally better, as the sample size increases the lower the marginal advantage becomes. For example, a sample of 30 observations enables you to use the Z distribution in statistical inference based on your sample and the population need not be normally distributed. A sample of at least 30 observations rather than just 20 observations is therefore of benefit. The marginal advantage of a very large sample of, for example, 200 observations compared to a sample of 100 observations is not as substantial, in fact is of debatable benefit, given the extra time and effort involved.

If you want inference results to a specific degree of precision and level of confidence you should work out the minimum sample size to use. Sections 16.3.2 and 16.3.6 explain this.

If you intend to use the contingency analysis we considered in section 17.5 to test association between categories of qualitative variables, you must take account of the number of categories involved. In asking respondents from five different organisations about five different product types the contingency table that you draw up for your results will require five rows and five columns, a total of 25 cells. If there are only 100 respondents the spread of sample data among the cells will be too sparse, on average just four a cell. You will either need to reduce the number of categories or collect more data for your results to be substantial enough to enable you to draw valid conclusions.

Bear in mind that the sample size is not the number of people or organisations you approach; it is the number that respond. Some of them may be unwilling or unable to meet your request for data. The response rate is the proportion of enquiries that are successful.

Your response rate will depend in part on how you collect your data. There are some things you can do to improve your chances of getting a good response rate which we will consider in the next section. The key issue for now is that in planning data collection you should factor in a figure for the likely response rate.

Response rates vary considerably and are difficult to anticipate. The best way of getting some idea of the response rate you are likely to achieve is to look for the response rates achieved by researchers who have undertaken similar investigations to your own. As a very general guide, in business research a response rate of 40% or more, i.e. 40% or so of the requests made are successful, is good but a response rate of 20% or less is poor.

To ensure you get enough responses to meet your required sample size multiply the sample size by three, or even four if you anticipate that your requests will be challenging for the respondents. For instance, if you want a sample of 30, then you should approach 90 or even 120 respondents.

18.3.2 Methods of collecting primary data

If you will be gathering your primary data from experiments in laboratory-style facilities, the planning of the collection process boils down to managing your time and gaining access to the facilities. You have considerable control over the collection of the data. Allow enough time for the experiments and some additional time in the event that things don't go according to plan. If you do this, completing the work in time for the data to be of use should be possible even if you run into problems.

If you will be gathering data from other people take account of the fact that you don't control their time or actions. You need to think carefully about how and when you will approach them for data. You should allow enough, indeed more than enough, time in your plan for the people you intend to ask for data to respond to your request, especially if you want them to complete a questionnaire.

In the first place you have to be clear about what data you require from those surveyed. If you are not clear about what you want, you cannot expect them to second guess your requirements. One thing you shouldn't do is write to them telling them about your project and ask vaguely if they can provide you with any information. The best you'll get is reference to a website or a leaflet about what they do which will be too general to be of much use. You'll be lucky to get a reply at all; if they think you can't be bothered to be clear about what you want from them, why should they go out of their way to help you?

Be clear about your data requirements but also about who can provide you with the necessary data, and how you propose to approach them. You need to be specific about what you need, to ensure that you will be asking the people who can help and to approach them in a way that makes it as easy as possible for them to provide you with what you need.

If your target respondents are individuals, perhaps buyers of a certain product, ensure you have the correct contact details for each one. If your target respondents are certain types of post-holders within organisations, for instance marketing managers, you need to obtain their correct names, job titles and contact information. If you get these details right you will probably achieve a higher response rate. The best way to get a request deleted or thrown away is if it is not directed to the appropriate named individual.

Deciding on your distribution mode, in other words how you will send out your requests, can be tricky. There is no simple answer; it depends on the nature of your targets. Probably the best way of maximising your response rate is to do it directly by visiting your respondents and asking them for the data or to fill in your questionnaire. If this is not viable but they are easy to access by email, maybe because they work for the same company or participate in a social network, it may be best to contact them electronically. If this is feasible and you intend to use a questionnaire to harvest your data there is questionnaire design software that you can use to design and lay out your material and send it.

If your targets are older and not part of an organisational or social network, a postal approach may be better. Burkey and Kuechler (2003) look at the technical issues involved in electronic surveys and Sax, Gilmartin and Bryant (2003) conducted a comparative study of response rates from electronic and non-electronic distribution.

Whether you send it electronically or physically your request should follow the style of a business letter to the individual. Use respectful opening and closing formalities. Your message should explain who you are, the research you are doing and exactly how they can help. In the last paragraph thank them in anticipation of their helping you.

You will probably be inclined to send your request by email. This is certainly faster and cheaper than by post. A possible drawback is that it is easy for recipients to dismiss it as a junk email and so delete it without reading it. To minimise the risk of this put something succinct about your research topic in the subject line e.g. 'Green marketing study'. At this stage it is also worth including the ethical terms under which you are conducting the research.

What you need your respondents to do depends on the amount and nature of the data that you want from them. If you are only after a few pieces of data just ask for them in your message. Be as precise as possible, for example if you need data about a specific year or location, say so.

If you want deeper information like opinions and attitudes then conducting interviews with your respondents will probably be the best way of raising useful data. Request an interview in your message and describe the issues you would like to explore with them. If your interviews are structured, in other words all of them have the same sequence of primary and supplementary questions, it will be easier to compare the data from different respondents.

If you are after breadth rather than depth then you should consider using a questionnaire. This is a single document consisting of a series of questions and means by which respondents can provide answers to them. The advantage of them is that because you are asking all your respondents the same questions the results are directly comparable.

Designing a good questionnaire is not particularly easy and using one is time-consuming. So before you embark on questionnaire research it is worth giving a second thought to whether it really is the best way of gathering the data you require. Many final year students go for questionnaire research without doing this and end up wasting time. One student was researching how useful corporate events such as receptions at Wimbledon were in increasing sales. She circulated a questionnaire to all the sales staff of a prominent computer company. Respondents were asked how many new leads had been generated from such events. A kindly office manager replied to her saying that she already had this information and would be happy to share it. A single email would probably have yielded results much faster than the considerable number of questionnaires she sent round let alone saving her much time and trouble.

If there are no other ways of going about it a questionnaire is often the best way of getting responses to a lot of questions from a lot of respondents. Go about it the right way and questionnaire research can generate the data you require relatively cheaply. What is more, the data from the different respondents is comparable which makes analysis of the data more straightforward. On the other hand, if it isn't done well questionnaire research can lead to a low response rate and data of little use.

So, what makes good questionnaire research? The most important thing is the design of the questionnaire and testing it before using it on your respondents. Put time and effort into designing a questionnaire that is comprehensive enough to produce the data you require. Make it as straightforward as possible for respondents to use and you are likely to get a better response rate.

If you are sending your questionnaire it should be accompanied by a covering note asking your respondents to help. If you are distributing it directly, include a message at the top of the questionnaire outlining the purpose of the research and say thank you to the respondent for helping. If you are distributing your questionnaire by post including a stamped and addressed envelope will probably improve your response rate.

Another way that can improve the response rate is offering enticements such as entering respondents who complete and return the questionnaire into a raffle for a prize, or offering them a summary of your results. The best one to use depends on the nature of your respondents. A raffle prize is better if your respondents are participating purely as individuals, but a summary of results may be better if your respondents all have a particular type of post within different organisations and share an interest in your topic.

As far as the length of your questionnaire is concerned, try to limit it to two sides. Any longer and completing it will be onerous for your respondents let alone making the collation and analysis more difficult for you. Treat the space on your questionnaire as valuable; every question you include must deserve its place.

Give careful consideration as to how you will set out the document, including font style and size, line spacing and indentation. Keep it clear and uncluttered to avoid respondents being distracted by over-elaborate or poor layout.

Think about the sequence of your questions. You will probably need some personal information from your respondents, for instance what qualifications they have or how long they have held their current job. On balance it is probably better to put such questions first. They should be straightforward for the respondents and hence encourage them to continue. This is good because once they start they are more likely to finish and thus boost the response rate.

It is possible to argue that personal questions should be at the end of the questionnaire because if you put intrusive questions that ask, for example, about income or marital status at the start this will deter respondents from filling in the questionnaire at all. You will have to exercise your own judgement about this but, as a guide, if the personal questions are not likely to seem to your respondents to be intrusive ask them first.

To help your respondents your questions should be asked in a logical sequence. Don't jump from one issue to another and back, which will frustrate and confuse respondents. If there are several different issues divide the questionnaire into sections, and have questions dealing with a specific issue in their own section.

Try to write questions that are as easy as possible for your respondents to understand and as easy as possible for you to process. With open-ended questions such as '*What is your opinion of the autocratic style of management*?' respondents may be put off answering them because it takes much more effort to write a sentence or two than to tick a box. The responses you get will be hard to analyse because they will be so disparate and not easy to present beyond broad categorisation.

Questions that offer response categories generate data that is much easier to collate and analyse. Sometimes the categories to use are self-evidently obvious like female or male for gender. For other questions, for example types of job, you may have to compile your own categories.

There are standard types of question that are used by organisations like market research agencies, which use questionnaires for commercial purposes. Sometimes they will use open-ended questions, especially for exploratory purposes, when they are trying to formulate alternatives to offer respondents by piloting the questionnaire before proceeding to the full survey. More generally they use closed or *closed-ended* questions of three types: dichotomous, multichotomous and scaled.

Dichotomous questions, whose name is derived from the word dichotomy which means a division into two, offer a choice between two alternative and mutually exclusive responses. An example is:

Do you have a current driving licence?   Yes ☐   No ☐

These types of question are often used as *filter* questions. Depending on the answer the respondent gives they may be directed to proceed straight to a subsequent section of the questionnaire.

Multichotomous questions offer more than two alternative responses, either where only one is required or where more than one is possible. An example of the former is:

Which party did you vote for in the last general election?

Conservative ☐   Labour ☐   Liberal ☐   Other ☐   None ☐

An example of a question which allows for more than one response is:

Which of the following types of places of entertainment have you visited in the past seven days?

Cinema ☐   Concert hall ☐   Night club ☐   Public house ☐

Restaurant ☐   Theatre ☐

When you use a multichotomous question you should indicate that the respondent should select only one, or all that apply, as appropriate.

Scaled questions are designed to assist respondents to record their attitudes in a form that you can analyse systematically. One form of scaled question invites respondents to rank a number of factors in relation to each other. An example is:

When choosing a holiday destination which criteria matter to you? Please rank the following in order of importance to you with 1 as the most important and 4 as the least important:

Cost ☐   Sunshine ☐   Scenery ☐   Nightlife ☐

Questions like these enable you to compare the rankings of different respondents quite easily, but do be careful not to ask your respondents to rank too many factors. Beyond six or so the respondent will reach the point of indifference between factors, if not about completing your questionnaire!

Likert scales offer a standard set of responses to a statement making an assertion, for instance:

Joining the euro will benefit the UK economy.

Strongly agree ☐   Agree ☐   Neither agree nor disagree ☐

Disagree ☐   Strongly disagree ☐

A variation of this is to ask them to indicate their opinion by giving a rating on a scale of 1 to 5, where 1 is strong agreement with the statement and 5 is strong disagreement with the statement. When you use this style of question try to make the statement as clear as possible otherwise you may get respondents who register indifference but actually are giving that response because they do not fully understand the statement. Semantic differential questions offer respondents a linear scale between two polar positions on which to indicate their attitude to a statement. An example is:

The prospect of a new type of cricket tournament is

Interesting _____ Boring

Stapel scale questions ask respondents to make an assessment of a statement by indicating how strongly the adjective describes their attitude. For instance:

I think the promotion procedures in my company are

+3

+2

+1

FAIR

−1

−2

−3

Data from rating scale questions is sometimes referred to as 'soft' data, which suggests it can be erratic or vague. In contrast 'hard' data is more likely to be consistent and clear.

The softness of rating scale data arises because of the different ways in which respondents can interpret it. Perceptions of terms like 'Strongly agree' differ. Two respondents can have the same opinion but one may put down that they 'Strongly agree' and the other may say they 'Agree'. There is no such difficulty with questions like 'To the nearest year how long have you been in your current post?' This would produce hard data.

In general it is better to use questions that generate hard data than those that generate soft data, although sometimes you won't have such a choice. Suppose your topic is gym membership. Rather than ask respondents whether they visit a gym 'Often', 'Seldom' or 'Never', asking them if they are a member of a gym and the last time they visited their gym would produce harder data.

If you use scaled questions, bear in mind that the results they generate are *ordinal* data, data whose order of responses is consistent, for instance 'Strongly agree' is more forceful than 'Agree', but there is no consistent unit of measurement. There is no basis for saying that the interval on the scale between, say, 'Strongly agree' and 'Agree' is larger or smaller than the interval between 'Agree' and 'Neither agree nor disagree'. This is true even if you use numerical scales, for instance where respondents are asked to make a selection between '1' for strong agreement and '5' for strong disagreement. You might be tempted to employ arithmetic measures, such as the mean, to summarise the results, but this would be quite wrong because even though the results are numerical the scale on which they are based is not arithmetically consistent. You may like to refer back to section 4.4 for more on types of data and the analytical tools that are appropriate for each.

We have assumed so far that any questionnaire you design will be sent to the respondents either electronically or by post. As an alternative you might consider asking your questions more directly, either by means of face-to-face interviews or by telephone. The advantages are that you can clarify misunderstandings and the response rate will probably be improved because you have the attention of the respondent and you don't have to rely on them to send the document back to you. The disadvantage is that it is easy to introduce bias unwittingly by the way in which you ask the questions and put the responses.

There are a number of very good specialist texts on questionnaire design including Converse and Presser (1986), Dillman *et al.* (2009), Fowler (2009), Gillham (2008), Hague (1993), Munn and Drever (2004), Oppenheim (2000) or Saris and Gallhofer (2007).

After writing your questionnaire it really is essential to test it. This is to ensure that respondents can understand it fully and therefore answer appropriately. You can't test it yourself: after all you wrote it, so it should it makes sense to you. The real question is whether it will make sense to your respondents.

Ask several people to test or 'pilot' your questionnaire independently. Preferably they should be similar to your target respondents in your sample in terms of age, level of education and so on. If this is not possible ask relatives or friends. Whoever it is ask them to complete the questionnaire and discuss it with them after they have done so. Find out whether they thought any questions were hard to understand or answer, whether the sequence was logical, whether the document was well-presented and so on. Improve the questionnaire by making appropriate modifications then test the revised version, ideally with different people. Refine it through testing until it is as easy to use as possible, yet still enables you to harvest the data you need.

Testing questionnaires is a tedious business, especially if you are certain that your questionnaire is one that an utter fool should be able to understand. The truth is, your opinion doesn't matter. The crucial issue is whether your respondents will be able to understand it and supply you with the data you want. Unless *they* can the whole exercise will be pointless. Be patient. Listen to the feedback from your questionnaire testers. What they tell you can enhance both the response rate and the quality of data you obtain when you use the questionnaire.

18.4   Presenting your analysis

Once your data collection and analysis is complete you will have to consider how to include your analysis in your report or dissertation. You need to make some important editorial decisions about what will be included, how it will be presented and where it will be put. These issues need to be considered when you design the structure of your report.

If you gathered primary data you must say how you did this. Explain it in a 'Research methods' section that should be put after the introduction. The reader should be clear from this section why you used the sample size you did, how the sample items, be they things or people, were selected, and how you collected your data.

You probably won't be required to include your raw data in your final report. Readers seldom want to wade through pages of letters, completed questionnaires etc. Having said that it is a good idea to put one example document, such as a blank questionnaire in an appendix and refer to it in your methods section to illustrate how the data was gathered.

You should use statistical software for your analysis. If you are entering data from a pile of questionnaires number each one of them before you start. Enter the data from the questionnaire numbered 1 in the first row of the worksheet, data from questionnaire 2 in the second row etc. This is a good idea because if you need to correct data entry errors or refer back to the answers from a particular respondent you will be able to connect the completed questionnaire to the data entered from it easily.

If your data has been generated by a questionnaire that includes scores respondents have given in answer to scaled questions you may be advised to include an assessment of the reliability of your data. One measure of this that you may hear of is Cronbach's α. Lee Cronbach was an eminent American education professor who specialised in psychological testing. He developed what he called the Coefficient α, which is based on measuring correlation, to measure the internal consistency of responses to separate questions designed to generate scores that could be combined to give an overall assessment of the respondents' abilities or attitudes. In his original work (Cronbach, 1951) he gives examples of tests of mechanical reasoning and morale. Researchers are often tempted to use Cronbach's α because it appears to give an overall and easily understandable reliability check on an entire data set: on a scale of 0 to 1, perfect reliability yields an α value of one. However, be wary of employing the coefficient; it is only of any use if you have reason to expect reliability between sets of responses in the first place.

The results you put in your final document should be the ones that constitute useful findings for your research objectives and questions. Sometimes things don't go according to plan;

respondents may not have been able to provide the data or gave the wrong data. For various reasons data collection can be disappointing. If this has happened during your project there isn't much you can do about it. Don't include inappropriate data in your report just because you have it. The results you put in your final document need to play their part in your discussion not leave the reader wondering why you included them.

If some aspect of your data collection hasn't worked out then it is probably worth discussing why, especially if it was an important part of the project. This is an important finding and could constitute a valid contribution to knowledge of the topic if others can learn from your experience.

As well as deciding which results to include you need to decide how you will present them. Remember that readers will read your work without taking the journey through your research with you. To help them follow your findings introduce the results gradually beginning with a simple presentation before leading them through the more sophisticated analysis.

Early on you need to explain the composition of your sample. Use simple tables and diagrams to illustrate the balance of respondents by basic divisions such as gender and age category. After this you can illustrate the responses given to the other questions you posed with more simple tables and diagrams. If your results include quantitative data use summary measures to present an overview of them to your readers.

At a later stage you can discuss any associations between categories of respondents such as gender or the type of job they have on the one hand and the facts they provide or attitudes they hold on the other. For this you should use bivariate techniques, specifically contingency analysis with qualitative data, and scatter diagrams, regression and correlation with quantitative data.

In most good projects that are based on data there are propositions or hypotheses that are tested using the data. To do this use the methods of statistical inference we covered in Chapters 16 and 17. These methods enable you to use your sample results to draw conclusions about the population your sample comes from.

Suppose for example you want to assess the proposition that successful clothing brands are marketed via the internet. To explore this we could test the association between whether or not clothing brands are marketed via the internet and the market share they have. To test the hypothesis that the numbers of hours drivers work in road haulage exceed the maximum hours in working time regulations we might use data from a random sample of haulage contractors.

Having decided what to include in your final document and how you will present it, you need to think about where you will put your tables, diagrams and numerical results in the document. It has probably taken you a considerable amount of time and effort to gather and analyse your data so make sure you weave them into your discussion effectively.

Make it as easy as possible for readers to locate the analysis you want them to see. With a diagram or table there are two choices: position it within your discussion or put it in an appendix. With numerical results there is a third possibility; you can report summary measures like means and standard deviations in your discussion. If you want to show readers how you produced them put the derivation in an appendix and refer readers to it.

In your project planning, leave yourself enough time to scrutinise the final document report before you hand it in. Check that all inserts are labelled, all appendices numbered and all sources acknowledged. If there is time, ask a friend to read through it in case you have missed something. Check that they have been able to locate the inserts and appendices when they were referred to.

Once you have written the document this last stage of checking and double-checking will feel exasperating; you've written it and can hardly bear to revisit it. Try to resist this sentiment, the time and effort you devote to checking and refining is well worth it. You want to maximise the marks you get for all your hard work so make sure that the tutors who assess it read as polished and professional a document as possible.

SELF-ASSEMBLY GUIDE

Positioning charts, diagrams and tables in a dissertation

◆ The key question is, how important is it for readers to see the chart, table or diagram?

◆ If it is so important that unless they look at it they won't be able to follow your argument, position it in the text. Put it as near as possible to the section of the discussion that refers to it. It is very frustrating for readers to have to rummage through the entire document for analysis that is referred to pages away.

◆ Label every inserted table or diagram (for example, 'Table 1' or 'Figure 2'), and refer to it using that label, e.g. '. . . the distribution of ages of respondents is shown in Figure 1'.

◆ If it is important but not essential for your readers to see put it in an appendix. Number the appendix and use the appendix number when you refer to the analysis it contains.

◆ If you have more than one appendix, sequence them so that the first one you refer readers to is Appendix 1, the second, Appendix 2 and so on.

◆ Don't use appendices as dumping grounds for every piece of analysis you produce. Any analysis that you do not refer to directly is superfluous to your argument and should be omitted altogether. If you include it just because you did it, at best it will be a distraction for your readers, at worst it will make them wonder if you really know what you're doing.

THE DEBRIEF

Key things to remember from this chapter

→ Find a topic that inspires you. You need to be motivated to research it for some months and this is very difficult if your heart is not in it.

→ Decide what data you will require at the early planning stage.

→ Remember to treat secondary data with caution; find out as much as you can about how it was gathered.

→ If you collect primary data be clear about your requirements before approaching respondents.

→ A questionnaire is rather like a gun with one bullet; you have one shot at using it so test it and refine it before you launch it on your respondents.

→ Good design and appropriate distribution can improve your response rate.

→ Give careful consideration to where you will place your analysis in your final document.

References

Bryman, A. and Bell, E. (2010) *Business Research Methods*, Oxford: Oxford University Press.

Burkey, J. and Kuechler, W.L. (2003) 'Web-based surveys for corporate information gathering: A bias-reducing design framework', *IEEE Transactions on Professional Communication*, 46(2), pp. 81–93 (abstract available at: http://ieeexplore.ieee.org/xpl/freeabs_all.jsp?arnumber=1202366).

Collis, J. and Hussey, R. (2009) *Business Research: A Practical Guide for Undergraduate and Postgraduate Students*, Basingstoke: Palgrave.

Converse, J.M. and Presser, S. (1986) *Survey Questions: Handcrafting the Standardised Questionnaire*, London: Sage.

Cronbach, L.J. (1951) 'Coefficient alpha and the internal structure of tests', *Psychometrika*, 16(3), pp. 297–334.

Dillman, D.A., Smyth, J.D. and Christian, L.M. (2009) *Internet, mail and Mixed-mode Surveys: The Tailored Design Method*, Hoboken, New Jersey: John Wiley.

Fisher, C. (2010) *Researching and Writing a Dissertation*, Harlow: Pearson Education.

Fowler, F.J. (2009) *Survey Research Methods*, Los Angeles: Sage.

Gillham, B. (2008) *Developing a Questionnaire*, London: Continuum International.

Hague, P.N. (1993) *Questionnaire Design*, London: Kogan Page.

Jankowicz, A.D. (2007) *Business Research Projects*, Filey: Thomson Learning.

Munn, P. and Drever, E. (2004) *Using Questionnaires in Small-scale Research: A Beginner's Guide*, Glasgow: SCRE Centre.

Oppenheim, A.N. (2000) *Questionnaire Design, Interviewing and Attitude Measurement*, London: Heinemann.

Saris, W.E. and Gallhofer, I.N. (2007) *Design, Evaluation and Analysis of Questionnaires for Survey Research*, Hoboken, New Jersey: Wiley.

Saunders, M., Lewis, P. and Thornhill, A. (2009) *Research Methods for Business Students*, Harlow: Pearson Education.

Sax, L.J. Gilmartin, S.K. and Bryant, A.N. (2003) 'Assessing response rates and nonresponse bias in web and paper surveys', *Research in Higher Education*, 44(4), pp. 409–32 (available at: http://www.springerlink.com/content/v71hp772066t1q85/fulltext.pdf)

APPENDIX 1

Statistical and accounting tables

Table 1 **Present values**

This table provides the present value of one unit of currency received in n years' time when the rate of interest is r%. To use this table to discount a future flow of cash find the figure in the row for the appropriate number of years until the cash flow takes place and in the column for the appropriate rate of interest, the discount rate. Multiply this figure by the sum of money involved.

EXAMPLE

Using a discount rate of 4%, find the present value of $5000 received in three years' time. The figure in the row for 3 years and the column for 4% is 0.889. $5000 multiplied by 0.889 is $4445, which is the present value of $5000 at a discount rate of 4%.

Year (n)	Discount rate (r)									
	1%	2%	3%	4%	5%	6%	7%	8%	9%	10%
1	0.990	0.980	0.971	0.962	0.952	0.943	0.935	0.926	0.917	0.909
2	0.980	0.961	0.943	0.925	0.907	0.890	0.873	0.857	0.842	0.826
3	0.971	0.942	0.915	0.889	0.864	0.840	0.816	0.794	0.772	0.751
4	0.961	0.924	0.888	0.855	0.823	0.792	0.763	0.735	0.708	0.683
5	0.951	0.906	0.863	0.822	0.784	0.747	0.713	0.681	0.650	0.621
6	0.942	0.888	0.837	0.790	0.746	0.705	0.666	0.630	0.596	0.564
7	0.933	0.871	0.813	0.760	0.711	0.665	0.623	0.583	0.547	0.513
8	0.923	0.853	0.789	0.731	0.677	0.627	0.582	0.540	0.502	0.467
9	0.914	0.837	0.766	0.703	0.645	0.592	0.544	0.500	0.460	0.424
10	0.905	0.820	0.744	0.676	0.614	0.558	0.508	0.463	0.422	0.386
11	0.896	0.804	0.722	0.650	0.585	0.527	0.475	0.429	0.388	0.350
12	0.887	0.788	0.701	0.625	0.557	0.497	0.444	0.397	0.356	0.319
13	0.879	0.773	0.681	0.601	0.530	0.469	0.415	0.368	0.326	0.290
14	0.870	0.758	0.661	0.577	0.505	0.442	0.388	0.340	0.299	0.263
15	0.861	0.743	0.642	0.555	0.481	0.417	0.362	0.315	0.275	0.239

Year (n)	Discount rate (r)									
	11%	12%	13%	14%	15%	16%	17%	18%	19%	20%
1	0.901	0.893	0.885	0.877	0.870	0.862	0.855	0.847	0.840	0.833
2	0.812	0.797	0.783	0.769	0.756	0.743	0.731	0.718	0.706	0.694
3	0.731	0.712	0.693	0.675	0.658	0.641	0.624	0.609	0.593	0.597
4	0.659	0.636	0.613	0.592	0.572	0.552	0.534	0.516	0.499	0.482
5	0.593	0.567	0.543	0.519	0.497	0.476	0.456	0.437	0.419	0.402
6	0.535	0.507	0.480	0.456	0.432	0.410	0.390	0.370	0.352	0.335
7	0.482	0.452	0.425	0.400	0.376	0.354	0.333	0.314	0.296	0.279
8	0.434	0.404	0.376	0.351	0.327	0.305	0.285	0.266	0.249	0.233
9	0.391	0.361	0.333	0.308	0.284	0.263	0.243	0.225	0.209	0.194
10	0.352	0.322	0.295	0.270	0.247	0.227	0.208	0.191	0.176	0.162
11	0.317	0.287	0.261	0.237	0.215	0.195	0.178	0.162	0.148	0.135
12	0.286	0.257	0.231	0.208	0.187	0.168	0.152	0.137	0.124	0.112
13	0.258	0.229	0.204	0.182	0.163	0.145	0.130	0.116	0.104	0.093
14	0.232	0.205	0.181	0.160	0.141	0.125	0.111	0.099	0.088	0.078
15	0.209	0.183	0.160	0.140	0.123	0.108	0.095	0.084	0.074	0.065

Table 2 Binomial probabilities and cumulative binomial probabilities

Use this table to solve problems involving a series of n trials each of which can result in 'success' or 'failure'. Begin by finding the section of the table for the appropriate values of n (the number of trials) and p (the probability of success in any one trial). You can then use the table in three ways:

1. To find the probability that there are exactly x 'successes' in n trials look for the entry in the $P(x)$ column and the row for x.

2. To find the probability that there are x or fewer 'successes' in n trials look for the entry in the $P(X \leq x)$ column and the row for x.

3. To find the probability that there are more than x 'successes' in n trials, $P(X > x)$, look for the entry in the $P(X \leq x)$ column and the row for x. Subtract the figure you find from one. The result, $1 - P(X \leq x)$ is $P(X > x)$.

EXAMPLE

The probability of success in a trial is 0.3 and there are 5 trials. The probability that there are exactly 2 successes, $P(2)$, is 0.309. The probability that there are two or fewer successes, $P(X \leq 2)$ is 0.837. The probability that there are more than two successes, $P(X > 2)$, is $1 - 0.837, 0.163$.

For 5 trials ($n = 5$)

	$p = 0.1$		$p = 0.2$		$p = 0.3$		$p = 0.4$		$p = 0.5$	
	$P(x)$	$P(X \leq x)$	$P(x)$	$P(X \leq x)$	$P(x)$	$P(X \leq x)$	$P(x)$	$P(X \leq x)$	$P(x)$	$P(X \leq x)$
x: 0	0.590	0.590	0.328	0.328	0.168	0.168	0.078	0.078	0.031	0.031
x: 1	0.328	0.919	0.410	0.737	0.360	0.528	0.259	0.337	0.156	0.187
x: 2	0.073	0.991	0.205	0.942	0.309	0.837	0.346	0.683	0.313	0.500
x: 3	0.008	1.000	0.051	0.993	0.132	0.969	0.230	0.913	0.313	0.813
x: 4	0.000	1.000	0.006	1.000	0.028	0.998	0.077	0.990	0.156	0.969
x: 5	0.000	1.000	0.000	1.000	0.002	1.000	0.010	1.000	0.031	1.000

For 10 trials ($n = 10$)

	$p = 0.1$		$p = 0.2$		$p = 0.3$		$p = 0.4$		$p = 0.5$	
	$P(x)$	$P(X \leq x)$	$P(x)$	$P(X \leq x)$	$P(x)$	$P(X \leq x)$	$P(x)$	$P(X \leq x)$	$P(x)$	$P(X \leq x)$
x: 0	0.349	0.349	0.107	0.107	0.028	0.028	0.006	0.006	0.001	0.001
x: 1	0.387	0.736	0.268	0.376	0.121	0.149	0.040	0.046	0.010	0.011
x: 2	0.194	0.930	0.302	0.678	0.233	0.383	0.121	0.167	0.044	0.055
x: 3	0.057	0.987	0.201	0.879	0.267	0.650	0.215	0.382	0.117	0.172
x: 4	0.011	0.998	0.088	0.967	0.200	0.850	0.251	0.633	0.205	0.377
x: 5	0.001	1.000	0.026	0.994	0.103	0.953	0.201	0.834	0.246	0.623
x: 6	0.000	1.000	0.006	0.999	0.037	0.989	0.111	0.945	0.205	0.828
x: 7	0.000	1.000	0.001	1.000	0.009	0.998	0.042	0.988	0.117	0.945
x: 8	0.000	1.000	0.000	1.000	0.001	1.000	0.011	0.998	0.044	0.989
x: 9	0.000	1.000	0.000	1.000	0.000	1.000	0.002	1.000	0.010	0.999
x: 10	0.000	1.000	0.000	1.000	0.000	1.000	0.000	1.000	0.001	1.000

Table 3   Poisson probabilities and cumulative Poisson probabilities

Use this table to solve problems involving the number of incidents, x, that occurs during a period of time or over an area. Begin by finding the section of the table for the mean number of incidents per unit of time or space, μ. You can then use the table in three ways:

1. To find the probability that exactly x incidents occur look for the entry in the $P(x)$ column and the row for x.

2. To find the probability that there are x or fewer incidents look for the entry in the $P(X \leq x)$ column and the row for x.

3. To find the probability that there are more than x incidents, $P(X > x)$, look for the entry in the $P(X \leq x)$ column and the row for x. Subtract the figure you find from one. The result, $1 - P(X \leq x)$ is $P(X > x)$.

EXAMPLE

The mean number of incidents is 4. The probability that there are exactly 2 incidents, $P(2)$, is 0.147. The probability that there are two or fewer incidents, $P(X \leq 2)$ is 0.238. The probability that there are more than two incidents, $P(X > 2)$, is $1 - 0.238, 0.762$.

	$\mu = 1.0$		$\mu = 2.0$		$\mu = 3.0$		$\mu = 4.0$		$\mu = 5.0$	
	$P(x)$	$P(X \leq x)$	$P(x)$	$P(X \leq x)$	$P(x)$	$P(X \leq x)$	$P(x)$	$P(X \leq x)$	$P(x)$	$P(X \leq x)$
x: 0	0.368	0.368	0.135	0.135	0.050	0.050	0.018	0.018	0.007	0.007
x: 1	0.368	0.736	0.271	0.406	0.149	0.199	0.073	0.092	0.034	0.040
x: 2	0.184	0.920	0.271	0.677	0.224	0.423	0.147	0.238	0.084	0.125
x: 3	0.061	0.981	0.180	0.857	0.224	0.647	0.195	0.433	0.140	0.265
x: 4	0.015	0.996	0.090	0.947	0.168	0.815	0.195	0.629	0.175	0.440
x: 5	0.003	0.999	0.036	0.983	0.101	0.916	0.156	0.785	0.175	0.616
x: 6	0.001	1.000	0.012	0.995	0.050	0.966	0.104	0.889	0.146	0.762
x: 7	0.000	1.000	0.003	0.999	0.022	0.988	0.060	0.949	0.104	0.867
x: 8	0.000	1.000	0.001	1.000	0.008	0.996	0.030	0.979	0.065	0.932
x: 9	0.000	1.000	0.000	1.000	0.003	0.999	0.013	0.992	0.036	0.968
x: 10	0.000	1.000	0.000	1.000	0.001	1.000	0.005	0.997	0.018	0.986
x: 11	0.000	1.000	0.000	1.000	0.000	1.000	0.002	0.999	0.008	0.995
x: 12	0.000	1.000	0.000	1.000	0.000	1.000	0.001	1.000	0.003	0.998
x: 13	0.000	1.000	0.000	1.000	0.000	1.000	0.000	1.000	0.001	0.999
x: 14	0.000	1.000	0.000	1.000	0.000	1.000	0.000	1.000	0.000	1.000
x: 15	0.000	1.000	0.000	1.000	0.000	1.000	0.000	1.000	0.000	1.000

Table 4 **Random numbers**

Use this table by starting from some point in the table (you could choose this by putting your finger down somewhere on the table without looking at the table). Use the random numbers in strict sequence from that point either down from it, up from it, to the right of it or to the left of it.

EXAMPLE

Suppose we start from the seventh entry in the tenth column and decide to go down from that point. The sequence of numbers we would use are: 37 58 52 01 etc.

1	2	3	4	5	6	7	8	9	10	11	12	13	14	15
42	25	33	31	02	09	45	22	47	43	82	42	00	93	54
45	19	83	72	21	31	13	13	98	52	69	96	85	66	10
77	97	33	52	62	74	22	88	53	91	52	34	54	82	81
38	03	38	43	40	71	31	13	90	95	55	16	44	75	60
98	28	37	30	52	41	79	75	95	25	31	97	72	82	23
59	01	27	34	52	61	33	75	64	88	87	79	40	94	91
14	26	71	56	76	51	00	42	95	37	25	73	74	42	18
92	16	76	70	23	98	06	69	76	58	89	43	58	29	23
35	34	09	18	17	34	11	32	78	52	07	05	39	98	25
84	22	97	30	02	34	93	15	59	01	97	43	10	90	66
07	72	31	79	66	18	01	80	90	84	93	85	61	46	17
50	37	30	61	42	01	53	02	93	82	59	25	90	81	51
30	39	71	29	65	19	95	34	61	91	00	92	35	55	92
36	54	68	01	91	97	95	89	82	75	68	95	40	58	37
15	75	66	52	73	69	32	00	25	89	44	56	60	42	58
28	30	77	44	16	16	90	76	32	38	86	55	81	00	04
03	41	28	95	96	19	71	56	86	99	59	10	61	31	81
20	83	85	13	43	03	09	41	69	31	08	66	01	78	23
06	51	04	97	18	68	73	25	76	94	57	04	08	53	13
39	77	12	45	53	48	52	69	72	05	02	77	88	37	16
81	35	60	28	48	21	75	17	50	88	96	78	01	65	01
72	50	45	71	90	99	67	01	12	37	05	43	44	24	77
83	15	08	28	66	16	72	13	10	68	26	61	59	06	92
66	46	23	38	37	08	71	76	22	79	79	11	68	25	08
09	02	24	39	40	77	71	97	70	50	13	98	32	46	02
94	82	36	40	08	12	08	98	41	99	87	54	54	71	73
64	95	39	07	49	32	12	51	84	75	96	44	64	55	94
76	39	06	67	66	36	61	66	46	95	08	26	04	36	78
54	15	15	22	37	25	63	62	61	79	33	52	98	45	15
61	45	16	62	79	84	18	12	25	90	98	12	05	93	91
21	74	66	52	01	96	26	29	04	58	14	97	89	06	75
13	12	32	82	23	99	19	57	73	94	69	31	03	89	00
60	19	52	31	55	90	92	27	61	75	24	26	10	22	96
08	78	10	09	73	45	00	51	13	00	74	76	35	23	50
01	01	19	39	72	27	49	78	62	14	72	45	39	66	18
09	09	58	93	31	33	33	85	79	93	02	30	27	39	51
45	67	71	94	64	80	24	35	39	41	37	48	05	48	54
44	03	31	59	42	84	09	23	09	60	89	38	69	98	60
47	19	04	04	43	65	21	36	19	88	35	54	04	29	08
48	36	42	24	17	96	09	03	77	43	74	78	41	35	39
73	60	54	56	80	79	97	78	62	32	16	00	32	40	54
69	32	50	14	43	38	04	66	17	53	26	59	77	52	77
38	81	23	56	78	59	43	98	08	87	30	54	87	66	85
09	36	85	37	60	80	54	74	16	98	67	21	03	22	88
60	67	85	05	80	22	59	89	12	43	46	04	53	52	12
55	11	45	15	35	41	25	45	40	12	73	04	65	95	77
86	23	12	64	73	37	37	43	51	19	12	46	30	84	03
02	61	75	96	96	84	06	92	14	46	83	77	24	32	76
78	40	58	13	07	36	48	38	81	21	71	39	23	88	10
30	10	85	02	44	44	48	91	20	34	59	79	36	03	98

Table 5 Cumulative probabilities for the standard normal distribution

This table describes the pattern of variation of the standard normal variable, Z, which has a mean, μ, of 0 and a standard deviation, σ, of 1. You can use this table to find proportions of the area of the distribution that lie either to the right or to the left of a particular value of Z, z.

To find the proportion of the area to the right of z, which represents the probability that Z is greater than z, $P(Z > z)$, find the row for the value of z to the first decimal place and then look across the columns until you reach the column associated with the second figure after the decimal place.

EXAMPLE 1

The probability that Z is greater than -1.61 is in the row for -1.6 and in the column labelled 0.01. $P(Z > -1.61) = 0.9463$.

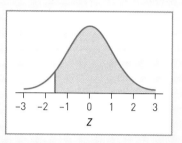

EXAMPLE 2

The probability that Z is greater than 0.58 is in the row for 0.5 in the column labelled 0.08. $P(Z > 0.58) = 0.2810$.

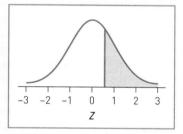

EXAMPLE 3

To obtain the probability that Z is less than -0.84, first find the figure in the row for -0.8 and in the column labelled 0.04. This is $P(Z > -0.84)$, 0.7995. $P(Z \leq 0.84) = 1 - 0.7995 = 0.2005$.

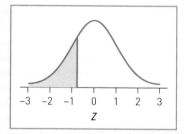

EXAMPLE 4

To obtain the probability that Z is less than 2.09, first find the figure in the row for 2.0 and in the column labelled 0.09. This is $P(Z > 2.09)$, 0.0183. $P(Z < 2.09) = 1 - 0.0183 = 0.9817$.

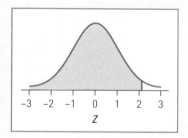

Z	0.00	0.01	0.02	0.03	0.04	0.05	0.06	0.07	0.08	0.09
−2.9	0.9981	0.9982	0.9982	0.9983	0.9984	0.9984	0.9985	0.9985	0.9986	0.9986
−2.8	0.9974	0.9975	0.9976	0.9977	0.9977	0.9978	0.9979	0.9979	0.9980	0.9981
−2.7	0.9965	0.9966	0.9967	0.9968	0.9969	0.9970	0.9971	0.9972	0.9973	0.9974
−2.6	0.9953	0.9955	0.9956	0.9957	0.9959	0.9960	0.9961	0.9962	0.9963	0.9964
−2.5	0.9938	0.9940	0.9941	0.9943	0.9945	0.9946	0.9948	0.9949	0.9951	0.9952
−2.4	0.9918	0.9920	0.9922	0.9925	0.9927	0.9929	0.9931	0.9932	0.9934	0.9936
−2.3	0.9893	0.9896	0.9898	0.9901	0.9904	0.9906	0.9909	0.9911	0.9913	0.9916
−2.2	0.9861	0.9864	0.9868	0.9871	0.9875	0.9878	0.9881	0.9884	0.9887	0.9890
−2.1	0.9821	0.9826	0.9830	0.9834	0.9838	0.9842	0.9846	0.9850	0.9854	0.9857
−2.0	0.9772	0.9778	0.9783	0.9788	0.9793	0.9798	0.9803	0.9808	0.9812	0.9817
−1.9	0.9713	0.9719	0.9726	0.9732	0.9738	0.9744	0.9750	0.9756	0.9761	0.9767
−1.8	0.9641	0.9649	0.9656	0.9664	0.9671	0.9678	0.9686	0.9693	0.9699	0.9706
−1.7	0.9554	0.9564	0.9573	0.9582	0.9591	0.9599	0.9608	0.9616	0.9625	0.9633
−1.6	0.9452	0.9463	0.9474	0.9484	0.9495	0.9505	0.9515	0.9525	0.9535	0.9545
−1.5	0.9332	0.9345	0.9357	0.9370	0.9382	0.9394	0.9406	0.9418	0.9429	0.9441
−1.4	0.9192	0.9207	0.9222	0.9236	0.9251	0.9265	0.9279	0.9292	0.9306	0.9319
−1.3	0.9032	0.9049	0.9066	0.9082	0.9099	0.9115	0.9131	0.9147	0.9162	0.9177
−1.2	0.8849	0.8869	0.8888	0.8907	0.8925	0.8944	0.8962	0.8980	0.8997	0.9015
−1.1	0.8643	0.8665	0.8686	0.8708	0.8729	0.8749	0.8770	0.8790	0.8810	0.8830
−1.0	0.8413	0.8438	0.8461	0.8485	0.8508	0.8531	0.8554	0.8577	0.8599	0.8621
−0.9	0.8159	0.8186	0.8212	0.8238	0.8264	0.8289	0.8315	0.8340	0.8365	0.8389
−0.8	0.7881	0.7910	0.7939	0.7967	0.7995	0.8023	0.8051	0.8078	0.8106	0.8133
−0.7	0.7580	0.7611	0.7642	0.7673	0.7703	0.7734	0.7764	0.7794	0.7823	0.7852
−0.6	0.7257	0.7291	0.7324	0.7357	0.7389	0.7422	0.7454	0.7486	0.7517	0.7549
−0.5	0.6915	0.6950	0.6985	0.7019	0.7054	0.7088	0.7123	0.7157	0.7190	0.7224
−0.4	0.6554	0.6591	0.6628	0.6664	0.6700	0.6736	0.6772	0.6808	0.6844	0.6879
−0.3	0.6179	0.6217	0.6255	0.6293	0.6331	0.6368	0.6406	0.6443	0.6480	0.6517
−0.2	0.5793	0.5832	0.5871	0.5910	0.5948	0.5987	0.6026	0.6064	0.6103	0.6141
−0.1	0.5398	0.5438	0.5478	0.5517	0.5557	0.5596	0.5636	0.5675	0.5714	0.5753
−0.0	0.5000	0.5040	0.5080	0.5120	0.5160	0.5199	0.5239	0.5279	0.5319	0.5359
0.0	0.5000	0.4960	0.4920	0.4880	0.4840	0.4801	0.4761	0.4721	0.4681	0.4641
0.1	0.4602	0.4562	0.4522	0.4483	0.4443	0.4404	0.4364	0.4325	0.4286	0.4247
0.2	0.4207	0.4168	0.4129	0.4090	0.4052	0.4013	0.3974	0.3936	0.3897	0.3859
0.3	0.3821	0.3783	0.3745	0.3707	0.3669	0.3632	0.3594	0.3557	0.3520	0.3483
0.4	0.3446	0.3409	0.3372	0.3336	0.3300	0.3264	0.3228	0.3192	0.3156	0.3121
0.5	0.3085	0.3050	0.3015	0.2981	0.2946	0.2912	0.2877	0.2843	0.2810	0.2776
0.6	0.2743	0.2709	0.2676	0.2643	0.2611	0.2578	0.2546	0.2514	0.2483	0.2451
0.7	0.2420	0.2389	0.2358	0.2327	0.2297	0.2266	0.2236	0.2206	0.2177	0.2148
0.8	0.2119	0.2090	0.2061	0.2033	0.2005	0.1977	0.1949	0.1922	0.1894	0.1867
0.9	0.1841	0.1814	0.1788	0.1762	0.1736	0.1711	0.1685	0.1660	0.1635	0.1611
1.0	0.1587	0.1562	0.1539	0.1515	0.1492	0.1469	0.1446	0.1423	0.1401	0.1379
1.1	0.1357	0.1335	0.1314	0.1292	0.1271	0.1251	0.1230	0.1210	0.1190	0.1170
1.2	0.1151	0.1131	0.1112	0.1093	0.1075	0.1056	0.1038	0.1020	0.1003	0.0985
1.3	0.0968	0.0951	0.0934	0.0918	0.0901	0.0885	0.0869	0.0853	0.0838	0.0823
1.4	0.0808	0.0793	0.0778	0.0764	0.0749	0.0735	0.0721	0.0708	0.0694	0.0681
1.5	0.0668	0.0655	0.0643	0.0630	0.0618	0.0606	0.0594	0.0582	0.0571	0.0559
1.6	0.0548	0.0537	0.0526	0.0516	0.0505	0.0495	0.0485	0.0475	0.0465	0.0455
1.7	0.0446	0.0436	0.0427	0.0418	0.0409	0.0401	0.0392	0.0384	0.0375	0.0367
1.8	0.0359	0.0351	0.0344	0.0336	0.0329	0.0322	0.0314	0.0307	0.0301	0.0294
1.9	0.0287	0.0281	0.0274	0.0268	0.0262	0.0256	0.0250	0.0244	0.0239	0.0233
2.0	0.0228	0.0222	0.0217	0.0212	0.0207	0.0202	0.0197	0.0192	0.0188	0.0183
2.1	0.0179	0.0174	0.0170	0.0166	0.0162	0.0158	0.0154	0.0150	0.0146	0.0143
2.2	0.0139	0.0136	0.0132	0.0129	0.0125	0.0122	0.0119	0.0116	0.0113	0.0110
2.3	0.0107	0.0104	0.0102	0.0099	0.0096	0.0094	0.0091	0.0089	0.0087	0.0084
2.4	0.0082	0.0080	0.0078	0.0075	0.0073	0.0071	0.0069	0.0068	0.0066	0.0064
2.5	0.0062	0.0060	0.0059	0.0057	0.0055	0.0054	0.0052	0.0051	0.0049	0.0048
2.6	0.0047	0.0045	0.0044	0.0043	0.0041	0.0040	0.0039	0.0038	0.0037	0.0036
2.7	0.0035	0.0034	0.0033	0.0032	0.0031	0.0030	0.0029	0.0028	0.0027	0.0026
2.8	0.0026	0.0025	0.0024	0.0023	0.0023	0.0022	0.0021	0.0021	0.0020	0.0019
2.9	0.0019	0.0018	0.0018	0.0017	0.0016	0.0016	0.0015	0.0015	0.0014	0.0014

Table 6 **Selected points of the *t* distribution**

This table provides values of the *t* distribution, with different numbers of degrees of freedom, which cut off certain tail areas to the right of the distribution, $t_{\alpha,v}$. To use it you will need to know the number of degrees of freedom, v, and the size of the tail area, α. Find the row for the number of degrees of freedom and then look to the right along the row until you come to the figure in the column for the appropriate tail area.

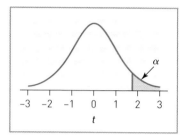

EXAMPLE

The value in the *t* distribution with 7 degrees of freedom that cuts off a tail area of 0.05, $t_{0.05,7}$ is in the row for 7 degrees of freedom and the column headed 0.05, 1.895.

v	0.10	0.05	0.025	0.01	0.005
1	3.078	6.314	12.706	31.821	63.657
2	1.886	2.920	4.303	6.965	9.925
3	1.638	2.353	3.182	4.541	5.841
4	1.533	2.132	2.776	3.747	4.604
5	1.476	2.015	2.571	3.365	4.032
6	1.440	1.943	2.447	3.143	3.707
7	1.415	1.895	2.365	2.998	3.499
8	1.397	1.860	2.306	2.896	3.355
9	1.383	1.833	2.262	2.821	3.250
10	1.372	1.812	2.228	2.764	3.169
11	1.363	1.796	2.201	2.718	3.106
12	1.356	1.782	2.179	2.681	3.055
13	1.350	1.771	2.160	2.650	3.012
14	1.345	1.761	2.145	2.624	2.977
15	1.341	1.753	2.131	2.602	2.947
16	1.337	1.746	2.120	2.583	2.921
17	1.333	1.740	2.110	2.567	2.898
18	1.330	1.734	2.101	2.552	2.878
19	1.328	1.729	2.093	2.539	2.861
20	1.325	1.725	2.086	2.528	2.845
21	1.323	1.721	2.080	2.518	2.831
22	1.321	1.717	2.074	2.508	2.819
23	1.319	1.714	2.069	2.500	2.807
24	1.318	1.711	2.064	2.492	2.797
25	1.316	1.708	2.060	2.485	2.787
26	1.315	1.706	2.056	2.479	2.779
27	1.314	1.703	2.052	2.473	2.771
28	1.313	1.701	2.048	2.467	2.763
29	1.311	1.699	2.045	2.462	2.756
30	1.310	1.697	2.042	2.457	2.750
50	1.299	1.676	2.009	2.403	2.678
100	1.290	1.660	1.984	2.364	2.626
∞	1.282	1.645	1.960	2.326	2.576

Note: as the number of degrees of freedom increases, the *t* distribution becomes more like the standard normal distribution. Look at the bottom row of this table and you will see a row of *t* values that are from the *t* distribution that has an infinite (∞) number of degrees of freedom. This 'extreme' *t* distribution is the standard normal distribution, and the figures along the bottom row here can also be found in Table 5: for example, look up the *z* value 1.96 in Table 5 and you will see the probability that *Z* is more than 1.96 is 0.025. In this table 1.96 is listed as the value of *t* with infinite degrees of freedom that cuts off a tail area of 0.025.

Table 7   **Selected points of the *F* distribution**

This table provides values of the *F* distribution, with different numbers of degrees of freedom for the numerator and denominator, which cut off tail areas of 0.05 and 0.01 to the right of the distribution, $F_{v1,v2,\alpha}$. To use it you will need to know the degrees of freedom of the numerator, v_1, the degrees of freedom of the denominator, v_2, and the size of the tail area, α. Find the column for the degrees of freedom for the numerator and the row for the degrees of freedom for the denominator. The upper figure in the cell you have located is the *F* value that cuts off a tail area of 0.05, the lower figure, in italics, is the *F* value that cuts off a tail area of 0.01.

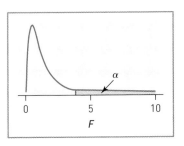

EXAMPLE

The value in the *F* distribution with 3 numerator degrees of freedom and 7 denominator degrees of freedom that cuts off a tail area of 0.05, $F_{3,7,0.05}$ is the upper figure in the column for 3 degrees of freedom and the row for 7 degrees of freedom, 4.35. The figure below it, 8.45, is $F_{3,7,0.01}$.

			v_1		
v_2	1	2	3	4	5
1	161.45	199.50	215.71	224.58	230.16
	4050.00	*5000.00*	*5040.00*	*5620.00*	*5760.00*
2	18.51	19.00	19.16	19.25	19.30
	98.50	*99.00*	*99.17*	*99.25*	*99.30*
3	10.13	9.55	9.28	9.12	9.01
	34.12	*30.82*	*29.46*	*28.71*	*28.24*
4	7.71	6.94	6.59	6.39	6.26
	21.20	*18.00*	*16.69*	*15.98*	*15.52*
5	6.61	5.79	5.41	5.19	5.05
	16.26	*13.27*	*12.06*	*11.39*	*10.97*
6	5.99	5.14	4.76	4.53	4.39
	13.75	*10.92*	*9.78*	*9.15*	*8.75*
7	5.59	4.74	4.35	4.12	3.97
	12.25	*9.55*	*8.45*	*7.85*	*7.46*
8	5.32	4.46	4.07	3.84	3.69
	11.26	*8.65*	*7.59*	*7.01*	*6.63*
9	5.12	4.26	3.86	3.63	3.48
	10.56	*8.02*	*6.99*	*6.42*	*6.06*
10	4.96	4.10	3.71	3.48	3.33
	10.04	*7.56*	*6.55*	*5.99*	*5.64*
11	4.84	3.98	3.59	3.36	3.20
	9.65	*7.21*	*6.22*	*5.95*	*5.32*
12	4.75	3.89	3.49	3.26	3.11
	9.33	*6.93*	*5.95*	*5.41*	*5.06*
13	4.67	3.81	3.41	3.18	3.03
	9.07	*6.70*	*5.74*	*5.21*	*4.86*
14	4.60	3.74	3.34	3.11	2.96
	8.86	*6.51*	*5.56*	*5.04*	*4.70*
15	4.54	3.68	3.29	3.06	2.90
	8.68	*6.36*	*5.42*	*4.89*	*4.56*

Table 8 Selected points of the chi-square distribution

This table provides values of the χ^2 distribution, with different numbers of degrees of freedom, which cut off certain tail areas to the right of the distribution, $\chi_{\alpha,\nu}^2$. To use it you will need to know the number of degrees of freedom, ν, and the size of the tail area, α. Find the row for the number of degrees of freedom and then look to the right along the row until you come to the figure in the column for the appropriate tail area.

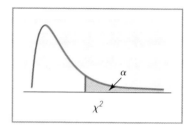

EXAMPLE

The value in the χ^2 distribution with 3 degrees of freedom that cuts off a tail area of 0.05, $\chi_{0.05,3}^2$, is in the row for 3 degrees of freedom and the column headed 0.05, 7.815.

ν	0.10	0.05	0.01
1	2.706	3.841	6.635
2	4.605	5.991	9.210
3	6.251	7.815	11.345
4	7.779	9.488	13.277
5	9.236	11.070	15.086
6	10.645	12.592	16.812
7	12.017	14.067	18.475
8	13.362	15.507	20.090
9	14.684	16.919	21.666
10	15.987	18.307	23.209

APPENDIX 2

Answers to review questions

Answers are either precise or accurate to at least three decimal places unless stated otherwise.

Fully worked solutions are on the supporting website (**www.pearsoned.co.uk/buglear**). These include the diagrams that feature in some questions but are not included here.

Chapter 1

To the right of the answer, in square brackets [ ], are the Chapter 1 Example or Examples that are most like the question. If you haven't obtained the right answer, look at them for guidance.

1.1 (i) (g), (ii) (h), (iii) (f), (iv) (e), (v) (a), (vi) (j), (vii) (d), (viii) (b), (ix) (c), (x) (i)   [1.15, 1.21]

1.2 (i) (b), (ii) (c), (iii) (h), (iv) (f), (v) (g), (vi) (a), (vii) (e), (viii) (d)   [1.13, 1.14]

1.3 (i) (e), (ii) (g), (iii) (a), (iv) (c), (v) (f), (vi) (b), (vii) (d)   [1.16, 1.17]

1.4 (a) (i) Total 6,875,000; Italy 1,440,000; USA 543,400; Australia 197,000
   (ii) Total 6,900,000; Italy 1,400,000; USA 540,000; Australia 200,000   [1.19]
   (b) Italy 0.209; USA 0.079; Australia 0.029   [1.20]

1.5 (a) 26, (b) 17 sales operatives, (c) £7010   [1.2, 1.22]

1.6 (a) 13.45, (b) 15.00 the next day   [1.7]

1.7 324   [1.16]

1.8 425   [1.8, 1.9]

1.9 Alexander 51%, Pass; Bukhtar 50%, Pass; Ciani 38.8%, Fail (less than 40%);
   Dalkiro 45.8%, Fail (exam less than 35%); Elchin 43.8%, Pass;
   Franklin 38.2%, Fail (less than 40%)   [1.16]

1.10 £2995.40   [1.16]

1.11 34.456   [1.9, 1.11]

1.12 (a) £2520, (b) £1890   [1.9, 1.11]

Chapter 2

To the right of the answer, in square brackets [ ], are the Chapter 2 Example or Examples that are most like the question. If you haven't obtained the right answer, look at them for guidance.

2.1 (a) Budget $= 35,000 + 500x$ where x is the number of corporate clients
  (b) (i) £56,500 (ii) £49,500 (iii) £68,000
  (c) Budget $= 20000 + 800x$; Ashford £54,400 (down £2100); Byfleet £43,200
     (down £6300); Carlton £72,800 (up £4800) [2.1, 2.2]

2.2 (a) $x = 1, y = 2$ (b) $x = 2, y = 3$ (c) $x = 5, y = -1$ (d) $x = 0.5, y = 4$ [2.10]

2.3 (a) 5,800 (b) £11,000; 3.333% [2.11, 2.12]

2.4 110 litres of Smazka and 70 litres of Neftianikov. Profit $=$ £830 [2.13 − 2.22]

2.5 25,000 [2.10]

2.6 (a) 32,000 scooters (b) 40,000 scooters [2.11]

2.7 (a) 1400 (b) Increases to 1120 [2.11]

2.8 No Houstons and 1,500 Soap Dishes giving a profit of £24,000 [2.13 − 2.22]

2.9 (a) 60,000 bottles of Volossy, 60,000 bottles of Sedina giving a profit of £36,000
  (b) Solidifier and licence are tight, colourant and commitments slack [2.13 − 2.22]

2.10 (a) 12 peak and 24 off-peak slots to reach an audience of 264m
  (b) 60 off-peak and no peak slots to reach an audience of 300m [2.13 − 2.22]

2.11 No pairs of Nelson and 200 pairs of Oldham giving a profit of £2400 [2.13 − 2.22]

2.12 18kg of Seelni-swine and 28kg of Vita-sosiska at a cost of £780 [2.23]

Chapter 3

To the right of the answer, in square brackets [ ], are the Chapter 3 Example or Examples that are most like the question. If you haven't obtained the right answer, look at them for guidance.

3.1 Own diagram [3.2]

3.2 £21m, £36m, £45m, £48m, £45m [3.2]

3.3 (a) 36 [3.6]
  (b) Second derivative is positive (1), so a minimum [3.8]
  (c) £652 [3.7]

3.4 40 litres [3.11]

3.5 (i) (f), (ii) (c), (iii) (g), (iv) (a), (v) (b), (vi) (j), (vii) (d), (viii) (e), (ix) (h), (x) (i) [3.6]

3.6 (a) £25
  (b) Second derivative is negative $(-2/5)$, so a maximum
  (c) £35,000 [3.9]

3.7 (a) Profit $= 480x - 4x^2 - 150$
  (b) Produce 60 and sell at £20 giving a profit of £14,250
  (c) Second derivative is negative (-8), so a maximum [3.9]

3.8 130kg [3.11]

3.9 (a) Profit $= 630x - 3.5x^2 - 450$
  (b) Sell 90, price $=$ £365, profit $=$ £27,900
  (c) Negative (-7), so a maximum [3.9]

3.10 (a) 320kg (b) Yes, maximum stock will be 320kg (c) 267.731kg [3.11]

3.11 (a) 208 litres (b) Not at all [3.11]

3.12 (a) 400 bags (b) 200 bags [3.11]

Chapter 4

To the right of the answer, in square brackets [ ], are the Chapter 4 Example or Examples that are most like the question. If you haven't obtained the right answer, look at them for guidance.

4.1   (a) (v), (b) (vi), (c) (i), (d) (ii), (e) (iii), (f) (iv)   [Table 4.1]

4.2

Type of transaction	Number of customers
Cash only	180
Balance check only	90
Deposit only	36
More than one transaction	54
Total	360

[4.3]

4.3

Number of bedrooms	Number of houses
2	6
3	5
4	7
5	2
Total	20

[4.6]

4.4

Number of trips	Number of executives
0–2	6
3–5	6
6–8	8
9–11	11
12–14	8
15–17	2
Total	41

[4.7]

4.5   Qualitative (b) (e); Discrete quantitative (d) (f); Continuous (a) (c)   [4.3]

4.6   (a) (iv), (b) (vii), (c) (v), (d) (ii), (e) (viii), (f) (iii), (g) (i), (h) (vi)

4.7

Experience	Females	Males	Total
No retail	19	9	28
Retail	23	22	45
Clothing retail	32	22	54
Total	74	53	127

[4.5]

4.8

Price (£)	Frequency
1000 and under 2000	6
2000 and under 3000	7
3000 and under 4000	5
4000 and under 5000	8
5000 and under 6000	1
Total	27

[4.7]

4.9   Nominal (d) (g); ordinal (a) (c) (f) (h); interval (i); ratio (b) (e)   [4.2]

4.10

Type of booking	One night	More than one night	Total
Business	672	141	813
Functions	162	23	185
Leisure	106	256	362
Total	940	420	1360

[4.5]

4.11

Wage (£)	Frequency
4.00–4.99	9
5.00–5.99	13
6.00–6.99	6
7.00–7.99	3
8.00–8.99	1
Total	32

[4.7]

4.12 (a) and (b)

Visit duration (minutes)	Redcar (%)	Skegness (%)	Torquay (%)
0 and under 20	2 (9.5%)	2 (11.1%)	17 (85.0%)
20 and under 40	12 (57.1%)	9 (50.0%)	3 (15.0%)
40 and under 60	3 (14.3%)	4 (22.2%)	0 (0.0%)
60 and under 80	4 (19.1%)	3 (16.7%)	0 (0.0%)
Total	21 (100.0%)	18 (100.0%)	20 (100.0%)

(c) 90.5% of visits in Redcar, 88.9% of visits in Skegness, and 15% of visits
in Torquay last at least 20 minutes   [4.7, 4.9]

Chapter 5

Most of the review questions require charts or diagrams. These are provided on the supporting web-site (**www.pearsoned.co.uk/buglear**). To the right of the question number, in square brackets [ ], are the Chapter 5 Example or Examples that are most like the question. If you are not sure how to do the question, look at them for guidance.

5.1   Own diagram   [5.3]

5.2   Own diagram   [5.7]

5.3 (a) Own diagram.
(b) Symmetrical   [5.8]

5.4

Stem	Leaves
3	2 5 6
4	1 3 4 8
5	1 1 4 7
6	2 2 5 7 7 7 8
7	0 2
	Leaf unit = 1 year

[5.15]

5.5 Own diagram. A direct relationship   [5.21]

5.6 Own diagram   [5.22]

5.7 Own diagrams   [5.3, 5.4, 5.6]

5.8 (a) Own diagram   [5.8]

(b)

Weight lost (kg)	Cumulative frequency
0 and under 2	3
2 and under 4	6
4 and under 6	10
6 and under 8	17
8 and under 10	41
10 and under 12	50

[5.11]

(c) Own diagram   [5.12]

5.9 (a)

Adventure holiday	Stem	Cruise
9 8 7 4 4 2 1	2	
9 7 6 5 4 2 2 2 0	3	2 5 6
6 5 2 0	4	1 3 4 8
3 1	5	1 1 4 7
	6	2 2 5 7 7 7 8
	7	0 2
		Leaf unit = 1 year

(b) Cruise passengers tend to be older

5.10 Own diagram   [5.23]

5.11

Stem	Leaves
1	95
2	00 05 10 30 45 68
3	10 25 40 50 64 75 89 90
4	00 09 12 25 45 60 75
5	00
	Leaf unit = £1000

5.12 (a) Engine size
(b) Own diagram   [5.21]
(c) Direct

Chapter 6

To the right of the answer, in square brackets [ ], are the Chapter 6 Example or Examples that are most like the question. If you haven't obtained the right answer, look at them for guidance.

6.1 (a) Mode = 2, Median = 2 [6.1, 6.3]
(b) Mean = 2.92 − higher, suggesting positive skew [6.5, 6.8]
(c) Own diagram [6.7]

6.2 (a) Mode = 1, Median = 2, Mean = 2.321. Mode is lowest, mean is highest [6.1, 6.3, 6.8]
(b) Own diagram [6.7]

6.3 Q1 = 1, Q3 = 4, SIQR = 1.5 [6.18, 6.19]

6.4 Mean = 25.118 (25,118 miles); Standard deviation = 6.451 (6.451 miles) [6.5, 6.27]

6.5 Females: Mode = 2, median = 2, mean = 2.030
Males: Mode = 1, median = 2, mean = 2.144
Females have higher mode, lower mean and more symmetrical distribution [6.6]

6.6 (a) Mode = 13, range = 28 [6.1, 6.17]
(b) Median = 13 [6.3]
(c) Q1 = 10, Q3 = 19 [6.18]
(d) SIQR = 4.5 [6.19]

6.7 Positive skewed [6.21]

6.8 Median is approximately 6150 litres, SIQR is approximately 475 litres [6.15, 6.30]

6.9 (a) Cyclists: Mean = 7.197 km, median = 7 km
Motorists: Mean = 14.467 km, median = 14.545 km [6.14, 6.16]
(b) Standard deviations: Cyclists = 4.496 km, Motorists = 5.345 km [6.31]
(c) Cyclists have a lower mean and spread

6.10 (a) False   (b) False   (c) True   (d) False   (e) False   (f) True

6.11 (a) False, (b) True, (c) True, (d) True, (e) False, (f) True, (g) True

6.12 Own diagram [6.32]

Chapter 7

To the right of the answer, in square brackets [ ], are the Chapter 7 Example or Examples that are most like the question. If you haven't obtained the right answer, look at them for guidance.

7.1 (a) positive, (b) negative, (c) negative, (d) negative, (e) positive,
(f) positive, (g) negative [7.1, 7.2]

7.2 (a) Own diagram
(b) 0.996; strong, positive [7.1, 7.4]

7.3 0.543; weak, positive [7.7]

7.4 Contamination level = −1.776 + 10.020 Hours worked [7.13]

7.5 (a) Cost
(b) Own diagram
(c) 0.907; strong, positive [7.3]

7.6 −0.762; fair, negative [7.7]

7.7 (a) League position
(b) Own diagram
(c) League position = 29.182 − 0.649 Goals scored   [7.13]
(d) AFC Wonderland; high league position for the number of goals scored

7.8 (a) 4320 units
(b) 6690 units
(c) 57,840 units   [7.14]
(d) 0.805   [7.6]

7.9 (a) 0.971   [7.5]
(b) Strong, positive

7.10 0.624; fair, positive   [7.6]

7.11 (a) Mean hourly wage
(b) Own diagram
(c) Mean hourly wage ($) = 10.333 + 0.338 Union membership (%)   [7.13]
(d) 0.713 (71.3%); the model explains 71.13% of the wage variation   [7.6]

7.12 (a) Own diagram
(b) Motorway network = 219.924 + 17.729 Land area   [7.13]
(c) 0.542 (54.2%); the model explains 54.2% of the network variation   [7.6]
(d) The country with land area of 337km^2 and network of 394 km

Chapter 8

To the right of the answer, in square brackets [ ], are the Chapter 8 Example or Examples that are most like the question. If you haven't obtained the right answer, look at them for guidance.

8.1 (a) (i) 143.478, (ii) 134.783, (iii) 113.793, (iv) 106.897   [8.1]

8.2 123.709 (2010), 134.247 (2011)   [8.2]

8.3 415.602 (2002), 437.836 (2004), 421.237 (2006), 396.415 (2008), 399.855 (2010).
Increases to 2004 then decreases   [8.5]

8.4 (a) 50%   [8.6]
(b) Half-way through the third year   [8.7]

8.5 (a) 149.580   [8.3]
(b) 144.265   [8.4]

8.6 (a) 72.971   [8.5]
(b) 27.638   [8.5]

8.7 (a) 3.75 years   [8.7]
(b) £2320   [8.11]
(c) −£2010   [8.11]

8.8 (a) −£7330   [8.12]
(b) £11,180; IRR is about 13%   [8.13]

8.9 (a) 120.070 (2008), 131.690 (2011)   [8.3]
(b) 120.454   [8.4]
(c) 131.819   [8.4]

8.10 L: 22.486 (2006), 21.096 (2007), 21.810 (2008), 25.516 (2009), 24.386 (2010)
Z: 18.900 (2006), 18.773 (2007), 18.503 (2008), 19.227 (2009), 17.946 (2010)

L: revenue in 2010 is approximately 12.4% higher than in 2005

Z: revenue in 2010 is approximately 2.5% lower than in 2005   [8.5]

8.11 (a) −$4.903m   [8.12]

(b) $3.632m; IRR is about 17%   [8.13]

8.12 (a) 4.111 years (Markets), 4.0 years (Riverside)   [8.7]

(b) £51,780 (Markets), £17,870 (Riverside)   [8.12]

(c) Markets; the payback is marginally longer but the NPV is much higher

Chapter 9

To the right of the answer, in square brackets [ ], are the Chapter 9 Example or Examples that are most like the question. If you haven't obtained the right answer, look at them for guidance.

9.1 (a) Own diagram

(b) 9, 10, 11, 12, 13, 13, 14   [9.2]

9.2 (a) Own diagram

(b) 14.0375, 14.3625, 14.3750, 14.6500, 15.3125, 15.8500, 16.0125, 16.1375   [9.3]

9.3 (a) 63, 57.4, 50.68, 46.136, 50.027, 38.805, 41.361, 37.872   [9.11]

(b) Own diagram

9.4 (a) Morning 4.556, Afternoon −3.611, Evening −0.944   [9.4, 9.5]

(b) 0.455   [9.6, 9.8]

9.5 (a) Morning 1.383, Afternoon 0.696, Evening 0.921   [9.9]

(b) 0.162, (c) Lower than 9.4 (b) so multiplicative model is more appropriate   [9.9]

9.6 (a) −1.514 (Q1), 1.936 (Q2), −6.045 (Q3), 5.623 (Q4)   [9.4, 9.5]

(b) 0.877   [9.6, 9.8]

9.7 (a) 0.904 (Q1), 1.128 (Q2), 0.595 (Q3), 1.373 (Q4)   [9.9]

(b) 0.549   [9.9]

(c) Multiplicative model   [9.9]

9.8 (a) Month 10 = 273.809   [9.11]

(b) Own diagram

9.9 21.667, 11.484, 15.964   [9.10]

9.10 15.402, 19.557, 10.494, 24.628   [9.10]

9.11 (a) Day 9 = 140.397, MSD = 2986.376   [9.11]

(b) Day 9 = 180.466, MSD = 1919.384 Better   [9.11]

9.12 (a) Week 10 = 405.547, MSD = 8307.63   [9.11]

(b) Week 10 = 349.935, MSD = 8648.863; model in (a) is better   [9.11]

Chapter 10

To the right of the answer, in square brackets [ ], are the Chapter 10 Example or Examples that are most like the question. If you haven't obtained the right answer, look at them for guidance.

10.1 (a) 0.552, (b) 0.295, (c) 0.154, (d) 0.448   [10.2, 10.5]

10.2 (a) 0.446, (b) 0.105, (c) 0.449   [10.2]

10.3 (a) (i) 0.208, (ii) 0.063, (iii) 0.275   [10.2]

(b) No   [10.12]

10.4 (a) (i) 0.353, (ii) 0.547, (iii) 0.147, (iv) 0.273   [10.3–10.6]
      (b) No   [10.12]

10.5 (a) 0.733, (b) 0.272   [10.3]
      (c) 0.121   [10.4]
      (d) 0.868   [10.6]
      (e) Country and recognition are not independent   [10.12]

10.6 (a) 0.344   [10.3]
      (b) 0.032   [10.4]
      (c) 0.656   [10.5]
      (d) 0.529, (e) 0.087   [10.6]
      (f) They are not independent   [10.12]

10.7 (a) 0.56, (b) 0.14, (c) 0.18, (d) 0.12   [10.11, 10.18]

10.8 0.0408   [10.18]

10.9 (a) 0.24, (b) 0.072   [10.18]

10.10 (a) 0.4725, (b) 0.4125, (c) 0.0075   [10.18]

10.11 0.95   [10.18]

10.12 (a) 0.199, (b) 0.551, (c) 0.722   [10.2, 10.5]

10.13 0.417   [10.16]

10.14 (a) 0.36176, (b) 0.11424, (c) 0.43952, (d) 0.07296, (e) 0.17568   [10.18]

10.15 (a) 0.315, (b) 0.450, (c) 0.235   [10.18]

Chapter 11

To the right of the answer, in square brackets [ ], are the Chapter 11 Example or Examples that are most like the question. If you haven't obtained the right answer, look at them for guidance.

11.1 $188,000   [11.2]

11.2 £280   [11.2]

11.3 (a) Ice cream, (b) Mix, (c) Mix, (d) Mix   [11.3–11.7]

11.4 (a) EMV (Cabin baggage only) = £12; pay extra £10 for hold baggage   [11.8]
      (b) EMV (Cabin baggage only) = £20; pay extra £10 for hold baggage   [11.8]
      (c) Take cabin baggage only   [11.8]

11.5 £12,800   [11.2]

11.6 (a) Fee, (b) No win no fee, (c) Fee, (d) Fee   [11.3–11.7]

11.7 (a) Own diagram
      (b) EMV (Vaccination) = £0.9m, EMV (No vaccination) = £0.8m; vaccinate   [11.8]
      (c) EMV (Vaccination) = £0.96m, EMV (No vaccination) = £1.04m; yes   [11.8]

11.8 (b) (i) Increased area, (ii) Same area, (iii) Decreased area   [11.8]

11.9 (a) EMV (A) = 6400, EMV (B) = 3750; choose A   [11.8]
      (b) EMV (A) = 3800; choose A   [11.8]

11.10 (a) Own diagram
       (b) EMV (S) = 2.05, EMV (P) = 4.5; choose Parooka   [11.8]
       (c) New EMV (S) = 4.6; choose Sloochai   [11.8]

11.11 (a) EMV (star) = 1, EMV (no star) = −2, EMV (bid) = 0.85;
bid for the rights and hire a star [11.10−11.12]
(b) If P (success without a star) > 0.275, don't hire a star [11.13]

11.12 (a) EMV (large-scale) = 0, EMV (small-scale) = 11, EMV (develop) = 7.75;
develop and start small-scale production if the tests are passed. [11.10−11.12]
(b) Choose large-scale production if P (approval) > 0.529 [11.13]

11.13 EMV (build if expert predicts failure) = 5.8, so sell
EMV (build if expert predicts success) = 20.2, so build
EMV (build if no advice is sought) = 13
EMV (seek expert advice) = 14.1
Get expert advice, build if prediction is success, sell if it is failure [11.14]

Chapter 12

To the right of the answer, in square brackets [ ], are the Chapter 12 Example or Examples that are most like the question. If you haven't obtained the right answer, look at them for guidance.

12.1 (a) 0.512, (b) 0.384, (c) 0.096, (d) 0.008 [12.1]

12.2 (a) 0.2401, (b) 0.4116, (c) 0.2646, (d) 0.0756, (e) 0.0081 [12.1]

12.3 (a) 0.007, (b) 0.265, (c) 0.762, (d) 0.133 [12.7]

12.4 (a) 0.018, (b) 0.073, (c) 0.238, (d) 0.371 [12.7]

12.5 (a) 0.006, (b) 0.633, (c) 0.111, (d) 0.055 [12.5]

12.6 (a) 0.070, (b) 0.322 [12.5]
(c) In (a) mean = 1, s.d = 0.949; in (b) mean = 2, s.d = 1.265 [12.6]

12.7 (a) 0.982, (b) Yes, to 0.950 [12.7]

12.8 Average number of unsatisfied customer per day = 6/10 = 0.6 [12.8, 12.9]

12.9 (a) 375, (b) 20; cope with capacity to spare on several days [12.8−12.11]

12.10 £5920 [12.8−12.11]

12.11 £10,790 [12.8−12.11]

12.12 £18,400 [12.8−12.11]

Chapter 13

To the right of the answer, in square brackets [ ], are the Chapter 13 Example or Examples that are most like the question. If you haven't obtained the right answer, look at them for guidance.

13.1 (a) 0.0475, (b) 0.5714, (c) 0.9864, (d) 0.0643, (e) 0.1952, (f) 0.3840, (g) 0.4396 [13.1]

13.2 (a) 0.0708, (b) 0.9984, (c) 0.5000, (d) 0.0708, (e) 0.6034 [13.3]

13.3 (a) 0.0031, (b) 0.0853, (c) 0.0853, (d) 0.9147, (e) 0.8294, (f) 0.9938 [13.3]

13.4 (a) 0.537, (b) 0.099, (c) 0.365 [13.5]

13.5 (a) 0.301, (b) 0.451, (c) 0.074 [13.5]

13.6 (a) 0.0329, (b) 0.0228, (c) Yes − fewer fail in less than 60,000 miles [13.3]

13.7 (a) (i) 0.3156, (ii) 0.0287, (iii) 0.6578 [13.3]
(b) (i) 0.2206, (ii) 0.1251, (iii) 0.5229 [13.3]

13.8 (a) (i) 0.0314, (ii) 0.0026, (iii) 0.7580, (iv) 0.5578 [13.3]
(b) 6750.4 litres, (c) 5492.65 litres [13.4]

13.9 (a) 0.8, (b) 0.328, (c) 0.133 hours = 8 minutes, (d) 3.2 [13.7]

13.10 (a) 0.6915 (B), 0.5714 (N), 0.3085 (P); choose Plankston [13.3]
(b) 0.3085 (B), 0.4286 (N), 0.6915 (P); choose Beamer [13.3]
(c) 0.4225 (B), 0.3453 (N), 0.5375 (P); choose Plankston [13.3]

13.11 (a) (i) 0.9564, (ii) 0.2148, (iii) 0.0029 [13.3]
(b) (i) 0.8461, (ii) 0.1271, (iii) 0.0023 [13.3]
(c) (i) 0.9906, (ii) 0.3300, (iii) 0.0040 [13.3]

13.12 (a) (i) 0.75, (ii) 2.25, (iii) 0.375 hours = 22.5 minutes [13.7]
(b) (i) 0.6, (ii) 0.9, (iii) 0.15 hours = 9 minutes [13.7]

Chapter 14

To the right of the answer, in square brackets [ ], are the Chapter 14 Example or Examples that are most like the question. If you haven't obtained the right answer, look at them for guidance.

14.1 (a) Own diagram
(b) Minimum duration = 23 days. Critical path: A, D, E, G [14.1, 14.3]

14.2 22 days, A−B−E−F [14.1, 14.3]

14.3 (a) Own diagram
(b) 30 days, A−B−D [14.1, 14.3]

14.4 (a) Own diagram
(b) 24 seconds; A−B−E−H−I [14.1, 14.3]

14.5 (a) 1.33pm, (b) D−F−G−H−I−J−K−L−M−O [14.1, 14.3]

14.6 (a) 23.333 days, 2.677 days, (b) 0.9936, (c) 25.582 [14.5−14.7]

14.7 (a) 24.883 seconds, 1.384 seconds, (b) 0.0202 [14.5, 14.6]

14.8 (a) 41 weeks, A−C−D−E−F−H−I [14.1, 14.3]
(b) (i) 41.833, 1.951, (ii) 0.1736, (iii) 46.371 weeks [14.5−14.7]

14.9 (a) Own diagram
(b) A−C−D−F−G−I−J−K, 13 days [14.1, 14.3]
(c) Crash D and F: £1100 [14.8]

14.10 (a) 23.167 days, 1.5 days, (b) 0.2177, (c) 25.635 days [14.5−14.7]
(d) (i) A = 0, B = 1, C = 1, D = 0, E = 0, F = 3 [14.4]
(ii) Crash costs per day: £200 for B, £150 for C, £300 for E and £200 for F
1: Crash E by 1 day cost £300, project duration 22 days
2: Crash E by a further day and C by 1 day cost £450, project duration 21 days
(iii) Crash to 22 days; cost (£300) < net loss (£400) [14.8]

14.11 (a) B−H−I−J−M, 37 days [14.1, 14.3]
(b) Crash B (2 days) and I (1 day): £1100 [14.8]

14.12 (a) 31 minutes, A−B−C−D−F [14.1, 14.3]
(b) 0.2033 [14.5−14.7]

Chapter 16

To the right of the answer, in square brackets [ ], are the Chapter 16 Example or Examples that are most like the question. If you haven't obtained the right answer, look at them for guidance.

16.1 (a) (i) 0.9292, (ii) 0.1635, (iii) 0.0708, (iv) 0.0071, (v) 0.6171, (vi) 0.9276   [16.1]
 (b) (i) 0.7257, (ii) 0.3446, (iii) 0.2743, (iv) 0.1587, (v) 0.3050, (vi) 0.6106

16.2 (a) (i) 0.1922, (ii) 0.0968, (iii) 0.7660   [16.1]
 (b) (i) 0.3085, (ii) 0.2266, (iii) 0.7745   [16.1]

16.3 (a) (i) 0.1190, (ii) 0.0091, (iii) 0.0384, (iv) 0.9616, (v) 0.8719, (vi) 0.1174   [16.2]
 (b) No

16.4 (a) (i) 1.956 inches to 1.984 inches, (ii) 1.953 inches to 1.987 inches
   (iii) 1.948 inches to 1.992 inches   [16.6–16.8]
 (b) (i) 1.954 inches to 1.986 inches, (ii) 1.950 inches to 1.990 inches
   (iii) 1.944 inches to 1.996 inches   [16.6–16.8]

16.5 (a) (i) 0.643 to 0.817, (ii) 0.616 to 0.844   [16.12]
 (b) Yes

16.6 Test statistic $= -1.265$, can't reject H_0 (i) at 5%, (ii) at 1%   [16.16, 16.17]

16.7 7 minuses, 3 pluses; can't reject H_0 [16.24]

16.8 (a) (i) 0.0062, (ii) 0.0228, (iii) 0.1026   [16.1]
 (b) (i) 0.1056, (ii) 0.1587, (iii) 0.1805   [16.1]

16.9 (a) 0.0548, (b) 0.0021, (c) (i) 0.2266, (ii) 0.0119   [16.1, 16.2]

16.10 (a) (i) £34,029.832 to £35,970.168, (ii) £33,844.055 to £36,155.945
   (iii) £33,480.758 to £36,519.242   [16.6–16.8]
 (b) (i) £31,140.754 to £32,859.246, (ii) £30,962.099 to £33,037.901
   (iii) £30,589.275 to £33,410.725   [16.11]
 (c) (i) 153, (ii) 217, (iii) 374   [16.9]

16.11 (a) (i) 0.228 to 0.304, (ii) 0.222 to 0.310, (iii) 0.208 to 0.324   [16.12]
 (b) (i) 423, (ii) 601, (iii) 1037   [16.13]

16.12 (a) (i) 78.435° to 79.365°, (ii) 78.346° to 79.454°, (iii) 78.171° to 79.629°   [16.6–16.8]
 (b) (i) 79.630° to 81.170°, (ii) 79.471° to 81.329, (iii) 79.139° to 81.661°   [16.11]
 (c) Temperatures are normally distributed
 (d) (i) 31, (ii) 14   [16.9]

16.13 (a) (i) 13.389 minutes to 15.011 minutes, (ii) 13.234 minutes to 15.166 minutes,
   (iii) 12.930 minutes to 15.470 minutes   [16.6–16.8]
 (b) (i) 10.684 minutes to 11.916 minutes, (ii) 10.557 minutes to 12.043 minutes,
   (iii) 10.293 minutes to 12.307 minutes   [16.11]
 (c) (i) 35, (ii) 60, (iii) 98, (iv) 139   [16.9]

16.14 (a) Test statistic $= -1.450$; can't reject H_0 at 5%   [16.21]
 (b) Test statistic $= -2.348$; reject H_0 at 5%   [16.22]
 (c) New system seems to be significantly faster when the sample is adjusted.
   Dispensing times should be normally distributed

16.15 Test statistic $= -2.775$; reject H_0 that $\pi = 0.08$ at 10%, 5% and 1%   [16.23]

Chapter 17

To the right of the answer, in square brackets [ ], are the Chapter 17 Example or Examples that are most like the question. If you haven't obtained the right answer, look at them for guidance.

17.1 Test statistic = 2.663; reject H_0 at 5% [17.1]

17.2 Test statistic = −4.134; reject H_0 at 1% [17.3]

17.3 Test statistic = −2.878; reject H_0 at 1% [17.7]

17.4 Test statistic = 11.25; reject H_0 at 5% [17.16–17.20]

17.5 Test statistic = 6.065; (i) reject H_0 at 5%, (ii) can't reject H_0 at 1% [17.16–17.20]

17.6 Test statistic = −2.130; reject H_0 at 5% [17.2]

17.7 (a) Test statistic = −8.198; reject H_0 at the 1% level [17.8]
(b) 32.728 mpg to 40.142 mpg [17.9, 17.10]
(c) 25.131 mpg to 47.739 mpg [17.12]

17.8 (a) Test statistic = 10.587; (i) reject H_0 at 5%, (ii) can't reject H_0 at 1% [17.16–17.20]
(b) A/B and 3 or more holidays, D/E and none; both higher than expected [17.21]

17.9 (a) Test statistic = 13.818; (i) reject H_0 at 5%, (ii) reject H_0 at 1% [17.16–17.20]
(b) 50 and over/Credit card, lower than expected; 50 and
over/Debit card, higher than expected [17.21]

17.10 (a) Test statistic = 6.697; (i) reject H_0 at 10%, (ii) can't reject H_0 at 5% [17.16–17.20]
(b) Test statistic = 5.522; (i) can't reject H_0 at 10%, (ii) can't reject H_0 at 5% [17.16–17.20]

17.11 Test statistic = 0.159; can't reject H_0 [17.5, 17.6]

17.12 Test statistic = 7.186; reject H_0 [17.5, 17.6]

17.13 Test statistic = 5.817; reject H_0 at 5% but not at 1% [17.5, 17.6]

17.14 (a) Test statistic = 9.306; reject H_0 [17.16–17.20]
(b) England/Seldom; higher than expected [17.21]
(c) Test statistic = 12.100; (i) reject H_0 at 10%, (ii) can't reject H_0 at 5% [17.16–17.20]

17.15 (a) No; Expected counts less than 5 [17.21]
(b) Test statistic = 5.368; (i) reject H_0 at 10%, (ii) can't reject H_0 at 5% [17.16–17.20]

Index

Page numbers in *italics* denote a diagram/table